OCEANSIDE PUBLIC LIBRARY
330 N. Coast Highway
Oceanside, CA 92054

200 Years of Dolls

SECOND EDITION

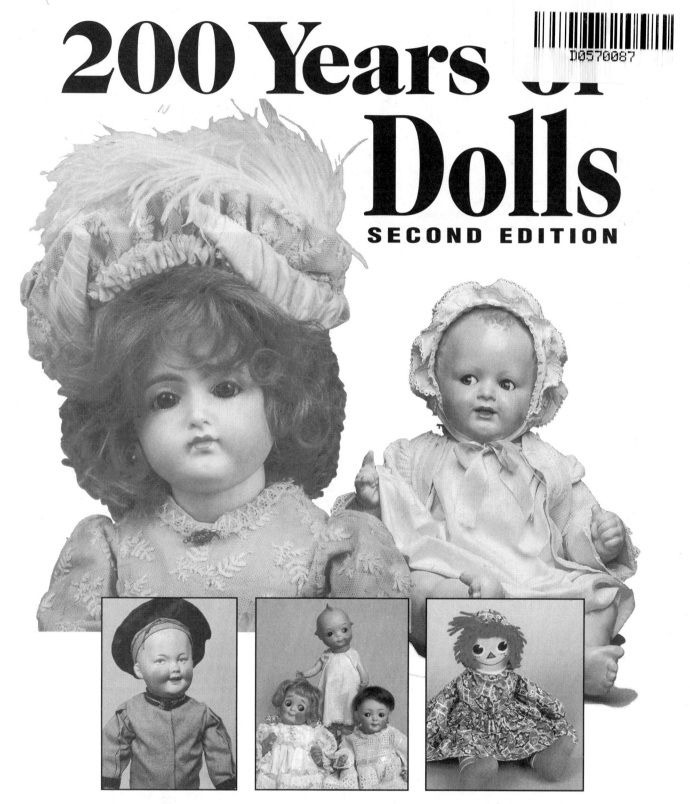

IDENTIFICATION AND PRICE GUIDE

25 More Doll Companies • 200 New Listings • All Updated Pricing

DAWN HERLOCHER

OCEANSIDE PUBLIC LIBRARY
330 N. Coast Highway
Oceanside, CA 92054

© 2002 by
Dawn Herlocher

All rights reserved.
No part of this publication may be reproduced or transmitted in any form
or by any means, electronic or mechanical, including photocopying,
recording, or by any information storage and retrieval system
without the permission in writing from the Publisher.

Published by

**krause
publications**

700 East State Street • Iola, WI 54990-0001
715/445-2214 • FAX: 715/445-4087   www.krause.com

Please call or write for our free catalog of publications.
Our toll-free number to place an order or obtain a free catalog is 800-258-0929
or please use our regular business telephone, 715-445-2214.

On the cover: (top) Simon & Halbig #989, courtesy of Helen Brooke; German composition baby with
flirty eyes, courtesy of Sandi Haroldson; (bottom) Gebrüder Heubach #7647, courtesy of David Cobb's
Doll Auctions; Group of Googly-Eyed Dolls, Armand Marseille #240, Kestner #221, Hertel Schwab
#165 courtesy of David Cobb's Doll Auctions; Molly-'es Baby Raggedy, courtesy of Rusty Herlocher.

Library of Congress Catalog Number: 2001097827
ISBN: 0-87341-886-7

3 1232 00866 6101

Printed in the United States of America

Acknowledgments

*F*irst and foremost I wish to thank David Cobb, of Cobb's Doll Auctions, Johnstown Ohio for his kindness and generosity. David shared with me his marvelous collection of dolls and photographs. As you peruse this book, you will surely notice that many, if not most, of the photographs are courtesy of David Cobb. Thank you David.

My deepest appreciation goes to the hundreds of doll dealers, auction houses, and auctioneers across the country that supplied me with information. In addition to David Cobb, I especially want to thank Sheri and Jim McMasters of McMaster's WorldWide Productions for once again proving to be the professionals with a heart; Becky and Andy Ourant of Village Doll and Toy Shop in Adamstown, Pa.; the staff at the Strong Museum, Rochester New York, what a wonderful day exploring your research library; Sandi Haroldson of Sandra Lee Products, www.sandralee.com. Sandi can truly do wonders with a composition doll.

I would like to express my thanks to the many doll collectors who loaned me their dolls for study and/or photography. Their generosity was overwhelming. My special thanks to Mrs. Adam Condo; Leah and Gene Patterson; Joyce and Harry McKeague; Helen Brooke; Dr. Georgia Kemp-Caraway; Barbara Williams; Alice Eldridge Taylor; Julia Burke; and Jean Campbell.

Thanks to Bill Neff for photographing so many dolls. Your talents are greatly appreciated. When I needed a skilled photographer, you were there.

Thank you to my staunch supporter, Harry Rinker of Rinker Enterprises, Inc. Harry was the first person to encourage me to write books. Over the years, Harry has maintained steadfast confidence in them and me, and remains my friend.

My appreciation goes to my new friends at Krause Publications: Don Gulbrandsen, Senior Acquisitions Editor, for never being too busy to help guide me; Jodi Rintelman, Associate Editor, who is without a doubt one of the brightest and sweetest souls that God ever created. She has somehow managed to decipher and perfectly interrupt my notes and ideas and does so with a smile! What an angel!

Two old friends that prodded me along, and for lack of a better word 'got the ball rollin', Ellen Schroy, Warman's Editor, and Allan Miller, both authors of extraordinary accomplishments.

I put my wonderful family last in these acknowledgments, but it goes without saying that they are first in my heart. Jennifer, Maribeth, and Ty—my own living dolls—are three of the greatest kids in the world. I'm proud to be their mom!

Pat and Bill Tyson, my mother and father, along with countless hours of proofreading, taught me a love for antiques and instilled in me the belief that a person can do anything she sets her mind to do. My sister Trina, her husband Billy, and their sons, Billy Grant and Jordan, offered me encouragement and always, without fail, are able to make me laugh.

Finally, my husband and best friend, Rusty. I could not have written this book without his constant and unwaver-

Table of Contents

Introduction

I've been a doll collector all of my life. I have, for as long as I can remember, loved my genteel silent companions. They have provided a presence on which, as a child, I could project my fantasies, and as an adult develop an appreciation for their artistic appeal.

There is probably no rational explanation for the feelings collectors have for their dolls. Perhaps it's because they awaken memories and dreams, stirring our feelings of nostalgia, or the simple pleasure gained in admiring the beauty of these present-day reminders of a long vanished era.

The attraction to dolls seems to be immediate and universal, made obvious by the thousands of new enthusiasts who have excitedly embraced the world of doll collecting in recent years.

It is our hope that this book will help both the beginning and the more advanced collector enjoy doll collecting as a rewarding experience by avoiding bad investments. In addition to information for identifying and evaluating a wide variety of dolls, we provide practical hints to help you recognize reproductions; identify the shortcomings of particular dolls; and heighten your awareness of superior and inferior examples of seemingly identical dolls, whether of early wood or contemporary vinyl.

No two dolls are exactly alike. A study of their various features indicates the factors that influence the value of a doll, including rarity, condition, quality of material, artistry, availability, originality, history of providence, and the ever-important visual appeal. All of these factors contribute to a doll's charisma.

To assist you further, we've included background information on social influences and technological improvements that have affected the doll-making industry. Brief histories of the manufacturers emphasize the importance of condition. Please take the time to thoroughly inspect a doll. An antique bisque doll head should be checked not only on the outside, but also from the inside, for at times a repair or hairline crack will only be visible from the inside. Remember not to confuse maintenance with repairs. Reset eyes, restrung bodies, and patched leather are examples of necessary maintenance and are not repairs to a doll. Modern dolls should always be in perfect, complete condition. Inspect the markings of a doll. You may find them on the back of the head, the torso, the bottom of a foot, or even on the derriere. Of course, many fine dolls will have absolutely no markings. Learn from every doll you see or handle, for there is almost as much fun in learning about a doll as there is in owning it. Visit doll shows and museums.

I encourage you to read and study as much as you can about dolls. The two volumes of Dorothy S., Elizabeth A., and Evelyn J. Coleman's *The Collector's Encyclopedia of Dolls* (Crown Publishing 1972 and 1986) are accurate guidebooks to doll manufacturing prior to 1930. *Antique Trader's Doll Makers and Marks* (Krause Publications, 1999) is a concise directory for doll identification. If you don't own a copy, visit a library that does.

Talk to other collectors. I have never met a doll collector that doesn't enjoy talking about their dolls. Consider joining a doll club. Clubs that are members of the United Federation of Doll Clubs (U.F.D.C.) "represent the highest standards of excellence for collectors to create, stimulate and maintain interest in all matters pertaining to doll collecting." Write the U.F.D.C. at P.O. Box 14146, Parkville, MO 64152 to obtain the address of a club near you.

The format of this book is really quite simple. Dolls are arranged by manufacturer or type. Within each section, there are generalized sub-headings presented by material or style. These are further described by particular doll model, either by name, mold number, or a visual clue that identifies a particular doll.

There are several aspects of this book I'm sure you'll find to be not only extremely informative but also quite unique. We give you the detailed clues needed to identify a doll; in-depth descriptions of categories to establish classification; and even share some "old doll secrets." However, we think you'll rank our new and distinctive approach to pricing—accomplished through easy-to-follow charts—among the most distinctive features in this volume. You will find them a quick and easy way to determine the value of a particular doll.

The astute collector or interim care-giver can use this book for comparative purposes when assessing and evaluating their dolls, whether building a new collection or researching an existing one of a thousand dolls.

Collecting Tips

The following procedures are provided to inform and educate. Neither the author nor publisher accept liability or responsibility in respect to any type of loss or damage caused, or alleged to be caused, directly or indirectly, by the information or products contained in this book. We simply intend to share some old tricks and methods that have been used over the years.

Like real children, dolls require tender loving care. They need to be repaired, restored, handled, displayed, and stored properly. The following tips will help you develop skills to ensure that your dolls receive the loving treatment they deserve.

When dealing with dolls, the best approach is to be a minimalist. Do only the bare minimum to bring a doll to display level—retain, rather than destroy. Period features count heavily in a doll's value. Plan any repairs in a step-by-step process, evaluating as you go along.

Always approach the cleaning or maintenance of dolls with the greatest of care and respect. If you're not sure how to perform a certain procedure, ask an expert. We have an obligation to future doll collectors to preserve the dolls in our care and to maintain them in as good or better condition than they were when we received them.

Care

Bisque, China, and Parian are all made of clay, feldspar, and flint. Differences between them are subtle. Parian is unglazed, untinted porcelain; china is glazed porcelain; and bisque is unglazed porcelain with a flesh color.

The earliest bisque, china, and parian dolls were pressed into a mold by hand; later examples were poured.

Cleaning porcelain is fairly simple. The decorations have been fired on, so it is highly unlikely that you will harm them by cleaning. Start with the least-abrasive technique—usually warm soapy water. If this is not sufficient, try a wet eraser. As a last resort, very, very gently clean with a low-abrasive cleaner such as Tilex® or Soft Scrub®. Use extreme caution, as some cleansers contain bleaching agents that are devastating to antique clothing, wigs, or bodies. When displaying a bisque, china, or parian doll, avoid the damaging ultraviolet rays of direct sunlight.

If placed on a doll stand, be sure that the doll is secure and that the stand is weighted sufficiently to support it.

Celluloid dolls are extremely perishable. They are easily broken and become quite brittle over time. Proper care and respect of a celluloid doll helps a perfect example remain in that condition. Heat is celluloid's worst enemy. Keep these dolls in a cool room with good ventilation, and never store celluloid in a sealed case—it is highly combustible.

Cloth dolls have a special place in every doll collector's heart. Even a well-loved rag doll tugs at one's heartstrings. Vintage, and even the not-so-vintage cloth art dolls can be valued at thousands of dollars. They deserve your best efforts to preserve them and prevent needless deterioration.

Clean fabric is a pre-requisite to preservation. Exposing a doll to any pollutants through storage or display weakens the fabric. Direct sunlight is an enemy of cloth dolls and should be avoided.

Inspect cloth dolls regularly for signs of insect activity. Insecticides designed especially for textiles are available under several brand names. When used according to the manufacturer's instructions, the results can be excellent.

If you decide to vacuum your doll, place a nylon screen over the fabric first to protect delicate fibers. Often, a thorough vacuuming is enough to restore a doll to display condition. Again, approach this procedure with appropriate caution. If a valuable or historically significant cloth doll is badly soiled, seek the advice of a professional who specializes in textile conservation.

Some stains on cloth dolls can be removed with an eraser—art gum or tapeten appear to give the best results. Use this technique with careful, gentle application. Frequently stains, such as ink, may be removed with hair spray. It is essential to test the fabric first on an inconspicuous location to assure that no damage will occur. Apply the hair spray with a cloth, then wipe in a light rubbing motion using a clean white cloth.

Lenci once advertised that a Lenci doll could be cleaned by rubbing it with a piece of bread!

To preserve and display cloth dolls. It is best to keep them in protective cases and inspect them regularly. Moth crystals should be placed near your dolls. Many collectors recommend making a small cloth pouch, filling it with moth crystals, cedar chips, or whole cloves and placing it under the doll's hat or tying it around its waist beneath the clothing.

Composition and papier-mâché dolls, being made from pulp-based materials, require similar care. They are particularly susceptible to damage from temperature changes. Never store composition or papier-mâché dolls in a hot or cold attic, or in a damp basement.

Most collectors will accept slight signs of aging on composition dolls—fine craze lines or crackled eyes, for example. Think long and hard before performing irreversible restorations that can compromise a doll's historical and practical value. Remember a true restoration can later be undone. Several temporary cover-ups are acceptable.

There are several popular methods for cleaning composition. Test any method first on an inconspicuous area of the doll. Work quickly. Never leave any substance on the surface for any length of time. Pond's® Cold Cream or Vaseline® and a soft tissue are favorites of many collectors. Another option is paste window cleaner—not the ammonia type, but the old fashioned paste available at most hardware stores.

Wigs can be restyled after lightly spraying with Johnson's® baby shampoo detangling formula, carefully working out the tangles. Faded or worn-off facial features can be touched up with artist's colored pencils; when moistened they are quite easy to apply. Crackled eyes are best left alone.

Hard plastic dolls are a favorite with collectors. Their sharp features and beautiful detailing are hard to resist.

Hard plastic is very resilient and can be cleaned with warm soapy water. Stubborn stains may be removed with cold cream or waterless hand cleaner. Avoid chlorine bleach and ammonia. Facial features may not be as durable, so approach painted surfaces with caution, checking paint stability before proceeding. Never use fingernail polish remover or lacquer thinner, which may eat into the plastic.

Many report excellent results using Oxy-10 to remove stains that are not close to painted surfaces. Moisten a cotton ball and allow it to sit on the stain for a few minutes. You may need to repeat this process several times. After each cleaning, wash the doll with mild soap and rinse well.

When displaying or storing hard plastic dolls, avoid direct exposure to ultraviolet light. Though seemingly indestructible, hard plastic can slowly oxidize and change color. Direct heat may also cause warping.

Rubber, early latex, or Magic Skin dolls will deteriorate no matter what precautions are taken, but you may be able to delay the process. Any form of grease is harmful and accelerates deterioration. Always wear cotton gloves when handling a Magic Skin doll. I practice the old trick of rubbing corn starch on these dolls twice a year—once on my March birthday and once on my dad's September birthday. As with all dolls, maintain an even temperature and relative humidity.

Tin dolls often have chipped paint. When the metal becomes very cold, the paint lifts easily from the surface. Store or display metal dolls in an environment with a relatively constant temperature.

Vinyl dolls are probably the most lifelike in appearance and touch. Special care is needed to keep them looking good. Extreme room temperatures are harmful. Even quality vinyl dolls subjected to heaters or air conditioners can be damaged in just a few months. Direct sunlight can be devastating. Vinyl is also sensitive to fluorescent lighting; use indirect non-fluorescent lights. Finally, avoid tightly sealed show cases or glass domes, as condensation can form and damage vinyl dolls.

Wooden dolls have withstood the test of time quite well, as proven by the sheer number that have survived the years. Chipping paint is a major problem with wooden dolls. Humidity and mistreatment are the two main culprits. Keep wooden dolls in a dry atmosphere. Expanding and contracting associated with high humidity causes paint to chip. Knocks and bumps can also chip paint, so take care in moving or displaying wooden dolls.

Wax dolls tend to intimidate many collectors. They do require special care, as do all types of dolls. Basic care and common sense will help preserve a wax doll in perfect condition. Of course, never place a wax doll in direct sunlight or near any heat source, such as a fireplace mantle.

A long-accepted practice for cleaning wax dolls is to start with the safest method and then gradually progress to more drastic measures until a suitable remedy is found. First, try a solution of cool water and Woolite®. Saturate a cotton ball or Q-tips® cotton swab, and wash the wax. If this is unsuccessful, try a dab of cold cream on a cotton swab, followed by a rinse of the Woolite solution and then clean, cool water. As a last resort, try denatured alcohol on a cotton ball, followed by a thorough rinsing. Never use turpentine to clean wax dolls, as it can soften the wax.

Repairs

Some long-time doll collectors recommend placing a drop of sewing machine oil in the crackled eyes of a composition doll. Although it does seem to make the eyes appear more clear for a time, the downside is that the oil dries and causes further deterioration. It is always evident when eyes have been treated in this manner.

Green deposits found around Barbie pierced ears can be removed by covering the ears with a small piece of cotton soaked in Tarn-X® silver cleaner. Wrap the head in plastic wrap to keep the application moist. Check after two days—if the ears are still green, replace the plastic wrap. If the ears are still green after four days, repeat the procedure with fresh cotton balls. Once the green in gone, rub a paste of baking soda and water over the treated areas. After several days, flake off the dried baking soda and clean the area with warm, soapy water on a cotton swab. Tarn-X causes a chemical reaction that acts as a bleach; the baking soda neutralizes the reaction, and the warm, soapy water removes any residue. It is important to perform each step as described, and to inspect the doll periodically throughout the process.

Bubble Cut Barbies often have sticky or greasy faces. This is due to an ingredient being emitted by the vinyl. To alleviate the problem, carefully remove the head from the body and clean inside and out with a cotton swab soaked in alcohol. Dry thoroughly, fill the head cavity with baking soda, and replace it on the body. The baking soda will neutralize the chemicals and absorb the extracted grease.

Some Very Old Tips

Here are some old-fashioned tips suggested by doll collectors. They are neither recommended nor condemned. I have included them for your enjoyment only.

• To remove mildew: soak in sour milk and salt, and then lay the doll in the sun. To remove the milk therapy, follow with a warm soapy water wash and rinse.

• To restore color to faded cloth: sponge with chloroform.

• To soften old kid: saturate an old woolen rag with kerosene and rub in the kid.

• To clean old ivory: scrub with Ivory soap; bleach in the sun for several days, re-applying the soapy solution often.

• To remove tar: clean first with turpentine, then clean with Lux soap.

• To remove paint: patient rubbing with chloroform.
• To restore faded calico: wash in water with a teaspoon of sugar of lead; soak for fifteen minutes and launder.
• Black taffeta is best washed in strong tea.

Dolls are a fascinating part of our culture and provide a look into our past. By scattering the seeds of doll collecting and furnishing basic information, I hope I've helped the reader build a collection that is enjoyable and profitable.

Doll Clubs

Doll clubs are wonderful. You meet and share knowledge with other people who are almost as obsessed with dolls as you! Whether you love and collect a particular type of doll, or, like Will Rogers, "ya' never met a soul ya' didn't like," there is a club that should fit your interests. Most clubs are well organized and in constant pursuit of information. They are often involved in community services, making wonderfully worthwhile contributions. Our club, for example, has kept our police department supplied with dolls and teddy bears to give to children involved in unfortunate situations. We've shipped boxes of refurbished dolls to orphanages in Bosnia, and make a practice of sending handcrafted cloth dolls and quilted lap robes to our local hospital and Women's Center. Many clubs have conventions, luncheons, sales, newsletters, swap meets, and other activities all centered around dolls. The following list hopefully will help you find a doll club in your area.

Annalee Doll Society
P.O. Box 1137
Meredith, NH 03253-1137

Antique Toy Collectors of America
Rt. 2, Box 5A
Parkton, MD 21120

Cabbage Patch Kids Collectors Club
P.O. Box 714
Cleveland, GA 30528

Chatty Cathy Collectors Club
2610 Dover St.
Piscataway, NJ 08854-4437

Doll Artisan Guild
35 Main St.
Oneonta, NY 13820
Doll Collectors of America
14 Chestnut Road

Westford, MD 01886

Effanbee Dolls
4701 Queensbury Road
Riverdale, MD 20840

GI Joe Collectors Club
150 S. Glenoaks Blvd.
Burbank, CA 91510

Ginny Doll Club
9628 Hidden Oaks Circle
Tampa, FL 33612

Ideal Doll Collector's Club
P.O. Box 623
Lexington, MA 02173

International Barbie Doll Club
P.O. Box 70
Bronx, NY 10464

International Doll Makers' Association
3364 Pine Creek Drive
San Jose, CA 95132

International Rose O'Neill Club
P.O. Box 668
Branson, MO 65616

Madame Alexander Fan Club
P.O. Box 330
Mundelein, IL 60060

National Institute of American Doll Artists
303 Riley St.
Falls Church, VA 22046

National Organization of Miniaturists and Dollers
1300 Schroder
Normal, IL 61761

United Federation of Doll Clubs (UFDC)
Becky Moncrief, Membership Chairman
2007 Sea Cove Court
Houston, TX 77058

Price Adjustment Factors

Prices in this book are based on dolls in good condition, appropriately dressed with no damage. Unfortunately, dolls frequently have a number of faults.

What follows is a method by which you can take the prices listed in this book and adjust them to fit the doll you are examining. Admittedly, some of these adjustments do require you to make a judgment call. When analyzing a doll, it's always best to use your head, not your heart. That may sound easy, but it is difficult to do. Over-grading a doll and, hence, over paying for it, are major problems in doll collecting circles. Hopefully, the suggestions offered here will make you a wiser, more savvy buyer and/or seller.

Bisque

Hairline crack or repair in back or under wig ...... **- 50%**
Hairline crack or repair to face .... **- 70%**
Very poor body (beyond normal wear) .... **- 35%**
Replaced body .... **- 45%**
Tinted or untinted ornamentation damage.......... **- 25%**
Original super-pristine condition and/or with original box .... **+ 200% or more**

China

Head cracked or repaired .... **- 75%**
Cracked or repaired shoulder............................... **- 50%**
Worn or replaced body .... **- 40%**
Exceptional, original doll...................... **+ 75% or more**

Cloth

Face stained or faded .... **- 50%**
Tears or large holes in face .... **- 80%**
Mint or excellent condition .... **+ 200%**

Metal

Lightly dented or lightly chipped head .... **- 50%**
Badly dented or badly chipped head .... **- 80%**
Bucherer Dolls are forgiven for some chips and damage. So desirable are these dolls that the adjustment would be only 20–30% depending on severity and location.

Composition and Papier-Mâché

Very light crazing .... **Acceptable**
Heavy crazing or cracking .... **- 50%**
Small splits at corners of eye and/or mouth........ **- 10%**
Heavy chipping to face... **- 75%**
Face repainted .... **- 80%**
Major cracks, splits, and peeling......................... **- 30%**
Redressed or undressed.. **- 25%**
Mint and/or boxed .... **+ 200% or more**

Wax

Minor cracks or minor warp to head.................... **- 20%**
Major cracks or major warp to head .... **- 50%**
Softening of features .... **- 20%**
Rewaxed.. **- 70%**
All original with sharp features and good color
.... **+ 200% or more**

Celluloid

Cracks .... **- 80%**
Discolored.. **- 70%**
Mint .... **+ 50%**

Wood

Light crazing or minute paint touch-up...... **Acceptable**
Repainted head or heavy splits
(depending on severity and location)..... **- 50% to - 80%**
Mint ....**+ 100%**

Plastic

Cracks or discoloration .... **- 75%**
Hair combed... **- 40%**
Shelf dirt.. **- 10%**
Redressed or missing accessories .... **- 50%**
1950s, mint, boxed..**+ 150%***
1960s, mint, boxed..**+ 100%***
1970s, mint, boxed... **+ 50%***
1980s, mint, boxed... **+ 10%**
1990s, mint, boxed..................................**List Value**
* Or more, depending on the desirability of the doll

Acme Toy Company

Early glass-eyed composition Acme Mama doll. Courtesy of David Cobb's Doll Auctions

premium dolls without a premium price." Time has proven this statement to be true. Acme dolls have a much better aging appearance than many other dolls produced at that time. The familiar Peek-A-Boo infant, Honey Baby, and Marilyn, all originally costumed in silks, crepe de chine, and other fine fabrics, are prized additions to many collections.

Popular mama and baby dolls with soft cloth bodies and nicely modelled composition heads were not their only specialty. Along with the all composition character dolls, it is believed they also produced a portion of the Kiddie Joy line for Hitz, Jacobs, and Kassle.

Acme Toy Company was a formidable competitor to many larger manufacturers. Horsman, in fact, sued Acme for infringement of copyright of their Tynie Baby. Horsman lost the suit. The courts determined that the Tynie Baby was not sufficiently labeled. At the time Horsman marked their dolls only with the initials E.I.H., instead of their whole name. Needless to say, it was a practice that was soon amended.

Prices listed are for appropriately costumed dolls in good condition. Slight crazing is acceptable and does not greatly affect the price. If badly crazed, cracked, peeling, or repainted, expect the value to be less than half the amount listed.

Mama Doll: composition head; cloth body; molded and painted hair or good wig; painted or sleep eyes; open or closed mouth; appropriately dressed; typically marked "ACME TOY."

Child Doll: all composition; jointed at neck, shoulder, and hip; human hair wig; tin sleep eyes; closed, slightly-smiling mouth; appropriately dressed; typically marked "ACME TOY Co" (the o may be positioned within the C, thereby making the Co appear as a solid circle).

Lady Doll: all composition; slim, flapper-type body jointed at neck, shoulder, and hip; thin legs; human hair wig; tin sleep eyes; closed mouth; appropriately dressed; typically marked "ACME TOY CO" (the o may be positioned within the C, thereby making the Co appear as a solid circle).

The Acme Toy Company was located in New York City from 1908 until the 1930s. They quickly earned a reputation for producing fine quality composition dolls and were soon supplying doll parts to other manufacturers. Advertisements for the company included the slogan "We sell

Acme Composition Value Comparison				
Size	Painted Eye, Mama	Glass Eye, Mama	Child	Lady
14"	300.00	350.00	450.00	
16"	350.00	375.00		
18"	400.00	450.00	600.00	
24"		500.00		
27"				900.00

Aetna Doll Company

Between 1901 and 1925, the small Brooklyn, New York based company, Aetna, changed doll-manufacturing history. In 1909, Aetna purchased The First American Doll Factory (also known, and doing business as "Goldstein & Hoffman" and "The Hoffman Co." and "American Doll and

Toy Company"—all one and the same owned by Saloman D. Hoffman). The significance of the merger is composition. In 1892, Saloman D. Hoffman, a Russian citizen, obtained the U. S. patent for "Can't Break Em" composition. When Aetna acquired The First American Doll Factory, they also acquired

Aetna's all-composition doll made for Horsman. Courtesy of McMaster's Doll Auction

Hoffman's secret process for making composition doll heads. About this same time, Aetna entered a binding contract with E. I. Horsman and Company. Horsman became the sole recipient of Aetna dolls in exchange for their guaranteed commitment to purchase 4,000 doll heads a day. This business agreement continued until Horsman and Aetna merged in 1925.

Prices listed are for appropriately costumed dolls in good condition. Slight crazing is acceptable and does not greatly affect the price. If badly crazed, cracked, peeling, or repainted, expect to pay less than half the amounts listed.

Early Marked Dolls: composition socket or shoulder head; composition or cloth body; molded and painted hair or good wig; painted or sleep eyes; closed mouth; appropriately dressed; typically marked "F. A. D. F." or "E. I. H © A. D. Co."

Aetna Doll Co. Value Comparison		
Size	**All Composition Character**	**Cloth-Bodied Baby**
10"		300.00
15"		500.00
17"	800.00	575.00

Aich, Menzel & Co.

A ich, Bohemia, later to become Czechoslovakia, was the home of Aich, Menzel & Co., once known as Porzellanfabrik Aich. Founded by A. C. Anger in 1848, Aich, Menzel and Co. continued operations until 1930.

The limited information and existing records account for part of the confusion concerning this particular porcelain factory. Documents confirm that by the late 1800s, M. J. Moehling was the owner. In 1918, the first year that doll heads were made, the firm officially became Aich, Menzel & Co.

Over the years, the porcelain factory continued to change owners and partners, however, the characteristics of their dolly-faced dolls remained consistent.

Even the most experienced collectors often incorrectly interpret the marks on Menzel dolls. The "AeM Austria" or "A&M Austria" is mistakenly referred to as Austria's AM or Armand Marseille. It must be pointed out that Armand Marseille has no ampersand between his first and last name, and that his porcelain factory was in Germany not Austria.

To further complicate identification, many dolls are found bearing a 1904 mark. The 1904 mark is only a mold number, not the year of manufacture, since dolls were not produced until after 1918. Another mark frequently found is "Eduardo Juan." It has been suggested that this may have been for Eduard Wolf, one of the many owners.

Prices listed are for appropriately dressed dolls in good condition. Normal wear, slight damage, or well-made repairs to the body do not greatly affect the price. If the bisque is damaged or

Dolly-Face bisque doll by Aich Menzel. Courtesy of McMaster's Doll Auction

repaired, expect the value to be less than half the amounts listed. It is perfectly acceptable to show a missing or repaired finger or a mended body.

Dolly-Face: bisque socket head; jointed composition body; good wig; glass eyes; painted lashes; stenciled or single stroke brows; open mouth; appropriately dressed; typically marked "1904 AeM/Made in Austria" or "Eduardo Juan/Made in Austria."

Aich, Menzel & Co. Value Comparison	
Size	Dolly-Face*
14"	400.00
20"	450.00
24"	550.00

* Add an additional $150.00 for an exceptionally pretty face with soft coloring and feathered brows.

Alexander Doll Company

The Alexander Doll Company was founded in 1923 by Beatrice Alexander Behman and her sisters Rose Alexander Schrecking, Florence Alexander Rapport, and Jean Alexander Disick. The Alexander sisters, daughters of Maurice and Hannah Alexander–the owners and operators of the first doll hospital in the United States–had been raised to appreciate beauty along with a love of dolls. It was through the ambition and creativity of Beatrice that the company grew into the giant doll manufacturer it has become.

Originally sold in their father's shop, the first dolls were made of cloth and had flat faces. Molded faces with painted features soon replaced these earlier renditions.

In 1929, a high quality line of dolls appeared in the trade catalogs advertised as "Madame Alexander." The following year the Alexander sisters expanded this new line, now commonly known as "Madame Alexander Dolls."

Madame Alexander Dolls must be preserved in their original costumes, for herein lies the individuality of the doll. While over 6,500 different Madame Alexander personality dolls were introduced, a relatively small number of faces were developed. It is essential to have the original costume and/or wrist tag in order to identify the doll.

Alexander Doll Company's reputation for high quality has earned the respect of doll lovers of all ages. The dolls are outfitted in exquisitely trimmed silks, velvets, satins, and other fine fabrics, with beautiful accessories completing the costume.

In 1988, the still active, 93-year-old Madame Alexander sold the company to Jeff Chodorow and Ira Smith, both attorneys and business men. The Alexander Doll Company changed ownership again in 1995 when it was acquired by The Kalzen Breakthrough Partnership, a private capital fund managed by Gefinor Acquisition Partners.

The Alexander Doll Company continues to produce quality dolls, albeit in larger quantities than in the past. Although Madame Alexander (Beatrice) has passed away, her endless reservoir of creativity provides the company with a vast supply of beautiful creations from which to draw in the future.

In the early years of hard plastic (late 1940s), a common factory was used by Alexander Doll Company, American Character Doll Company and Arranbee Doll Company. This factory produced the same body and limb molds, and very similar faces, for all three companies. Though not reproductions, they are very similar. Special attention must be given to authentacating a Madame Alexander doll. No marked reproduction dolls, tags, or labels are known to exist.

When purchasing a Madame Alexander Doll look carefully and critically at the condition. Check for a nice bright color on the face as well as even, unblotched coloring on the body. Pay particular attention to areas adorned with jewelry, as contact occasionally resulted in stains to the body. Determine if the hair retains its original set. Clothing should be original and in excellent condition. Check body and head seams for splitting, often a result of the dolls being strung too tightly. Cissy dolls tend to crack at the leg seams and below the ears. Lissy tends to crack around the ears.

Prices listed are for originally costumed dolls in good condition.

Early Madame Alexander cloth "David Copperfield" and "Pip." Courtesy of McMaster's Doll Auction

Cloth

Prices listed are for appropriately costumed dolls with good color and little or no fading. Slight wear and signs of aging such as a settled body do not greatly affect the price. If a doll is stained, torn, badly mended, or faded, expect the value to be less than half the amounts listed.

Early cloth: 7", 9", 10", 12", 13", 14", 16", 18", 20", 22", 24", and 30"; flat or molded face socket head; pink cloth body; log-type legs (no shape or joint seams); slightly bent arms; mohair wig; painted, side-glancing eyes; white highlights; red eye-corner dots; single stroke brows, high on face give a startled look; round, apple-cheek blush; closed heart-shaped mouth; costumes primarily cotton with one-piece organdy undergarments; typically unmarked; clothing tag with character name/"MADAME ALEXANDER/NEW YORK USA," gold octagon wrist tag with "character name/ALEXANDER DOLL COMPANY."

Examples of early cloth dolls introduced are: Red Riding Hood, Tippit Toe, Pitty Pat, Grace Alice, Laughing Allegra, Edith With Golden Hair, Hiawatha, McGuffey Ann, Dickens Characters, Playmates, Cherub Babies, Little Women, Susie Q., Bobbie Q., Little Shaver, Bell & Beau Brummel, Goldilocks, Alexander Rag Time, So-Lite, Country Cousins, Dionne Quintuplets, Cuddly, Evangeline, Priscilla, Tweedle-Dum, Tweedle-Dee, Doris Keane, Little Lord Fauntleroy, Baby Genius, Baby Blue Boy, Pinky, and others.

Modern Cloth: 12" and 14"; stitched facial features; typically marked with cloth label "MADAME ALEXANDER/N.Y.N.Y."; clothing tag "MADAME ALEXANDER"; booklet-type wrist tag.

Examples of modern cloth dolls introduced are: Pechity Pam, Funny, Muffin, Pechity Pepper, Good Little Girl, and Carrot Top.

21" Madame Alexander composition Sonja Henie with original box. Courtesy of McMaster's Doll Auctions

the price. If badly crazed, cracked, peeling, or repainted, expect the value to be less than half the amounts listed.

Tiny Betty Face Doll: 7" and 8" one-piece, composition body and head; mohair wig; painted, side-glancing eyes; light peach blush; very-red, closed, heart-shaped mouth; painted-on, black shoes and white socks. Typically marked "MmE. ALEXANDER" or "WENDY ANN"; clothing tag with character name "MADAME ALEXANDER/NEW YORK USA"; gold, octagon wrist tag with character name "ALEXANDER DOLL CO."

Examples of the more than eighty Tiny Betty dolls introduced are: Bo Peep, Cinderella, Carmen, McGuffey Ana, Bride Belgium, Pan American, Heidi, Ding Dong Dell, Little Women, and Topsy-Turvy.

Little Betty Face Doll: 9" and 11"; all composition; jointed at neck, shoulder, and hip; molded hair or wig; painted side-glancing eyes; light pink blush; closed, bow-shaped mouth; typically marked "MmE. ALEXNADER NEW YORK"; clothing tag with character name "MADAME ALEXANDER/NEW YORK USA"; gold, octagon wrist tag with character name "ALEXANDER DOLL CO. N.Y./USA."

Examples of the more than fifty Little Betty dolls introduced are: Hansel and Gretel, Virginia Dare, Dill Dolly Sally, Bridesmaid, Swiss, Princess Elizabeth, Red Cross Nurse, Bo Peep, McGuffey Ana Peasant, and Little Colonel.

Betty Face Doll: 13", 17", and 22", all composition; jointed at neck, shoulder, and hip; mohair wig; tin or glassene sleep eyes; painted upper and lower or only lower lashes; light pink blush; distinguishing tiny dimples on each side of closed, bow-shaped mouth; typically unmarked; clothing tag with character name/"Madame Alexander/New York," rectangle or octagon wrist tag with character name/"Created by Madame Alexander/New York New York."

Examples of the more than thirty Betty dolls introduced are: Little Colonel, Little Betty, Nurse Leroux (Yvonne Leroux was the nurse for the Dionne Quintuplets and later made promotional tours for the Alexander Doll Company), and Princess Elizabeth.

Wendy Ann Face Doll: 11", 13", 18", and 21"; all composition; jointed at neck, shoulder, and hip; may have swivel waist; slightly round face; molded hair or wig; painted or sleep eyes; light pink blush; closed mouth shows less of a smile; typically marked "WENDY ANN" or "WENDY ANN/MmE. ALEXANDER"; clothing tag with character name "MADAME ALEXANDER/NEW YORK USA"; or a green foil, clover-shaped wrist tag with "WENDY ANN/ALEXANDER DOLL CO." and occasionally the character name. **Note:** *An extensive wardrobe could be purchased separately.*

Examples of the more than fifty-five Wendy Ann dolls introduced are: Queen Alexanderine, Carmen, W.A.V.E., Annie Laurie, Little Lord Fauntleroy, Mary Louise, Mother and Me, Dickens Characters, Suellen Sally, Rosetta, Fairy Queen, Princess, and Little Women. **Note:** *Add an additional $300.00 for Scarlett O'Hara (also spelled Scarlet) and Sonja Henie dolls.*

Alexander Cloth Value Comparisons

Size	Vintage Cloth	Modern Cloth
7"	550.00	
10"	525.00	
12"	550.00	75.00
14"	600.00	85.00
16"	700.00	
18"	725.00	
20"	750.00	
24"	900.00	
30"	1,600.00	

Composition

Prices listed are for appropriately costumed dolls in good condition. Slight crazing is acceptable and does not greatly affect

7" and 10" Alexander's composition Dionne Quintuplets. The 10" Cecile is missing her green embroidered bib. Courtesy of David Cobb's Doll Auctions

Princess Elizabeth Face Doll: 13", 14", 15", 16", 17", 21", 24", and 27"; all composition; jointed at neck, shoulder, and hip; round face; mohair or human hair wig; tin or glassene sleep eyes; open, slightly-smiling mouth with inset upper teeth and felt tongue; typically marked "PRINCESS ELIZABETH/ALEXANDER DOLL CO."; clothing tag with character name "MADAME ALEXANDER NY/USA RIGHT RESERVE"; gold, octagon wrist tag with character name/"ALEXANDER DOLL CO. NY." **Note:** *Some 13" and 17" closed-mouth Princess Elizabeth dolls used the Betty face.*

Examples of the many Princess Elizabeth dolls introduced are: Snow White, Kate Greenaway, McGuffey Ana, Miss Victoria, Margaret Rose, Girl Scout, Flora McFlimsy, Cinderella, and Princess Elizabeth. **Note:** *Add an additional $100.00 for Flora McFlimsy with red hair and freckles.*

Margaret Face Doll: 14", 18", and 21"; all composition; jointed at neck, shoulder, and hip; mohair or human hair wig; single-stroke brows lower on face give a shy look; oval sleep eyes; real upper, and painted lower lashes; small turned-up nose; wider, barely smiling mouth; typically marked "ALEXANDER"; clothing tag with character name "Madame Alexander NY/USA"; green foil, clover-shaped wrist tag with "ALEXANDER DOLL CO. N.Y. U.S.A." and occasionally character name.

Examples of the many Margaret dolls introduced are: Margaret O'Brien, Karen the Ballerina, Alice in Wonderland, and Hulda. **Note:** *Add an additional $500.00 for Hulda doll.*

Character Baby Face Doll: 11", 12", 15", 19", 21", 23", and 24"; all composition; five-piece bent limb baby body or cloth body with composition head and limbs; molded and painted hair or fine mohair wig; sleep or painted eyes; open or closed mouth; clothing tag with baby's name/"MADAME ALEXANDER NEW YORK U.S.A."; gold octagon wrist tag with baby's name/

Size	Betty*	Wendy Ann*	Princess Elizabeth*	Margaret*	Character Baby*	Dionne Quints	Jane Withers	Jeannie Walker	Sonja Henie	Marionette
7"	350.00									
7 1/2"	400.00					400.00				
8"	425.00									300.00
9"	400.00									
10"						525.00				325.00
11"	450.00	475.00			350.00					
12"										350.00
13"	550.00	575.00	550.00				1,200.00			
14"			750.00	1200.00		750.00		850.00		
15"			600.00		425.00	800.00	1,500.00		900.00	
16"			650.00							
17"	600.00		675.00			600.00	1,700.00			
18"		700.00		1,700.00					1,200.00	1,200.00	
19"					500.00	900.00				
20"							1,900.00			
21"		1,800.00	800.00	1,900.00	525.00				1,600.00	
22"	700.00									
23"					550.00	800.00				
24"			900.00		600.00					
27"			1,300.00							

Alexander Composition Value Comparisons

* The more famous characters and elaborately-costumed dolls will command higher prices.

"ALEXANDER DOLL CO. NEW YORK USA" or green foil, clover-shaped wrist tag with "ALEXANDER DOLL CO. NEW YORK USA."

Examples of the many Character Babies introduced are: Princess Alexander, Precious, Little Genius, Cookie, McGuffey Ana, Slumbermate, Genius Baby, and Kitty Baby. ***Note:*** *Add an additional $50.00 for Pinky Baby doll.*

Individual Personalities

Occasionally, a personality was so popular that it merited its own face. Dolls that fall into this catagory include:

Dionne Quintuplets: 7 1/2", 10 1/2", 14", 17", 19", and 23 1/2", all composition; toddler body or cloth body with composition head and limbs; molded and painted hair or wig; typically marked "Dionne" and/or the individual name, "Dionne Alex," "Alexander," and possibly others. ***Note:*** *Ferris wheel, crib, bed, basket, swing, high chair, chair, and "Quintmobile" were also available. Accessories had the quintuplet's name and her particular color: Annette, yellow; Cecile, green; Emelle, lavender; Marie, blue; and Yvonne, pink.*

Dr. Dafoe: 14", Dionne Quintuplets doctor; cloth, chubby body; composition limbs; swivel composition head and shoulder plane; gray, mohair wig; painted blue eyes with upper lashes only; smiling mouth; chin dimple; typically unmarked; white jumpsuit and doctor's coat; tagged "DR. DAFOE/MmE. ALEXANDER"; gold octagon Dr. Dafoe wrist tag. $1,800.00

Minister: Dr. Dafoe body and face; identified by clothing and/or wrist tag. $1,200.00

Priest: Dr. Dafoe body and face; identified by clothing and/or wrist tag. $1,300.00

Baby Jane: 16", named for child star Juanita Quigley; all composition; jointed at neck, shoulder, and hip; chubby cheeks; brown, human-hair wig; brown sleep eyes; long, painted upper and lower lashes; open, smiling mouth with four teeth, felt tongue; typically marked "BABY JANE/ALEXANDER"; clothing tag "BABY JANE/MmE. ALEXANDER." ... $1,200.00

Jane Withers: 13", 15", 17", and 20" child star of radio and films; all composition; jointed at neck, shoulder, and hip, or cloth body with composition head and limbs; mohair wig; sleep eyes; long, painted upper and lower lashes; closed or open smiling mouth with four teeth, felt tongue; typically marked "JANE WITHERS/ALEX DOLL CO."; clothing tag "JANE WITHERS/ALL RIGHTS RESERVED MADAME ALEXANDER"; gold script name pin.

Jeannie Walker: 14" and 18"; all composition; jointed body; advertised as "able to sit in lady like fashion"; wooden walking mechanism, worked by pulley and levers, first of its kind in the U.S.; oval-shaped face; human hair wig; sleep eyes; closed, puckered mouth; typically marked "ALEXANDER DOLL CO./PAT NO. 2171271"; clothing tag "JEANNIE WALKER/MADAME ALEXANDER NY USA."

Sonja Henie: 15", 18" and 21", named for three-time Olympic gold-medallist and film star; all composition; body may have swivel waist, less curved arms, jointed at neck, shoulder, and hip; round faces; blond mohair wig; sleep eyes; real eyelashes with dark eye shadow; dimples; open mouth with four teeth; typically marked "SONJA HENIE/MADAME ALEXANDER." Clothing tag "SONIA HENIE MmM ALEXANDER/ALL RIGHTS RESERVED N.Y. U.S.A."; wrist tag with picture of Sonja Henie. ***Note:*** *The registration for Sonja Henie dolls reads "to be dressed in elaborate skating costumes in assorted styled, skates attached to high skate shoes." Some smaller, closed-mouth Sonja Henie dolls used the Wendy Ann face.*

Marionettes: 8", 10", and 12" composition character face, torso, and lower limbs; connected by cloth joints; typically marked "Tony Sarg/Alexander" on back and "Tony Sarg" on head; clothing tag "Madame Alexander" or may include character name. Tony Sarg designed and endorsed the marionettes including a special series commissioned for Walt Disney's Silly Symphonies and Snow White.

Examples of the more than forty marionettes introduced are: Hansel, Gretel, Witch, Red Riding Hood, Gretchen, Mr. Archibald, Gnome, Sambo, Ring Master, Ballet Dancer, Alice, Tweedle Dum, and Tweedle Dee. ***Note:*** *Marionettes marked "Walt Disney's Marionettes" can easily demand two to three times the values given.*

Hard Plastic

Health regulations of the 1950s forbade the use of human hair wigs. Saran (a filter that could have a permanent set baked in) and nylon (which could be washed and set) were viable alternatives. Original costumes included a gold medallion necklace, boasting the Gold Medal for Fashion Award presented to Alexander Doll Company for the years 1951, 1952, and 1953.

Prices listed are for dolls in near-mint, original condition. If damaged, redressed, or undressed, expect the value to be less than one half to one fourth the amounts listed.

Margaret (O'Brien) Face Doll: the bridge doll used the same mold for both composition and hard plastic. 14", 18", and 22" all hard plastic; jointed at the neck, shoulder, and hip; mohair, floss, human hair, saran, or nylon wig; single-stroke brows lower on the face give a shy look; sleep eyes with real upper and painted lower lashes; pert, little nose; slightly smiling mouth; typically marked "ALEXANDER"; clothing tag with character name.

Examples of the more than fifty-five Margaret face dolls introduced are: Alice in Wonderland, Snow White, Story Princess, Cinderella, Majorette, Peter Pan, Little Women, Prince Charming, Me and My Shadow—an 18" portrait doll with a 7 1/2" matching miniature, which must have matching tags and

Hard plastic Alexander-Kins "Spring Holiday" and "Shopping with Auntie." Courtesy of McMaster's Doll Auction

labels—Renoir, Lady and Winston Churchill, Margot, Karen the Ballerina, Little Men, Century of Fashion, Civil War, Hedy Lamar, and Glamour Girls. *Note: Godey, Renoir, Victoria, Queen Elizabeth, and Me and My Shadow Series can easily command twice the values given. Add an additional $200.00 for black version Cynthia.*

Maggie Face Doll: 15", 18", and 23" all hard plastic; jointed at neck, shoulder, and hip; round faced young child; mohair, floss, human hair, saran, or nylon wig; single-stroke brows, higher on face give a wide-awake look; pug nose; closed, non-smiling, puckered mouth; advertised as "she walks when you lead her by the hand." After the mid-1950s, the phrase "and moves her head from side to side" was added. Typically marked "ALEXANDER"; clothing tag character name/"ALEX-ANDER N.Y., N.Y." *Note: In the 1950s, the Maggie face was used only for the Little Women series.*

Examples of the more than thirty Maggie faced dolls introduced are: Kathy, Garden Party, Picnic Day, Cherie, Alice in Wonderland, Beau Art Dolls, Little Men, Glamour Girls, Me and My Shadow, Betty, Maggie, Teenager, Evening Gown, Victorian, and Century of Fashion. *Note: Me and My Shadow Series, Century of Fashion, and Glamour Girls can easily command twice the values given.*

Mary Ellen: 31"; all hard plastic; walker body; jointed at neck, shoulder, hip, elbows, and knees; pretty teenage, oval-shaped face; rooted nylon hair; single-stroke brows lower on the face; pert nose; pink blush lower on cheeks; wider smiling mouth; typically marked "MME ALEXANDER."

Wendy-Ann/Wendy/Wendy-Kins/Alexander-Kins and Billy (the boy): 7" to 8"; made continuously for the past forty years; molded and named for Madame Alexander's grandchildren, William and Wendy Ann. When the real Wendy Ann passed away in 1955, Ann was dropped from the doll's name. All have chubby round faces with thin chins; single-stroke brows; sleep eyes with molded upper, and painted lower lashes; small, closed, unsmiling, almost pouty mouth; synthetic wigs; typically unmarked or marked "ALEX," after 1976 "ALEXANDER"; clothing tag "ALEXANDER-KINS," character name/"BY MADAME ALEXANDER REG U. S. PAT. OFF NY NY," or Character name/"MADAME ALEXANDER/ALL RIGHTS RESERVED NEW YORK USA."

Hundreds of personalities have been introduced. Location, rarity, appeal, and demand all help direct the ever-fluctuating doll market. Most of the demure little Alexander-Kins will fall within the following chart, however, there are rare and desirable paragons that have a greater value. *Note: Baby Clown, Little Minister, Parlor Maid, Indian Girl, Agatha, Aunt Pitty Pat, Cousin Grace, Easter Wendy, Little Madeline, Little Victoria, My Shadow, Prince Charles, Princess Ann, Wendy in Easter Egg, and the Bible Characters can easily command two to three times the values given.*

Very rare 1961 Lissy Cissy. Courtesy Frasher's Auctions

Madeline: 18", hard plastic; body jointed at neck, shoulder, elbows, wrist, hip, and knees; vinyl head; rooted nylon or saran hair; single-stroke brows; sleep eyes; light dimples; open/closed, smiling mouth; typically marked "ALEXANDER."

Penny/Barbara Jane: 29", 34", and 42"; soft cloth body; vinyl stuffed head, legs, and straight arms; advertised as "made to appeal to boarding-school and college girls"; happy, chubby cheek, longer-shaped face; synthetic "Newtar" saran wig; single-stroke, very pale brows lower on the face; sleep or painted eyes; turned up nose; wide smiling mouth; typically marked "ALEX-ANDER."

Cissy Face Dolls (Winnie and Binnie Walker): 15", 18", 20/21", and 23/25"; introduced in 1953 as Winnie Walker with walker child body, and in 1954 as Binnie Walker. Cissy was introduced in 1955 using the Winnie and Binnie face with an adult figure; high heel feet; jointed elbows, vinyl-over-hard-plastic arms on a walker body.

The flat-footed Winnie and Binnie walkers are identified by their hairstyle. Winnie had a glued-wig with a feather cut, combed in all directions. Binnie's hair is rooted to a vinyl skull-cap with bangs. Identical square-shaped face; brows slightly raised; oval sleep eyes with real upper, and painted lower lashes;

Wendy/Alexander-Kins Value Comparisons

Date	Body Type	Body Color	Eyes	Mouth	Current Est. Value
1953	Straight legs, non walker	Tannish	Oval sleep	Dark red	550.00
1954	Straight legs, walker	Tannish, slightly shiny	Oval sleep	Dark red	500.00
1955	Slightly bent legs, walker body	Tannish, shiny bisque look	Oval sleep	Red	400.00
1956	Jointed knees, walkers with turning heads	Pink	Very oval sleep	Dark pink	300.00
1965	Slightly bent or jointed knees, non-walker	Soft pink	Oval sleep	Dark pink	350.00
1974*	Straight legs, jointed above knees	Very matte finish	Rounder	Orange mouth, high blush	250.00
1982	Straight leg	Matte pale pink	Very round	Dark pink pinched	65.00

* In 1974, a new series was introduced called "United States." Tags may have a misspelled "United States," adding an additional $100.00.

Hard Plastic Value Comparisons

Size	Margaret*	Maggie*	Mary Ellen	Madeline*	Penny*	Cissy*	Lissy*	Elise*	Cissette*	Maggie Mix-Up
8"										650.00
10"									500.00	
11"							650.00			
14"	1,200.00									
15"		700.00				600.00				
16"								500.00		600.00
18"	1,400.00	900.00		550.00		650.00				
21"						800.00				
23"	1,800.00	1,000.00								
25"						925.00				
29"					500.00					
31"			700.00		600.00					
34"					700.00					

* The more famous characters and elaborately costumed dolls will command higher prices.

straight nose tapers at the bridge; blush lower on the cheek gives a sculptured, almost debutante look; closed, unsmiling mouth. Typically marked "ALEXANDER"; clothing tag "CISSY, WINNIE, BINNIE," or character name. **Note:** *Cissy was produced for nine years. In 1962, Cissy was used only for Queen.*

Examples of the many Cissy faced dolls introduced are: Flora McFlimsey, Agatha, Debutante Series, Mary Louise, Active Miss, Margot Ballerina, Skater's Waltz, and Princess. **Note:** *Lady in Red, Godey Portrait, Victoria, Lady Hamilton, Renoir, Gainesborough, Ice Capades Series, or elaborately accessorised costumes can easily command three to four times the values given.*

Two 21" dolls (Shari Lewis and Sleeping Beauty) were released using the Cissy body, but with different faces. They also came in smaller sizes, on different bodies.

Shari Lewis: 21" hard plastic and vinyl body; jointed at shoulder, elbows, hip, and knees; high heel feet; heart-shaped face; synthetic, dark blond pony tail; feathered brows; blue, sleep eyes; real upper, painted lower lashes; very, very turned-up nose; pierced ears; closed, unsmiling full mouth; typically marked "MmE 19©58 ALEXANDER." $1,000.00

Sleeping Beauty: 21" hard plastic and vinyl body; jointed at shoulder, elbows, hip, and knees; high heel feet; beautiful round-shaped face; synthetic, very blond wig; lightly feathered and shaped brows; blue, sleep eyes; real upper, painted lower lashes; original satin gown trimmed in gold; gold tiara with rhinestone stars; gold brocade net floor-length cape; rhinestone necklace and ring. Typically marked "ALEXANDER"; clothing tag "MADAME ALEXANDER PRESENTS WALT DISNEY'S AUTHENTIC SLEEPING BEAUTY." $1,500.00

Lissy Face Doll: 11" hard plastic; medium high heeled feet; small bosom; jointed elbows and knees; round face; advertised as "Sub-Deb" and "Cissy's saucy younger sister"; large oval sleep eyes; real upper, and painted lower lashes; very slight pug nose; blushed cheeky look; closed, unsmiling, slightly puckered mouth; typically unmarked; clothing tag with Lissy or character name; booklet-type wrist tags. **Note:** *An extensive wardrobe could be purchased separately.*

Examples of the many Lissy faced dolls introduced are: Ballerina, Bride, Bridesmaid, Little Men, Classic Group, and Cinderella. **Note:** *Katie, Tommy, Southern Belle, McGuffey Ana, or the trouseau sets can easily command twice the values given.*

Elise Face Doll: 16"; hard plastic body with vinyl arms; jointed elbows, knees, and ankles; oval face; single-stroke brows lower on face; oval sleep eyes with real upper, painted lower lashes; pierced ears; closed, unsmiling mouth; typically marked "ALEXANDER" and "MmE ALEXANDER"; clothing tag with "ELISE/MeM ALEXANDER" or character name/"MeM ALEXANDER"; booklet-type wrist tag. An extensive wardrobe could be purchased separately.

Examples of the many Elise faced dolls introduced are: Going Visiting, Bride, Lucy Bride, Bridesmaid, Scarlett O'Hara, Ball Gown, Queen, and Renoir. Another doll introduced using the Elise body, but with her own face, was Sleeping Beauty. (The 21" Sleeping Beauty used the Cissy body.)

Sleeping Beauty: 16"; hard plastic, fully-jointed body; beautiful round face; very blond, synthetic wig; lightly feathered brows; blue, sleep eyes with real upper, and painted lower lashes; straight nose; very full, wide, slightly-smiling mouth; original satin gown trimmed in gold; gold tiara with rhinestone stars; gold brocade net floor length cape; rhinestone necklace and ring; typically marked "ALEXANDER"; clothing tag "MADAME ALEXANDER PRESENTS WALT DISNEY'S AUTHENTIC SLEEPING BEAUTY." $1,200.00

Cissette Face Doll: 10" or 11"; all hard plastic; jointed at neck, shoulder, hip, and knees; high heel feet; advertised as "porcelain-like finish"; heart-shaped face with broad forehead, full cheeks, tapering chin; single-stroke brows higher on face, give a wide-eyed look; oval sleep eyes with real upper, painted lower lashes; most with pierced ears; small, pug, turned-up nose; full, very slightly smiling, closed mouth; typically marked "MmM ALEXANDER" or unmarked; clothing tag with character name or "CISSETTE" in turquoise, except blue in 1963; booklet-type wrist tag.

Examples of the many Cissette faced dolls introduced are: Gainsborough, Ballerina, Barbary Coast, Gibson Girl, Liesl & Brigitta, Jenny Lind, Lady Hamilton, Klondike Kate, Margot, Tucker Bell, Portette, Southern Belle, Queen, Gold Rush, Fairy Princess, Godey, and Renoir. **Note:** *Gold Rush, Lady Hamilton, and Klondike Kate can easily command four to five times the values given.*

Maggie Mix-Up: 8" and 17"; 8" all hard plastic body with jointed knees; 17" hard plastic body with vinyl arms, jointed at elbows, knees, and ankles; easily identified by straight, orangish-red hair; freckles; sleep eyes; typically marked "ALEX"; clothing tag "Maggie"; booklet-type wrist tags.

Vinyl

Vinyl came into its own in the late 1950s and continued to be the doll manufacturers' material of choice. Some vinyl trademarks of 1957 were not actually made until 1958.

Prices listed are for dolls in near-mint, original condition. If damaged, redressed, or undressed, expect the value to be less than one half to one fourth the amounts listed.

Kelly Face Doll: 12", 15", 17", and 22" rigid vinyl bodies and limbs; soft vinyl head; fully jointed, including the waist; square-shaped face; rooted, synthetic hair; single-stroke brows lower on face; round sleep eyes with molded lashes; small button nose; open/closed mouth with somewhat down-turned lip; typically marked "MME ALEXANDER" 1958; (same date used in 1958 and 1965); booklet-type wrist tag. *Note: Add an additional $200.00 for "Marybel the Doll That Gets Well" in suitcase with sick child accessories.*

Jacqueline Face Doll: 21", new face with jointed Cissy body. In 1962, White House Press Secretary, Pierre Salinger, requested that the Alexander Doll Company not make reference to the First Lady, Jacqueline Kennedy, in advertising this doll. That year the Jacqueline doll was dropped, but was re-introduced as the Portrait Series in 1965 and continues to be used. Brown, short-rooted hair combed to side; brown, sleep eyes with thick lashes; eyeliner; shaped brows; soft blush on lower cheeks;

closed, smiling mouth; typically marked "ALEXANDER 1961" (1961 remains in marking); booklet-type wrist tag.

Caroline Baby Face Doll: 15"; five-piece, jointed hard plastic body; vinyl-head character baby; rooted, shiny blond hair, parted on side; big blue sleep eyes with lashes; soft single-stroke brows; dimpled, open, smiling mouth; typically marked "ALEXANDER/1961" and "ALEX. 1959/13"; booklet-type wrist tag.

Joanie Face Doll: 36"; hard plastic jointed body; vinyl head; rooted saran hair; big, round, flirty eyes with long curly lashes; single-stroke slanted brows; closed, large smiling mouth; typically marked "ALEXANDER/1959"; booklet-type wrist tag.

Mimi Face Doll: 30"; rigid, hard plastic body jointed in twelve places; soft vinyl head and hands; more grown-up look; rooted hair in various styles, from long curls to short bob cut; almond-shaped, sleep eyes; molded lashes; single-stroke sweeping brows; small, closed unsmiling mouth; typically marked "ALEXANDER/1961"; booklet-type wrist tag.

Smarty Face Doll: 12" hard plastic; jointed, toddler-type, pigeon-toed body; vinyl head; short, rooted hair; oval sleep eyes; molded lashes; single-stroke brows; lightly blushed chubby cheeks; open/closed smiling mouth; typically marked "ALEXANDER/1962"; booklet-type wrist tag. *Note: Add and additional $200.00 for Katie (black version) and $100.00 for Brother (dressed as a boy).*

Janie Face Doll: 12" Smarty body with chubby, character, occasionally-freckled face; round eyes; pugged nose; closed,

Larger-size vinyl Sound of Music. Courtesy of McMaster's Doll Auction

19" Madame Alexander McGuffey Ana with the Princess Elizabeth face. Courtesy of McMaster's Doll Auction

smiling mouth; typically marked "ALEXANDER/1964"; booklet-type wrist tag. **Note:** *Add an additional $100.00 for Lucinda, Rosy, or Suzy (identified by clothing label).*

Melinda Face Doll: 16" and 22"; hard plastic or vinyl body; swivel waist; sweet character face; almost white, rooted hair with full bangs; big, round, sleep eyes; open/closed smiling mouth with two teeth molded in top; typically marked "ALEXANDER/1962"; booklet-type wrist tag.

Brenda Starr (Yolanda): 12"; hard plastic; jointed adult body; Alexander's response to Barbie®, advertised as "long stemmed American Beauty Doll"; blond hair with one long lock on top; sleep eyes; long, molded lashes; crescent-shaped brows higher up on forehead; closed, unsmiling mouth; typically marked "ALEXANDER/1964" and "ALEXANDER."

Polly Face Doll: 17"; all vinyl; jointed at neck, shoulder, and hip; long, thin arms and legs with flat feet; narrow face; rooted, long nylon hair; sleep eyes; closed, smiling mouth; typically marked "ALEXANDER DOLL CO. INC./1965"; clothing tag "Mary Ellen Playmate (Polly)"; booklet-type wrist tag. **Note:** *Add an additional $200.00 for Leslie (black version) and $100.00 if wearing a ring on the right hand (this accessory was included only in 1965, the year Polly was introduced).*

Mary Ann Face Doll: 14"; vinyl head; hard plastic body; jointed at neck, shoulder, and hip; slightly-bent, chubby limbs; rooted nylon hair; sleep eyes with molded upper and painted side and lower lashes; pale complexion with rosy cheeks; closed, slightly-smiling mouth; typically marked "ALEXANDER/19©65"; booklet-type wrist tag.

Coco: 21"; vinyl head and limbs; plastic body; jointed at waist, one piece lower torso with bent right leg; rooted, blond shoulder length hair; dramatic face with full cheeks; pointed chin; dark sleep eyes; blue shadow; black eyeliner; feathered brows; beautiful, original costume; carrying a clear plastic wig box with extra hairpiece, rollers, comb, and hairpins; typically marked "ALEXANDER/1966." **Note:** *Fashioned after Paris designer Coco, this was one of Madame Alexander's finest creations. Patented in 1966 and never used again, she is understandably one of the most desirable and hardest to find modern dolls.*

First Lady Series: 14", Martha or Mary Ann face:
First Series	$700.00
Second Series	400.00
Third Series	350.00
Fourth Series	350.00
Fifth Series	350.00
Sixth Series	350.00

Peter Pan Series:
Michael, 12"	$400.00
Peter Pan, 14"	350.00
Tinker Bell, 10"	450.00
Wendy, 14"	350.00

Sound of Music Series
(all but the Kurt doll are available in two sizes):
Brigitta, 10" or 14"	$200.00
Frederick, 8" or 11"	200.00
Gretl, 8" or 11"	200.00
Kurt, 11" only	400.00
Lisel, 10" or 14"	200.00
Louisa, 10" or 14"	250.00
Maria, 12"	250.00
Maria, 17"	300.00
Martha, 8" or 11"	200.00

Vinyl Value Comparisons

Size	Kelly	Jacqueline*	Portrait*	Caroline	Joanie	Mimi	Smarty	Janie	Melinda	Brenda Starr	Polly	Mary Ann	Coco
12"	300.00						250.00	350.00		350.00			
14"												250.00	
15"	350.00			450.00									
16"									300.00				
17"	550.00										325.00		
21"		800.00	1,200.00										2,700.00
22"	575.00								400.00				
30"						600.00							
36"					500.00								

* The more famous characters and elaborately costumed dolls will command higher prices.

Henri Alexandre

H enri Alexandre, Paris, France, was named for its founder. The doll company, registered in 1888, was in existence for only a few years before being purchased by Tourrell Company, which ultimately merged with Jules Steiner in 1895. Henri Alexandre is best known for designing and registering the line of Phenix Bébés, of which there were thirty models. Phenix Bébés were manufactured for many years, eventually by Jules Steiner. A beautiful, closed mouth doll, often referred to as a H. A. Bébé, was also produced. The company's many mergers account for the confusion that has occurred concerning the maker of the lovely Phenix Bébé and H. A. Bébé.

Prices listed are for appropriately costumed dolls in good condition. Normal wear, slight damage, or well-made repairs to the body do not greatly affect the price. If the bisque is damaged or repaired, expect the value to be less than half the amounts listed. It is perfectly acceptable to show a missing or repaired finger or joint or a mended body.

Closed Mouth H. A. Bébé: bisque socket head; jointed wood-and-composition body; straight wrists; good wig; paperweight eyes; pierced ears; appropriately dressed; marked "H.A. Bébé."

Closed Mouth Phenix Bébé: bisque socket head: jointed wood-and-composition body; straight or jointed wrists; good wig; paperweight eyes; pierced ears; appropriately dressed; marked "Phenix Bébé."

Open Mouth Phenix Bébé: bisque socket head; jointed wood-and-composition body; good wig; paperweight eyes; appropriately dressed; marked "Phenix Bébé."

Alexandre Bébé Value Comparisons

Size	Closed Mouth H. A. Bébé	Closed Mouth Phenix Bébé	Open Mouth Phenix Bébé
10"		2,500.00	
12"	5,500.00	2,800.00	
14"	6,000.00	3,400.00	1,900.00
16"	6,200.00	3,800.00	2,100.00
17"	6,500.00	4,200.00	2,400.00
18"	7,100.00	4,700.00	2,500.00
20"	7,500.00	5,100.00	2,700.00
22"	8,000.00	5,300.00	3,000.00
23 1/2"	8,500.00	5,700.00	3,100.00
25"	10,000.00	6,000.00	3,400.00

17" H. A. Bébé #7 in original costume. Courtesy of David Cobb's Doll Auctions

All Bisque

Bisque, china, parian, and porcelain are all forms of ceramics derived from a clay-based material to which feldspar and flint have been added. This mixture is molded, fired, painted, and fired again. Quality can range from the finest porcelain with beautifully detailed decoration to coarse and crudely painted "stone bisque." Factors determining a doll's quality include: the texture of the porcelain, the artistry applied in decorating the piece, the subject model, and the presence or absence of a glaze.

Reproductions are found at almost every flea market and secondhand shop. When attempting to identify All-Bisque Dolls, first look for markings in the bisque. Most reproductions are marked only with a small, paper label that is easily removed. Many older German and Japanese dolls are marked in the middle of the back, on the head, or at the crotch with a number or the country of origin. Early bisque dolls may have numbers incised on the limbs at the joints. If the arms or legs are separate, gently pull one away from the body. Does it look old? Arms on reproductions are often attached with aluminum wire, which frequently has been made to look old. The aluminum can leave telltale signs of gray at the opening. Most French All-Bisque

Dolls are unmarked. However, their superior quality helps to differentiate an authentic example from a reproduction.

Prices listed are for appropriately costumed dolls in good condition. Normal wear, such as slight rubs or minute flakes at

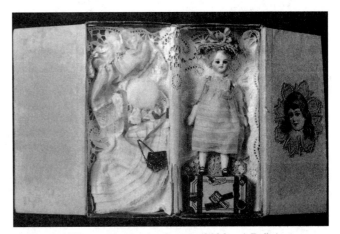

French All-Bisque with accessories. Courtesy of McMaster's Doll Auction

French All-Bisque Value Comparisons

Size	Kid-lined jointed body, molded shoes, thin legs, glass eyes	Kid-lined jointed body, extra joints at elbows, glass eyes	Kid-lined jointed body, extra joints at elbows and knees, glass eyes	Kid-lined jointed body, wrestler-type legs, glass eyes	S.F.B.J., Unis, or later dolls	Painted eyes
4"						750.00
5"	1,900.00	3,000.00		2,300.00		800.00
6"	2,500.00	3,500.00	4,200.00		700.00	1,000.00
7"	3,600.00	4,000.00	5,000.00	2,800.00	800.00	1,100.00
8"	5,200.00	5,000.00	6,100.00	3,100.00	900.00	1,200.00
9"	5,500.00	6,500.00	6,800.00	3,700.00	950.00	1,500.00
10"	5,900.00		7,200.00		1,000.00	1,700.00
11"						1,900.00
12"					1,200.00	2,200.00

Add an additional $500.00 for molded bare feet.

the joint openings, does not greatly affect the price. If chipped, cracked, broken, or repaired, expect the value to be much less. The value of a damaged All-Bisque Doll should directly reflect the degree of damage.

Also see Kewpie.

French

The lovely, little French All-Bisque Dolls are extremely desirable and very costly. Most are unmarked, making positive identification difficult. They are made from excellent quality bisque, which appears smooth and delicate. A unique "French Loop" or "Bell Top," a molded loop found at the base of the neck, enabled the head to be strung to the body. The dolls are jointed at neck, shoulder, and hip, occasionally elbows and/or knees. Limbs are connected by tiny wooden pegs, wire, or elastic, and they're lined with kid. Most have slender legs and barefoot or painted shoes and/or socks. Some have wrestler-type legs, which are very wide at the top and thin at the ankle. Although some French All-Bisque Dolls have painted eyes, most have glass eyes. Facial decoration is outstanding, with beautifully feathered brows; long eyelashes; solid dome or cork pate and good wig; closed mouth.

German

German bisque quality can range from outstanding to quite poor. Extremely popular dolls may be modeled as flappers, babies, comic characters, or huminals (dolls having both human and animal characteristics).

Sizes range from less than one inch to well over a foot, the most common being in the 4" to 8" size. Many dolls are found with the head and body as one piece. If the head is a swivel neck, it may be attached to the body with a small, wooden neck plug, or the neck may be molded with holes on either side and strung with elastic. The German dolls have molded and painted hair or a mohair wig; painted or glass eyes; open or closed mouth. They are typically marked "Germany," mold or size number or paper label on chest.

The many types of All-Bisque Dolls can make categorization staggering. Most, however, fall into the groups shown. Pay close attention to detail when evaluating a doll, as condition and fineness of decoration are extremely important.

Group of All-Bisque, including from top: 10" #134 German with closed mouth and glass eyes; 9" unmarked French-type with closed mouth and paperweight eyes; 9" & 10" #102 German with open mouth and glass eyes; 9" Gebrüder Heubach #10499 with closed mouth and intaglio eyes; 6" #620 German with closed mouth and painted eyes; 8" unmarked German with molded hair bows, closed mouth, and painted eyes; 6" Bonnie Baby with open mouth and glass eyes; 5" Baby Bo-Kaye with stomach label; 4" Happifat; 6" Kestner #130 with closed mouth and glass eyes; 7" original olive bisque oriental with slanted glass eyes and queue; 4" original olive bisque oriental with slanted, painted eyes and queue. Courtesy of David Cobb's Doll Auctions

German All-Bisque Value Comparisons

Size	Painted Eyes, Molded Clothes	Painted Eyes, Stationary Neck, Jointed Arms, Jointed or Stationary Hips*	Glass Eyes, Stationary Neck, Jointed Hip and Arms	Glass Eyes, Jointed Neck, Hip, and Arms	Glass Eyes, Jointed Neck, Hip, and Arms, Molded Bare Feet	Extraordinary Appeal, Glass Eyes, Fine Decoration, May Have Joints at Waist or Knees
1 1/2"	75.00	100.00				
2"	75.00	125.00	300.00	350.00		
3"	150.00	175.00	325.00	375.00		
4"	200.00	225.00	350.00	450.00		
5"	225.00	250.00	375.00	550.00	2,400.00	3,500.00
6"	250.00	300.00	425.00	650.00		4,200.00
7"	300.00	325.00	475.00	850.00		4,600.00
7 1/2"	325.00	350.00	525.00	1,000.00		5,000.00
8"	350.00	450.00	600.00	1,200.00	3,700.00	5,500.00
9"	425.00	500.00	850.00	1,300.00		6,200.00
10"	500.00	575.00	1,200.00	1,500.00	4,600.00	7,000.00
11"		625.00	1,400.00	1,800.00		
12"		700.00	1,600.00	1,900.00		

*Add an additional $100.00–200.00 for swivel neck.

All-Bisque Character Babies Value Comparisons

Size	Baby Bo-Kaye	Bonnie Baby	Bye-Lo, Glass Eyes	Bye-Lo, Painted Eyes	Didi, Mimi, Veve, Fefe, Glass Eyes	Didi, Mimi, Veve, Fefe, Painted Eyes	Little Annie Roomie
4"							350.00
5"	1,700.00	1,200.00	725.00	450.00	1,900.00	1,200.00	
6"	2,200.00		900.00	550.00	2,100.00	1,400.00	
7"		1,400.00				1,700.00	
8"	3,500.00	1,500.00	1,250.00	800.00			

All-Bisque Character Babies Value Comparisons

Size	HeBee, SheBee	Max, Moritz	Mibs, Baby Peggy	Scootles or Our Fairy	Sonny, Glass Eyes	Sonny, Painted Eyes
4"	700.00	1,900.00	450.00	750.00		
5"	750.00	2,400.00	500.00			
6"	850.00		625.00		3,100.00	925.00
7"	1,000.00			1,200.00	3,500.00	1,250.00
9"	2,000.00			2,000.00		

All-Bisque Googly-Eyed Value Comparisons

Size	879 Crawling Baby, Painted Eyes	218, 222, 217 Glass Eyes, Elaborate regional costume	292, 189 Glass Eyes	899 Round Face Painted Eyes Top Knot	897 Painted Eyes	320 Glass Eyes	Sad Mouth	65 Glass Eyes
4"			900.00				700.00	500.00
5"	600.00	900.00	1,400.00		800.00	1,200.00		
6"		1,300.00						
7"		1,400.00	2,900.00	3,500.00				

Add an additional $1,500.00 to any all bisque Googly with jointed elbows and knees.

Babies and Characters

A few character dolls stand out as being very desirable, usually because of the "character" portrayed, rather than superior quality. While purest collectors assign value to quality of artistry, the popularity of these dolls cannot be disputed.

Baby Bo-Kaye: swivel neck; glass eyes; typically marked with paper label.

Bonnie Baby: swivel neck; glass eyes; very distinctive character face; molded teeth; typically marked with paper label.

Bye-Lo: typical Bye-Lo face; glass or painted eyes; typically marked with paper label or "Germany."

Didi, Mimi, Veve, Fefe: open/closed mouth; molded teeth; glass or painted eyes; typically marked with paper label or Orsini.

Hebee and Shebee: cute, oversized face; molded clothes and shoes with holes for ribbons.

Max (123) and Moritz (124): 5"; very distinctive character smiling face; typically marked "K ★ R."

Mibs, Baby Peggy, L. Amberg: sweet character face; typically marked "1921," or with paper label.

Our Fairy #222: swivel neck; glass, side-glancing eyes; open/closed mouth with painted upper teeth; paper label.

Sonny: swivel neck; glass or painted eyes; round open/closed mouth; bare feet; typically marked with paper label.

Scootles: jointed shoulder and hip; molded wavy hair; painted, side-glancing eyes; closed, smiling mouth; typically marked "Germany."

Little Annie Rooney: jointed shoulders or no joints; yarn-braided wig; molded and painted dress and jacket; big eyes; wide, smiling, closed mouth; typically marked "Germany."

Googly Eyed: jointed shoulder and perhaps hip and neck; molded and painted hair or mohair wig; painted or glass eyes; closed mouth; typically marked "Germany" or a mold number.

Frozen Charlotte

The various German porcelain factories that made these figurines called them "Nacktfrosch" or "Naked Baby." The names Charlotte and Charlie are believed spawned from "Young Charlotte," a popular 1860s ballad.

Small Frozen Charlottes and Frozen Charlies were baked into birthday cakes as prizes. Larger 4" to 5" dolls were placed in fine china cups to absorb the heat and prevent the cup from cracking. Divers searching for the Titanic wreckage knew they were in the right location when they saw a Frozen Charlie looking up at them from the bottom of the sea.

Frozen Charlottes. Courtesy of David Cobb's Doll Auctions

During the 1970s, German-made, 15" Frozen Charlie reproductions flooded the market. The well-made reproductions have no permanent markings. Some, but not all, have a hole between their legs large enough to insert a pencil point. Another indication of age is a very clean slip. Most old bisque dolls have peppering, or tiny black specks, in the slip.

Frozen Charlotte and Frozen Charlie: glazed or unglazed; solid, one-piece body, distinctive, bent arms; straight legs separated to knees; molded and painted hair; delicate facial features; undressed or rare molded clothing, hats, and/or boots; typically marked "Germany," mold number, or unmarked.

Later Examples

The later examples were popular from the 1920s through the early 1940s. In addition to adult, child, and baby, characters such as Aviatrix, flappers, and even dolls with animal characteristics are found.

Pink Bisque: the bisque is not painted, but tinted pink, rather like adding food coloring to clay; jointed shoulder and hip; molded and painted bobbed hair or mohair wig; nicely painted facial features; textured stockings and single strap black shoes; typically marked "Germany."

Frozen Charlotte Value Comparisons					
Size	Charlotte or Charlie	Pink Tinted	Black Tinted	Molded Clothes or Boots	Unusual Hair
2"	75.00	275.00	165.00	265.00	350.00
3"	85.00	300.00	185.00	285.00	375.00
4"	150.00	350.00	210.00	335.00	400.00
5"	175.00	400.00	235.00	385.00	425.00
6"	210.00	450.00	265.00	425.00	450.00
7"	235.00	475.00	285.00	450.00	475.00
8"	285.00	500.00	325.00	475.00	500.00
9"	335.00	525.00	375.00	500.00	525.00
10"	360.00	550.00	425.00	525.00	575.00
11"	500.00	600.00	525.00	575.00	600.00
12"	600.00	650.00	565.00		
14"	700.00	700.00	675.00		
15"	750.00	800.00	775.00		

Complete set of Snow White and the 7 Dwarfs Japanese Immobiles. Courtesy of David Cobb's Doll Auctions

Painted Bisque: thin layer of flesh-colored paint applied over the entire doll, but not fired on. Please note the difference between "cold painted," which has only particular parts painted and "painted bisque," which is an all-over coating or wash. Jointed shoulder and hip; molded and painted hair or mohair wig; painted facial features; socks and single strap black shoes; typically marked "Germany."

Pink Bisque/Painted Bisque Value Comparisons

Size	Adult/Child/ Baby, Glass Eye*	Adult/Child/ Baby, Painted Eye*	Unusual Character or Jointed Waist	Painted Bisque
2"				60.00
3"	165.00	115.00	350.00	100.00
4"	200.00	135.00	400.00	
5"	250.00	165.00	450.00	150.00
6"	300.00	220.00	500.00	
7"	400.00	275.00	700.00	

*Add an additional $100.00 for unusual footwear.

Immobiles and Nodders

The apparent characteristic of most Immobiles and Nodders is the lack of artistry and the cold-painted method of decoration. Cold painting is the absence of firing after the decoration is applied. It is not unusual to find pieces with the paint worn off.

Young girls of the 1920s spent hours in shops analyzing each doll in order to find just the right one. Quality was as important then as it is today. Smaller dolls were called "Penny Dolls," and the larger ones "Quarter Dolls." Bisque can range from good to very poor, and decoration can range from cute to crude. Prices listed are for average quality dolls. Extremely inferior or superior doll values fluctuate accordingly.

Immobiles: no joints; molded and cold-painted features and clothing. Do not confuse Immobiles with German bisque figurines or Frozen Charlottes. Immobiles used an inferior-quality bisque. The cold-painted decoration is brightly colored and poorly applied, and it may result in a worn appearance to facial features and clothing. Typically marked "Germany," a mold number, or unmarked.

Nodders: also known as Knotters; solid, one-piece body, joined at the neck by elastic knotted through hole at top of head; stringing enables doll's head to nod; molded and painted features; nodders representing people have molded and painted clothes; most animal Nodders have molded and painted fur; animal nodders with molded clothes are rare; typically unmarked.

Immobiles Value Comparisons

Size	Adult or Child	Comic/Personality Characters
2"	60.00	165.00
3"	85.00	185.00
5"	130.00	225.00
7"	185.00	250.00

Nodder Value Comparisons

Size	Adult or Child	Comic Characters	Personalities	Animals	Dressed Animals
3"	75.00	135.00	250.00	185.00	290.00
4"	85.00	150.00	285.00	200.00	315.00
5"	100.00	175.00	300.00	215.00	335.00

Japanese All-Bisque Value Comparisons

Size	Betty Boop	Character Baby	Shirley Temple or Kewpie Type	Popular Comic Character*	Child or Adult	Two-Faced Dolls
2"		60.00		50.00		
3"			90.00	60.00		
3 1/2"	30.00	85.00	100.00	65.00		
5"	35.00	95.00	125.00	70.00	65.00	225.00
6"					70.00	250.00
7"	450.00					

*Add an additional $100.00 for known Disney characters.

Japanese

The various types of Japanese All-Bisque Dolls range in size from 1" to 8". Most have molded and painted hair and facial features, and they are unjointed or jointed only at the shoulder. Rare examples have glass eyes, wigs, and/or additional joints. They may have molded and painted clothes or no clothing.

Good quality Japanese All-Bisque Dolls are rare. The painted features are usually very crude. The bisque is often grainy—called "stone bisque" or "sugar bisque"—and seams are seldom cleaned. Occasionally, a good quality Japanese All-Bisque is found.

The most familiar type is probably the Betty Boop with bobbed, wavy, molded hair; big, round, side-glancing eyes; spiked lashes; one-piece solid body; and head with shoulder joint. She is often found wearing a crepe paper dress.

Another common type is the "Candy Baby," premiums given away with the purchase of candy. Typically marked "JAPAN" or "NIPPON" or with a paper label.

Japanese Immobiles Value Comparisons

Size	Child/Adult	Animal	Characters	Boxed Character Sets*
3"	5.00	40.00	60.00	
4"	10.00	45.00	65.00	250.00
5"	25.00	55.00	70.00	
6"	35.00	65.00	75.00	300.00

*Add an additional $100.00–200.00 for known Disney characters.

Bathing Dolls

Bathing Dolls were made in Germany and the United States. All-Bisque Bathing Dolls are actually bisque figurines, however they tend to be popular with many doll collectors.

Bathing Dolls range in size from a few inches to one foot. They are found sitting, reclining, or standing, usually with very graceful arms and legs. The beautiful little nymphs have an Art Deco-style appearance and at times seem almost risqué. They have painted facial features or, very rarely, a jointed neck and tiny glass eyes. They come in a molded and painted bathing suit, draped toga, or as delicately detailed nudes.

Bathing Dolls may be beautiful and graceful, or comical in appearance. An extremely lovely Bathing Doll could easily bring two or three times the price listed. Check carefully for chipped fingers and toes—a common fault of these delicate dolls. They are typically unmarked, "Germany" or a number.

Bathing Beauties, top row: 3 1/2" long German tinted-bisque nude; 6 1/2" long German tinted-bisque nude; 3 1/2" tall German tinted-bisque nude, dressed in tutu; middle row: 5 1/2" long German tinted-bisque with molded and painted striped bathing suit, cap, and shoes; 3 1/4" tall German #4103 glazed bisque with molded and painted bathing dress, cap, and shoes, leaning on a shell; bottom row: 9" tall German tinted-bisque with molded and painted bathing suit; 5" tall china mermaid, riding a sea horse; 3 1/4" tall German #5662 tinted-bisque nude, kneeling on a snail; 3 1/2" tall bisque with molded and painted dress and large hat, riding a fish; 10" tall German untinted bisque with molded bathing suit. Courtesy of David Cobb's Doll Auctions

Bathing Dolls Value Comparisons

Size	Fine, Delicate, & Graceful	Standard Quality	Unusual Pose, 2 Dolls Molded as 1
3"	400.00	200.00	1,900.00
6"	600.00	275.00	
9"	900.00	350.00	2,400.00
12"	1,400.00		

Add an additional $250.00 for glass eyes.

Half Dolls or Pincushion Dolls

Half Dolls have been included in this edition because so many doll collectors are drawn to them. Early examples were made by some of the most prestigious German porcelain factories. Later Half Dolls were made in the United States, and poorer imitations were commonly from Japan.

Half dolls, including top row: 7 1/2" Goebel; 5-1/2" German #5432; 7" unmarked German; 6 1/2" German 13370; middle row: 5" Karl Schneider # 15272; 5 1/2" Dressell & Kister #23146; 4 1/2" rare French #3893 with jointed arms; 5" German #3392; bottom row: 5" German #4761; 5" unmarked; 5" German 9301, and 5" German 4625. Courtesy of David Cobb's Doll Auctions

Half Dolls are a classic example of the range of quality to be found in a single doll category. Even within the same factory and using the same mold, one can be exquisite while another is crudely executed. Craftsmanship varies from doll to doll. One may have an elaborate hair style, beautifully painted features, fancy molded clothing with delicate hands extending gracefully from the body. Another may have splotchy paint and heavy mitt-type hands attached to the body.

The most beautiful Half Dolls graced ladies' dressing tables at the turn of the century. Half Dolls were used on pincushions, powder boxes, music boxes, clothes brushes, jewelry boxes, and letter boxes. Occasionally, a Half Doll has a companion bottom half with legs. They are typically marked "Germany," "Japan," porcelain factory, or unmarked.

Half Dolls Value Comparisons

Size	Arms and Hands Attached	One Arm Attached or Arms Extended, Hands Attached	Both Hands Extended	Detailed or Fancy Application
2"	20.00			
3"	30.00	150.00	450.00	
4"	50.00	175.00	475.00	650.00
5"	55.00	200.00	500.00	700.00
6"	60.00	250.00	525.00	750.00
8"	65.00	300.00	575.00	800.00
10"	70.00		700.00	
12"	100.00			

German Piano Babies. Courtesy of David Cobb's Doll Auctions

Piano Babies

What doll collector can resist the charm of these All-Bisque figurines? These unjointed babies come in various positions; with deeply molded and painted hair; painted, often intaglio, eyes; character face with smiling, open/closed or pouty mouth; and molded and painted clothes. It is understandable that most Victorian homes had one—or better yet a pair—of Piano Babies resting on the piano scarf. Several of the better German porcelain factories such as Kestner, Limbach, Dressel, and Gebrüder Heubach produced superior quality Piano Babies. It is important to examine Piano Babies carefully, as lesser-quality examples do exist.

Buyer Beware! Reproduction Piano Babies are everywhere! With some practice, reproductions are easy to spot. Authentic Piano Babies are often, but not always, marked with the name or symbol of the porcelain factory where they were made. Reproductions have no factory markings, but many have a red number painted on the bottom. A red number alone is not a sure sign of a reproduction; some antique Piano Babies are also marked in this way. Many reproductions have a large hole (about the diameter of a pencil point) in the bottom. Old Piano Babies may also have a hole, but it is generally much smaller. Subtle but distinct differences are found in flesh tone. Antique Piano Babies have a soft, human flesh color; the arms and legs of reproductions often exhibit a chalky pallor.

Piano Babies Value Comparisons

Size	Excellent	Unusual	Standard
4"	500.00		185.00
7"	700.00	1,200.00	325.00
9"	800.00	1,500.00	350.00
11"	1,000.00	1,700.00	450.00
16"	1,500.00	2,200.00	

Snow Babies and friends. Courtesy of David Cobb's Doll Auctions

Snow Babies

Although Snow Babies were produced as early as the 1880s, they did not reach their peak of popularity until after the turn-of-the-century. This surge of popularity is due to the birth of Marie Ahnighito Peary, daughter of Admiral Peary. Marie was affectionately called a "Snow Baby" by the Eskimos with whom she lived. In 1901, Mrs. Peary wrote a book showing a picture of her daughter wearing a white snow suit and referred to her as a "Snow Baby." Suddenly the German-made figurines were in demand.

Usually small, unjointed All-Bisque figurines, the Snow Babies are covered with tiny bits of ground porcelain that resemble snow. Despite being produced as simple Christmas novelties or party favors, Snow Baby faces have lifelike detail with excellent coloring.

Hertwig & Company of Thüringia, Germany, is believed to have made the first Snow Baby. Other German manufacturers soon followed suit.

Value is dependent upon detail and workmanship.

Reproductions of the German Snow Babies exist in two distinct forms. The Japanese industry produced Snow Babies of inferior quality, typically marked with only a paper label. Now collectible in their own right, Japanese Snow Babies do not command the higher price of the fine German examples. Common sense and careful study will enable the buyer to recognize differences between the two. German manufacturers produced superior Snow Babies; the facial decorations and mannerisms are extremely appealing.

A more recent model has been imported for Department 56®. These fine quality Snow Babies are posed well and have a delightful look. They are easily identified by their marking. Ironically, unmarked copies of the contemporary figurines are being made. No attempt is being made to make them appear old. A casual glance is sufficient to distinguish the somewhat-yellowed, modern Snow Babies from the earlier, very white German and Japanese examples.

Snow Babies Value Comparisons						
Size	Japanese	German Standing, Lying, or Sitting on a Sled	German Shoulder Head Cloth Body	German Tumbling or with Musical Instruments	German, with Animals	German Snow Man, Santa, or Other
1 1/2"	50.00			150.00	250.00	
2"	100.00	200.00		200.00	325.00	
3"	110.00	225.00		250.00	400.00	450.00
4"	120.00	250.00	350.00	300.00		
9"	135.00	350.00	375.00	400.00		600.00

Add an additional $100.00 to any Snow Baby with jointed shoulder or hip.

Allied Imported

*A*llied Imported, circa 1950s, was an eastern company manufacturing mainly larger-sized vinyl and hard plastic fashion dolls. The mass produced dolls were sold in bulk to smaller companies, which in turn marketed them under several different names, often referred to as "knock-offs." Due to their affordability and impressive size, the dolls were extremely popular, particularly the bride doll.

Prices listed are for dolls in near-mint, original condition. If damaged, redressed, or undressed, expect the value to be less than one half to one fourth the amounts listed.

Child: one-piece vinyl body; painted, side-glancing eyes; molded hair with top knot; appropriately dressed; typically marked "Allied Grand Doll Mfg. Inc., 1958" or "A."

Teen: vinyl head; hard plastic adult body; jointed at neck, shoulder, elbows, hip, knees, and ankles; special ball rotation above elbows and at waist; rooted hair; sleep eyes; heavy makeup; long lashes; appropriately dressed; typically marked "KT" or "Made by Allied Doll Co."

Bride: all heavy vinyl; high heel feet; rooted hair; sleep eyes; blue eye shadow; very red lips; pierced ears with pearl earrings; original bridal gown with lace overlay; typically marked "AE."

Buffalo Bill by Allied. Courtesy Busby and Company Doll Auctions

Allied Imported Value Comparisons			
Size	Child	Teen	Bride
10"	40.00		
15"	50.00	125.00	150.00
21"	75.00	150.00	200.00
24"		200.00	250.00
28"		250.00	300.00

Alma, Italian Felts

*A*lma, Turin, Italy manufactured beautiful felt dolls resembling the popular Lenci dolls. Although many companies copied Lenci in concept, few could rival their quality. Alma is the exception. The dolls were exceptionally well made and exquisitely costumed.

Identifying characteristics include a hollow torso covered in light flesh-colored felt; ladder-like stitched seams; attached ears made of folded and gathered material. The most unique construction aspect is the method used to attach the limbs. Unlike other cloth dolls that have limbs sewn onto the body, Alma dolls are jointed by elastic stringing.

Prices listed are for original costumed dolls with good color and little or no fading. Slight wear and signs of aging, such as loose or wobbly joints, do not greatly affect the price. If a doll is stained, torn, mended, or faded, expect the value to be less than half the amounts listed.

Child/Character Dolls: all felt; socket head; covered hollow torso; limbs with no top stitching, attached with elastic; mohair sewn onto head in strips; painted side-glancing eyes; white dot highlights; painted outside-corner lashes; attached ears; closed or open mouth with teeth; beautifully costumed; typically unmarked or with wrist tag only.

Alma Felt Child. Courtesy of McMaster's Doll Auction

Alma Felt Doll Value Comparison		
Size	Child	Character*
9"	450.00	
11"	500.00	
13"	550.00	
16"	700.00	900.00
18"	800.00	
20"	900.00	1,400.00
22"	1,000.00	
26"	1,300.00	
28"		2,000.00
30"		2,500.00

* Exceptional or elaborately costumed characters, such as Russian Cossack Dancer, can easily double the amounts listed.

Alt, Beck & Gottschalck

Alt, Beck & Gottschalck was located in Nauendorf, near Ohrdruf, Thuringia, Germany, from 1854 until 1930. Along with the traditional bisque child and character babies, A.B.G., as it's commonly known, is credited by most doll historians with producing a series of beautifully detailed glazed and unglazed shoulder heads. More than fifty mold numbers, all between 639 and 1288, have been identified. While it is assumed these fine quality dolls were made by A.B.G., there are other possible manufacturers, such as Kestner and Simon & Halbig. Notably, the #639 mold has a very "Kestner look," as do several others. Many of the mold numbers correspond exactly to gaps in the sequence of known registered mold numbers of Simon & Halbig.

Reproductions are numerous, for there are molds available to today's doll maker for almost every doll credited to Alt, Beck & Gottschalck. The majority of reproduction dolls are made for the pleasure or profit of a legitimate doll maker. Check markings carefully. Lightly run your fingers over the cheek or shoulder of the doll. Old bisque will have a slightly rough feel. The new bisque of a reproduction will feel satiny smooth.

Bisque Shoulder Head: bisque shoulder head or socket head and separate shoulder plate; kid or cloth body; cloth, kid, or bisque limbs; short neck; molded and painted hair or wig; may have bonnet, hat, scarf, or other molded ornamentation; painted or pierced ears; open or closed mouth ("1/2" after the mold number indicates open mouth); appropriately dressed; typically marked "693," "698," "772," "882," "890," "889," "911," "916," "926," "974," "978," "980," "990," "996," "998," "1000," "1002," "1024," "1028," "1044," "1054," "1056," "1062," "1064," "1123," "1127," "1142," "1154," "1214," "1218," "1222," "1226," "1234," "1235," "1254," "1288," and possibly

Closed mouth Alt, Beck & Gottschalck #689 child doll. Courtesy of McMaster's Doll Auction

Alt, Beck & Gottschalck #1008 and 1000. Courtesy of David Cobb's Doll Auctions

others, followed by "XX" (double X's misaligned), "#," "No.," "1/2," size number, and/or "Germany."

China Shoulder Head: china shoulder head extends over tops of arms; kid or cloth body; cloth, kid, or china limbs; short neck; molded and painted hair; many with molded bonnet, scarf, or other headwear; painted eyes, but at least one china head (mold 1008) has been found with glass eyes; many with pierced ears; closed mouth; appropriately dressed; typically marked "784," "880," "882," "1000," "1008," "1028," "1030," "1046," "1056," "1112," "1142," "1210," or "1214," followed by "XX" (double X's misaligned), "#," "No.," and size number.

Closed Mouth Child: bisque socket head; composition and wood ball-joint body; good wig; glass eyes; appropriately dressed; typically marked "630," "911," "938," "989," and possibly others.

Dolly Face: bisque socket head; composition-and-wood ball-joint body; good wig; glass eyes; appropriately dressed; typically marked "630," "1326," "1357," "1358," "1359," "1361," "1362," or "1367."

Character Baby: bisque socket head; composition bent-limb baby body; good wig; glass eyes; may have pierced nostrils; open mouth with teeth and tongue; appropriately dressed; typically marked "1322," "1352," or "1361."

Shoulder Head Value Comparisons

Size	Molded Hair, Painted Eye, Closed Mouth	Molded Hair, Glass Eyes, Closed Mouth	Molded Elaborate Hair, Closed Mouth*	Molded Cap, Hat, or Scarf, Closed Mouth*	Wearing Wig, Glass Eyes, Closed Mouth	1/2 Mold Number, Open Mouth	China Shoulder Head**
12"	450.00	700.00	1,100.00	900.00	900.00	650.00	350.00
14"	500.00	750.00	1,200.00	1,000.00	1,000.00	700.00	450.00
16"	550.00	875.00	1,400.00	1,100.00	1,150.00	750.00	500.00
18"	600.00	1,000.00	1,700.00	1,300.00	1,200.00	850.00	550.00
22"	650.00	1,250.00	1,850.00	1,500.00	1,400.00	950.00	675.00
24"	800.00	1,500.00	2,100.00	1,750.00	1,750.00	1,200.00	750.00
27"	1,100.00	1,750.00	2,300.00	1,950.00	1,950.00	1,450.00	825.00
29"	1,300.00	2,000.00	2,800.00	2,300.00	2,300.00	1,800.00	900.00

* Add an additional $100.00 for pierced ears.
** Add and additional $300.00 for glass eyes.

Child and Baby Character Doll Value Comparisons

Size	Closed Mouth 911, 630, 1322	Closed Mouth 938, 989	Rare Smiling Character 1450	Dolly-Face 1362, 1367	Open Mouth, Unique Face 630, 1357, 1358, 1359	Character Baby 1322, 1352, 1361*
10"						550.00
12"	2,200.00	3,500.00	15,000.00			600.00
14"	2,500.00	3,800.00		550.00	1,200.00	700.00
16"	2,800.00	3,900.00	19,000.00		1,750.00	
18"	3,000.00	4,300.00		675.00	1,800.00	775.00
20"	3,250.00	4,700.00	22,000.00	800.00	2,000.00	900.00
22"	3,500.00	5,000.00				1,200.00
24"	3,800.00	5,500.00		1,000.00		1,550.00
26"	4,500.00	6,000.00				
30"				1,500.00		2,400.00
36"				2,700.00		

* Add an additional $150.00 for flirty eyes, and $700.00 for jointed toddler body.

Louis Amberg & Son

Louis Amberg & Son was located in Cincinnati, Ohio in 1878, and in New York City from 1893 until 1930. Louis Amberg imported and manufactured both bisque and composition dolls. In 1907, Louis' son, Joshua, joined the firm, and it became Louis Amberg & Son. In 1909, Louis Amberg was listed as the artist and owner of "Lucky Bill," the first known American copyrighted composition doll head. By 1928, Louis Amberg advertised over 600 style numbers available (including some imported from Germany and France). Louis Amberg & Son was sold to E. I. Horsman in 1930.

Molds for several Amberg Dolls are still available. The intent is not to forge reproductions, but for the legitimate doll maker of today to make "reproduction" dolls for pleasure or profit. Although these dolls are usually dated and signed by the artist, bear in mind two things: the doll world has its share of unscrupulous individuals who are not above deliberately omitting the date and signature; and to assume the responsibility of thoroughly inspecting any doll you may be interested in. Dolls made for and by Louis Amberg & Son were well made, reasonably priced dolls. While the workmanship was good, the dolls were not intended to be works of art.

Vanta Baby, made in Germany for Amberg.
Courtesy of McMaster's Doll Auction

made by Armand Marseille; brown mohair wig with bobbed style; glass eyes; closed mouth with smiling or serious expression; appropriately dressed; typically marked "19 c 24/LA & S/Germany/-50-/ (style number)." ***Note:*** *Socket head on jointed body with a sad expression "972"; shoulder head on a kid body with a smile "983"; shoulder head on a kid body with a sad expression "982."*

Fulper: bisque socket head; jointed composition-and-wood body; good wig; glass sleep eyes; thick upper and lower lashes; open mouth; two upper teeth; appropriately dressed; typically marked "Amberg Dolls the World Standard Fulper Made in USA."

Newborn Baby (a.k.a. "Bottle Baby" or "My Playmate"): designed by Jeno Juszko to represent a two-day old infant; heads made by Armand Marseille, Racknagel, Herm Steiner, and possibly others; bisque flange neck; cloth body; solid dome; lightly spray-painted hair; flat, broad nose; sunken chin; full cheeks; small, flat ears; closed mouth; appropriately dressed; typically marked "L. A. & S. 1914/No.G45520," "L.A.S. 371 DRGM Germany," or "Newborn Baby 45520."

Vanta Baby: bisque flange neck; cloth body; bent, composition limbs; lightly spray-painted hair; glass sleep eyes; real lashes; open mouth; two teeth; original Vanta Baby undergarments; with rattle, Baby's Record Book, and gift card; marked "Vanta Baby/LA & S 3/0 D.R.G.M Germany."

Bisque

Prices listed are for appropriately costumed dolls in good condition. Normal wear, slight damage, or well-made repairs to the body do not greatly affect the price. If the bisque is damaged or repaired, expect the value to be less than half the amounts listed. It is perfectly acceptable to show a missing or repaired finger or joint, or a mended body.

Baby Peggy: bisque shoulder or socket head; jointed composition-and-wood or kid body; happy or sad expression; heads

Composition

Prices listed are for appropriately costumed dolls in good condition. Slight crazing is acceptable and does not greatly affect the price. If badly crazed, cracked, peeling, or repainted, expect the value to be less than half the amounts listed.

Babies: all composition; bent-limb baby body; molded and painted hair; painted eyes; closed mouth; appropriately dressed; typically marked "L.A.S. c/414/1911."

	Amberg Bisque Doll Value Comparisons					
Size	**Baby Peggy Kid Body**	**Baby Peggy Composition Body**	**Standard Quality Fulper**	**Better Quality Fulper**	**Newborn Baby**	**Vanta**
8"					425.00	
10"					475.00	
12"					575.00	
14"			350.00	450.00	725.00	
17"					950.00	
18"	2,400.00	2,800.00				1,200.00
20"	2,600.00	3,000.00	400.00	600.00		1,400.00
22"	2,800.00	3,200.00				1,600.00
24"	3,200.00	3,500.00	450.00	700.00		1,700.00

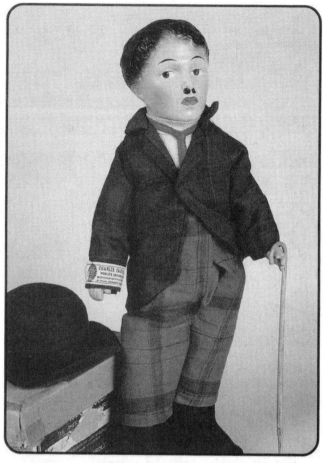

Charlie Chaplin composition portrait doll with label on sleeve. Courtesy of McMaster's Doll Auction

cally marked with cloth label "Charlie Chaplin Doll/Worlds Greatest Comedian/Made Exclusively by Louis Amberg & Son N.Y./By Special Arrangement with Essanay Film Co."

Lucky Bill: composition boy's character face; teddy-bear-type body. This rare doll's desirability is due more to its historical significance than artistic value.

Mibs: composition shoulder head and limbs cloth body; slightly bowed legs; molded and painted strawberry blond hair with wave falling down the center of the forehead; perplexed expression; detailed, painted blue eyes looking down; thick lashes; slightly feathered brows; closed mouth; appropriately dressed; typically marked "L. A. & S. 1921/Germany" or unmarked; clothing tag "Amber Dolls/Please Love Me/I'm Mibs"; wrist tags "Amberg Dolls/Please Love Me/I'm Mibs" or "Please Love Me/I'm Mibs."

Sis Hopkins: composition shoulder or socket head on shoulder plate; cloth body; composition or sateen arms; character face of laughing child; molded hair with pigtails or wig with two braids; painted, side-glancing eyes; open/closed mouth, grinning with top and bottom teeth, or molded tongue sticking out; appropriately dressed; marked "SIS HOPKINS."

Sunny Orange Blossom: composition shoulder head; cloth body and limbs; molded and painted bonnet, resembling an orange with holes for ribbon to tie under chin; painted eyes; closed mouth; original orange organdy dress with "Sunny Orange Blossom" ribbons; painted socks and shoes; typically marked "L.A. & S./1924."

Vanta Baby: composition shoulder head and bent limbs; cloth body with crier; molded and painted hair; tin sleep or painted eyes; open mouth with two teeth; original Vanta baby undergarments; celluloid baby rattle, gift card, and Dolly Record Book; typically marked "Vanta Baby" or "Vanta Baby/Trade Mark Reg./An Amberg Doll."

Victory Doll: composition socket head, jointed wood-and-composition body; good wig; glass, sleep eyes; open mouth; appropriately dressed, typically marked "Amberg Victory Doll."

Edwine/IT/Peter Pan/Sue/Tiny Tots: all composition; one-piece upper body and head, separate lower body; straight arms and legs; body-twist joint at waist; constructed with a rounded ball in the lower half of the body and a socket in the upper waist; appropriately dressed; typically marked "Amberg/Pat. Pend/L.A.S. R.C.P. 1928."

Baby Peggy: composition shoulder head and limbs; (more closely resembles a child) cloth body; molded and painted brown hair in bobbed style or mohair wig; painted eyes; open/closed mouth with teeth showing; appropriately dressed.

Charlie Chaplin: composition portrait head and hands; cloth body; dark molded and painted hair; painted, side-glancing eyes; closed mouth below molded and painted mustache; typi-

Amberg Composition Value Comparisons											
Size	Baby	Baby Peggy	Charlie Chaplin	Lucky Bill	Mibs	Sis Hopkins	Sunny Orange Blossom	Vanta Baby	Victory	Edwine/IT Peter Pan/ Sue/ Tiny Tots
8"										300.00
10"				900.00						
12"	275.00									
14"	325.00		700.00	500.00		600.00	800.00	375.00		600.00
16"					1,300.00	750.00			325.00	
18"								400.00		
20"	450.00	950.00	900.00			1,100.00		425.00	300.00	
22"	600.00									
24"								500.00	475.00	
25"								700.00		

Felt

Prices listed are for appropriately costumed dolls with good color and little or no fading. If a doll is stained, torn, badly mended, or faded, expect the value to be less than half the amounts listed.

Louis Amberg responded to the public's desire for Lenci-style dolls, producing various sizes and at least fourteen different styles. The dolls were jointed at the neck, shoulder, and hip. They had washable faces, and they were nicely dressed with bonnets or hats and single-strap shoes. When Horsman bought Louis

Amberg & Son in 1930, the Amfelt doll was the only doll excluded from the sale. Instead, it was purchased by Paul Cohen Co. with the trade name "Art Felt Dolls."

Amfelt Value Comparisons	
Size	
16"	600.00
18"	800.00
24"	900.00

American Character

The American Character Doll Company was located in New York City from 1919 until 1968. The design and quality of the American Character Dolls help to explain their popularity among today's collectors.

Early in the company's history, sixteen styles of composition dolls were made with the trade name Aceedeecee (A C D C for American Character Doll Co.).

The first dolls marketed by American Character were composition bent-limb babies with cloth bodies. By 1923, the trade name "Petite" was adopted. In 1928, two years after moving to Brooklyn, American Character received exclusive permission from the Campbell Soup Company to make Campbell Kids.

Composition

Prices listed are for appropriately costumed dolls in good condition. Slight crazing is acceptable and does not greatly affect the price. If badly crazed, cracked, peeling, or repainted, expect the value to be less than half the amounts listed.

Campbell Kids: all composition; character face; (similar to Averill's Dolly Dingle designed by Grace G. Drayton) bent arms; straight legs, slightly pigeon-toed; short, molded and painted hair; painted, round, side-glancing eyes; pug nose; smiling, closed mouth; original outfits resemble those in Campbell Soup advertisements; typically marked "A/Petite/Doll."

Puggy: all composition; character face; male companion to the Campbell Kids; frowning expression; molded and painted hair; small, painted eyes; appropriately costumed; typically marked "A/Petite/Doll."

Character Babies: petite Babies and Mama Dolls; composition head; cloth body; bent limbs; molded and painted hair or good wig; sleep eyes; open or closed mouth; appropriately dressed; typically marked "Petite American Character," "Amer. Char. Doll Co.," "AC," or "Wonder Baby."

Tots: composition shoulder or socket head on shoulder plate; cloth or composition body; good wig; tin or glassine sleep eyes; real lashes; open or open/closed mouth with teeth; appropriately dressed; typically marked "Petite Am. Char."

Child: composition socket head on shoulder plate; composition limbs; cloth body; molded and painted hair or good wig; painted or glassene sleep eyes; appropriately dressed; typically

marked "Amer. Char.," "Petite Sally," or "Sally" below a horseshoe with an embossed doll standing in the center.

Older Child/Teen: all composition; jointed at neck, shoulder, and hip; molded and painted hair and eyes or good mohair wig and glassene sleep eyes; appropriately dressed; typically marked "AmCharacter."

American Character's vinyl Betsy McCall and her big brother Sandy McCall. Courtesy of McMaster's Doll Auction

Size	Campbell Kid	Puggy	Character Babies, Petite Baby, Mama	Tots	Child	Older Child/Teen*
12"	750.00	700.00		225.00		
14"			275.00		325.00	350.00
16"			300.00	325.00	375.00	400.00
18"			325.00			
20"			350.00	350.00		
22"			375.00		450.00	
24"			435.00	375.00	550.00	600.00
28"			550.00			

*Add an additional $200.00–300.00 for original Carol Ann Berry with special crown braided hair.

Vinyl and Hard Plastics

American Character vinyl and hard plastic dolls are as varied as their composition predecessors. The babies that dominated in the 1930s and 1940s were slowly being replaced by older child and teen dolls.

Prices listed are for dolls in near-mint, original condition. If damaged, redressed, or undressed, expect the value to be less than one half to one fourth the amounts listed.

Ben Cartwright: solid vinyl; fully jointed; molded hair; painted features; molded clothes; typically marked "C/American Character."

Betsy McCall: hard plastic, vinyl, or combination of both; socket head; rooted hair; sleep eyes with lashes; closed mouth, slightly smiling expression; appropriately dressed; typically marked "McCall Corp" in a circle, "McCall 1958," or unmarked. *Note: smaller size particularly susceptible to splitting at the knees.*

Cricket/Teessy: plastic and vinyl teenage body; bendable limbs; hair grows when stomach button is pushed, shortens when metal key is inserted and turned in back; painted eyes; closed mouth; appropriately dressed; typically marked "American Character."

Eloise: all cloth; yellow yarn hair; painted, almond-shaped eyes; darling character molded face; tiny nose; closed, smiling mouth; appropriately dressed; typically marked with hangtag only "Amer. Char. Doll/Corp." (Bette Gould interpretation of Kay Thompson's fictional character, Eloise, who lived at the Plaza Hotel in N.Y.)

Freckles: small, two-faced girl changes expression when left arm is moved up (happy) and down (sad); rooted hair; painted eyes; mouth either open/closed smiling, or closed sad expression; freckles painted across nose; marked "Amer. Char. Inc./1966."

Hedda Get Bedda: all vinyl; hard plastic bonnet; three-sided vinyl head; knob on top of bonnet rotates molded faces (awake and smiling, asleep and grinning, or sick child); appropriately dressed; marked "American Doll and Toy Corp. 1961" and "Whimsie/Amer. Doll and Toy Corp. 1960"; Hedda Get Bedda is one of the few dolls issued with two dates.

Little Miss Echo: hard plastic, recorder doll; battery operated recorder housed within the torso allows the doll to repeat whatever is said to her.

Little Ricky Jr.: vinyl socket head; one-piece, stuffed vinyl body; molded and painted hair; blue, plastic sleep eyes; open nurser mouth; appropriately dressed; typically marked "Amer. Char. Doll." *Note: the introduction of the Little Ricky Jr. doll, inspired by the "I Love Lucy Show," was as eagerly anticipated in 1956 as Ricky Jr.'s birth.*

Sweet Sue in authentic Annie Oakley costume. Courtesy of McMaster's Doll Auction

Sandy: vinyl head; hard plastic, jointed body; advertised as "Sandy McCall, Betsy McCall's big brother"; molded and painted hair; sleep eyes; open/closed mouth; appropriately dressed; typically marked "Amer-Char," "McCall Corp.," or "American Character."

Sweet Sue and Toni: hard plastic socket head; plastic and vinyl or all hard plastic body (walker or non-walker); arms slightly bent; well manicured hands; may have painted nails; jointed shoulder and hip; various combinations of jointed elbows, waist, knees, and ankles; wig or rooted hair; sleep eyes with real lashes; closed mouth; (Toni had high heel feet and pierced ears); beautifully dressed; typically marked "Amer. Char.

Doll," "American Character Doll," "Amer Char," "A.C.," or unmarked. **Note:** *Sweet Sue and Toni costumes are some of the loveliest ever made—gowns of chiffon, silk, or satin, trimmed with lace, ruffles, and rhinestones. A boy version, called "Groom," had a lamb's wool wig and was dressed in a tuxedo.*

Tiny Tears: all vinyl; jointed at neck, shoulder, and hip; rooted or molded and painted hair; sleep eyes with lashes; nicely molded fingers and toes; open nurser mouth; tiny holes at corners of eyes for tear ducts; appropriately dressed; typically marked "American Character Doll/Pat." **Note:** *dressing table/tub, monogrammed towel for bathing, high chair, stroller, and other accessories could be purchased.*

Toodles: all quality vinyl; chubby, bent-limb baby body; "rolling joint" at elbows and knees; advertised as "… Toodles can kneel, sit, play with her toes and fingers, and assume 1000 different positions"; rooted or molded hair; sleep eyes; open nurser mouth; older toddler version with molded teeth and open smiling mouth; appropriately dressed; typically marked "AM," "Amer-9," "American Char.," "Toodles," or unmarked; mark is sometimes obscured by the holes on rooted-hair dolls.

Whimsies: one-piece vinyl body; face with elf-like quality; rooted hair; very large eyes; full, smiling, closed mouth; appropriately dressed; marked "Whimsies/1960/American Doll & Toy"; many different Whimsies were introduced, including "Wheeler the Dealer," "Dixie the Pixie," "Lena the Cleaner," and others.

American Character Vinyl and Hard Plastics Value Comparisons

Size	Ben Cartwright	Betsy McCall/Sandy	Cricket/Teessy		Eloise	Freckles	Hedda Get Bedda	Little Miss Echo	Little Ricky Jr.	Sweet Sue/Toni*	Tiny Tears	Toodles	Whimsies
7 1/2"	90.00	275.00											
8"													
10"			75.00										
10 1/2"										350.00			
13"											200.00		
14"		350.00	135.00			55.00			125.00	400.00		250.00	
16"					500.00				200.00				
17"											350.00		
18"										425.00		300.00	
20"		450.00				95.00			265.00	450.00			
21"												325.00	
22"		500.00			700.00	100.00	200.00			500.00	450.00		225.00
23"												350.00	
24"										550.00		375.00	
25"												400.00	
30"		650.00						300.00				450.00	
31"										700.00			
36"		800.00											
39"		850.00											

*Add an additional $150.00–200.00 for groom or elaborately costumed dolls, and add $300.00–500.00 for authentically costumed character dolls, such as Annie Oakley or Alice.

Max Oscar Arnold

❖

Max Oscar Arnold manufactured various types of dolls from 1878-1930 in Neustadt, Germany. Most noted for their patented mechanical dolls, Arnold dolls included walking or talking dolls and even a bathing doll. The first mechanical doll patented by Arnold in 1904 moved on wheels, said "Mama" and "Papa," turned its head from side to side, and swung its arms forward and backwards.

Arnold's interest grew to include phonograph dolls, made with bodies that separated above the hips so that a phonograph could be placed inside. A metal front amplified the sound.

Arnold obtained several patents for talking dolls. "Arnoldia" was the trade name for a 1906 doll that talked and sang. Patented in both Germany and France, Arnoldia could count, do arithmetic, pray, talk, and sing in three languages—English, German, and French. Advertising boasted "children could learn their lessons and foreign languages with only Arnoldia as teacher." Fifty-one English records, twenty-eight German, and twenty French were available. Record titles included: *The Dead Doll, Dolly's Funeral, Mr. Nobody, Bald-headed Billy, My One Legged Doll, The Groo Groo Man, The Gobles 'uns and The Little Girl, Seein' Things at Night,*

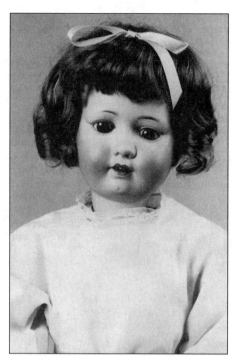

Dolly-Face Max Oscar Arnold bisque doll.
Courtesy of McMaster's Doll Auction

A Terrible Tale, and *There's Another Picture in My Mama's Frame*. If nothing else, Arnoldia was certainly a morbid doll.

Prices listed are for appropriately costumed dolls in good condition. Normal wear, slight damage, or well-made repairs to

the body do not greatly affect the price. If the bisque is damaged or repaired, expect the value to be less than half the amounts listed. It is perfectly acceptable to show a missing or repaired finger or joint, or a mended body.

Also see Automata.

Dolly-Face: bisque shoulder or socket head; jointed composition-and-wood or kid body; good wig; glass eyes, painted lashes; feathered brows; open mouth with upper teeth; appropriately dressed; typically marked "MOA" within star, helmeted man inscribing block "MOA," or "MOA" with sunburst and eagle.

Arnoldia: bisque socket head; jointed composition-and-wood; phonograph body; mohair wig; sleep eyes; painted upper and lower lashes; feathered brows; open mouth with upper teeth; appropriately dressed; typically marked "Arnoldia 54/14"; Arnoldia stood 30" high and came beautifully dressed with matching socks, shoes, and hat.

Max Oscar Arnold Value Comparisons			
Size	Dolly-Face Composition Body	Dolly-Face Kid Body	Arnoldia Phonograph Doll
15"	425.00	350.00	
17"	450.00		
18"	475.00	375.00	
22"	500.00	400.00	
24"	550.00	425.00	
28"	600.00	500.00	
30"	700.00		3,000.00

Arranbee Doll Company

The Arranbee Doll Company was founded in New York in 1922 and operated until 1959. In its early years, the company imported dolls, doll heads, doll parts, and doll hospital supplies. Arranbee originally assembled imported doll parts but later manufactured its own doll heads. Miss Ruby Hopf, Georgene Averill's sister, was Arranbee's principal designer. As with so many of the earlier American doll companies, Arranbee was absorbed by another larger company. Vogue bought out Arranbee in 1959 but continued to use the "R & B" marking until early in 1961. Arranbee produced excellent quality dolls, explaining their highly collectible status today.

Bisque

Prices listed are for appropriately costumed dolls in good condition. Normal wear, slight damage, or well-made repairs to the body do not greatly affect the price. If the bisque is damaged or repaired, expect the value to be less than half the amounts listed. It is perfectly acceptable to show a missing or repaired finger or joint, or a mended body.

My Dream Baby: bisque flange neck; cloth body or socket head; composition, bent-limb baby body; solid dome head made

9" composition Nursery Rhyme pair in original box with printed rhyme:
"A Little Dutch Boy and a Little Dutch Girl
Lived by a tulip-covered hill.
They were much in love with one another
And with the surrounding land.
Every day they strolled to the mill.
Over the hill hand and hand."
Courtesy of David Cobb's Doll Auctions

Arranbee Bisque Doll Value Comparisons					
Size	Mold 351, Open Mouth, Cloth Body	Mold 341K, Open Mouth, Composition Body	Mold 341, Closed Mouth, Cloth Body	Mold 351K, Closed Mouth, Composition Body	Dolly Face Composition Body
9"	300.00	350.00	375.00	450.00	
12"	500.00	550.00	575.00	650.00	
15"	700.00	775.00	800.00	875.00	
18"	800.00	875.00	900.00	975.00	950.00
20"	900.00	975.00	1,000.00	1,100.00	1,000.00
24"	1,100.00	1,200.00	1,250.00	1,400.00	1,200.00

by Armand Marseille; lightly spray-painted hair; small, glass sleep eyes; open mouth (mold 351) or closed mouth (mold 341); appropriately dressed; typically marked "AM Germany/341/3/1/2K," "Germany/Arranbee," or "AM 351/4 Germany Arranbee."

Dolly-Face: bisque socket head; jointed composition body; good wig; glass eyes; open mouth; appropriately dressed; typically marked "Simon & Halbig/Arranbee/Patent/Germany." ***Note:*** *Although Arranbee did not requisition a great many bisque child dolls, occasionally a lovely, German, dolly-face doll made for, and imported by, Arranbee is found. The quality of bisque is always of the utmost importance, therefore pay careful attention to the supplying manufacturer. The quality of any doll head produced by a particular company will be similar. For instance a bisque socket head made by Simon & Halbig, whether imported for Arranbee or used on a Simon & Halbig Doll, will have a comparable value.*

Composition

Composition Arranbee Dolls are generally quite lovely and were so well made that they have survived in better condition than many other dolls from the same period.

Prices listed are for appropriately costumed dolls in good condition. Slight crazing is acceptable and does not greatly affect the price. If badly crazed, cracked, peeling, or repainted, expect the value to be less than half the amounts listed.

Nursery Rhyme: all composition; jointed neck, shoulder, and hip; molded and painted hair; painted eyes; closed mouth; original character costume; typically marked "R & B Doll Co." or "R & B." ***Note:*** *The character and nursery rhyme are printed on elaborate suitcase-style box.*

Mama or Character Baby: composition shoulder or socket head; cloth or composition body; molded and painted hair; painted or tin sleep eyes; closed or open mouth; appropriately dressed; typically marked "R & B," "Arranbee," or "Little Angel R & B."

Child Dolls: older child or teenager; all composition; jointed at neck, shoulder, and hip; molded and painted hair or good wig;

painted or sleep eyes; closed mouth; appropriately dressed; typically marked "Nancy/Arranbee/Dolls," "R & B," or "Debu-Teen." ***Note:*** *examples of child dolls include Nancy, Nancy Lee, Debu-Teen, Girls From The Southern Series, Nancy Jean, and Princess Betty Rose. All these lovely young ladies have beautiful faces and are made from the highest quality composition.*

Kewty: all composition; jointed at neck, shoulder, and hip; molded hair with swirl across forehead and deep part; sleep eyes; open or open/closed mouth; appropriately dressed; marked "Kewty." ***Note:*** *due to similarities in hairstyle to the Nancy Doll, it is generally accepted that Kewty is an Arranbee product. However, some believe Kewty is actually a carnival doll produced by the small Pennsylvania factory of Domec.*

Magic Skin/Latex

Arranbee made a few rubber-type dolls in the late 1940s. Collectors often referred to this type of doll as "Magic Skin," perhaps because it can vanish right before your eyes. When considering the purchase of a Magic Skin doll, remember that the rubber will get sticky and rot. The process may be slowed by regularly rubbing cornstarch into the doll. Eventually, however, age will triumph and the doll will deteriorate. A rubber doll is only a temporary addition to your collection.

Child or Baby: all magic skin or vinyl head on magic skin body; molded and painted hair or wig; painted or plastic eyes; closed mouth; appropriately dressed; typically marked "A & B," "Arranbee," "210 Pat/Pen," or "Made in USA."

Magic Skin Value Comparison	
Size	Child or Baby
10"	95.00
14"	125.00
18"	150.00
22"	175.00
25"	200.00

Hard Plastic/Vinyl

Arranbee's most popular hard plastic dolls are Nanette and Nancy Lee, cousins to the composition Nancy Lee and Debu-Teen. Production of hard plastic dolls began in the 1940s. Although similar to composition in appearance, the thinner consistency of hard plastic allows a sharpness of detail that could not be achieved with composition.

During the 1950s, vinyl babies, toddlers, children, and teenage style dolls were introduced. The later Arranbee are quickly becoming collectibles.

Prices listed are for dolls in near-mint, original condition. If damaged, redressed, or undressed, expect the value to be less than one half to one fourth the amounts listed.

Arranbee Composition Dolls Value Comparisons				
Size	Nursery Rhyme*	Mama Dolls	Child Dolls	Kewty
7"		250.00		
9"	275.00			
10"	295.00			
12"			350.00	
14"		350.00	400.00	375.00
16"		400.00		450.00
17"			450.00	
18"		450.00	500.00	
21"		500.00	600.00	
23"				

Littlest Angel in original box, shown with additional boxed outfit. Courtesy of McMaster's Doll Auction

Hard Plastic Nancy Lee. Courtesy of McMaster's Doll Auction

Littlest Angel: all hard plastic, jointed walker body with chubby bent arms and short stocky legs; synthetic wig; sleep eyes with molded or real lashes; closed mouth; appropriately dressed; typically marked "R & B," "Arranbee," or "Made in USA."

Nanette and Nancy Lee: all hard plastic; jointed neck, shoulder, and hip; long, thin legs; synthetic wig; sleep plastic eyes with molded or real lashes; closed, smiling mouth; appropriately dressed; typically marked "R & B," "Arranbee," "210 Pat/Pen," or "Made in USA." ***Note:*** *teenage-style dolls were known as Angeline, Dream Bride, Taffy (wearing a caracul wig), Prom Queen, and Francine.*

Little Dear: socket-head baby; stuffed vinyl body; bent, chubby, baby-type arms and legs; rooted synthetic hair; sleep eyes with molded lashes; open/closed mouth; appropriately dressed; typically marked "R & B" or "Arranbee."

Nancy Lee: older child socket head; stuffed vinyl body, saran wig; sleep eyes with molded lashes; distinctive eyebrows shaped like an "S" on its side; closed mouth; appropriately dressed; typically marked "Arranbee" or "R & B."

Susan: older child socket head; stuffed vinyl body; straight arms, toddler legs; synthetic wig; sleep eyes with molded lashes; open/closed mouth; appropriately dressed; typically marked "Arranbee" or "A & B."

Angel Baby: socket head; vinyl baby body; curly, rooted synthetic hair; sleep eyes; open drink and wet mouth; appropriately dressed; typically marked "R & B" or "Arranbee."

My Angel Walking Doll: socket head; jointed, hard polyethylene vinyl walker body; rooted straight hair; sleep eyes with molded lashes; smiling, rosebud mouth; appropriately dressed; typically marked "Arranbee," "R & B" or "Made in USA."

Arranbee Hard Plastic/Vinyl Doll Value Comparisons

Size	Little Dear	Nancy Lee	Susan	Angel Baby	My Angel	Littlest Angel	Nanette Family
8"	50.00						
10"						200.00	
12"	75.00					250.00	
14"		275.00	125.00				500.00
16"			150.00				
17"							600.00
18"	350.00						
20"				100.00	300.00		
21"							700.00
23"							800.00
24"			125.00				
36"					500.00		

Arrow Novelty Company

The Arrow Novelty Company, founded in New York City in 1920, is best known for its Skookum Indian Dolls, designed by Mary McAboy of Montana. Early doll heads were made of dried apples and later of composition. Indian blankets were wrapped around wooden frames, leaving very little of the bodies to be seen. The dolls' costumes were made to represent various tribes, with sizes ranging from a few inches to several feet. Most are marked with a paper label on the foot that reads "Skookum Bully Good Indian."

Because Skookum Dolls were produced for the souvenir trade rather than as playthings, most Skookum Dolls are found in good condition. Look for nicely painted dolls with good color and no crazing.

Prices listed are for original dolls in good condition. If cracked, repainted, stained, torn, body mended, moth-eaten, or faded, expect the value to be less than one half to one fourth the amounts listed.

Composition: composition head; wrapped body; wooden feet with leather moccasins; typically marked "Skookum Bully Good Indian."

Hard Plastic: hard plastic head; later production with plastic feet and leather or plastic moccasins.

Skookum Indian Value Comparisons		
Size	Composition	Hard Plastic
8"	175.00	100.00
18"	600.00	200.00
20"	900.00	
36"	2,000.00	

Skookum Indian dolls, top row: hard plastic; bottom row: composition. Courtesy James D. Julia Auctions, Inc. Fairfield Maine

36" Skookum Indian dolls used for store display. Courtesy James D. Julia Auctions, Inc. Fairfield Maine

Artist Dolls

*I*ndividually designed, crafted, and produced works of art, the high investment potential of the Artist Doll encourages a relatively safe existence, as few are purchased as toys.

Many of the artists listed are members of either the National Institute of American Doll Artists (N.I.A.D.A.) or Original Doll Artists Council of America (O.D.A.C.A.). Material, workmanship, subject matter, and visual or decorative appeal are all contributing aspects that assure a wise investment rather than a speculative acquisition.

Prices listed are for dolls in mint, original condition. If damaged, undressed, or compromised in any way, expect the value to be less than one fourth of the amounts listed. Please, do not confuse the original artist dolls listed here with the more commonly found, moderately priced, commercially produced dolls designed by many of the same artists.

Also see Modern Collectible Dolls

Wooden artist dolls by Nancy Burns.
Courtesy of David Cobb's Doll Auctions

Artist Original Doll Value Comparison		
Adair-Kertzman, Linda	Porcelain; magical miniature fairies	600.00–900.00
Adams, Christine	Oilcloth; painted-featured tiny tots; appropriately costumed	200.00–350.00
Angel, Cindy	Porcelain; child or portrait with vintage accessories	300.00–700.00
Aprile, Paulette	Wax or porcelain; detailed lady or child portrait	3,000.00–4,500.00
Armstrong-Hand, Martha	Porcelain; expressively sculptured adult, child, or baby	2,800.00–3,500.00
Barrie, Mirren	Cloth; historical characters	200.00–500.00
Beckett, Bob and June	Wooden; smiling impish child	500.00–700.00
Bello, Yolanda	Porcelain; one of a kind or extremely limited edition	1,500.00–3,500.00
Blakely, Halle	Porcelain; realistic historical portrait; wearing artist-designed authentic costumes	1,500.00–3,500.00
Brahms, Abigail	Wax or porcelain; child or adult	1,000.00–3,000.00
Brandon, Elizabeth	Porcelain; child	400.00–700.00
Bringloe, Frances	Wooden; small early American child	400.00–600.00
Brouse, Mary	Porcelain; original designed child or adult	200.00–250.00
Bruns, Nancy	Wooden; child with nicely detailed facial features	700.00–900.00
Bruyere, Muriel	Molded; cloth; hand painted facial features	700.00–1,200.00
Bullard, Helen	Wooden; adult or child	300.00–500.00
Burnell, Patricia	Clay-based composition; character modelled, wearing authentically-detailed period costumes	900.00–1,500.00
Cameron, Beth	Santa	1,200.00–1,700.00
Campbell, Astry	Porcelain; child; finely modelled and costumed	900.00–1,500.00
Clear, Emma	Porcelain or china; original design; adult	700.00–1,500.00
Crees, Paul	Wax; finely detailed and beautifully executed portrait dolls with magnificent costumes	1,800.00–3,000.00
Dengel, Dianne	Cloth; young child or baby with stitch-shaped, painted facial features	250.00–500.00

Artist Original Doll Value Comparison		
Deval, Brigette	Wax or porcelain; one of a kind or extremely limited edition	3,500.00–5,500.00
Ellis, Cathy	Super Sculpey; charming character face child	300.00–600.00
Fisher, Ruth	Porcelain; oriental child	300.00–500.00
Fox, Madelaine	Clay-like composition; historical portrait in elaborate costumes designed and made by the artist	1,200.00–2,500.00
Goodnow, June	Porcelain; American Indian with authentic tribal costuming	1,200.00–2,800.00
Gunzel, Hildegard	Porcelain or wax over porcelain; expressive, beautiful, life-like children	1,500.00–3,000.00
Hale, Patti	Wooden; charming in their simplicity	400.00–600.00
Heighton, Jean	Cloth, latex, or porcelain; fantasy folks wearing appealing costumes	400.00–700.00
Heiser, Dorothy	Cloth; finely detailed stitch-sculptured portrait magnificently costumed	2000.00–4000.00
Helm, Anne	Gesso over wood; adult or child reminiscent of early wooden with painted facial features	200.00–400.00
Hesner, Dorothy	Porcelain; "Fruit Head" characters child with comic appeal	100.00–350.00
Holmes, Barbara	Sculpey, porcelain, or wax; historical portrait and fairy tale characters	300.00–500.00
Johnson, Sharon	Porcelain; child	200.00–300.00
Kane, Maggie Head	Porcelain; character portrait adult or child	400.00–700.00
Koerling, Cindy	Native American babies in authentic costume	600.00–800.00
Lafitte, Desirat	Wax; portrait with exquisite period costumes	1,000.00–1,500.00
Ling, Tita	Wooden; oriental child or adult	700.00–900.00
Little, Virginia	Wooden; artistically carved and historically significant character	400.00–700.00
Mark, Suzanne	Porcelain; miniature child uniquely styled to suggest movement, animation, and playfulness	250.00–400.00
McLean, Jan	Porcelain; hauntingly beautiful child wearing appealing artist-designed costumes	3,000.00–5,000.00
Motter, Jennifer Berry	Cloth; beautifully detailed, hand painted features with a three dimensional look wearing layers of aesthetically pleasing costumes of vintage fabrics	500.00–1,500.00
Nelson, Bill	Modelled character faces on cloth covered wire armature bodies	2,500.00–4,500.00
Oldenburg, Mary Ann	Porcelain; child	350.00–700.00
Park, Irma	Wax; tiny characters posed in delightful settings with accessories and props	200.00–400.00
Parker, Ann	Wax or wax over; miniature historical or fictional portrait dolls in authentic artistically designed costumes	300.00–900.00
Port, Beverly	Porcelain, cloth, wax, or composition; fanciful animal people	500.00–750.00
Price, Jeanette	Porcelain or sculpey; appealing Santa Claus and gnomes	300.00–700.00
Randolf, Patricia Gene	Porcelain or ceramics; artsy characters with fantastically modelled facial features	600.00–1,200.00
Redmond, Kathy	Porcelain; portrait modelling with fine attention to detail	900.00–2,000.00
Robinson, Pat	Porcelain; life-like, finely detailed, articulated adult, figures	400.00–900.00
Sandreuter, Regina	Wooden; child; delicate features and natural finish	1,500.00–2,500.00
Saucier, Madeline	Cloth	400.00–500.00
Scattolini, Laura	Cernit; sculpted, pensive child; appropriately costumed.	700.00–1,800.00
Smith, P. D.	Composition; character child with expressive facial modelling	2,000.00–3,700.00
Smith, Sherman	Wooden; Grodnertal-type; some with porcelain heads; valued for the artistic body construction	400.00–1,000.00
Sorensen, Lewis	Gibson Girl created with less attention to detail (see below for other examples)	400.00–700.00
	Wax, porcelain or papier mâché; highly detailed character portrait	1,500.00–3,500.00
Stafford, Joyce	Porcelain; small child	200.00–400.00
Thanos, Charleen	Porcelain; beautifully sculptured children	2,000.00–3,500.00
Thompson, Martha	Hand pressed porcelain or cultured glass; beautifully detailed features	1,000.00–3,000.00
Treffeisen, Ruth	Porcelain; child	2,000.00–3,000.00
Tuttle, Eunice	Porcelain or wax; miniature child, angel, or character	600.00–800.00
Wallace, Shelia	Wax; realistic portrait with inserted hair, historically correct costume and great attention to detail	3,000.00–5,000.00
Walters, Beverly	Porcelain; miniature; flawlessly designed fashion portrait	700.00–1,400.00
Walters, Helen	Cloth; Folk Art; hand painted and embroidered characters	600.00–900.00
Webster, Mary Hortence assisted by Loredo Taft	Composition; character with whimsical costume	400.00–700.00

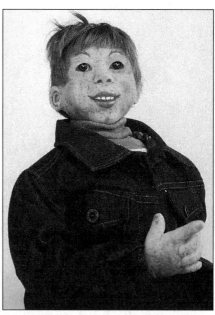

Original bisque artist dolls by Kathy Redmond. Queen Victoria; Edward VIII as a baby; Young Queen Victoria; Prince Albert and the Royal Princess in her bassinet. Courtesy of McMaster's Doll Auction

A 1991 original "Brad" by Pat Kolesar, valued at $600.00. Photograph courtesy of Bill Neff

Artist Original Doll Value Comparison		
Wick, Faith	Porcelain; historic or fictional character wearing artist designed detailed costume	700.00–1,500.00
Wilson, Lita	Porcelain; beautifully designed petite portrait	1,000.00–1,500.00
Witherspoon	Cloth; hand painted studio characters from New Orleans	1,000.00–2,500.00
Wright, Phyllis	Porcelain; child with expressive hand painted eyes	300.00–500.00
Wyffels, Berdine	Porcelain; child	250.00–300.00
Zeller, Fawn	Porcelain; one of a kind	2,500.00–3,500.00

Automata

Automata are French, German, or American-made mechanical dolls. Although references to automated dolls can be found dating as early as the mid-17th century, Automata's peak popularity spanned the years from 1860 to 1900.

There are several types of Automata, including: Automatons; Animated dolls; Autoperipatetikos; Cymbalers; Marottes; Pull toys; Phonograph dolls; Gigoteur; walking; talking; or swimming dolls. The most popular and actively sought examples are the lavishly costumed French Automatons.

The criteria for evaluating Automata is originality, costuming, condition, visual appeal, and the intricacy of its movements. Generally, value increases in direct relation to the doll's complexity. The more intricate the movements and the greater their number, the more valuable the Automata. Working condition is extremely important. Animated repairs can be very costly, and sometimes impossible to make.

Prices listed are for appropriately costumed dolls in perfect working condition with all parts, accessories, and, when applicable, keys.

Automaton

Automatons are charming, musical, mechanical dolls. The music box consists of a revolving cylinder with a series of small pins that strike a metal comb. The music box and/or clockwork mechanism is usually hidden in a velvet-covered platform base. When wound, the music plays and the doll performs a series of movements. Most Automatons were intended for the amusement of adults rather than children. Well-known manufacturers of Automatons include Rousselot, Phalibois, Vichy, Fleischmann and Blodel, Lambert, Roullet, and Decamps. Marks may be found on keys or on the inside of the housings. Doll heads were supplied by various doll manufacturers and were marked accordingly.

Broken Polichinelle by Lambert (French c. 1890): 19"; velvet-covered base conceals mechanism; rare bisque character head doll (marked "211/ Déposé Tete Jumeau") with very narrow squinting glass eyes and open/closed wailing mouth perfectly depicts emotions of an unhappy child crying over a broken

*Lady Bru in a Chariot by Roullett and Decamps Musical Automaton. 19"
tall and 22" long with closed mouth; Bru Jne swivel head on molded-breast
shoulder plate; when activated, arms move up and down, head turns side to
side, and chariot rocks back and forth while the music plays and the bird
flutters his wings ($32,000.00). Courtesy of David Cobb's Doll Auctions*

toy; carton moule legs and torso, wire upper arms, bisque forearms; nicely dressed in original silk dress with matching bonnet;
when activated, doll turns head from side to side, looks down at
dismembered marionette, brings head up and wipes at eyes with
handkerchief in one hand while the other lifts the Polichinelle'
papier-mâché head still connected to the broken body that lies
on the floor at her feet; plays two tunes........................$18,000.00

Flower Peddlar by Leopold Lambert (French c. 1900):
21"; velvet-covered base conceals mechanism; bisque head doll
(marked "S & H 1159/Germany 4") glass eyes and open mouth;
carton moule legs and torso, wire upper arms, bisque forearms;
authentic gypsy costume with bright satin blouse, black velvet
cummerbund, dark wool skirt and paisley scarf; when activated,
doll turns head, blinks eyes, brings one hand holding flowers to
her nose, simultaneously nods head to smell flowers, as she lowers the flowers her head turns and looks towards a cone-shaped
flower arrangement sitting on a table before her, she lifts the
cone to reveal a hidden surprise – a tiny dancing all bisque doll
that spins to the music; key marked "LB".....................$15,000.00

**Girl with a Pocket Watch by Leopold Lambert (French
c. 1890):** 18"; velvet-covered base conceals mechanism; bisque
head doll (marked "Déposé Tete Jumeau"); paperweight eyes
and closed mouth; carton moule legs and torso, wire upper arms,
bisque forearms; beautiful, velvet-trimmed dress with applied
ribbon roses; when activated, doll turns head from side to side
while alternately looking at time on watch and bringing other
hand, holding lace-edged hanky, to face while music plays
....$6,700.00

Jester with Mandolin by Renou (French c. 1895):
15 1/2"; velvet-covered base conceals mechanism; bisque character head doll (marked "S & H," a 1300 series Simon & Halbig);
white Parian complexion with brightly painted clown decoration,
glass eyes, closed smiling mouth; carton moule legs and torso,
wire upper arms, bisque forearms; colorful satin costume with

jester's cap, adorned with silk pom-poms; when activated, doll
turns head from side to side, nods forwards and back, strums
aptly-decorated mandolin, and moves other hand realistically up
and down the neck of the instrument while the music plays; key
marked "Renou"..$4,600.00

**Laundress at the Ironing Board by Leopold Lambert
(French c. 1890):** 19"; velvet-covered base conceals mechanism;
bisque head doll (marked "Déposé Tete Jumeau/1"); paperweight eyes and closed mouth; carton moule legs and torso, wire
upper arms, bisque forearms; appropriately dressed in domestic
uniform, mob cap, and apron; when activated, doll looks down
at the ironing board, adjusts the lace-edge garment, lifts her arm
holding a miniature flat-iron, presses the material in realistic circular motions, lifts her head, turns to the side, and glances
towards a laundry basket full of linens sitting off to the side,
while the music plays $8,750.00

Performing Clown (Germany c. 1885): 18"; brightly colored, decorative base with lithographed design of Victorian children conceals mechanism; papier-mâché clown with painted
facial decorations; padded wire body and upper limbs with
papier-mâché feet and hands; ornate silk costume; when activated, clown turns head side to side, shakes tambourine, taps his
foot, and appears to sway while music plays.................$3,200.00

**Spanish Mandolin Player by Leopold Lambert (French
c. 1890):** 23"; wooden pedestal sits atop a velvet-covered base,
concealing mechanism; bisque head doll (Jumeau, marked "8");
paperweight eyes and closed mouth; carton moule legs and
torso, wire upper arms, bisque forearms; beautifully dressed in
original, elaborately-detailed silk and velvet costume; when activated, doll strums and plucks ebony and ivory inlay mandolin
with finely manicured bisque hand, turns head from side to side,
looks down at instrument, then slowly brings head back, tilts to
the side as if listening, all the while keeping perfect time to the
music by tapping her dainty foot; plays two tunes; key marked
"LB"...$35,000.00

Waltzing Couple by Gustave Vichy (French c. 1890): 23";
couturier-costumed couple in formal dance position; mechanism
concealed within a metal cone under the lady's gown; pale bisque
heads, paperweight eyes and closed mouths; gentleman unobtru-
sively attached to the lady at the waist by hidden wires, his feet
ever so slightly raised from the floor; carton moule torsos, wire
upper arms, bisque forearms; magnificent silk gown and suit
embellished with tiny, covered buttons, ruche, lace, and glass
beads; when activated, the couple glides and parades about the
room in an elaborate performance; they turn, pause, promenade,
and continue to strut to the music; marked "G. Vichy Paris"
....$38,000.00

Waltzing Couple by Gustave Vichy (French c. 1865): 13";
couple in conventional evening attire; perched atop a three-
wheeled tin platform with mechanism sheltered within a box
beneath; bisque head dolls with glass eyes, man with closed
mouth, lady with open mouth (lady's head appears to have been
replaced, dating c. 1890); joined by entwined bisque arms; gentleman's feet clearly raised from the floor in an awkward position; carton moule torsos, wire upper arms; when activated, the
couple moves around in circles, pauses, reverses, repeats, and
continues to dance to the music; marked "G Vichy Fils Paris";
(please note the many obvious and subtle differences between
this and the preceding Waltzing Couple by Vichy; the height difference of ten inches; the detailed couturier costuming versus
common evening attire; the quality of the doll heads; the manner
in which the couples are joined; the unrealistic positioning of the
bodies and feet; and finally the movements and complexity of
the dance—satisfying the key elements to evaluating an automata, namely originality, costuming, condition, visual appeal and
the intricacy of the movements) $54,000.00

Wonderful group of Automata, back row: bisque head Pull Toy, when pulled along, his arms go up and down, causing the bells to ring; all original bellows-type Cymbaler jester; front row: Animated Platform dolls, when cranked, toy plays or shakes instruments. Courtesy of David Cobb's Doll Auctions

Animated Dolls

Animated Dolls were first introduced in Germany and share some similarities with Automatons. The spring clock work of the Automaton is replaced by a rotating mechanism. Turning a crank causes the figure to move in a somewhat stiff and awkward style. Generally the value of an animated doll is determined more by charm and visual appeal than from the complexity of their movements.

Prices listed are for appropriately costumed dolls in perfect working condition, with all parts and accessories.

Children at Play: 12" high x 7" deep; lithographed-designed, paper-covered base conceals mechanism with wooden knob; five bisque head dolls (marked with Heubach trademark and various style numbers); painted facial features; wooden block bodies with wire armature limbs and papier-mâché, stub-like hands; wearing simple, lace-trimmed muslin gowns and bonnets; when cranked, two dolls perched upon a wooden see-saw ride up and down, a single doll with a garland of flowers spins round and round, while the fourth doll pushes a metal filigree carriage, containing a tiny all-bisque baby, back and forth as the music box plays..**$4,600.00**

Musical Mandolin Player (French c. 1870): 18" doll; carton moule torso houses mechanism with porcelain turning knob protruding from back (hidden beneath cape); bisque head (marked "4" attributed to Gaultier); paperweight eyes; closed mouth; wire armature arms; carved wooden hands; standing on sturdy, composition, un-jointed legs; appropriately dressed in bright satin jester costume with long velvet cape and matching calotte; when cranked, doll briskly strums the mandolin as music box plays..**$5,000.00**

The Bandleader (Germany c. 1890): 13" overall height; lithographed-designed, paper-covered base conceals mechanism with porcelain turning knob; bisque head doll (marked "Germany// 7/0") with glass eyes and open mouth; carton moule torso; wire armature arms, papier-mâché hands and legs; nicely costumed in silk suit with long jacket, gold braid epaulets and matching fez; when cranked, doll vigorously turns head from side to side and waves baton up and down as music box plays **$3,600.00**

Three Gypsy Musicians, probably by Zinner and Sohne (Germany c. 1890): 13" high x 11" deep; lithographed-designed, paper-covered base conceals mechanism with porcelain turning knob; three rare amber-tinted bisque character head dolls; glass eyes; accurately-detailed sculpted wrinkles, brows, and moustache over closed mouth; wooden block torso; wire armature limbs with carved wooden hands and feet; appropriately outfitted in knickers, full sleeved shirts, vests, cravat, and felt caps; when cranked, dolls turn heads from side to side, center conductor doll raises and lowers baton while other two gypsies perform on musical instruments as music box plays **$4,900.00**

Two Babies on the Telephone by Zinner and Sohne (Germany c. 1910): 12" high x 12" deep; lithographed-designed, paper-covered base conceals mechanism with wooden turning knob; partition-like curtain divides stage into separate rooms; two bisque head dolls with nicely painted hair and facial features; wooden block bodies with wire armature arms and papier-mâché hands; appropriately dressed as children with lace-trimmed bonnets; when cranked, dolls (one standing on a stool) move heads back and forth while talking on the phone as music box plays...**$2,800.00**

Autoperipatetikos

Autoperipatetikos were made in France, Germany, and America, representing children, ladies, and gentlemen complete with mustache and goatee. A clockwork mechanism within a walking body caused the pressed metal feet, to move back and forth. Most are about 10" high and typically marked "Patented July 15th 1862 also in England."

Prices listed are for appropriately costumed dolls in good working condition with no damage.

Pressed cloth face: molded and painted hair and facial features; leather or papier-mâché arms **$1,400.00**

Composition head: molded and painted hair and facial features; composition arms **$1,600.00**

China head: molded and painted hair and facial features; leather or china arms...**$2,200.00**

Bisque head: molded and painted hair or good wig; glass or painted eyes; papier-mâché arms **$2,700.00**

Note: *Add an additional $300.00 to any Autoperipatetikos styled as a man.*

Cymbalers

Cymbalers contain a pressure activated bellows mechanism within their bodies. When compressed the arms come together. Heads are usually made of bisque and commonly resemble a baby or clown less than ten inches tall.

Prices listed are for appropriately costumed dolls in good working condition with no damage.

Common Pat-a-Cake: 10"; doll or clown; wooden block bellows body; wire armature limbs; hands come together when tummy is pressed **$800.00**

Blinking Eye Clown: 12"; wooden block bellows body; wire armature limbs; hands come together and eyes blink rapidly when tummy is pressed **$2,400.00**

Marottes

Marottes from France and Germany fall somewhere between a doll and a toy. By definition a marotte is a doll's head on a stick. Most, however, are bisque heads sitting atop music boxes concealed within lavishly dressed carton moule drum-shaped torsos perched atop carved and decorated handles. When waved a musical movement is activated as the doll twirls, creating a lovely effect. Frequently Marottes are made of papier-mâché and decorated to represent a variety of characters from clowns to animals.

Prices listed are for appropriately costumed marottes in good working condition with no damage.

Bisque Head: 12"; good wig; glass or paperweight eyes; open or closed mouth; beautifully costumed **$1,500.00**

Papier-Mâché: 12"; molded and painted hair and facial features; appropriately costumed **$1,000.00**

31" open mouth Jumeau holds a 12" all-original Marotte with ivory handle; when twirled, bells ring and music plays. Courtesy of David Cobb's Doll Auctions

Pull Toys

France and Germany produced the entertaining pull toys. Usually found with one or more small bisque dolls fixed to a wooden platform on wheels. The dolls are stationary, or simple movements are incorporated into the toy's design, with the drive initiated via the axis of the wheel.

Recently, thousands of reproduction pull toys have been imported. Doll markings may be the best defense against a fake, although remember that some genuine antiques are unmarked. The platform of reproductions have rounded, smooth corners and heavy, molded, cold-cast metal wheels. A final clue may be in the size. Reproductions tend to be made on a larger scale. Most antique pull toys are more petite, usually less than 15" long.

Prices listed are for appropriately costumed, visually appealing toys with no damage. Condition, charm, and appeal are equally important components of a pull toy's value.

Boy on a Horse, attributed to Zinner & Shone (Germany c. 1890): 10" long; lithograph-designed, paper-covered wooden platform on four metal wheels; bisque head doll (marked "S H 1079//0 DEP") with glass eyes and open mouth; wooden block torso, wire armature upper arms with papier-mâché hands and molded boots; beautifully made satin and velvet riding costume, elaborately decorated by gold braid and brass buttons; carrying a small French horn; seated upon a felt-covered horse, complete with saddle blanket, leather harness and tiny silver bells; stationary, however, when pulled, the wire construction of the arms allows the doll to appear to be riding while the miniature bells tinkle softly **$3,800.00**

Normandy Girl with Swans (France c. 1915): 14" long; painted 'grass' and 'lake' wooden platform on four metal wheels with simple push-rod mechanism; bisque head doll (marked "Limoges/France") with glass eyes and open mouth; wooden block torso, wire armature upper arms with wooden legs and stub-like hands; original Normandy folklore costume with matching hat and cleverly painted shoes; three papier-mâché flocked-flannel-down geese with glass eyes, applied feather tails, and painted blue and white dotted vests with red ribbon neckties (perhaps a distant ancestor of Donald Duck); when pulled, the geese vibrate and flutter as though running away while the girl nods her head and waves her arm **$4,000.00**

Polichinelle and a Dancing Dog (France c. 1890): 11" long; painted 'flowered garden path' wooden platform on four tin wheels with simple push-rod mechanism; bisque head doll with glass eyes and open mouth; wooden block torso, wire armature upper arms, papier-mâché hands and legs, molded pointed-toe clog shoes; beautifully detailed Polichinelle costume with humped back and broad hat, embellished with gold trim and tiny brass bells; faces white plush poodle standing upright on hind legs upon a small decorated table; when pulled, dog twirls around while Polichinelle arms wave; also a small bellows-type voice box is positioned beneath the platform so that as the dog spins a squeak or bark sound is made..............................**$4,800.00**

The Parade by Zinner and Sohne (Germany c. 1900): 11" long; lithograph-designed, paper-covered wooden platform on four metal wheels with simple push-rod mechanism; two bisque head dolls with wooden block torsos, wire armature upper arms with carved wooden hands and papier-mâché legs; front doll with glass eyes and open mouth, holding an accordion, dressed in lace-trimmed jester's costume, hat decorated with tiny bells; rear character doll with painted clown face, glass eyes and closed grinning mouth stands behind a brightly painted bass drum, wears a traditional clown's outfit and cap; when pulled, the dolls play their instruments and turn their heads from side to side **$3,800.00**

Mary and Her Lamb, probably by Zinner and Shone (Germany c. 1890): 9" long; lithograph-designed, paper-covered wooden platform on four tin wheels with simple push-rod mechanism, bisque head doll (marked "4600/S pb H/ 11") with glass eyes, open mouth; wooden block torso, wire armature upper arms with papier-mâché hands and legs; dressed in school-girl style pinafore over cotton dress with lace trim; holding harness to plush covered papier-mâché lamb; when pulled, Mary's arm moves up and down and she taps her foot **$2,700.00**

Phonograph Dolls

Finding an antique Phonograph Doll is truly a rare treat. Be sure that the mechanical parts are in working condition and the doll itself is not damaged.

Edison Phonograph Doll: In 1878, Thomas A. Edison invented and patented a "phonographic doll." Initially the arms and head were attached to a tube-shaped body. The first dolls bore little resemblance to the Edison Talking Doll patented in 1888 by William Jacques, assembled at the Edison Phonographic Works in New Jersey. The Edison Phonographic Toy Company records indicate that there were two manufacturers of bisque heads for these dolls, although the only known are from Simon & Halbig. Metal torso containing hand-cranked talking mechanism; jointed wooden arms and legs; German made bisque head **$7,000.00**

Bébé Phonographe by Jumeau with original box and talking wax cylinders. Courtesy of David Cobb's Doll Auctions

Bébé Phonographe by Jumeau: bisque head; ball-jointed composition body; beautiful paperweight eyes; open mouth with molded teeth. The cylinders were made of white wax to talk and sing in French, English, and Spanish **$10,000.00**

Max Oscar Arnold: bisque head; jointed composition body. The body separated above the hips with a phonograph placed inside. The bodies were later improved with a metal front for the speaker **$3,000.00**

Primadonna made by Giebeler-Falk: aluminum head and body; human hair wig. The crown of the head was hinged and lifted forward. The horn and turntable were in the head and the mechanism was in the body. The doll would sing or talk when a record was placed in the head **$1,700.00**

Dolly Record by Madame Hendren/Averill and MAESTARR by Effanbee: composition head; metal eyes; phonograph mechanism housed in body; appropriately dressed**$900.00**

Talking Terri Lee: hard plastic and vinyl; painted eyes; special adapter assembly that installed to any record player; receptacle in back of doll head to connect to record player with adapter cord; speaker within torso; advertised as "I will tell you stories and sing you songs. I will tell you many wonderful things. My stories and songs are called Terri Tales and Terri Tunes at Terri Time"; appropriately dressed..**$800.00**

Walking and Talking Dolls

Walking and Talking Dolls are often found with chain mechanisms. Others have wire arrangements connecting the arms and feet, a technique first used by Schoenhut wooden dolls. The talking device in early Talking Dolls consists of a bellows in the body that was activated by pulling strings, exerting pressure, or moving some part of the body. The body was cut in two, the bellows were placed inside, and the body was rejoined with strips of kid. Different sounds could be produced with different tubes and objects placed in the bellows. The reeds-and-bellows type mechanism made Mama dolls of the 1920s very popular. Regardless of the type of talking device, a simple "Mama" or "Papa" was all that was achieved.

Boy Pulling a Cart: 16" overall length, boy 12" ; bisque socket head; mohair wig; glass eyes; open mouth; papier-mâché torso with clockwork mechanism; jointed shoulder and hip; bisque hands screwed to handles of cart; when activated, boy walks briskly forward, pulling wooden two-wheeled cart; marked "1078/Simon Halbig" **$4,200.00**

Talking Madame Hendren Dolly Record Dolls, holding boxes of record cylinders. Courtesy of David Cobb's Doll Auctions

Walking, Kiss Throwing, Talking, Flirting Doll: 22"–24"; bisque socket head; composition straight limbed, pin-jointed body; good wig; glass, flirty eyes; open mouth; when 'walked,' doll's head turns, causing eyes to move side to side; simple pull-cords control kissing and talking; appropriately dressed; various doll manufacturers' markings **$2,000.00–3,500.00**

Walking Doll: 14"–22"; bisque socket head; composition straight limbed, pin-jointed or hinged body; clockwork mechanism in torso with permanently set-in key; good wig; glass eyes; open mouth; appropriately dressed; when key-wound, doll alternately lifts each leg and walks; various doll manufacturers' markings ....**$2,500.00 and up**

Creeping Baby: 12"–14"; papier-mâché head, torso, and lower limbs with metal pivot-joints; key-wound, teeth-edged gears protrude from body (the Creeping Baby was originally patented by Robert Clay in 1871, but the teeth-edged gears were not used until later that year by George Clark, considered by most to be the superior model); mohair wig; painted features; when wound, the baby crawls forward in a realistic fashion....**$1,700.00**

Gigoteur

First patented in September 1855 by Jules Steiner, walking, kicking, crying, and talking dolls, known as Gigoteur, were modified several times over the following twenty years. The body houses the flywheel regulator and clockwork mechanism. Typically marked "1," "2," "3," or unmarked.

Prices listed are for appropriately dressed undamaged dolls in good working condition. Slight wear to the body does not affect the value.

Bébé Gigoteur: 17"–24"; solid domed, flat cut, bisque socket head; mechanism within carton moule torso, papier-mâché arms and lower legs, jointed with leather or kid strips; skin or mohair wig; small, almond-cut enamel or paperweight eyes, finely lined in black; open mouth with tiny porcelain teeth; appropriately dressed; winding and releasing lever causes doll to wave arms, kick legs, move head from side to side, and cry "mama"

17"	$2,800.00
20"	3,600.00
24"	4,500.00

Swimming Doll

Swimming Doll, also known as Ondine, was once advertised as "Parisian Mechanician for Adult Amusement." Made with either a bisque or celluloid head and a cork body with jointed wooden arms and legs that simulated swimming when wound by a key.

Swimming Doll: 12"; bisque head.............................**$1,900.00**
Swimming Doll: 12"; celluloid head **$900.00**

Averill Manufacturing Company

Bisque Bonnie Babies. Courtesy of McMaster's Doll Auction

Averill Manufacturing Company was located in New York, N.Y. from 1913 until 1965, when operations ceased and assets were liquidated.

Headed by the husband and wife team of Georgene and James Paul Averill, Georgene's brother, Rudolph A. Hopf, served as president of the Averill Manufacturing Company. The variety of dolls produced was vast and bridged the gap from bisque to vinyl.

Georgene and James Averill branched out in 1923, forming Madame Georgene Inc. Doll Company, with James Paul as president. They later went on to form Georgene Novelties, Inc.

In addition to promoting her own line of dolls, Georgene Averill also did design work for George Borgfeldt (her most popular doll being the Bonnie Baby) and served as superintendent of Borgfeldt's toy department.

Madame Hendren is a trademark used by Averill Manufacturing Company.

Also see All-Bique, Automaton, Raggedy Ann & Andy.

Bonnie Babe

Bonnie Babe resembles a one-year-old baby; bisque or celluloid head; cloth body with composition limbs, or composition bent-limb baby body; molded and painted hair; sleep eyes; open, smiling, slightly-crooked mouth with two lower teeth; appropriately dressed; marked "Copr. By/Georgene Averill/Germany/

1005-3653/1386" (or "1402"). **Note:** *Bisque heads were produced in Germany by Alt, Beck & Gottschalk or Kestner. They were distributed by George Borgfeldt. Georgene registered a U.S. trademark of Bonnie Babe in 1926 and quickly transferred it to G. Borgfeldt. A renewal of U.S. trademarks indicates that Bonnie Babes were still being produced in 1946.*

Bonnie Babe Value Comparisons

Size	Bisque Head, Cloth Body	Bisque Head, Composition Body	Celluloid Head
10"		1,600.00	
12"	1,500.00	2,200.00	500.00
14"	1,700.00	2,400.00	600.00
16"	1,950.00	2,900.00	900.00
18"	2,100.00	3,200.00	950.00
20"	2,300.00	3,400.00	975.00
22"	2,400.00	3,600.00	1,000.00
24"	2,700.00	3,800.00	1,100.00

Composition

Prices listed are for appropriately costumed dolls in good condition. Slight crazing is acceptable and does not greatly affect the price. If badly crazed, cracked, peeling, or repainted, expect the value to be less than half the amounts listed.

Mama Doll: composition head and limbs; cloth body; molded and painted hair or good wig; painted or tin sleep eyes; closed or open/closed mouth with teeth; appropriately dressed; typically marked "Genuine Madam Hendren Doll 1717 Made in USA."

Bobby and Dolly Dolls: composition head and limbs; cloth body; molded and painted hair; round, painted, side-glancing eyes; round, pug nose; closed, smiling, single-lined, painted mouth; appropriately dressed; typically marked "G.G. Drayton"; neither the Averill nor the Hendren names appear on this doll

Whistling Dolls (Nell, Dan, or Sailor): composition head; cloth body; molded and painted hair with rows of curls in back; painted, side-glancing eyes; puckered mouth with hole for whistling; cloth-covered spring legs are part of whistling mechanism; whistling sound is made when feet are pushed; appropriately dressed; typically marked "USA" or unmarked; hang tag "I whistle when you dance me on one foot/and then the other/Patented Feb. 2, 1926. A Genuine Madame Hendron Doll."

Costumed Character: composition head and lower limbs; cloth body; molded and painted hair or mohair wig; painted eyes; closed mouth; tagged; appropriate costume; typically unmarked.

Body Twist (Dimmie and Jimmie): all composition; jointed neck, shoulder, and hip; large ball joint at waist; advertised as "pleasingly plump, and able to stand and pose a thousand ways"; molded and painted hair; painted eyes with large pupils and eye shadow; appropriately dressed; unmarked; wrist tag "Dimmie/Jimmie, Another Madame Hendren Doll/Made in

Composition Mama baby in original box. Courtesy of David Cobb's Doll Auctions

USA" or "Jimmie/Dimmie's Boy Friend/Another Madame Hendren Doll/Made in USA."

Val-encia: composition shoulder head and limbs; slim body with voice box; low center of gravity allows the doll to walk; face flocked to resemble felt (imitates Lenci Dolls); mohair wig; big, painted eyes surrounded by dark eye shadow; dressed in felt or combinations of felt and organdy; typically stamped "Genuine/Madame Hendren/Doll/1714 Made in U.S.A."

Harriet Flanders: all composition; jointed at neck, shoulder, and hip; molded tufts of hair; painted eyes; three eyelashes above each eye; open mouth with painted tongue; appropriately dressed; typically marked "Harriet Flanders/1937."

Celluloid

Prices listed are for appropriately costumed dolls in good condition. If cracked, warped, or badly discolored, expect the value to be less than one fourth the amounts listed.

Sunny Boy or Sunny Girl: celluloid head; composition arms and legs; slender cloth body; molded hair; glass eyes; appropriately dressed; marked "Sunny Girl" with a turtle and a sun burst;

Averill Composition Value Comparisons

Size	Mama Baby	Bobby Dolly	Whistling Doll*	Body Twist	Val-encia	Harriet Flanders
10"	200.00					
12"						350.00
14"		600.00	450.00	650.00		
15"	400.00				500.00	
16"		450.00				450.00
17"	450.00					
22"	600.00					
24"	650.00					

* Add an additional $100.00 for Black Rufus.

wrist tag "Sunny/Girl [Boy]/the doll with the/beautiful bright eyes, Averill Manufacturing Co. USA."

Averill Celluloid Value Comparisons

Size	Sunny Boy or Sunny Girl
14"	550.00
17"	575.00
19"	600.00
22"	700.00

Cloth

Prices listed are for appropriately costumed dolls with good color and little or no fading. Slight wear and signs of aging, such as a settled body, do not greatly affect the price. If a doll is stained, torn, badly mended, or faded, expect the value to be less than half the amounts listed.

Grace G. Drayton (Dolly Dingle, Chocolate Drop, Happy Cryer, Sis, Baby Bunny, Mah-Jongg Kid, Kitty Puss, and Susie Bear): cloth doll; movable limbs; painted, flat face; large, round, side-glancing eyes; pug nose; single line, smiling mouth; removable clothing; typically marked "Dolly Dingle/Copyright By/G. G. Drayton."

Maud Tousey Fangel (Snooks and Sweets): printed cloth doll; flat, painted face; painted or yarn hair; very big eyes with long lashes; little nose; closed, smiling mouth; printed clothing and flesh-colored body; typically marked "MTF" at seam on side of head or unmarked (mark may be sewn into seam); hang tag "Soft Baby Doll/Created Exclusively for us by/Maud Tousey Fangel/America's Foremost Baby Painted/Georgene Novelties, Inc. New York, N.Y." An article in a 1936 edition of *Toys and Novelties* reads: "Snooks and Sweets are new creations in novelty dolls. These dolls are accurate reproductions from the works of the celebrated artist Maud Tousey Fangel, whose drawings have appeared as cover designs on many important magazines of wide circulation. (Her work is in demand by national advertisers.) These dolls are soft and cuddly, distinctly baby-type, washable and waterproof. Anyone familiar with the work of Maud Tousey Fangel knows the lovable expressions and natural baby charm she puts into her creations. It is the irresistible appeal [that] the manufacturers have captured and reproduced with such convincing accuracy. The dolls are copied from pastel drawings preserving all the color value of the originals. The Maud Tousey Fangel Dolls are made in two faces and in four sizes. The brunette is Snooks and the blonde is Sweets."

Child or Baby Doll: mask face; cloth body; yarn hair; painted features; or all sateen with beautifully applied facial deco-

ration and elaborate costuming; some with real eyelashes; appropriately dressed; typically unmarked; Bridesmaid, Ring Bearer, Flower Girl, Mary Had a Little Lamb, Girl Scout Brownie, and international dolls are more common than sateen character dolls. One clue to identifying an Averill cloth doll is that the body is hand-sewn with an overcast stitch.

Comic Character Doll: swivel head; mask face; yarn hair; painted eyes; applied ears; closed mouth; original, appropriate character costumes of cotton, felt, knit, or a combination of the three; typically unmarked; hang tag character name "Georgene Novelties, Inc. New York City, Exclusive Licensed Manufacturers Made in U.S.A." ***Note:*** *Identified by their striking resemblance to the characters they portray. Comic characters include Alvin, Little Lulu,*

Cloth Comic Characters with original boxes, including Alvin, Little Lulu, and Tubby Tom. Courtesy of McMaster's Doll Auction

Averill Cloth Value Comparisons

Size	Grace G. Drayton*	Maud T. Fangel	Character Sateen	International/ Mask-Face Series	Comic Characters	Characters
11"	850.00					
12"		800.00	300.00	185.00	1,500.00	
14"	750.00	900.00			1,500.00	
15"				200.00		
16"	950.00	1,000.00	450.00			
18"		1,100.00				
21"						750.00
22"		1,400.00	500.00			
24"				300.00		

* Add an additional $100.00 for Chocolate Drop (Black cloth doll).

Nancy, Sluggo, Tubby Tom, and Becassine. Check carefully for damage. Mask faces are vulnerable to indentations.

Character Doll: all cloth; shaped face and body; painted features; original costume; typically unmarked; hang tag "Georgene Averill." Nurse Jane and Uncle Wiggily are among the most popular.

Vinyl

Prices listed are for dolls in near-mint, original condition. If damaged, redressed, or undressed, expect the value to be less than one half to one fourth the amounts listed.

Aver Baby: vinyl head and gauntlet hands; cloth body; molded hair; painted eyes; wide open, smiling mouth; original outfit; typically marked "Averill."

Baby Dawn: all vinyl; chubby baby body; rooted, synthetic hair; large, sleep eyes; dimpled cheeks; open/closed, slightly-smiling mouth; original outfit; typically marked "AVERILL."

Averill Vinyl Value Comparison		
Size	**Baby Dawn**	**Aver Baby**
18"		350.00
20"	450.00	
24"		400.00
26"		425.00

Babyland Rag

*B*abyland Rag is the trade name of various types of cloth dolls produced and/or distributed by Horsman. The earliest Babyland Rag Dolls had simple hand-painted features with little detail—single-stroke brows, nice eyes, pug nose, and slightly-smiling bow-type mouth. Later dolls had lithographed faces.

Prices listed are for appropriately dressed dolls with good color and little or no fading. Slight wear and signs of aging such as a settled body do not greatly affect prices. If a doll is stained, torn, badly mended, or faded, expect the value to be less than half the value listed.

Oil-Painted Face

Painted Babyland Rag: painted cloth; mitt-type hands; mohair sewn on front of head or detailed, painted hair; flat face with painted features; removable, appropriate clothing; typically marked "Genuine Babyland Trade Mark" or unmarked. ***Note:*** *Black versions of Painted Babyland Rag dolls were also produced, as was a Topsy-Turvy model with one white face and one Black face.*

Lithograph Babyland Rag Doll

Printed Babyland Rag: cloth doll; printed, life-like features and hair; removable, appropriate clothing; typically unmarked. ***Note:*** *Black versions of Printed Babyland Rag Dolls were also produced, as was a Topsy-Turvy model with one white face and one Black face.*

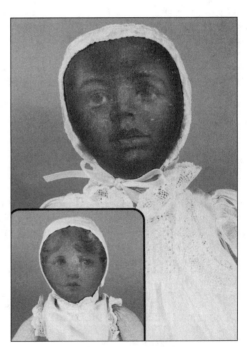

Lithograph Topsy Turvy Babyland Rag doll. Courtesy of McMaster's Doll Auction

Babyland Rag Value Comparisons						
Size	Oil-Painted Face	Black Oil-Painted Face	Topsy-Turvy Oil-Painted	Lithograph	Lithograph Black	Lithograph Topsy-Turvy
13"	1,200.00			750.00		
15"	1,400.00	1,600.00	1,200.00	850.00	900.00	1,000.00
17"		1,800.00				
18"			1,500.00	950.00		
22"	1,800.00	2,100.00		1,000.00	1,100.00	1,400.00
26"		2,600.00				
28"	2,500.00	3,000.00		1,200.00		

Bähr & Pröschild

Bähr & Pröschild #604 Character Baby on a jointed toddler body. Courtesy of McMaster's Doll Auction

Bähr & Pröschild was a porcelain factory in Ohrdruf, Germany. Founded in 1871, it continued operating until 1910. The original owners, George Baehr and August Proeschild, changed the spelling of their names in order to facilitate correspondence with American customers. Bähr & Pröschild made some of the loveliest German dolls.

Dating a Bähr & Pröschild doll is relatively easy. The earliest dolls were marked with only a mold number. In 1988, "dep" was added. Around 1895, the initials "B & P" were included. In 1900, a crossed swords symbol was added. Finally in 1919, when Bruno Schmidt purchased the business, The Bähr & Pröschild dolls adopted a heart as a trademark and incorporated it into the markings.

Mold numbers registered by Bähr & Pröschild included: 201, 204, 207, 209, 212, 213, 217, 219, 220, 224, 225, 226, 227, 230, 239, 244, 245, 247, 248, 251, 252, 253, 259, 260, 261, 263, 264, 265, 269, 270, 273, 275, 277, 278, 281, 283, 285, 287, 289, 292, 297, 300, 302, 305, 306, 309, 313, 320, 321, 322, 323, 324, 325, 330, 340, 342, 343, 348, 350, 374, 375, 376, 378, 379, 380, 381, 389, 390, 393, 394, 424, 425, 441, 482, 499, 500, 520, 525, 526, 529, 531, 534, 535, 536, 537, 539, 541, 546, 549, 554, 557, 562, 568, 571, 581, 584, 585, 587, 600, 604, 619, 620, 624, 640, 641, 643, 644, 645, 646, 678, 707, and 799.

Molds 529, 534, 536, 537, and 539 are among the molds made for Bruno Schmidt and have a 2000 series number (e.g. 537/2033). The three-digit number is the Bähr & Pröschild number; the four-digit number is the registered Bruno Schmidt number. The name Buporit was registered for celluloid.

Some Bähr & Pröschild mold numbers identify specific dolls. For example, 217 is a Black doll, 220 is Oriental, 244 is an Indian character, and 678 is a closed-mouth Googly. Other mold numbers are not so definitive. The same mold number may be found with either open or closed mouth and open pate or Belton-style dome head. Descriptions and classifications are listed as pricing comparisons.

Prices listed are for appropriately costumed dolls in good condition. Normal wear, slight damage, or well-made repairs to the body do not greatly affect the price. If the bisque is damaged or repaired, expect the value to be less than half the amounts listed. It is perfectly acceptable to show a missing or repaired finger or joint, or a mended body.

Bähr & Pröschild Value Comparisons

Size	Closed Mouth, Belton-Type, Composition Body	Closed Mouth, Socket Head, Composition Body	Closed Mouth, Shoulder Head, Kid Body	Dolly-Face, Composition Body	Dolly-Face, Kid Body	Character Baby, Bent-Limb Body*	#244 Character Socket head Closed Mouth Glass Eyes	#520 Character Socket Head Closed Mouth Painted Eyes	#536 Character Socket Head Closed Mouth Painted Eyes	#562 Character Socket Head Closed Mouth Glass Eyes
10"	2,000.00			700.00	350.00	650.00				
12"	2,400.00	1,100.00	900.00	800.00		700.00	3,200.00			6,500.00
14"			1,400.00			850.00	3,800.00	3,900.00	6,700.00	
16"		1,600.00			700.00	1,000.00				
18"	3,200.00			1,100.00		1,200.00				
20"	3,600.00	2,000.00	1,800.00	1,200.00	750.00	1,400.00				
22"				1,400.00	800.00	1,700.00				
24"	4,500.00	2,600.00	2,300.00	1,500.00		1,900.00				

* Add an additional $700.00 for jointed toddler body.

Also see Oriental Dolls, Googly-Eyed Dolls, and All Bisque.

Belton-Type Doll: bisque solid dome or flat top, usually with two or three holes; jointed composition, often French, wood body; good wig; paperweight eyes; pierced ears; closed mouth; appropriately dressed; typically marked in 200 series.

Closed Mouth Child Doll: bisque shoulder or socket head; kid or jointed straight wrist composition body; good wig; glass eyes; pierced ears; closed mouth; appropriately dressed; typically marked in 200 or 300 series.

Dolly-Faced: bisque shoulder or socket head; kid or jointed-wood-and-composition body; good wig; glass eyes; pierced ears; open mouth; appropriately dressed; typically marked in 200 or 300 series.

Character Babies: bisque socket head; composition bent-limb baby body; solid dome; painted hair or good wig; sleep eyes; open mouth; appropriately dressed; typically marked "585," "587," "604," "619," "620," "624," and "678."

Character Dolls: bisque socket head; jointed-wood-and-composition body; solid dome; painted hair or good wig; sleep or painted eyes; open/closed or closed mouth; appropriately dressed; typically marked "244," "520," "536," "562," and possibly others.

Barbie® & Friends

The Barbie era began in 1958 when Ruth Handler, wife of the co-founder of Mattel, decided that a fashion doll with an expensive wardrobe would be a wonderful idea. Her intuition could not have been more correct. Mattel's Barbie has been so successful that there is now a third generation of children playing with Barbie and her friends.

Barbie has changed with the times. There have been at least two instances in which Mattel has instigated a trade-in program. The first was in May of 1967. A new Twist 'N Turn Barbie could be had in exchange for $1.50 and a used Barbie doll in any condition. Over 1.4 million Barbies were traded that month. The second trade-in program was for Living Skipper in 1970.

Barbies can twist, walk, dance, wink, kiss, grab things, hunch their shoulders, and talk. Barbie's "A" list of friends, costumes, and accessories seems endless.

Mattel released a talking Barbie, programmed to say four different phrases that had been randomly selected from a total of 270 recorded by Mattel. Of the 350,000 dolls produced, an estimated 3,500 uttered a controversial line "Math class is tough." This seemingly innocuous phrase proved to be offensive to many people who claimed it reinforced the stereotype that girls do not do well in math. The phrase was dropped from future production, and Mattel offered to exchange any of the "offensive" dolls already purchased. For Barbie collectors, this was a dream come true. The limited production run, coupled with the number of dolls returned to Mattel, meant Teen Talk Barbie would be a fairly rare find. Additionally, there was nothing on the box to indicate which Teen Talk Barbie spoke the offensive phrase. One had to buy the doll and listen to her. What a time Barbie collectors had trying to acquire a "politically incorrect" Barbie. The original price of Teen Talk Barbie was under $20. Today, collectors will happily pay $300.00 to add this Barbie to their collections.

When examining a Barbie doll, check condition carefully. Any doll in less than very good condition will quickly drop in value. Vinyl fading and spotting is acceptable to collectors as it is a normal aging process and therefore does not greatly affect value. A damaged or played with Barbie, or one missing accessories, should be valued at less than half the prices listed.

Barbie #1: 1959; vinyl; heavy, solid body, most likely faded to a very pale or whitish color; vinyl usually has an aroma of crayons, chocolate, or wax; soft, silky floss blond or brunette hair, styled in ponytail with curly bangs; highly arched (upside down V-shaped) eyebrows; painted black and white eyes with heavy black eyeliner and a thin line of blue on the eye lid; bright red lips and nail color may be faded to orange-red; holes in balls of feet with copper tubes running up into legs to accommodate prongs

Barbie dolls, back row: on left Barbie #2, on right Barbie #1. Front row: Barbie #3. Courtesy of McMaster's Doll Auction

of posing stand; wearing one-piece black and white striped swimsuit, gold hoop earrings, and black high heel plastic shoes with holes in the soles that correspond to holes in feet. Marked "Japan" on the arch of the foot; marked on the hip:

Barbie T. M.
Pats. Pend.
©MCMLVIII
by
Mattel Inc.

The #1 doll stand is a round, black plastic base with two prongs and a cross bar underneath for support. It is marked "Barbie T.M." The fashion booklet has Barbie's profile on the cover and is marked "Barbie T.M." The box is marked "Barbie T.M." and "850."

Barbie #2: made for three months in 1959-1960; identical in appearance to Barbie #1, but without holes in the feet, and most have pearl stud earrings. The Barbie #2 stand is a round, black plastic base with a "T" wire support placed one inch from the edge of the stand. The wire was designed to fit under Barbie's arms. Barbie #2 is marked the same as #1. Most fashion booklets and boxes were also marked the same, although a few #2 Barbies have been found with the "Barbie®" mark.

Barbie #3: 1960; same heavy, solid body, usually faded to a very pale or whitish color with same familiar "waxy" smell; blond or brunette soft floss hair, styled in a ponytail with curly bangs; rounded and tapered eyebrows, blue eyes, most with dark brown eyeliner, some with blue eyeliner on upper eye lid; bright red lips and nails that may have faded to orange-red; most #3 Barbies do not have holes in their feet, although a few transitional models were made; wearing one-piece black and white striped swimsuit, pearl earrings, black plastic high heel shoes; marked in the same manner as #1 and #2 Barbies. The major differences between Barbies #1 and #2 and the 1960 Barbie #3 are the eyebrows and eyes. Mattel felt that the earlier Barbies were too Asian in appearance, so the eyebrows were softened and given a more rounded and tapered look without the arch. Another distinction is the addition of eye color. Barbie #3 was the first to have real eye color.

Barbie #4: 1960; vinyl; heavy, solid body retains its nice flesh-tone color; same hair and hair style; softly rounded and tapered eyebrows, blue eyes with blue eyeliner on lids; original bathing suit, earrings, and shoes. The vinyl used for Barbie #4 has a tendency to turn green at the earring holes. The stand is a round, black plastic base hollowed out underneath and with the "T" wire support and stand placed 1/4" from the edge of the stand; marked "Barbie®" on fashion booklet and box. There may be some overlap in stands supplied with Barbie #3 and #4,

but value is unaffected. Barbie #4 is marked in the same manner as #1, #2, and #3.

Barbie #5: 1961; first hollow-body doll, much lighter in weight than the earlier Barbies; blond, brunette, or red saran hair, styled in the same ponytail and curly bangs; hair texture is sturdier and firmer than floss; longer eyebrows; smaller pupils show more blue eye color; blue eyeliner; most with red lips, some with a more delicate lip and nail color; original swimsuit, earrings, and shoes. Black wire stand with square base. Fashion booklet and box marked "Barbie®"; gold-colored wrist tag with "Barbie" written in script across the front; first box to offer red hair. Barbie #5 is marked in the same manner as #1, #2, #3, and #4, or may have T.M. replaced with ®.

Barbie #6: 1962–67; hollow body; transitional-style ponytail; lip and nail colors include pink, coral, and peach (which often fades to yellow or white); earlier Barbie #6 with dark royal blue eye color, models produced from 1963 on have aqua blue eye color; blond, brunette, red, ash blond, or platinum hair colors; one-piece red swimsuit. Typically marked on hip:

Barbie T.M.		MIDGE		1960
Pats. Pend.	*or*	©1962	*or*	By
©MCMLVIII		BARBIE®		Mattel Inc.
by		1958		Hawthorne
Mattel Inc.		by		Calif, USA
		Mattel, Inc.		

Bubble Cut Barbie: 1962–67; hollow body; sturdier, firmer saran hair, styled in full bubble cut; brunette, light brown, blond, or red hair; various lip and nail colors, often faded to yellow or white; one-piece red swimsuit and red plastic high heels. Typically marked:

Barbie T. M.	MIDGE
Pats. Pend.	©1962
©MCMLVIII	BARBIE®
by	1958
Mattel Inc.	by
	Mattel Inc.

See Doll Care for helpful tips concerning Barbie problems.

Barbie	Mint with Box*	Doll Only Very Good to Near Mint	Doll Only Good to Fair	Doll Only Played with to Poor	Doll Stand
#1	9,800.00	6,000.00	3,000.00	700.00	1,500.00
#2	9,000.00	5,000.00	2,500.00	600.00	1,000.00
#3	2,500.00	1,200.00	550.00	150.00	100.00
#4	1,200.00	700.00	250.00	100.00	600.00
#5	700.00	400.00	200.00	60.00	100.00
#6	400.00	200.00	75.00	40.00	
Bubble Cut	600.00	350.00	150.00	50.00	

* Add $1,000.00 for brunette.

Barbie and friends, back row: #4 Barbie; TnT Barbie; #4 Barbie; Midge; Ken; Francie, and TnT Christie. Front row: #5 Barbie, Ricky, Ken, #3–4 Transitional Barbie, #5 Barbie, and Skipper. Courtesy of McMaster's Doll Auction

Barbie and friends, back row: Bubble Cut Barbie, Swirl Ponytail Barbie, American Girl Barbie, Bubble Cut Barbie, Ken, Francie, and Allan. Front row: # 6 Barbie, Growing Hair Francie, Skipper, Midge, Living Barbie, and TnT Skipper. Courtesy of McMaster's Doll Auction

Date	Name	Description	Mint
1959	Barbie #1	Vinyl, heavy solid body; soft silky floss or saran hair, blond or brunette, ponytail with curly bangs; very arched eyebrows, painted black and white eyes, heavy eyeliner; bright red lips and nails; holes in feet, one-piece black and white swimsuit; with box	9,800.00
1959-60	Barbie #2	Sames as Barbine #1; no holes in feet; pearl stud earrings; change to stand; with box	9,000.00
1960	Barbie #3	Vinyl, heavy solid body; blond or brunette ponyail, curly bangs; changes to eyebrows; with box	2,500.00
1960	Barbie #4	Vinyl, heavy solid body; same hair and style; blue eyes; same swimsuit, earrings, and shoes; slight change to stand; with box	1,200.00
1961	Barbie #5	Hollow body; sturdier saran hair in ponytail and curly bangs, blond, brunette, and red head; original swimsuit; with box	700.00
1962-67	Barbie #6	Hollow body; dark royal blue eyes until 1963, then more aqua blue; blond, brunette, red head, ash blond, or platinum hair; with box	400.00
1962-67	Bubble Cut Barbie	Hollow body; sturdier saran hair, bubble-cut style brunette, light brown, blond, red; lip and nail colors vary; one-piece red swimsuit; red shoes; with box	600.00
1963	Fashion Queen	Egyptian-style gold and white swimsuit and head covering; 3 interchangeable wigs and wig stand	700.00
1964	Miss Barbie (Sleep Eye Barbie)	Open/close eyes; 3 interchangeable wigs; lawn swing, swimming cap, pink swimsuit	1,700.00
1964	Swirl Ponytail Barbie	Rooted hair, long sweeping bang crosses forehead; one-piece red swimsuit	900.00
1965	Bendable Leg Barbie, center part	4 different hairstyles; swimsuit with striped top, teal green bottom	3,000.00
1965	Bendable Leg Barbie, Doris Day-style side part	Specially rooted hair; swimsuit with striped top, teal green bottom	7,000.00
1965	Color Magic	Blond hair changes to scarlet red; swimsuit changes color	2,000.00

Group of Barbie and friends, from top: Moon Goddess by Bob Mackey, Empress Bride by Bob Mackey, Ken, #3 Barbie, Bubble Cut Barbie, Transitional # 4 Barbie, Midge, Bob Mackey Platinum, Molded Hair Midge, Bob Mackey Gold, Skipper, Francie, Christie, American Airlines Bubble Cut Barbie, Stacy, Fashion Queen Barbie, and Tutti. Courtesy of David Cobb's Doll Auctions

Date	Name	Description	Mint
1965	Color Magic	Midnight Black hair changes to ruby red; swimsuit changes color (hair fails to return to black)	3,000.00
1966	Twist 'N Turn "TNT"	Real rooted eyelashes	500.00
1968	Talking Barbie, Spanish Barbie	Ponytail to one side; pull-string at back	400.00
1969	Talking Truly Scrumptious	Pink gown; pull-string at back (from the movie, *Chitty Chitty Bang Bang*)	800.00
1969	Non-talking Truly Scrumptious	Pink gown; hair pulled straight back	1,000.00
1970	Living Barbie	Jointed wrists, bendable elbows and ankles	400.00
1971	Malibu Barbie	Tanned-tone vinyl	45.00*
1971	Live Action Barbie	Battery operated stage moves Barbie in a dancing motion	250.00
1971	Growing Pretty Hair Barbie	Pink dress; hair piece, hair ornaments	500.00
1971	Hair Happening Barbie (Limited Edition offered exclusively through Sears.)	Red haired Twist 'N Turn, several hair pieces to add; wearing pink skirt, white blouse	1,500.00
1972	Walk Lively Barbie	Red jumpsuit; Miss America; battery operated walker stand	200.00
1972	Busy Barbie with Holding Hands	Hands open and close to hold things, 5 accessories for holding	400.00
1972	Ward's Anniversary Barbie	Montgomery Ward exclusive; copy of Barbie #5 or #6; surprised look, brows high on forehead	600.00
1973	Quick Curl Barbie		85.00
1974	Sun Valley Barbie	Mint on card; no box	300.00*
1975	Gold Medal Sports Barbie		150.00
1976	Beautiful Bride Barbie		250.00
1976	Ballerina Barbie	Hair pulled back, stands on toes	65.00
1976	Super Star Barbie	Wear and Share accessories	225.00
1984	Le Nouveau	Theatre de la Mode by Billy Boy	500.00
1986	Feelin' Groovy	Designed by Billy Boy	300.00
1987	Mardi Gras	1st American Beauty Series	100.00
1988	Pink Jubilee	1st Jubilee Series	1,800.00
1992	My Size	36" tall	145.00
1994	Evergreen Princess	From Winter Princess LE	125.00
		With red hair LE/Disney Convention	500.00
	Peppermint Princess	From Winter Princess LE	100.00
	Snow Princess	1st Enchanted Season	175.00
1995	Gold Jubilee	2nd in Jubilee Series/celebrate 35 years	900.00
	Christian Dior	1st in Series	125.00
1996	Christian Dior	2nd in Series	100.00
1980s	International Barbie	Eskimo	100.00
		Canadian	95.00
		German	65.00
		Greek	45.00
		Hawaiian	45.00
		Indian	150.00
		Irish	85.00
		Italian	200.00
		Japanese	125.00
		Parisian	75.00
		Peruvian	45.00
		Scottish	100.00
		Swiss	65.00
1986	Blue Rhapsody	Porcelain	600.00
1987	Enchanted Evening	Porcelain	500.00
1988	Benefit Performance	Porcelain	400.00
1989	Wedding Party	Porcelain	400.00
1990	Solo In The Spotlight	Porcelain	250.00
1990/1991	Sophisticated Lady	Porcelain	225.00
1991	Gay Parisian	Porcelain (1st in Treasury Collection)	200.00
1992	Plantation Bell	Porcelain	300.00
1993	Royal Splendor	Porcelain	200.00
1994	Star Lilly	Porcelain	200.00
1988	Happy Holiday	Red gown with silver trim	600.00
1989		White gown with fur trim	200.00
1990		Fuchsia gown with silver trim	150.00
1991		Green velvet gown with sequins	125.00
1992		Silver gown with beading	100.00

* No original box.

Date	Name	Description	Mint
1993		Red gown with gold	100.00
1994		Gold gown with fur	75.00
1990	Bob Mackie	Gold	600.00
1991		Platinum	550.00
		Starlight Splendor	500.00
1992		Empress Bride	600.00
		Neptune Fantasy	600.00
1993		Masquerade Ball	300.00
1994		Queen of Hearts	250.00
1995		Goddess of the Sun	175.00
1996		Moon Goddess	125.00
1992	Classique Line	Benefit Ball by Carol Spencer	200.00
1993		Opening Nite by Janet Goldblatt	125.00
		City Style by Janet Goldblatt	150.00
1994		Uptown Chic by Kitty Black Perkins	100.00
1994		Evening Extravaganza by Kitty Black Perkins	100.00
1995		Midnight Gala by Abbe Littleton	125.00
1996		Starlight Dance by Cynthia Young	100.00
1989	FAO Schwarz	Golden Greetings	225.00
1990		Winter Fantasy	200.00
1991		Night Sensation	175.00
1993		Rockettes	195.00
	Little Debbie	Little Miss Debbie	65.00
1994	Bloomingdale's	Nicole Miller	100.00
	Hallmark	Victorian Elegance	110.00
	FAO Schwarz	Silver Screen	175.00
	Wal-Mart	Tooth Fairy	20.00
1995	Spiegel	Shopping Chic	95.00
	FAO Schwarz	Jeweled Splendor	300.00
		Circus Star	125.00
	Bloomingdale's	Donna Karan	125.00
	Airport/Duty Free	Traveler	75.00
1996	Bloomingdale's	Calvin Kline	85.00
	Bloomingdale's	Ralph Lauren	95.00
	J. C. Penney	Royal Enchantment	60.00
	FAO Schwarz	Statue of Liberty	95.00
1997	Toys-R-Us	Pink Ice	100.00
1990	Stars and Stripes	Air Force	60.00
1991		Navy	55.00
1992		Marine	55.00
		Marine Gift Set	100.00
1993		Army Gift Set	95.00
1994		Air Force Gift Set	75.00
1993	Great Eras	Gibson Girl	150.00
		1920s Flapper	175.00
1994		Egyptian Queen	145.00
		Southern Bell	125.00
1995		Medieval Lady	75.00
		Victorian Lady	95.00
1996		Grecian Goddess	75.00
		French Lady	55.00
1997		Chinese Empress	60.00

Gift Sets

Boxed outfits with dolls. All sets in mint condition in original boxes or packages.

Date	Name	Doll	Value
1962	Mix and Match Set	Barbie	1,500.00
1963	Sparkling Pink Gift Set	Barbie	1,200.00
1964	Party Time Gift Set	Skipper	500.00
1964	Round The Clock Gift Set	Barbie	1,400.00
1964	Wedding Party Gift	Barbie in Bride's Dream, Ien in tuxedo, Midge in Orange Blossom, Skipper as Flower Girl	3,200.00
1967	Cut 'N Button	Skooter	500.00
1964	On Parade Gift Set	Barbie, Ken, and Midge	2,100.00
1964	Little Theatre	Barbie, Ken with production costumes and accessories	8,000.00

Other Accessories

Barbie's life has been filled with accessories of all kinds. Here is a sampling of current prices for mint accessories.

Barbie's Fashion Shop	700.00
Barbie & Ken Little Theatre	900.00
Barbie & Skipper School	600.00
Skipper Dream Room	500.00
Barbie's Dream Kitchen and Dinette	800.00
Barbie's Music Box Piano and Bench	500.00
Barbie's Lawn Swing and Planter	200.00
Barbie's Sports Car	500.00

Little Theatre Costume Sets

Set in original Mint condition with props.

Gwenevere & King Arthur	900.00
Poor & Rich Cinderella & Prince	1,200.00
Arabian Nights	700.00
Red Riding Hood & The Wolf	1,400.00

Barbie's Friends and Family

Date	Name	Description	Mint in Box
1961	Ken	Boyfriend, #1, flocked hair	300.00
		Bendable Leg	450.00
1963	Midge	Best friend	350.00
		Bendable Leg	600.00
1964	Allan	Ken's friend, Midge's boyfriend	350.00
		Bendable Leg	550.00
1964	Skipper	Barbie's Little Sister	250.00
1965	Ricky	Skipper's friend	300.00
1965	Skooter	Skipper's friend	300.00
		Bendable Leg	350.00
1966	Francie	Cousin, white	400.00
		Cousin, white, no bangs	2,000.00
1966	Tutti	Baby Twin, Bendable vinyl body	200.00

Barbie's Friends and Family

Date	Name	Description	Mint in Box
1966	Tutti	Package set, Me & My Dog	450.00
1966	Todd	Baby Twin, Bendable vinyl body	200.00
1966	Todd	Packaged set, Sundae Treat	500.00
1967	Casey	Francie's friend, clear plastic stand	400.00
		Twist 'N Turn	250.00
1967	Chris	Tutti & Todd's friend	150.00*
1967	Francie	Cousin, Black	1,900.00
1968	Christie	Barbie's Black friend	300.00*
		Talking	425.00
		Twist 'N Turn	450.00
1968	Stacey	Barbie's British Friend, long hair	350.00
		Short hair	500.00
		Twist 'N Turn	400.00
1969	P.J.	Barbie's friend	300.00*
		Twist 'N Turn	350.00
1970	Brad	Ken's friend, Christie's boyfriend, black	100.00*
1971	Fluff	Skipper's friend	125.00*
1972	Tiff	Skipper's friend, Pose 'N Play	300.00
1972	Steffie	Barbie's friend	350.00
		Walk Lively	250.00
1973	Kelley	Barbie's friend, Yellowstone	225.00
		Quick Curl	100.00
1974	Cara	Friend, black	50.00*
		Ballerina	50.00
1975	Curtis	Cara's boyfriend, black	75.00
1975	Casey	Francie's friend, packed in plastic	65.00*

*No original box

Barbie's Outfits

Barbie outfits must be complete and in excellent condition. Values shown are for outfits mint in the original package (MIP). Very good, complete condition, unpackaged outfits would be valued at half of the MIP prices. Incomplete outfits or those in played-with condition are valued at one-quarter the MIP prices.

Easter Parade #971: tight black dress; multicolored donut print; black coat; hat; bag; and shoes $3,000.00

Gay Parisian #968: blue bubble dress, fur cape, gold bag, blue shoes..$2,500.00

Roman Holiday #964: Straight dress, gray skirt, striped top, matching red and white striped coat, red hat, shoes, and bag $3,500.00

Solo in the Spotlight #982: very tight, black, sparkly dress; net kick flounce; long, black gloves; long scarf; black shoes; plastic microphone $2,000.00

Enchanted Evening #983: beautiful, long, pink gown with long attached train; long, white, opera-length gloves; fluff shoulder cape; matching shoes $900.00

Collection of Barbie clothing in mint condition. Courtesy of David Cobb's Doll Auctions

Plantation Belle #966: pink, dotted, Swiss dress with lace inserts, fitted to waist, full skirt; pink, net, wide-brim hat; straw bag; short, white gloves; pink shoes..................$700.00

Picnic Set #967: red and white checked blouse; blue jean pedal pushers; straw hat and bag; fishing line and plastic fish $400.00

Busy Gal #981: red suit; red and white striped blouse; glasses; hat; portfolio; red shoes $400.00

Commuter Set #916: dark, two-piece suit with white blouse and pearls; large, red, flowered hat; shoes; hat box; and extra blouse..$1,800.00

Wedding Day Set #972: wedding gown with layers of lace; head piece with net veil; holding flowers; white shoes; white gloves $700.00

Sophisticated Lady #993: pink gown; deep pink, long coat; head piece; matching shoes; long white gloves.................$600.00

Midnight Blue #1617: gown with sleeveless, blue, long coat with white fur collar; long, white gloves; gold evening bag and shoes..$900.00

Reception Line #1654: pretty blue dress, fitted to waist with lace over skirt; blue, pillbox-style hat; white, long gloves; white shoes..$600.00

Here Comes The Bride #1665: long, straight gown, somewhat fitted, lace overlay; very long veil; white gloves; flowers; shoes..$1,200.00

Golden Glory #1645: gold gown; matching coat with mink collar; white gloves; evening bag; shoes $600.00

Nighty Negligee #965: pink nightie and chiffon robe; pink felt dog; slippers..$300.00

Sheath Sensation #986: red sheath dress, square neck; white straw hat; short, white gloves, shoes..................................$200.00

Fun at the Fair #1624: red skirt; print blouse; matching scarf with red shoes; cotton candy on a wooden stick..............$500.00

Riding in the Park #1668: tan riding pants; plaid jacket; white shirt; riding hat; high boots; riding crop.................$500.00

Stormy Weather #0949: yellow, belted rain coat; rain hat; umbrella; high boots $200.00

Sporting Casuals #1671: blue slacks; knit sweater with cowl neck; blue shoes $250.00
Saturday Matinee #1615: stylish suit with matching hat, fur trim; tan gloves; shoes; bag $1,300.00
Gold 'N Glamour #1647: gold, two-piece suit with scarf and matching hat, all with fur trim; tan gloves and shoes $1,600.00
Japan Outfit #0821: red kimono; fan; head ornament; musical instrument; sandals.....................................$1,900.00

Miss Astronaut #1641: silver space suit; head gear; American flag..$1,000.00
Skaters Waltz #1629: peach skating dress, fur trimmed; skates..$1,300.00
Fashion Luncheon #1656: pink suit, matching, satin-color hat; gloves; pink shoes...$500.00
Silken Flame #977: strapless, red bodice gown; white satin full skirt; gold belt & purse $200.00

E. Barrois

E. Barrois, located in Paris from 1844–1877, was one of the earliest manufacturers of porcelain-head dolls in France. Barrois dolls tend to be quite pale, with delicate blush and brow decorations. Mouths are small, with just a hint of a smile. Eyes are either glass or finely painted with long lashes. Their China heads have painted eyes and hair. The pressed method was used in making E. Barrois doll heads. Most are a shoulder head, although a few socket heads on bisque shoulder plates can be found. Lady bodies are made of kid or cloth. Hands are either kid with stitched fingers, or wooden upper arms with bisque hands. Sizes range from 9 to 23 inches with the sizing codes of 3/0 to 7. Typical markings include "E (size number) B," "E (size number) Déposé B," and "EB."

Prices listed are for beautifully costumed dolls in good condition. Normal wear, slight damage, or well-made repairs to the body do not greatly affect the price. If the bisque is damaged or repaired, expect the value to be less than half the amounts listed. It is perfectly acceptable to show a missing or repaired finger or joint, or a mended body.

"EB" bisque doll with glass eyes. Courtesy of David Cobb's Doll Auctions

E. Barrois Value Comparisons

Size	Painted Eyes	Glass Eyes	Black Lady
9"	2,200.00	2,800.00	
11"	2,700.00	3,200.00	
13"	3,300.00	3,600.00	
15"	3,600.00	4,000.00	
17"	3,900.00	4,300.00	
19"	4,300.00	4,600.00	37,000.00
21"	4,600.00	4,900.00	
24"	4,800.00	5,200.00	

Add an additional $500.00 to any doll with jointed, wooden body.

Beecher Baby

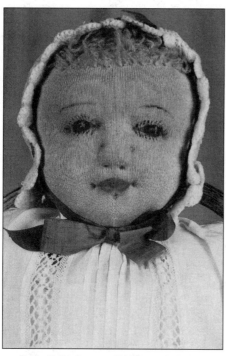

Beecher Baby. Courtesy of McMaster's Doll Auction

Julia Jones (Mrs. Thomas) Beecher produced Beecher Baby Dolls in Elmira, N.Y. between 1893 and 1910. She was the granddaughter of Noah Webster, the sister-in-law of Henry Ward Beecher and Harriet Beecher Stowe, and the wife of a Congregational Church pastor. Mrs. Beecher's first doll was made for her niece Daisy Day. These charming dolls, made of pink or black cotton or silk with needle-sculptured and painted features, had hand-stuffed bodies and looped-wool yarn hair. Devoted ladies of the Church's Sewing Circle made the dolls, with all proceeds used for missionary work, which explains why these dolls are often referred to as Missionary Rag Babies. Dressed in simple, cotton, homespun outfits, they are typically unmarked.

When considering a Beecher Baby for your collection, consider yourself lucky just to find one! Their irresistible charm accounts in part for their scarcity and usually well-loved condition.

Prices listed are for appropriately costumed dolls in good condition. Slight wear and signs of aging do not greatly affect the price.

	Beecher Baby Value Comparisons					
Size	Caucasian Extra Clean Condition	Caucasian Good Condition	Caucasian Fair Condition	Black Extra Clean Condition	Black Good Condition	Black Fair Condition
15"	4,500.00	3,000.00	2,000.00	5,000.00	3,500.00	2,500.00
21"	7,500.00	6,000.00	5,000.00	8,500.00	7,000.00	5,500.00

Belton-Type

Although Belton-Type Dolls are generally regarded as French, the beautiful bisque dolls were probably manufactured in Germany after 1870. A distinguishing characteristic of the Belton doll is the uncut pate section with one, two, or three small holes. The top of the head may be concave, flat, or convex. Over the years, almost every doll manufacturer has been suggested as a possible source for this type of doll. To date, no firm evidence has surfaced confirming any one company. Other common factors include a good wig; closed mouth; quality paperweight eyes with long painted lashes; and pierced ears. They range in size from nine to twenty-four inches. Bodies are usually jointed composition with straight wrists, small hands, and long wooden stick-type upper legs. Occasionally, they are found with a shoulder head on a kid body, with fine quality bisque hands. Beautifully dressed, they are typically unmarked or marked with a size or mold number.

There are variations in the faces and the quality of the bisque and decoration. Evaluate dolls carefully. Check feathering of the eyebrows; better examples will be applied with several single strokes. The bisque should have a pale rather than ruddy complexion with delicately applied blush.

Later # 7 Belton Type. This face if often referred to as an Owl-Faced Belton. Courtesy of David Cobb's Doll Auctions

Early pale bisque # 11 Belton Type. Courtesy of David Cobb's Doll Auctions

Prices listed are for appropriately costumed dolls in good condition. Normal wear, slight damage, or well-made repairs to the body do not greatly affect the price. If the bisque is damaged or repaired, expect the value to be less than half the amounts listed. It is perfectly acceptable to show a missing or repaired finger or joint, or a mended body.

Also see Oriental.

Belton-Type Value Comparison		
Size	Very Good Quality	Standard Quality
9"	1,400.00	900.00
12"	2,800.00	1,750.00
14"	3,100.00	2,000.00
16"	3,500.00	2,200.00
18"	3,800.00	2,400.00
20"	4,000.00	2,700.00
22"	4,400.00	3,000.00
24"	4,800.00	3,500.00

C. M. Bergmann

*A*s a young man, C. M. Bergmann lived and worked in America as a miner and later as a cowboy. Upon his return to Waltershausen, Germany in 1877, he spent eleven years learning the doll-making business. Bergmann launched his own company in 1888 with just two employees. He specialized in ball-jointed composition bodies with bisque heads from the factories of Armand Marseilles, Simon & Halbig, Alt, Beck & Gottshalck, William Gobel, and perhaps other German companies. Bergmann's dolls were distributed in the United States by Louis Wolf, who registered several Bergmann trademarks, including Cinderella Baby, Baby Belle, and Columbia. C. M. Bergmann filed for bankruptcy in 1931.

C. M. Bergmann Dolly-Faced dolls, all marked "1916." Courtesy of David Cobb's Doll Auctions

Prices listed are for appropriately costumed dolls in good condition. Normal wear, slight damage, or well-made repairs to the body do not greatly affect the price. If the bisque is damaged or repaired, expect the value to be less than half the amounts listed. It is perfectly acceptable to show a missing or repaired finger or joint, or a mended body.

Standard Quality Dolly Face: bisque shoulder or socket head by Armand Marseilles or other unknown manufacturer; composition or kid body; good wig; glass eyes; open mouth; appropriately dressed; typically marked "C. M. Bergmann Waltershausen Germany 1916; "A. M. Columbia."

Better Quality Dolly Face: bisque socket head by Simon & Halbig and others; jointed composition body; good wig; glass eyes; open mouth; appropriately dressed; typically marked "C. M. B. Simon & Halbig"; "Eleonore."

Standard Quality Character Baby: bisque socket head by Armand Marseilles or other unknown manufacturer; composition bent-limb baby body; good wig; glass eyes; open mouth; appropriately dressed; typically marked "A. M. C. M B."

Better Quality Character Baby: bisque socket head by Simon & Halbig, William Goebel, and possibly others; composition bent-limb baby body or stockinet torso with composition limbs (may have rubber hands); good wig; glass eyes; open mouth; appropriately dressed; typically marked "C B Bergmann B 4" or "S H C M B."

612 Character Baby: bisque socket head by Simon & Halbig; composition bent-limb baby body; open/closed mouth; appropriately dressed; typically marked "Simon & Halbig/612/C M Bergmann."

C.M. Bergmann Value Comparisons

Size	Dolly Face on Kid Body	Dolly Face Standard Quality Composition Jointed Body	Dolly Face Better Quality Composition Socket Head, Jointed Body	Marked Eleonore	Standard Character Baby*	Better Character Baby*	S.H. 612 Character Baby*
10"	350.00	500.00	750.00				
12"	375.00	525.00	775.00				
14"	400.00	550.00	800.00		700.00	1,400.00	2,700.00
16"	425.00	575.00	825.00	900.00			
18"	450.00	600.00	850.00				2,900.00
20"	500.00	650.00	875.00	1,000.00	900.00	2,500.00	
22"	525.00	700.00	900.00	1,100.00			
24"	600.00	750.00	1,000.00	1,200.00	1,300.00		
26"		900.00	1,100.00	1,300.00			
28"		1,000.00	1,200.00	1,400.00			
30"		1,100.00	1,450.00				
32"		1,300.00	1,650.00				
34"		1,700.00	2,050.00	2,000.00			
36"		2,000.00	2,500.00				

C.M. Bergmann Value Comparisons							
Size	Dolly Face Kid Body	Standard Quality Dolly Face Composition Jointed Body	Dolly Face Better Quality Composition Socket Head, Jointed Body	Marked Eleonore	Standard Character Baby*	Better Character Baby*	S.H. 612 Character Baby*
38"		2,600.00	2,900.00				
40"		2,800.00	3,200.00				
42"		3,000.00					

*Add an additional $700.00 for jointed toddler body.

"1916" Dolly-Face C. M. Bergmann doll.
Courtesy of McMaster's Doll Auction

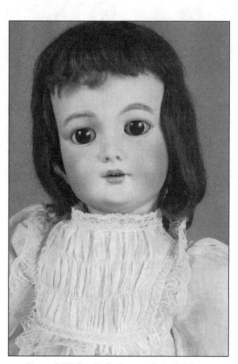

Simon & Halbig Dolly-Face, made for C. M.
Bergmann. Compare the application of brows and
facial coloring of this, and the previous "1916" doll.
Courtesy of McMaster's Doll Auction

Bing Brothers

Bing Brothers, later known as Bing Werke and Bing Wolf Corp., was a large corporation operating from 1882 until 1932. In addition to its home office in Nuremberg, they had headquarters all over the world. John Bing was the American representative. By 1920, Bing Werke was a large conglomerate consisting of thirty-one subsidiary companies, including Bing, Kämmer & Reinhardt, Max Oscar Arnold, Welsch & Co., and Louis Wolf. Bing Corp. was the only toy factory in Nuremberg that remained open during World War I. The company went bankrupt in 1932.

Prices listed are for appropriately costumed dolls with good color and little or no fading. Slight wear and signs of aging, such

Bing Art doll in original costume.
Courtesy of McMaster's Doll Auction

as a settled body, do not greatly affect the price. If a doll is stained, torn, badly mended, or faded, expect the value to be less than half the amounts listed.

Art Doll (resembles Kathe Kruse doll): heavily painted, mask-type face; cloth body; mitt hands with stitched fingers and separate thumb; painted hair; molded and painted features in the "Kathe Kruse style"; appropriately dressed; typically marked "Bing."

Felt Doll (resembles Lenci doll): pressed face; felt wool body; mohair wig; painted, side-glancing eyes; molded and painted features in the "Lenci-style"; appropriately dressed; typically marked "Bing."

Bing Cloth Doll Value Comparisons		
Size	Art Doll	Felt Doll
7"	500.00	
10"	600.00	600.00
15"	1,100.00	750.00

George Borgfeldt & Co.

George Borgfeldt & Co., located in New York City from 1881 through the 1950s, was an international importing company, not a doll manufacturer. Borgfeldt was responsible for importing thousands of dolls into America. The Germans described Borgfeldt as a "Verlegers" meaning assembler. Several famous designers were employed by Borgfeldt, as were various companies who made the heads or complete dolls.

Before World War I, Borgfeldt had exclusive American and Canadian rights to many dolls, including Kestner, Kämmer & Reinhardt, Handwerck, Steiff, Kathe Kruse, and Buschow & Beck. George Borgfeldt & Co. did not ignore American-made dolls. Some of the companies that distributed through Borgfeldt were Aetna Doll Co., K & K Toy, Dreamland Doll, Cameo Doll Co., and Bergfeld & Son. Borgfeldt was responsible for commissioning two of the most successful dolls ever made—Rose O'Neill's Kewpie and Grace Putnam's Bye-Lo.

Trademarks registered by Borgfeldt include: Alma, Bonnie Baby, Lilly, Skookum, Celebrate, Uwanta, Juno, Florodora, Dutchess, Kidlyne, My Playmate, My Dearie, Pansy Doll, Little Bright Eyes, My Girlie, Happifat, Cubist, Peero, Butterfly, Prize Baby, September Morn Doll, Mamma's Angel Child, Little Sister, Bettijak, Nobbikid, Rastus, Skating Charlotte, Preshus, Em-Boss-O, Hollikid, Come-A-Long, Bye-Lo Baby, Mimi, Daisy Doll, Rosemarie, Felix, Bringing Up Father, Whatsmatter,

George Borgfeldt bisque Dolly-Face dolls. Courtesy of David Cobb's Doll Auctions

Ko-Ko, Little Annie Rooney, Jackie Coogan, Buttercup, Featherweight, Rolly-I-Tot, Bonton, Jolly Jester, Rag & Tag, Fly-Lo, Gladdie, Mignonne, Nifty, Rosy Posy, Sugar Plum, Just Me, Babykins, Mary Ann, and Mary Jane.

Also see All Bisque, Averill, Googly-Eyed Dolls, Kewpie, and Cameo Dolls.

Bisque

Prices listed are for appropriately costumed dolls in good condition. Normal wear, slight damage, or well-made repairs to the body do not greatly affect the price. If the bisque is damaged or repaired, expect the value to be less than half the amounts listed. It is perfectly acceptable to show a missing or repaired finger or joint, or a mended body.

Dolly-Face Shoulder Head: bisque shoulder head; kid, cloth, or imitation kid body; good wig; glass eyes; open mouth; appropriately dressed; typically marked "G. B.," "Florodora," "My Playmate," or "Alma." ***Note:*** *Imported by the thousands by George Borgfeldt Co.*

Dolly Face Socket Head: bisque socket head; jointed composition body; good wig; glass eyes, open mouth; nicely painted or haphazardly applied features; appropriately dressed; typically marked "My Dearie," "Pansy," "My Girl," "Florodora," "My Playmate," or "G.B."

Note: *Judge quality objectively whether standard or better quality*

Character Baby: bisque socket head; composition bent-limb baby body; good wig; glass or painted eyes; open or open/closed mouth; appropriately dressed; typically marked "251/248," "326," "327," "329," or "G.B." ***Note:*** *Mold "251/248" is a charming character with open/closed mouth and molded tongue. The mold number is 251, and 248 is the German registration number.*

Bye-Lo Baby (a.k.a. Million Dollar Baby): designed by Grace Storey Putnam with Borgfeldt as sole distributor; bisque heads by Alt, Beck & Gottschalck, Kestner, Kling, and Hertel, Schwab & Co.; specially designed cloth "frog" body with celluloid hands, or five-piece bent-limb baby body; solid dome; painted hair; tiny glass eyes; closed mouth; appropriately dressed; typically marked "1923 Grace S. Putnam/Made in Germany" or "1369 Grace S. Putnam." ***Note:*** *A black version was also produced, along with a composition head Bye-Lo by Cameo Doll Co., and a rare bisque with painted eyes and smiling mouth typically marked "1415."*

14", 12", and 11" solid dome Putnam Bye-Lo bisque babies on cloth frog bodies with celluloid hands. Courtesy of David Cobb's Doll Auctions

Fly-Lo (a.k.a. Baby Aero): designed by Grace S. Putnam; bisque flange neck; cloth body; molded and painted hair; glass sleep eyes; closed, slightly-smiling mouth; non-removable satin suit with wings, wire is attached from wing to doll's wrist; typically marked "Grace S. Putnam Germany 1418/#."

Baby Bo-Kaye: designed especially for George Borgfeldt by Joseph Kallus; bisque baby head by Alt, Beck & Gottschalck; sweet, wistful, almost pouting expression; cloth body; composition limbs; molded and painted hair; glass, oval sleep eyes; open/closed full mouth with two lower teeth; appropriately dressed; typically marked "Copr. by J. L. Kallus, Germany 1394." ***Note:*** *Supposedly, after Kallus designed this doll, he went to the office of Fred Kolb (President of George Borgfeldt) with the sculpted head. The two men were considering names when the secretary entered with a bouquet of flowers. The problem was solved. "Bo-Kaye" was the perfect name for Bo (Borgfeldt) and Kaye (Kallus).*

Gladdie: designed by Helen W. Jensen; biscaloid (imitation bisque composition) or bisque flange head; cloth body; composition limbs; deeply molded and painted hair; glass eyes; open/closed, laughing mouth with molded upper teeth; appropriately dressed; typically marked "1410 Germany" or "Gladdie Copyriht by Helen W. Jensen/Germany." The word "copyright" may be misspelled as "copyriht."

Borgfeldt Bisque Value Comparisons

Size	DollyFace, Shoulder Head, Kid Body	Standard Quality, DollyFace, Socket Head, Composition Body	Better Quality, DollyFace, Socket Head, Composition Body	Character Baby	Bye-Lo Cloth Body*	Bye-Lo Composition Body*	#1415 Painted eye, Fly-Lo and Bye-Lo	#251 Character and Baby Bo-Kaye	Gladdie Bisque	Gladdie Biscaloid
12"	375.00	525.00	600.00	550.00	700.00		4,400.00	1,800.00		
14"		550.00	625.00	650.00	900.00	1,400.00	4,900.00			
16"	425.00	575.00	675.00		1,100.00	1,800.00	6,000.00			
18"	450.00	600.00	750.00	900.00	1,700.00	2,400.00		3,000.00	4,500.00	1,200.00
20"	500.00	650.00	850.00		1,900.00			3,500.00	5,500.00	1,400.00
22"	525.00	700.00	925.00	1,100.00						
24"	600.00	750.00	1,100.00	1,200.00					6,800.00	2,400.00
26"		900.00	1,300.00							
30"		1,100.00	1,500.00							
32"		1,300.00	1,900.00							
34"		1,700.00	2,300.00							
36"		2,000.00	2,700.00							

*Add an additional $100.00 for black version.

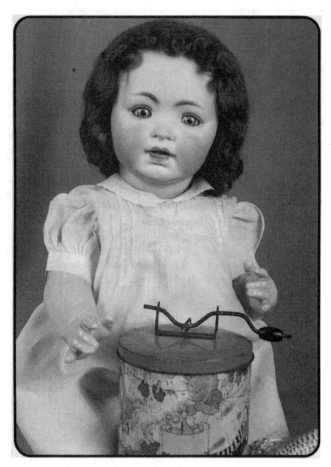

"G. B." Character Baby. Courtesy of McMaster's Doll Auction

Biscaloid Gladdie. Courtesy of David Cobb's Doll Auctions

Composition

Prices listed are for appropriately costumed dolls in good condition. Slight crazing is acceptable and does not greatly affect the price. If badly crazed, cracked, peeling, or repainted, expect the value to be less than half the amounts listed.

Many composition dolls were distributed by George Borgfeldt, both German and American made. Examples include: Mamma's Angel Child, Hollikid, Com-A-Long, Daisy, Bye-Lo, Fly-Lo, and Baby Bo-Kaye. Most have cloth bodies. Characteristics and markings are identical to those of their bisque counterparts; appropriately dressed; typically marked "My Playmate," "Borgfeldt," or "G.B." identical to the bisque dolls.

Composition Value Comparisons

Size	Characters	Bye-Lo	Fly-Lo	Baby Bo-Kaye
10"		350.00		
12"	400.00	450.00	1,100.00	700.00
14"	425.00	475.00	1,400.00	900.00
17"	450.00	700.00		
20"	500.00			

Tin

Prices listed are for appropriately costumed dolls in good condition. If dented, chipped or repainted expect the value to be less than one half to one fourth the amounts listed.

At least one metal head was imported by George Borgfeldt from Germany. Known as Juno, it was designed by Karl Standfuss.

Juno: tin shoulder head; cloth body; molded and painted hair, or mohair wig; painted or sleep eyes; closed mouth; appropriately dressed; typically marked "Juno" in an oval.

Tin Value Comparisons

Size	Molded Hair, Painted Eyes	Molded Hair, Glass Eyes	Mohair Wig, Glass Eyes
12"	160.00	185.00	265.00
15"	185.00	200.00	295.00
20"	225.00	245.00	345.00

Boudoir Dolls

oudoir Dolls, also known as Flapper or Sofa dolls, acquired their name because of their use as decorations on beds and divans. They were made in France, Italy, and the United States from 1915 through the 1930s. Paris doll artists developed boudoir dolls into an art form.

Boudoir Dolls were never intended as children's toys. The ever important costuming and presentation can be elaborate or outrageous: silk pantsuit, ruffled gowns, patriotic attire, or theatrical costumes complete with headware, exaggerated high heeled shoes, and even cigarettes dangling from their mouths. Celebrities such as Marlene Dietrich, Joan Crawford, and Josephine Baker were often used as models.

Prices listed are for dolls in near-mint, original condition. If damaged, redressed, or undressed, expect the value to be less than one half to one fourth the amounts listed.

Boudoir Dolls: cloth bodies; exaggerated long limbs; heads of cloth, composition, wax, china, or suede; mohair or silk floss wigs; painted facial features; fashionable costumes; typically unmarked.

Mask face Blossom Pierrot Boudoir Dolls dressed in pink silk costumes. Courtesy of McMaster's Doll Auction

Boudoir Doll Value Comparisons

Size	Extraordinary QualityCloth, 1920s Art Deco-Style or Elaborately Costumed	Standard Quality Cloth, 1930s, Mohair or Floss Wigs	Lesser Quality Cloth or Composition, 1940s Heavily Painted	Lenci	Wax
14"	300.00	150.00	75.00		
18"	350.00	175.00	90.00		
20"	450.00	200.00	100.00		700.00
26"	600.00	225.00	120.00	2,400.00	900.00
30"	700.00	250.00	130.00	2,600.00	1,200.00
36"	900.00	300.00	150.00	3,000.00	1,700.00

Jne Bru & Cie

ne Bru & Cie, commonly known as Bru, is one of the most famous bisque doll manufacturers known to collectors. The company was located at Paris and Montreuil-sous-Bois, France from 1866 to 1899.

There is no doubt that the delicately molded, limpid-eyed bébés produced by Bru during the last quarter of the 19th century are among the most treasured prizes of the doll world. An

1872 catalog provides the following information: "Without clothes a number 4 doll will cost $1.20 to $2.10. If this doll was dressed in wool and had a kid body it cost $4.40 and with a wooden body it was $4.60. But if a number 4 doll was dressed in silk it cost $6.00 to $100.00 depending on the outfit." Imagine a doll in 1872 costing $100.00!

After 1899, S.F.B.J. (Society Francaise de Fabrication de Bébé & Jouets), of which Bru was a charter member, made Bru Dolls and Bébés. In fact, S.F.B.J. renewed the trademark for Bru in 1938 and again in 1953. A 1952 *DOLL NEWS* Magazine advertised Bru dolls that were then being produced.

There are three basic types of Bru Dolls: The Fashion Lady; The Bébé on a kid body with beautifully made shoulder plate and hands; and the Bru Doll on a wood-and-composition body.

Beware of reproductions! Reproductions can be very convincing. In 1989, a reproduction of a Black Bru Jne won a national doll competition in which it was entered. This doll fooled several experts. A few tips to help distinguish an authentic Bru from a reproduction are:

	Reproduction	Authentic
Head Mark	Bru Jne	Bru Jne (plus size #)
Body	Hand sewn	Machine sewn
Stuffed	Sawdust	Ground cork & grass
Elbows	Bisque arms put directly into kid	Hinged joint
Cutting of Leather	Scalloped	Scalloped with pinking
Arms	Hang straight	Graceful curve
Head	Poured rim cut off	Pressed
Ear Piercing	Into the head	Through the lobe

Carefully examine size numbers, ever mindful that dolls will shrink in size when copied.

There are more reproduction Bru Jne Dolls than other doll types. Genuine copies made by doll makers will have the artist's name, and usually the date, marked in order to prevent mis-identification.

Prices listed are for appropriately costumed dolls in good condition. Normal wear, slight damage, or well-made repairs to the body do not greatly affect the price. If the bisque is damaged or repaired, expect the value to be less than half the amounts listed. It is perfectly acceptable to show a missing or repaired finger or joint, or a mended body.

Also see Oriental.

Fashion Lady

Poupée de Modes (Fashion Ladies): bisque swivel head; shoulder plate; gusseted kid lady body with pinking around top of leather; human, mohair, or skin wig; paperweight or painted eyes; pierced ears; small, closed, somewhat-smiling mouth; beautifully dressed; shoulder plate occasionally marked "B. Jne & Cie"; typically marked with incised number of letter size. (Size chart: A-11", D-14", G-19", K-25") ***Note:*** *In 1869, a patent was obtained by Bru for a wooden body with joints at the waist and ankles in addition to the usual shoulder, elbow, hip, and knee joints.*

Bébé Bru

Brevete Bébé: bisque socket head; kid-lined bisque shoulder plate; kid body pulled high on shoulder plate and straight cut (leather pinked where cut); bisque lower arms; skin wig; cork pate; paperweight eyes; delicately shadowed eye lids; long lashes painted on upper and lower lids; lightly feathered brows; pierced

Lovely Bréveté Bébé. Courtesy of David Cobb's Doll Auctions

Circle Dot Bru. Courtesy of David Cobb's Doll Auctions

ears; full cheeks; closed mouth with white space between lips; appropriately dressed; typically marked with size number only; body stamped "Bébé Brevete SGDG Paris." (Size chart: 5/0-10 1/2", 1-16", 3-19") ***Note:*** *Bébé Modele was produced for 1 or 2 years around 1880, with articulated all wood body, pin and dowel joints at shoulder, elbows, waist, hip, knees, and ankles.*

Circle Dot: bisque socket head; kid-lined bisque, deep shoulder plate with molded breasts; kid gusseted body; bisque lower arms with no joints at the elbows; fine mohair wig; cork pate; paperweight eyes finely lined in black; somewhat heavier feathered brows; pierced ears; plump cheeks; closed mouth with slightly parted lips and suggestion of molded and painted teeth; appropriately dressed; typically marked with a dot within a circle or crescent over a dot. (Size chart: 2/0-14", 4-17", 12-30")

31" #12 Jne Bébé. Courtesy of David Cobb's Doll Auctions

Bru Jne R Bébé. Courtesy of David Cobb's Doll Auctions

Jne Bébé: bisque socket head; kid-lined, deep shoulder plate with molded breasts; kid body with scalloped edge at shoulder plate; bisque lower arms with graceful hands; kid-over-wood upper arms, hinged elbows; may have wooden lower legs; good wig; cork pate; paperweight eyes; long lashes, finely lined in black; pierced ears; closed mouth with suggestion of molded tongue; appropriately dressed; typically marked "Bru Jne" and a size number; body labeled "Bébé Bru" and "BTE SGDG." (Size chart: 0-11", 2-13", 3-14") ***Note:*** *Add an additional $700.00 for a wooden jointed body, provided the markings are not that of Bru Jne R. If there is an "R" in the marking, a wooden body is appropriate.*

Bru Jne R Bébé: bisque socket head; wood-and-composition jointed body; good wig; paperweight eyes; pierced ears;

open or closed mouth; (quality of bisque ranged from beautiful with fine decoration to less attractive standard quality, which greatly affects the value); appropriately dressed; typically marked "Bru Jne R" and size number, stamped "Bébé Bru." (Size chart: 4-13", 8-20 1/2", 12-27")

Bébé Teteur (Bru Nursing Bébé): bisque socket head; kid-lined bisque shoulder plate; kid body with bisque lower arms; kid-covered, metal upper arms and legs; carved wooden lower legs or jointed wood-and-composition body; skin wig; paperweight eyes; mouth opened in to an "O" with hole for nipple; mechanism in head sucks liquid as key is turned; appropriately dressed; typically marked "Bru June N T." ***Note:*** *Manufactured from 1876-1929; dolls made prior to 1899 are generally of better quality.*

			Bru Value Guide			
Size	Poupée de Mode with Number*	Poupée de Mode with Letter*	Brevete Bébé*	Circle Dot Bébé	Black Circle Dot Bébé	Bru Jne Bébé
11"	2,800.00	3,100.00	13,000.00	12,500.00		
12"	3,000.00	3,400.00	14,000.00			18,000.00
13"			15,000.00	16,000.00		20,000.00
14"	3,400.00	4,200.00	17,000.00		30,000.00	
16"	4,000.00	4,800.00	19,000.00	19,000.00		20,500.00
17"		5,500.00	20,000.00		35,000.00	
18"	4,800.00		21,500.00	22,000.00		21,000.00
19"	5,200.00	6,000.00	23,000.00			
20"	5,400.00	6,700.00	24,000.00	25,000.00		
22"	6,000.00	7,200.00	25,000.00		40,000.00	22,000.00
24"			27,000.00	29,000.00		25,000.00
25"	6,800.00	7,800.00	28,000.00			
26"			29,000.00			
28"	7,600.00	8,500.00		38,000.00		35,000.00
30"			35,000.00			

* Add an additional $2,000.00 for original jointed wooden body.

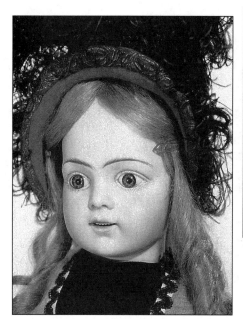

Open mouth Bru Jne R Bébé. Courtesy of David Cobb's Doll Auctions

Size	Closed Mouth Bru Jne R Exceptional	Closed Mouth Bru Jne R Standard	Open Mouth Bru Jne R	Early Nursing Bru Exceptional	Later Nursing Bru Standards
11"	4,000.00	3,000.00			
13"			2,000.00	9,500.00	6,500.00
14"	6,500.00	5,900.00			
16"	7,300.00	6,400.00		11,000.00	8,000.00
19"		7,200.00			
22"	9,500.00	7,400.00	5,300.00		
25"	11,500.00				
26"			6,500.00		
28"	15,500.00	10,000.00			
33"	22,000.00				
35"			8,000.00		

Albert Brückner

"1901" marked Albert Brückner mask-type cloth doll. Courtesy of McMaster's Doll Auction

New York City and Jersey City, New Jersey, were the homes for this doll manufacturer from 1901 until 1930. Doll maker, Albert Brückner, was joined in his business by his sons several years before his death, resulting in the name "Albert Brückner's Sons." Albert's 1926 obituary provided the following information: "In 1901, while watching one of his friends working through the tedious process of stuffing and shaping the faces then used on rag dolls, he conceived the idea of giving form and expression to the faces by stamping out or embossing the features into a mask. His knowledge of lithographing and printing trades enabled him to perfect his idea and he obtained a patent for it in July 1901. His earlier days had been spent with the Gray Lithographing Co. In 1901, he proceeded with the manufacture of doll faces and within a few months had a small factory established for the manufacture of a full line of rag dolls. He held several patents pertaining to the manufacture of dolls and at the time of his death, he was treasurer of the Up-To-Date Manufacturing Co., manufacturers of cry voices for dolls...He had a 'Museum' [that] contained samples of the various dolls produced from 1901–1926, showing their changing dress styles."

Several of Brückner's rag dolls were released through Horsman and sold as part of Horsman's Babyland Rag Doll series. These dolls are particularly prone to dents and rubs.

Prices listed are for appropriately costumed dolls with good color and little or no fading. Slight wear and signs of aging, such as a settled body, do not greatly affect the price. If a doll is stained, torn, badly mended, or faded, expect the value to be less than half the amounts listed.

Mask-type: all cloth; pressed mask; painted hair and facial features; appropriately dressed; typically marked "Pat'd July 8th 1901."

Topsy-Turvy (a.k.a. "Tu-N-One"): two dolls in one; mask-type faces; one white and one black mask-type face; white doll with blond hair, blue eyes, and wearing dress and bonnet; Black doll with black mohair wig, painted large eyes with white highlights, laughing mouth with two rows of teeth, and wearing dress and kerchief. When correctly positioned, the skirt of one doll completely covers the unused doll; typically marked "Pat'd July 8th 1901."

Brückner Value Comparisons

Size	White Cloth*	Black Cloth*	Topsy-Turvy
12"	350.00	400.00	650.00
14"	400.00	450.00	750.00

* Add an additional $50.00 for Dollypop with cry box.

A. Bucherer

Bucherer, Amriswil, Switzerland, 1921-1930, made dolls with a patented metal ball-jointed body. Advertised as having changeable heads, the dolls represented comic characters and celebrities as well as everyday civilians such as chauffeurs, policemen, and firemen. Many were dressed in regional costumes with outfits sewn directly onto the doll.

Cabinet-sized dolls are popular with today's collectors. Comic characters are generally valued higher than common examples. Because clothing is sewn onto the body, it may be difficult to inspect the doll. Prices listed are for originally costumed dolls in good condition. If stained, torn, faded, or if the composition is badly crazed or chipped, expect the value to be less than half the amounts listed.

Character Doll: 6 1/2" to 9"; composition head, hands, and feet; metal-jointed body; painted hair and features; appropriately dressed; typically marked "Made in Switzerland Patents Applied For" embossed on front of torso.

Bucherer Value Comparisons

Size	Regional Costumes	Civilian-Type	Characters and Animals	Comic Characters
6-1/2" to 9"	250.00	325.00	350.00	450.00

Bucherer dolls. Courtesy of James D. Julia Auctions Inc., Fairfield, Maine

Cabbage Patch Dolls

Cabbage Patch dolls were delivered at the Babyland Hospital in Cleveland, Georgia, first by Coleco Industries and later by Hasbro Toys. Their creation evoked a frenzied level of demand by children and collectors.

The Cabbage Patch fantasy was created in 1977 in the mountains of Georgia. The original hand-stitched Cabbage Patch dolls, designed by Xavier Roberts, were known as "Little People." They were so popular at craft shows that Roberts borrowed $400.00 on a VISA Card and started the Babyland Hospital, with local women helping to stitch the faces. Roberts visited yard sales to obtain clothing for his creations. The first Little People were not signed. Right from the start, Roberts' dolls had to be adopted rather than bought. In exchange for a signature and adoption fee, the new "parent" received a baby and birth certificate. To quote Roberts, "from the very beginning, the whole concept was for the babies to be different." Their popularity led Roberts to license many adoption centers to make babies available for adoption. More than 500,000 of the Little People were adopted.

In 1982, Coleco was granted a license to mass produce the babies, renaming them Cabbage Patch Kids, a smaller version of the original Little People. Worldwide, fifty-seven million Cabbage Patch Kids were adopted. Despite the tremendous popularity of Cabbage Patch Kids, Coleco closed its doors in 1989. That same year, Hasbro was licensed to mass produce Cabbage Patch Kids.

Each year, a Cabbage Patch Convention is held in Cleveland, Georgia. At a recent convention, over 7,000 people celebrated the adoption of more than seventy-five million Kids.

The reported estimated values are from collectors and devotees of Cabbage Patch Kids and Little People. Remember that the Birth Certificate, Adoption Papers, and Name Tags are important components. Use the Current Estimated Value as a tool to help you determine values. The secondary market for contemporary dolls is extremely volatile. Prices given are for dolls in mint condition with boxes and papers.

Money can't buy Love ...

Adoption Fees
Start at $125.00
Up For Adoption!

We know where you can Adopt it

The Little People™ soft sculptured babies are handstitched to birth and designed by Xavier Roberts. They are ready to move into your loving home with their Birth Certificates, Adoption Papers and magnetic personalities. Also available in signed and limited Collector's Edition.

A 1979 advertisement for the original Xavier Roberts Little People.

Cabbage Patch Value Comparisons

Year	Edition	Birth Mark	Estimated Number Issued	Current Estimated Value
1978	Helen Blue	Signed	1,000	2,000.00
1978	"A" blue papers	Signed	1,000	1,500.00
1978	"B" red papers	Signed	1,000	1,200.00
1979	"C" burgundy papers	Signed	5,000	800.00
1979	"D" purple papers	Signed	10,000	700.00
1979	"X" Christmas, Limited Edition	Signed	1,000	1,200.00
1979	"E" bronze papers	Signed	15,000	600.00
1980	"SP" Preemie	Signed	5,000	500.00
1980	Christmas Set, Nicholas, Noel	Signed	2,500	500.00
1980	Grand Edition	Signed	1,000	700.00
1981	"U" Unsigned	Stamped	73,000	200.00
1981	New Ears Edition	Stamped	15,000	200.00
1981	"PR" II Preemie	Stamped	10,000	175.00
1981	Standing Edition	Stamped	5,000	200.00
1982	"PE" New Ears, Preemie	Stamped	5,000	250.00
1982	"U" Unsigned	Stamped	21,000	100.00
1982	Christmas Set, Christy, Nicole, Baby Rudy Cabbage Patch Kids Editions	Stamped	1,000	600.00
1982	Cabbage Patch Kids 10 Character Kids Set	Stamped	2,500	400.00 each; Set 4,000.00
1983	Cleveland Green	Stamped	2,000	300.00
1983	"KP" dark green	Stamped	2,000	400.00
1983	"KPR" red	Stamped	2,000	400.00
1983	"KPB" burgundy	Stamped	10,000	150.00
1983	Oriental	Stamped	1,000	600.00
1983	Indian	Stamped	1,000	500.00
1983	Hispanic	Stamped	1,000	400.00
1983	Powder Scent	Stamped	Mass	75.00
1983	Bald Babies	Stamped	Mass	75.00
1983	Baby with pacifier	Stamped	Mass	100.00
1983	White with freckles	Stamped	Mass	75.00
1983	Black with freckles	Stamped	Mass	100.00
1983	Red fuzzy haired boy	Stamped	Mass	100.00
1984	"KPP" purple	Stamped	20,000	200.00
1984	"KPG" bronze	Stamped	30,000	150.00
1984	"KPF" turquoise	Stamped	30,000	150.00
1984	"KPG" coral	Stamped	35,000	150.00
1984	Single tooth	Stamped	Mass	200.00
1984	Popcorn hairdo	Stamped	Mass	200.00
1984	Gray eyed Kid	Stamped	Mass	100.00
1984	Champagne, Maderia, Andre	Signed	1,000	600.00
1984	Sweetheart, Candi, Beau	Stamped	750	250.00
1984	Bavarian Set	Stamped	1,000	1,000.00
1984	World Class Set	Stamped	2,500	600.00
1984	Daddy's Darlin's, Pun'kin, Tootsie, Princess, Kitten	Stamped	500	400.00
1984	Christmas, Carole, Chris	Stamped	1,000	100.00
1984	Green Signature	Stamped	Mass	75.00
1985	Blue Signature	Stamped	Mass	65.00
1985	Christmas, Sandy, Claude	Stamped	2,500	100.00
1985	Emerald	Stamped	35,000	75.00
1985	Four Seasons, Crystal, Morton, Sunny, Autumn	Stamped	2,000	100.00
1985	Gold	Stamped	50,000	75.00
1985	Iris	Stamped	N/A	100.00
1985	Irish	Stamped	4,000	100.00
1985	Ivory	Stamped	45,000	60.00
1985	Preemie Show Baby	Stamped	15,000	75.00
1985	Preemie Twins, set	Signed	3,000	400.00
1985	Rose	Stamped	40,000	65.00
1985	Sapphire	Stamped	35,000	65.00

Cabbage Patch Value Comparisons

Year	Edition	Birth Mark	Estimated Number Issued	Current Estimated Value
1986	Amethyst	Screened	10,000	75.00
1986	Christmas, Hillary, Nigel	Monogram	2,000	100.00
1986	Corporate Kids	Signed	2,000	400.00
1986	Georgia	Monogram	4,000	100.00
1986	Identical Twins, set	Stamped	5,000	100.00
1986	Mark Twain, Tom Sawyer, Huck Finn, Becky Thatcher	Monogram	2,500	400.00
1987	Baby Otis	Monogram	2,000	200.00
1987	Big Top Clown, Baby Cakes	Monogram	2,000	250.00
1987	Christmas, Katrina, Misha	Monogram	2,000	200.00
1987	Iddy Buds	Monogram	750	500.00
1987	Polynesian, Lokelina, Ohana	Monogram	1,000	300.00
1987	Sleeping Beauty, Prince Charming	Monogram	1,250	250.00
1987	Topaz	Screened	5,000	100.00
1988	Aquamarine	Screened	5,000	100.00
1988	Christmas, Kelly, Kane	Monogram	1,000	200.00
1988	Nursery Edition, Baby Marilyn, Suzann, Baby Tyler Bo, Baby Dorothy Jane, Baby Sybil Sadie	Monogram	2,000	75.00
1989	Amber	Screened	3,000	75.00
1989	Christmas Joy	Monogram	500	300.00
1989	Fourth of July	Signed	3,000	100.00
1989	Lapis	Screened	2,000	75.00
1989	Mother's Day	Signed	5,000	65.00
1989	Ruby	Screened	1,325	75.00

There are over twenty-five different faces, many hairstyles, and a wide array of outfits. It would be impossible to list them all, but these examples should prove helpful. Most of the Cabbage Patch Kids not listed fall in the $60.00 to $100.00 range for dolls made before 1989. Dolls made after 1989 have a $60.00 retail value; typically marked:

Copy R 1978 _ 1982
ORIGINAL APPALACHIAN ART WORKS, INC.
MANUFACTURED BY COLECO IND. INC.
MADE IN HONG KONG
3

Compare these two dolls. The taller doll in back is an impostor doll, marked CBS Toys, not a Cabbage Patch doll. The smaller doll in front is a licensed, marked Coleco Cabbage Patch doll. Note the differences in the hands and finger stitching

Cameo Doll Company

The Cameo Doll Company operated in Port Allegheny, Pa., from 1922 until 1970. In 1970, the entire Cameo Doll Company, including equipment, was acquired by the Strombecker Corporation of Chicago. Joseph Kallus, the founder and president, gained notoriety through his work with Rose O'Neill in the modeling of dolls she created, especially the Kewpies. Cameo Doll Company became the sole manufacturer of composition Kewpies in the United States. George Borgfeldt & Company distributed them along with other dolls by Cameo such as Bye-Lo, Baby Bo-Kaye, and Little Annie Rooney.

Doll collectors are fascinated with dolls produced between World War I and World War II. The dolls of Cameo and Joseph Kallus are among the most avidly sought. They are not only charming, but in terms of artistry and construction, they are among the finest quality American dolls made in the 20th century.

It is common for early Cameo Dolls to be unmarked, or have only a wrist tag. Later dolls were usually well marked and, after 1970, "S71" was added.

Also see Kewpie, Borgfeldt, and All-Bisque.

Cameo composition "Giggles." Courtesy of McMaster's Doll Auction

Composition

Prices listed are for appropriately costumed dolls in good condition. Slight crazing is acceptable and does not greatly affect the price. If badly crazed, cracked, peeling, or repainted, expect the value to be less than half the amounts listed.

Scootles: all composition; jointed at neck, shoulder, and hip; deeply-molded, wavy hair; painted, side-glancing eyes; closed, smiling, watermelon mouth; appropriately dressed; typically marked with "Scootles" wrist tag only.

Dog (Ginger, Bones, and Streak): composition dog head; wooden, fully-jointed body; typically marked with paper label "Des & Copyright by J. L. Kallus."

Pete the Pup: composition character dog head; segmented wood body; ball hands; large feet; large, side-glancing eyes; round nose; wide, smiling mouth; typically marked "Pete the Pup" label on chest, "Cameo" on foot.

Joy/Pinkie: composition head and hands; segmented body; molded and painted hair; side-glancing eyes; tiny pug nose; closed, smiling mouth; appropriately dressed; typically marked "Joy" or "Pinkie" label on chest.

Margie: composition head; separate neck piece, attached by hook to eighteen-piece wood-segmented body; painted hair and head band; side-glancing eyes, upper lashes, no lower lashes; open, smiling mouth with four teeth; appropriately dressed; typically marked "Margie" label on chest.

Betty Boop: composition head, hands, upper torso, and skirt; segmented body; molded and painted black hair; side-glancing eyes; molded and painted red swimming suit; typically marked "Betty Boop/Des & Copyright by Fleischer/Studios" label.

Champ: composition freckled-face boy; jointed at shoulder and hip; molded and painted hair falling across forehead; large eyes; closed, smiling mouth; original jersey with "CHAMP" printed across front.

Giggles: starfish hands; painted hair with bun in back and bangs in front; side-glancing eyes; closed, smiling mouth; appropriately dressed; typically marked "Giggles/Designed and copyrighted/Rose O'Neill/Cameo Doll Co." wrist tag.

Marcie: all composition; painted hair; side-glancing eyes, closed slightly; puckered mouth; dressed in original young girl's French-style outfit (copied from clothing in Lord and Taylor's); molded and painted socks and shoes; typically unmarked or wrist tag only.

Sissy: all composition; jointed at shoulder and hip; balanced to stand alone; painted hair; painted eyes; smiling mouth; appropriately dressed; typically unmarked or wrist tag only.

Little Annie Rooney: all composition; one-piece head and torso; jointed shoulder and hip; long, thin legs with molded shoes; orange yarn hair; big, oval, painted, side-glancing eyes; small nose; closed, smiling mouth; wearing original green dress and felt jacket tagged "Little Annie Rooney/trademark/copyright 1925 by Jack Collins/pat applied for."

R.C.A. Radiotrons: composition head; separate neck piece attached by hook to wood-segmented body; molded and painted top hat in shape of radio tube; boots and facial features; marked "R.C.A. Radiotrons" across the hat and on a band across the chest.

Cameo Composition Value Comparisons													
Size	Scootles	Black Scootles	Dog	Pete the Pup	Joy & Pinkie	Maggie or Marcie	Betty Boop	Giggles	Champ & Sissy	Little Annie Rooney	RCA Radiotrons & Bandmaster	Popeye & Crownie	Baby Blossom
8"	525.00		500.00	400.00									
10"	550.00	750.00	600.00	450.00	375.00	350.00							
12"	625.00	900.00					750.00	800.00	350.00				
13"	725.00	1,000.00											
15"	875.00				550.00	500.00		1,000		900.00		500.00	
16"	1,000.00										900.00		
18"									700.00		1,000.00	700.00	
20"	1,200.00												900.00

Pop-Eye: faithful reproduction of cartoon Popeye; composition head; wooden, segmented body, finished in bright colors; molded sailor cap; no hair; small eyes; very full cheeks; wooden pipe in closed mouth; wood painted to represent clothing; marked "King Features/Syn, Inc. 1932" on foot.

Bandmaster (Drum Major or Bandy): composition head; wooden, segmented body (twenty segments assembled with coil spring); molded high shako head; humorously-cheerful, painted facial features; red and white painted drum major's uniform; carries wooden baton; medal molded around neck; marked "G.E." (General Electric trademark); "Mfg. Cameo Prod. Inc./Port Allegany, Pa./Des. & by JLK."

Crownie: composition head; wooden, segmented body; molded and painted long, wavy hair with crown; painted, closed eyes; jolly, laughing open/closed mouth; brightly painted body, representing clothing; wearing felt cape; holding wooden baton; typically marked "Mfg. Cameo Prod. Inc./Port Allegany, Pa./ Des. & by JLK."

Baby Blossom: composition head and bent limbs; cloth body; molded and painted hair in short style with lock coming down over forehead; baby-type face with painted, side-glancing or sleep eyes; pug nose; dimpled, fat cheeks; dressed; typically marked "Baby Blossom" hang tag, and appropriately "Des. & Copyright/by I. L. Kallus/Made in USA."

Vinyl

Prices listed are for appropriately costumed dolls with good color and little or no fading. Slight wear and signs of aging such as a settled body do not greatly affect the price. If a doll is stained, torn, badly mended, or faded, expect the value to be less than half the amounts listed.

Scootles: all vinyl; fully jointed; molded and painted hair and eyes; closed, smiling, watermelon mouth; appropriately dressed; typically marked "R7234 Cameo JLK."

Miss Peep: all vinyl; pin-hinged joints at shoulder and hip; painted hair; inset, good-quality plastic eyes; nurser/open mouth (drink and wet baby); appropriately dressed; typically marked "CAMEO."

Baby Mine: all vinyl; pin-hinged, jointed at shoulder and hip; painted hair; sleep eyes; open/closed mouth with molded tongue; appropriatly dressed; typically marked "CAMEO."

Cameo vinyl Miss Peep and Kewpie. Courtesy of McMaster's Doll Auction

Plum: one-piece latex body; two squeakers, one in bottom for spanking, one in tummy for hugging; painted hair; sleep eyes; open/closed mouth; appropriately dressed; typically marked "Cameo."

Margie: all vinyl; ball-and-socket universal joints at neck, shoulder, hip, elbows, and waist; rooted hair; sleep eyes; slightly parted lips; appropriately dressed; typically marked "Cameo T.M." or "9093/60" or "9013/60."

Cameo Vinyl Value Comparisons				
Size	Scootles	Margie and Miss Peep	Baby Mine	Plum
14"	225.00			
15"		225.00		
16"			250.00	
18"		300.00		175.00
19"	350.00		300.00	
21"		400.00		
24"				250.00
27"	700.00			

Campbell Kids

Various manufacturers have produced Campbell Kids. Grace Drayton originally designed the Kids in 1909 for Campbell's advertising cards. They immediately became popular with children. Within a year, dolls were being manufactured not only as premiums, but also for over-the-counter sales.

The earliest Horsman composition heads on cloth bodies were made with a flange neck. In 1914, a shoulder head was used so the dolls could wear clothes with lower necklines. Outfits copied the Campbell Soup advertisements and were labeled, "The Campbell Kids/Trademark by/Joseph Campbell/Mfg. by E. I. Horsman Co." In 1929, American Character Company acquired the license for Campbell Kids. Their all-composition version was slightly pigeon-toed. They are marked with raised lettering on the neck "A Petite Doll." Outfits were familiar Campbell Soup advertising costumes.

Horsman began to manufacture Campbell Kids again in the late 1940s. The dolls were unmarked, except for hang tags that read, "Campbell Kid/A Horsman Doll." The Canadian company of Dee and Cee purchased the rights for the Campbell Kids in the late 1940s. The Dee and Cee dolls are similar to the Horsman Campbell Kids, with a few exceptions. The quality of the composition is not as fine as Horsman's; eyelashes tend to be heavier and thicker; and the hair color is more orange than brown.

Ideal created vinyl and latex Campbell Kids during the 1950s. Campbell Kids continue to be popular collectibles and have been produced most recently in porcelain by Collectible Concepts, Corp.

Composition

Prices listed are for appropriately costumed dolls in good condition. Slight crazing is acceptable and does not greatly affect the price. If badly crazed, cracked, peeling, or repainted, expect the value to be less than half the amounts listed.

All composition Campbell Kids share a similar face with molded and painted, bobbed hair; round, side-glancing eyes; chubby cheeks; pug nose; and closed smiling mouth. Distin-

Horsman's composition Campbell's Kid Boy and Girl in original costumes. Courtesy of McMaster's Doll Auction

guishing characteristics are body types and markings that include:

Premium Kid: flange neck; cloth body; stub hands; appropriately dressed; unmarked; offered as magazine subscription premium.

Early Horsman: flange neck; cloth body; composition arms; appropriately dressed; marked "E. I. H. © 1910."

Later Horsman: all composition; jointed at neck, shoulder, and hip; appropriately dressed; unmarked.

American Character: all composition; jointed at neck, shoulder, and hip; appropriately dressed; marked "A Petite Doll."

Modern

Prices listed are for dolls in near-mint, original condition. If damaged, redressed, or undressed, expect the value to be less than one half to one fourth the amounts listed.

Magic Skin: latex body; appropriately dressed; marked "Campbell Kid/made by Ideal Toy Corp."

Bicentennial Campbell Kid: all vinyl; molded and painted features; colonial costume.

Porcelain: in a soup can; military costumes; 100% Happiness and Joy; sequence costumes; wrist tag "1998 T.M. Collectible Concepts."

Campbell Kid Value Comparisons

Size	Premium Campbell Kid	Early Horsman, All Cloth Body	Later Horsman, All Composition	Dee & Cee, All Composition	Am. Char., All Composition	Magic Skin	Bicentennial	Porcelain in a Can	100% Hap & Joy
10"	300.00	350.00				60.00	200.00		75.00
12"		400.00	775.00	600.00	750.00	85.00		95.00	
14"		500.00							

Catterfelder Puppenfabrik

31" Catterfelder Puppenfabrik bisque Dolly-Face child, holding a bisque head squeaker toy marked 4700 by Schoenau and Hoffmeister. Courtesy of McMaster's Doll Auction

Catterfelder Puppenfabrik manufactured dolls in Walterhaussen, Germany from 1894 until the 1930s. Kestner supplied most of the heads for Catterfelder, generally representing babies, although child dolls were also produced. Several rare character dolls are credited to Catterfelder, namely molds 207, 217, 219, and 220. Dolly-face mold numbers assumed to have been used on Catterfelder Dolls are 264, 270, 1100, 1200, and 1357. Mold numbers 205 and 206 were registered in 1909, but to date no doll with either number has ever been reported. Catterfelder is probably best known for its bisque character babies, including the mold numbers 200, 201, 208, 209, 218, 262, and 263.

Bisque

Prices listed are for appropriately costumed dolls in good condition. Normal wear, slight damage, or well-made repairs to the body do not greatly affect the price. If the bisque is damaged or repaired, expect the value to be less than half the amounts listed. It is perfectly acceptable to show a missing or repaired finger or joint, or a mended body.

Dolly-Face: bisque socket head; jointed wood-and-composition body; good wig; glass eyes; short, painted lashes; feathered brows; open mouth with teeth; appropriately dressed; typically marked "Catterfelder Puppenfabrik," "270," "264," and probably "1100," "1200," & "1357."

Character Baby: bisque socket head; composition bent-limb baby body; molded and painted hair or good wig; painted or glass eyes; open or open/closed mouth; appropriately dressed; typically marked "CP 200," "201," "208," "262," "263/Depoiert," or "Catterfelder Puppenfabrik."

Character Child: bisque socket head; jointed wood-and-composition body; good wig; painted eyes with line indicating eye lid; small pug nose; closed, slightly-pouting mouth; appropriately dressed; typically marked "207" or "219."

Character Child: bisque socket head; jointed wood-and-composition body; good wig; painted or sleep eyes; open/closed mouth with two molded teeth; appropriately dressed; typically marked "220" or "217."

Celluloid

Prices listed are for appropriately costumed dolls in good condition. If cracked, warped, or badly discolored, expect the value to be less than one fourth the amounts listed.

Child: all celluloid; molded and painted hair; painted eyes; molded and painted socks and shoes; appropriately dressed; typically marked with mermaid in shield.

Size	DollyFace	200, 201, 208 Character Baby	262, 263 Character Baby	207, 219 Character	220, 217 Character	Celluloid
8"						115.00
10"		500.00	800.00			
12"						165.00
14"		650.00	1,200.00			
16"	900.00	800.00	1,400.00		11,000.00	
18"				6,200.00		
20"	1,000.00	1,050.00	1,600.00		14,000.00	
22"	1,100.00	1,200.00	2,000.00			
24"	1,300.00	1,400.00	2,600.00			
26"	1,800.00					
36"	3,000.00					

Catterfelder Puppenfabrik Value Comparisons

* Add an additional $700.00 for jointed toddler body or $200.00 for black version.

Celluloid Dolls

Celluloid was produced in Germany, France, United States, Japan, England, Poland, and other countries from 1869 until about 1950. Many companies produced celluloid dolls or celluloid doll parts; for example, Le Minor, Parsons Jackson, Kämmer & Reinhardt, Petitcollin, Kestner, Averill, Irwin, Marks, and Rheinische Gummi, who claimed it was the first to manufacture celluloid dolls. Marking may include an embossed stork (Parsons-Jackson), turtle (Schutz), Indian head (American), mermaid (Cellba), beetle or lady-bug (Hernsdorfer-Germany), star (Hollywood), SNF (Société Nobel Francaise), ASK (Zast of Poland), or others. For additional marks, refer to *Antique Trader's Doll Makers and Marks.*

In 1908, Playthings Magazine reported, "...prior to 1905, celluloid dolls were clumsy looking and could not withstand the knocking about that children gave them. Between 1905 and 1908, celluloid dolls improved in appearance and durability. Most of the Celluloid Dolls were made in Germany but many of them were painted by girls in Italy. All types of boys and girls were represented in celluloid dolls."

Production of celluloid became illegal in the United States during the 1940s because it burned or exploded if placed near an open flame or high heat.

Celluloid Dolls are grouped into several categories rather than by manufacturer. When considering a Celluloid Doll, check

17" Turtle Mark celluloid twins with painted features; 16" Japan all celluloid with sleep eyes, and a 14" Schutz mark celluloid with sleep eyes. Courtesy of David Cobb's Doll Auctions

French celluloid babies. Courtesy of McMaster's Doll Auction

condition carefully and evaluate quality critically. Discoloration is considered damage.

Prices listed are for appropriately costumed dolls in good condition. If cracked, warped, or badly discolored, expect the value to be less than one fourth the amounts listed.

See Kewpie.

All Celluloid: molded in one-piece or jointed at shoulders only; molded and painted hair and facial features; dressed, undressed, or molded clothing; often pink in color; marked or unmarked.

All Celluloid: jointed at neck, shoulder, and hip, or bent-limb baby body; molded hair or good wig; painted eyes; dressed or undressed; marked or unmarked.

Celluloid, Shoulder Head: cloth or kid body; celluloid or composition arms; molded and painted hair or good wig; glass or painted eyes; closed mouth or open mouth with teeth (often made of cardboard); appropriately dressed; marked or unmarked.

Better Quality, Socket Head: dolly, character, or baby face; composition-and-wood body; mohair or human hair wig; glass eyes; applied lashes and brows; closed or open mouth with teeth; appropriately dressed; typically marked by various manufacturers, such as Käthe Kruse, Kämmer & Reinhardt, and others.

Käthe Kruse: celluloid child doll; socket head; jointed at neck, shoulder, and hip; molded and painted hair or good wig; painted or sleep eyes; closed mouth; appropriately dressed; typically marked with turtle.

Flocked: socket head flocked to resemble felt; flocked jointed body; mohair wig; painted, side-glancing eyes; closed mouth; appropriately dressed; marked or unmarked.

Celluloid Value Comparisons

Size	Lesser Quality, Painted Eyes, Carnival Doll	All Celluloid Socket Head, Jointed Body, Painted Eyes	All Celluloid Socket Head, Jointed Body, Glass Eyes*	Celluloid Shoulder Head, Cloth/ Kid Body, Painted Eyes	Celluloid Shoulder Head, Cloth/ Kid Body, Glass Eyes	Standard Quality Celluloid Socket Head, Composition Body, Glass Eyes	Better Quality Celluloid Socket Head*	Käthe Kruse	Flocked Painted Eyes
4"	25.00	75.00							
6"	35.00	85.00							
8"	45.00	115.00							350.00
10"	50.00	135.00							
12"	60.00	165.00	250.00	185.00	235.00		500.00		
14"			300.00	195.00	250.00	300.00	550.00		
16"		250.00				350.00	650.00	700.00	550.00
18"			450.00	220.00	265.00	400.00	750.00	900.00	
20"		275.00		250.00	285.00	425.00	850.00		
22"			550.00	275.00	325.00	450.00			
24"						500.00	1,000.00		

* Add an additional $200.00 for black version.

Century Doll Company

The Century Doll Company was located in New York City from 1909 into the 1930s. It was founded by Max Scheuer and his sons, Bert and Harold. Max retired in 1926, and in 1929 his sons merged the company with Domec to become the Doll Corporation of America. Century Doll Company manufactured a wide variety of composition dolls in the mama doll, child doll, and baby doll categories. Its most popular doll was a bisque infant designed and produced by Kestner to compete with the Bye-Lo Babies. Mold numbers for the Kestner babies include 277 and 281.

Century Bisque Baby in original costume. Courtesy of McMaster's Doll Auction

Bisque

Prices listed are for appropriately costumed dolls in good condition. Normal wear, slight damage, or well-made repairs to the body do not greatly affect the price. If the bisque is damaged or repaired, expect the value to be less than half the amounts listed. It is perfectly acceptable to show a missing or repaired finger or joint, or a mended body.

Character Baby: bisque solid dome; flange neck; cloth body; composition limbs; molded and painted hair; tiny sleep eyes; open/closed mouth; two upper teeth; appropriately dressed; typically marked "Century Doll Co./Kestner, German 281" or "277."

Composition

Prices listed are for appropriately costumed dolls in good condition. Slight crazing is acceptable and does not greatly affect the price. If badly crazed, cracked, peeling, or repainted, expect the value to be less than half the amounts listed.

Romper Boy: composition shoulder head and limbs; cloth body; molded and painted hair; painted eyes; chubby cheeks; closed smiling mouth; appropriately dressed; typically marked "Century Doll Co./1921 Made/by Grace Corey."

Mama Girl: composition shoulder head and limbs; cloth body; good wig; tin sleep eyes; open mouth; appropriately dressed; typically marked "Century Doll Co., NY."

Century Doll Value Comparisons				
Size	Bisque #281	Bisque #277	Composition Romper Boy	Mama Doll
10"		700.00		250.00
12"		800.00		
13"		900.00	300.00	
14"	750.00	1,000.00		300.00
16"				350.00
18"		1,200.00		400.00
22"	900.00	1,400.00		500.00
26"				600.00
30"				1,000.00

Chad Valley, Ltd.

Chad Valley was located in Harbonne, England, and manufactured toys as early as 1897. The company was a part of England's National Scheme for Employment of Disabled Men and Contractors for His Majesty's Government. Chad Valley, Ltd. began producing dolls in 1917 and continued into the 1940s. Various types of cloth dolls were made, the earliest predominately with stockinette faces. Around 1924, the company began producing hand-painted felt faces on dolls made of velvet or velveteen.

Chad Valley pressed face Bo Peep and Boy Blue. Courtesy of McMaster's Doll Auction

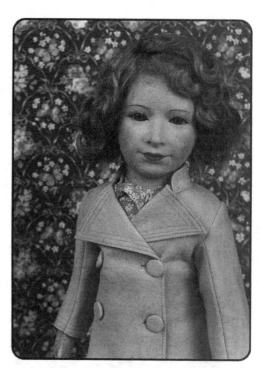

Chad Valley Princess Elizabeth with glass eyes, in original clothing. Courtesy of McMaster's Doll Auction

The quality of Chad Valley Dolls also varied. Less expensive examples were cloth dolls with printed clothes. Better dolls had combable wigs, threaded glass eyes, molded hand-painted faces, and removable clothing. Dresses and suits were extremely short, exposing long legs.

In the 1929-1930 period, the Chad Valley catalog offered hundreds of dolls, but only four models of babies. Most of the dolls manufactured by Chad Valley were children. The royal children dolls were extremely popular. They included a representation of Princess Elizabeth, Princess Margaret Rose, Prince Edward, and Princess Alexandria.

A series of six Black dolls with outfits representative of different ethnic cultures was also produced. One example was a black boy wearing tweed, knicker-type pants, a large cap, and red suspenders. Carolina wore a grass skirt, beads, bracelets, and a headband. Rajah wore an East Indian outfit with turban and full trousers. Nabob and others were also dressed with great detail.

Prices listed are for originally costumed dolls in good condition. If stained, torn, mended, faded, or moth-eaten, expect the value to be less than half to a quarter of the amounts listed.

Character Dolls: velvet face and body; plush wig; glass or painted side-glancing eyes; painted facial features; typically labeled "Hygienic Toys/Made in England by/Chad Valley Co. Ltd.," "Chad Valley/Hygienic/Toys/Made in/England/The Seal of Purity"; hang tag "Chad Valley Hygienic Fabric Toys."

Child Dolls: felt mask; velvet body; good wig; double thickness of felt for ears; glass eyes or painted, side-glancing eyes; molded and painted facial features; appropriately dressed; typically labeled "Hygienic Toys/Made in England by/Chad Valley Co. Ltd.," and celluloid button "Chad Valley/British/Hygienic Toys," hang tag "Chad Valley Hygienic Fabric Toys."

Royals: felt mask; velvet body; mohair wig; glass eyes; nicely modeled features in portrait likeness; appropriately dressed; typically marked "HRH (Name)/British made Doll/By permission of/Her Majesty The Queen/Sole makers/The Chad Valley Co. Ltd./Harbonne/England."

Chad Valley, Ltd. Value Comparisons

Size	Character Doll, Glass Eyes	Character Doll, Painted Eyes	Child Doll, Glass Eyes	Child Doll, Painted Eyes	Royals
10"		300.00		400.00	
12"		400.00		500.00	
14"	1,000.00	500.00	800.00	650.00	
16"	1,200.00	700.00	850.00	800.00	1,700.00
18"	1,600.00	800.00	950.00	900.00	1,900.00
20"	2,200.00				

Martha Chase

Martha Chase Dolls were made in Pawtucket, Rhode Island, from about 1880 to 1938. They were made of stockinette fabric stretched over a mask with raised features. The head and limbs were sized with a coating of glue and paste, dried, and painted with oils. Features were hand-painted, the rough brush strokes of the hair providing a realistic texture. Ears and thumbs were applied separately. The earliest Chase Dolls had pink sateen bodies. Later bodies were made from heavy, white cotton cloth stuffed with cotton batting. Legs and arms were painted to above the knees and elbows, and an unstuffed area was left at each joint to facilitate movement. Many of the Chase Dolls were jointed at the shoulder, elbows, hip, and knees. Later dolls were jointed only at the hip and shoulder.

Mrs. Chase was quoted in the 1917 issue of *Toys and Novelties*: "I first made the dolls about 28 years ago (1889) as an amusement and to see what I could do. For several years I did this and gave the dolls away to the neighborhood children. Then by chance a store buyer saw one and insisted upon my taking an order. That was about 20 years ago, and since then there has been a gradual increase in the business. The dolls gained recognition by their merits, as I have advertised them very little. Then someone who knew about them asked me to make one adult size to use in the hospital training schools, and from that has developed another new industry. Now (1917) we are making dolls that can be immersed in water and used in child welfare work."

In 1911, Gimbles advertised Martha Chase Dolls as twice as expensive as the finest bisque head doll.

Prices listed are for appropriately dressed dolls in good condition. Slight wear and signs of aging, such as a settled body, do not greatly affect the price. If a doll is stained, torn, dented, cracked, peeling, or repainted, expect the value to be less than half the amounts listed.

Adult: stockinette adult face; cloth body; heavily oil-painted head, arms, and legs; molded and painted hair; painted eyes; thick lashes; closed mouth; appropriately dressed; typically marked "Made by Martha Chase" under arm, "Chase Hospital Doll," or hang tag "Made by hand/Chase Stockinette Doll."

Baby: stockinette baby face; cloth body; heavily oil-painted head, arms, and legs; molded and painted hair; painted eyes; chubby cheeks; slightly-smiling mouth; appropriately dressed; typically marked with paper label "The Chase Stockinette Doll/Made of Stockinette and Cloth/Stuffed with cotton/Made by Hand/Painted by Hand/Made by Especially Trained Workers" or stamped "Made by Martha Chase" or "Chase Hospital Doll."

Martha Chase dolls with their Teddy Bears. Courtesy of David Cobb's Doll Auctions

Child: stockinette child face; cloth body; heavily oil-painted head, arms, and legs; molded and painted hair; attached ears; painted eyes, thick lashes; slightly-smiling mouth; appropriately dressed; typically marked "Chase Hospital Doll" or "Made by Martha Chase."

Portrait Character: stockinette, cloth body; character features raised and heavily oil-painted; good wig or molded and painted hair; painted eyes, attached ears; closed mouth; appropriately dressed; typically marked "The Chase Stockinette Doll/ Made of stockinette and cloth."

Hospital Doll: all stockinette; entire body and head are heavily oil-painted; molded and painted hair and facial features; appropriately dressed; typically marked "Chase Stockinet Hospital Doll/Pawtucket, R.I./Made in USA."

Martha Chase Value Comparisons

Size	Chase Adult, Female	Chase Adult, Male	Chase Baby	Child	Hospital Doll
14"	1,600.00	3,200.00	700.00		
16"			750.00	1,700.00	
18"	2,200.00	3,500.00	800.00	2,000.00	
20"			850.00	2,200.00	900.00
22"	2,500.00	3,800.00	900.00	2,300.00	
24"			950.00	2,800.00	
26"			1,100.00	3,000.00	
30"				3,400.00	
62"					1,400.00

Size	Duchess	Frog Footman	Mad Hatter	Tweedle Dee	Tweedle Dum	Alice in Wonderland	George Washington	Black ethnic
6"	7,000.00	7,200.00	7,000.00	7,500.00	7,500.00			
18"						9,000.00		
23"								10,000.00
25"							9,500.00	
27"								15,000.00

China Heads

Rare glass-eyed French china head. Courtesy of McMaster's Doll Auction

China Heads of glazed porcelain were made primarily in Germany from 1840 to the 1940s. Identifying China Heads according to manufacturer is nearly impossible. Facial features vary little. China Heads characteristically have painted blue eyes; a red line, indicating eyelids; full cheeks; and a small, closed, smiling mouth.

Very rare early china heads were attached to commercially made, jointed, wooden bodies with china limbs. Most china heads, however, were sold separately. The consumer either purchased a body or made one.

Several terms are used to describe china heads. The most commonly found models are named for their hairstyle. Occasionally, unique characteristics suggest additional classification. Glass-eyed china head dolls are referred to as "French China." Flesh-colored or pink luster china heads with wigs, rather than painted hair, are known as "English China." "Kinderkopf" is applied to any style of china head representing a child. A "China Socket" style head attached to a china shoulder plate is very rare and desirable.

Familiar to collectors are the "Pet Name" dolls with painted gold letters across the molded yoke. They gave a final, but short-lived, boost to the china head market until permanently losing ground to the lovely bisque dolls around the turn of the century.

Germany continued to produce china heads through the 1940s, and thereafter in other countries. Reproduction and modern China Heads are plentiful and can be difficult to spot. Most are unmarked, making authentication that much more difficult. Although reproductions are very similar in appearance to the originals, some differences are evident. Reproductions usually have a good, clean slip, where antique China Heads are often found with tiny black flecks called peppering. Antique China Heads often have a red line above the eyes; reproductions usually do not. Obtaining the doll's history or provenance may be helpful.

Prices listed are for nicely dressed dolls in good condition. Normal wear or well-made repairs to the original body do not greatly affect price. If the porcelain is damaged or repaired, expect the value to be less than half the amount listed. A china head without a body commands about sixty-five percent of the list value.

Also see Alt, Beck & Gottschalk, Kling, Rohmer, and Huret.

Adelina Patti: elaborate hairstyle with center part and rolled curls; appropriately dressed. (1860s)

Alice (in Wonderland): hair styled with molded headband; appropriately dressed. (1850s)

Biedermeier: bald or solid dome head, some with top of head painted; good wig; appropriately dressed. (1840s)

Bun China Head: hair styled in bun, braid, or roll in back; appropriately dressed. (1840s)

Countess Dagmar: pierced ears; various, finely decorated elaborate hairstyles; appropriately dressed. (1840s)

Covered Wagon: hair styled flat on top with sausage curls around head; appropriately dressed. (1840s)

Curly Top: hair styled with ringlet curls over entire head; appropriately dressed. (1850s)

Currier & Ives: hair styled with long bangs and molded headband; appropriately dressed. (1860s)

Dolly Madison: all over curls with molded ribbon; appropriately dressed. (1870s)

English China Head: flesh-tinted china; solid dome head or small slit to insert good wig; appropriately dressed. (1840s)

Covered Wagon china head; Curly Top china head; Dolly Madison china head; Covered Wagon china head; Modified Low Brow china head and Boy-Styled china head. Courtesy of David Cobb's Doll Auctions

English china head; Exposed ears china head, and another English china head. Courtesy of David Cobb's Doll Auctions

Exposed Ear: hair pulled back from face in curly bun; exposed ears; appropriately dressed. (1850s)

Flat Top, a.k.a. Civil War or High Brow: hair styled with part in middle and short curls around head; appropriately dressed. (1850s)

French China Head: glass or beautifully painted eyes; feathered brows; open crown with cork pate; good wig; shapely kid body; appropriately dressed. (1850s)

Glass Eyed: painted hair with exposed ears; glass eyes; appropriately dressed. (1870s)

Greiner Style: high forehead; hair styled with middle part, wavy sides, and comb marks; exposed ears; appropriately dressed. (1850s)

Highbrow: very round face and high forehead; hair styled with center part, flat top, and sausage curls around head; appropriately dressed. (1870s)

Highland Mary: hair styled with straight top and curls at sides; appropriately dressed. (1860s)

Jenny Lind: high forehead, hairstyle parted in middle and pulled back into bun; appropriately dressed. (1860s)

K. P. M.: delicate, fine Meissen porcelain; appropriately dressed; marked "KPM" or crossed swords; handwritten mold number inside shoulder pate. (1840s)

Kinderkoff: obvious childlike modeling; appropriately dressed. (1840s)

Lowbrow: common, wavy, painted blond or black hairstyle; appropriately dressed. (1890s)

Bun china head and Spill Curl china head.

Man or Boy: masculine-styled china head; appropriately dressed. (1840s)

Mary Todd Lincoln: wearing snood of varying combinations, including: black hair with luster snood, blond hair with black snood, elaborate decoration at the crown with flowers or ruffles; appropriately dressed. (1860s)

Morning Glory: high forehead; exposed ears; flowers molded at nape of neck; appropriately dressed. (1860s)

Pet Name China Head: common hairstyle; name printed in gold on shoulder plate. (Names include Agnes, Bertha, Daisy, Dorothy, Edith, Esther, Ethel, Florence, Helen, Mabel, Marion, Pauline, and Ruth) appropriately dressed. (1905)

Sophia Smith: hair styled with straight sausage curls, not curved to head; appropriately dressed. (1860s)

Spill Curl: individual curls over forehead and shoulders; appropriately dressed. (1870s)

China Heads Value Comparisons

Size	French China Head	English China Head	Lowbrow China Head	Covered Wagon China Head*	Bun China Head**	Biedermeier or Greiner China Head	Flat Top China Head	Currier & Ives or Alice	Curly Top	Exposed Ear
8"			175.00		1,000.00		250.00		600.00	
12"	3,500.00	1,900.00	250.00	650.00	2,300.00	1,400.00	300.00			
14"	3,700.00	2,100.00		800.00	2,900.00	1,500.00	325.00	550.00	800.00	
16"		2,300.00	300.00	900.00	3,200.00		365.00		900.00	4,200.00
18"	4,200.00				3,700.00	1,700.00		700.00	1,100.00	
20"	4,900.00	2,600.00		1,100.00	5,000.00	2,000.00	400.00	1,000.00	1,300.00	
22"	5,500.00	3,800.00	400.00	1,300.00				1,200.00	2,000.00	6,500.00
24"		3,800.00	425.00	1,500.00	6,200.00	2,300.00	550.00			
30"				1,700.00			900.00			
36"			1,600.00	1,900.00				2,000.00	3,000.00	

* Add an additional $300.00 for brown eyes.

** Add an additional $500.00 for fancy bun.

China Heads Value Comparisons

Size	Sophia Smith China Head	Jenny Lind China Head	Mary Todd Lincoln	Morning Glory	Dolly Madison or Adelina Patti	Kinderkoph	China Socket Head	Countess Dagmar
6"		900.00			300.00			
12"			850.00		450.00	2,400.00	2,600.00	
14"					600.00			800.00
16"	2,700.00	1,700.00			650.00			
18"		1,800.00	1,100.00		775.00		4,500.00	1,200.00
20"	3,800.00	2,000.00	1,200.00	8,000.00		3,000.00		
22"	4,200.00		1,800.00		950.00			1,700.00
24"		2,600.00		12,000.00		3,800.00	9,000.00	

China Heads Value Comparisons

Size	Spill Curl	Highland Mary	K.P.M.	Man or Boy	Pet Name
6"	700.00				
12"				1,200.00	
14"	950.00	450.00			350.00
16"	1,100.00	500.00	5,500.00	1,500.00	400.00
18"		550.00		2,000.00	
20"	1,500.00	600.00	7,000.00	2,700.00	500.00
22"	1,700.00	650.00			600.00
24"		750.00	10,000.00		
28"		900.00		4,000.00	900.00
30"	3,500.00				

Add an additional $300.00 for pierced ears, $1,000.00 for glass eyes, $1,000.00 for unusual or elaborate decoration, $300.00 for molded necklace, or $1,500.00 for wooden articulated body with China lower limbs.

Cloth Dolls

Uncut lithographed Arnold Print Works characters from Palmer Cox Brownies. Courtesy of McMaster's Doll Auction

From the earliest pioneering days until the present, cloth dolls of all types have been produced in the United States. The two most popular types are Pillow or Rag dolls and Vintage Folk Art Dolls.

Pillow or Rag dolls were early printed or lithographed dolls, designed to be cut, sewn, and stuffed at home. Detailed instructions were printed alongside the figures. Most early printed dolls were produced in New England, the center of American textile manufacturing in the 1880s.

The inexpensive Cloth Dolls were a perfect advertising medium and were used to promote various products.

Toy manufacturers were slower to realize their commercial value. Although a few patents were issued in the 1860s and 1870s, it was not until the mid-1880s that patented and perfected rag dolls appeared in any great quantity in the United States.

The war years, 1914 and 1920, meant sacrifices for everyone. Doll manufacturing was limited to materials not essential to the war effort. Consequently, rag dolls enjoyed a boom.

Vintage Folk-Art dolls, handmade by known or unknown artists, are extremely popular with today's collectors. There are vast differences in quality, depending on the talent and skill of the maker. Uniqueness makes general pricing difficult. Several sample listings are provided in order to help gauge the current market. Charm and appeal is often a more crucial factor than condition.

Care must be given when purchasing a Cloth Doll. Craft shows offer hundreds of "aged" dolls. Some even have an "attic odor." Intended as accent pieces, they are well made and authentic looking. One particular copy that has caused some confusion is the reprint of Palmer Cox Brownies. These convincing reprints even bear the original 1892 copyright date. A clue to spotting the reprints is their washed out or faded appearance. They also measure 7" tall. The original Brownies measured 8" and were brightly colored.

Prices listed are for appropriately costumed dolls with good color and little or no fading. Slight wear and signs of aging, such as a settled body, do not greatly affect the price. If a doll is stained, torn, badly mended, or faded, expect the value to be less than half the amounts listed.

Vintage Pillow or Rag Doll (1880-1930)

American Beauty Doll: Empire Art Company; pretty child with hair ribbon; printed with undergarments, socks, and shoes, separate soles to feet.

Baby: Cocheco; printed muslin; circus elephant with red blanket labeled "Baby"; seamed in middle of back and head; separate double sided legs; unmarked.

Beauty the Cat: Varden Fabric; yellow, tan, and white calico cat print; separate oval bottom with paws.

Brownies: Arnold Print Works; "Irishman" with yellow cap, red band, green jacket, red pants, gray-blue socks, and dark orange slippers. Marked on right foot "Copyrighted 1892 by Palmer Cox."

Buster Brown: Art Fabric Mills/Knickerbacher; printed blond hair in Dutch boy style; happy smiling face; brown suit with knickers, white shirt, blue tie, white stockings, brown ankle strap shoes.

The Aunt Jemima family lithographed rag dolls by Davis Milling Co. includes: Uncle Mose, Aunt Jemima, Diana Jemima, and Wade Davis. Courtesy of McMaster's Doll Auction

Goldilocks and the Three Bears contemporary printed cloth advertising dolls. Courtesy James D. Julia Auctions, Inc., Fairfield Maine

Columbian Sailor Doll: Arnold Print Works; printed brown hair; very attractive face; red cap, blue coat, red striped pants, brown boots; marked along rim of cap "Arnold Print Works Pat Jan. 13, 1893." This commemorative doll was issued for the Columbian Exposition of 1912.

Crackles: Quaker Oats Co.; Quaker boy; smiling; bright green and violet suit; box of Quaker Oats in back pocket.

Darky Doll: Cocheco Mfg. Company; black boy; unusual feature of seam down center of face gives doll a three-dimensional look; printed tan cap, red jacket, black pants, tan socks, and brown shoes.

Foxy Grandpa: Art Fabric Mills/Knickerbacher; bald head, gray hair at sides; round wire rim glasses; smiling mouth; suit and vest, white shirt, bold tie, pocket watch hanging from side pocket; bunny tucked under his arm; printed spats, black shoes; made to look as though his hands are in his pockets.

Liberty Belle: Annin & Company; silk-screened brown hair; red and white striped hat, blue band with stars and stripes and "Liberty Belle" across front; dressed in jumper in shape of Liberty Bell and "150 Years of American Independence 1776–1926 Sesquicentennial" printed on skirt, red shirt with white star trimmed cuff, red and white striped socks, blue shoes; marked on back "Pat. Appl'd for Annin & Co. NY."

Little Red Riding Hood: Arnold Print Works; printed blond hair; red hooded cape over cream-colored dress with black trim; white socks, brown shoes; holding daisies in one hand, basket in other; made to look as though doll is standing in grass; marked on oval base "Patented July 5, 1892 & Oct. 4, 1892. Arnold Print Works North Adam, Mass. Incorporated 1876."

Pitty Sing: Arnold Print Works; lithographed oriental lady with fan and parasol; pink and blue; separate oval base; unmarked.

Punch & Judy: Art Fabric Mills; complicated cutting and sewing; some seams go down sides and others down front of dolls. Punch has characteristic hooked nose, jutting chin, wide grin, hunched back, lace trimmed plaid jacket, red pants, blue shoes, and blue and red peaked hat. Judy has sharp-featured profile, black hair, smiling character face, plaid gown, white collar, lace trim, and red, blue, and white bonnet.

Roosevelt Bear: Selchow & Righter; bear in sitting position; attached limbs and ears; printed brown wavy fur; open mouth, red tongue.

St. Nicholas/Peck's Santa: New York Stationery and Envelope Company; printed gray beard and hair; closed eyes; red nose; pipe in mouth; pocket watch peeking out from under fur-edged jacket; American flag tucked into belt; holding armful of toys including Chinese doll, pinwheel, hobbyhorse, drum, girl doll, ball, stuffed animal, bell, sword, and wagon; marked "Patent Applied for Santa Claus," printed under his hand near flag.

Tommy Trim: Horsman; smiling boy; blue "Little Lord Fauntleroy" suit with wide, white collar; red socks; black shoes; pattern sheet marked "E.I.H. Co."

Topsy Doll: Art Fabric Mills; Black child with extra piece for foot; short curly hair; exaggerated ethnic features; wearing union suit; printed "Topsy Doll," directions, and "Here's something to entertain 'em/to help'em in their play/Mama can make 'em/Baby can't break 'em/and they will last for many a day."

Vintage Pillow or Rag Doll Comparisons

Size	Child	Black	Character	Animals
8"	150.00			
12"	175.00			250.00
14"	200.00			300.00
15"	200.00	300.00		350.00
16"	225.00	350.00	250.00	
18"	250.00	400.00	275.00	
20"	275.00	450.00	300.00	
24"	300.00		400.00	

Uncut sheets are valued at twice the amount listed.

Collectible and Contemporary Printed Cloth Dolls (1940-1970)

Archie: orange hair; dark, thick eyebrows; wide open eyes; freckles across nose; printed red shirt; orange and black bell bottom pants; marked "Archie"; (c. 1960)................................**$175.00**

Beatles Forever: John, Paul, George, and Ringo; 21"; printed; instruments; signature stands; wrist tag "Applause" ....**$500.00 set**

Campbell Kids: life-like character with red and white familiar outfit; (c 1980) **$35.00**

Petite Bébé: various sweet child or doll face "by the yard to sew at home"; marked "circa 1860"; (c.1980) **$30.00**

Snow White and the Seven Dwarfs: dwarfs with character faces; Snow White with black hair and red ribbon; the 8" doll set; (c.1970) **$150.00**

Vintage Folk Art Dolls

Black Lady: all cloth, handmade, black stockinette limbs; stockinette head shows considerable skill in its making; hand-stitched, molded features; red, painted lips; black, shoe-button irises on painted, white eyes; black wool wig with red ribbons; brass rings sewn to side of head for earrings; wearing original printed cotton dress with apron; none of the typical "Mammy doll" qualities found on many Black dolls; (late 1800s) **$700.00**

Child: all cloth, handmade, one-piece; rather naive ink drawn features; touches of red on lips and cheeks; horse hair sewn to head for hair; wearing original brown cotton dress; feather stitched, red satin insert at bodice; white apron, hand-knitted stockings, straw hat; (mid-late 1800s) **$800.00**

Child: all cloth, handmade, two-piece head and torso (front and back) joined at side seams; legs attached to body at hips; stub hands; painted head, arms and booted legs; nicely done features; dressed in cotton dress with ruffled trim; (early 1900s) **$450.00**

Couple: all cloth; mask-pressed and heavily oil-painted facial features; shaped ears; well made Pilgrim or Quaker style costumes; pair; (1920s) **$1,200.00**

Family: all black cotton; stitch jointed body; fleeced yarn hair; embroidered and painted facial features; well-detailed; "salt-of-the-earth" costuming; mother, father, sister, and brother; (c. 1900)..**$1,500.00**

Vintage and collectible folk art dolls. Courtesy of David Cobb's Doll Auctions

Gentleman: all cloth, handmade, artistically-made man doll; cotton stuffed body; very long limbs; stitched fingers; oil-painted head, arms, and booted feet; extremely well done facial features, shading and accents giving great charm; original finely-made blue wool suit, brocade vest, white shirt, and red tie; carrying black top hat; (late 1800s) **$900.00**

Photo Doll: all cloth, handmade; face is picture-cut from paper and covered with gauze; poorly proportioned body with long arms and short legs; rather large bosom; wearing original print cotton dress, net and lace bonnet; (c.1930s)............**$200.00**

Pouty Baby: stockinette; stitched-shaped face with well-defined ears; shoes; button eyes; painted brown lashes; pouty mouth; yarn hair; home-spun dress and shoes; (turn of the century) **$700.00**

Toddler: all cloth, handmade, cotton stuffed, one-piece; hands and head completely painted over; facial features embroidered in red and black thread; twisted thread hair knotted to head; original old woolen clothes; hand knitted stockings; appealing face, sweet smile; (c.1920s) **$400.00**

Collectible Folk Art Dolls

Dolly: 15"; all cloth; stuffed body, attached head, arms and legs jointed to allow movement; yarn hair styled in braids; felt and embroidered facial features; handmade pink dress with rows of lace; white socks, white leather handmade shoes with pink bows; unmarked...**$200.00**

Nancy and Her Doll: Marla Florio; 12"; all cloth; one-of-a-kind; stiff cloth legs; clutching armful of cloth mini babies; yarn hair; needle-sculptured features; blue sweater, print slacks, white socks, blue shoes...**$350.00**

Nursing African Doll: Ann Fisher; 24"; brown cloth doll; large head; long arms attached to body; well developed bosom; black yarn hair tied up in a big red bow; felt eyes, large, round, white circles with black centers; wide, red, felt mouth; brass rings sewn on sides of head as earrings; removable twin babies attached to bosom with snaps; brightly colored print skirt................**$175.00**

Topsy Turvy Doll: Mamie Tyson; 16"; all cloth; head at both ends, attached at mid-section; one head is white with yellow yarn hair, beautifully embroidered wide awake facial features, nicely stitched fingers, and pink flowered dress with eyelet trim; doll flips over and dress falls to reveal black doll with black yarn hair, embroidered sleeping facial features, nicely stitched fingers, and white nightie with eyelet trim; exceptional quality and workmanship..............................**$500.00**

Dewees Cochran

The story of Dewees Cochran's life and doll making career is fascinating, yet bittersweet. Dewees was the only child of affluent parents. She was educated in private schools before attending the School of Industrial Art in Philadelphia and the Pennsylvania Academy of Fine Arts. After completing her studies in the United States, she traveled to Europe where she studied and taught art and art history.

Dewees met Paul Helbeck while studying at the International People's College in Elsinore, Denmark. They were married in her parents' home in September of 1924. After the wedding, Paul and Dewees returned to Europe to pursue the artistic life of artist and writer. Situations changed drastically and their ideal life together ended. The stock market crash, the rise of Nazi power in Germany, and the death of her father in March of 1933 made it necessary for the couple to return to America. Dewees' mother was forced to sell her home and furnishings in order to pay off the mortgages. Dewees decided to stay in the United States to help her mother, rather than return to Europe as she and Paul had planned.

Settling in New Hope, Pennsylvania, Dewees began creating dolls. Her first dolls were sold at local gift shops. Later, she traveled to New York City to peddle her dolls at fashionable shops such as Saks. Dewees eventually created meticulously sculpted and beautifully dressed living portrait dolls. Orders poured in within days of their introduction. The early portrait dolls featured carved balsa wood heads, perfectly proportioned stuffed silk bodies, and beautiful costumes.

Following the success of her portrait dolls, Dewees and Paul moved to New York. Realizing that the wealthy were not alone in desiring her portrait dolls, Dewees set out to produce quality dolls at more affordable prices. In 1936, she developed six basic face shapes, believing that, given the proper eye and hair color, any child could be captured in a portrait doll using one of six basic shapes. The basic Look-Alike faces were: Cynthia, an oval happy smiling face with teeth showing; Abigail, a rather square face with slightly smiling expression; Lisa, with a triangular face barely smiling; Deborah, with a heart-shaped face, slightly smiling; Melanie, a very thin, long face with a slight smile; and Jezebel, a round face with a slightly-pouting mouth. A customized portrait doll could be likened to nearly any child.

Paul who had been supportive and a source of inspiration, felt that his own career was being neglected. He desperately wanted to return to Europe to resume his writings. It was decided that Paul would return, and Dewees would join him later. Unfortunately, Dewees' financial situation, coupled with responsibilities to her mother, prevented her reunion with Paul. Although she remained Mrs. Paul Helbeck, Dewees and Paul never saw each other again; a circumstance they came to accept as they concentrated on their individual careers.

Angela Appleseed depicted as a child and as an adult from the Grow-up series by Dewees Cochran. Courtesy of McMaster's Doll Auction

The war years all but brought an end to Dewees Cochran doll production. Dewees became Art Director for the R. H. Donnelley Corporation, and later Design Director for the School of American Craftsmen. When the war ended and materials were once again available, she formed a small doll company—Dewees Cochran Dolls, Inc.—and in 1947, the Cindy Doll was introduced.

The contract for the fabrication of the Cindy Doll was awarded to Molded Latex Company of New Jersey, owner of the patented latex process. The doll was transported from the New Jersey factory to the workshop at 10 E. 46th Street, New York City, where it was assembled, wigged, dressed, packed, and shipped. Although she was originally satisfied with the doll, the molded Latex Company failed to meet the high standards set by Dewees. After less than a year and fewer than 1,000 Cindy Dolls, Dewees withdrew from the company. Molded Latex Company continued marketing unmarked dolls of lesser quality following Dewees' departure. Authentic Cindy dolls have a written production number and "Dewees Cochran Dolls" embossed on their torso.

In 1951–1952, Dewees developed the famous "Grow-Up" series of dolls. Susan Stormalong (Stormie) had red hair; Angela Appleseed (Angel) had blond hair; and Belinda Bunyan (Bunnie) was a brunette. The three girls were portrayed as grand nieces of famous American folklore characters—Bullhead Stormalong, a Cape Cod fisherman; Johnny Appleseed; and Paul Bunyan. In 1957, two little boys, Peter Ponsett, a blond extrovert, and Jefferson Jones (Jeff) a brunette introvert, joined the Grow-Up family. The Grow-Up Series was an instant success. For the next five years, a new version of each doll was produced with features representing various stages of development. A child of five could watch her doll progress through ages 5, 7, 11, 16, and 20 over the span of five years. Grow-Up Dolls matured from childhood to adulthood in face and figure, growing from 12 1/2 to 18 inches.

When interviewed some years ago by the Valley Press in California, Dewees explained her choices. "I've never wanted to put my art into large production. I suppose I could have made more money, but your soul gets twisted by the things you have to do for that kind of success. What I do has to do with people, with children, and the love of children. It has nothing to do with the commercial side."

Beware of the Molded Latex Company Cindy copy, easily recognized by the absence of a Dewees Cochran mark.

Prices listed are for original dolls in near mint condition. If damaged, cracked, warped, crazed, dented, or repainted, expect the value to be less than one half to one fourth the amounts listed.

Also see Effanbee.

Cindy: all latex; jointed at neck, shoulder, and hip; human hair wig; painted eyes; human hair or painted lashes; closed, slightly-smiling mouth; marked "Dewees Cochran Dolls" within oval; production number written above mark.

Grow-Up Series Dolls (Stormie, Angel, Bunnie, Peter, or Jeff ages 6-20): all latex; jointed at neck, shoulder, and hip; human hair wig; painted eyes, human hair or painted lashes; beautifully dressed. Marked "DC" and signed around initials on back; typically marked: "DC/BB-54 #9," "DC/SS 58/1," and "DC/JJ 60/2."

Look-Alike Portrait Dolls: (1 of 6 faces); custom order portrait doll; all latex; joined at neck, shoulder, and hip; human hair wig; painted eyes; human hair or painted lashes; open/closed mouth; beautifully dressed; marked "Dewees Cochran Dolls 19__" in script on small of back.

Individual Portrait: carved or sculptured face; silk body; human hair wig; beautifully painted facial features; nicely costumed; typically marked "Dewees Cochran" signature under arm or behind ear...**$4,000.00–6,000.00**

Dewees Cochran Value Comparisons			
Size	Look-Alike	Grow-Up Series	Cindy
12 1/2"		2,400.00	
15"			1,200.00
15 1/2"		2,600.00	
17"	2,700.00		
18"		2,800.00	

Columbian Dolls

Emma and Marietta Adams, sisters living in Oswego, N.Y., made and dressed cloth dolls in their home from 1891 until about 1910. Columbian Dolls were named for the Columbian Exposition, the World's Fair held in Chicago in 1893, where the dolls were exhibited. The Miss Columbia Doll traveled around the world as an ambassador of good will and, in 1902, was presented to President William Howard Taft.

Faces of early Columbian Dolls were skillfully painted by Emma. Following her death in 1900, Marietta continued the business for another ten years, hiring less talented artists to take Emma's place. Columbian Dolls were outfitted by Marietta and wore simple cotton dresses, bonnets or caps, and hand-sewn kidskin slippers or booties.

Columbian Dolls were not patented, but they were marked with a "Columbian Doll" stamp on their backs.

Prices listed are for appropriately costumed dolls with good color and little or no fading. Slight wear and signs of aging, such as a settled body, do not greatly affect the price. If a doll is stained, torn, badly mended, or faded, expect the value to be less than half the amounts listed.

Early Columbian Doll: All cloth; stitched joints at shoulder, hip, and knees; stitched fingers and toes; painted, flesh-colored lower limbs; painted hair and eyes; heart-shaped nostrils; rosebud mouth; rosy cheeks; appropriately dressed; marked "Columbia Doll/Emma E. Adams/Oswego Centre/N.Y."

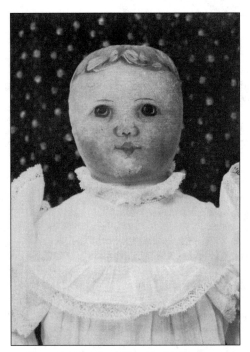

Rare early Columbian doll in original clothing. Courtesy of David Cobb's Doll Auctions

Later Columbian Doll: All cloth; stitched joints at shoulder, hip, and knees; stitched fingers and toes; painted, flesh-colored lower limbs; painted hair and eyes; rather long mouth; slight blush on cheeks; appropriately dressed; marked "The Columbian Doll/Manufactured by/Marietta Adams Ruttan/Oswego N.Y." on back.

	Columbian Cloth Doll Value Comparison			
Size	Early Mark White	Early Mark Black	Later Mark White	Later Mark Black
15"	7,000.00	10,000.00	4,200.00	6,200.00
18"	7,500.00		4,900.00	
20"	8,000.00	16,000.00		
22"	9,000.00		6,900.00	
24"	12,000.00			
29"	17,000.00		10,000.00	

Composition Dolls

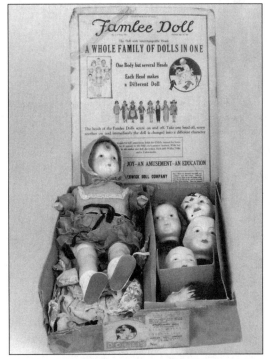

Complete Famlee doll set with interchangeable screw-on heads and matching outfits with original box. Courtesy of David Cobb's Doll Auctions

Composition Dolls were made by countless manufacturers in various countries from 1912 until about 1940. Many are unmarked and/or unidentified. The earliest composition was made from rags, bones, hides, and other waste materials, which were boiled and molded. Later composition was a pulp-based mixture of sawdust and glue.

When World War I halted imports, American doll makers seized upon the opportunity to market dolls without foreign competition. Hundreds of small companies began production and after a year or two quietly went out of business. Thousands of these Composition Dolls with no marks or unknown marks were produced and sold.

Composition is susceptible to damage caused by the environment. Heat, dampness, and temperature changes are extremely harmful. The dolls have reached the time in which signs of aging, such as the fine stress lines at the eyes and mouth openings, crackling of the eyes, and crazing, are expected. Considering that many of the dolls were manufactured between two world wars and during a depression, it is rather amazing that they have survived as well as they have.

Prices listed are for appropriately costumed dolls in good condition. Slight crazing is acceptable and does not greatly affect the price. If badly crazed, cracked, peeling, or repainted, expect the value to be less than half the amounts listed.

Flange Neck Child: cloth body; composition limbs; painted features; appropriately dressed; unmarked or marked by a small or unknown manufacturer.

Monica Studio Doll: exceptional quality; all composition; jointed at neck, shoulder, and hip; implanted human hair with widow's peak; beautifully painted features; original costume; unmarked or wrist tag "Monica Doll Hollywood."

Novelty Composition: all composition; various body joints; painted features; foreign costumes; fairy tale or wedding attire; intended as display dolls not as toys; unmarked or marked by small or unknown manufacturer.

Shoulder Head Mama: cloth body; composition limbs; good wig; glass, tin, or glassene eyes; open mouth with teeth; appropriately dressed; unmarked or marked by a small or unknown manufacturer.

Socket Head Baby: composition bent-limb baby body; molded hair or wig; sleep or painted eyes; open or closed mouth; appropriately dressed; unmarked or marked by a small or unknown manufacturer.

Socket Head Child: dolly-face; composition jointed body; good wig; sleep or flirty eyes; open mouth with teeth; appropriately dressed; unmarked or marked by a small or unknown manufacturer.

Socket Head Loop Type: molded loop for hair bows; composition body jointed at shoulder and hip, or tightly stuffed cloth torso with composition limbs; painted facial features; appropriately dressed; unmarked or marked by a small or unknown manufacturer.

Socket Head Patsy-Type: all composition; jointed at neck, shoulder, and hip; slightly bent right arm; long, thin legs; molded and painted bobbed hair; painted or sleep eyes; appropriately dressed; unmarked or marked by a small or unknown manufacturer.

Monica doll in original gown with wrist tag. Note inserted human hair forming a widow's peak. Courtesy of McMaster's Doll Auction

Character Dolls

Buddy Lee: 13"; all composition; jointed, molded, and painted features; large, side-glancing eyes; originally dressed in one of the several different advertising costumes; typically unmarked or "Buddy Lee."

Lee Jeans	$600.00
Coca-Cola (tan suit with red stripes)	750.00
Coca-Cola (white suit with red stripes)	700.00
Other soft drink outfits	500.00
Cowboy	600.00
Engineer	500.00
Gas Station	550.00
John Deere	650.00

Carmen Miranda: 14"; all composition; jointed at neck, shoulder, and hip; mohair wig; sleep eyes; original, red taffeta and black lace gown with mantilla; unmarked or wrist tag only (Uneeda) $600.00

Also a simlar version by (Eegee)

15"	$350.00
20"	450.00

Dennie Dimwit or Bobbi Mae: 11"; all composition; molded head mounted on stick fastened to top of legs, attached to hollow body with metal rod; when doll is touched, it sways back and forth; marked "Pat. Pending" inside dress; (Toy Craft Inc.) ....$200.00 each

Famlee Doll: 16"; "A Whole Family of Dolls in One"; set of at least one body and several interchangeable heads; matching costumes; set with heads, shoulder plates, cloth body; unmarked; (Berwick Doll Co.)..................................$1,400.00

Gene Carr Kids: 14"; very character faced; cloth body; composition hands; unmarked (Horsman)

Blink: squinting eyes; open/closed mouth; one tooth $450.00

Jane: round eyes; freckles; open/closed mouth; two upper teeth $450.00

Mike: round eyes; freckles; open/closed mouth; two upper teeth $450.00

Skinny: squinting eyes; open/closed mouth; one tooth $450.00

Snowball: black; round, painted eyes; open/closed mouth; two upper teeth..............$700.00

Jackie Robinson: 20"; black; socket head; jointed at shoulder and hip; molded and painted hair; black, side-glancing eyes; open/closed mouth with teeth; wearing Dodger's uniform; unmarked; (Allied Grand)..$900.00

Johnny: composition head; cloth body with felt-stitched finger hands; modelled characterization with large, open, downcast eyes; wide open/closed "Call for Phillip Morris" mouth with molded teeth; dressed in detailed bell hop uniform and cap; unmarked (advertising doll)......................................$900.00

Kewpie-Type: 12"; jointed at neck, shoulder, and hip; star-shaped hands; no wings on back; molded hair in top knot; painted, side-glancing eyes; closed mouth; unmarked.......$300.00

Lone Ranger or Tonto: 21"; composition socket head, hands, and feet; cloth body and limbs; molded and painted black hair; painted brown eyes; closed mouth; original costume; hang tag reads "The Lone Ranger and Tonto/Manufactured by Dollcraft Novelty Co./Sole Licensees/New York City," "Lone Ranger" in rope script, "Official Doll copyright T.L.R. Co., Inc.," or unmarked

Lone Ranger	$1,800.00
Tonto	1,500.00

Ming Ming: 11"; all composition; jointed at neck, shoulder, and hip; painted suggested-oriental facial features; solid dome

Unmarked composition in original case with wardrobe. Courtesy of McMaster's Doll Auction

painted or yarn hair; original taffeta oriental costume and painted shoes; unmarked (Quan Quan)..**$250.00**

Pinocchio: 12"; all composition, jointed at neck, shoulder, and hip; molded and painted hair; round eyes; large nose; closed, smiling mouth; unmarked (Crown).....................................**$400.00**

Puzzy, Sizzy: 15"; "Good Habit Kids"; all composition; character faces with full cheeks; painted hair; appropriately dressed; marked "H of P USA," "Sizzy H of P USA." (Herman Cohen)...**$450.00**

Smith, Mrs. P. D.: 20"-22"; distinctive modeling; character socket head; cloth or recycled jointed body; good wig; glass eyes; wide, beaming smile with molded teeth; unmarked

Early doll with great attention to detail.....................**$3,700.00**
Later less skillfully decorated...................................**$2,000.00**

Trudy: 15"; composition head and arms; cloth body; three faces, smiling, sleeping, and crying; knob at top of head turns head; painted features; appropriately dressed; unmarked (Three In One Doll Corp.) **$400.00**

Two Face: 16"; composition head; cloth body; one face laughing and one crying; molded and painted hair and features; appropriately dressed; unmarked...**$300.00**

Composition Doll Value Comparisons

Size	Flange Neck Child	Shoulder Head Mama Doll	Socket Head Baby Doll, White	Socket Head Baby Doll, Black	Socket Head Child Doll Exceptional
11"-12"		300.00			225.00
13"-14"	250.00				400.00
15"-16"		350.00	450.00	525.00	
17"-18"	350.00		475.00		500.00
19"-20"	400.00	400.00	500.00		550.00
21"-22"	450.00	450.00			650.00
23"-24"		500.00			800.00
25"-26"	650.00	550.00			

Size	Socket Head Child Doll Standard	Socket Head Loop-Type	Socket Head Pasty-Type	Teen-type	Monica Studio	Novelty Costume
11"-12"	200.00				600.00	200.00
13"-14"	250.00	200.00	400.00	350.00		
15"-16"		225.00	450.00	400.00	700.00	250.00
17"-18"	300.00			450.00	750.00	
19"-20"	325.00		500.00	500.00	900.00	
21"-22"	350.00			550.00	1,100.00	
23"-24"	375.00				1,200.00	

Danel & Cie

Early Paris Bébé. Courtesy of David Cobb's Doll Auctions

Later Paris Bébé with somewhat thinner face and a slightly aquiline nose. Courtesy of David Cobb's Doll Auctions

Danel & Cie was located in Paris and Montreuil-sous-Bois, France from 1889 until at least 1895. Before starting his own company, Danel served as director of the Jumeau doll company.

The location of the Danel factory, just across the street from Jumeau, proved to be troublesome. In 1890, Jumeau sued Danel for infringement. Court records show that Jumeau claimed Danel had "borrowed" molds and tools from his factory and had enticed workers to "leave the employment of Jumeau and join Danel & Cie." Danel of course denied the charges, but the courts ruled in favor of Jumeau.

In 1892, Jumeau began using the names "Paris Bébé" and "Français Bébé," both previously used by Danel. This led to the assumption that Jumeau took over the Danel Company. However, several years later, in 1899, Danel & Cie is known to have been a charter member of S. F. B. J. (The Société de Fabrication de Bébés & Jouets). It is more likely that part of the settlement award gave Jumeau the right to use the names "Pairs Bébé" and "Français Bébé."

Perhaps the most important contribution Danel & Cie made to the doll industry was the introduction of exquisite mulatto and gorgeous black dolls.

Prices listed are for appropriately dressed dolls in good condition. Normal wear, slight damage, or well-made repairs to the body do not greatly affect the price. If the bisque is damaged or repaired, expect the value to be less than half the amounts listed. It is perfectly acceptable to show a missing or repaired finger or a mended body.

Also see Jumeau.

Early Paris Bébé: (before 1892, appears very similar to a Jumeau Bébé) bisque socket head; wood and composition French body, may have straight wrist; good wig; paperweight eyes; heavy feathered brows; pierced ears; closed mouth; appropriately dressed; marked "Tête Déposé/Paris Bébé," also may have the Eiffel Tower trademark.

Later Paris Bébé: (after 1892, narrow face with aquiline nose) bisque socket head; wood and composition French body; good wig; paperweight eyes; feathered brows; pierced ears; closed, slightly-smiling mouth; appropriately dressed; marked "Tête Déposé/Paris Bébé," also may have the Eiffel Tower trademark.

Bébé Français: (occasionally attributed to Ferte of Paris) bisque socket head; wood and composition French body; good wig, paperweight eyes; feathered brows; pierced ears; closed mouth; appropriately dressed; marked "B (size number) F."

Français by Danel & Cie. Courtesy of David Cobb's Doll Auctions

Danel & Cie Value Comparison				
Size	Early Paris Bébé	Later Paris Bébé	Bébé Francais	Black Paris Bébé
13"	4,100.00			
15"	4,800.00		5,400.00	5,900.00
17"		6,300.00		
19"		6,800.00	5,900.00	6,800.00
22"	5,700.00			
24"		7,600.00	6,800.00	
27"	6,300.00			
31"			7,700.00	
33"	6,900.00			

Dean's Rag Book Company

Dean's Rag doll, holding a smaller identical rendition. Courtesy of David Cobb's Doll Auctions

Dean's Rag Book Co., of England has made cloth books, toys, and dolls since its conception in 1903. Founder, Samuel Dean, claimed that he started the company for "children who wear their food and eat their clothes." In 1920, the company introduced the first molded, pressed, and painted three-dimensional dolls called "Tru-To-Life" rag dolls.

Prices listed are for appropriately costumed dolls with good color and little or no fading. If a doll is stained, torn, badly mended, or faded, expect the value to be less than half the amounts listed.

Child Doll: All cloth; felt head and arms; dark pink cloth body, long slender legs; mohair wig; painted eyes; white highlight dot at upper eye pupil; two-tone, closed mouth; appropriately dressed; marked "Hygenic Al Toys"/picture of two dogs having a tug-of-war over a book/"Made in England/Dean's Rag Book Co. Ltd." within an oval on bottom of foot.

Printed Flat Face Doll: stuffed cotton bodies; appropriately dressed; marked "Hygenic Toys/Dean's Rag/Made in England" within an oval.

Other Dean's Dolls

Wolley Wally: Dean's Golliwog.
Dancing Boy and Girl: hugging; bobs up and down on a golden string.

Filly on a Trike: velvet arms, legs, and dress, which is part of the body; mohair wig; beautifully painted eyes; attached to metal tricycle.

Mickey Mouse: brown velvet; brown velvet pants with buttons on front; large, white felt hands.

Minnie Mouse: brown velvet; large, white felt hands.

Peter Pan: molded felt face; velvet body; wearing gold velvet suit.

Wendy: molded felt face; velvet body; wearing white nightgown.

Dean's Rag Doll Value Comparisons

Size	Child Doll	Flat Face	Wolley Walley	Dancing Dolls	Filly on Trike	Mickey	Minnie	Peter Pan	Wendy
9"		200.00							
10"	450.00								
12"			450.00	800.00	1,500.00				
14"	700.00								
15"	800.00	275.00							
16"			600.00			2,900.00	2,700.00		
17"	1,050.00	350.00						2,500.00	2,300.00
20"	1,300.00	400.00							

DEP Dolls

DEP Dolls originated in the 1880s. These bisque dolls should not be confused with dolls commonly found with the addition of the letters "DEP" to a registered mold number. On a French doll, the "DEP" stands for "Déposé," and on a German doll it's "Deponirt." In both instances, "DEP" indicates a claim of registration, and will be found with a mold number, manufacturer, or both. The DEP Dolls described here are marked only "DEP" and a size number incised into the bisque.

The early, closed-mouth DEP Dolls were made with exceptionally fine bisque and delicately applied decoration, showing great artistry. Later open-mouthed models, although generally very good in quality, lack the striking beauty of the earlier dolls.

DEP Dolls are generally regarded as French. Early dolls have a striking resemblance to Jumeau Bébés. Some French bodies are even stamped "Jumeau." The later dolls are widely considered to be German. Most likely all were of German origin. Simon & Halbig seems the obvious source, as indicated by the deeply molded and cut eye socket.

Prices listed are for appropriately costumed dolls in good condition. Normal wear, slight damage, or well-made repairs to the body do not greatly affect the price. If the bisque is damaged or repaired, expect the value to be less than half the amounts listed. It is perfectly acceptable to show a missing or repaired finger or joint, or a mended body.

Closed Mouth: bisque socket head; composition-and-wood jointed body, good wig; paperweight eyes; heavy feathered brows; long, thick eyelashes; pierced ears; closed mouth; appropriately dressed; marked "DEP" and a size number.

Open Mouth: bisque socket head; composition-and-wood jointed body; good wig; deeply molded eye sockets; glass or paperweight eyes; painted lower, and real upper lashes; feathered brows; pierced ears; open mouth with upper teeth; appropriately dressed; marked "DEP" and a size number.

DEP doll with original human hair wig and factory chemise. Courtesy of McMaster's Doll Auction

Dep Dolls Value Comparisons

Size	Closed Mouth	Open Mouth	Black
12"	2,400.00	950.00	
14"		1,000.00	
16"	3,200.00	1,100.00	2,900.00
18"	3,800.00	1,200.00	
20"	4,000.00	1,300.00	
22"	4,800.00	1,400.00	
24"	5,200.00	1,700.00	4,200.00
28"		2,400.00	
30"		2,900.00	
34"		3,400.00	

Doll House Dolls

*P*etite dolls made to roam the halls of Victorian doll-houses originated in the 1880s for the enjoyment of both adults and children. Most dollhouses boasted of a wife, husband, several children, two or three maids, a butler, and at least a few visiting friends. Early bisque Doll House Dolls were made in Germany. They are often unmarked or marked with a number or letter only.

Qualities to consider when evaluating a Doll House Doll are condition, visual appeal, and costuming. Prices listed are for desirable and charming, appropriately costumed dolls with no damage.

Adult or Child: bisque head; cloth, composition, papier-mâché; or bisque body; mohair or molded and painted hair; painted or tiny glass eyes; appropriately dressed.

Adult or Child: china head; cloth body; china stub arms; high heel feet, painted shoes; molded and painted common hairstyle; rosy cheeks; painted eyes; closed mouth; appropriately dressed.

Also see Effanbee.

Shown from top: 7" Man with mutton chops, 6 1/2" Woman #487, 5 1/2" Chauffeur in original costume, 5 3/4" Woman with molded bun, 6 1/2" Man with mustache, and a 5 3/4 Woman in original gown. Middle row: 4 3/4" Doorman, 4 3/4" Bellhop, 6 1/2" Woman, 3 3/4" Little brother # 325, 3 3/4" Little sister # 341, and a 4 1/2" Girl. Bottom row: 5 3/4" stern faced man, 5 3/4" Woman with molded high heel shoes # 440, 4 1/4" child, 3 1/2" child, and a 3 1/4" baby. Courtesy of David Cobb's Doll Auctions

Doll House Dolls Value Comparisons

Size	Painted Eyes, Adult or Child	Glass Eyes, Adult or Child	China Head	Black	Elderly Character	Molded Military Figures*	Chauffeur Molded Cap
4"	200.00						
5"	250.00						450.00
6"	275.00	500.00	200.00				
7"	350.00	650.00	225.00	900.00	900.00	1,000.00	600.00
8"	300.00	550.00	200.00				

*Add an additional $500.00 for molded hat, goatee, and mustache.

Door of Hope Dolls

Door of Hope Mourner and Widow. Courtesy of McMaster's Doll Auction

Door of Hope dolls include an Amah and baby, a Kindergarten child, and a Small boy. Courtesy of McMaster's Doll Auction

Door of Hope Dolls were made from 1901 to 1949 in Shanghai and Canton, China. A Protestant mission called the Door of Hope was founded in Shanghai in 1901 to rescue destitute children and slave girls.

At the Door of Hope Mission, the girls were taught needlework, embroidery, knitting, and other skills. Their skills were put to good use in the dressing of the Door of Hope Dolls. A girl working five days a week could make only one doll a month. The head, hands, and arms to the elbow were carved of pearwood. Men in Ning Po probably did the doll carving. The wood was as smooth as satin and needed no paint or varnish to mirror the ivory-yellow Chinese skin tone. The hair, eyes, and lips were painted. A few of the dolls had fancy buns or flowers carved into their heads. Most have hands with rounded palms and separate thumbs, although some have been found with cloth stub hands. Cloth bodies were stuffed with raw cotton donated to the Mission by local textile factories. The elaborate handmade costumes are exact copies of clothing worn by the Chinese people.

Examples of Door of Hope Dolls include:

Boy in Silk: wearing velvet, sleeveless jacket and brocaded silk outfit with tunic and trousers. The long, full sleeves ended well below the hands, indicating a member of the upper class who did not work with his hands.

Manchu Lady: wearing beautifully-detailed, carved headdress.

Grandmother: carved wrinkles; "bound" feet with constricting shoes; wearing winter hat.

Grandfather: carved wrinkles; dressed as well-to-do elderly man.

School Boy; Table Boy; and School Girl: all dressed in cotton.

Young Lady and Husband: dressed as members of the upper class.

Small Boy: wearing holiday dress of silk.

Young Man: dressed for father's funeral; three balls on his hat to catch tears; paper wand for driving off evil spirits.

Widow: wearing sack cloth; bonnet acts as veil covering her face.

Bridegroom: wearing official royal purple and blue robe with embroidered squares on front and back.

Bride: wearing traditional, red, hand-embroidered old-style costume, with tri-colored tassels.

Farmer: with grass raincoat for working in wet weather.

Temple Clerk: long yellow gown with no buttons; shaved head.

Municipal Policeman: Shanghai police uniform of dark blue woven jacket with brass buttons.

Kindergarten Child: wearing cap with ears, and "cat" (tiger) slippers to scare away evil spirits.

Cantonese Amah: nurse with baby on her back; Amah are also found without babies.

Buddhist Priest: twelve scars at top of bald head, signifying completion of training; black cotton tunic over blue trousers; black silk cap or white mandarin tunic with blue trim.

Mourners: drab, unadorned robe of rough linen with cord rope trim; ragged edged cloth symbolizes the need to hurry to prepare the cloth for mourning.

The Mission workers also filled special orders; therefore, other examples do exist.

Condition and costuming are important factors when determining value. Prices listed are for undamaged dolls in original costume. If the doll is undressed or redressed, expect the value to be less than one third of the amounts listed.

Door of Hope Value Comparisons

Size	Child/Adult*	Amah with Baby	Bride, Groom/Man- chu Lady	Priest
6"	900.00			
7 1/2"	800.00			
10 1/2"		1,100.00	1,900.00	
11 1/2"	1,000.00			1,200.00
16"			2,300.00	

*Add an additional $300.00 for specially carved hair ornamentation.

Dressel & Koch

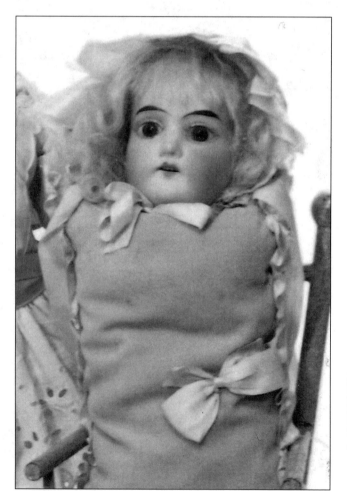

Dressel & Koch was a rather short-lived porcelain factory that operated in the Köppelsdorf area of Germany from 1892 until 1897. In 1897, Dressel & Koch collaborated with Kratky Weithase (also spelled Weithause) and formed Koch and Weithause, before closing their doors permanently in 1905. The mediocre quality of the socket and shoulder head dolls produced may explain the limited success they enjoyed.

Care must be used to not confuse an uninspired Dressel & Koch with a beautiful, artistically designed Dressel, Kister & Co. doll. Both markings may include the initials D. K., but a Dressel, Kister & Co. mark also has a spiked spiral on a stick in addition to D. K.

Prices listed are for appropriately dressed dolls in good condition. Normal wear, slight damage, or well-made repairs to the body do not greatly affect the price. If the bisque is damaged or repaired, expect the value to be less than half the amounts listed. It is perfectly acceptable to show a missing or repaired finger or joint or a mended body.

Dolly-Face: bisque socket or shoulder head; composition, kid, or papier mâché body; mohair wig; glass eyes; single stroke or stenciled brows; open mouth; appropriately dressed; typically marked "D & K No." or "D & K dep."

Dressel & Koch Dolly-Face child made into a pillow. Courtesy of David Cobb's Doll Auctions

Dressel & Koch Value Comparison

Size	Shoulder Head	Socket Head
14"	200.00	225.00
17"	300.00	350.00
20"	350.00	400.00

Cuno & Otto Dressel

The Dressel family operated a toy business in Sonneberg, Germany from the 1700s until 1942. It is the oldest toy manufacturer for which there are conclusively accurate business records. The firm passed from one generation of Dressels to the next, and in 1873 it became known as Cuno & Otto Dressel. The toys sold by Cuno and Otto Dressel were not all original products. The company purchased bisque doll heads from Armand Marseille, Simon & Halbig, Ernst Heubach and Gebrüder Heubach. It also depended upon cottage industries to help stock the incredible assortment of 30,000 different toys and dolls in its inventory.

The partnership of the Dressel brothers proved to be immensely successful. They expanded to three factories: one in Sonneberg for dolls; one in Nurnberg for the production of metal toys; and one in Grunhainichen for wooden toys.

Mold numbers known as, and attributed to, Cuno & Otto Dressel are: 93, 1348, 1349, 1468, 1469, 1776, 1848, 1849, 1893, 1896, 1898, 1912, 1914, 1920, 1922, and 2736.

Additional trademarks include Holz-Masse (wooden composition), Admiral Dewey, Admiral Sampson, Bambina, Die Puppe de Zukunft (Doll of the Future), Fifth Ave. Doll, Jutta, Jutta-Baby (named for Countess Jutta, the Patroness of Sonneberg), McKinley, M. Miles, Poppy, Uncle Sam, and Victoria.

Reputable doll makers have made reproductions of many Cuno & Otto Dressel Dolls, especially character dolls. Most of these reproductions are marked with the artist's name and date. A careful inspection should be sufficient to distinguish an authentic Cuno & Otto Dressel Doll from a reproduction.

Bisque

Prices listed are for appropriately costumed dolls in good condition. Normal wear, slight damage, or well-made repairs to the body do not greatly affect the price. If the bisque is damaged or repaired, expect the value to be less than half the amounts listed. It is perfectly acceptable to show a missing or repaired finger or joint, or a mended body.

Dolly-Face: bisque socket or shoulder head; kid body or jointed composition body; good wig; glass eyes; feathered brows; open mouth; appropriately dressed; typically marked "COD 93DEP," "AM 1893COD," "1896," "1898," "1776," or "COD1912."

Character Baby: bisque shoulder or socket head; bent-limb baby or cloth body; molded and painted hair or good wig; painted or glass eyes; appropriately dressed; typically marked "COD341," or Heubach Koppelsdorf 1922/Jutta Baby/Germany."

Jutta Character Baby: bisque socket head by Simon & Halbig; bent-limb baby body; good wig; glass eyes; open mouth; appropriately dressed; marked "Jutta 1914," or "Jutta 1920." **Note:** *Simon & Halbig Jutta character babies are always marked with mold number 1914 or 1920.*

Jutta Child: bisque head by Simon & Halbig; jointed composition body; good wig; glass eyes; pierced or unpierced ears; open mouth; appropriately dressed; marked "1349/Jutta/S & H," "S & H/1348/Jutta," or "1348 Dressel." **Note:** *Simon & Halbig Jutta child dolls are always marked with mold number 1348 or 1349.*

Prominent German manufacturers such as Gebrüder Heubach and Simon & Halbig produced Cuno and Otto Dressel's Character Dolls. They can be whimsical and charming, or simply beautiful. Their three main categories include:

Early Cuno & Otto Dressel bisque shoulder head with heavily feathered brows. Courtesy of McMaster's Doll Auction

Three lovely Cuno & Otto Dressel brown bisque child dolls marked #1349, known as Jutta. Courtesy of David Cobb's Doll Auctions

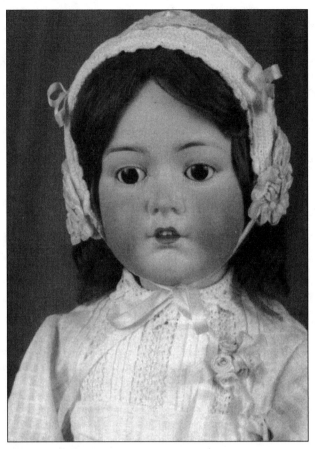

Unusual face marked only Cuno & Otto Dressel/Germany. Courtesy of McMaster's Doll Auction

Character Portrait: modelled to represent military, political, or legendary figures; bisque socket head; jointed composition body; painted or glass eyes; appropriately dressed; typically marked "S," "D," "R," or "A."

Character Child: bisque socket head; jointed composition body; molded and painted hair or wig; painted or glass eyes; open or closed mouth; appropriately dressed; typically marked "Germany," "C.O.D.," "C.O.D./S.H.," and perhaps a size number.

Character Lady: lovely, slim young woman; bisque socket head; shapely, jointed-composition lady's body with graceful arms and legs; feet molded for high heel shoes; good wig; glass eyes; closed mouth; appropriately dressed; typically marked "1469/C O Dressel Germany," "1468 COD," "SH1468," or "S & H/COD/1469."

Composition

Prices listed are for appropriately costumed dolls in good condition. Slight crazing is acceptable and does not greatly affect the price. If badly crazed, cracked, peeling, or repainted, expect the value to be less than half the amounts listed.

Character Lady: composition limbs and shoulder head; cloth body; good wig; glass eyes; closed mouth; appropriately dressed; typically marked "C.O.D."

Character Child: composition socket head; jointed composition body; painted hair with brush marks; glass or painted eyes; closed, puckered mouth; appropriately dressed; typically marked "C.O.D."

Dolly-Face: composition socket head; jointed composition body; good wig; glass eyes; open mouth; appropriately dressed; typically "M & S.," "C.O.D.," or "Jutta."

C.O.D. Bisque Value Comparison:

Size	Dolly Face Kid Body	Dolly Face Composition Body	Character Baby Heubach or COD*	S & H Jutta Baby 1914/1920*	S & H Jutta/Child 1348/1349*
12"	450.00		475.00	750.00	
14"	475.00	550.00	600.00	900.00	800.00
16"	500.00	600.00	700.00	1,000.00	850.00
18"	550.00	700.00	800.00	1,200.00	900.00
20"	650.00	800.00	900.00	1,600.00	1,000.00
22"	700.00	850.00	1,000.00		1,200.00
24"	750.00	900.00	1,200.00	2,000.00	1,400.00
26"	800.00	950.00		2,400.00	2,000.00
28"	900.00		1,800.00		2,300.00
30"		1,200.00			2,500.00
36"		2,800.00			3,500.00
40"					4,200.00

Size	Uncle Sam/ Admiral Dewey	Old Rip Farmer Buffalo Bill	Character Child Closed Mouth/Painted Eyes*	Character Child Closed Mouth/Glass Eyes*	Character Lady**
12"	1,800.00	1,200.00	3,000.00	3,200.00	3,800.00
14"	2,000.00	1,400.00	3,200.00	3,400.00	4,500.00
16"	2,400.00		3,400.00	3,800.00	5,000.00
18"			3,800.00		5,800.00
20"			4,200.00		6,200.00
22"				4,500.00	
24"				5,000.00	

* Add an additional $700.00 for jointed toddler.

** Add an additional $300.00 for high knee flapper body.

Papier-Mâché

Papier-mâché was made from powdered or torn bits of paper and paste. Turn-of-the-century composition was often merely a papier-mâché base with additives.

Prices listed are for appropriately costumed dolls in good condition. Slight crazing is acceptable and does not greatly affect the price. If badly crazed, cracked, peeling, or repainted, expect the value to be less than half the amounts listed.

Shoulder Head: papier-mâché shoulder head and limbs; cloth body; molded and painted hair or good wig; painted or glass eyes; feathered brows; closed mouth; entire head and shoulder plate with varnish-like coating; appropriately dressed; typically marked with winged helmet and "HOLZMASSE."

Wax

Prices listed are for appropriately costumed dolls in good condition. If damaged or re-waxed, expect the value to be less than one half to one fourth of the amount listed.

Reinforced Wax: rare, usually poured and reinforced with plaster or composition; wax shoulder head; cloth body; wax over composition arms; good wig; glass eyes; appropriately dressed; typically marked with winged helmet and "ED"; body stamped "HOLZMASSE" or "Dressel."

Wax-Over Composition: composition shoulder head coated with layers of wax; cloth body; wax-over composition limbs; good wig; painted or glass eyes; closed mouth; appropriately dressed; typically marked "ED Patent DE HOLZ-MASSE" inside back shoulder plate and "XXXVIII" painted in gold.

			C.O.D. Composition, Papier-Mâché, and Wax Value Comparisons					
Size	Composition Lady	Composition, Closed Mouth, Chracter Child	Composition, Open Mouth, Dolly-Face	Papier-mache Painted Eye	Papier-mache Glass Eye	Reinforced Wax Dolls	Wax-Over Composition
14"	1,200.00		450.00	425.00		900.00	
18"	1,700.00	2,200.00	475.00	550.00	550.00	1,200.00	500.00
20"		2,500.00		575.00	650.00	1,700.00	
24"		2,800.00	600.00	700.00	750.00	1,800.00	600.00
26"				800.00	900.00		
28"						2,000.00	

Edmund Edelmann

E dmund Edelmann was a small doll business in Sonneberg, Germany between 1921 and 1933. The Edelmann Company purchased doll heads from Armand Marseille and Schoenau & Hoffmeister. Edelmann also served as a supply agent for doll hospitals. Admittedly small and in business a short time, Edelmann was nevertheless responsible for the popular Melitta doll. Melitta, with familiar baby-face characteristics, was commonly advertised and distributed on a five-piece composition toddler body.

It's interesting to note that Edmund Edelmann is mentioned several times in historical documents concerning the "Art Doll Movement," made famous by Marion Kaulitz. Although records are rather inconclusive and lack particulars, the contributions from less known individuals, such as Edelmann, certainly helped to revolutionize the doll industry of the early twentieth century.

Bisque

Prices listed are for appropriately costumed dolls in good condition. Normal wear, slight damage, or well-made repairs to the body do not greatly affect the price. If the bisque is damaged or repaired, expect the value to be less than half the amounts listed. It is perfectly acceptable to show a missing or repaired finger or a mended body.

Melitta character toddler.
Courtesy of David
Cobb's Doll Auctions

Character Baby: bisque socket head; five-piece composition body, jointed at neck, shoulder, and hip; good wig; sleep eyes; real lashes; pierced nostrils; open mouth; appropriately dressed; typically marked "Melitta" or "Melitta A. Germany M."

Composition

Prices listed are for appropriately costumed dolls in good condition. Slight crazing is acceptable and does not greatly affect the price. If badly crazed, cracked, peeling, or repainted, expect the value to be less than half the amounts listed.

Character Baby: all composition; socket head; bent limb baby body; molded and painted hair or good wig; sleep eyes;

open mouth; occasionally pierced nostrils; appropriately dressed; typically marked "Melitta Germany," "A. M.," "SPBH Mona," or "Mine."

Edelmann Value Comparison		
Size	Bisque*	Composition
16"	1,500.00	
20"	1,700.00	
24"		1,000.00

*Add an additional $700.00 for a jointed toddler body.

Eden Bébé

❧

$\mathcal{E}$den Bébé, a trade name, is more familiar than the manufacturer, Fleischmann and Bloedel Doll Factory. The company was established in 1873 in Fürth, Bavaria, and Paris, France. In 1899, Saloman Fleischmann formed and became director of the S.F.B.J. (Societe Francaise de Febrica-tion de Bébés & Jouets), making the Fleischmann and Bloedel Doll Factory its first charter member.

Unwilling to forfeit his German citizenship, Fleischmann left France during World War I and returned to Germany. He died soon after in Spain. Consequently, the firm changed directors and ownership many times and eventually filed for bankruptcy in the early 1920s.

Prices listed are for appropriately costumed dolls in good condition. Normal wear, slight damage, or well-made repairs to the body do not greatly affect the price. If the bisque is damaged or repaired, expect the value to be less than half the amounts listed. It is perfectly acceptable to show a missing or repaired finger or joint, or a mended body.

Eden Bébé: bisque socket head; five-piece or jointed wood and composition body; good wig; cork pate; paperweight eyes, feathered brows; long eyelashes; pierced ears; open or closed mouth with a hint of a molded tongue; appropriately dressed; typically marked "Eden Bébé" or "Eden Bébé Paris."

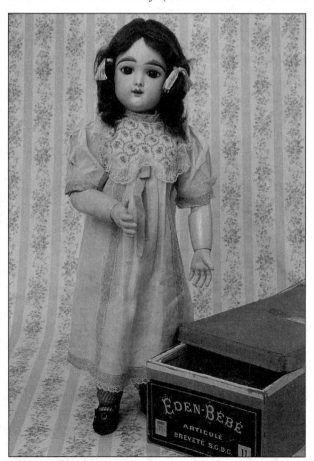

Open mouth Eden Bébé with original box. Courtesy of David Cobb's Doll Auctions

Eden Bébé Value Comparisons				
Size	Closed Mouth	Open Mouth	Black	Composition
11"	2,200.00	1,500.00		
12"	2,400.00	1,600.00		
14"	2,600.00	1,700.00		
16"	3,000.00	1,900.00	3,900.00	600.00
18"	3,100.00	2,000.00		
20"	3,300.00	2,300.00		
22"	3,500.00	2,500.00		
24"	3,800.00	2,800.00		
26"	4,000.00	3,000.00		
28"	4,400.00			
30"	5,200.00	3,700.00		
34"		4,000.00		

Eegee

*M*r. and Mrs. E. Goldberger founded this famous doll company in 1917 in Brooklyn, New York. The trademark EEGEE was adopted in 1923. Early dolls were marked "EG," followed by "E. Goldberger," and finally "Eegee" or occasionally "Goldberger." Eegee is one of the longest-running continuously operating manufacturers of dolls in the United States. Although the company never achieved the level of fame acquired by many other doll companies, Eegee constantly produced innovative and appealing quality dolls.

Also see Composition dolls.

Composition

Prices listed are for appropriately costumed dolls in good condition. Slight crazing is acceptable and does not greatly affect the price. If badly crazed, cracked, peeling, or repainted, expect the value to be less than half the amounts listed.

Child: composition socket head; jointed composition body; molded and painted hair or good wig; painted or sleep eyes; open/closed mouth; appropriately dressed; typically marked "EEGEE," "E. Goldberger," or "E.G."

Baby: composition limbs and flange neck; cloth body; molded and painted hair or good wig; tin sleep eyes; open/closed mouth with molded teeth; appropriately dressed; typically marked "E. Goldberger," "E.G.," or "EEGEE."

Early Latex

Early latex was a synthetic material that looked and felt like human skin. Over time it becomes unstable and deteriorates, becoming badly discolored. The process may be slowed by regularly rubbing cornstarch into the doll.

Prices listed are for appropriately dressed dolls in good condition.

Child: early latex head with wooden plug neck flange; one-piece latex body; molded and painted hair; sleep eyes; open/closed mouth; appropriately dressed; typically marked "EEGEE" or "EE-GEE."

Hard Plastic & Vinyl

Prices listed are for dolls in near-mint, original condition. If damaged, redressed, or undressed, expect the value to be less than one half to one fourth the amounts listed.

Gigi Perreaux (child actress): vinyl head; jointed, hard plastic body; dark brown synthetic wig; brown sleep eyes, feathered brows; open/closed mouth with molded teeth; appropriately dressed; typically marked "E.G."

Child: vinyl socket head; jointed or walker hard plastic body; rooted saran hair; sleep eyes; closed mouth; appropriately dressed; typically marked "E.G." or "EEGEE."

Baby: vinyl socket head; molded plastic body; rooted hair; painted or sleep eyes; closed mouth; appropriately dressed; typically marked "Eegee."

Teen: all vinyl; jointed at neck, shoulder, and hip; rooted hair; painted or sleep eyes; closed mouth; appropriately dressed; typically marked "20/25M," "EEGEE," or "20 HH."

"Miss Charmin," an obvious Shirley Temple look-alike and a wonderful example of the fine quality composition dolls produced by Eegee. Courtesy of David Cobb's Doll Auctions

Musical Dimples: vinyl head and hands; cloth body containing music box; rooted hair; painted eyes; open/closed mouth; body and clothing as one; typically marked "14 BD/ Eegee Co."

Dolly Parton: vinyl head; jointed plastic woman's shapely body; painted eyes; open/closed mouth with molded teeth; orig-inal gown; marked "DOLLY PARTON/EEGEE CO./HONG KONG/Goldberger Mfg. Co."

Granny: plastic and vinyl; rooted, long, gray hair pulled into bun; painted facial features; closed mouth; original cotton "homespun" dress; typically marked "Eegee/3."

Eegee Value Comparisons

Size	Composition Child	Composition Baby	Gigi Perreaux	Vinyl and Hard Plastic Child	Early Latex	Vinyl Baby	Vinyl Teen	Musical Dimples	Dolly Parton	Granny
10"						25.00				
12"						45.00	75.00	50.00	75.00	
14"		300.00		100.00	100.00	50.00				150.00
16"	400.00	350.00								
18"	450.00	400.00	750.00			65.00	100.00	85.00	150.00	
20"	525.00		900.00	150.00	150.00					
22"		475.00		200.00						
28"				250.00				135.00		
36"								175.00		

Effanbee Doll Company

Effanbee composition dolls, includeing from back: 22" Patsy Lou in original dress, 19" Patsy Ann in original dress, 14" Patricia in original dress and replaced shoes, 11" Patsy Jr. in original dress and replaced skates, all original 6" Wee Patsy, and an unnamed marked F&B original girl. Courtesy of David Cobb's Doll Auctions

Effanbee is an acronym for Fleischaker & Baum, who founded this prolific doll company in New York City around 1910. Effanbee has been a creative pioneer in the American doll industry, responsible for many significant innovations. Patsy was the first realistically proportioned American-made doll designed to resemble a real child. She was also the first doll for which companion dolls were created, and the first to have a wardrobe and fan club. Patsy's fan club, reportedly, had over 275,000 members. In 1934, Effanbee enhanced its modernistic image with the introduction of "Dydee," the first drink-and-wet doll.

Effanbee dolls will undoubtedly remain popular. While maintaining its excellence in the play doll field, Effanbee also became a leader in the collector dolls phenomena. By enlisting talented doll artists, initiating the Limited Edition Doll Club, and producing realistic celebrity and personality dolls, Effanbee has secured their position of excellence for future generations of doll collectors.

Also see Automaton.

Composition

Prices listed are for appropriately costumed dolls in good condition. Slight crazing is acceptable and does not greatly affect the price. If badly crazed, cracked, peeling, or repainted, expect the value to be less than half the amounts listed.

Character Doll (Chubby Boy Bud, Baby Grumpy, Pouting Bess, Coquette, Harmonica Joe, Katie Kroose, and Whistling Jim): cloth body; sewn-on shoes; painted facial features; appropriately dressed; typically marked "Effanbee," "176," "Deco," "172," "174," "Baby Grumpy," "166," "162," "462," or "116."

Child and Baby (Baby Dainty, Sweetie Pie, Mickey, Baby Bright Eyes, Lovums, Rosemary, and Marilee): composition limbs and shoulder head; cloth body; molded hair or good wig; painted or tin sleep eyes; open/closed mouth; appropriately dressed; typically marked "Effanbee/Lovums/c Pat No.," "Effanbee/Rosemary Talks Walks Sleeps," "Effanbee/Baby Dainty," "Effanbee/Marilee/CopyR/Doll," or possibly others.

Dolly-Face (Mary/Ann/Jane/Lee): composition socket head; jointed wood-and-composition body; good wig; sleep eyes; open mouth; appropriately dressed; typically marked "Effanbee," "MaryAnn," or possibly others.

Mama (Bubbles and Lambkin): composition head and limbs; cloth body, molded hair or good wig; sleep eyes; open/closed mouth, most say "Mama"; appropriately dressed; typically marked "Effanbee/Bubbles/Corp 1924/Made in U.S.A.," "Effanbee/Dolls/Walk, Talk, Sleep/Made in U.S.A.," "1924/Effanbee/Dollys/Walk, Talk, Sleep/Made in USA," or "EFFANBEE."

Patsy and Patsy's Family: one of the most popular 20th century dolls; all composition; jointed at neck, shoulder, and hip; painted and molded hair or good wig; painted or sleep eyes; closed mouth; appropriately dressed; typically marked "EFFANBEE PATSY DOLL," "EFFANBEE PATSY BABY," or with other variations of the Patsy family (see chart).

Skippy: newspaper character drawn by Percy Crosby and produced as playmate for Patsy; all composition or composition head and limbs; cloth body; molded and painted hair; painted, round, side-glancing eyes; closed mouth; appropriately dressed; typically marked "Patsy Pat./Pending" or "Effanbee Skippy/P.L. Crosby"; original pin "I am Skippy The All American Boy."

Ventriloquist Doll (Charlie McCarthy, W. C. Fields, Lucifer): composition and cloth; pull string activates mouth; typically marked "Lucifer/V. Austin/EffanBEE," "Fleischaker & Baum," "W. C. Fields/EffanBEE," or "EDGAR BERGEN CHARLIE McCARTHY EFFANBEE." *Note: Ventriloquist dolls were expensive to produce, transport, and display; therefore, relatively few were made. Today they are a rare find. Puppeteer Virginia Austin designed and patented a number of Effanbee's puppets. She also gave marionette demonstrations and founded the "Clippo Club" as part of the Effanbee marionette promotion.*

American Children: composition socket head; jointed composition body; human hair wig; beautifully detailed painted eyes; closed mouth; original, well-made outfit; typically marked "Effanbee/American Children" or "Effanbee/Ann Shirley." *Note: Lovely dolls designed by Dewees Cochran. Dewees met Bernard Baum and Hugo Fleischaker in 1935. They were impressed with her work and commissioned her to produce six dolls for the upcoming 1936 Toy Show. Effanbee signed a three-year contract with Dewees to produce the designs of her American Children portrait dolls. When the three-year contract expired, it was not renewed.*

Child/Lady (Suzanna, Tommy Tucker, Ann Shirley, and Little Lady): all composition, jointed at neck, shoulder, and hip; good wig; sleep eyes; closed mouth; appropriately dressed; typically marked "EFFANBEE USA" or "EFFANBEE/ANN SHIRLEY."

Open Mouth American Children (Barbara Joan, Barbara Ann, Barbara Lou, and Peggy Lou): all composition; jointed at neck, shoulder, and hip; human hair wig; sleep or painted eyes; open mouth; original well-made outfit; typically marked "EffanBEE/Ann Shirley" or unmarked.

Historical/Historical Replica Dolls: designed by Dewees Cochran; Effanbee produced three sets of thirty dolls depicting changing American styles. The 20" dolls were exhibited around the country. They had an Ann Shirley body and the American Children head with painted eyes. Original costumes were made from satins, velvets, and silks. Effanbee produced a smaller and less elaborately costumed 14" version known as a Historical Replica Doll. They were an accurate representation with beautifully painted eyes and historically correct cotton costumes.

Doll House Doll: 6"; composition head and hands; cloth-covered wire armature body; molded and painted shoes; molded and painted hair; painted blue eyes; closed mouth; original, detailed costume; typically marked "EFFanBEE"............**$100.00**

Button Nose: 8"; all composition; jointed at neck, shoulder, and hip; molded and painted hair; painted, round, side-glancing

Patsy & Patsy's Family Composition Value Comparisons

Size	Wee Patsy	Baby Tinyette	Tinette Toddler	Patsy Babyette	Patsyette*	Patsy Baby/Babykins*	Patsykins/Patsy Jr.*
6"	500.00						
7"		400.00					
8"			450.00				
9"				450.00	500.00		
10"						450.00	
11"							550.00

Size	Patsy/Patricia	Patsy Joan*	Patsy Ann*	Patsy Lou	Patsy Ruth	Mae	Skippy*
14"	650.00						700.00
16"		650.00					
19"			700.00				
22"				750.00			
27"					1,500.00		
30"						1,800.00	

* Add an additional $300.00 for black or Oriental versions.

eyes; closed, slightly-smiling mouth; original detailed costume; typically marked "Effanbee" $400.00

Oriental facial features $600.00

Little Sister and Big Brother: 12" and 16"; composition socket head; shoulder plate and hands; cloth body and limbs; floss hair; painted eyes; small closed mouth; original Little Sister's pink and white and Big Brother's blue and white outfits; typically marked "Effanbee."

Little Sister: 12" $300.00

Big Brother: 16" $350.00

Candy Kid: 13"; all composition, jointed at neck, shoulder, and hip; chubby child figure; molded and painted hair; painted eyes; pointed eyebrows; closed mouth; original gingham outfit; holding small stuffed monkey; typically marked "EFFANBEE" $500.00

Hard Rubber

Prices listed are for original or appropriately dressed dolls in good condition. If damaged or showing signs of deterioration, expect the value to be less than one fourth the amounts listed.

Dy-Dee Baby: hard rubber, drink-and-wet doll; hard rubber or plastic socket head; hard rubber body; jointed at shoulder and hip; attached soft rubber ears; molded and painted hair; sleep eyes; open nurser drink and wet mouth; appropriately dressed; marked "Effanbee/DyDee Baby/U.S. Pat. 1-857-485/England-880-060/France-723-980/Germany-585-647/Other Pat. Pending." The rubber heads (and eventually bodies) were replaced with hard plastic.

Cloth

Gaining in popularity are the charming cloth display or souvenir-type dolls made in Spain by Klumpe, imported and distributed by Effanbee.

Prices listed are for dolls in near mint, original condition. If damaged or undressed, expect the value to be less than one fourth the amounts listed.

Klumpe: 10"–12"; all firmly stuffed cloth; wire armature body; felt or floss hair; amusing pressed and painted facial features; wide-open eyes; expressive mouth; authentically designed, sewn-on costumes; typically marked with hang or wrist tag only, "I am a Klumpe doll/hand made in Spain//distributed by EFFANBEE," "Klumpe Made in Spain," "Klumpe/Patented Barcelona" may also have a production or style number ....$175.00–250.00, **depending upon characterization**

Hard Plastic/Vinyl

Prices listed are for dolls in near-mint, original condition. If damaged, redressed, or undressed, expect the value to be less than one half to one fourth the amounts listed.

Howdy Doody: hard plastic character head and hands; cloth body, molded and painted hair; sleep eyes; open/closed mouth; original cowboy costume with scarf printed "Howdy Doody"; marked "Effanbee."

Klumpe character doll. Courtesy Dr. Georgia Kemp Caraway

Honey: all hard plastic; jointed at neck, shoulder, and hip; synthetic wig; sleep eyes; closed mouth; appropriately dressed; typically marked "Effanbee," hang tag "I am Honey An Effanbee Durable Doll." ***Note:*** *the Honey series of dolls includes famous characters such as Cinderella and Prince Charming, and elaborately costumed dolls such as those from the Schiaparelli Collection, designed by famous Paris designer, Madame Schiaparelli.*

Fluffy: 8"; all vinyl; jointed at neck, shoulder, and hip; molded and painted hair with long curls; sleep eyes; closed mouth; appropriately dressed; typically marked "©Fluffy/Effanbee"$100.00

Happy Boy: 10"; all vinyl; jointed at neck and shoulder; character face; molded and painted hair; molded and painted closed eyes; open/closed mouth; molded upper tooth; freckles; appropriately dressed; typically marked "1960/Effanbee" or "Effanbee"$100.00

Half Pint: 11"; all vinyl; jointed at neck, shoulder, and hip; rooted short hair; large, side-glancing sleep eyes; closed grinning mouth; appropriately dressed; typically marked "IOME/Effanbee/19©66"....................$125.00

Mickey The All American Boy: 11"; all vinyl; jointed at neck, shoulder, and hip; molded hat and hair; painted eyes; closed smiling mouth; freckles; appropriately dressed; typically marked "Mickey/Effanbee"....................$175.00

Patsy Ann: 15"; all vinyl; jointed at neck, shoulder, and hip; rooted hair; sleep eyes; closed smiling mouth; appropriately dressed; typically marked "Effanbee Patsy Ann/1959"....$250.00

Twinkie: 15"; all vinyl; jointed at neck, shoulder, and hip; rooted hair or molded and painted hair; sleep eyes; open nurser drink and wet mouth; appropriately dressed; typically marked "Effanbee/1959"....................$200.00

Sugar Plum: 16"; vinyl head and limbs; cloth body, rooted hair; sleep eyes; closed smiling mouth; appropriately dressed; typically marked "141 Effanbee/1969/1949"; or "F & B/1964" $125.00

Suzie Sunshine: 18"; all vinyl; jointed at neck, shoulder, and hip; rooted hair; sleep eyes; closed, pouty mouth; freckles; appropriately dressed; typically marked "Effanbee/1961".........$150.00

Miss Chips: 18"; all vinyl; jointed at neck, shoulder, and hip; rooted hair, full bangs; very large, side-glancing sleep eyes; closed mouth; appropriately dressed; typically marked "Effanbee/19©65/1700"....................$125.00

Thumbkin: 18"; vinyl head and limbs; cloth body; rooted, short hair; round, side-glancing eyes; open/closed mouth; appropriately dressed; typically marked "Effanbee/1965/9500 UI"....................$150.00

Rootie Kazootie: 19"; vinyl hands and character flange neck; cloth body; molded and painted hair, long curl coming down forehead; round, painted eyes; open/closed laughing mouth; appropriately dressed; typically marked "Rootie/Kazootie/Effanbee"....................$350.00

Candy Ann: 20"; all vinyl; jointed at neck, shoulder, and hip; rooted hair; sleep eyes; closed, smiling mouth; appropriately dressed; typically marked "Effanbee"....................$150.00

Honey Walker: 20"; vinyl head; hard plastic walker body; jointed at shoulder and hip, just above the knees, and at ankles; feet molded for high heel shoes; rooted hair; sleep eyes; pierced ears; closed mouth; appropriately dressed; typically marked "EFFanBEE"....................$450.00

Effanbee Doll Company Composition Value Comparisons

Size	Character Dolls*	Child/Baby Face	Dolly Face	Mama	Ventriloquist* Dolls	American Children	Child/Lady	Unmarked Child	Historical/ Historical Replica
7"	250.00								
10"	300.00			350.00					
11"							275.00		
12"	350.00	350.00		450.00			325.00		
14"	400.00	400.00					400.00		750.00
16"	500.00	450.00	400.00	600.00			475.00		
17"		500.00		650.00		2,200.00		900.00	
18"			450.00		1,400.00		500.00		
20"		600.00	550.00	675.00		2,500.00	550.00	1,200.00	2,200.00
22"				750.00			700.00		
24"		650.00	600.00				725.00		
25"		700.00		850.00					
27"		750.00		900.00			800.00		

* Add an additional $200.00 for black dolls.

Lil Darling: 20"; vinyl limbs and flange neck head; cloth body; molded and painted hair; small, slit-like, painted eyes; molded underlying pouches; wrinkled brow; pug nose; open/closed mouth, molded tongue; appropriately dressed **$250.00**

Vinyl Mark Twain and Huck Finn from Effanbee's Great Moments in Literature collection.

My Fair Baby: 21"; all vinyl; jointed at neck, shoulder, and hip; rooted hair; sleep eyes; open nurser mouth; body has crier; appropriately dressed; typically marked "EFFanBEE/1960" **$125.00**

Precious Baby: 21"; vinyl limbs and flange neck head; pink cloth body; rooted hair; sleep eyes; open/closed mouth; appropriately dressed; typically marked "Effanbee 19©69".......**$125.00**

Mary Jane: 30"; vinyl socket head; plastic body; jointed at shoulder and hip; rooted hair; sleep/flirty eyes; closed, slightly-unsmiling mouth; freckles over nose; appropriately dressed, typically marked "Effanbee/Mary Jane"......................................**$450.00**

Limited Edition Dolls

Effanbee produced dolls for series, collections, and clubs. Initiated in 1975, the Effanbee Limited Edition Doll Club introduced a new doll each year. A unique feature of the club was that each doll, produced in a pre-announced limited quantity, was available only through Effanbee's Limited Edition Doll Club.

Doll Club Series

Precious Baby: 1975...**$550.00**
Patsy: 1976...450.00
Dewees Cochran Self Portrait: 1977 ....225.00
Crowning Glory: 1978..200.00
Skippy: 1979...375.00
Susan B. Anthony: 1980.......................................175.00
Girl with Watering Can: 1981 ....175.00
A Royal Bride: Diana, 1982..................................250.00
Sherlock Holmes: 1983 ....150.00
Bubbles: 1984..150.00
Red Boy: 1985...150.00
China Head: 1986...100.00

Legends Series

W.C. Fields $200.00
John Wayne: soldier 150.00
John Wayne: cowboy 150.00
Mae West 150.00
Groucho Marx 100.00
Judy Garland as Dorothy 125.00
Lucille Ball 100.00
Liberace 150.00
James Cagney 75.00
Humphrey Bogart...85.00
Carol Channing 75.00
George Burns 100.00
Gracie Allen..100.00

Presidents Series

George Washington $100.00
Abraham Lincoln...100.00
Theodore Roosevelt..125.00
Franklin D. Roosevelt...100.00
John F. Kennedy 200.00
Dwight D. Eisenhower...75.00

Great Moments in History

Winston Churchill $200.00
Eleanor Roosevelt...100.00

Great Moments in Literature

Huck Finn..$100.00
Mark Twain 100.00
Becky Thatcher 60.00
Tom Sawyer 65.00

Great Moments In Music

Louis Armstrong..$100.00

Great Moments In Sports

Babe Ruth..$300.00
Muhammad Ali...200.00

International Collection

Grand Dames Collection $85.00
Currier & Ives Collection 75.00
Soft & Sweet Collection 45.00
Keepsake Collection 65.00
Age of Elegance Collection 75.00
Gigi Through the Years Collection 125.00
Passing Parade Collection 75.00
Day by Day Collection 60.00
Innocence Collection..60.00

Storybook Collection

Dorothy $75.00
Cowardly Lion 75.00
Tin Man...75.00
Straw Man..75.00
Santa Claus 60.00
Mrs. Claus..50.00
Old Woman in the Shoe 50.00
Little Milk Maid..45.00

Craftsman Corner Collectible Dolls

Jan Hagara: Christian $225.00

Effanbee Doll Company Hard Plastic/Rubber Value Comparison					
Size	Dy-Dee Baby	Howdy Doody	Honey	Cinderella/Prince	Madame Schiaparelli
9"	325.00				
12"	400.00				
14"	425.00		400.00	600.00	650.00
16"	450.00		450.00		
18"	500.00		500.00		
19"		450.00			
20"	550.00		550.00	800.00	900.00
23"	600.00	650.00			
24"	700.00		600.00		
27"			800.00		

Eisenmann & Co.

The firm of Eisenmann & Co., known as Einco, was located in Bavaria and London from 1881 until 1930. Einco produced and distributed dolls for which Gebrüder Heubach supplied bisque heads. Joe Eisenmann, the founder of the company, was called "King of the Toy Trade."

There are reproduction dolls very similar to Eisenmann's. They do not, however, bear the Einco markings. A careful examination should eliminate any doubt you may have concerning an Einco doll's authenticity.

Prices listed are for appropriately costumed dolls in good condition. Normal wear, slight damage, or well-made repairs to the body do not greatly affect the price. If the bisque is damaged or repaired, expect the value to be less than half the amounts listed. It is perfectly acceptable to show a missing or repaired finger or joint, or a mended body.

Also see Googly-Eyed Dolls.

Character Baby: bisque character socket head; composition bent-limb body; molded and painted hair; intaglio painted eyes; open/closed mouth; appropriately dressed; typically marked "Germany Einco."

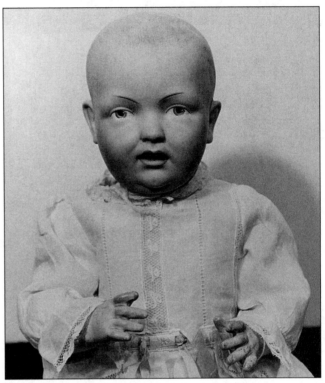

18" Eisenmann & Co. character baby marked EINCO/ Germany. Courtesy of David Cobb's Doll Auctions

Einco Value Comparisons	
Size	Character Baby
12"	800.00
15"	900.00
18"	1,100.00
20"	1,400.00

Joel Ellis

Joel Ellis operated the Co-Operative Manufacturing Company in Springfield, Vermont, from 1873 to 1874. Ellis patented and manufactured wooden dolls and employed about sixty people, most of them women. The Joel Ellis Doll is considered one of the earliest commercially-made American dolls. It embodies many technical innovations. The doll's unique mortise-and-tenon construction allowed a complete range of movement. Pewter hands and feet were attached to rock maple limbs. The wooden heads were cut into a cube, steamed until softened, and shaped in a hydraulic press with steel dies to form the features. The body and limbs were turned on a lathe and connected to the head by a dowel. The hair was molded in a prim 1860s-style and painted either black or blond. Joel Ellis Dolls were made in three sizes, 12", 15", and 18". Many prefer to display the dolls undressed, as this is how they were originally sold.

Although Joel Ellis Dolls are unmarked, their unique mortise-and-tenon joint construction, metal hands, and distinct facial features make them easy to identify.

Joel Ellis Dolls tend to age rather poorly. They are particularly prone to peeling and flaking. As a result, collectors are a bit more tolerant of worn or age-stricken dolls. The desirability rests in the

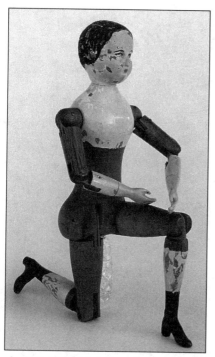

12" Joel Ellis doll. Courtesy of Bill Neff

doll's design and historical significance rather than any artistic decoration.

Prices listed are for dolls in fair to good original condition with normal wear. Badly damaged or repainted dolls would be valued much less. Parenthetically, a well preserved example will easily command twice the values listed.

Joel Ellis Doll: wooden head and body; painted metal hands and feet; molded and painted hair; heavily-painted facial features; closed mouth; undressed; unmarked.

Joel Ellis Wooden Doll Value Comparisons	
Size	Price
12"	1,200.00
15"	1,600.00
18"	2,000.00

J. K. Farnell & Company

The J. K. Farnell & Company was founded in 1871 in England. In the 1920s, Farnell's Alpha Toys began producing dolls made of felt, velvet, stockinette, and other types of cloth. Farnell Dolls are found with a label sewn in the foot.

Farnell's dolls feature felt faces, side-glancing eyes, and smiling mouths. Chubby stockinette bodies have seams at the front, back, and sides of each leg. Hair consists of mohair sewn in a circular pattern on the head or a human hair wig. Dolls with velvet faces and bodies, usually native dolls, were also made.

Farnell produced a King Edward VIII Coronation Doll that was quickly withdrawn from the market following his abdication. Today, this rare doll commands double or even triple the price of other Farnell dolls of comparable quality. Farnell also marketed a similar King George VI Doll, but it does not enjoy the same status awarded the Edward VIII Doll.

Prices listed are for appropriately costumed dolls with good color and little or no fading. If a doll is stained, torn, badly mended, or faded, expect the value to be less than half the amounts listed.

Child Doll: pressed felt mask; pink cotton body; velvet arms and legs; stitched joints; good wig; painted facial features; appropriately dressed; tagged "Farnell's/Alpha Toys/Made in England."

Novelty and International Doll: velvet face; clothing is part of body construction; stitched joints; slightly-molded, painted features; appropriate articles or accessories; tagged "Farnell/Alpha Toy Co./Made in England."

King George VI pressed felt personality doll by J. K. Farnell & Co. in authentic Royal Air Force uniform. Courtesy of McMaster's Doll Auction

Portrait Doll: pressed felt mask face; stockinette body; jointed neck, shoulder, and hip; painted facial features; appropriately dressed; tagged "H. M. The King (or character name)/ Made in England/J. K. Farnell & Co./Action London."

J. K. Farnell Value Comparisons

Size	Child Doll	Novelty	Portrait	King Edward*
8"		100.00		
12"		150.00		
13"			600.00	1,200.00

J. K. Farnell Value Comparisons

Size	Child Doll	Novelty	Portrait	King Edward*
14"	400.00	250.00		
15"	500.00	300.00		
16"	600.00		700.00	
20"		400.00		
22"		500.00		

* Only King Edward VIII.

French Bébés

There are many French socket-head Bébés found in the marketplace today that were produced by small or unknown manufacturers or not attributed to any specific maker.

Prices listed are for beautifully dressed dolls in good condition. Normal wear, slight damage, or well-made repairs to the body do not greatly affect the price. If the bisque is damaged or repaired, expect the value to be less than half the amounts listed. It is perfectly acceptable to show a missing or repaired finger or joint, or a mended body.

Bébé: fine quality bisque, socket head; wood-and-composition French body; good wig; paperweight or good enamel eyes; pierced ears; closed mouth; beautifully dressed; marks are listed below. The # indicates a size number.

30" French Bébé with beautiful paperweight eyes, marked E 13 D Déposé, holding a closed mouth French Bébé marked only "2/0 Bte. S. G. D. G." Courtesy of David Cobb's Doll Auctions

26" Petit & Dumontier marked "PD 5." Courtesy of David Cobb's Doll Auctions

Bébé Value Comparisons

Size	A L #	A # V	B. F.	B. L. / B # L	C.P.
15"			4,800.00		
20"		7,000.00		6,500.00	
22"	38,000.00		6,200.00		65,000.00

Size	E D Déposé*	F. R.	J	J M	M #
15"	4,800.00	8,000.00	7,500.00		
20"				23,000.00	6,000.00
22"	5,600.00		11,000.00		

Size	P. D.	PAN	R # R
15"	17,000.00	14,000.00	
20"			5,400.00
22"	27,000.00	17,000.00	

*If the word "Déposé" is not included in the marking, see Jumeau. An E. D. Bébé produced by the Jumeau factory while Emile Douillet was director (1892–1899) was marked only E. D.

French Fashion-Type

18" unmarked bisque swivel head Fashion-type and 12" bisque swivel head Fashion-type marked "0," both with kid bodies. Courtesy of David Cobb's Doll Auctions

French Fashion-Type Dolls, known as Poupée de Mode, were manufactured between 1860 and 1930. Whether produced in France, Germany, or Austria, collectors use the term, "French Fashion" or "Fashion Doll" for a lady doll with fashionably formed cloth, kid, and/or wooden body. There is ample evidence that this type of doll was intended to be a play doll. Quoting from an 1869 *Harper's Bazaar*, "The chief French toy is a doll—not a representation of an infant—but a model of a lady attired in the heights of fashion." There are hints, however, that these lovely ladies were also used to model the latest fashions. An advertisement from *Hannah Teats of Boston* states "The mannequin dolls could be seen at her shop for 2 shillings or could be dispatched to a lady's home for 7 shillings, seeing the newest fashions of dress, nightdress and everything pertaining to women's attire, lately arrived on the Captain White from London."

According to the United Federation of Doll Clubs (U.F.D.C.) "The term French Doll is to be applied only to dolls made entirely in France—according to this definition any doll with an unmarked or unrecognizably marked head cannot be called French." To further the controversy is the argument that a fashion doll is not a type of doll, but rather describes a functional use. Nearly any type of doll could be dressed in the latest adult or child's fashions. Although many dealers and collectors apply the term "Fashion" to this type of doll, serious students reject it. Whether mannequin, milliner, lady, fashion, or play doll, the little Poupée de Mode presents a perfect example of the beauty and splendor of Parisian life and fashionable attire.

Reproductions frequently surface. Study the doll carefully. If marked, examine the markings closely. Be wary of bisque with a bit of a shine; it may be a clue that the doll is not authentic. French Fashion-Type Dolls have very good quality paperweight

14" unmarked Bru-style smiling Fashion-type, 12" Francois Gaultier Fashion-type with painted eyes, and 11" Simonne swivel head Fashion-type. Courtesy of David Cobb's Doll Auctions

16" bisque head Fashion-type on Gesland swivel jointed wood body, all original with trunk containing additional dresses, hats, ivory parasol, wigs, books, slate board, boots, and jewelry.

or finely detailed painted eyes, and nicely featured brows. Look for subtle differences in markings. For example, F. G. should not be F+G. Spotting a reproduction French Fashion Doll often requires piecing together several minute clues. Seldom are there obvious signs of a fake. One must learn to recognize the subtle differences that distinguish authentic dolls from reproductions.

Prices listed are for beautifully dressed dolls in good condition. Normal wear, slight damage, or well-made repairs to the body do not greatly affect the price. If the bisque is damaged or repaired, expect the value to be less than half the amounts listed. It is perfectly acceptable to show a missing or repaired finger or joint, or a mended body.

Wooden Body Poupée de Mode: pale, fine bisque swivel head; kid-lined bisque shoulder plate; attached with kid to fully articulated wooden body; wooden peg joints; good wig; paperweight eyes, finely lined in black; painted, long lashes; softly feathered brows; pierced ears; small, closed mouth; appropriately dressed; typically marked with size number only or unmarked.

Kid Body Poupée de Mode: pale, fine bisque swivel head; kid-lined bisque shoulder plate; fine gusseted kid body; bisque or kid arms with stitched fingers; good wig; exquisitely painted or paperweight eyes, finely lined in black; painted lashes; feathered brows; pierced ears; closed mouth; appropriately dressed; typically marked with size number only or unmarked.

Rochard Jeweled Stanhope: bisque shoulder plate; kid body, bisque lower arms; photographic scenes of Paris and religious figures can be seen through the glass jewels of the necklace, known as a Stanhope Bodice, when doll is held to the light; good wig; stationary eyes, finely lined in black; short lashes; thin, feathered brows; closed mouth; appropriately dressed; marked "Ed. Rochards Brevete S.G.D.G. France Patented 1867." ***Note:*** *Only twelve examples have been documented and are known to exist to date.*

French Fashion-Type (Poupée De Mode) Value Comparisons

Size	Wooden Body Poupée de Mode	Kid Body Poupée de Mode	Black Poupée de Mode on Wooden Body	Rochard Jeweled Stanhope Poupée de Mode
12"	5,300.00	2,700.00		
14"	5,500.00	2,900.00		
15"	6,000.00	3,200.00	13,000.00	
16"	6,500.00	3,400.00		
18"	7,000.00	3,600.00		50,000.00
20"	7,500.00	3,800.00		
22"	9,000.00	4,200.00		
24"	9,300.00	4,800.00	26,000.00	
30"	12,000.00	6,200.00		
34"	18,000.00	8,800.00		

Accessories

Accessories to complete the Poupée de Mode's wardrobe include tiny parasols, reticules, kid gloves, toilette sets, opera glasses, embroidered handkerchiefs, corsets, stationery, watches, tea sets, and even a miniature all-bisque French doll of her very own.

Album à photographies pour poupées (photo album for dolls) $450.00–700.00
Boites à chapeaux (hat box) 350.00–600.00

Buvard (writing case) 300.00–700.00
Cartes de bureau (business cards) 300.00–500.00
Cartes de Toilette (social cards) 150.00–300.00
Courroies pour châles et waterproofs (straps to carry rain covers) 100.00–150.00
Cerceau (hoop) 200.00–450.00
Complet costume sur mesure (tailor made men's suit) 1,500.00–4,500.00
Cordes à sauter (jump rope).........................75.00–175.00
Cravaches (horse whip)...........................350.00–600.00
Damier (checker-board) 300.00–500.00
Démâloirs (large hair comb) 150.00–350.00
Des Bas (stockings) 100.00–200.00
Des Bottinés (boots)...............................400.00–1,500.00
Dominos (dominos) 200.00–400.00
Epingles à cheveux (hairpins) 35.00–65.00
Eventails (fans) 200.00–500.00
Formes, tulle pour chapeaux (forms and stands for hat) 200.00–400.00
Gants peau et fil (leather gloves) 125.00–500.00
Hamac (hammock) 100.00–300.00
Jarretières (garters) 50.00–150.00
Jeu de loto (Loto game) 350.00–600.00
Jeu de nain-jaune (Pope Joan card game) 250.00–350.00
Livre de messe (book of Mass)........................350.00–600.00
Lunettes, lorgnons, binocles (eye glasses, longnette, opera glasses)..300.00–800.00
Malles pour Poupée (trunk for doll) 200.00–1,200.00

Malles pour trousseaux (trunk for trousseau) 175.00–600.00
Medaillon (locket) 100.00–400.00
Montres avec chaine (watch and chain)........250.00–800.00
Moufle (mittens)................................150.00–800.00
Nécéssaires de toilette (toiletries) 150.00–800.00
Ombrelles et En-tou-cas (umbrellas or parasols) 400.00–2,500.00
Paniers de voyage (baskets for travel)............150.00–300.00
Pantoufles (slippers) 100.00–500.00
Papeterie (stationery) 75.00–250.00
Peignes à chigons (combs with trim) 100.00–250.00
Peignes, brosses (combs and brushes) 100.00–200.00
Perruque (wig)................................200.00–1,200.00
Pied ou support pour la poupée (vintage doll stand) 75.00–600.00
Resilles (mantilla)................................75.00–150.00
Sacs à ouvrage (work bag) 125.00–250.00
Souliers (shoes) 250.00–3,000.00
Un Chapeau (hat) 400.00–900.00
Un corsage blanc (white waist) 150.00–400.00
Un Costume de Fantaisie (a fancy outfit) 1,200.00–5,000.00
Un jupon (petticoat)..............................125.00–300.00
Un pantalon (drawers) 75.00–200.00
Une chemise (chemise)...............................75.00–200.00

This is not a complete list of all the accessories available. Hopefully, it will serve as a guide to help you get a feel for prices commanded by quality Poupée de Mode accessories. Values are given as ranges. Consider each accessory carefully, and evaluate its individual appeal and condition.

Poupée de Mode's accessories.

Ralph A. Freundlich, Inc.

Ralph A. Freundlich, Inc., was founded in 1929 in New York City. The company is best known for its composition, novelty-type dolls.

Most Freundlich dolls are unmarked; therefore accurate identification is difficult. Collectors researching the company have relied largely on old advertisements and catalogs for positive identification. Listed below are dolls that have been attributed to Freundlich. In time, more dolls will undoubtedly be identified and added to the list. The quality of the dolls produced over the years varies from very good to very poor. Recently, Freundlich character dolls have become extremely popular and prices have risen sharply.

Prices listed are for appropriately costumed dolls in good condition. Slight crazing is acceptable and does not greatly affect the price. If badly crazed, cracked, peeling, or repainted, expect the value to be less than half the amounts listed.

Baby Sandy: all composition; jointed at neck, shoulder, and hip; molded and painted hair; tin sleep eyes; open mouth with two upper teeth, felt tongue; appropriately dressed; typically marked "Baby Sandy."

Baby Sandy: 7 1/2"	$350.00
Baby Sandy: 11"	450.00
Baby Sandy: 16 1/2"	700.00
Baby Sandy: 19 1/2"	1,000.00

Baby with Scale: 9 1/2"; all composition; jointed at neck, shoulder, and hips; molded and painted hair and facial features; wearing diaper; unmarked; in basket on working scale; advertised in June, 1934 *PLAYTHINGS* **$300.00**

Douglas MacArthur: 18"; all composition; right arm bent to salute; molded hat; character face with painted features; dressed in beautifully detailed full military uniform; unmarked; original hang tag "General MacArthur/The Man of the Hour/Manufactured by Freundlich Corp., New York" **$700.00**

Dummy Dan: 15"; composition head and limbs; cloth body; molded and painted facial features very similar to Charlie McCarthy; unmarked; advertised as "Dummy Dan The Ventriloquist Man" in 1938 Sears & Roebuck catalog.....................**$300.00**

Feather Weight Doll: 28"; composition shoulder head and limbs; cloth body with crier box; molded and painted hair; painted eyes; closed mouth; appropriately dressed; unmarked; advertised in February, 1930 *PLAYTHINGS* **$400.00**

Goo Goo Eva: 15"; composition head; pink, cloth body and limbs; square hands with no finger details; mohair wig with stitched side part; round, celluloid, googly-type eyes with floating disks; closed mouth; original flowered percale dress and matching bonnet; unmarked; advertised in 1938 Sears & Roebuck catalog **$200.00**

Little Orphan Annie and Sandy: 11 1/4", 6 3/4"; all composition; Annie is jointed at neck, shoulder, and hip; molded and painted hair; painted, round eyes; closed mouth; appropriately dressed; Sandy is molded and painted with no joints; character dog face with painted large round eyes; unmarked; advertised in 1938 store catalog..**$700.00**

Military Dolls: 18"; Marine, Sailor, Soldier, W.A.A.C., or W.A.V.E.; unmarked; original hang tag "Praise The Lord and Pass The Ammunition".......................................**$400.00**

Princess: 22"; all composition; jointed at neck, shoulder, and hip; long, slim limbs; mohair wig; sleep eyes; open mouth with teeth, felt tongue; appropriately dressed; unmarked; advertised in July, 1937 *Toys and Bicycles*.....................................**$800.00**

Quintuplets and Nurse: 6 3/4", 9"; all composition; jointed at neck, shoulder, and hip; molded and painted hair; painted eyes; appropriately dressed; unmarked; advertised in the November 1935 *PLAYTHINGS* **$900.00**

Red Riding Hood, Grandma, and Wolf: 10"; all composition; jointed at neck, shoulder, and hip; molded and painted hair and facial features; Grandma has a nicely molded character face; white mohair at front of scarf tied to head; painted, side-glancing eyes; closed mouth molded to look as though she has no teeth. Wolf has molded and painted fur; character wolf face; face and body painted brown; all appropriately dressed; unmarked; advertised in 1934 Sears & Roebuck catalog................................**$950.00**

9 3/4" Freundlich Red Riding Hood Set. Courtesy of McMaster's Doll Auction

Fulper Pottery Company

20" Fulper marked "67 Fulper/Made in USA."
Courtesy of McMaster's Doll Auction

19" Fulper marked "2-B Fulper/Made in USA."
Courtesy of McMaster's Doll Auction

The Fulper Pottery Company, founded in 1805 and located in Flemington, New Jersey, is well known for its art pottery and utilitarian wares. Due to import shortages caused by World War I, Fulper produced bisque dolls and doll heads from 1918 to 1921. The quality of Fulper Dolls ranges from very poor to very good. Their historical value is perhaps more significant than their aesthetic value.

Fulper made doll heads using German molds, as well as those from American companies such as Amberg and Horsman. It is not uncommon to find a doll marked "Fulper" alongside a specific company for whom the heads were produced.

Prices listed are for appropriately costumed dolls in good condition. Normal wear, slight damage, or well-made repairs to the body do not greatly affect the price. If the bisque is damaged or repaired, expect the value to be less than half the amounts listed. It is perfectly acceptable to show a missing or repaired finger or joint, or a mended body.

Dolly-Face Socket Head: bisque socket head; jointed composition body; good wig; glass eyes; open mouth with molded teeth; appropriately dressed; typically marked "Fulper Made in USA."

Dolly-Face Shoulder Head: bisque shoulder head; kid body, bisque or composition lower arms; good wig; glass eyes; open mouth with molded teeth; appropriately dressed; typically marked "Fulper Made in USA."

Character Baby: bisque character socket head; composition body; good wig; celluloid, metal, or glass sleep eyes; open mouth with molded teeth; appropriately dressed; typically marked "Fulper Made in USA."

Fulper Bisque Doll Value Comparisons

Size	Dolly-Face Composition Body, Exceptional Quality	Dolly-Face Composition Body, Standard Quality	Dolly-Face Kid Body, Exceptional Quality	Dolly-Face Kid Body, Standard Quality	Character Baby Exceptional Quality*	Character Baby Standard Quality*
13"	700.00	450.00	500.00	350.00		400.00
14"	750.00	475.00	600.00	400.00		
15"	800.00	500.00	650.00	450.00	800.00	600.00
16"	850.00	550.00	700.00	500.00		
18"	900.00	600.00	750.00	550.00	950.00	700.00
20"	925.00	625.00	850.00	650.00	1,100.00	
22"	950.00	650.00	900.00	700.00	1,400.00	1,000.00
24"	1,000.00	700.00	1,000.00	750.00	1,700.00	1,300.00
26"	1,500.00	900.00	1,200.00	850.00		

* Add an additional $700.00 for jointed toddler body.

Luigi Furga & Company

*I*n 1872, the Luigi Furga doll factory was established in Canneto, Sull' Oglio, Mantua Province, Italy. A quote from *Pupeide* tells the company's early history: "In the 1870s Luigi Furga, an Italian nobleman, who owned property in Canneto, decided to begin making dolls with the help of Ceresa, who had acquired the art of making papier-mâché masks in Germany…" The first dolls offered by Furga were made of papier mâché and wax. Later, bisque heads were imported from Germany.

When World War I interrupted the import business, Furga's solution to the doll shortage was to build his own porcelain factory. In 1929, the trade magazine *Plaything* reported that "Furga bisque head dolls rivaled the German's." Giving evidence to the problems facing European manufacturing the article goes on to say, "when one is able to find them on the market."

Furga also produced a limited number of pressed-felt dolls, undoubtedly in competition with Lenci.

In the span of over 125 years, Furga has examined, experimented, and applied all possible techniques known to the doll industry. They made all types of composition, hard plastic, and vinyl dolls. The early bisque and felt dolls were exported only to England, Brazil, and other South American countries; of course later dolls were imported to the United States as well.

It is the lovely vinyl and hard plastic dolls that are the best known to today's collector. In order to meet the tremendous demand, Furga currently produces over 25,000 dolls a day.

11" Furga bisque marked "Furga, Canneto, J. Oglio B28." Courtesy of McMaster's Doll Auction

Vinyl and Hard Plastic

Prices listed are for original dolls in near-mint condition. If damaged, redressed, or undressed, expect the value to be one half to one fourth the price listed.

Babies: all vinyl, or vinyl head and limbs; cloth body; jointed at shoulder and hip; rooted hair; sleep eyes; open or closed mouth; original costume; typically marked "Furga" or "Furga/Italy."

Child/Teen: all vinyl or vinyl head and limbs; cloth body; jointed at neck, shoulder, and hip; rooted hair; closed mouth; original costume; typically marked "Furga" or "Furga/Italy."

Lady: all hard plastic or combination hard plastic and vinyl; rooted hair or good wig; sleep eyes; heavy make-up; open or open/closed mouth; original costume; typically marked "Furga" or "Made in Italy/Furga."

Bisque

Prices listed are for appropriately costumed dolls in good condition. Normal wear, slight damage, or well-made repairs to the body do not greatly affect the price. If the bisque is damaged or repaired, expect the value to be less than half the amounts listed. It is perfectly acceptable to show a missing or repaired finger or a mended body.

Dolly-Face: Bisque socket head; jointed composition body; good wig; sleep eyes; open mouth with teeth; appropriately dressed; typically marked with a stick figure within a box and "Furga Italy."

Furga Value Comparison				
Size	Vinyl Baby	Vinyl Child or Teen	Hard Plastic Lady	Bisque Dolly-Face
7"	65.00			
13"	150.00	200.00		
16"	175.00	225.00	250.00	
19"		250.00	300.00	
22"				900.00
25"			325.00	1,000.00

Francois Gaultier

Francois Gaultier, along with Jumeau, Bru, and Steiner, earned a reputation as a manufacturer of elegantly modelled and exquisitely crafted bisque French dolls. As a result, Gaultier produced doll heads for several well-known doll companies including Gresland, Jullien, Rabery & Delphieu, Simonne, and Thiller. The 1860 Francois Gaultier factory was located in St. Maurice and Charenton in the province of Seine, on the outskirts of Paris, France. Francois Gaultier continued to produce dolls up until at least 1916, the later years as a part of S.F.B.J. (Societe Francaise de Fabrication de Bébé & Jouets).

A Francois Gaultier Bébé is more difficult to find than a Poupee de Modes. The elusive Bébés are characterized by their subtle pale complexions; delicately shadowed eyelids; large, wide-set, lustrous, paperweight eyes, finely lined in black; plump cheeks; and fully outlined, slightly parted lips; features highly valued by collectors.

Reproductions can be spotted with little difficulty. Carefully check the markings. Most copies are marked with the artist's name and possibly a date.

Be aware of Fashion-Type Dolls marked F + G, which are reproductions and intentional frauds. Check seams of the kid body. Reproductions will be snowy white at the seams. Lightly run your finger over the doll's cheek. Avoid very smooth, perfectly clean bisque, for although Gaultiers have fine quality bisque, it is not satiny and silk-like as the porcelain used in reproductions.

Prices listed are for beautifully dressed dolls in good condition. Normal wear, slight damage, or well-made repairs to the body do not greatly affect the price. If the bisque is damaged or

24" Later scroll mark, closed mouth Gaultier Bébé #10. Courtesy of David Cobb's Doll Auctions

11-1/2" Early block mark Francois Gaultier Petite Bébé #2. Courtesy of David Cobb's Doll Auctions

26" scroll mark, open mouth Gaultier Bébé # 9.

repaired, expect the value to be less than half the amounts listed. It is perfectly acceptable to show a missing or repaired finger or joint, or a mended body.

French Fashion Poupee de Mode: bisque swivel head; kid-lined bisque shoulder plate; kid, lady body; bisque lower arms; good wig; paperweight or beautifully painted eyes, finely lined in black; long lashes; feathered brows; pierced ears; closed mouth; appropriately dressed; marked "F.G."

Block Letter Bébé: bisque socket head; jointed composition, French, straight-wrist body, or kid-lined shoulder plate kid body; good wig; paperweight eyes, finely lined in black; delicately shadowed eye lids; pierced ears; slightly parted closed mouth; appropriately dressed; marked with early block letters "F.G."

Scroll Mark Bébé: bisque socket head; composition, jointed French body; good wig; paperweight eyes, finely lined in black; long lashes; feathered brows; pierced ears; closed mouth; appropriately dressed; marked "F.G." within a scroll.

Open Mouth Bébé: bisque socket head; composition jointed French body; good wig; paperweight eyes; long lashes; feathered brows; pierced ears; open mouth with teeth; appropriately dressed; marked "F.G." within scroll.

Gaultier Value Comparisons

Size	Fashion Type Poupée de Mode, Glass Eyes*	Fashion Type Poupée de Mode, Painted Eyes	Block Letter Bébé Composition Body	Block Letter Bébé, Kid Body	Scroll Mark, Closed Mouth, Exceptional	Scroll Mark, Closed Mouth, Standard	Open Mouth Bébé
8"	1,400.00	1,000.00				1,500.00	
10 1/2"	2,000.00	1,300.00					
11 1/2"	2,300.00	1,500.00	4,700.00	5,600.00	3,800.00	2,300.00	
13 1/2"	2,500.00	1,800.00	4,900.00	6,000.00	4,000.00	2,700.00	1,800.00
15"	2,700.00	2,000.00	5,000.00	6,400.00	4,200.00	3,000.00	2,000.00
17"	2,900.00	2,400.00	5,200.00	6,700.00	4,600.00	3,400.00	
19"	3,300.00		5,400.00				2,300.00
20"	3,500.00		5,700.00	7,200.00	4,900.00	3,700.00	2,400.00
21"			5,800.00		5,000.00		3,000.00
23"	3,800.00		6,200.00	7,800.00		4,000.00	
25"	4,400.00		6,600.00		5,800.00	4,300.00	3,300.00
27"			7,800.00		6,000.00	4,500.00	3,500.00
29"					6,200.00	4,700.00	3,600.00
31"	7,000.00		8,400.00		6,700.00	5,000.00	3,800.00
35"	8,500.00		9,500.00		7,000.00	5,200.00	4,200.00

*Add an additional $1,200.00 for fully articulated wooden body.

German Bisque Dolls

Various small or unknown German doll manufacturers, operating after 1880, produced bisque dolls. The questions and mysteries concerning a doll can be endless. Who made it? What does the mark mean? Where does it come from? How old is it? What is it worth? In an industry that is really only a little over a hundred years old, you would think that we could easily find answers to these questions. Unfortunately, this is not always the case. Obstacles to identification include an ocean to limit our research; two world wars responsible for the destruction of many records; a country that had been divided for decades, with vital information often on the wrong side of a wall; language barriers; and the fact that hundreds of dolls were produced with little or no documentation ever recorded. These all help to explain why it is virtually impossible to answer all the questions or solve all the mysteries. We are forever grateful to the pioneers in doll research: the Cielsliks, Colemans, Smith, Foulkes, St. George, Holbrook, Theriault, Leuzzi, King, Johnson, Fraser, Miller, and countless others, who have spent years pursuing the curriculum of dolls.

In building a doll collection, one often encounters a bisque doll with no markings or with an unidentified mark. Don't be discouraged simply because you cannot put a label on a particu-

A pair of 25" German Dolly-Face dolls marked only "Germany 8." Courtesy of David Cobb's Doll Auctions

20" open mouth German "495" lady with molded bosom and slim waist. Courtesy of David Cobb's Doll Auctions

13" closed mouth German bisque marked only with a size number, 4-1/2", and 14" unmarked solid dome German bisque. Courtesy of David Cobb's Doll Auctions

lar doll. The following charts will help you place a value on unidentified or unlisted German bisque dolls. The final analysis is yours. Evaluate the quality, workmanship, and condition.

Prices listed are for appropriately costumed dolls in good condition. Normal wear, slight damage, or well-made repairs to the body do not greatly affect the price. If the bisque is damaged or repaired, expect the value to be less than half the amounts listed. It is perfectly acceptable to show a missing or repaired finger or joint, or a mended body.

Also see Doll House Dolls.

Dolly-Face: bisque socket or shoulder head; jointed composition or kid body; good wig; glass eyes; open mouth; appropriately dressed; typically marked "G. B.," "L. H. K.," "GS," "BJ," "Girlie," "K," "CK701," "PR," "1907," "ROMA," "2210," "TR," and surely others.

Closed Mouth: bisque socket or shoulder head; jointed composition or kid body; good wig; glass eyes; finely painted lashes; feathered brows; pierced or unpierced ears; closed mouth may have white space between lips; delicate coloring; appropriately dressed; typically marked "R 806," "50," "132," "51," "136," "503," "506," "WD," "TR," "104," "HL" "510," "ELISA," "100," "121," "300," "101," "G.L.," "B," "N.," "86," "120," "126," "179," "183," "6," and surely others.

Character Baby: bisque socket or shoulder head; composition bent-limb baby or cloth body; molded and painted hair or good wig; glass eyes; appropriately dressed; typically marked "Made in Germany, 44611," "HVB," "PM," "800," "SAH," "TH," "EB," "Sweet Baby," and surely others.

13" closed mouth German bisque marked "5" socket head on marked "5" shoulder plate with pierced ears and kid body. Courtesy of David Cobb's Doll Auctions

German Bisque Value Comparisons

Size	Dolly Face Kid Body, Standard Quality	Dolly Face Kid Body, Very Good Quality	Dolly Face Composition Body, Standard Quality	Dolly Face Composition Body, Very Good Quality	Closed Mouth, Kid Body	Closed Mouth, Composition Body	Character Baby*	Character Child*
10"							500.00	1,800.00
12"	450.00	600.00	500.00	800.00	1,400.00	2,800.00	600.00	
14"	500.00	700.00	550.00	850.00	1,800.00	3,200.00	700.00	
16"	600.00	800.00	600.00	900.00	2,100.00		750.00	2,800.00
18"	650.00	850.00	650.00	950.00	2,500.00	3,600.00	800.00	
20"	700.00	900.00	700.00	1,000.00		3,900.00	1,000.00	4,500.00
22"	750.00	1,000.00	800.00	1,100.00	3,000.00	4,300.00		5,000.00
24"	800.00	1,100.00	900.00	1,200.00	3,400.00	4,900.00	1,500.00	5,700.00
26"	900.00	1,200.00	1,000.00	1,400.00		5,200.00		
28"	1,100.00	1,400.00	1,200.00	1,700.00				
30"	1,300.00	1,600.00	1,400.00	1,900.00				
34"	1,400.00	1,800.00	1,500.00	2,200.00				
36"				2,800.00				

* Add an additional $700.00 for jointed toddler body.

German Bisque Value Comparisons

Size	Molded Bonnet Painted Eye	Molded Bonnet Glass Eye
8"	275.00	
10"	350.00	750.00
12"	450.00	800.00
14"	500.00	900.00
16"	600.00	1,000.00
18"		1,200.00

Character Child: bisque socket head; jointed composition body; molded and painted hair or good wig; glass or painted eyes, may have line above lid to indicate lid; closed mouth; appropriately dressed; typically marked "HJ 1," "GK 223," "216," "230," 820," "660," "500," "WSK," "130," and surely others.

Molded Bonnet: bisque shoulder head; cloth body; painted or glass eyes; closed mouth; appropriately dressed; typically unmarked or marked with size number only.

Other German Bisque Dolls

De Fuisseaux was a Belgian doll artist who produced dolls with outstanding modelling and distinctively freckled bisque for a few years just prior to World War I. The wonderfully expressive modelling has an uncanny resemblance to the Van Rosen style, another Belgian doll designer.

De Fuisseaux: freckled bisque socket or shoulder head with extended plate; composition, cloth, or kid body; bisque hands or lower limbs; stunning, cameo-shaped character face; elongated neck; artfully sculptured nose and throat hollow; good wig; painted, blue or gray eyes; defined eyelids; closed, solemn mouth; appropriately dressed; typically marked "DF/B/F," "F," or "B" along with a size number.

15"	**$2,000.00**
18"	2,400.00
20"	2,600.00

The Sonneberg movement was responsible for many beautiful simulations of popular French dolls. The modelling and decoration often mirrors the French dolls to perfection. Along with the Bébés that were duplicated, a very convincing Bébé Teteur was produced.

Nursing Baby: (Sonneberg's rendition of Bru's Bébé Teteur); 19"; bisque socket head; early 8-ball jointed wood and composition body; good wig; beautiful glass eyes, finely lined in black; feathered brows; open 'O' mouth with nursing mechanism extending to the back of the head; appropriately dressed; marked "86" **$4,900.00**

Fritz Bierschenk acquired the established doll firm of E. Escher in 1906 and continued to produce dolls until filing for bankruptcy shortly after an explosion destroyed his factory during the late 1920s.

F. Bierschenk Character: 20"; slender-faced bisque socket head; five-piece composition body; good wig; intaglio eyes; detailed, eye-corner modelling; open/closed mouth with tiny upper beaded teeth; appropriately dressed; marked "F B 616" **$18,000.00**

16" German bisque character marked "111/5," often attributed to Kämmer & Reinhardt. Courtesy of David Cobb's Doll Auctions

E. Gesland

31" Bébé on marked Gesland stockinette body with composition shoulder plate, metal frame padded with wound cotton, wooden lower arms, composition hands and lower legs. Courtesy of McMaster's Doll Auction

12" Fashion type on a stamped Gesland body.

facilitate movement. The framework was wrapped with kapok or cotton to give it a natural shape, and then covered with stockinette or fine lambskin. Hands and feet were either bisque or painted wood. The dolls could be posed in a variety of lifelike positions. Most were marked with the Gesland stamp or label.

Prices listed are for appropriately costumed dolls with good color and little or no fading. If a doll is stained, torn, badly mended, or faded, expect the value to be less than half the amounts listed.

Poupee de Mode: bisque swivel head; kid-lined bisque shoulder plate; Gesland covered metal frame body; bisque or wooden hands and feet; good wig; paperweight eyes, finely lined in black; long lashes; feathered brows; pierced ears; closed mouth; appropriately dressed; typically marked "F.G.," "R.D.," and stamped "E. Gesland Bte F.G.," "E. Gesland Bte S.G.D.G./Paris" on body.

Bébé: bisque socket head; jointed French composition or Gesland covered metal frame body; bisque or wooden hands and feet; good wig; paperweight eyes; long lashes; feathered brows; pierced ears; closed mouth; appropriately dressed; typically marked "R. # D.," "F. G.," "A. Gesland Fave De Babes/& Tetes incassables, Bte S.G.D.G./Reparations en tous genres/5 & 5 Rue Beranger/En Boutique/Paris."

E. Gesland produced, exported, distributed, and repaired bisque dolls from about 1860 until 1928. Gesland advertised that from his Paris factory he could "repair in ten minutes Bébés and dolls of all makes and replace broken heads." Gesland purchased bisque heads from F. Gaultier, Verlingue, Rabery & Delphieu, and possibly others.

Early Gesland dolls had outstanding body features. The body and limb frame was steel covered with tin. Joints were riveted to

Size	Early Beautiful Poupée de Mode Gesland Body*	Later, Familar Poupée de Mode Gesland Body	Bébé	Exceptionally Beautiful Face
10"			3,800.00	
13"	4,800.00	3,600.00	3,600.00	
14"	5,200.00	3,900.00	3,700.00	6,200.00
15"	5,600.00	4,200.00	3,800.00	6,900.00
17"	6,000.00	4,400.00	4,000.00	
19"	6,400.00	4,700.00	4,300.00	
21"	7,000.00	4,900.00	4,500.00	7,500.00
23"	7,400.00	5,200.00	5,000.00	
25"	7,800.00	5,700.00	5,200.00	8,500.00
27"	7,200.00	6,200.00	5,700.00	
29"			6,200.00	
31"	8,500.00	7,400.00	6,800.00	

E. Gesland Value Comparison

* Double the amount for man with molded derby and masculine features.

Giebeler-Falk Doll Company

A New York City based company, manufacturing dolls from 1918 until 1921, Giebeler-Falk may be a rather unfamiliar name to many collectors (despite a 1919 advertisement claiming they produced 1,000 dolls a week). One must wonder, with the very few that emerge onto the collector's market, whatever happened to the others?

Giebeler-Falk dolls were made with aluminum heads and well-made wooden bodies, frequently with unusual rubber joints. The names "Gie-Fa" and "Primadonna" were registered in 1918 as trademarks.

The Primadonna Phonograph Doll has gained a respected position within the doll collecting community. Not only does she have a very appealing face, but also the mechanism is really quite fascinating. The clockwork is located in the torso. A crank coming out the neck rotates a turntable placed within the head. Access to the turntable (through top of the hinged-head) facilitates changing records, played by a needle. The total configuration gives the impression that the "voice" comes out the mouth.

Prices listed are for appropriately dressed dolls in good condition. Normal wear or slight crazing is to be expected and does not greatly affect the price. If the head is peeling, dented, chipped, or repainted, or if the phonograph is damaged and inoperable, expect the value to be less than one half to one fourth the amounts listed.

Gie-Fa: aluminum socket head; wooden body; may have aluminum hands and feet; good wig; tin sleep eyes; nicely feathered brows; open/closed mouth; appropriately dressed; typically marked "25G (within a star) U.S. Pat" or "Gie-Fa/Trademark/New York/Aluminum Heads & Hands/Guaranteed Unbreakable."

Primadonna Phonograph Doll: aluminum socket head; wooden body; may have rubber joints and aluminum hands and feet; working phonograph with records; good wig; tin sleep eyes; nicely feathered brows; open/closed mouth; appropriately dressed; typically marked "25 (star around G) U.S. Pat."

26" fully marked Giebeler-Falk child doll with metal head, hands, and feet.
Courtesy of Barbara Williams

Giebeler-Falk Aluminum Doll Value Comparison		
Size	Gie-Fa	Primadonna Phonograph
15"	450.00	
20"	500.00	
25"	600.00	
30"		1,700.00

Godey Lady Dolls

S everal dolls have enjoyed the title "Godey Doll"; in fact not long ago all China Head Dolls were referred to as "Godey Dolls." The Godey Lady Dolls described and listed here are the charming dolls made by Ruth Gibbs and the Charlotte Eldridge originals.

The term Godey Lady Doll comes from the popular *Godey's Lady's Book*—the "Victorian Bible of the Parlor"—for which generations of American women depended upon for guidance in how to be "real ladies." "The aim of a real lady," Godey's told them, "is always to be natural and unaffected and to wear her tal-

ents, her accomplishments, and her learning as well as her newest and finest dresses, as if she did not know she had them about her."

Prices listed are for dolls in near-mint, original condition. If damaged, redressed, or undressed, expect the value to be less than one half to one fourth the amounts listed.

Charlotte Eldridge's Godey Lady Dolls: 1940s; very rare individually crafted; papier-mâché heads, beautifully hand painted facial features; embroidery floss wigs, caught with small stitches and tightly wound curls; cloth covered wire armature

Original Charlotte Eldridge Godey doll "Skating Costume" from 1859 Godey's Magazine. Courtesy of Alice Eldridge Taylor

Ruth Gibbs "Godey's Little Lady Dolls" shown with a Bliss dollhouse and a vintage Steiff bear. Courtesy of David Cobb's Doll Auctions

body; sculptured ceramic hands; elaborate, authentically detailed costume; typically unmarked; clothing tag signed "Frances Jennings" (Ms. Eldridge's pen name). ***Note:** Ms. Eldridge's mother, Susan Blakley, helped with the costuming, which faithfully followed sketches from* Godey Lady's Book.

Ruth Gibbs' Godey's Little Lady Dolls: 1940s; pink or white china shoulder head; cloth body; rather crude china limbs; lightly molded and painted hair or skin wig; painted facial features with very little detail; original, simple costume; typically marked "R.G."; clothing tag "Godey's Little Lady Dolls."

Godey's Little Lady Dolls Value Comparisons

Size	Eldrige's Godey's	Eldrige's Diorama 2 Dolls	Eldrige's Diorama 4 Dolls	Ruth Gibbs Godey's	Ruth Gibbs with Skin Wig	Ruth Gibbs 5 Little Women Set	Ruth Gibbs Fairy Tale Doll
7"				145.00			
10"	2,100.00	3,800.00	5,400.00	200.00	375.00	1,000.00	700.00
12"				300.00			

William Goebel

❧❦❧

*I*n 1876, Franz D. Goebel and his son William built a porcelain factory in Oesleau, Bavaria. William Goebel became sole owner in 1893, changing the name to William Goebel.

Early Goebel bisque objects were marked with a triangle and a quarter moon. After 1900, a crown above an intertwined "W & G" was introduced. Mold numbers registered include 30, 34, 46, 54, 60, 73, 77A, 77B, 80, 91, 92, 102, 106, 107, 110, 111, 114, 120, 121, 123, 124, 125, 126, 317, 319, 320, 321, 322, 330, 340, 350, 501, and 521.

Prices listed are for appropriately costumed dolls in good condition. Normal wear, slight damage, or well-made repairs to the body do not greatly affect the price. If the bisque is damaged or repaired, expect the value to be less than half the amounts listed. It is perfectly acceptable to show a missing or repaired finger or joint, or a mended body.

Dolly Face: bisque shoulder or socket head; jointed composition or kid body with bisque arms; good wig; glass eyes; feathered brows; open mouth; appropriately dressed; typically marked with Goebel trademark and "36," "350," "521" "120," "89," "330," "80," and possibly others.

Character Baby: bisque character baby socket head; composition bent-limb baby body; good mohair wig; glass eyes; open mouth; molded teeth; appropriately dressed; typically marked with trademark, "B/Germany," "120," "123," or "124."

Cabinet Doll: bisque character socket head; five-piece papier-mâché body; molded and painted hair; may have molded ornamentation; painted eyes; closed or open/closed mouth; appropriately dressed; typically marked with trademark "73," "84," or "34." **Note:** the letters "S," "B," "A," "K," "M," "C," "H," "SA," "G," or "T," may appear alone or with a mold number. For example "K" is the abbreviation for "Knabe" (German for boy), and "M" for "Madchen" (German for girl).

William Goebel Value Comparisons

Size	Dolly-Face Kid Body	Dolly-Face Composition Body	Character Baby, Bent-Limb Baby Body*	Cabinet Dolls
7"				400.00
12"	500.00			
14"	600.00	700.00	650.00	
16"	700.00	750.00	750.00	
18"	750.00	800.00	850.00	
20"	800.00	900.00	1,000.00	
22"		950.00	1,200.00	
24"		1,000.00	1,500.00	
26"		1,200.00		

* Add an additional $700.00 for jointed toddler body.

22" William Goebel toddler marked WG, B5/Germany. Courtesy of McMaster's Doll Auction

Googly-Eyed Dolls

11" Armand Marseille #323 Googly. Courtesy of David Cobb's Doll Auctions

Most early twentieth century doll manufacturers produced Googly-Eyed Dolls between 1912 and 1938. The term "Googly-Eyed" is probably from the German "Guck Augen," meaning eyes ogling to one side.

The impish little characters are so endearing that few collectors can resist their charm. The small comedians demonstrate their youthful exuberance with pugged noses, rounded faces, and wide alert eyes.

Reproductions abound in the Googly-Eyed Doll market. Be thorough and meticulous in examining the markings; often a name or date is hidden under the wig or below the neck socket. Keep in mind the time period (1912-1938) in which Googly-Eyed Dolls were manufactured. The quality of the bisque made at that time ranged from mediocre to good quality. Very clean, silky-smooth bisque may suggest a reproduction.

Prices listed are for appropriately costumed dolls in good condition. Normal wear, slight damage, or well-made repairs to the body do not greatly affect the price. If the bisque is damaged or repaired, expect the value to be less than half the amounts listed. It is perfectly acceptable to show a missing or repaired finger or joint, or a mended body.

Googly-Eyes: bisque socket head; composition or papier-mâché body; molded and painted hair or good wig; round, googly, painted or glass eyes; smiling watermelon mouth; appropriately dressed; typically marked with mold number and/or manufacturer.

See All Bisque.

Googly-Eyed Value Comparisons

Armand Marseille

Size	200 G.E.	200 P.E.	210 P.E.	240 P.E.	240 G.E.	241 G.E.	252 P.E.	253 G.E.	254 P.E.	257 G.E.	310 G.F.	324/322 P.E.	323 G.E.	325 G.E.
7"	2,000.00			1,900.00	2,000.00		1,300.00	1,500.00		1,400.00	1,800.00	900.00	1,700.00	1,100.00
10"				3,700.00		3,400.00	1,600.00	2,900.00	1,200.00					
12"	2,900.00	2,500.00	3,200.00		4,400.00	5,200.00	2,200.00	3,800.00		2,200.00	3,200.00	1,400.00	3,000.00	1,600.00

Bahr Proschild	
Size	686 G.E.
7"	3,500.00
12"	4,900.00

Demalcol G.E.	
Size	Demalcol G.E.
10"	
14"	1,900.00

Butler	
Size	179 G.E.
9"	1,700.00

Gobel 82/83/84/85/86/87/88			
Size	9230 PE.	Molded Gap P.E.	G.E.
10"	2,100.00 (pair)	1,400.00	2,600.00

10-1/2" Armand Marseille #240 Googly, 11" Kestner #221 Googly, and 10-1/2" Hertel Schwab #165 Googly. Courtesy of David Cobb's Doll Auctions

Max Handwerk					
Size	Elite Bellhop G.E.	Elite 1 Helmet G.E.	Elite 2 Face G.E.	Elite Molded Hat G.E.	Elite Uncle Sam G.E.
12"	3,500.00	3,100.00	3,600.00	3,400.00	3,200.00
16"	4,900.00		5,300.00	4,900.00	5,100.00

Hertel, Schwab & Co.								
Size	163 G.E.	165 G.E.	172 Toddler G.E.	173 Baby G.E.	175 Winking One G.E.	178 Open Mouth G.E.	222 P.E.	222 G.E.
10"				4,100.00			2,100.00	2,700.00
12"	4,800.00	5,300.00						
14"				6,500.00			3,000.00	3,400.00
15"	7,500.00		7,900.00		5,400.00	6,500.00		
16"		6,800.00	12,000.00	7,900.00				
20"		7,900.00						

Size	Elisabeth G.E.	Eisenmann Einco 8723 G.E.	8589 P.E.	8606/8729 P.E.	8995 P.E.	9056/9081 P.E.	9085 P.E.	9141 P.E.	9513/9572/9573 G.E.	9578 Tiss Me G.E.	9594 G.E.	10542 G.E.
Gerbruder Heubach												
9"	3,500.00	6,000.00	1,300.00	1,200.00	3,400.00	1,600.00	1,500.00	1,100.00	2,800.00	1,900.00	1,100.00	3,500.00
15"		8,500.00							5,000.00	2,000.00		
20"		18,000.00										

Ernest Heubach, Koppelsdorf						
Size	322 G.E.	219/260/261/262/263/264 P.E.	255/274/289 P.E.	318 P.E.	319 Tearful P.E.	310 G.E.
7"	2,300.00	900.00	1,100.00	1,000.00	1,400.00	3,700.00

Kämmer & Reinhardt	
Size	S & H / K ★ R 131 G.E.
9"	6,500.00
16"	13,000.00

Kestner		
Size	111/122/208/G.E.	221 G.E.
14"	3,000.00	9,600.00
16"		15,000.00

P.M. Porzellanfabrick Mengersgeruth		
Size	255 G.E.	950 G.E.
7"	2,700.00	
12"		5,200.00

Schieler (August)	
Size	G.E.
10"	2,900.00
15"	3,200.00

Kley & Hahn	
Size	180 G.E.
9"	2,400.00
16"	4,000.00

Rechnagel	
Size	R 50A/R 47 A/R 43 A P.E.
7"	1,400.00

S.F.B.J.	
Size	245 G.E.
11"	6,000.00
17"	12,000.00

Herm Steiner		
Size	133 G.E.	223/242/247 Disc. Pupils
7"	900.00	
10"		1,500.00
14"		1,800.00
17"		2,000.00
20"		2,200.00

Strobel & Wilkin	
Size	S&W 250/405 G.E.
7"	2,100.00

Morimura Brothers	
Size	Copy of Hertel, Schwab & Co.'s 173 G.E.
14"	3,700.00

Composition Face				
Size	Composition Hug-Me (Cloth Body) G.E.	Composition 94-7/Am 323	LaPrialyline Hansi/Gretel P.E.	Black Composition Unmarked, Disc Pupils	DRGM 954647 Disk Pupils
8 1/2-10			3,400.00		
10"	900.00				
12"	1,200.00	1,200.00	2,900.00	1,700.00	
14"					3,200.00

G.E.—Glass Eyes
P.E.—Painted Eyes
Disc Pupils—Insert Movable Disc Pupils Under Glass

12" Samstag Hilder "Hug Me Kiddy" composition mask face Googly and 14" Kämmer & Reinhardt #131 Googly. Courtesy of David Cobb's Doll Auctions

Ludwig Greiner

Records show Ludwig Greiner was listed as a toy maker in Philadelphia, Pennsylvania, as early as 1840. In 1858, Greiner received the first known United States patent for a papier-mâché doll's head. The patent reads: "1 pound of pulped white paper, 1 pound of dry Spanish Whiting, 1 pound of rye flower [sic] and 1 ounce of glue reinforced with linen (strips of linen or silk lined the inside of the head adding strength), painted with oiled paint so that children may not pick off the paint." The heads were then given a layer of varnish, which has served to protect the labels. A doll with the '58 patent date is known as "Early Greiner," whereas an 1872 extension date is known as a "Later Greiner."

Greiner papier-mâché heads are easily identified. The molded, wavy hair gives the appearance of a high forehead and rather broad face. A snub nose and tight mouth suggest a sober expression.

Prices listed are for appropriately costumed dolls in good condition. Slight crazing is acceptable and does not greatly affect the price. If badly crazed, cracked, peeling, or repainted, expect the value to be less than half the amounts listed.

Early Greiner: papier-mâché shoulder head; cloth body and legs; kid arms; stitched fingers; molded and painted hair, parted in center and drawn back to expose ears; painted black eyes; closed mouth; appropriately dressed; marked with label on back of shoulder plate "Greiner Improved Patent Heads/Pat. March 30th '58."

Later Greiner: papier-mâché shoulder head; cloth body and legs; kid arms; stitched fingers; molded and painted hair with center part; painted eyes; closed mouth; appropriately dressed; marked with label on back of shoulder plate "Greiners Patent Doll Heads, No. 7 Pat. Mar. 30 '58, Ext. '72."

Pre-Greiner: papier-mâché shoulder head; cloth body; leather, wood, or cloth limbs; molded and painted hair with center part; black, pupil-less, glass eyes; closed mouth; appropriately dressed; typically unmarked.

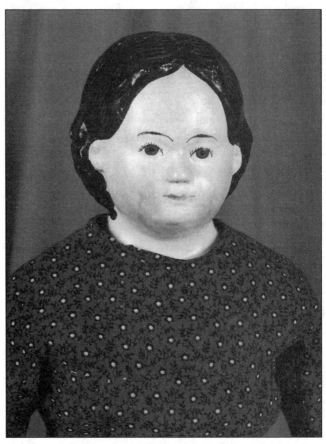

23" Early Greiner marked "Greiner's Improved Patent Heads, Pat. March 30th '58." Courtesy of McMaster's Doll Auction

Greiner Value Comparison

Size	Early Greiner '58	Later Greiner '72	Labeled Greiner Glass Eye	Later Greiner on Marked Jacob Lachmann Body	Pre-Greiner Glass Eye
15"	1,100.00	550.00			1,100.00
17"	1,200.00	600.00			1,300.00
19"	1,300.00	650.00	2,500.00		1,500.00
21"	1,400.00	700.00	2,900.00	1,000.00	1,700.00
23"	1,600.00	800.00			2,100.00
25"	1,900.00	900.00			2,300.00
27"	2,000.00	1,000.00	3,800.00	1,400.00	
29"	2,000.00	1,100.00			2,500.00
31"	2,200.00	1,200.00			2,600.00
33"	2,400.00	1,400.00			2,900.00
35"	2,600.00	1,500.00			
37"	2,900.00	1,700.00			3,400.00
39"	3,400.00	1,900.00			

H Mold Dolls

The H mold, a particular doll made from the late 1870s to the early 1880s, is attributed to A. Halopeau of Paris. A. Halopeau was listed as a doll maker in the Paris annual register from 1881 until 1889. Of course, this is only an assumed manufacturer and production date for this elusive mystery doll. It was once believed the Bébé was produced to celebrate the opening of a major department store in Paris, but that theory has been abandoned.

Certain facts are obvious and accepted by all doll enthusiasts. H mold dolls are of exceptional quality. The creamy, pale bisque, magnificent paperweight eyes, and delicately applied artistry resulted in one of the most exquisite dolls ever created.

There are many reproduction H mold dolls. Most were made to satisfy collectors longing for the 'look,' but unable to purchase an authentic antique Bébé. The legitimate copy will be well marked, usually with the doll makers' name or initials and possibly a date. There are also reproduction dolls that were made to deliberately deceive the consumer. A total and complete examination should identify an impostor. Carefully check the marking. An authentic Bébé will be marked only with a size number, a dot, and the letter "H." For example, a 21-inch Bébé would be marked 3●H. The original pate was cork. Only the finest quality deep-crystal paperweight eyes were used. The French bodies, usually stamped "Jumeau," were jointed wood and composition with straight wrists. The pressed, not poured, bisque was sumptuous and creamy, but not satiny and silk-like. The most helpful clue may be in the doll's height. Reproductions tend to be shorter than the incised number would indicate, for example #0 = 16 1/2", #2 = 19", #3 = 21", and #4 = 24". Any deviation of more than one-inch should be considered suspicious.

Prices listed are for beautifully dressed dolls in good condition. Normal wear, slight damage, or well-made repairs to the body do not greatly affect the price. If the bisque is damaged or repaired, expect the value to be less. The H mold Bébé is so rare and desirable that serious collectors will forgive fine hairlines or professional repairs that do not jeopardize the integrity of the doll. The price should reflect the degree and extent of damage. It is perfectly acceptable to show a missing or repaired finger or a mended body.

H Mold Bébé: beautiful, pale pressed bisque socket head; jointed wood and composition French body with straight wrists; good human or fine mohair wig; cork pate; paperweight eyes, finely lined in black; long lashes; nicely feathered brows; pierced ears; closed mouth with white space between two-toned lips; appropriately dressed; marked (size number) (dot) "H."

Rare H mold. Photo by Richard Withington. Courtesy of Ellen Schroy

| H Mold Bébé Value Comparison ||
Size	Bébé
16 1/2"	69,000.00
19"	73,000.00
21"	78,000.00
24"	82,000.00

Hamburger & Company

Hamburger & Company was founded in New York City in 1889 as an importer of dolls and toys. The company later opened offices in Berlin and Nuremberg, Germany. Although dolls made for and imported by Hamburger & Company are quite well known to collectors, they are usually attributed to their respective manufacturers.

Prices listed are for appropriately costumed dolls in good condition. Normal wear, slight damage, or well-made repairs to the body do not greatly affect the price. If the bisque is damaged or repaired, expect the value to be less than half the amounts listed. It is perfectly acceptable to show a missing or repaired finger or joint, or a mended body.

Dolly Dimple: character face with molded dimples by Gebrüder Heubach; bisque shoulder or socket head; jointed composition or kid body; good wig; glass eyes; open mouth with teeth; appropriately dressed; typically marked "Dolly Dimple," "5777," and the Heubach trademark.

Santa: unique dolly-face by Simon & Halbig; bisque socket head; jointed composition body; good wig; glass eyes; open mouth with teeth; appropriately dressed; typically marked "S & H Germany," "1248," or "1249."

Dolly-Face: bisque socket head; jointed composition body; good wig, glass eyes; open mouth with teeth; appropriately dressed; typically marked "H & Co.," "Viola," or "Marguerite."

Hamburger & Co. Value Comparisons

Size	Dolly Dimple, Kid Body	Dolly Dimple, Composition Body	Santa*	Dolly-Face
14"			1,300.00	600.00
15"	1,200.00			
16"		3,300.00	1,500.00	650.00
17"	1,600.00			
18"		3,500.00	1,600.00	700.00
19"	2,000.00			
20"		3,900.00	1,750.00	800.00
21"	2,700.00			
22"			2,000.00	850.00
24"		4,200.00	2,100.00	950.00
26"			2,300.00	
28"		4,700.00	2,500.00	1,000.00
30"			2,700.00	1,500.00
32"			2,800.00	
36"			3,500.00	
38"			3,700.00	2,000.00

* Add an additional $500.00 for black version.

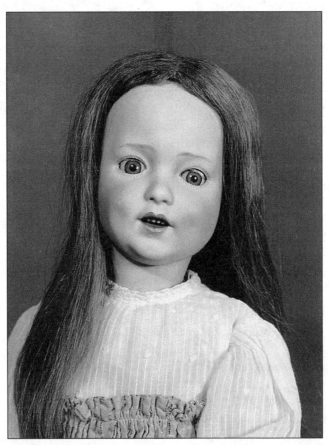

22" Dolly Dimple by Gebrüder Heubach for Hamburger & Co. Courtesy of David Cobb's Doll Auctions

Heinrich Handwerck

Heinrich Handwerck Sr. and his wife Minna started producing dolls amidst humble beginnings in Gotha, near Waltershausen, Thüringia, Germany, in 1876. They managed to build one of the most prolific firms in Germany during the flourishing years of the doll industry, before closing in 1930.

They quickly developed a working relationship with Simon & Halbig, which produced doll heads designed by Handwerck. Pretty, dolly-faced child dolls and babies were Heinrich Handwerck's forte. Character dolls apparently were not included in their repertoire. Consistently meeting the highest standards, Handwerck's dolls were made of exceptionally fine quality bisque.

Heinrich Handwerck Sr. suffered with an incurable disease and passed away in 1902 at the age of forty-four. The business was purchased by Kämmer & Reinhardt of Walterhausen, following Handwerck's posthumous guidelines. The acquisition made Kämmer & Reinhardt world famous. It also afforded K & R the opportunity to negotiate a contract with the prestigious porcelain factory of Simon Halbig of Gräfenhain.

To the delight of today's collectors, Heinrich Handwerck marked the majority of his dolls "Heinrich Handwerck" and frequently included a two or three digit mold number ending in "9" (69, 79, 89, 99, 109, 119, 139, and 189). Other marks include "W" at the top of the forehead, "Hch H," "Baby Cut," "Bébé Cosmopolite," "Bébé de Reclame," "Bébé Superior," "LaBelle," "LaBonita," and "Lotti."

Prices listed are for appropriately costumed dolls in good condition. Normal wear, slight damage, or well-made repairs to the body do not greatly affect the price. If the bisque is damaged or repaired, expect the value to be less than half the amounts listed. It is perfectly acceptable to show a missing or repaired finger or joint, or a mended body.

Dolly-Face: bisque shoulder head; kid body; bisque arms; good wig; glass eyes; open mouth with teeth; appropriately dressed; typically marked "Hch H Germany" or "139."

Un-Numbered Dolly-Face: bisque socket head; jointed composition body; good wig; glass eyes; feathered brows; pierced ears; open mouth with teeth; appropriately dressed; typically marked "Heinrich Handwerck," "W," "HANDWERCK," "H," "HHW," "HH," "Hch H" or "HW."

Numbered Dolly-Face: bisque socket head; jointed composition body; good wig; glass eyes; feathered brows; pierced ears; open mouth with teeth; appropriately dressed; typically marked "Handwerck Germany/99," "109," "89," "79," "69," "119," or "W."

Closed Mouth: bisque socket head; jointed composition body; good wig; glass eyes; feathered brows; pierced ears; closed mouth with slight space between lips; appropriately dressed; typically marked "89" or "79."

Character Baby: bisque socket head; composition bent-limb baby body; good wig; glass eyes; open mouth; appropriately dressed; typically marked "Germany HW," "LaBelle," or "Baby Cut."

37" un-numbered Dolly-Face child, 32" #99 child. Courtesy of David Cobb's Doll Auctions

32" Heinrich Handwerck dolly-face. Courtesy Mr. and Mrs. Gene Patterson

Heinrich Handwerck Value Comparisons						
Size	Dolly-Face Kid Body	Dolly-Face Composition Body No Mold #	Dolly-Face, Composition Body With Mold #	Closed Mouth, Child Doll	Character Baby	Black Dolly-Face
10"		600.00	600.00			
12"		650.00	700.00			
14"		700.00	800.00			
16"	500.00	750.00	850.00		1,200.00	
18"	550.00	850.00	950.00	2,800.00	1,500.00	
20"	600.00	900.00	1,000.00	3,000.00		
22"	650.00	1,000.00	1,100.00	3,500.00	2,200.00	
24"		1,200.00	1,400.00	3,800.00		3,600.00
26"		1,300.00	1,500.00			
28"		1,500.00	1,700.00			
30"			2,200.00			
36"		2,800.00	3,200.00			
42"		4,500.00	4,700.00			

Max Handwerck

17" marked Max Handwerck. Courtesy of McMaster's Doll Auction.

The firm of Max Handwerck, located in Walterhausen, Thüringia, Germany, was originally owned by Heinrich Vortmann and Max Handwerck in 1899. Henrich Vortmann left in 1902 and, after Max Handwerck's death, the business was owned by his widow, Anna.

Max Handwerck designed and modelled their facial molds, many of which were produced as bisque doll heads by William Goebel. One of the most popular character babies was Bébé Elite. Poured by Goebel, the head bears the Goebel trademark of a triangle within a half moon, in addition to the name "Bébé Elite." This combination suggests that the heads were produced before 1900, the year Goebel changed their trademark. The doll industry, however, did not produce character babies until 1910. Therefore either Goebel re-introduced the half moon symbol for the production of Baby Elite after 1910, or Max Handwerck, and not Kämmer & Reinhardt, may actually be responsible for ushering the character baby into the doll industry. It is a fact that in 1901 Max Handwerck registered the trademark "Bébé Elite" and advertised, "…Bébé Elite, finest ball joint dolls with first class bisque heads after our own models…." Regardless of the mysteries surrounding its conception, the Bébé Elite is unquestionably a darling character baby.

In addition to "Elite," other mold markings include: "283," "285," and "296."

Prices listed are for appropriately costumed dolls in good condition. Normal wear, slight damage, or well-made repairs to the body do not greatly affect the price. If the bisque is damaged or repaired, expect the value to be less than half the amounts listed. It is perfectly acceptable to show a missing or repaired finger or joint, or a mended body.

Also see Googly-Eyed Dolls.

Bébé Elite Character: bisque socket head; composition, bent-limb baby body; good wig; glass eyes; finely painted lashes; feathered brows; open mouth with two upper teeth; appropriately dressed; typically marked "Max Handwerck Bébé Elite Germany" and triangle within a half moon trademark.

Dolly-Face: bisque socket head; jointed composition body; good wig; glass eyes; painted lashes; feathered brows; open mouth with teeth; appropriately dressed; typically marked "283 Max Handwerck Germany," "285," "297," "286."

Max Handwerck Value Comparisons		
Size	Baby Elite*	Dolly-Face
16"	800.00	500.00
18"	900.00	550.00
20"	1,100.00	
22"	1,300.00	650.00
24"	1,600.00	700.00
26"	1,800.00	
28"		850.00
30"		1,200.00
34"		1,800.00
38"		2,500.00
40"		2,700.00

* Add an additional $700.00 for jointed toddler body.

Carl Hartmann

Carl Hartmann was a doll exporter in Neustadt, near Coburg, Germany, in 1899.

Hartman registered the trade names Erika, Globe-Baby, Hanson, Palodian Baby, and Thüringia. Of these, the small bisque Globe-Babies, often dressed in regional costumes, are the most commonly found. Kämmer & Reinhardt supplied many of the doll heads. Hartmann advertised that he could supply and export "dolls without the brand mark and without any hint of the producer," which may help to explain the origin of at least some of the many unmarked dolls found.

Prices listed are for appropriately costumed dolls in good condition. Normal wear, slight damage, or well-made repairs to the body do not greatly affect the price. If the bisque is damaged or repaired, expect the value to be less than half the amounts listed. It is perfectly acceptable to show a missing or repaired finger or joint, or a mended body.

Globe Baby: bisque or papier-mâché socket head; five-piece composition body; good wig; glass eyes; open mouth with tiny teeth; appropriately dressed; typically marked "Globe Baby/ DEP/Germany/CH."

Carl Hartmann Value Comparisons	
Size	Globe Baby
5"	425.00
7"	475.00
9"	550.00

10" all original Carl Hartmann Globe Baby.
Courtesy of David Cobb's Doll Auctions

Karl Hartmann

25" Karl Hartmann #30 bisque socket head child. Courtesy of McMaster's Doll Auction

Karl Hartmann operated a doll factory and export business in Stockheim, Upper Franconia, Germany, from 1911 until 1926. Hartmann's lovely bisque dolls have a sophisticated, worldly look, going a step beyond the delicate, wholesome expression often found on German dolly-faced dolls. This cosmopolitan look may be the reason Karl Hartmann dolls are a favorite with so many.

Prices listed are for appropriately costumed dolls in good condition. Normal wear, slight damage, or well-made repairs to the body do not greatly affect the price. If the bisque is damaged or repaired, expect the value to be less than half the amounts listed. It is perfectly acceptable to show a missing or repaired finger or joint, or a mended body.

Child Doll: bisque socket head; jointed composition body; good wig; glass eyes; feathered brows; open mouth with teeth; appropriately dressed; typically marked "K" inside "H."

Karl Hartmann Value Comparisons	
Size	**Child Doll**
14"	450.00
16"	500.00
18"	600.00
22"	700.00
24"	850.00
26"	1,000.00
28"	1,200.00
30"	1,500.00

Hasbro®, Inc.

Hasbro, Inc., originally known as Hassenfeld Bros., was founded by Henry and Hillel Hassenfeld in Pawtucket, Rhode Island, in 1923. The family owned and operated toy business adopted the familiar Hasbro name following a division in the company. One branch went into the pencil box business, the other into the toy business.

Although Hasbro was primarily a toy manufacturer, its journey into the doll world was an interesting one. The extremely popular G.I. Joe®—called an "action figure" by manufacturer, consumers, and collectors—has developed an almost cult-like following among male enthusiasts. In addition to dolls and action figures, Hasbro also manufactures Playskool® Toys and Milton Bradley® games.

Prices listed are for dolls in near-mint, original condition. If damaged, redressed, or undressed, expect the value to be less than one half to one fourth the amounts listed.

Also see Raggedy Ann & Andy.

G.I. Joe: The first G.I. Joe was introduced in 1964. In 1962, Hasbro's creative director, Don Levin, was approached by a television producer to develop a line of toys based on a pending television program about soldiers. The first G.I. Joe had twenty-one movable parts and realistic hair. He was named after the title

Japanese Imperial Soldier from "G. I. Joe Action Soldiers of the World."
Courtesy of McMaster's Doll Auction

French Resistance Fighter from "G. I. Joe Action Soldiers of the World."
Courtesy of McMaster's Doll Auction

character in the movie *The Story of G.I. Joe*. From the start, realism, simplicity, price, and an endless supply of play accessories contributed to the success of the G.I. Joe figures. There are reportedly more than 500 G.I. Joe figures, vehicles, and auxiliary items.

Production was discontinued in 1978 due to an increase in the price of petroleum, a major component in the manufacturing of G.I. Joe. Kirk Bozigian, Hasbro's Vice President of Boys' Toys Marketing, offers an explanation for G.I. Joe's collectible appeal: "Joe has become a timeless classic because he stands for heroism and the power of imagination."

Sequence of development and changes in G.I. Joe:
1st Series: 1964; 11 1/2"; identified by letters "TM" in mark; marked on lower back:

> G.I. Joe TM
> Copyright 1964
> By Hasbro®
> Patent Pending
> Made in U.S.A.

2nd Series: 1965; 11 1/2"; "TM" replaced by "®"; First black G.I. Joe introduced; marked on lower back:

> G.I. Joe®
> Copyright 1964
> By Hasbro®
> Patent Pending
> Made in U.S.A.

3rd Series: 1966; 11 1/2"; identified by the lack of scar; same mark as 2nd Series.

Nurse Jane: only female member of series; green eyes; short blond wig; marked "Patent Pend. 1967 Hasbro Made in Hong Kong."

4th Series: 1967; 11 1/2"; identified by lack of scar and addition of patent number; marked:

> G.I. Joe®
> Copyright 1964
> By Hasbro®
> Pat. No. 3,277,602
> Made in U.S.A.

5th Series: 1968; 11 1/2"; identified by return of scar with same patent number marking; mark remains the same as 4th Series.

6th Series: 1970; 11 1/2"; peace time adventures in response to anti-war feelings; flocked hair introduced; same mark as 4th and 5th Series.

7th Series: 1974; 11 3/4"; new "Kung Fu Grips" allows G.I. Joe to grasp objects; same mark as 4th, 5th, and 6th series.

8th Series: 1975; 11 1/2"; Mike Power model only, identified by see-through right arm and leg and mark on back of head "Hasbro Inc. 1975/Made in Hong Kong." Mark on lower back same as 4th, 5th, 6th, and 7th series.

9th Series: 1975; 11 1/4"; more muscular body with molded-on swimming trunks; new mark introduced:

> 1975 Hasbro®
> Pat. Pend. Pawt. R.I.

10th Series: 1976; 11 1/2" same mark as Series 9, or "Hasbro Ind. Inc. 1975 Made in Hong Kong."

11th Series: 1977; 8" Action Figures.

G.I. Joe Value Comparisons

Series 1, 11 1/2", Mint Condition:
Action Soldier, Molded Black Hair, Blue Eyes $600.00
Action Sailor or Marine, Molded Brown Hair, Brown Eyes
.... $700.00
Action Pilot, Molded Blond Hair, Brown Eyes $950.00

Series 2, 11 1/2", Mint Condition:
Action Soldier, Molded Black Hair, Blue Eyes $600.00
Action Sailor or Marine, Molded Brown Hair, Brown Eyes
.... $700.00
Action Pilot, Molded Blond Hair, Brown Eyes $750.00
Black Action Soldier, Molded Black Hair, Brown Eyes $900.00

Series 3, 11 1/2", Mint Condition:
Action Soldier, Molded Black Hair, Blue Eyes $600.00
Action Sailor or Marine, Molded Brown Hair, Brown Eyes
.... $700.00
Action Pilot, Molded Blond Hair, Brown Eyes $750.00
Black Action Soldier, Molded Black Hair, Brown Eyes ...$1,800.00
Talking Commander, Blond Molded Hair, Brown Eyes $700.00
Nurse Jane, Blond Wig, Green Eyes $4,500.00
Australian Jungle Fighter, Molded Hair $1,200.00
British Commando, Molded Hair $2,000.00
French Resistance Fighter, Molded Hair $1,500.00
German Soldier, Molded Hair $1,900.00
Japanese Imperial Soldier, Molded Hair $2,400.00
Russian Infantry Man, Molded Hair $1,900.00

Series 4, 11 1/2", Mint Condition:
Action Soldier, Molded Black Hair, Blue Eyes $600.00
Action Sailor or Marine, Molded Brown Hair, Brown Eyes
.... $700.00
Action Pilot, Molded Blond Hair, Brown Eyes $700.00
Black Action Soldier, Molded Black Hair, Brown Eyes $900.00
Talking Commander, Molded Blond Hair, Brown Eyes $900.00

Series 5, 11 1/2", Mint Condition:
Action Soldier, Molded Black Hair, Blue Eyes $350.00
Action Sailor or Marine, Molded Brown Hair, Brown Eyes
.... $300.00
Action Pilot, Molded Blond Hair, Brown Eyes $300.00
Black Action Soldier, Molded Black Hair, Brown Eyes $350.00
Talking Commander, Molded Blond Hair, Brown Eyes $800.00

Series 6, 11 1/2", Mint Condition:
Adventure Team Talking Commander, Flocked Blond Hair and
Beard $900.00
Black Adventure Team Talking Commander, Flocked Black
Hair and Beard $900.00
Adventure Team Talking Commander, Flocked Blond Hair,
No Beard $1,200.00
Land Adventurer, Flocked Brown Hair, No Beard $450.00
Sea Adventurer, Flocked Red Hair and Beard $450.00
Air Adventurer, Flocked Blond Hair and Beard $450.00
Black Adventurer, Flocked Black Hair, No Beard $450.00
Astronaut, Flocked Blond Hair, No Beard $700.00
Talking G.I. Joe $450.00

Series 7, 11 3/4", Mint Condition:
Adventure Team Talking Commander, Flocked Brown Hair
and Beard $400.00
Black Adventure Team Talking Commander, Flocked Black
Hair and Beard $400.00
Land Adventurer, Flocked Black Hair and Beard $350.00
Sea Adventurer, Flocked Red Hair and Beard $350.00
Air Adventurer, Flocked Blond Hair and Beard $350.00
Black Adventurer, Flocked Black Hair, No Beard $400.00
Man of Action, Flocked Black Hair, No Beard $400.00
Talking Man of Action, Flocked Brown Hair, No Beard ...$450.00

Series 8, 11 1/2", Mint Condition:
Mike Power Atomic Man, Molded Brown Hair, No Beard, Blue
Eyes $700.00

Series 9, 11 3/4", Mint Condition:
Life-Like Talking Commander, Flocked Brown Hair and
Beard, Blue Eyes $400.00
Life-Like Talking Man of Action, Flocked Brown Hair, No
Beard, Blue Eyes $400.00
Life-Like Black Talking Commander, Flocked Black Hair and
Beard, Brown Eyes $400.00
Life-Like Land Adventurer, Flocked Brown Hair and Beard,
Blue Eyes $300.00
Life-Like Sea Adventurer, Flocked Red Hair and Beard, Brown
Eyes $300.00
Life-Like Air Adventurer, Flocked Blond Hair and Beard,
Brown Eyes $300.00
Life-Like Black Adventurer, Flocked Black Hair, No Beard,
Brown Eyes $300.00
Life-Like Man of Action, Flocked Brown Hair, No Beard, Blue
Eyes $300.00

Series 10, 11 1/2", Mint Condition:
Eagle Eye, Bullet Man, The Intruder $250.00
The Defender $300.00

Series 11, 8", Mint Condition: $100.00

Accessories, Mint In The Box Condition:
Armored Car $300.00
Desert Jeep $2,500.00
Foot Locker $75.00
General's Jeep $700.00
Helicopter $600.00
Motorcycle with Side Car $700.00
Space Capsule $700.00
Tank $400.00

**Outfits, Unopened Packages, Complete with Clothing
and All Accessories:**
Action Sailor $500.00
Air Cadet $1,600.00
Annapolis Cadet $1,600.00
Astronaut $350.00
Deep Freeze w/sled $350.00
Dress Parade Uniform $450.00
Fire Fighter $400.00
Frogman $575.00
Green Beret $800.00
Marine Jungle Fighter $1,300.00
Military Police blue $1,700.00
Military Police brown $600.00
Rescue Diver $350.00
Shore Patrol $350.00
Ski Patrol $350.00
West Point Cadet $1,900.00

Other Hasbro Dolls

Dolly Darling Series: 4 1/2"; plastic and vinyl; molded hair; painted eyes; closed mouth; molded-on shoes; marked "1963/ Hasbro/Japan" $45.00

Little Miss No Name: 15"; vinyl and hard plastic; jointed at neck, shoulder, and hip; rooted hair; very big plastic eyes; real tears; closed sad mouth; original patched burlap dress; marked "1965 Hasbro" $300.00

Sweet Cookie: 18"; plastic and vinyl rooted hair; painted eyes; freckles across nose; open/closed mouth; molded and painted teeth; original short dress; white pinafore with "Sweet Cookie" printed across front; marked "Hasbro, Inc./Pat. Pend. 1972" on head and "Hasbro/Made in USA" on back $75.00

That Kid: 21"; plastic and vinyl; jointed; rude talking; battery operated; reposition arm to repeat phrases; built-in sling shot in hip pocket; rooted hair; sleep eyes; freckles; open/closed mouth; two upper teeth; original cotton shorts outfit; marked "Hasbro/ 1967" on head and "Patent Pending/1967 Hasbro." **Note:** *"Put me down," "You're funny looking" are examples of phrases* $225.00

Aimee: 16" and 18"; vinyl head; plastic body; jointed at neck, shoulder, and hip; rooted hair; sleep eyes; long lashes; closed, smiling mouth; original, floor-length dress; gold sandals and "designer original" jewelry; typically marked "Hasbro Inc. 1972." *Note: Only produced for the one year, 1972.*

16"...	$75.00
18"	95.00

World of Love Dolls: 9"; portraying a classic "flower child"; vinyl head; plastic body; bendable knees; jointed waist; rooted hair; painted, heavily made-up eyes; closed, smiling mouth; original "groovy" costumes; typically marked "Hasbro/US Pat.Pend/1968," "Made in Hong Kong/Hasbro US Pat. Pend/1971" or "Hong Kong/Hasbro/US Patented"

Music..	$100.00
Peace...	100.00
Flower...	100.00
Soul (Black).......................................	125.00
Love..	100.00
Adam (male with molded hair)............	55.00

Leggy Series: 10"; vinyl head; plastic body; extremely long, very thin arms and legs; rooted hair; painted eyes; closed, smiling mouth; original "mod" outfits; typically marked "1972 Hasbro/Hong Kong"

Leggy Sue (Black version)	$100.00
Leggy Nan (Brown hair)	75.00
Leggy Jill (Blond hair)	75.00
Leggy Kate (red or orange hair)	100.00

Bonnie Breck: 9"; vinyl head; plastic body; bendable knees; high heeled feet; rooted, long hair; large, painted eyes; closed mouth; original, long dress; typically marked "Made In/Hong Kong"; wrist tag "Beautiful Bonnie Breck/Made in Hong Kong 1972"...$65.00

Charlie's Angels: 8 1/2"; vinyl head; plastic body; rooted hair; painted facial features; original jump-suit and boots; typically marked "1977/Spelling Goldberg/ Productions/All rights/Reserved/Made in Hong Kong//Hasbro Pat. 3740894" and model number; clothing tag "1977 Hasbro/Made in Hong Kong"

Kelly (Jaclyn Smith) model number "1862"
.... $100.00

Sabrina (Kate Jackson) model number "1861"
....100.00

Jill (Farrah Fawcett) model number "1860"
....100.00

Boxed Gift Set	400.00
Packaged Fashion with accessories:	
Black Magic (4877)	$50.00
Moonlight Flight (4873)	45.00
Night Caper (4871)	40.00
Pleasantry (4872)	45.00

Jem Series: 12 1/2"; all vinyl; rooted hair; painted facial features; original fashion and stage costume; typically marked "Hasbro/Hong Kong//Pat. Pend. 1986"

Jem...	$75.00
Kimber..	100.00
Aja...	125.00
Bambe...	135.00
Shana..	150.00
Roxy...	100.00
Pizazz...	150.00
Stormer...	100.00
Rio...	75.00

The Mamas and The Papas: 4"; realistic characterization; all vinyl; wire armatures; rooted hair; nicely-detailed, painted eyes; open/closed mouth; original classic '60s costumes of bell bottom pants, vests, mini skirts and boots; typically marked "1967/Hasbro®/Hong Kong"

Cass Elliot..	$150.00
John Phillips......................................	100.00
Michelle Phillips................................	125.00
Denny Doherty	75.00
Complete Set	600.00

The Monkees: 4"; realistic characterization; all vinyl; wire armatures; rooted hair; nicely-detailed, painted eyes; open/closed mouth; original brown corduroy jackets, yellow and brown striped pants; typically marked "1967/Hasbro ®//Hong Kong"

Peter Tork	$75.00
Mickey Dolenz...................................	100.00
Davy Jones	100.00
Mike Nesmith.....................................	50.00
Complete Set	400.00

Real Baby: 20"; vinyl head and floppy limbs; cloth body; rooted hair; insert or molded sleep eyes; open/closed mouth; original baby or sleeper outfit; typically marked "Real Baby/H-23/1985 Hasbro Bradley Inc."; clothing tag "1984 J. Turner/Hasbro Inc." $85.00

The Mamas and The Papas. Courtesy Hasbro, Inc.

Hertel, Schwab & Company

Hertel, Schwab & Company operated a porcelain factory in Stutzhaus, near Ohrdruf, Thüringia, Germany, from 1910 until at least 1930. The company was founded by August Hertel and Heinrich Schwab, sculptors who designed the dolls, and a minor partner, porcelain painter Hugo Rosenbush.

Several models were produced exclusively for the American market, including the Bye-Lo Baby for Borgfeldt; Our Baby and Our Fairy for Louis Wolf, and the Jubilee Dolls for Strobel & Wilken.

Known Hertel, Schwab & Company mold numbers include: 111, 125, 126, 130, 132, 133, 134, 135, 136, 138, 140, 141, 142, 143, 147, 148, 149, 150, 151, 152, 157, 158, 159, 160, 161, 162, 163 165, 166, 167, 169, 170, 172, 173, 175, 176, 179, 180, 181, 200, 208, 217, 220, and 222, many of which are character faces.

Most dolls are marked with their mold number and "Made in Germany" or the mark of the company for whom the head was made, such as Louis Wolf or Kley & Hahn.

Prices listed are for appropriately costumed dolls in good condition. Normal wear, slight damage, or well-made repairs to the body do not greatly affect the price. If the bisque is damaged or repaired, expect the value to be less than half the amounts listed. It is perfectly acceptable to show a missing or repaired finger or joint, or a mended body.

Also see Googly-Eyed Dolls.

Character Baby: bisque socket head; composition, bent-limb body; molded and painted hair or good wig; painted or glass eyes; winged brows; open/closed mouth with tongue and upper teeth; appropriately dressed; typically marked "130," "142," "150," "151," or "152."

Dolly Face: bisque socket head; jointed composition body; good wig; glass eyes; feathered brows; open mouth with teeth; appropriately dressed; typically marked "Made in Germany 136" or "132."

Character Child: bisque socket head; from the Art Character Series; jointed composition body; painted or glass eyes; open or closed mouth; appropriately dressed; typically marked "148," "143," "111," "125," "126," "127," "134," "141," "169," "154," "140," or "157."

17" Hertel Schwab #136 child doll. Courtesy of David Cobb's Doll Auctions

29" and 12" Hertel Schwab character baby # 152. Courtesy of David Cobb's Doll Auctions

Hertel, Schwab & Co. Character Baby Value Comparisons

Size	Character Baby*	Dolly-Face	Open/Closed Mouth Character 148*	Closed Mouth Character 143*	Open/Closed Mouth Character 140*	Open Mouth Character 154, 125, 126, 127*	Closed or Open/Closed Mouth Character 134, 141, 149*
10"	600.00						
12"	800.00						
14"	850.00		3,700.00				
16"	900.00	700.00		2,700.00	9,000.00	2,800.00	8,000.00
18"	950.00	750.00					9,000.00
20"	1,000.00	800.00				3,500.00	
24"	1,400.00	1,000.00					1,200.00
26"	1,700.00	1,200.00					

* Add an additional $700.00 for jointed toddler body.

Hertel, Schwab & Co. Character Child Value Comparisons

Size	Closed Mouth Pouty 111*	Closed Mouth Character 169*	Open Mouth Character 169*	Closed Mouth Character 154*
18"	23,000.00	4,000.00	1,200.00	2,800.00

* Add an additional $700.00 for jointed toddler body.

Hertwig & Company

Hertwig & Company produced Snow Babies and "Nanking Dolls" in its porcelain factory in Katzhütte, Thüringia, Germany. Nanking Dolls have bisque heads and limbs, and cloth bodies stuffed with cotton (nanking). The company also made the "Pet Name" china heads exclusively for the United States market.

Many Hertwig & Company dolls have molded clothing and are either unmarked or marked only "Germany." The dolls are often among the first acquisitions made by doll collectors. Their charming vintage appearance and easy accessibility makes them a logical first step in the "antique doll collecting" journey.

Prices listed are for appropriately costumed dolls in good condition. Normal wear, slight damage, or well-made repairs to the body do not greatly affect the price. If the bisque is damaged or repaired, expect the value to be less than half the amounts listed. It is perfectly acceptable to show a missing or repaired finger or joint, or a mended body.

Also see All Bisque, China Heads.

Molded Clothing: all bisques jointed at shoulder, occasionally hip; molded and painted facial features and detailed clothing; typically marked "Germany" or unmarked.

Shoulder-Head Child: bisque shoulder head; cloth body; bisque arms and legs; nicely molded and painted hair and facial features; closed mouth; appropriately dressed; typically marked "Germany," "140," "150," "175," 385," "386," and possibly others or unmarked.

Hertwig & Co. Value Comparisons

Size	Molded Clothes	Bisque Shoulder-Head Child
8"	375.00	300.00
10"	425.00	325.00
12"		350.00

8 1/2" and 7" Hertwig bisque child dolls with molded clothing. Courtesy of McMaster's Doll Auction

Ernst Heubach

*I*n 1887, Ernst Heubach began manufacturing bisque dolls in his porcelain factory in Köppelsdorf, near Sonneberg, Germany.

The structure of the European doll industry at the end of the 19th century was shaped by the traditions of an earlier time, when businesses were bound by strong family ties. Ernst Heubach's company is a classic example of the interconnection. Undoubtedly related to the Heubach porcelain factory in Thüringia, Ernst Jr. added to the complexities by marrying Beatrice Marseilles, daughter of Armand Marseilles, unquestionably one of the leading doll manufacturers of the time. One of Ernst Heubach's sculptors, Hans Homgberger, was a brother to the senior sculptor for Armand Marseilles. Such family connections help explain the similarities so often found in early bisque character dolls.

In 1919, Ernst Heubach and Armand Marseilles merged to become "Vereinigte Köppelsdorfer Porzellanfabrik vorm Armand Marseilles and Ernst Heubach" (United Porcelain Factory of Köppelsdorf). The new company split into two separate entities once again in 1932.

Dolls incised "Heubach Koppelsdorf" were produced between 1919 and 1932. Other marks include a horseshoe, the intitials "E.H," and various three or four digit mold numbers.

Prices listed are for appropriately costumed dolls in good condition. Normal wear, slight damage, or well-made repairs to the body do not greatly affect the price. If the bisque is damaged or repaired, expect the value to be less than half the amounts listed. It is perfectly acceptable to show a missing or repaired finger or joint, or a mended body.

Also see Googly-Eyed Dolls, Oriental.

Character Baby: bisque socket head: bent-limb baby body; some with pierced nostrils; good wig; glass eyes; open mouth; appropriately dressed; typically marked "Heubach Köppelsdorf," a horseshoe, "300," "320," "342," and possibly others.

Infant: bisque flange neck; cloth body; composition or celluloid hands, painted hair; glass eyes; closed mouth; appropriately dressed; typically marked "Heubach/Köppelsdorf/Germany,"

horseshoe, "338," "339," "340," "349," "350," "399," and possibly others.

Dolly-Face: bisque socket or shoulder head; kid or composition body; good wig; glass eyes; open mouth; appropriately dressed; typically marked "Heubach/ Köppelsdorf," "Germany," "H/K," horseshoe, "1900," "1901," "1902," "1906," "1909," "205," "251," "275," "302," "312," and possibly others.

Character Child: bisque socket head; jointed, composition body; ethnic and charming character dolls; molded and painted hair or good wig; painted or glass eyes; open or closed mouth; appropriately dressed; typically marked "Heubach/Köppelsdorf/Germany," a horseshoe, "269," "399," "414," "463," "452," "445," "SUR 312," and possibly others.

Greif Puppenkunst: ebony-black bisque character head flange neck; cloth body; fantastic modelling; made for Erich Reiser's Fily-Plüshpuppen; solid dome; glass eyes; wide, smiling, open/closed mouth; molded upper and lower teeth; appropriately dressed; typically marked "Greif Puppenkunst/Germany."

Ernst Heubach character babies #267 with treble tongue and #300. Courtesy of David Cobb's Doll Auctions

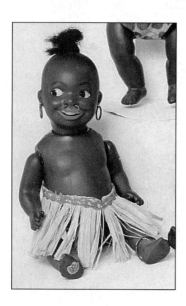

14" Ernst Heubach #463 black bisque character. Courtesy of David Cobb's Doll Auctions

Ernst Heubach Value Comparisons

Size	Character Baby*	Infant	Dolly-Face Kid Body	Dolly-Face Composition Body	269 Character	Gypsy #452
6"	325.00				900.00	
8"	350.00			300.00		
10"	375.00			325.00		
12"	500.00	900.00	300.00	350.00		
14"	550.00	1,000.00	325.00	400.00	2,000.00	
16"	600.00	1,200.00	350.00	450.00		1,600.00
18"	700.00		375.00	500.00		
20"	750.00		400.00	550.00		
22"	850.00		450.00	600.00		
24"	1,000.00		600.00	700.00		
26"	1,200.00			800.00		
28"				900.00		
30"				1,200.00		

Size	2-Face Doll #445	Character Clown	Black 444	399, 414, 452*	312**	Black, 316, 418, 463	Greif Puppenkunst Black Character
8"			750.00	650.00		950.00	
10"			800.00	700.00	450.00	1,200.00	
12"			850.00	750.00		1,300.00	
14"						1,500.00	
16"			1,000.00		600.00		
18"	2,400.00			1,000.00	700.00	2,300.00	
20"					750.00		
24"					800.00		7,500.00
26"					900.00		
28"					1,200.00		9,000.00
30"		3,200.00			1,500.00		
36"					2,500.00		
42"					3,500.00		
46"					3,900.00		

*Add an additional $700.00 for jointed toddler body.

**Add an additional $300.00 for high knee flapper body.

Gebrüder Heubach

The Heubach family bought an established porcelain factory in Lichte, Thüringia, Germany, in 1840 and began producing porcelain figurines shortly thereafter. Heubach is not known to have made doll heads until around 1910. With the introduction of character dolls, doll makers in America and Europe seized upon the new interest for the exotic. Rarely could others compete with the skill and attention to detail used to produce the amusing and extraordinary Gebrüder Heubach character dolls.

One secret to Heubach's success was the location of an art school for sculptors located near the factory. The school trained the especially skilled artists and sculptors responsible for creating many beautiful porcelain figurines and dolls. Several of the artists known to have modelled doll heads for Gebrüder Heubach were Zitzmann, Zeiller, Holwein, Krieger, Niemeyer, and Wera von Bartels. Occasionally their initials were included in the markings.

The enormous quantity and range of character doll heads produced by Gebrüder Heubach has, at times, made positive

Gebrüder Heubach 20" closed, pouty mouth with glass eyes #7246; and 17" closed mouth #7603 solid dome, fleece hair, and intaglio eyes. Courtesy of David Cobb's Doll Auctions

identification difficult. Due to their heavy use, the molds became worn, causing identifying numbers to become unreadable. Many heads never had mold numbers; they were simply marked "S" (for sun) or "Q" (for square). No logical numbering system has been deciphered, further impeding attempts to precisely identify many dolls.

The socket or shoulder heads had either molded hair or wigs, and sleeping eyes or the famous painted intaglio eyes. Heights range from four inches to at least twenty-eight inches. Mold numbers appear to be from 5,625 to 12,386. Most in the 5,000s, 6,000s, and 7,000s have the sunburst mark, while the mold numbers in the 8,000s and beyond are more likely to have the square mark. Many of the firm's doll heads were made for other German companies as well, including Cuno & Otto Dressel, Eisenmann, Hamburger & Company, Gebrüder Ohlhaver, and Wagner & Zetsche. Several small doll factories in and around Sonneberg also used Gebrüder Heubach heads.

Reproductions are numerous. A legitimate copy of a Gebrüder Heubach doll will be marked with the artist's name and date. It may also have the name of the company that produced the mold. Examine the doll's patina. Inspect the body. Authentic Gebrüder Heubach bodies are often rather crude. While Gebrüder Heubach dolls were charming character dolls, their bisque does not have the satiny smoothness so often found in reproductions.

Prices listed are for appropriately costumed dolls in good condition. Normal wear, slight damage, or well-made repairs to the body do not greatly affect the price. If the bisque is damaged or repaired, expect the value to be less than half the amounts listed. It is perfectly acceptable to show a missing or repaired finger or joint, or a mended body.

Also see Googly-Eyed Dolls.

The following listing should enable you to evaluate mold numbers not listed by using comparables. With the thousands of dolls made by Gebrüder Heubach, it is impossible to list each. The examples are indicative of the character dolls' current popularity.

Gebrüder Heubach Character Value Comparisons

Size	5626 O/CM Laughing, Glass Eyes	5636 O/CM Laughing 2 Lower Teeth, Intaglio Eyes	5636 O/CM Laughing, Glass Eyes	5689 OM Smiling, Glass Eyes	5730 OM Smiling, Glass Eyes	5777 OM Smiling, Glass Eyes Socket Head	5777 OM Smiling, Glass Eyes Shoulder Head
9"		1,000.00	1,800.00				
12"	1,700.00	1,500.00	2,200.00				
14"					1,700.00		
16"	2,300.00		3,200.00	3,000.00		3,300.00	1,300.00
20"				3,800.00	2,500.00	3,900.00	2,600.00

Size	6692 CM Pouty Shoulder Head, Intaglio Eyes	6736 Laughing, Intaglio Eyes	6774 CM Whistling, Intaglio Eyes	6894, 6898 CM Pouty, Socket Head, Intaglio Eyes	6969 CM Pouty, Glass Eyes	6970 Pouty, Glass Eyes	6971 O/CM Lower Teeth Smiling, Intaglio Eyes
8"				900.00			
10"		1,400.00					2,400.00
12"	900.00		1,000.00		3,000.00	1,900.00	
16"	1,200.00	2,200.00	1,700.00	1,400.00	4,200.00	2,900.00	
22"					6,200.00		

Size	7054 CM Smiling, Intaglio Eyes	7109 O/CM Intaglio Eyes	7246, 7374, 7407, CM Pouty, Glass Eyes	7247 CM Glass Eyes	7407 CM Full Lips, Intaglio Eyes	7550 O/CM Molded Tongue, Glass Eyes
8"		800.00				
12"	900.00	1,000.00	3,000.00			2,200.00
16"	1,200.00		4,200.00	3,200.00	2,700.00	3,000.00
22"			6,200.00			

Size	7602 CM Pouty, Intaglio Eyes	7603 CM Fleece Hair	7604 O/CM Laughing, Intaglio Eyes	7616 O/CM Molded Tongue, Glass Eyes	7620 O/CM Protruding Ears, Intaglio Eyes	7622 CM Wide Lipped Pouty, Intaglio Eyes	7623 O/CM Molded Tongue, Intaglio Eyes
8"	900.00						
10"			900.00				
12"	1,000.00	1,900.00					1,000.00
14"	1,200.00		1,300.00	2,400.00	1,500.00	1,300.00	
16"				3,100.00			1,700.00
20"			1,900.00		1,900.00	1,800.00	

Size	7631 CM Intaglio Eyes	7644 O/CM Intaglio Eyes	7646 O/CM Wide Grin, Intaglio Eyes	7661 O/CM Crooked Mouth, Squinting Eyes	7665 O/CM Smiling, Glass Eyes	7669 O/CM Molded Tongue, Glass Eyes	7679 O/CM Whistler, Itaglio Eyes
8"	800.00						
10"	900.00	900.00					1,200.00
12"			2,200.00			2,500.00	
14"							1,600.00
16"				6,000.00	2,300.00		
20"				7,500.00			

Size	7681 CM Wide-awake Painted Eyes	7684 O/CM Screaming, Intaglio Eyes	7686 O/CM Wide Mouth, Glass Eyes	7701 CM Pouty, Intaglio Eyes	7711 OM Glass Eyes	7743 O/CM Protruding Ears, Glass Eyes
10"	1,500.00					
12"					2,400.00	
14"			3,200.00			6,000.00
16"		3,200.00			2,900.00	
18"			5,900.00			7,500.00
20"		3,800.00		2,900.00		

Size	7745 O/CM Molded Teeth, Intaglio Eyes	7746 O/CM Lower Teeth, Intaglio Eyes	7748 Wide O/CM Fatty Neck, Teeth, Tiny Intaglio Eyes	7749 CM Nearly Closed Painted Eyes	7751 O/CM Squinting Glass Eyes
8"	900.00				
10"				2,900.00	
12"	1,600.00				
14"		1,600.00			4,000.00
16"			7,000.00		
18"		2,400.00	8,000.00		6,000.00

Gebrüder Heubach 15" #7788. Coquette with open-closed smiling mouth, painted teeth, side-glancing intaglio eyes, and molded hair bow; and 17" #7602 closed mouth with intaglio eyes. Courtesy of David Cobb's Doll Auctions

Size	7759 CM Pouty, Intaglio Eyes	7761 O/CM Squinting, Painted Eyes	7764 Singing, Intaglio Eyes	7768 CM, Hair Molded in Bun, Intaglio Eyes	7781 O/CM Yawning, Painted Eyes	7788, 7850 CM Coquette Smiling, Intaglio eyes	7802 CM Pouty, Intaglio Eyes
8"	475.00						
10"	500.00						
12"				1,200.00	1,800.00	1,100.00	
14"			10,000.00	1,400.00		1,400.00	2,000.00
16"		6,800.00	12,000.00		2,400.00		
18"		7,000.00	15,000.00				
20"		7,500.00				1,900.00	

Size	7820 O/CM Laughing Intaglio Eyes	7843 O/CM, Yawning, Squinting	7847 O/CM Grinning, Tiny Intaglio Eyes, Oversized Ears	7849 CM Intaglio Eyes	7851 CM Molded Hair Bow, Intaglio Eyes	7852 CM Coiled Braids, Intaglio Eyes
10"	900.00	1,200.00		600.00		
12"					1,500.00	
14"				1,000.00		2,500.00
16"	1,300.00	2,200.00			1,900.00	
18"						3,400.00
20"	1,900.00		4,900.00			

Size	7853 CM Downcast Painted Eyes	7862 CM Coiled Braided Hair, Intaglio Eyes	7865 Glass Eyes	7877 CM Molded Bonnet, Intaglio Eyes	7877 7977 Baby Stewart, Glass Eyes
12"		1,800.00	3,400.00	1,500.00	2,600.00
14"	2,300.00				
16"		2,500.00		1,900.00	2,900.00
18"					
20"					4,000.00

Size	7911 O/CM, Grinning Intaglio Eyes	7920 Glass Eyes	7925 OM, Smiling Lady, Glass Eyes	7926 OM, Smiling Lady, Painted Eyes	7959 O/CM Molded Bonnet, Intaglio Eyes	7975 CM, Removable Bonnet, Glass Eyes
12"	1,200.00					2,500.00
14"				3,700.00	4,500.00	
16"	1,500.00			4,000.00		3,200.00
18"		3,200.00	4,700.00		5,200.00	
20"						
22"					6,500.00	

Size	7977 CM, Baby Stewart Molded Bonnet, Intaglio Eyes	8017 Pouty, Glass Eyes	8107 CM, Pouty, Intaglio Eyes	8035 CM Full Lips, Intaglio Eyes	8050 O/CM Hair Ribbon, Laughing, Intaglio Eyes	8053 CM Glancing, Intaglio Eyes	8058 O/CM Rows Teeth, Intaglio Eyes
8"			700.00				
12"	1,500.00	3,000.00	1,100.00				
14"					9,000.00	7,000.00	
16"		4,200.00				9,000.00	12,000.00
18"					15,000.00		
20"		6,000.00		9,000.00			

Size	8145 CM Side-Glancing, Intaglio Eyes	8191 O/CM Laughing Boy, Intaglio Eyes	8192 OM Child/Glass Eyes	8197 CM Molded Hair Loop, Glass Eyes	8306 O/CM Molded Teeth, Intaglio Eyes	8316 O/CM Molded Teeth, Glass Eyes	8381 CM Princess Julianna Exposed Ears, Intaglio Eyes
12"		1,100.00	600.00		1,300.00		
14"	1,700.00	1,300.00	900.00	8,200.00	1,500.00		
16"				9,000.00		3,900.00	
18"	1,900.00		1,300.00				15,000.00
20"						4,800.00	

Size	8413 O/CM With Tongue, Intaglio Eyes	8420 CM Pouty, Glass Eyes	8459 O/CM Laughing, Glass Eyes	8467 CM Character Indian	8469 O/CM Laughing, Glass Eyes	8550 CM Protruding Tongue, Intaglio Eyes	8555 CM Bulging, Painted Eyes
10"					2,600.00		
12"	1,200.00	1,900.00	2,700.00			1,400.00	3,000.00
14"					3,400.00		
16"		2,700.00	3,200.00	4,800.00		1,700.00	5,000.00

Size	8556 O/CM, Molded Hair, Ribbon, and Teeth	8578 CM Molded Tongue, Intaglio Eyes	8590 CM Puckered Mouth, Intaglio Eyes	8596 CM, Smiling, Intaglio Eyes	8648 CM Very Pouty, Intaglio Eyes
10"		1,100.00			
12"		1,400.00			
14"			1,500.00	1,000.00	
16"				1,200.00	2,500.00
18"	15,000.00		2,000.00		3,200.00

Size	8724 CM Smiling, Intaglio Eyes	8774 O/CM Whistling Intaglio Eyes	8793 CM Slight Dimple, Intaglio Eyes	8868 CM Short Chin, Glass Eyes	8991 O/CM Molded Tongue, Intaglio Eyes	9027 CM Tentative Smile, Intaglio Eyes
10"		1,400.00				
14"			2,200.00		3,500.00	
16"			2,600.00	2,700.00		4,600.00
18"	1,900.00					
20"				3,500.00		

Size	9102 Cat Socket Head, Wide Smile, Upward Glancing Intaglio Eyes	9114 Intaglio Eyes	9114 Glass Eyes	9189 O/CM Hair Bow, Intaglio Eyes	9355 OM, Shoulder Head Glass Eyes
10"		1,200.00	1,700.00		
12"				1,700.00	
16"	6,500.00			2,300.00	
18"					1,400.00
22"					2,000.00

Size	9457 CM Wrinkled Character	9467 Character Indian	9591 CM Fretful Frown Intaglio Eyes	9891 CM Aviator, Intaglio Eyes	9891 CM Farmer, Intaglio Eyes	9891 CM Sailor, Intaglio Eyes
12"	2,800.00	3,000.00	2,800.00	2,200.00	1,900.00	2,000.00
14"					2,300.00	

Size	10532 OM Character, Glass Eyes	10586 Baby, Glass Eyes	10511 CM Smiling, Intaglio Eyes	10617 OM Baby, Small Squinting Eyes	10633 OM Shoulder Head, Glass Eyes
12"		750.00	1,900.00		
14"					850.00
20"		1,100.00		1,200.00	1,100.00
22"	1,700.00				

Size	11173 Tiss Me Indented Cheeks, Glass Eyes	11173 Tiss Me Indented Cheeks, Intaglio Eyes	12886 OM Laughing, Dimpled, Glass Eyes	No Mold # CM Socket Head, (Looks similar to K ★ R 114) Intaglio Eyes
8"	2,400.00			
10"			2,200.00	
12"	2,700.00	1,900.00		4,500.00
16"				5,400.00

Size	No Mold # O/CM Socket Head, Two Teeth Resting on Tongue	No Mold # O/CM Socket Head Grinning, Side-Glancing, Intaglio Eyes	Animals, Bisque Body	Animals, Bisque Heads, Composition Body	Black Character Molded Curly Hair, Intaglio Eyes
8"			3,500.00	3,000.00	
12"					3,200.00
16"		4,700.00			
20"	5,200.00				

O/CM = Open/Closed Mouth

OM = Open Mouth

CM = Closed Mouth

Hollywood Dolls

*D*ominick Ippolite founded the Hollywood Doll Manufacturing Company of Glendale, California in 1941. Until closing their doors in the 1960s, Hollywood Dolls supplied more dolls to the public than any other manufacturer.

The demure Hollywood ladies were made of painted bisque, composition, or hard plastic. They stand a mere five to eight inches tall and are jointed at the shoulder, hip, and eventually neck.

Dolls released include: Princess Series, Lucky Star Series, Nursery Rhyme Series, Little Friends, Playmates, Toyland Series, Sweetheart Series, Lullaby Series, Rock-A-By Baby, Western Series, Everyday Series, Cradle Series, Baby Buggy Series, Lucky Star, Queen for a Day, Wishes, Old Mother Witch, Nun, Peter Rabbit, Bunny Rabbit, Bridegroom, Little One, Ballerina, Bedtime Dolly, Little Snow Baby, and even a doll to dress at home!

Hollywood also produced accessories such as doll stands, cradles, and carriages. Most dolls and accessories carry the "Hollywood Doll" mark and occasionally ★. To correctly identify a particular character, however, it is imperative to have the original star-covered box printed with the name or a wrist tag.

Composition or Painted Bisque

It may be difficult to distinguish between the two. Fortunately, they have a shared value.

Prices listed are for originally costumed dolls in good condition. If damaged, repaired, redressed, or undressed, expect the value to be less than one half the amounts listed.

All composition or painted bisque: one-piece head and body; jointed shoulder and hip; mohair glued onto head; painted eyes; long, painted lashes; closed mouth; original costume; typically marked "Hollywood Doll," "Hollywood," or unmarked.

Hard Plastic or Vinyl

Prices listed are for dolls in near-mint, original condition. If damaged, redressed, or undressed, expect the value to be less than one quarter the amounts listed.

All hard plastic: jointed neck, shoulder, and hip; molded hair or mohair glued onto head; sleep eyes; closed mouth; original costume; typically marked "Hollywood Dolls," "Hollywood" within a circle, ★, or unmarked.

All Flexible Vinyl: all vinyl; jointed at neck, shoulder, and hip; thin face and limbs; nice wig; exotic sleep eyes; closed mouth; original costume; typically marked "Hollywood Doll."

	Hollywood Doll Value Comparison		
Size	Composition/ Painted Bisque	Hard Plastic	Vinyl*
5"–6"	95.00	45.00	
7"–8"	135.00	85.00	150.00

* Add an additional $100.00 for "Little One" in original, special Picture Frame Box.

Painted bisque Hollywood doll with original box and booklet. Courtesy of Bill Neff

E. I. Horsman & Company

E. I. Horsman & Company was founded in New York City by Edward Imeson Horsman in 1865. In 1859, at the age of sixteen, Horsman worked as an office boy for $2.00 a week. Just six years later, he opened a company that was to become a leader in the doll industry.

Beginning in the early 1900s, Horsman produced a variety of popular composition dolls. The dolls had painted hair or wigs, forward or side-glancing, painted or sleep eyes, open or closed mouths, with or without teeth. As time went on, even more variations were incorporated. Often, a doll was manufactured with a concoction of parts, entirely different from the norm, or the same mold was given more than one name. Obviously consistency was not one of Horsman's virtues.

Around 1890, a Russian inventor, Solomon D. Hoffmann, brought his formula for "unbreakable" composition doll heads to America. Doll manufacturers showed little interest, overlooking one of the biggest opportunities in the doll industry. To his credit, Horsman saw the great potential of composition and through a series of acquisitions he was able to secure the rights to Hoffmann's secret formula.

With his keen sense of marketing, Horsman recognized the charm of the Billiken character and the appeal of a soft cuddly teddy bear, and he concluded that a doll made from a combination of the two would be irresistible to the public. How right he was! It is reported that during the first six months of production, Horsman sold more than 200,000 Billikens. It should be mentioned that the Billiken was originally created by Florence Pretz of Kansas City who patterned him after Joss the Chinese god of "things as they ought to be."

Also see Babyland Rag, Campbell Kids, Composition, Aetna, and Modern Collectible.

12" Billikin by Horsman with composition head and mohair body. Courtesy of David Cobb's Doll Auctions

Bisque

Prices listed are for appropriately costumed dolls in good condition. Normal wear, slight damage, or well-made repairs to the body do not greatly affect the price. If the bisque is damaged or repaired, expect the value to be less than half the amounts listed. It is perfectly acceptable to show a missing or repaired finger or joint, or a mended body.

Tynie Baby: bisque flange neck; cloth body; composition hands; molded and painted hair; glass eyes; closed mouth; appropriately dressed; typically marked "1924/E.I. Horsman Co./ Made in Germany/U."

Composition

Prices listed are for appropriately costumed dolls in good condition. Slight crazing is acceptable and does not greatly affect the price. If badly crazed, cracked, peeling, or repainted, expect the value to be less than half the amounts listed.

Baby Bumps: composition flange neck; cloth body; sateen limbs; painted hair and eyes; open/closed mouth; appropriately dressed; labeled "Genuine/Baby Bumps/Trademark."

Baby Butterfly: composition shoulder head and hands; cloth body; painted, black hair; painted, Oriental facial features; appropriately dressed; typically marked "E. I. H."

Baby Chubby: composition shoulder head and limbs; cloth body; molded and painted hair; glassine sleep eyes; real lashes; closed mouth; appropriately dressed; typically marked "A/Horsman."

Baby Dimples: composition limbs and flange neck; cloth body; molded and painted hair; tin sleep eyes; open, dimpled mouth with two teeth and molded tongue; appropriately dressed; typically marked "E.I.H. Co., Inc."

Biliken: composition head; beige, plush body; jointed at shoulder and hip; stitched claw hands and feet; molded and painted top knot hair; slanted, slit eyes and brows; pug nose; closed, impish watermelon grin mouth; labeled "Licensed Stamp Copyright 1909 by The Billiken Company."

Character Baby: composition shoulder head and hands; jointed cloth body; molded and painted hair; painted eyes; nicely molded, closed mouth; appropriately dressed; typically marked "1910 by E. I. Horsman Co."

Child Doll: all jointed composition or composition socket head, shoulder plate, and limbs; cloth body; good wig; tin sleep eyes; open mouth; appropriately dressed; typically marked "Horseman, Rosebud."

Ella Cinders: composition character shoulder head and limbs; cloth body; molded and painted black hair with center part; painted wide eyes; freckles; closed mouth; appropriately dressed; typically marked "©/1925/M. N.S."

HeBee and SheBee: all composition oversized head; spray-painted hair; painted eyes; rosy cheeks and nose; tiny, closed mouth; molded chemise and booties; holes in booties for ribbon ties; paper label on foot "Trademark Charles Twelvetrees/Copyrighted 1925."

Jackie Coogan: composition shoulder head and limbs; cloth body; molded and painted brown hair; and side-glancing eyes;

closed mouth; appropriately dressed; marked "E.I.H. Co./ 19©21."

Mama Doll: composition shoulder head and limbs; cloth body; good wig; tin sleep eyes; open mouth with upper teeth and felt tongue; appropriately dressed; typically marked "E. I. Horsman."

20" Horsman composition Rosebud in original condition. Courtesy of David Cobb's Doll Auctions

Peterkins: all composition; molded and painted hair with forehead curl on left side; painted eyes with large pupils; tiny, arched eyebrows; tiny, closed, watermelon mouth; appropriately dressed; typically marked "E. I. Horsman Inc." or unmarked.

Raggedy Man Character Doll: composition, well-molded shoulder head; cloth body; nicely shaped hands; molded and painted hair; painted brown eyes; closed mouth; original patched pants, shirt, jacket and floppy hat; marked "The Raggedy Man/ Trademark/Under License From L. P. Tucks/Mfgd by E. I. Horsman."

Whatsit Doll: all composition; jointed at neck, shoulder, and hip; molded and painted hair; side-glancing eyes; open/closed mouth with molded tongue; appropriately dressed; typically marked "Naughty Sue/©1937, Roberta/1938 Horsman."

Hard Plastic and Vinyl

Prices listed are for dolls in near-mint, original condition. If damaged, redressed, or undressed, expect the value to be less than one half to one fourth the amounts listed.

Child: all hard plastic; jointed at neck, shoulder, and hip; saran wig; sleep eyes; open mouth with upper teeth; appropriately dressed; typically marked "170," "170 Made in USA," "Bright Star," or "Horsman/All Plastic."

Cindy: vinyl head; swivel waist; rigid vinyl, jointed body; high heeled feet; rooted, red hair; painted nails; sleep eyes; pierced ears; closed mouth; original stylish costumes with accessories; typically marked "Horsman/83," "Horsman," "88//Horsman," or "818 Pat. 2736135."

Tweedie: 14"; used in advertising "Tweedie Toiletries" by Lenthneric; vinyl head; rigid vinyl body; rooted hair; sleep eyes; closed mouth; designer costumes included Bambury Coats, Love Dresses, Geisha Robes, Regan Swimwear, and Mr. John Juniorette hats; typically marked "38/Horsman" or "Horsman" $110.00

Horsman Bisque and Composition Value Comparisons

Size	Bisque Tynie Baby	Baby Bumps, White	Baby Bumps, Black	Baby Butterfly	Baby Chubby	Baby Dimples	Billiken
9"	700.00	300.00	350.00				
10"		350.00	400.00				
12"	950.00	450.00	500.00				475.00
13"				900.00			
14"	1,200.00				350.00		
16"					400.00	475.00	600.00
18"		600.00	650.00			525.00	
20"						650.00	
24"					500.00	725.00	

Size	Character Baby	Child Dolls	Ella Cinders	Hebee/ SheBee	Jackie Coogan	Mama Dolls	Peterkins	Raggedy Man	Whatsit Doll
10"				900.00		300.00			
11"	475.00						600.00		
12"		375.00				350.00			
13"					700.00				
14"		425.00				475.00			600.00
16"	600.00	550.00			900.00	525.00		900.00	700.00
18"		575.00	900.00			550.00			
20"		625.00				600.00			
22"		675.00							

Disney's Cinderella Gift Set: 11 1/2"; used to help celebrate Horsman's "Century of Quality 1865-1965"; vinyl heads and arms; hard plastic body; rooted hair; painted, side-glancing eyes; pierced ears; closed mouth; included in the set, with the Cinderella doll in silver trimmed pink satin ball gown, an additional "poor Cinderella" head with dress of yellow skirt, green and blue blouse, and brown suede weskit, glass slipper perched upon a velvet pillow, pail, mop, cardboard clock and instruction to "...change Cinderella's head and clothes to her scullery outfit"; typically marked "H" **$200.00**

Mary Poppins: vinyl head; plastic body; rooted hair; painted, side-glancing eyes; slightly open/closed mouth; appropriately dressed; typically marked "H."

Jane: 7"; all vinyl; rooted hair; painted eyes; closed mouth; nicely dressed; typically marked "Horsman Doll Inc. 6681" **$175.00**

Michael: 9"; all vinyl; rooted hair; painted eyes; closed mouth; nicely dressed; typically marked "9/Horsman Doll/ 6682" **$175.00**

Patty Duke: vinyl head; plastic body; rooted, blond hair with bangs; painted blue eyes; closed mouth; appropriately dressed; typically marked "Horsman Doll/6211."

Ruth's Sister: vinyl head and arms; plastic body; rooted hair; sleep eyes with lashes; open/closed mouth; appropriately dressed; typically marked Horsman/T-27."

Zodiac Baby: all vinyl; jointed at neck, shoulder, and hip; long, rooted, pink hair; black eyes; open/closed mouth; original star-shaped dress; charm bracelet with signs of the zodiac; and "Your Individual Horoscope" booklet; typically marked "Horsman Dolls Inc./1968."

Black Character: vinyl head; one-piece, stuffed vinyl body; molded hair; painted, squinting eyes; open/closed mouth; appropriately dressed; typically marked "Horsman" on back of head.

Poor Pitiful Pearl: vinyl head; one-piece, stuffed vinyl body; rooted, long, straight hair; sleep eyes; closed, slightly-smiling, thin line mouth; protruding ears; original, patched cotton dress and scarf; typically marked "©1963/Wm. Steig/Horsman."

Couturier: all vinyl; pose-able, soft, stuffed vinyl body; unusual ball joints at neck, shoulder, and elbows; individual fingers; long neck; high heeled feet; rooted, unusual-color hair; sleep eyes; real lashes; closed mouth; original, beautifully designed costume of satin and lace; typically marked "82/Horsman."

Jackie: soft vinyl head; rigid vinyl body; jointed at neck, shoulder, and hip; rooted black hair; sleep eyes; pronounced, arched

36" Mary Poppins in original condition.
Courtesy of McMaster's Doll Auction

eyebrows; pierced ears; closed mouth; original, white, Schiffli embroidered dress; cotton shawl; pearl earrings, necklace, and bracelet; typically marked "Horsman, 19©61/JK/25/4."

BiLo: vinyl head and swivel limbs; cloth body; molded and painted hair; painted eyes; open/closed mouth; original, long gown with lace inserts and matching cap; typically marked "Horsman Doll/1972."

Pippi Longstocking: vinyl head and limbs; cloth body; rooted, braided, orange hair; painted eyes; freckles; open/closed mouth; typically marked "25-3/Horsman Dolls Inc./1972."

Squalling Baby: soft vinyl head and limbs; cloth body; softly molded hair; painted, squinting, blue eyes; wide, open/closed, yawning mouth; appropriately dressed; typically marked "Corp. Lastic Plastic 49."

Horsman Plastic Value Comparisons

Size	Hard Plastic Child	Mary Poppins	Patty Duke	Ruth's Sister	Zodiac Baby	Black Character	Poor Pitiful Pearl	Cindy or Couturier
6"					50.00			
10"								125.00
12"		75.00	150.00			350.00	200.00	
15"	450.00							
16"		150.00					250.00	
17"	500.00							
19"								300.00
26"		300.00		200.00				

Size	Jackie	BiLo	Pippi Longstocking	Squalling Baby
14"		125.00		
17"			100.00	
19"				175.00
23"	225.00			

Mary Hoyer Doll Manufacturing Company

The Mary Hoyer Doll Manufacturing Company, named for its founder, was located in Reading, Pennsylvania, from 1925 until the 1970s. Mary Hoyer owned and operated a yarn shop. She sold a wide variety of yarns and craft supplies through her mail order business. As a designer of knit and crochet fashions for infants and children, it was a natural transition to begin designing costumes for dolls. Mary Hoyer wanted a small, slim doll to use as a model for her clothing designs. She then concluded that a doll could be sold along with a pattern book of instructions for a knitted and crocheted wardrobe.

While the Ideal Novelty & Toy Company showed initial interest in marketing Hoyer's idea, nothing was accomplished. Instead, the company offered to supply large quantities of dolls directly to the Hoyers at wholesale prices. The early dolls bear only the Ideal Doll markings. In 1937, Ideal ended this arrangement. Mary Hoyer then approached Bernard Lipfert, a well-known doll sculptor, to design a doll for her. Following Hoyer's specifications, Lipfert created the "perfect" doll. The Fiberoid Doll Company in New York produced the composition dolls until 1946, when hard plastic became available.

The Mary Hoyer Doll Manufacturing Company ceased production during the 1970s, closing the door on an American success story. Recently, the Mary Hoyer family reintroduced a beautiful vinyl Mary Hoyer Doll. The doll was warmly embraced by contemporary doll collectors and caused a renewed interest and demand for the original Mary Hoyer dolls.

Many collectors reject some Mary Hoyer Dolls because they assume that the doll has been given a hair cut. This is a mistake. Hoyer produced a boy doll that had either a fur wig or a regular wig with a ragged haircut. For positive identification of fashions, see Mary Hoyer's book, *Mary Hoyer and Her Dolls* (Hobby House Press, Inc., 1986). It is an invaluable source of information.

Composition

Prices listed are for original factory tagged, or authentic "Mary Hoyer Make-At-Home" costumed dolls in good condition. Slight crazing is acceptable and does not greatly affect the price. If badly crazed, cracked, peeling, or repainted, expect the value to be less than half the amounts listed.

Mary Hoyer: all composition; jointed at neck, shoulder, and hip; slim body; mohair wig; sleep eyes; real lashes; painted lower lashes; closed mouth; typically marked "The/Mary Hoyer/Doll."

Hard Plastic

Prices listed are for near-mint dolls in original factory tagged or authentic "Mary Hoyer Make-At-Home" costumes. If damaged, redressed or undressed, expect the value to be about one half the amounts listed.

Mary Hoyer: all hard plastic; jointed at neck, shoulder, and hip; synthetic wig; sleep eyes; real lashes; lower painted lashes; closed mouth; typically marked "Original/Mary Hoyer/Doll."

Mary Hoyer Value Comparisons			
Size	Composition	Hard Plastic	Boy Doll
14"	600.00	700.00	800.00
18"		2,000.00 (Gigi)	

Hard Plastic Mary Hoyer in tagged Hoyer gown with original box. This doll has remained with the original owner and was signed by Mary Hoyer at her shop during the early 1950's. Photograph courtesy of Bill Neff

Adolf Hülss

14" Adolf Hülss #156 bisque toddler. Courtesy of McMaster's Doll Auction

The Adolf Hülss doll factory began operating in Waltershausen, Germany, in 1913. It is generally accepted that the bisque heads were supplied by Simon & Halbig.

The good quality Hülss dolls are modelled as either dolly-face child dolls or character babies. Markings include the AHW trademark, which was registered in 1925, "Germany," and possibly a mold number.

Prices listed are for appropriately costumed dolls in good condition. Normal wear, slight damage, or well-made repairs to the body do not greatly affect the price. If the bisque is damaged or repaired, expect the value to be less than half the amounts listed. It is perfectly acceptable to show a missing or repaired finger or joint, or a mended body.

Character Baby: bisque socket head; composition, bent-limb baby body; good wig; glass eyes; open mouth with upper teeth; appropriately dressed; typically marked "Simon & Halbig/ AHW" within a circle "Made in Germany 156."

Dolly Face: bisque socket head; jointed wood-and-composition body; good wig; glass eyes; open mouth with upper teeth; appropriately dressed; typically marked "176" "A7H/Germany/ AHW" within a circle "Made in Germany."

Adolf Hülss Value Comparisons		
Size	Character Baby*	Dolly-Face Doll**
10"	600.00	
12"	700.00	
14"		850.00
16"	850.00	900.00
18"	950.00	950.00
20"	1,100.00	1,000.00
22"	1,400.00	1,200.00
24"	1,600.00	
26"		1,500.00
30"		1,800.00

* Add an additional $700.00 for a jointed toddler body.

** Add an additional $200.00 for flirty eyes or $300.00 for a high knee flapper body.

Maison Huret

Located in Paris, France, Huret was already an established toy company when, in the 1850s under the creative force of Mele Calixte Huret, it emerged as a French doll manufacturer. Huret was known for its beautifully made, gusseted kid and articulated wooden bodies. The firm pioneered numerous innovations, including the important socket swivel neck, patented in 1861.

Huret reportedly produced about 1,500 dolls a year, a rather modest figure when compared to other doll makers. Although child dolls were produced, Maison Huret is best known for its Mele Calixte's lady dolls.

Huret Dolls have a full, somewhat youthful face made of bisque or china, with glass or painted eyes; bodies were compo-

 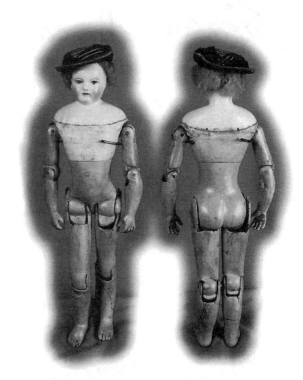

17" Huret Man and Lady. The man has a gutta percha body stamped "Brevet D'Inv: S. G. D. G. Masion Huret, Boulevard Montmartre, 22 Paris: Exposition Universelle de 1855, Napoleon III Empereur." The lady has a wooden jointed body with illegible stamp. Courtesy of McMaster's Doll Auction

sition, gutta-percha, kid, or wood with hands of bisque, china, composition, or metal. Huret first used astrakhan fur for wigs, later switching to the more satisfactory mohair. Dolls were dressed as ladies or children, in a workshop on the Rue de Choiseul.

Huret Dolls can often be dated by their markings. Those made in the 1850s bear the address "2 Boulevard des Italienos." Dolls produced from the mid- to late-1860s are marked "22 Boulevard Montmartre," and after 1870 "68 Rue de la Boetier." Unfortunately, stamped markings are sometimes worn away.

Reproduction Hurets have been reported. Check markings carefully. Ask questions. The doll's owner may know its history. Examine both the inside and the outside of the head. Many Huret Dolls have pressed, rather than poured, bisque heads. Beware of very clean and silky smooth bisque. The porcelain of an authentic Huret Doll will have a slightly textured and often peppered appearance.

Prices listed are for beautifully costumed dolls in good condition. Minimal wear to the body does not greatly affect the price. If the bisque is damaged or repaired or the integrity of the original body has been compromised, expect the value to directly reflect the degree of damage. The value of a Huret doll depends not only upon the porcelain head, but also the unusual body construction. It is perfectly acceptable to show a missing or repaired finger or joint, or other necessary maintenance.

Bébé: delicate bisque socket head; outstanding modelling; wooden-pin-and-dowel jointed body; articulated at neck, shoulder, hip, elbows, waist, knees, and ankles; well defined fingers and toes; wonderfully-detailed painted or almond-shaped paperweight eyes; softly shadowed eye lids; rouged cheeks; multi-stroked, feathered brows; pierced ears; outlined and shaded, closed mouth; beautifully dressed; typically marked "Huret 68 Rue de la Boetier" or other Paris address; body impressed "Huret."

Poupée: china, delicately tinted porcelain, or bisque; plump-cheeked socket or shoulder head; kid body; gutta percha, china, or stitched fingered kid forearms; skin or mohair wig; wonderfully-detailed painted or paperweight eyes; finely drawn, softly feathered brows; rouged cheeks; closed mouth; beautifully dressed; typically marked "Brevet D Inv. SGCG/Maison Huret/ Boulevard Monte Marte 22/Paris," "Huret 68 Rue de la Boetier," or other Paris address; body impressed "Huret."

Swivel Neck: bisque, swivel head; wooden body and limbs; metal spring joints; swivel waist; metal hands; good wig; paperweight or wonderfully-detailed painted eyes; soft, feathered brows; rouged cheeks; closed mouth; beautifully dressed; typically marked "Huret 68 Rue de la Boetier" or other Paris address; body impressed "Huret."

Huret Value Comparison						
Size	**Bébé, Wooden Body**	**Bébé, Gutta Percha Body**	**China Poupée, Kid Body**	**China Poupée, Gutta Percha Body**	**Bisque or Tinted Porcelain Poupée de Mode (Fashion-type), Kid Body**	**Bisque Swivel Neck Poupée on wooden body**	**China, Tinted Porcelain or Bisque Shoulder head Poupée de Mode (Fasion-type), Gutta Percha Body**
15"	35,000.00						22,000.00
17"		75,000.00	11,000.00	16,000.00	19,000.00	35,000.00	
18–18 1/2"		80,000.00			23,000.00	39,000.00	
19"	40,000.00						27,000.00
22"					30,000.00	45,000.00	

Ideal ® Novelty and Toy Company

*I*n 1902, Morris Mitchom and A. Cohn founded the Ideal Novelty and Toy Company for the express purpose of producing Mitchom's teddy bears. Mitchom's wife had made a pair of handmade stuffed bears for a window display for the small stationery store they owned in Brooklyn, New York. A newspaper cartoon concerning President Theodore Roosevelt's 1903 hunting trip in Mississippi served as her inspiration. The cartoon featured a frightened bear cub that had stumbled into Roosevelt's camp. Mitchom sent the President a sample of his "Teddy" and asked permission to name his stuffed bear after him. The President answered in a handwritten note: "I doubt if my name will mean much in the bear business, but you may use it if you wish." The rest is, as they say, Teddy Bear history. The Ideal Novelty and Toy Company was off to a tremendous start, and that was only the beginning.*

The 1930s were prime years for Ideal. The popularity of the Shirley Temple, Judy Garland, and Deanna Durbin dolls placed the company firmly in the forefront of the industry.

Ideal was one of the few large companies that made its own composition dolls. The company was a pioneer in making "unbreakable" dolls in America. They were so proficient that they supplied other manufacturers in addition to meeting their own needs. American Character, Arranbee, Eugenia, and Mary Hoyer were among Ideal's customers.

Ideal began experimenting with hard plastic in 1936 and was the first to market a hard plastic doll. Soon the wonderful Toni Dolls and the Play Pal Family of dolls brought as much recognition to Ideal as its earlier attempts at perfection. Play Pal children were sculpted according to measurements issued by the U.S. Bureau of Standards of Specifications. They could wear actual clothing of a child at the age of three months, one year, two years, three years, and an older child of ten or eleven years.

Also see Shirley Temple and Steiff.

Note: *The facts and information for this introduction were furnished by Ideal. There may be seemingly conflicting facts and information elsewhere about "Teddy Bears."*

Early composition Uneeda Biscuit Kid in original costume. Courtesy of David Cobb's Doll Auctions

Cloth

Prices listed are for appropriately costumed dolls with good color and little or no fading. If a doll is stained, torn, badly mended, or faded, expect the value to be less than half the amounts listed.

Cloth Character (Seven Dwarfs, Queen of Hearts, Snow White, Bo Peep, or Oz's Scarecrow): pressed oil cloth mask; cloth body; wool hair; painted facial features; appropriately dressed; typically marked with character's name printed on clothing.

12" $400.00
16" 800.00

Composition

Many composition dolls were made for various themes such as patriotism, comedy, literature, and the theater.

Prices listed are for appropriately costumed dolls in good condition. Slight crazing is acceptable and does not greatly affect the price. If badly crazed, cracked, peeling, or repainted, expect the value to be less than half the amounts listed.

Deanna Durbin: all composition; jointed at neck, shoulder, and hip; very dark brown, human hair wig; brown, sleep eyes; dark gray eye shadow; dimples on cheeks; open mouth with five teeth; appropriately dressed; marked "Deanna Durbin/Ideal toy Co."

Betty Jane: all composition; jointed at neck, shoulder, and hip; mohair wig; sleep eyes; open mouth with five teeth; appropriately dressed; typically marked "Ideal 18."

Judy Garland: all composition; jointed at neck, shoulder, and hip; dark brown, human hair wig; brown, sleep eyes; open mouth with six teeth; appropriately dressed; typically marked "Ideal Doll," "18/Ideal Doll/Made in USA" on back, "11/18" on upper left arm, "10" on upper right arm, and "18" on inside of both legs.

Snow White: all composition; jointed at neck, shoulder, and hip; black mohair wig; brown, flirty eyes; open mouth with four teeth; appropriately dressed; typically marked "Shirley Temple."

Child (Rosy, Teen Star, Little Princess, Pigtail Sally, or Ginger): all composition; jointed walker or non-walker body; good wig; sleep eyes; open or closed mouth; appropriately dressed; typically marked "IDEAL DOLL," "MADE IN USA/IDEAL DOLL."

Baby Mine: all composition; ball jointed body; wig; sleep eyes; open mouth with teeth; appropriately dressed; typically marked "Ideal" within a diamond/"U.S.A."; wrist tag "Baby Mine/USA IDEAL." **Note:** *Very similar in appearance and construction to the German dolly-face dolls.*

Snow White: composition shoulder head and limbs; cloth body; molded and painted black hair with molded blue or red bow; painted, side-glancing eyes; closed, smiling mouth; appropriately dressed; typically marked "IDEAL DOLL."

Mama/Child Doll (Bronco Bill (rodeo costume), **Buster** (sailor suit), **Dolly Varden** (low-waisted school dress), **Jenny Wren** (nicely designed dress and matching hair bow), **Sanitary Baby** ("can-wash," oilcloth body), **Columbia Kids** (four styles 12"–24", all patriotic red, white, and blue stars and stripes), **Flossie Flirt** (squared-off crier body), **Pretty Peggy** (smiling child, long lashes and flirty eyes)**):** composition head and limbs; cloth body; good wig; tin sleep eyes; closed mouth; appropriately dressed; typically marked "Ideal" within a diamond/"U.S.A." or "Ideal Doll/Made in USA."

Uneeda Biscuit Boy: composition head and limbs; cloth body; molded and painted hair; painted, blue eyes; closed mouth; original, yellow sateen rain slicker and hat; striped romper; molded and painted, black rain boots; marked with label on raincoat "Uneeda Biscuit/Pat'd Dec 8, 1914/Mfd by Ideal Novelty & Toy Co."

Snoozie: composition head and lower limbs; cloth body; molded and painted hair; celluloid over tin eyes; open, yawning mouth with molded tongue; appropriately dressed; typically marked "B. Lipfert."

Gorgeous: composition head, shoulder plate, and limbs; cloth body; good wig; sleep eyes; black eye shadow; closed mouth; appropriately dressed; typically marked "Ideal."

Babies (Hush-a-baby (orange hair and gray eyes), **Ticklette** (crier in each leg))**:** composition head; cloth body; rubberized limbs (advertised as "washable and soft as a baby's own"); molded and painted hair; sleep eyes; open mouth with teeth; appropriately dressed; marked "Ideal" within a diamond/ "U.S.A.," "USA Patents 1621434," and other Patents, "By B. Lipfert."

Baby Bi-Face (Soozie Smiles): composition hands and two-sided head; cloth body; character tearful and crying, or happy and smiling; molded and painted hair and facial features; appropriately dressed; typically marked "Ideal" within a diamond/"U.S.A."

Characters (Mr. Hooligan (plush body), **Dandy Kid, Ty Cobb** (1911 Baseball uniform), **Naughty Marietta** (molded hair bow), **The Country Cousins** (copyrighted and trademark registered with over fifty models within the series, all well designed, "farm costumes," and no shoes), **Russian Boy, Arctic Boy** (knit snow suit), **Admiral Dot** (sailor clad character from Barnum and Bailey Circus), **Jack Horner, Captain Jinks** (red-trimmed khaki suit), **ZuZu Kid** (clown))**:** composition head and hands; cloth body; molded and painted hair and facial features; appropriately dressed; typically marked "IDEAL" within a diamond and "US of A" at each point.

Betsy Wetsy: composition (Idonite) head; rubber (Truflesh), drink-and-wet body; molded and painted hair; sleep eyes; open nurser mouth; appropriately dressed; typically marked "Ideal."

12" Ideal Fanny Brice and Mortimer Snerd Flexy dolls. Courtesy of McMaster's Doll Auction

Wood Segmented Character (8 1/4" Jiminy Cricket, 10 1/2" Pinocchio, 11" Gabby, 13" Superman, and 14" King Little): composition character heads; wooden spool or segmented body, painted to represent the character's costume; occasionally, felt ornamentation was added; typically marked "Ideal."

Flexy Character (Mortimer Snerd, Sunny Sam, Sunny Sue, Fannie Brice, Baby Snooks, or Soldier): composition hands, feet, and character head; wooden, flexible, spring-jointed body; molded and painted hair; painted eyes; closed, smiling mouth; appropriately dressed; typically marked "Ideal Doll/Made in USA"; hang tag "The Doll of a Thousand Poses/Made in USA/A Flexy Doll (character name)."

Magic Skin

Ideal also manufactured dolls with "Magic Skin," an early synthetic material that looked and felt like human skin. Over time, Magic Skin becomes unstable and deteriorates, becoming badly discolored. The process may be slowed by regularly rubbing cornstarch into the doll. Early vinyl dolls produced in the late 1940s were a bit more stable, but still far from the durability of today's vinyl.

21" Ideal composition Deanna Durbin with original box. Courtesy of McMaster's Doll Auction

Sparkle Plenty, Plassie, Joan Palooka, Babies, Baby Brother and Sister, Coos, Pete and RePete: all latex (Magic Skin) or hard plastic head; Latex (Magic Skin) body; may have arms attached with metal disc at shoulder; yarn or molded and painted hair; insert or sleep eyes; closed mouth; appropriately dressed; typically marked "Made in U.S.A./Pat. No. 2252077."

Magic Skin Value Comparisons	
Size	Value
14"	125.00
18"	150.00
22"	235.00
25"	300.00

Hard Plastic & Vinyl

The first plastic doll was manufactured by Ideal in 1940, but was discontinued shortly thereafter due to war restrictions on materials. Ideal was a leader in the doll industry during the Hard Plastic era. Ideal's patent number for hard plastic was #2252077, and many different dolls can be found marked with this number.

Prices listed are for dolls in near-mint, original condition. If damaged, redressed, or undressed, expect the value to be less than one half to one fourth the amounts listed.

Toni Dolls (Miss Curity Nurse, Mary Hartline, Harriet Hubbard Ayer, and Betsy McCall): all hard plastic; jointed at neck, shoulder, and hip; synthetic wig; sleep eyes with real upper lashes; painted lower lashes; appropriately dressed; typically marked "P90-14," "P91-16," "P92-16," "P93-21," or "P94-22 1/2."

Sara Ann: another member of the Toni family, identical to Toni in every way—without the original box or hang tag, it is impossible to tell the dolls apart; Ideal manufactured Sara Ann in an attempt to save the royalties that went to the Toni Home Perm Co. for each Toni Doll sold. Sara Ann demanded no such royalties.

Saucy Walker: all hard plastic; walker body; jointed at neck, shoulder, and hip; synthetic wig; flirty, sleep eyes; open mouth with two upper teeth; appropriately dressed; typically marked "Ideal Doll."

Brother Coos: hard plastic head; cloth body; composition arms; molded and painted, curly hair; sleep eyes; closed mouth; appropriately dressed; typically marked "Ideal Doll/Made in USA."

Plassie: hard plastic head; cloth body; latex limbs; good wig; sleep eyes; open mouth with two upper teeth; felt tongue; appropriately dressed; typically marked "P-50/Ideal/Made in U.S.A.," "Ideal Doll/Made in U.S.A./Pat. No. 2252077."

Play Pal Family (24" Bonnie, Johnny, or Susy; 25" Miss Ideal; 32" Penny; 36" Pattie; 38" Peter; and 42" Daddy's Girl): vinyl head; plastic body; rooted hair; sleep eyes; smiling

Ideal Composition Value Comparisons										
Size	Deanna Durbin	Betty Jane	Judy Garland	Snow White All Composition	Child	Baby Mine	Snow White Composition and Cloth	Mama/Child Doll*	Uneeda Biscuit
12"				700.00					
13"							550.00	425.00	
14"	900.00			400.00				450.00	
15"	1,000.00	450.00					600.00		
16"			1,800.00			500.00		525.00	650.00
17"	1,100.00								
18"		600.00	2,300.00	900.00	600.00			550.00	
19"	1,200.00								
21"	1,400.00							600.00	
22"						600.00		700.00	
24"	1,800.00								1,000.00

*Add an additional $200.00 for original character costumes.

Size	Snoozie	Gorgeous	Babies	Baby Bi-Face	Characters*	Betsy Wetsy	Wood Segmented	Flexy Characters
8 1/4"							550.00	
10 1/2"							600.00	
11"					500.00	175.00	700.00	
12"								450.00
13"							750.00	
14"				550.00	550.00	225.00	800.00	
16"	500.00		500.00	650.00	600.00	275.00		
17"		500.00						
21"	600.00				700.00		1,200.00	
22"		600.00						

* Add an additional $300.00 for original Ty Cobb doll.

Ideal 30" Betty Big Girl marked "1968 / Ideal Toy Corp / HD 31 – H – 121," valued at $400.00; and 32" vinyl head Saucy Walker with rooted hair. Courtesy of David Cobb's Doll Auctions

mouth; appropriately dressed; typically marked "Ideal Doll O.E.B-24-3-/Ideal" or "Ideal Toy Corp./SP-#" (# = height of doll).

Growing Hair Crissy: vinyl head; plastic body; rooted, auburn hair with center ponytail; lengthen hair by pulling ponytail; big, dark brown eyes; smiling, open/closed mouth with molded teeth; appropriately dressed; typically marked "1968/Ideal Toy Corp/GH-17-H 129," "1969/Ideal Toy Corp/GH-18 US Pat Pend. # 3,162,976." ***Note:*** *Crissy series includes her cousins Velvet and Cinnamon; her friends Cricket, Tara, Kerry, Brandi, and Tessy; Velvet's friends Mia and Dina; and Baby Crissy.*

Miss Revlon: vinyl head; solid vinyl body; jointed at neck, shoulder, hip and waist; rooted hair; sleep eyes; pierced ears; closed, unsmiling mouth; polished fingernails and toenails; marked "Ideal Doll/VT" and size number

Thumbelina: vinyl head and hands; cloth body; rooted hair; painted eyes; open/closed mouth; appropriately dressed; mechanism in center back makes her wiggle; marked "Ideal Toy Corp/©TT-19."

Sara Lee: black vinyl head and limbs; cloth body; life-like features; molded and painted hair; brown, sleep eyes; open/closed mouth; appropriately dressed; typically marked "Ideal Doll." Doll was named after designer Sara Lee Creech.

Kiss Me: vinyl head and limbs; cloth body; molded, brown hair; painted, squinting eyes; frowning expression with wide open/closed mouth; mouth opens and closes when back is pressed; appropriately dressed; typically marked "S3/Ideal Doll/Pat. Pending."

Judy Splinters: vinyl character head and limbs; cloth body; yarn hair; large, painted eyes; wide, open/closed, smiling mouth; appropriately dressed; typically marked "Ideal Doll."

National Velvet: (Lori Martin from NBC TV series); beautifully modelled vinyl head; hard plastic body; jointed at neck, shoulder, hip, ankles, and swivel or non-swivel waist; graceful

Ideal Hard Plastic & Vinyl Value Comparisons

Size	Toni/Sara Ann	Betsy McCall and Miss Curity	Mary Hartline	Harriet Hubbard Ayer	Saucy Walker	Brother Coos	Plassie	Play Pal Family
14"	500.00	500.00	450.00	250.00		300.00		
15"					175.00			
16"	600.00		600.00	300.00	200.00			
17"							200.00	
18"					250.00	350.00		
19"	750.00			350.00			225.00	
20"					300.00			
21"	900.00			450.00				
22"						300.00	250.00	
22 1/2"	1,100.00		900.00					
24"								350.00
25"								600.00
27"					400.00			
32"								450.00
36"								650.00
38"								800.00
42"								1,500.00

Size	Growing Hair Crissy	Black Growing Hair Crissy	Cinnamon	Cricket/Tara	Kerry/ Brandi/ Tressy	Mia & Dina	Velvet	Black Velvet	Baby Crissy
11 1/2"			75.00						
15 1/2"				60.00		100.00	75.00	100.00	
17 1/2"	125.00	175.00			80.00				
24"									100.00

Ideal Vinyl and Vinyl Combination Value Comparisons

Size	Miss Revlon	Thumbelina	Black Thumbelina	Sara Lee	Kiss Me	Judy Splinters	National Velvet
10"	200.00						
11"		150.00	200.00				
15"		175.00					
17"			250.00	500.00			
18"	300.00			550.00	250.00	300.00	
20"		200.00				500.00	
21"					275.00		
22"	350.00						
30"							1,200.00
36"	400.00					600.00	
38"							1,700.00

hands; rooted, long, dark hair; blue, sleep eyes; closed, slightly-smiling mouth; original plaid blouse, jeans, boots, and scarf; marked "Metro-Goldwyn-Mayer Inc./MFG by/IDEAL TOY CORP./38//G-38" or "/30//G30."

Little Lost Baby: 22"; three-faced, vinyl head; foam stuffed suit encased body; one face smiling awake, one sleeping, and one crying, all with molded and painted features; lever at base of neck turns head; marked with tag "Little Lost Baby/1968 Ideal Toy Corp" $175.00

Cuddly Kissy: 17"; vinyl head; cloth body; rooted hair; sleep eyes; open/closed mouth; appropriately dressed; press stomach, and hands come together, head tilts forward, lips pucker, and doll makes a kissing sound; marked "Ideal Toy Corp/KB-17-E" $175.00

Bonnie Braids: 13"; vinyl head; hard plastic body; jointed at shoulder and hip; molded and painted hair with saran braids coming through holes on each side of head; blue, sleep eyes with real lashes; open mouth with three painted teeth; original dress; typically marked "1951/Chicago Tribune/Ideal Doll" $350.00

Dorothy Hamil: 11 1/2"; vinyl head and arms; plastic body; bendable legs; rooted hair; painted eyes; open/closed mouth with painted teeth; appropriately dressed; typically marked "1977 DH/Ideal" within oval, "H-282/Hong Kong" on head, "1975/Ideal" in oval on hip, and "U.S. Pat. No. 3903640/Hollis NY 11423/Hong Kong P" $75.00

Tammy: 12"; vinyl head and arms; plastic body; jointed at neck, shoulder, and hip; rooted hair; painted, side-glancing eyes; closed mouth; appropriately dressed; typically marked "Ideal Toy Corp./B-5 12," "Ideal Toy Corp/B-5 12-1/2" $150.00

Tammy's family:

Big Brother Ted: 12 1/2"; typically marked "B-12 1/2 M-2" $175.00

Mother: 12 1/2"; typically marked "W-1 3 L" or "W-13" 225.00

Father: 13"; typically marked "M13–2" or "B–12 1/2" 175.00

Little Sister Pepper: 9"; typically marked "6-9 W/2," "G9W," or "P-9DD-9-6" 100.00

Little Brother Freckled-Face Pete: 8"; typically marked "P-8" 250.00

Peppers Friend Patti: 9"; typically marked "P-9" or "G-9-W" 300.00

Peppers Friend Dodi: 9"; typically marked "DO-9-E" 100.00

Peppers Freckled-Face Friend Salty: 8"; original baseball cap, glove, bat, ball, and catcher's mask; typically marked "P-8" 350.00

Tammy's Boyfriend Bud: 12 1/2"; typically marked "B-12 1/2 M-2" 300.00

007 James Bond: 12 1/2"; vinyl head and arms; plastic body; molded and painted hair and facial features; appropriately dressed; typically marked "Ideal Toy Corp/B-12-1/2-2".$150.00

Tiffany Taylor: 14"; vinyl head; shapely plastic body; jointed at neck, shoulder, and hip; swivel cap wig (spins to change hair color from blond to brunette); painted eyes; closed mouth; appropriately dressed; typically marked "1974/Ideal" in an oval, "Hollis, NY 11423/2M 5854 01/2" "1973/CG-19-H-230" $100.00

Bye-Bye Baby: 25"; vinyl head; plastic body; nicely molded, lifelike hands and feet; softly molded and painted hair; sleep eyes; open nurser mouth; appropriately dressed; typically marked "Ideal Toy Corp./HB-25" $500.00

Kissy: 22"; vinyl head; plastic body; rooted hair; sleep eyes; open/closed mouth; appropriately dressed; typically marked "® IDEAL/IDEAL CORP./K-21-L//IDEAL TOY CORP. K-22 PAT. PEND." **Note:** *Kissy dolls made a kissing sound, advertised as "Go get Kissy if you want a little kiss, do her arms like this [squeeze arms together] she'll give a little kiss."* $250.00

Kissin Cousins: 11 1/2" $100.00
Tiny Kissy Baby: 16" $150.00

Ideal Tammy in original condition. Courtesy of McMaster's Doll Auction

Posey (Posie): 17"; vinyl head; hard plastic, walker body; rooted hair; sleep eyes; closed mouth; appropriately dressed; typically marked "VP17 Ideal Doll" $250.00

Baby Ruth: 16"; vinyl head and limbs; waterproof cloth body; rooted hair; sleep eyes; open/closed mouth; beautiful, organdy outfits; typically marked "16/IDEAL DOLL"...$350.00

Giggles: 16"; vinyl head; plastic body; giggles and moves loosely-jointed arms; rooted hair; sleep eyes; open/closed, smiling mouth; appropriately dressed; typically marked "1966 Ideal Toy Corp./G G 18 H 17" $125.00

Little Boy: 23"; all vinyl; bent legs; beautifully molded, curly hair; sleep eyes; closed mouth; appropriately dressed; typically marked "IDEAL DOLL/B 23" $300.00

Little Girl: 18"; vinyl head; rigid, vinyl body; rooted hair; sleep eyes; dimpled, closed, grinning mouth; appropriately dressed; typically marked "Ideal Doll/B-19-1" $250.00

Liz: 15"; vinyl head; rigid, vinyl body; rooted hair; dramatically painted and lined, side-glancing eyes; closed mouth; original undergarments; typically marked "©/IDEAL TOY CORP./M-15-1"..$200.00

Patti Playful: 15"; vinyl head and limbs; cloth body; turn-knob activates movements of head, arms, yawning, clapping hands, waving, sucking thumb, opening and closing eyes; rooted hair; dark sleep eyes; open/closed mouth with molded tooth; original outfit embroidered "Patti Playful"; typically marked "1970/Ideal Doll Corp./LL-16-H-162" $225.00

Belly Button Baby: 9"; vinyl head and limbs; rigid vinyl body; rooted hair; painted eyes; 3 types: **Me So Silly:** closed mouth with tongue out; **Me So Glad:** closed, smiling mouth, black or white version; **Me So Happy:** open/closed, laughing mouth; appropriately dressed; typically marked "1970/Ideal Toy Corp./E-9-5-H159/Hong Kong//Ideal Toy Corp 2-A-0156" $125.00

Lazy Dazy: 11"; white or black vinyl head and hands; cloth body; in sitting position; slowly goes to sleep and falls onto pillow; rooted hair; sleep eyes; closed mouth; original nightie and matching pillow; typically marked "© 1971/Ideal Toy Inc. Corp. L B-12-H-197"...$100.00

Illfelder Spielwaren

*I*llfelder was an export company with offices in Furth, Germany and New York City. From 1869, the German distributor, Max Illfelder, assembled and exported all types of toys and dolls to the United States. In 1918, Illfelder stopped buying better German bisque and began using more affordable Japanese bisque. Soon after (sometime during the early 1920s), Illfelder went out of business.

Trade names registered by Illfelder include Rosebud, My Sweetheart, Merry Widow, Billy Possum, and Bumble Puppy.

Prices listed are for appropriately dressed dolls in good condition. Normal wear, slight damage, or well-made repairs to the body do not greatly affect the price. If the bisque is damaged or repaired, expect the value to be less than half the amounts listed. It is perfectly acceptable to show a missing or repaired finger or a mended body.

Better Quality Dolly-Face: bisque socket head; jointed wood and composition body; good wig; glass eyes; feathered or shaped brows; open mouth; appropriately dressed; typically marked "Germany," "101," "My Sweetheart," Merry Widow," "Rosebud A M," "B J & Co," or "B J."

Standard Quality Dolly-Face: bisque socket head; jointed wood and composition body; mohair wig; glass eyes; single stroke or stenciled brows; open mouth; appropriately dressed; typically marked "My Sweetheart/Nippon," "Nippon 501," "Merry Widow," or "B J Nippon."

20" Illfelder child doll marked "BJ & Co. 101 My Sweetheart / Germany." Courtesy of David Cobb's Doll Auctions

	Illfelder Value Comparison	
Size	**Better Quality, Dolly-Face**	**Standard Quality, Dolly-Face**
16"	575.00	300.00
20"	650.00	350.00
24"	750.00	450.00
30"	1,400.00	

Japanese Dolls

15" earlier Yamato Ningyo, 13" later Ischimatus May Ling in case with accessories, 15" Later Yamato Ningyo, and a pair of traditional babies. Courtesy of David Cobb's Doll Auctions

*I*n Japan, the art of doll making is a tradition that has been handed down from one generation to the next. Many dolls are created to be more than just children's playthings. There are more than 300 different types of Japanese dolls, some of which were commercially produced as early as the 16th century. Most Japanese dolls originally had a ritual significance with religious associations, and they were made for decorative purposes. For example, the Boys' Day and Girls' Day Festival dolls are part of the Japanese culture, symbolizing chivalry, bravery, and loyalty to country and emperor.

The Girls' Day Festival (Hina Matsuri), celebrated as early as the 1400s, was intended to instill the virtues of patriotism and domesticity in young girls and to honor the Imperial family. The holiday is still celebrated in Japan on March 3, the peak of the peach blossom season. Several days before the festival, mothers and daughters take their dolls from storage and display them on steps (hina dan) covered with red silk. A set of dolls traditionally consists of fifteen figures. The Emperor and Empress are placed on the top with the court musician, ladies in waiting, guard, and dancers on lower steps.

The Boys' Day Feast of Flags Festival (Tanono Sekka) is celebrated on May 5. Banners in the shape of a carp—the fish signifying fortitude—are flown outside the houses of young boys. Inside, an array of fierce-looking dolls, symbolizing strength, valor, and adventure, are displayed on a cloth-covered, tiered stand. The dolls represent warriors such as Monotaro, Yoshitsumen, and Kato Kiyomasa, as well as commanders, generals, and wrestlers. Each year a boy receives a new doll to add to his set, reminding him of the vestiges of Japanese chivalry and the Samurai.

Antique Festival Dolls are treasured family heirlooms. Newer versions along with play dolls (Ichimatsu) and child dolls (Yamato Ningyo) are popular collectibles.

The exceptionally beautiful, unmarked Japanese dolls have perfectly white faces. The porcelain-like finish is made of polished gofun, a fine white composition of pulverized oyster shell and glue. It is not unusual for a doll's head to have twenty to thirty coats of gofun. All dolls are gorgeously costumed in nonremovable clothing made from materials specially woven in miniature patterns. When appropriate, they are equipped with armor and weapons. The traditional glass-eyed Japanese dolls portray three distinct classes—the Royal group, the Samurai, and the peasants.

In the early years of the 20th century, many dolls with Oriental faces and costumes were made in Europe and the United States. Those dolls should not be confused with the classic Japanese dolls made in Japan.

Later Yamato Ningyo of standard quality are commonly found. In 1927 alone, more than 10,000 dolls were sent to the United States as part of a good-will exchange. The dolls, depicting children ages six or seven, were dressed in costumes representing different regions of Japan.

The labor-intensive workmanship needed to achieve the look of the gofun, and the dolls' intricate costuming, make them unsuitable for the reproduction market. There are, however, levels of quality of authentic Japanese dolls.

Prices listed are for dolls in near-mint, original condition. If damaged, redressed, or undressed, expect the value to be less than one half to one fourth the amounts listed.

Early Hina-Ningyo (Festival Dolls): c. 1870; beautiful composition head, coated with several layers of highly polished gofun; straw body; long-fingered, composition hands, painted white to match face; hair stippled around face; silk thread wig; glass eyes; closed mouth; original, elaborate robe; obi and headdress; seated on fret worked, lacquered, or silk-covered wooden platform; unmarked.

Later Hina-Ningyo (Festival Dolls): c. 1920; composition head, coated with gofun; paper-wound body in permanent position; long-fingered, composition hands, painted white; silk thread hair; glass eyes; feathered brows; finely-painted lower lashes; closed mouth; original silk robes and tin headdress; seated on painted or cloth-covered wooden platform; unmarked.

Early Ichimatus (Play Dolls): c. 1850; papier-mâché socket head, coated with gofun; papier-mâché shoulder plate extending to chest area; papier-mâché hips, lower legs, and lower arms, connected with cloth (floating joints); hair stippled around face; fine human hair wig; black, glass eyes; finely-painted, feathered brows; no lashes; pierced ears and nostrils; closed mouth; original, elaborate costume; wooden, painted sandals with silk tassels; unmarked.

Later Ichimatus (Play Dolls): c. 1920, papier-mâché socket-head, coated with gofun; composition body and limbs, painted pink; jointed at shoulder and hip; black, silk hair; brown, glass eyes; feathered brows; no lashes; pierced nostrils; closed mouth; original, multi-colored, floral kimono with large obi and silk slippers; unmarked.

Early Sakura-Ningyo (Cherry Dolls/Traditional Lady Statue Dolls): c. 1890; beautiful, oyster shell composition socket head; layers of highly polished gofun; well-shaped torso with rounded belly and molded bosom; composition lower limbs, painted to match head; cloth upper arms and thighs; hair stippled around face; floor length human hair wig, styled around gilt metal comb, adorning hair; insert glass eyes; painted brows; no lashes; closed mouth, finely outlined with deep red; original, long, silk kimono over white damask shorter Kimono; carrying wooden fan with hand-painted decorations; unmarked.

Later Sakura-Ningyo (Cherry Dolls/Traditional Lady Statue Dolls): c. 1920; oyster shell composition socket head, coated with gofun; slim, straw-stuffed body; graceful hands with long fingers; black, silk wig in elaborate style with ornate hair combs; black, glass eyes; feathered brows; very fine lower lashes; closed mouth; original silk kimono with long sleeves, wide obi, and silk jacket; holding painted umbrella or fan; unmarked.

Modern Sakura-Ningyo (Cherry Dolls/Traditional Lady Statue Dolls): silk, mask-type face; wire armature body, padded with strips of cotton; black floss wig in upsweep style; painted eyes; closed mouth; original kimono with wide sleeves; often holding red, disk-type hat or fan; on varnished wood; stamped "Made in Japan."

Early Benkei Warrior: c. 1875; papier-mâché head, coated with several layers of gofun and painted flesh color; straw and paper body; long-fingered, composition hands, painted to match face; molded feet; glass eyes; winged brows; long, black silk beard; closed mouth; original silk brocade kimono, silk obi, and hooded brocade headdress and kabuto; holding weapon; unmarked.

Later Benkei Warrior: c. 1900; composition head, coated with gofun and painted flesh color; body with padded, non-removable costume; black, silk wig; glass eyes; winged brows; closed mouth; original, padded silk brocade robes; holding weapons; on cut-out, painted, and lacquered wooden platform; unmarked.

Early Yamato Ningyo (Japanese Child) Mitsuore: c. 1890; composition socket head, coated with a gofun and painted flesh color; composition body and arms; molded male sex organs portrayed in detail; hair delicately stippled with fine writing brush; brown, glass eyes; closed mouth; large, molded ears; original, brocade kimono tied with silk obi; unmarked.

Later Yamato Ningyo (Japanese Child) Mitsuore: c. 1920; composition head, coated with gofun and painted flesh color; composition body, lower arms, and legs, connected to body with cloth (floating joints); black, silk hair; brown, glass eyes; closed mouth; original kimono with large obi and silk tie sandals; unmarked.

Baby: c. 1910–1930; composition socket head, coated with gofun and painted flesh color; jointed wooden or bent-limb composition baby body; painted hair or short, silk wig; glass eyes; pierced nostrils; open/closed mouth with molded tongue; appropriately dressed; unmarked.

Japanese Dolls Value Comparisons

Size	Hina-Ningyo Early	Hina-Ningyo Later	Ichimatus Early	Ichimatus Later	Sakura-Ningyo Early	Sakura-Ningyo Later
10"	1,500.00	400.00	700.00	200.00		
12"			800.00	225.00	800.00	400.00
14"	2,000.00	600.00	1,000.00	275.00	1,000.00	500.00
16"	2,500.00	700.00	1,200.00	300.00	1,200.00	550.00
18"	3,500.00	750.00	1,400.00	375.00	1,400.00	
20"			1,450.00			
22"			1,600.00	400.00		
24"			1,800.00	450.00		
26"			2,000.00	475.00		
28"				500.00		
30"			2,500.00	600.00		

Size	Sakura-Ningyo Modern	Warrior Early	Warrior Late	Yamato Ningyo Early	Yamato Ningyo Later	Baby
10"	70.00					
12"	80.00					300.00
14"	90.00	1,300.00	500.00	2,500.00	250.00	350.00
16"	100.00	1,400.00	550.00	2,700.00	300.00	400.00
18"		1,700.00	600.00	3,000.00	325.00	
20"				3,200.00	350.00	
22"		2,500.00		3,600.00	400.00	

Jullien

The beautiful Jullien Bébés were made in Paris, France, from about 1863 until 1904. Research concerning Jullien Bébés is inconclusive. There appears to have been more than one factory operating under the name "Jullien." More than likely they were interconnected, perhaps one was the porcelain factory, another decorated the heads, and yet another assembled the dolls. It is also unclear exactly when Jullien began to produce bisque doll heads, although it is assumed that Jullien was one of the early French doll makers. Records confirm that Jullien purchased at least some doll heads from Francois Gaultier. The lovely bisque heads are marked "Jullien." Dolls have also been found marked "JJ," but it is not known with any certainly whether these are Jullien, Jeune, Jules Jeanson, or Joseph Joanny dolls.

While reproduction French Bébés abound, Jullien Bébés do not seem to be as plagued by this misfortune as other dolls. A routine inspection should be sufficient to dispel any doubt.

Prices listed are for appropriately costumed dolls in good condition. Normal wear, slight damage, or well-made repairs to the body do not greatly affect the price. If the bisque is damaged or repaired, expect the value to be less than half the amounts listed. It is perfectly acceptable to show a missing or repaired finger or joint, or a mended body.

Early Closed Mouth Bébé: bisque socket head; jointed wood-and-composition body; good wig; paperweight eyes, long painted lashes; nicely feathered, multi-stroke brows; pierced ears; closed mouth with slight white space between lips; very softly blushed; appropriately dressed; marked "Jullien."

Later Closed Mouth Bébé: bisque socket head; jointed wood-and-composition body; good wig; paperweight eyes; long, sparse lashes; single stroke or poorly applied brows; pierced ears; closed mouth; appropriately dressed; marked "Jullien."

Open Mouth Bébé: bisque socket head; jointed wood-and-composition body; good wig; paperweight eyes; long, painted lashes, feathered brows; pierced ears; open mouth; appropriately dressed; marked "Jullien."

Open mouth Jullien. Courtesy of David Cobb's Doll Auctions

Early closed mouth Jullien. Photograph by P. Byron. Courtesy of Ellen Schroy

Jullien Bébé Value Comparisons

Size	Early Closed Mouth	Later Closed Mouth	Open Mouth
15"	3,900.00	2,500.00	1,500.00
17"	4,100.00	2,800.00	1,800.00
19"	4,500.00	3,100.00	2,000.00
21"	4,900.00	3,500.00	2,200.00
23"	5,100.00	3,900.00	2,400.00
25"	5,400.00	4,000.00	2,700.00
27"			3,000.00
29"			3,500.00

Jumeau

Pierre Francois Jumeau began manufacturing dolls in Paris and Montreuil-sous-Bois, France, about 1842, in a partnership called Belton & Jumeau. Although the death of Belton brought the partnership to an end, Jumeau continued creating exquisite bisque Bébés. Pierre Jumeau planned to have his eldest son, George, take over the business upon his retirement. However, George died very suddenly, and when Pierre retired in 1877–1878, his second son, Emile Jumeau assumed the responsibilities. Emile had studied to be an architect, but when forced to take over the family doll making business, he resolved to make France the world leader in the doll industry. Collectors eagerly seek his magnificent Bébés—true works of art, even a casual observer would have to be impressed by their elegant beauty. The Metropolitan Museum of Art defines art as "including objects that had a true sense of time and place." According to this definition, antique dolls can be considered perfect examples.

When attempting to date or authenticate a doll, remember that bisque doll heads made prior to 1890 were pressed into molds; after 1890 liquid slip was poured.

Today's sophisticated collector has more accurately defined the distinction between spectacular and mediocre quality dolls. Hence, prices for seemingly identical dolls can vary a great deal. When evaluating a Jumeau Bébé or Poupée de Modes, remember the ever important "visual appeal factor."

Jumeau doll head markings vary considerably. The most commonly found mark is the "Tete Jumeau" stamp and a red artist check mark. Earlier Jumeaus can be found marked "E. J." with a size number. The rare, long faced Jumeau, as well as other portrait Jumeaus, are marked with a size number only. Recent reports indicate that Maison Jumeau released Bébés that did not meet his impeccable standards of excellence. These lesser-quality Bébés were sold as "seconds" and were unmarked. It is also known that during the 1890s several Paris stores sold less expensive dolls made by Jumeau, which were unmarked.

Reproduction Jumeau dolls are common. Being armed with some basic information should help eliminate any confusion. Check the marking for a doll artist's name, initials, or a date. Copies are often made for the enjoyment of the doll maker, never intended as a fraud, and will be well marked. Markings on the body should match those on the head. Examine the inside of the doll's head. Early bisque will show evidence of being pressed. On dolls larger than 20", the ears were applied, not molded. When evaluating an antique doll, attention must be paid to details.

Prices listed are for beautifully dressed dolls in good condition. Normal wear, slight damage, or well-made repairs to the body do not greatly affect the price. If the bisque is damaged or repaired, expect the value to be less than half the amounts listed. It is perfectly acceptable to show a missing or repaired finger or joint, or a mended body.

See Daniel et Cie., Automator, and Oriental.

Poupée de Modes (Fashion-Type Dolls): bisque socket head; kid-lined shoulder plate; kid body; slender waist; kid arms; stitched fingers; good wig; paperweight eyes; finely feathered brows; pierced ears; closed mouth; pronounced lip bow; beautifully dressed; body stamped in blue "JUMEAU/Medaille D'Or PARIS"; head marked with a size number only, or a red artist check mark.

19" Jumeau Fashion Lady. Courtesy of David Cobb's Doll Auctions

Portrait Jumeau Bébé: pressed bisque socket head; French, straight-wrist, wood-and-composition body; eight separate balls at joints; good wig; large, almond-shaped, beautiful, spiral, threaded enamel, paperweight eyes; may have tri-color irises; feathered brows; pierced ears; closed mouth; beautifully dressed; body stamped in blue "JUMEAU/Medaille D'Or/PARIS"; head marked with a size number only. "Déposé" and a size number, or a size number only (do not confuse with Déposé Jumeau, Déposé Tete, or Déposé E. J.—this particular bébé was marked only "Déposé" along with a size number). ***Note****: The Portrait Déposé Bébé has recently been given several distinct classifications. The following chart should help you distinguish between the types.*

16" second series or duet Portrait Jumeau marked only "7." Courtesy of David Cobb's Doll Auctions

17" Portrait Déposé Jumeau marked "Déposé 7" with original skin wig. Courtesy of David Cobb's Doll Auctions

	Standard or Premiere	Bébé Duet or Second Series	Almond Eyed	Déposé Sized
Bisque	Very pale, peppering is common	Delicately blushed	Delicately blushed	Delicately blushed
Paperweight Eyes	Deep cut	Defined eye lid	Very almond shaped, spiral threaded enamel	Oval shaped
Brows	Wide spaced, thin and feathered	Wide spaced, semi-full and feathered	Wide spaced, nicely shaped and feathered	Wide spaced, slightly full and feathered
Face shape	Round	Very full cheeks, almost square-shaped	Full cheeks, oval-shaped	Full cheeks, oval-shaped
Size number	#1-9", #3-16", expect variations in size numbers	#6-14", #8-19", #10-21", #12-25"	#4/0-12", #0-16", #3-20", #5-25"	#3-12", #6-16", #9-21", #11-25"

Long Face Triste: pressed bisque socket head; French, straight-wrist, wood-and-composition body; eight separate balls at joints; good wig; luminous, oval paperweight eyes; wide-spaced, feathered brows; applied pierced ears; closed mouth; beautifully dressed; typically marked with size number (9–16) only; stamped in blue ink "JUMEAU/Medaille D'OR/PARIS."
Note: *Designed by Carrier Belleuse, the chief designer for Sévres. Referred to as "Triste" because of the doll's sad, solemn, pensive expression.*

E. J. Jumeau Bébé: bisque head; jointed, wood-and-composition body; good wig; beautiful paperweight eyes; feathered brows; pierced ears, applied on larger sizes; closed mouth; appropriately dressed.

> **Early:** pressed bisque; substantial, almost chubby; straight wrists; eight separate balls at joints; marked with size number above "E.J."; body stamped in blue "JUMEAU/Medaille D'Or/Paris."
>
> **Mid:** poured or pressed bisque; trimmer, French bodies with jointed wrists and attached ball joints; marked with size number between "E" and "J"; body stamped in blue "Jumeau/Medaille D'Or/

Paris," or with oval paper label "Bébé Jumeau/ Diplome d'Honneur."
> **Late:** poured bisque; trimmer, French bodies; straight or jointed wrists; attached ball joints; marked with "DÉPOSE" above "E. J."; body stamped in blue "JUMEAU/Medaille D'Or/ Paris," or with oval paper label "Bébé Jumeau/ Diplome d'Honneur."

E. J. A. Bébé: bisque socket head; composition-and-wood chubby bodies with straight wrists; narrow, almond-shaped eyes; closely resembles the portrait Jumeau; 25"–26"; closed mouth; beautifully dressed; marked "E.J.A."; body stamped "JUMEAU/ Medaille D'Or/PARIS."

Déposé Jumeau Bébé: bisque socket head; French, straight- or jointed-wrist, wood-and-composition body; separate balls at joints; good wig; paperweight eyes with deep sockets; softly feathered brows; pierced ears; closed mouth with slight space between lips; beautifully dressed; marked "DÉPOSÉ/ JUMEAU"; body stamped in blue "JUMEAU/Medaille D'Or/ PARIS."

28" Long Face Triste Bébé marked "13." Courtesy of David Cobb's Doll Auctions

18" Early E. J. Bébé, note applied ears marked "6" above "EJ." Courtesy of David Cobb's Doll Auctions

26" EJA Jumeau Bébé in original dress marked "EJA 12." Courtesy of David Cobb's Doll Auctions

20" Incised Déposé Jumeau Bébé, note the deep eye sockets, marked "Déposé Jumeau 9." Courtesy of David Cobb's Doll Auctions

20" closed mouth Tete Jumeau, all original with box. Courtesy of David Cobb's Doll Auctions

23" open mouth Jumeau Bébé #10. Courtesy of David Cobb's Doll Auctions

Rare laughing character incised "208" and stamped "Déposé Tete Jumeau/ Bte SGDG 10," open-closed mouth with molded teeth and tongue, applied pierced ears, wig not original. Photograph Sotheby's of New York. Courtesy Ellen Schroy

Tete Jumeau Bébé: poured bisque socket head; French, straight- or jointed-wrist, wood-and-composition, ball-jointed body; good wig; large, lustrous, paperweight eyes; heavy, feathered brows; pierced ears; closed mouth; beautifully dressed; marked with red stamp "Déposé Tete Jumeau Bte SGDG"; body stamped in blue "Jumeau/Medaille D'Or/Paris," or with oval paper label "Bébé Jumeau/Diplome d'Honneur." *Note: Adult-faced Tete Jumeau with shapely woman's body; stamped with red "Tete Jumeau" mark.*

ED Bébé: produced while Emile Douillet was director (1892–1899); bisque socket head; French, wood-and-composition, ball-jointed body; good wig; paperweight eyes; feathered brows; pierced ears; closed mouth; beautifully dressed; marked "ED" and a size number only. *Note: If the word "Déposé" is included in the marking, see French Bébé.*

Paris Bébé/Français: (after the 1892 judgment) lovely, heart-shaped, bisque socket head; French, wood-and-composition, ball-jointed body; distinct aquiline nose; good wig; paperweight eyes; pierced ears; closed, slightly-smiling mouth; beautifully dressed. Marked "B F" or "Paris Bébé"; body may be stamped or have a paper label.

Open Mouth Bébé: poured bisque socket head; French, wood-and-composition, ball-jointed body with jointed wrists; good wig; large, paperweight eyes; heavy, feathered brows; molded, pierced ears; open mouth with molded upper teeth; beautifully dressed; marked with red stamps "Tete Jumeau," "Déposé Tete Jumeau Bte SGDG," and/or incised "1907"; body may have paper label "Bébé Jumeau Diplome d'Honneur."

S.F.B.J. Dolls (such as 221, 230, and 301): may be marked "Jumeau."

Jumeau Character Doll: expressive character face; glass eyes; French, jointed-composition body; most are marked with the red Tete stamp. Dolls numbering from 201 to 225 are assumed to be German origin but released as Jumeau Character Dolls; character dolls with mold numbers higher than 226 are generally marked "S.F.B.J."; Jumeau characters include a mischievous child, a laughing child, a gorgeously-sculptured lady with a heart-shaped face, an African woman with worry lines, and so on.

Jumeau Value Comparisons

Size	Poupée de Modes Kid Body*	Poupée de Modes Kid Body Extraordinary*	Standard or Premiere	Bébé Duet or Second Series	Almond-Shaped Eyes	Déposé Size
10"	2,000.00		5,400.00			
11"			6,000.00			
12"					17,000.00	
13"	3,500.00			9,000.00		
14"		5,000.00	7,000.00			
15"						8,000.00
17"	4,400.00	6,000.00		10,000.00	23,000.00	
19"	4,800.00	7,200.00	9,000.00			10,000.00
20 1/2"				12,500.00	38,000.00	
22"	5,000.00					
23"			11,000.00			
24"	5,500.00			22,000.00	58,000.00	
26"		11,000.00				

*Add an additional $1,500.00 for Jumeau Poupée de Modes with stamped wooden bodies.

Size	Long Face Triste, Closed Mouth, Jointed Body	Early E.J. Jumeau Bébé, Closed Mouth, Jointed Body	Mid E.J. Jumeau Bébé, Closed Mouth, Jointed Body	Later E.J. Jumeau Bébé, Closed Mouth, Jointed Body
10"			6,300.00	5,000.00
12"		9,000.00		5,500.00
13"				
14"		10,000.00	7,200.00	5,900.00
17"		12,000.00		6,400.00
19"			8,000.00	7,000.00
20 1/2"	24,000.00		8,700.00	7,700.00
22"			9,500.00	8,000.00
23"		19,500.00		
24"	26,000.00	24,000.00	11,000.00	

Jumeau Value Comparisons

Size	Long Face Triste, Closed Mouth, Jointed Body	Early E.J. Jumeau Bébé, Closed Mouth, Jointed Body	Mid E.J. Jumeau Bébé, Closed Mouth, Jointed Body	Later E.J. Jumeau Bébé, Closed Mouth, Jointed Body
25"				9,100.00
26"			12,000.00	
28"				9,700.00
30"	30,000.00		15,000.00	10,500.00
32"	32,000.00			
34"	35,000.00			

Size	E.J.A. Bébé	Déposé Jumeau, Closed Mouth, Jointed Body	Tete Jumeau Bébé, Closed Mouth	Black Tete Jumeau Bébé, Closed Mouth	Tete Lady	E.D. Bébé	Paris Bébé
11"		6,000.00	5,900.00				
13"			4,700.00				
14"		6,500.00	4,800.00				
15"			5,000.00				
16"							6,000.00
17"		7,000.00	5,700.00	9,000.00		5,600.00	
18"							6,500.00
19"		7,500.00				6,400.00	
20 1/2"			6,000.00		6,200.00		
22"		8,000.00	6,500.00	12,000.00		7,100.00	7,200.00
24"		8,500.00			8,000.00		
25"	37,000.00	9,500.00	7,000.00				8,000.00
28"			7,600.00				
30"			8,200.00				
34"			9,000.00				

Size	Open Mouth Tete or 1907	Great Ladies S.F.B.J. 221	230	301	208 O/C, Wide, Laughing Mouth Squinting Eyes	203/211 2-Face Character	200 Series Rare Expressive Characters
11"		800.00					
14"	3,000.00			900.00			
15"	3,200.00						
17"	3,500.00						
18"			2,000.00				
19"	3,700.00						75,000.00
20 1/2"	3,900.00						
22"					50,000.00		
24"	4,200.00			1,300.00		115,000.00	100,000.00
25"							135,000.00
26"			2,600.00				
28"	4,500.00						
34"	4,900.00						

K & K Toy Company

22" and 18" K & K bisque babies in an original condition Joel Ellis buggy. Courtesy of David Cobb's Doll Auctions

K & K Toy Company was founded in New York City in 1915. Like many doll manufacturers, they imported bisque heads from Germany. K & K also supplied cloth and composition bodies to several doll companies, including George Borgfeldt. Composition bodies were often marked "bisquette" or "fiberoid." Many K & K dolls were distributed by Butler Bros.

While most bisque doll heads marked K & K are found on cloth bodies with composition limbs, occasionally one is found on a kid body with bisque arms. The dolls' happy, smiling faces and big, shining eyes make them irresistible to doll collectors.

Bisque

Prices listed are for appropriately costumed dolls in good condition. Normal wear, slight damage, or well-made repairs to the body do not greatly affect the price. If the bisque is damaged or repaired, expect the value to be less than half the amounts listed. It is perfectly acceptable to show a missing or repaired finger or joint, or a mended body.

Character Child: bisque shoulder head; kid or cloth body; bisque or composition arms; good wig; glass eyes; open, smiling mouth; two upper teeth and felt tongue; appropriately dressed; typically marked "K & K Made in Germany" or "K & K Germany/Thuringia."

Composition

Prices listed are for appropriately costumed dolls in good condition. Slight crazing is acceptable and does not greatly affect the price. If badly crazed, cracked, peeling, or repainted, expect the value to be less than half the amounts listed.

Rose Marie: composition shoulder head; cloth body; slim legs; good wig; sleep eyes; open mouth with upper teeth and felt tongue; appropriately dressed; typically marked "K & K/Fiberoid/USA."

K & K Toy Company Value Comparison		
Size	Bisque	Composition
18"	600.00	
20"	700.00	475.00
22"	750.00	500.00
23"	800.00	
24"	850.00	550.00
25"	900.00	

Kamkins

The Louise R. Kampes Studio of Atlantic City, New Jersey produced dolls from 1919 until 1928. Kamkins were charming art dolls that were sold on the boardwalk at Atlantic City. Patented in 1920, the dolls were made of heavy cloth treated with rubber, a combination that made the face appear similar to composition. The production of Kamkins dolls was conducted as a cottage-type industry, where the studio supplies patterns and materials to home sewers. A line of doll clothing that could be purchased separately was also produced.

The most common characteristic of the Kamkins is the heavy, molded, mask-type face. Most of the character doll faces were painted a deep, healthy color and seldom had eyelashes. The stuffed cloth bodies usually had seams down the front of the legs. Kamkins range in size from eighteen to twenty inches. Because many Kamkins were marked with only a heart-shaped paper label on the chest, which was often lost, Kamkins art dolls are often found with no markings. Other Kamkins are stamped "Kamkins A Dolly Made To Love" or signed "Kamkins Studio."

The heavy, rubberized, mask-type face is difficult to duplicate, eliminating reproduction problems.

Prices listed are for appropriately costumed dolls with good color and little or no fading. Slight wear and signs of aging, such as a settled body, do not greatly affect the price. If a doll is stained, torn, badly mended, or faded, expect the value to be less than half the amounts listed.

Kamkins Art Doll: all treated cloth; molded and painted, mask-type face; flange neck; solidly stuffed body; jointed at shoulder and hip; good wig; painted eyes; closed mouth; appropriately dressed; typically marked with paper, heart-shaped label on chest "Kamkins A Dolly Made To Love/Patented from L. R. Kampes Studios/Atlantic City, N.J.," stamped "Kamkins A Dolly Made To Love," signed "Kamkins Studio," or unmarked.

Kamkins Value Comparisons	
Size	Price
18"	1,700.00
19"	1,700.00
20"	1,800.00

* Add an additional $500.00 for articulated body joints or exceptional modelling and decoration.

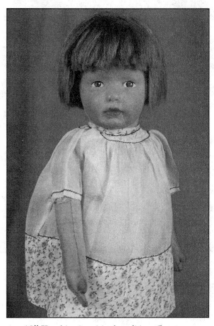

18" Kamkins in original condition. Courtesy of McMaster's Doll Auction

Kämmer & Reinhardt

Kämmer & Reinhardt was founded by Ernst Kämmer and Franz Reinhardt in 1886 in Waltershausen, Thüringia, Germany. Kämmer was a designer and modeller. When he died in 1901, Karl Krausser took over his position. About the same time, Henrich Handwerck, another great German doll manufacturer, also passed away. Shortly thereafter, in 1902, the company bought the Handwerck factory and began the important collaboration with Simon & Halbig. Kämmer & Reinhardt designed doll heads, but, having no porcelain factory, they did not actually manufacture them. This fact surprises many doll collectors. Simon & Halbig made most of the bisque heads and was a part of the company by 1920. Before Kämmer & Reinhardt's many mergers and acquisitions, Kling, Scheutzmeister & Quendt, and possibly others supplied bisque heads.

From 1886 to 1909, Kämmer & Reinhardt made only dolly-face dolls. They claimed they were the first company to include teeth in doll heads. While teeth had been used on dolls produced much earlier, they may have been among the first to use them in bisque doll heads. The "W" found on the forehead of some Kämmer & Reinhardt dolls is probably a reference to the Waltershausen region. Another point of confusion is a number between 15 and 100 found low on the doll's neck. This is actually a size number, in centimeters, not a mold number.

Kämmer & Reinhardt has long been credited with popularizing character dolls. The company was undoubtedly influenced by Marion B. Kaulitz, the instigator of the 1908 "Puppen Reform."

20" Kämmer & Reinhardt closed mouth, painted eye #101 Peter.
Courtesy of David Cobb's Doll Auctions

21" Kämmer & Reinhardt closed pouty mouth, painted eye #107 Carl.
Courtesy of David Cobb's Doll Auctions

Kämmer & Reinhardt caused quite a stir when it introduced its K ★ R character dolls on bent-limb baby bodies at the 1909 Munich Exhibit. The company later boasted to the media that it "had brought out our one model and influenced the market with it." The development of character dolls, which were modelled after real children, was an innovative progression of the German doll industry. While Kämmer & Reinhardt may have been the first company to commercialize the character doll, other firms soon joined in.

Reproduction Kämmer & Reinhardt are produced. While many are legitimate copies, whose express purpose is to add visual excitement to a collection, others are made as frauds. As always, check the markings carefully. Look for names and dates that would not be present on an authentic doll. Inspect the bisque. Bisque used for Kämmer & Reinhardt dolls was of good quality, but not smooth and creamy, nor was the decoration precisely executed. Many reproductions will have just such an "exact" look.

Also see Googly-Eyed Dolls.

Bisque

Prices listed are for appropriately costumed dolls in good condition. Normal wear, slight damage, or well-made repairs to the body do not greatly affect the price. If the bisque is damaged or repaired, expect the value to be less than half the amounts listed. It is perfectly acceptable to show a missing or repaired finger or joint, or a mended body.

Closed Mouth Child: bisque socket head; jointed wood-and-composition body; good wig; glass eyes; feathered brows; pierced ears; closed mouth; appropriately dressed; typically marked "K & R 191," "K & R 192," "192G," or "191G."

Dolly-Face Socket-Head: bisque socket head; jointed wood-and-composition body; good wig; glass eyes; feathered brows; pierced ears; open mouth; appropriately dressed; typically marked

"K ★ R Simon & Halbig 403," "Halbig/ K ★ R" "K ★ R 191," "192," "290," or "402."

Dolly-Face Shoulder Head: bisque shoulder head; kid body; bisque arms; good wig; glass eyes; open mouth; appropriately dressed; typically marked "SH/ K ★ R" or "377 K ★ R."

Characters: bisque socket or shoulder head; kid, composition, jointed or bent-limb baby body; molded and painted hair or good wig; sleep or painted eyes; closed or open/closed mouth; appropriately dressed; typically marked "K ★ R" and possibly a mold number.

Kämmer & Reinhardt Value Comparisons

Size	Closed Mouth Child*	Open Mouth Child	Open Mouth #192	Shoulder Head with Kid Body
5"		600.00		
6"	800.00			
8"	900.00	800.00	850.00	
9"	1,200.00		800.00	
12"	2,000.00	850.00	900.00	
14"	3,100.00	900.00	1,100.00	
16"	3,300.00	1,000.00	1,200.00	650.00
18"	3,600.00	1,100.00	1,400.00	800.00
20"	3,800.00	1,200.00	1,700.00	900.00
22"	4,000.00	1,400.00	2,000.00	1,000.00
24"	4,200.00	1,500.00	2,500.00	1,050.00
28"		1,700.00	2,700.00	
30"		2,000.00		
32"		2,500.00		
34"		2,700.00		
36"		3,200.00		
40"		4,000.00		
42"		4,700.00		

*Add an additional $200.00 for flirty eyes; $300.00 for flapper, or walker body; $300.00 for black version.

Character Value Comparisons

Size	100 O/CM, Glass Eyes	100 O/CM, Painted Eyes	115 CM, Solid Dome, Glass Eyes	115A CM, Glass Eyes	116 O/CM, Glass Eyes	116A O/CM, Glass Eyes	118-118A OM, Glass Eyes
12"		900.00	6,500.00			2,900.00	2,300.00
15"	2,200.00	1,200.00	7,500.00	5,200.00	6,000.00	3,500.00	2,800.00
20"	3,500.00	1,700.00	9000.00	6,000.00	7,900.00	4,500.00	3,400.00

Size	119 O/CM, Glass Eyes	121 OM, Glass Eyes	122 OM, Glass Eyes	122 (probably by S&Q) and 126 OM, Glass Eyes	127 OM, Glass Eyes	128 OM, Glass Eyes	135 OM, Glass Eyes
12"		1,100.00	1,200.00	700.00	1,800.00		1,700.00
15"	13,000.00	1,300.00	1,400.00	800.00	2,200.00	1,500.00	2,200.00
18"				900.00			
20"	18,000.00	1,800.00	1,800.00	1,200.00	2,900.00	1,800.00	3,500.00
24"				1,500.00	3,500.00	2,700.00	

Size	Klein Mammi 171, 172, O/CM, Glass Eyes	173, 175 Infant Cloth Body	200 Cloth Body, OM, Painted Eyes	926 Composition Socket Head, OM, Sleep Eyes	Klein Mammi 175, Painted Bisque, Cloth Body, Sleep Eyes
12"	3,400.00	1,400.00			1,500.00
15"	3,900.00	1,800.00	700.00		
18"				900.00	1,800.00
24"				1,000.00	

Add an additional $700.00 for jointed body; $300.00 for Black version; $200.00 for flirty eyes

Size	101 CM, Painted Eyes, Peter/Marie	101 CM, Glass Eyes	102 CM, Painted Eyes, Walter or Elsa	103 CM, Painted Eyes	104 CM/ Laughing, Painted Eyes	105 O/CM, Painted Eyes	106 CM, Painted Eyes
12"	3,500.00	12,000.00				100,000.00	
14"	4,500.00	18,000.00		75,000.00	80,000.00	150,000.00	145,000.00
20"	6,700.00		75,000.00	80,000.00	100,000.00	200,000.00	158,000.00

Size	107 CM, Painted Eyes, Carl	108 CM, Painted Eyes	109 CM, Painted Eyes, Elisa	109 CM, Glass Eyes	112-112X, O/CM, Painted Eyes	112A O/CM, Glass Eyes	114 CM, Painted Eyes, Gretchen/Hans
12"	23,000.00		6,200.00		17,000.00		3,900.00
14"			12,500.00	20,000.00	19,000.00	25,000.00	5,400.00
20"	65,000.00		19,000.00	26,000.00	25,000.00		7,500.00
25"		290,000.00					

Size	114 CM, Glass Eyes, Hans/Gretchen	117-117A, CM, Glass Eyes, Mein Liebling	117 No "N", OM, Glass Eyes	117 N, OM, Glass Eyes, Mien Neuer Leibling	123, 124, CM, Laughing, Glass Eyes Max/Moritz	201 CM, Cloth Body, Painted Eyes	214 CM, Painted Eyes
12"		4,400.00					
14"	13,000.00			1,500.00		1,900.00	3,500.00
15"					24,000.00		
16"						2,600.00	4,100.00
17"					27,000.00		
19"		6,200.00	3,200.00				
20"		6,800.00		1,900.00			
22"					45,000.00		
23"	24,000.00	7,500.00	4,700.00				
24"				2,000.00			

Add an additional $700.00 for jointed toddler body; $300.00 for Black version; $200.00 for flirty eyes to any character.

O/CM = Open/Closed Mouth

OM = Open Mouth

CM = Closed Mouth

Cloth

Kämmer & Reinhardt also made cloth dolls. Their wire-armature bodies were covered with cloth and had painted features. Authentically dressed in perfect miniature felt costumes, they represented various professions and stations in life such as dude, soldier, sailor, porter, clerk, bellhop, professor, chauffeur, gentleman, cook, and servant. At least twenty-five male character dolls were created, along with a maid (the only female character thus far documented). The dolls are very rare, and their value is as much dependent upon visual appeal as condition. A doll in generally good condition would be valued at $300.00 or more.

All original, closed pouty mouth, painted eye, Kämmer & Reinhardt #114, 13" Hans and 11" Gretchen. Courtesy of David Cobb's Doll Auctions

23" closed mouth Kämmer & Reinhardt #117, A Mein Liebling. Courtesy of David Cobb's Doll Auctions

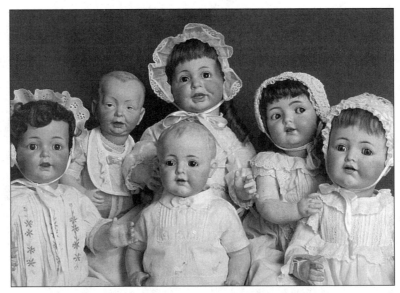

Kämmer & Reinhardt Babies, back row: #100 painted eyes Kaiser Baby, #116A with open-closed smiling mouth, #121 with flirty eyes. Front row: #122, #127 with molded hair, and #128. Courtesy of David Cobb's Doll Auctions

21" Madame Alexander Coco Portrait dolls including Renoir; Scarlett; Lissy. Courtesy of McMaster's Doll Auctions

All bisque babies, including from top: 9 1/2" Kestner solid dome with open/closed mouth and sleep eyes; 15" swivel head with painted eyes; 8 1/2" Kestner with painted eyes; 6 1/2" Hertel, Schwab & Co. #142; 7 1/2" marked "Japan" with painted eyes. Courtesy of David Cobb's Doll Auctions

Group of bisque half dolls, including from top: Dressel & Kister with crossed arrows; Karl Schneider #14495; Germany #34382; unmarked with jointed arms; bottom row: #22680; #9549 with wig; #7114; #51-B 8/0.9 with jointed arms; unmarked. Courtesy of David Cobb's Doll Auctions

26" Alt, Beck & Gottschalck; 23" Alt, Beck & Gottschalck #698; 20" German bisque solid dome turned head; 19" Alt, Beck & Gottschalck #639; 16" Kling #123. Courtesy of David Cobb's Doll Auctions

16" Alt, Beck & Gottschalck #1361; 12" Kley & Hahn #161; 12" Gebrüder Heubach #7602. Courtesy of David Cobb's Doll Auctions

27" Alt, Beck & Gottschalck #1367 breather and 18" Bähr & Pröschild #585 character babies. Courtesy of David Cobb's Doll Auctions

30" C. M. Bergmann Dolly-Face; 22" Bye-Lo baby; 24" S. F. B. J. character Laughing Jumeau; 25" H Mold Bébé; 10" Morimura Brothers baby, and a 22" K & K toddler.

15" Jules Steiner Automation Walking Lady, key wind causes arms to move up and down as doll rolls on a three-wheeled base; 9" Gebrüder Heubach #7804 Automaton Walking Baby, key wind causes baby to roll on a three-wheeled base while crying sound is made. Courtesy of David Cobb's Doll Auctions

19" Oriental Automaton Tea Server. All original rare brown bisque. Key wind causes right arm to raise to pour tea; left arm then moves cup from side to side; head nods up, down, forward, and back while music plays. Courtesy of David Cobb's Doll Auctions

19" Guitar Player Automaton; beautiful, marked Tete Jumeau Bébé #4; key wind causes right arm to strum wooden guitar; left hand moves up and down the neck; head moves side to side while music plays. Courtesy of David Cobb's Doll Auctions

32" C. M. Bergmann (Simon & Halbig); 21" Bähr & Pröschild #585 character baby in antique, bent-wood buggy.
Courtesy of David Cobb's Doll Auctions

*27" Bru Jne R Bébé #12; 24" Bru Jne Bébé #9.
Courtesy of David Cobb's Doll Auctions*

*19" Bru Jne Bébé #6; note beautifully persevered
original bisque hands. Courtesy of David Cobb's
Doll Auctions*

17" Bru; smiling, fashion "Poupée de Mode" type. Courtesy of David Cobb's Doll Auctions

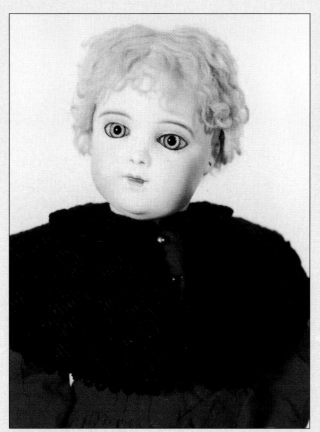

21" all original Bru Brevete. Courtesy of David Cobb's Doll Auctions

Group of china dolls, including from back: 24" black hair Currier & Ives; 25" curly black hair with exposed ears; 21" black hair Kling #188; middle row: 19" blonde wavy bangs; 19" blonde Highland Mary; 18" blonde Kling #189; 17" black hair Flat top with sausage curls; front: 11" and 15" frozen Charlies. Courtesy of David Cobb's Doll Auctions

Group of beautiful German composition babies from the collection of Sandra Lee. Compliments Sandra Lee Products, Inc., sandralee.com

18" Chad Valley Princess Elizabeth; 16" Chad Valley Margaret Rose. Courtesy of Ellen Schroy

All original composition dolls, including: 16" Effanbee Baby Brother; 16" Madame Alexander McGuffey Ana; 12" Effanbee Baby Sister; 14" Madame Alexander Alice. Courtesy of David Cobb's Doll Auctions

American Composition, including: 19" Arranbee Debuteen with box; 19" Effanbee Patsy Ann with box; 20" Effanbee Ann Shirley with box; 13" Ideal Shirley Temple in original tagged NRA dress; 11" Effanbee Patsy Jr. with box; 12" Cameo Scootles with box; 8" Effanbee Baby Tinyette; and 9" Patsyette on skates. Courtesy of David Cobb's Doll Auctions

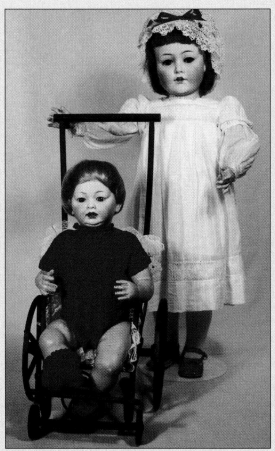

24" unmarked composition twins with hair bow loops; 22" A. D. C. composition boy doll shown with antique wash rack, tin tub, and laundry basket. Courtesy of David Cobb's Doll Auctions

29" Cuno & Otto Dressel dolly-face child; 18" Hertel, Schwab & Co. #150. Courtesy of David Cobb's Doll Auctions

22" Danel & Cie BF Bébé #9; 20" J. D. Kestner Gibson Girl. Courtesy of David Cobb's Doll Auctions

29" Cuno & Otto Dressel Jutta #1349; 28" Koenig & Wernicke; 19" Swaine & Co. Courtesy of David Cobb's Doll Auctions

20" Effanbee composition painted-eyed American child; 27" Ideal composition Shirley Temple with original box; 21" Dollcraft Novelty composition Tonto and Lone Ranger; 17" Effanbee composition Anne Shirley; 13" Ideal composition Howdy Doody with wood-segmented body; 13" Madame Alexander Snow White; 11" Ideal composition Shirley Temple. Courtesy of David Cobb's Doll Auctions

20" composition American Child boy doll designed by Dewees Cochran for Effanbee with painted eyes; 20" Effanbee composition child with sleep eyes; 17" Series 1 Käthe Kruse; 14" Contemporary Käthe Kruse with painted hair and features; 14" Hard Plastic Käthe Kruse. Courtesy of David Cobb's Doll Auctions

19" early, pale Francois Gaultier Fashion "Poupée de Mode" type. Courtesy of David Cobb's Doll Auctions

16" Francois Gaultier early bisque swivel head on marked shoulder plate. Courtesy of David Cobb's Doll Auctions

20" open mouth Fleischmann & Bloedel Eden Bébé #9; 18" open mouth Jumeau 1907 Bébé. Courtesy of David Cobb's Doll Auctions

Good things come in small packages. 11" French Bébé; 10-1/2" Belton type; 9-1/2" Kestner #150, and 7-1/2" A.M. #323 Googly. Courtesy of David Cobb's Doll Auctions

Group of G. I Joe from back: Annapolis Cadet in dark blue with white hat; Nurse Jane; West Pointe cadet in gray with red sash; Air Force Cadet in royal blue, saluting; from front: Action Marine in fatigues; Action Pilot in orange jump suit; Sea Adventurer with shoulder holster; Action Pilot with hip hostler and air vest. Courtesy of McMaster's Doll Auctions

16" Heubach Köppelsdorf #300; 15" Fulper character baby; 16" Fulper character baby. Courtesy of David Cobb's Doll Auctions

24" Gebrüder Heubach #7602 solid dome pouty and a 20" S. F. B. J. character #236 with molded tongue and teeth. Courtesy of David Cobb's Doll Auctions

17" Gebrüder Heubach #6970 with closed mouth and intaglio eyes; 15" Kestner #182 with closed mouth and painted eyes; and 15-1/2" Kestner character with closed mouth and glass eyes. Courtesy of David Cobb's Doll Auctions

11" Gebrüder Heubach #8191; 18" Bonnie Baby; 12" and 14" Kämmer & Reinhardt #100 character babies. Courtesy of David Cobb's Doll Auctions

15″ Ideal hard plastic Toni complete with original box and play wave set. Courtesy of McMaster's Doll Auctions

19″ Jules Steiner Bébé. Courtesy of David Cobb's Doll Auctions

13″ Jullien Bébé #3; 14″ Tete Jumeau Bébé #5. Courtesy of David Cobb's Doll Auctions

36" scrub mark Jumeau Bébé. Courtesy of David Cobb's Doll Auctions

21" Jumeau Portrait Fashion-type; 15-1/2" Bru swivel head Fashion-type; and a 22" Francois Gaultier Fashion type. Courtesy of David Cobb's Doll Auctions

25" DEP #12 Bébé; 20" open mouth Tete Jumeau; 20" closed mouth E. J. Jumeau #7 Bébé

Fait Dodo

Fais Dodo, Pierrot mon p'tit frère,
fais Dodo mon petit Pierre.

Maman est là-haut qui fait des
gâteaux pour le petit Pierrot.

Fais Dodo, Pierrot mon p'tit frère;
Fais Dodo, mon petit Pierrot.

Go to sleep, Pierre, my little brother.
Go to sleep my little Pierre.

Mama is upstairs. She is making
cakes for little Pierre.

Go to sleep Pierre, my little brother.
Go to sleep my little Pierre.

*25" Phonographe Jumeau with "Fait Dodo" cylinder.
Courtesy of McMaster's Doll Auctions*

*12" all original Jumeau "E3J" Bébé. Courtesy of David Cobb's
Doll Auctions*

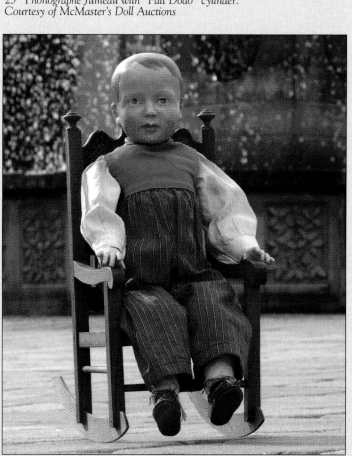

*Painted hair Munich Art Doll. Courtesy of Village Doll and Toy Shop,
Becky and Andy Ourant, Adamstown, Pa.*

*36" open mouth Jumeau #1907 with rare bisque hands holding 5"
all bisque Bye Lo. Courtesy of David Cobb's Doll Auctions*

22" rare, original portrait Jumeau fashion 'Poupée de Mode' type with applied ears.

26" Kämmer & Reinhardt #117 Mein Liebling open mouth character. Courtesy of David Cobb's Doll Auctions

11" E3J Deposé Jumeau; 13" Steiner Fire A; 10 3/4" Schmitt & Fils Bébé. Courtesy of Sotheby's Auctions

29" Kämmer & Reinhardt #126 character baby with treble tongue; 24" Schoenau & Hoffmeister #169 Burggraub Baby. Courtesy of David Cobb's Doll Auctions

23" Kämmer & Reinhardt #126 character toddler; 22" Heinrich Handwerck #109 dolly face child. Courtesy of David Cobb's Doll Auctions

15 1/2" Kämmer & Reinhardt #131 Googly; 13" Bru Jne Bébé #2; 15" almond-eyed Jumeau Bébé #4. Courtesy of David Cobb's Doll Auctions

20″ Kämmer & Reinhardt #126; 19″ Kley & Hahn #167; 16″ Hertel Schwab & Co #152. Courtesy of David Cobb's Doll Auctions

25″ Kämmer & Reinhardt #116A character; 14″ Kestner #211 character. Courtesy of David Cobb's Doll Auctions

25″ Kämmer & Reinhardt #126 toddler; 21″ Kley & Hahn #160 toddler. Courtesy of David Cobb's Doll Auctions

27″ Kämmer & Reinhardt #70; 21″ Kämmer & Reinhardt #53; 21″ Schoenau & Hoffmeister #4000. Courtesy of David Cobb's Doll Auctions

23″ Kämmer & Reinhardt #62 with flirty eyes; 18″ Heinrich Handwerck #119; 20″ Cuno & Otto Dressel Jutta # 1349. Courtesy of David Cobb's Doll Auctions

31″ Kestner #211 character boy and 32″ Kestner #260 character girl. Courtesy of David Cobb's Doll Auctions

13" Kestner #243 Oriental; 15" Kämmer & Reinhardt #100 character and 12" A.M. open mouth #971. Courtesy of David Cobb's Doll Auctions

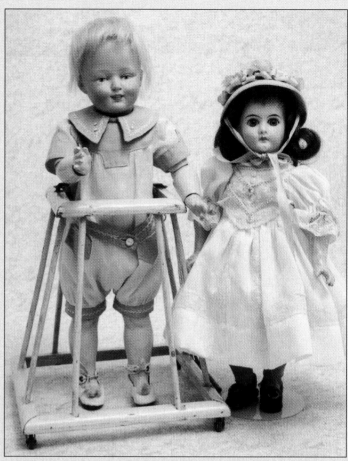

12" very rare Kestner automaton #185 with metal torso attached to wooden walker on wheels, the key wind mechanism causes legs to move back and forth and doll to roll about as though walking; 10" Bähr & Pröschild 'owl face' Belton type #200. Courtesy of David Cobb's Doll Auctions

22" Kestner closed mouth pouty #13; 21" Simon & Halbig black #1078; 20" Kestner #214. Courtesy of David Cobb's Doll Auctions

23" closed mouth Kestner with turned shoulder head; 22" closed mouth German with turned shoulder head, marked only "1." Courtesy of David Cobb's Doll Auctions

21" J. D. Kestner closed mouth #8; 21" Alt, Beck & Gottschalck #912 closed mouth, solid dome shoulder head.

Rare and irresistible bisque Kewpies. Courtesy Frasher's Auctions

16" Kley & Hahn character #536 with closed mouth and intaglio eyes and a 17" Kestner #143 child. Courtesy of David Cobb's Doll Auctions

27" Biedermeier solid dome with applied ears; 33" modified Flat Top china head. Courtesy of David Cobb's Doll Auctions

22" Kley & Hahn #282; 22" Armand Marseille Queen Louise; 11" JDK Kestner Character Baby #7 sitting on antique stick and ball oak rocking bed. Courtesy of David Cobb's Doll Auctions

23" German bisque closed mouth shoulder head; 25" G.K. #2429 tinted bisque with molded hair and painted eyes. Courtesy of David Cobb's Doll Auctions

24" Jolie & Jacques, 1996 Limited Edition porcelain dolls by Fayzah Spanos. Photo courtesy of the artist

Faith Wick's wonderfully whimsical Wonderland characters including: 28" Queen of Hearts; 27" Alice; 26" Duchess; 24" Mad Hatter; 21" Cheshire Cat; 25" March Hare; 11" Pig Faced Baby; 26" White Rabbit; 24" Tweedle Dee and Tweedle Dum. Courtesy of David Cobb's Doll Auctions

15 1/2" Gene Marshall in Somewhere Summer ensemble designed by Mel Odon for Ashton Drake Gallery. Photo courtesy Ashton Drake

23" Morimura Brothers; 21" Armand Marseille #390; 18" Schoenau & Hoffmeister dolly-face child dolls. Courtesy of David Cobb's Doll Auctions

20" Parian type with glass eyes, pierced ears, hair bow, and necklace; 16" Parian type with glass eyes, pierced ears, beautifully detailed ruffled bodice, and elaborate hair style. Courtesy of Ellen Schroy

22″ Emma Clear, Tiara Parian type with glass eyes, pierced ears, and gold luster hair comb; 21″ High Brow china head; 20″ china head with molded hair ribbon and snood with hand stippled hair line; 18″ Flat Top china head with sausage curls; 17″ Covered Wagon pink tint china head; 15″ Princess Augusta Victoria Parian type with beaded head band, pierced ears, and beautifully molded bodice with cross necklace. Courtesy of David Cobb's Doll Auctions

16″ open mouth Rabery & Delphieu #3/0; 12″ S. F. B. J. #60. Courtesy of David Cobb's Doll Auctions

19″ Rabery & Delphieu Bébé; 19″ Belton type; 19″ Francois Gaultier; 19″ Henri Alexandre Phenix; and a 19″ Jules Steiner Figure A Bébé. Courtesy of David Cobb's Doll Auctions

19" Rohmer fashion "Poupée de Mode" type with trunk full of accessories. Courtesy of David Cobb's Doll Auctions

15" S. F. B. J. #251 all original character. Courtesy of David Cobb's Doll Auctions

S. F. B. J. characters including from back 15" #236; 12" #251; 8" #60 with painted eyes. Courtesy of David Cobb's Doll Auctions

24" S. F. B. J. #230 character; 24" S. F. B. J. Bébé.
Courtesy of David Cobb's Doll Auctions

26" Bruno Schmidt #2097 and 23" Franz Schmidt #1272 with retractable tongue. Courtesy of David Cobb's Doll Auctions

29" Bruno Schmidt #2097 flirty eyes; 30" C. M. Bergmann; 23" Simon & Halbig #949; Kämmer & Reinhardt #58 flirty eyes. Courtesy of David Cobb's Doll Auctions

Schoenhut character circus figures including from top: animal trainer, lady bareback rider, Ringmaster (2), monkeys (2), Negro Dude (3), Chinese acrobat, clowns (4), and wooden props. Courtesy of David Cobb's Doll Auctions

12" Simon & Halbig #965; 12" German bisque known as American School Boy. Courtesy of David Cobb's Doll Auctions

17" Franz Schmidt #1310; 9" Armand Marseille #590 character with antique horse pull toy. Courtesy of David Cobb's Doll Auctions

22" Schützmeister & Quendt #201 character baby with treble tongue; 16" Kestner #257 character baby with group of Steiff animals. Courtesy of David Cobb's Doll Auctions

24" Schmitt & Fils #4 Bébé with shield mark. Courtesy of David Cobb's Doll Auctions

21" Simon & Halbig #1079 black child; 16" Kestner black child with square cut teeth; 13" German brown bisque by Herman Heyde. Courtesy of David Cobb's Doll Auctions

13" Simon & Halbig #1448; 12" Bruno Schmidt #2033 with glass eyes. Courtesy of David Cobb's Doll Auctions

29" Simon & Halbig #1009; 28" square cut teeth Kestner; 33" Heinrich Handwerck. Courtesy of David Cobb's Doll Auctions

*31" Simon & Halbig #1079; 30" Simon & Halbig #1248; 28"
Karl Hartman. Courtesy of David Cobb's Doll Auctions*

18" vintage Steiff felt child. Courtesy of Sotheby's Auctions

*13" and 15" S. F. B. J. #60; 12" Swaine & Co.
marked "DV3"; 10" Swaine & Co. marked
"DIP2." Courtesy of David Cobb's Doll Auctions*

*23" Germany Special; 23" Adolf Wislizenus dolly-faced child dolls with 16" Madame
Alexander mask face child and 11" black fold art doll sitting in an antique doll trunk.
Courtesy of David Cobb's Doll Auctions*

18" Poured wax; 21" Lenci #300; 18" Martha Chase with applied ears. Courtesy of David Cobb's Doll Auctions

Kenner Parker Toys, Inc.

Original Kenner Star Wars Luke Skywalker.
Courtesy of McMaster's Doll Auction.

*I*n 1985, Kenner became an independent company with two divisions, Parker Brothers and Kenner products. Kenner was once a subsidiary of General Mills. They produced many dolls as well as popular figures.

Prices listed are for dolls in near-mint, original condition. If damaged, redressed, or undressed, expect the value to be less than one half to one fourth the amounts listed.

Dolls

Boy Scout Bob (white), Steve (black): 9"; vinyl and plastic; molded and painted hair; painted eyes; closed, smiling mouth; beautifully detailed, authentic Boy Scout uniform; gives Boy Scout salute when right arm is raised. Marked "1974 G.M.F.G./ Kenner Prod/Cinti. Ohio/NO 7000/Made in Hong Kong" **$145.00**

Blythe: 12"; oversized, hard plastic head; tiny, fully-jointed body; rooted hair; eyes change color as ring is pulled; green, blue, brown, purple (some Blythe dolls have amber in place of purple); closed mouth; original "mod"-type dress and high plastic boots; marked "Blythe TM/Kenner Products/Cincinnati, Ohio/1972 General Mills/Fun Group Inc./Patents Pending/Made in Hong Kong" **$165.00**

Baby Alive: 16"; all vinyl; jointed at neck, shoulder, and hip; rooted hair; painted eyes; open, feeding mouth; original romper and disposable diaper; comes with packets of food, bottle, dish, and spoon, which activates chewing motion; doll smacks her lips after spoon or bottle is removed from mouth; bubbles like a real baby, and fills her diaper; requires two batteries; marked "1973 G.M.F.G. Inc./KENNER PRODUCTS DIV/Cinti,O/Made in Hong Kong"..**$100.00**

Gabbigale: 18"; vinyl head; fully-jointed, plastic body; rooted, blond hair; painted blue eyes; open/closed, smiling mouth; pull string in chest; battery operated; repeats spoken words; original, red, jumper-type dress; marked "1972 Kenner Products Co/99" on head and "Gabbigale/1972 Kenner Products/General Mills Fun Group Inc./Patents Pending" **$95.00**

Baby Won't Let Go: 17"; vinyl head; vinyl and hard plastic body; hand grips when arm is lifted; rooted hair; painted eyes; open/closed mouth; original baby outfit; typically marked "4046 Taiwan K002 GMFGI 1977 93//1977 Kenner Prod. Div. Cin't/ Ohio 45202 26150," "45202/28100," or "26150//1977/96" **$65.00**

Stretch Armstrong: 13"; all heavy, stretch vinyl; jointed at neck; will stretch to over four feet and return to original shape; molded and painted hair and expressive facial features; unmarked **$100.00**

Shawn Cassidy: 12"; all solid vinyl; jointed at neck, shoulder, and hip; realistic characterization; original, classic 70s outfit; marked "1978 USCI//GMFGI 1978 Kenner Prod./Cincinnati Ohio 45202//Made in Hong Kong" **$75.00**

Parker Stevenson: 12"; all solid vinyl; jointed at neck, shoulder, and hip; realistic characterization; original, classic 70s outfit; marked "GMFGI 1978 Kenner Prod./CINCINNATI Ohio 45202//Made in Hong Kong"..**$65.00**

International Velvet: 11 1/2"; (Tatum O'Neal); vinyl head; plastic body; jointed at neck, shoulder, hip, and waist; bendable knees; rooted, long hair; painted eyes; open/closed, wide, smiling mouth; original riding habit; marked "43/Hong Kong/1976 USCI//1978 GMFGI Kenner Prod./Cincinnati Ohio 45202/ Made in Hong Kong//Metro-Goldwyn-Mayer".................**$65.00**

Cover Girl Darci: 12 1/2"; all pose-able vinyl; rooted hair; painted features; original fashion costume; marked "140 Hong Kong/GMFGI 1978" **$125.00**

Cover Girl Erica: 12 1/4"; (Darci's best friend); all pose-able vinyl; rooted, red hair; painted features; original fashion costume and gold mask; marked "CRG PRODUCTS CORP./1978 Kenner Cincinnati 47400 Made In Hong Kong" **$225.00**

Black Cover Girl Dana: 12 1/2"; all pose-able vinyl; rooted black hair; painted features; original fashion costume; marked "56 Hong Kong/GMFGI 1978" **$150.00**

Dusty: 11 1/2"; all vinyl; wonderful character face; spring-loaded arms and body; plays golf or tennis; rooted platinum "shag-style" hair; painted eyes; freckles; open/closed, smiling mouth with molded upper teeth; original sports outfits; typically marked "Kenner" "GMFGI/1974" **$165.00**

Original Kenner Star Wars Princess Leia Organa. Courtesy of McMaster's Doll Auction

Figures

Most Star Wars figures were re-issued during the 1990s. Check figures carefully; prices given are for original 1970s figures.

Star Wars: large size; marked "GMFGI 1978" on head and "GMFGI 1978 Kenner Prod/Cincinnati, Ohio 45202/Made in Hong Kong," "GMIFGI 1974//1974 GMGI KENNER PROD. 33, 862, 512."

Strawberry Shortcake Collection: vinyl head; rigid vinyl or hard plastic body; bendable limbs; rooted hair; darling characterizations; dolls originally had fragrance of "fruit-character-name" (Lemon, Grape, Strawberry, Green Apple, etc.); painted features; original costumes appropriate to character, with accessories; marked "AMERICAN GREETING CORP. 1982//AGC/1982.

Kenner Value Comparisons						
Size	Small Figures	C3PO	Chewbacca	Darth Vader	Boba Fett	Yoda
3"	60.00–100.00					
9"						145.00
12"		175.00				
13"					350.00	
15"			200.00	225.00		

Size	Han Solo	IG 88	Jawa	Leia	Luke Skywalker	Obi Wan Kenobi	R2D2	Stormtrooper
7 1/2"							225.00	
8 1/2"			150.00					
11 1/2"				300.00				
12"	600.00					200.00		275.00
13"					350.00			
15"		850.00						

Size	Strawberry Shortcake and Other Typical Figures	Sour Grapes, Purple Pieman
5"	200.00	
15"		275.00

J. D. Kestner

Johann Danie Kestner, the charismatic founder of the Kestner empire, started in business by trading with the soldiers of the Napoleonic wars as early as 1805. He traded small necessary items in exchange for the wastes from their slaughtered cattle, such as kid, fat, horns, and bones. This operation was so successful that he was able to open his own factory in 1816. Originally intended to be a manufacturer of papier-mâché notebooks, he soon expanded to shirt buttons. Needing a lathe to make buttons, it only seemed natural to him that he could also make wooden, jointed dolls. By 1820, Kestner was manufacturing a complete line of toys and dolls made from both wood and papier-mâché. In 1840, Kestner participated in the Leipzig Fair as the first toy maker of Waltershausen, an impressive feat when one considers the toy capital that area was to become.

The German government granted Kestner a monopoly on the production of papier-mâché. In exchange for this exclusive right, and being charged a nominal annual tax of only 3 Taler, Kestner agreed to provide food and employment to the poverty-stricken people of Waltershausen. The arrangement must have been successful, for he held the monopoly for more than twenty-five years and employed over three-quarters of the total population in and around Waltershausen. The doll industry was of utmost importance in Germany, and Kestner was the head of this industry, thus he was bestowed the nickname "King Kest-

ner." Kestner's influence was so great and far reaching that he received permission to practice polygamy from the Ducal Government, and kept two wives in his home. Kestner's obituary gives credibility to this story by stating: "His two women continue the business." Upon his death in 1858, the company kept operating until his grandson Adolf (J. D.'s only son had preceded him in death by ten years) was trained and able to assume the responsibilities of running the company.

Kestner Dolls, as we think of them today, were introduced following Kestner's acquisition of the Ohrdug porcelain factory in 1860. Kestner was one of the few firms that produced complete dolls with all their parts. The company also supplied doll heads to several other doll manufacturers.

The century-old firm used a wide assortment of markings, including its name, initials, various mold numbers, and a series of letters. Many dolls have been attributed to Kestner simply because the marking "Made in Germany" is written in the distinctive Kestner manner, a practice started in 1892, when mold numbers were assigned. Another familiar word associated with Kestner is "Excelsior," a trade name of Kestner dolls distributed in the United States. The bisque head dolls may be found with various body types.

Common characteristics to verify an authentic Kestner include: heavy and somewhat shiny brows; high "bow," upper lip turned up at each end; did not have pierced ears; closed-mouth dolls have a darker line to separate lips. Also the nostril and inner-corner-eye dots were a soft orange, and usually matched the lip color. Kestner used good quality, blown glass eyes. The crown opening is commonly covered by a plaster pate, rather than cardboard or cork. Check carefully for the size letter/number. For a complete size listing, see *Antique Trader's Doll Makers and Marks* (Krause Publications, 1999).

Prices listed are for appropriately costumed dolls in good condition. Normal wear, slight damage, or well-made repairs to the body do not greatly affect the price. If the bisque is damaged or repaired, expect the value to be less than half the amounts listed. It is perfectly acceptable to show a missing or repaired finger or joint, or a mended body.

Also see All-Bisque, Googly-Eyed Dolls, and Oriental.

Closed Mouth, Shoulder Head: bisque shoulder head, may be slightly turned; kid body; bisque forearms; plaster dome; good wig; glass eyes; long eyelashes; heavy brows; closed mouth; appropriately dressed; typically marked "Germany," letter, or size number only.

Closed Mouth, Socket Head: bisque socket head; ball-jointed, wood-and-composition body; straight wrists; plaster dome; good wig; glass eyes; feathered brows; closed mouth; appropriately dressed; typically marked "128," "169," letter, or size number only.

Closed, Pouty Mouth: bisque socket head; ball-jointed, wood-and-composition body; straight wrists; plaster dome; good wig; glass eyes; heavy, feathered brows; closed, pouty mouth; appropriately dressed; typically marked "X," "XI," "103," letter, or size number.

Closed Mouth, French-Look: bisque socket head; jointed body, may have additional ankle joints, or kid body with matched bisque shoulder plate; jointed body; plaster dome; good wig; large, oval or almond-shaped glass eyes; long lashes; feathered brows; closed mouth; full, slightly parted lips with a hint of a

15" closed mouth Kestner marked "10 XI" and 12" closed mouth marked only "7." Courtesy of David Cobb's Doll Auctions

24" classic closed mouth Kestner marked "K / 14." Courtesy of David Cobb's Doll Auctions

33" Kestner #196 Dolly-Face child with fur brows. Courtesy of David Cobb's Doll Auctions

26" Kestner #143 open mouth character child. Courtesy of David Cobb's Doll Auctions

molded tongue or teeth; appropriately dressed; typically marked with letter or size number only.

Open Mouth, Carved Square-Teeth: bisque shoulder head and forearms; kid body; plaster dome; good wig; glass eyes; feathered brows; open mouth with carved square-teeth (cut or carved into the lip—not separate teeth); appropriately dressed; typically marked "Made in Germany" and/or letter or size number.

Open Mouth, Turned Head: bisque, slightly-turned shoulder head and forearms; kid body; plaster dome; good wig; glass eyes; featured brows; open mouth with teeth; appropriately dressed; typically marked "Made in Germany" and/or letter or size number.

Tiny Doll: bisque socket head; five-piece composition or papier-mâché body; molded and painted shoes; plaster dome; good wig; glass eyes; open mouth with tiny teeth; appropriately dressed; typically marked "155," "170," or "133."

Dolly-Face: bisque socket head; ball-jointed, wood-and-composition body; plaster dome; good wig; glass eyes; feathered brows; open mouth with teeth; appropriately dressed; typically marked "Made in Germany"/"141," "142," "144," "146," "164," "167," "168," "171," or "196." ***Note:*** *18", only mold #171, known as Daisy*..**$1,600.00**

Unique Dolly-Face: bisque socket dolly-face with unique, almost character face; ball-jointed, wood-and-composition body; plaster dome; good wig; glass eyes; feathered or fur brows; open mouth; chubby cheeks; appropriately dressed; typically marked "Made in Germany JDK/," "128," "129," "149," "152," "160," "161," "173," "174," "214," "215," "249."

Dolly-Face Shoulder Head: bisque shoulder head and forearms; kid body; plaster dome; good wig; glass eyes; feathered or fur brows; open mouth with upper teeth; appropriately dressed;

24" Kestner #245 Hilda. Courtesy of David Cobb's Doll Auctions

Kestner character babies, 23" #211 and 16" #226. Courtesy of David Cobb's Doll Auctions

typically marked "Made in Germany"/"145," "147," "148," "154," "159," "166," or "195."

Solid Dome Character Baby: bisque socket head; sweet, fat-cheeked face; composition bent-limb baby body; softly painted hair; glass eyes; feathered brows; open or open/closed mouth; appropriately dressed; typically marked "J.D.K." size number only. ***Note:*** *Often called Baby Jean, Sally, or Sammy.*

Character Baby Shoulder Head: bisque shoulder head; rivet-jointed, kid body; composition limbs; solid dome; glass eyes; open/closed mouth; appropriately dressed; typically marked "Made in Germany/J.D.K./" "210," "234," "235," or "238."

Character Baby Socket Head: bisque socket head; composition, bent-limb baby body; plaster dome; good wig; glass eyes; winged, feathered brows; open mouth with teeth; appropriately dressed; typically marked "Made in Germany J.D.K./" "211," "226," "236," "262," "257," or "263."

Hilda Character Baby: bisque socket head; composition, bent-limb baby body; softly molded and lightly painted hair or good wig; glass eyes; open mouth with two upper teeth; appropriately dressed; typically marked "J.D.K./ges.gesch K 14 1070/ Made in Germany," "237," "245," and "Hilda." ***Note:*** *The marking on the head of a Hilda Baby does NOT have to include the name "Hilda" to be authentic. The wigged version must be marked "237" or "245." The solid dome may be marked "1070"; the wigged version may also have the "1070" in addition to "237" or "245"; 1070 most likely is a registration number.*

Cunning Character: exceptional character face with beautiful modelling; bisque socket head; composition, jointed or bent limb baby body; molded wind-swept hair or good wig; glass eyes; open mouth with teeth, appears to have a slight overbite or

molded tongue; appropriately dressed; typically marked "Made in Germany/J.D.K.," "247," "JDK," or "267."

Flange Neck Character Baby: bisque character face; cloth body; solid dome with painted hair; glass eyes, appropriately dressed; typically marked "255/O.I.C." or "Siegfried 272." ***Note:*** *Kestner registered #255 as "Grotesquely Molded."*

Lady Character Face: bisque socket head; very shapely, composition woman's body; cinched waist; molded bosom; good wig; glass eyes; open mouth with teeth; appropriately dressed; marked "162."

Gibson Girl: bisque shoulder head and forearms; kid body; good wig in Gibson style; glass eyes; closed mouth; head with very stylish, regal bearing and upward-glancing eyes; appropriately dressed; marked "172."

Character Child: bisque socket head; memorable character modelling; jointed wood-and-composition body; good wig; glass or painted eyes; typical mold numbers include "143," "178," "179," "180," "181," "182," "183," "184," "185," "186," "187," "189," "190," "202," "203," "206," "208," "212," "220," "239," "241," "260," size number only.

Kestner Value Comparisons		
Size	**162 Lady**	**172 Gibson Girl**
10"		1,400.00
16"	2,500.00	3,100.00
18"	2,900.00	
20"	3,200.00	
22"		4,800.00

12" Kestner #185 closed mouth character. Courtesy of David Cobb's Doll Auctions

18" Kestner # 172 closed mouth Gibson Girl. Courtesy of David Cobb's Doll Auctions

JDK/no mold number: 18"; open/closed mouth; glass eyes; outstanding quality expression and modelling **$8,500.00**
143: 18"; open mouth; glass eyes; pug nose.................**2,200.00**
178: 18"; open/closed mouth; painted eyes; overbite **6,300.00**
178: 18"; open/closed mouth; glass eyes; overbite.....**7,400.00**
179: 18"; open/closed mouth; painted eyes; molded tongue; hint of upper teeth...**7,000.00**
179: 18"; open/closed mouth; glass eyes; molded tongue; hint of upper teeth...**7,400.00**
180: 18"; open/closed mouth; painted eyes; four molded upper teeth and tongue...**6,300.00**
181: 18"; open/closed mouth; painted eyes; slightly-parted lips with four molded upper teeth.....................................**6,900.00**
182: 18"; fully closed mouth; painted eyes **7,000.00**
183: 18"; open/closed mouth; glass eyes; smiling with molded teeth; light brows **6,400.00**
184: 18"; small closed mouth; glass eyes; fly-a-way brows **6,900.00**
185: 18"; wide open/closed mouth; smiling; painted eyes; temple dimples; fully molded teeth **7,000.00**
186: 18"; open/closed mouth; grinning; molded upper and lower teeth; full cheeks; double chin.................................**7,500.00**

187: 18"; closed mouth; painted eyes; slight grin; full cheeks; plump, double chin **7,200.00**
189: 18"; closed mouth; glass eyes; pensive expression; cheek dimples...**6,800.00**
190: 18"; open/closed mouth; painted eyes; hint of a tongue **6,300.00**
190: 18"; open/closed mouth; glass eyes; hint of a tongue **7,400.00**
203: 18"; smiling closed mouth; glass eyes; molded tongue **6,200.00**
206: 18"; closed mouth; tiny glass eyes; chin dimple**29,000.00**
208: 18"; closed mouth; painted eye character..........**28,000.00**
212: 18"; closed mouth; pouty; small glass eyes .....**12,000.00+**
220: 18"; open mouth; broad smile; glass eyes; full cheeks with dimples; double chin.....................................**8,000.00**
239: 18"; open mouth; glass eyes; full cheek; double chin **7,500.00**
241: 18"; open mouth; glass eyes; overbite and slightly pulled back as if about to speak **7,800.00**
260: 18"; open mouth; glass eyes; overbite **1,700.00**
Note: *For characters, 18" was used as a comparison base, but the dolls actually came in a wide range of sizes, from 8" up to 42" or more.*

Kestner Value Comparisons

Size	Closed Mouth, Shoulder Head, Kid Body	Closed Mouth, Socket Head, Composition Body	Closed Pouty Mouth, Socket Head, Composition Body	X or XI Composition Body	Closed Mouth, Socket Head, French Look
10"	900.00	2,200.00	3,400.00		
12"	1,000.00	2,400.00	3,300.00		
14"	1,200.00	2,700.00	3,900.00		
16"	1,400.00	2,900.00	4,000.00	5,200.00	10,000.00+
18"	1,500.00	3,200.00	4,400.00		
20"	1,700.00	3,500.00	4,900.00		15,000.00+
22"	3,600.00				
24"	2,000.00	4,000.00	5,200.00		
26"	2,200.00	4,700.00			
28"			6,000.00		25,000.00+
32"		5,500.00			

Size	Open Mouth, Cut Square-Teeth, Shoulder Head, Kid Body	Open Mouth, Turned Shoulder Head, Kid Body	Tiny Doll*	Dolly-Face, Socket Head, Composition Body	Unique Dolly-Face, Composition Body	Dolly-Face, Shoulder Head, Kid Body
7"			1,000.00			
8"			1,200.00			400.00
10"				800.00	900.00	450.00
12"	1,400.00	600.00		1,000.00	1,400.00	500.00
14"	1,600.00	700.00		1,000.00	1,500.00	550.00
16"	1,800.00	800.00		1,100.00	1,600.00	650.00
18"	1,900.00	900.00		1,200.00	1,700.00	700.00
20"	2,100.00	1,000.00				750.00
22"	2,200.00	1,100.00		1,400.00	1,800.00	800.00
24"	2,400.00	1,200.00		1,500.00	1,900.00	1,000.00
26"					2,000.00	
28"				1,700.00	2,100.00	1,200.00
30"						1,400.00
32"				1,900.00	2,500.00	1,600.00
36"	5,000.00			3,000.00	3,500.00	2,200.00
40"				4,500.00	4,700.00	
42"				4,900.00	5,400.00	

*Add an additional $600.00 for fully jointed body.

Size	Solid Dome Character Baby, Socket Head, Bent-Limb Body*	Character Baby, Shoulder Head Kid Body	Character Baby, Socket Head, Bent-Limb Body*	Hilda Character Baby*	Cunning Character	Flange Neck Baby
10"			800.00	3,000.00	1,400.00	1,700.00
12"	1,500.00	1,200.00	1,000.00	3,700.00	1,700.00	2,100.00
14"	1,600.00	1,500.00	1,200.00	4,200.00	2,500.00	2,400.00
16"	1,800.00		1,400.00	4,600.00	3,000.00	2,700.00
18"	2,000.00	1,900.00	1,500.00	5,000.00		
20"	2,200.00		1,600.00	5,300.00	4,500.00	
22"		2,500.00	2,000.00	5,900.00		
24"	2,700.00		2,600.00	6,700.00	5,000.00	
26"				7,500.00		
28"				8,700.00	6,000.00	
30"				9,500.00		

*Add an additional $700.00 for jointed toddler body or $500.00 for black version.

Kewpies

These sweet, little elfin-like creatures made their debut in the December 1909 issue of *Ladies Home Journal*.. Famous illustrator, Rose O'Neill, designed the Kewpies and held the design patents for them until her death in 1944. According to O'Neill, Kewpies first danced across her bed and shared their name with her while she was napping in her art studio—The Bird Café—on the third floor of her family home. O'Neill always maintained that she did not invent Kewpies; she only introduced them.

George Borgfeldt held the manufacturing rights for many years, eventually passing them to Joseph Kallus, who retained them until 1984 when Jesco took possession of the rights to the Kewpie trademark and copyright. Over the years, there have been many legal battles fought over the manufacturing of Kewpies without consent of the copyright. The Kewpies were so popular that it was inevitable that a Kewpie Doll would be born. The first Kewpie Doll was designed by Kallus, a friend of Miss O'Neill. Early Kewpies were made of bisque and came from Germany. It is reported that at the peak of the Kewpie craze, thirty German factories were producing Kewpies in order to meet demand. Although imports from Germany ceased during World War I, Kewpies continued to be made in the United States. The Cameo Doll Company of Port Allegheny, Pennsylvania, manufactured composition Kewpies, and later plastic and vinyl. Again, the demand for Kewpies was too great for a single company to supply. Kallus, president of Cameo Doll Company, licensed several other doll companies to aid in the manufacturing of Kewpie, including Effanbee, Strombecker, Knickerbocker, and Amsco. To maintain quality control, Kallus required each licensed company to affix a Cameo label, in addition to its own marking, on all their Kewpie dolls.

Rose O'Neill passed away more than a half century ago, but she and her immortal Kewpies are by no means forgotten. There is a collectors' club exclusively for Kewpies, as well as the Bonniebrook Historical Society, the home and final resting place for Rose O'Neill. Bonniebrook, located near Branson, Missouri, is a wonderful place to visit. The Bonniebrook Historical Society established a lasting memorial to her genius.

Collectors avidly seek all forms of Kewpies. Determining an authentic O'Neill Kewpie can sometimes be tricky. The first area of concern should be the marking. O'Neill's signature is often found incised in the bisque. Check the bottom of the foot. Factory markings are often obscure because, with the absence of clothing, there was no place for it to be hidden. A paper label with a clear protective covering was attached to the doll; however, it has often been removed. In the absence of markings, collectors should rely on the following clues:

1. Licensed Kewpies were never made in Japan. A "Nippon" or "Japan" mark indicates that the Kewpie is not authentic.

2. Rose O'Neill and Joseph Kallus both insisted on top quality. If a doll is made of poor quality materials or the application of decoration is inferior, the Kewpie is not authentic.

3. All Kewpies have blue-tipped wings.

4. Authentic Kewpies have star-shaped hands.

Prices listed are for dolls and figurines in good condition. If damaged or repaired, expect to pay about half the amount listed.

Dolls

All Bisque: jointed at shoulder only; molded and painted, top-knot hair; painted, round, side-glancing eyes with white dot highlights; closed, smiling, watermelon mouth; blue-tipped wings; typically signed "O'Neill" on sole of foot; may also have German manufacture marking.

Bisque Head: composition body; jointed at shoulder, hip, and knees; extended arms; starfish hands; long torso with rounded tummy; light brown, molded and painted, top-knot hair; round, glass, side-glancing eyes; single dot brow; closed, smiling, watermelon mouth; tiny, blue-tipped wings on sides of neck; typically marked "Ges.gesch/O'Neill J.D.K."

Bisque Head: flange neck; cloth body; molded and painted, light brown, top-knot hair; painted or glass, round, side-glancing eyes; single dot brow; closed, smiling, watermelon mouth; appropriately dressed; typically marked "A.B. & G 1377/ O'Neill."

Celluloid: straight-standing doll or action figure; jointed arms; painted, round, side-glancing eyes; closed, smiling, watermelon mouth; blue wings; typically marked "JUNO," paper label "Germany," or unmarked.

Composition: jointed at shoulder and occasionally the hip; arms extended; starfish hands; molded and painted, top-knot hair; painted, round, side-glancing eyes; single dot brows; closed, smiling, watermelon mouth; blue-tipped wings on back; typically marked with red, paper, heart-shaped label "Kewpie/Des & Copyright/by/Rose O'Neill."

4" bisque Kewpie Traveler and 3 1/4" bisque Kewpie with a cat. Courtesy of McMaster's Doll Auction

Composition Head: flange neck; cloth body; composition starfish hands; molded and painted, top-knot hair; painted, round, side-glancing eyes; single dot brows; closed, smiling, watermelon mouth; typically marked "O'Neill," "Cameo," or unmarked.

Cloth Kuddle Kewpies: all cloth; satin or plush body; mask-type Kewpie face; typically marked with cloth label "Kruegar" or "King Pat. number 1785800."

Hard Plastic Kewpies: all plastic; one-piece head, body, and legs; jointed at shoulder only; painted features; typically marked "Cameo."

Hard Plastic Kewpies: fully jointed at neck, shoulder, and hip; sleep eyes; typically marked "Cameo."

Vinyl Jesco: made using Cameo's original molds; molded and painted, top-knot hair; side-glancing eyes; original clothing; typically marked "Jesco."

Vinyl Pin-Hinged Limbs: painted features; original, one-piece pajama outfit; typically marked "Cameo" on head and body, and "S1/61C2/63" on doll's bottom.

Vinyl Ragsy Kewpie: blue vinyl; molded to resemble stitching; painted features; typically marked "Cameo 65 JLK" on head and "Cameo 6S" on back.

Red Plush Kewpie: plush body; vinyl face; painted features; typically marked with cloth label "Knickerbocker Toy Co. Inc./N.Y. U.S.A./Kewpie/Designed and Copyrighted/by Rose O'Neill/Licensed by Cameo Doll Co. 1964."

Bisque Kewpie Figurines (known as "Action Kewpies"): Typically marked with a paper label; incised "O'Neill" on the bottom of the foot, "©," or unmarked.

13" cloth Kuddle Kewpie. Courtesy of McMaster's Doll Auction

Kewpie Value Comparisons

Size	All Bisque, Painted Eyes*	Bisque Head, Composition Body, Glass Eyes	Bisque Head, Cloth Body, Painted Eyes	Bisque Head, Cloth Body, Glass Eyes	Celluloid Shoulder Joints, Painted Eyes	Composition Head and Body, Painted Eyes	Composition Head, Cloth Body
2"	200.00				75.00		
3"	225.00				100.00		
4"	250.00				125.00		
5"	300.00				150.00		
6"	450.00				175.00		
7"	550.00						
8"	700.00				275.00	350.00	
9"	850.00						
10"	1,100.00	6,000.00			400.00		
12"	1,700.00	6,800.00	2,600.00	3,500.00	450.00	600.00	350.00
14"		7,500.00					
15"					600.00		
20"		16,000.00			750.00		

Size	Black	Cloth, Kuddle Kewpie	Hard Plastic, Jointed Shoulders Only	Hard Plastic, Fully Jointed	Vinyl Jesco	Vinyl, Pin Hinged	Vinyl Ragsy	Plush Knickerbocker
6"								75.00
8"			200.00				75.00	
9"					80.00			
10"		350.00	225.00				150.00	
12"	550.00	400.00	300.00	600.00	125.00			100.00
14"		450.00		650.00	175.00			
16"			450.00	700.00	200.00	350.00		
18"		675.00			225.00	450.00		
20"		750.00			250.00			
22"					275.00			
24"					300.00			
27"					350.00			

*Add an additional $400.00–500.00 for jointed hips or molded and painted shoes and socks.

Kewpie Figurines Value Comparisons

Figurine	Size	Value
Blunderboo*	4"	$800.00
Bride and Groom	4"	900.00
Driving a Chariot or Riding an Animal	5"	5,500.00
Farmer	4"	1,200.00
Gardener	4"	1,200.00
Governor	4"	1,400.00
Guitar Player	3 1/2"	650.00
Holding Cat	4"	800.00
Holding Pen	3"	650.00
Hottentot (Black Kewpie)	3 1/2"	600.00
Hottentot (Black Kewpie)	5"	900.00
In a Basket with Flowers	4"	1,700.00
In a Drawstring Bag or Egg	4 1/2"	900.00
Kewpie Doodle Dog	1 1/2"	1,200.00
Kewpie Doodle Dog	3"	2,800.00
On Bench with Doodle Dog	4"	4,800.00
On Stomach	3 1/2"	600.00
Reading a Book	3 1/2"	1,200.00
Sitting in High Back Chair	4"	800.00
Soldier	4 1/2"	1,400.00
Buttonhole Kewpies Attached to Wooden Disk to Fit Into Buttonhole.	1 3/4"	225.00
Soldier and Nurse	6"	2,400.00
Thinker	6"	700.00
Traveler with Suitcase	3 1/2"	500.00
Two Kewpies Hugging	3 1/2"	350.00
Two Kewpies Reading Book	5 1/2"	2,500.00
Wearing Helmet	6"	1,500.00
With Broom or Mop	4"	900.00
With Butterfly	4"	1,200.00
With Dog Doodle	3 1/2"	1,900.00
With Ink Well	3 1/2"	900.00
With Ladybug	4"	650.00
With Outhouse	3"	1,600.00
With Pumpkin	4"	700.00
With Rabbit	2 1/2"	750.00
With Rose	2"	550.00
With Tea Table	4"	3,500.00
With Teddy Bear	4"	1,100.00
With Turkey	2"	700.00
With Umbrella	3 1/2"	800.00
With Umbrella and Doodle Dog	3 1/2"	1,400.00
In a Bisque Swing	3"	4,500.00
Kewpie Mountain or Tree (25 or more figures)		28,000.00

*Tumbling Kewpies are also known as Blunderboo. They have less rounded eyes and wider smiles.

Rare Kewpie Mountain. Courtesy of Ellen Schroy

Kley & Hahn

Albert Kley and Paul Hahn began business in Ohrdruf, Thüringia, Germany in 1902, with just fifteen employees. They devoted most of their efforts to capitalizing on the character doll boom in the American market.

Mold numbers indicate that several porcelain factories contributed to the Kley & Hahn inventory. Molds in the 200 series, 680 series, and the Walküre dolls were made by J. D. Kestner; the 100 series by Hertel, Schwab & Company; the 500 series by Bahr & Pröschild; and several trade names were also registered: Dollar Princess, Durable, K, Majestic, Mein Einziges Baby (My Only Baby), Mein Einzige (My Only One), Princess, Schneewittchen (Snow White), Special and Walküre.

Prices listed are for appropriately costumed dolls in good condition. Normal wear, slight damage, or well-made repairs to the body do not greatly affect the price. If the bisque is damaged or repaired, expect the value to be less than half the amounts listed. It is perfectly acceptable to show a missing or repaired finger or joint, or a mended body.

Named Dolly-Face: bisque socket head; jointed wood-and-composition body; good wig; glass eyes; feathered brows; open mouth; appropriately dressed; typically marked "Special 65 Germany," "Dollar Princess," "Majestie," or "Princess."

Walküre: bisque socket head; jointed wood-and-composition body; good wig; glass eyes; molded, feathered brows; open mouth; appropriately dressed; typically marked "Walküre Germany," "250," or "282."

Character Baby: bisque head; composition, bent-limb baby body; solid dome with molded and painted hair or good wig; painted or glass eyes; open or open/closed mouth; appropriately dressed; typically marked "Germany K & H" within a ribbon "133," "135," "138," "158," "160," "167," "176," "292," "525," "531," "571," or "680." ***Note:*** *Mold 571 is known as Giant Baby with 27" head circumference and 32" waist.*

Character Child: bisque socket head; jointed, composition body; molded and painted hair or good wig; painted or glass eyes; appropriately dressed; typically marked with mold number "154," "159," "162," "166," "169," "520," "526," "536," "546," "547," "548," "549," "554," "568," "567," or "654."

28" Kley and Hahn Walkure with pierced ears. Courtesy of David Cobb's Doll Auctions

24" Kley and Hahn #680. Character Baby with flirty eyes. Courtesy of David Cobb's Doll Auctions

Kley & Hahn Value Comparisons

Size	Named Dolly-Face	250/282 Walküre	Character Baby*	154 Closed Mouth, Glass Eyes*	154 Open Mouth, Glass Eyes*	159 2-Faced Doll, Glass or Painted Eyes*	162 or 554 Crying Expression	166 Closed Mouth, Glass Eyes*
12"			800.00			2,300.00		
14"			850.00			2,500.00		2,900.00
16"		750.00	900.00	3,000.00	1,900.00	2,700.00		
18"		800.00	950.00				2,800.00	
20"	600.00	850.00	1,000.00	3,900.00				
22"	700.00	900.00	1,200.00					4,200.00
24"		1,100.00	1,400.00		2,500.00			
25"							3,900.00	
26"	900.00	1,200.00	1,700.00					
28"	950.00	1,400.00	1,900.00					
30"		1,600.00						
34"		1,800.00						
36"		2,000.00						
42"			4,700.00					

Size	166 Open Mouth, Glass Eyes*	169 Closed Mouth, Glass Eyes*	169 Open Mouth, Glass Eyes*	520 Closed Mouth, Painted Eyes*	526 Closed Mouth, Painted Eyes*	536/546 Closed Mouth, Glass Eyes*	547 Closed Mouth, Glass Eyes*	549 Closed Mouth, Painted Eyes*	567 Multi-Face, Glass or Painted Eyes*	568 O/C Mouth Glass Eyes*
14"	1,600.00	2,900.00		5,700.00				5,000.00	2,400.00	
16"				6,100.00		6,000.00	6,900.00			
18"		3,900.00		6,400.00	5,900.00		7,400.00	5,700.00	3,000.00	
20"					6,400.00	6,900.00				
22"	2,300.00		2,000.00	7,300.00	7,200.00			6,700.00		2,900.00

* Add an additional $700.00 for jointed toddler body.

C. F. Kling & Company

⟨ornament⟩

A German porcelain factory, founded by Christian Friedrich Kling and operating from 1836 to at least 1941, began producing dolls about 1870. Among the sculptors responsible for the intricate details of the shoulder head dolls are Kienlenz, Liedel, Horn, Hermann Schmidt, Hugo Lieberman, and Paul Walter. It is not unusual to find flowers, jewelry, lacy-ruffles, and elaborate hair ornamentation incorporated into the molds.

Early Kling dolls are marked only with a mold number; after 1880 a ⟨bell symbol⟩ (bell symbol) was added. It is interesting that a few examples also have "K & R" or "K ★ R" added to the marking. It is assumed that before 1902, Kling manufactured doll heads for Kämmer & Reinhardt. Notably mold number 377 is found with either "K ★ R" or a ⟨bell symbol⟩ (bell symbol).

Frequently the same mold number may be found with glass or painted eyes, and with an open or closed mouth made of either bisque or china. For example, mold number 190 was registered as "molded hair, painted eyes, closed mouth, shoulder head." However, mold 190 was also made with wig, glass eyes, and an open mouth. It is not unusual to find Mold 182 with an open or closed mouth, and mold 189 as either a china or bisque head. Understanding these abnormalities will help collectors identify and evaluate dolls. It is vital, therefore, to categorize Kling dolls by characteristics and not rely totally on mold numbers.

Prices listed are for nicely costumed dolls in good condition. Slight flakes from a delicate ruffle or petal of a flower would detract from the value in direct relation to the degree of damage. If the porcelain is damaged or repaired, expect the value to be less than half the amounts listed. It is perfectly acceptable to show a missing or repaired finger or joint or a mended body.

Also see All Bisque, China Head.

14" closed mouth Kling #123, shoulder head on a kid body. Courtesy of David Cobb's Doll Auctions

Bisque

Shoulder head/molded hair/glass eyes/closed mouth: bisque shoulder head; cloth or kid body; molded and painted hair; glass eyes; closed mouth; appropriately dressed; typically marked "119," "122," "128," "133," "188," and possibly others.

Bisque shoulder head; *molded bodice, often ornate*; cloth or kid body; molded and painted hair; glass eyes; closed mouth; appropriately dressed; typically marked "151," "106," "170," and possibly others.

Bisque shoulder head; *molded cap or bonnet*; cloth or kid body; molded and painted hair; glass eyes; closed mouth; appropriately dressed; typically marked "116," "160," "217," "247," and possibly others.

Bisque shoulder head; cloth or kid body; molded and painted *boy-styled* hair; glass eyes; closed mouth; appropriately dressed; typically marked "140," "254," and possibly others.

Shoulder head/solid dome/glass eyes/closed mouth: bisque shoulder head; cloth or kid body; solid dome; good wig; glass eyes; closed mouth; appropriately dressed; typically marked "166," "167," "190," "203," "214," and possible others.

Shoulder head/molded hair/painted eyes/closed mouth: bisque (or china) shoulder head; cloth or kid body; molded and painted hair, often beautifully styled; painted eyes; closed mouth; appropriately dressed; typically marked "129," "131," "141," "142," "148," "176," "185," "186," "188," "189," "190," "200," "202," "220," and possibly others.

Bisque shoulder head; *molded bodice, often ornate*; cloth or kid body; molded and painted hair; painted eyes; closed mouth; appropriately dressed; typically marked "135," "170," and possibly others.

Bisque shoulder head; *molded cap or military hat, often with goatee*; cloth or kid body; molded and painted hair; painted eyes; closed mouth; appropriately dressed; typically marked "303," "305," and possibly others.

Bisque shoulder head; cloth or kid body; molded and painted *boy style* hair; painted eyes; closed mouth; appropriately dressed; typically marked "131," "254," "285," and possibly others.

Shoulder head/solid dome/glass eyes/open mouth: bisque shoulder head; cloth or kid body; solid dome; good wig; glass eyes; open mouth; appropriately dressed; typically marked "123," "124," "190," and possibly others.

Shoulder head/open pate/glass eye/open mouth: bisque shoulder head; cloth or kid body; good wig; glass eyes; open mouth; appropriately dressed; typically marked "373," "377," and possibly others.

Socket head/closed mouth: bisque socket head; jointed wood and composition body; good wig; glass eyes; closed mouth; appropriately dressed; typically marked "182," and possibly others.

Socket head/open mouth: bisque socket head; jointed wood and composition body; good wig; glass eyes; open mouth; appropriately dressed; typically marked "370," "372," "182," and possibly others.

China

Shoulder head/molded hair/painted eyes/closed mouth: china (or bisque) shoulder head; cloth or kid body; molded and painted hair, often beautifully styled; painted eyes; closed mouth; appropriately dressed; typically marked "129," "131," "141," "142," "148," "176," "185," "186," "188," "189," "190," "200," "202," "220," and possibly others.

Kling China Head Value Comparison	
Size	Shoulder Head, Molded Hair, Painted Eyes, Closed Mouth
14"	450.00
16"	500.00
18"	550.00
20"	600.00
21"	650.00
23"	675.00
24"	750.00
25"	800.00
28"	900.00

Kling Bisque Value Comparison

Size	Shoulder Head, Molded Hair, Glass Eyes, Closed Mouth*	Shoulder Head, Solid Dome, Wig, Glass Eyes, Closed Mouth	Shoulder Head, Molded Hair, Painted Eyes, Closed Mouth*	Shoulder Head, Solid Dome, Wig, Glass Eyes, Open Mouth	Shoulder Head, Open Pate, Wig, Glass Eyes, Open Mouth	Exceptionally Beautiful Or Unusual Molding, Elaborate Hair-Style, Collars, Bodices, Or Other Ornamentation**	Socket Head, Closed Mouth	Socket Head, Open Mouth
8"			300.00	400.00				
10"				500.00				
12"	850.00	800.00	450.00					
14"	900.00	850.00	500.00	700.00	550.00	1,800.00	2,000.00	650.00
16"	925.00		575.00					
18"	950.00	900.00	625.00			2,000.00	2,800.00	
20"	1,000.00		750.00		600.00	2,400.00		800.00
22"		1,200.00						900.00
24"	1,200.00		900.00		700.00			1,000.00
28"								1,400.00

* Add an additional $200.00 for boy-style hair.

** Add an additional $500.00 for glass eyes.

Knickerbocker Doll & Toy Company

The Knickerbocker Doll & Toy Company was established in New York City in 1925. Leo L. Weiss was the president, and A. S. Ferguson was the company's representative. Disney characters are among the premium products of this well-known American firm. Value is not only based on the condition of the doll, but also upon the popularity of the character portrayed.

Knickerbocker had exclusive rights to surprisingly few dolls; most were made by other toy companies as well. Also see Raggedy Ann & Andy.

Cloth Dolls

Prices listed are for appropriately costumed dolls with good color and little or no fading. If a doll is stained, torn, badly mended, or faded, expect the value to be less than half the amounts listed.

Dwarf: heavy oilcloth-type, pressed mask face; seam at sides of head; velveteen body in various colors with clothing being part of the body structure; cardboard in bottom of feet; arms stitched at shoulders; cotton gauntlet hands; mohair wig and beard; painted, expressive character face; slightly-pointed, brown, velveteen feet curved upwards; original cap with name printed in front in all capital letters, some letters printed on a slant; marked with wrist tag only, "Walt Disney's/Snow White and/The Seven Dwarves//America's/Premier Line of Stuffed Toys/Walt Disney's/Mickey Mouse/and/Donald Duck/Manufacturers/Knickerbocker Toy Co. Inc./New York City."

Disney Characters: all cloth; stuffed body; applied oil cloth eyes; appropriately dressed; typically marked on foot "Walt Disney's (character name) Knickerbocker Toy Co./Design Patent No. 82862"; hang tag "(Character Name) Mfg. Knickerbocker." **Note:** *All characters are comparable in quality. Value is based on the popularity of the character.*

10" Knickerbocker cloth, swivel head, pie-eyes, Mickey Mouse. Courtesy of McMaster's Doll Auction

Cloth Knickerbocker Value Comparisons

Size	Dwarf (each)	Mickey Mouse*	Pinocchio	Donald Duck	Jiminy Cricket	Minnie Mouse	Snow White	Katzenjammer Kid	Holly Hobbie
10"									65.00
13"		2,000.00	700.00	900.00	950.00	1,000.00		700.00	
14"	400.00							900.00	
16"						1,700.00	750.00	1,000.00	85.00
24"									135.00

* Mickey in original cowboy outfit with sheepskin chaps, guns, lasso, and hat is quite rare and valued at $4,000.00 or more.

Katzenjammer Kids (Hans, Mama, Captain, or Inspector): all cloth; applied and painted hair; cloth stitched on ears; glass button bug-eyes; bulbous, stuffed nose; painted facial accent features; closed mouth; appropriately dressed; marked with wrist tag only "Katzenjammer/Kids/Fritz/Knickerbocker/Toy Co. Inc./New York Toy Co. Inc./New York/Licensed by King Features Syndicate Inc."

Holly Hobbie: all cloth; stitched at shoulder and hip; mitt-type hands; yellow yarn hair; printed facial features; blue eyes; lashes; small, smiling mouth; original, calico dress and matching bonnet; marked with tag sewn into dress "Holly Hobbie/Knickerbocker Toy Co. Inc"; tags may vary.

Composition

Prices listed are for appropriately costumed dolls in good condition. Slight crazing is acceptable and does not greatly affect the price. If badly crazed, cracked, peeling, or repainted, expect the value to be less than half the amounts listed.

Dwarf: all composition; jointed at neck and shoulder; painted or mohair hair, beard; eyes and expressive facial features; dressed in velvet plush outfit; name printed on front of cap in all capital letters, some letters slanted; typically marked "Walt Disney Knickerbocker Toy Co."

Snow White: all composition; jointed at neck, shoulder, and hip; mohair wig or molded and painted black hair with molded and painted blue ribbon; painted brown, side-glancing eyes; closed mouth; original satin and velvet dress with matching cape; typically marked "Snow White Walt Disney//Knickerbocker Toy Co./New York" on body.

Girl: all composition; jointed at neck, shoulder, and hip; mohair wig; sleep eyes; light gray eye shadow; open mouth; appropriately dressed; typically marked "Knickerbocker Toy Co./New York" on back.

Character (Blondie, Dagwood, Alexander, Cookie, Jiminy Cricket, Pinocchio, and Donald Duck): all composition; jointed at neck, shoulder, and hip; realistic character face and body modelling; painted facial features; detailed authentic costumes; typically marked "(character name) W. D. PR. KN. T. Co. USA," "Walt Disney//Knickerbocker," "(character name) King Syndicated/Knickerbocker," and perhaps others.

Vinyl

Prices listed are for dolls in near-mint, original condition. If damaged, redressed, or undressed, expect the value to be less than one half to one fourth the amounts listed.

Annie: 7"; vinyl character head; (Aileen Quinn); plastic body; rigid vinyl limbs; rooted hair; painted eyes; smiling mouth; original, red cotton dress with white collar, white socks, and black shoes; marked "1982 CPI Inc. 1982 CTNYNS, Inc/1982 Knickerbocker Toy Co. Inc. H-15" **$85.00**

Daddy Warbucks: 7"; (Albert Finney); vinyl character head; plastic body; rigid vinyl limbs; solid dome; painted eyes; closed mouth; original, black suit and tie; white shirt and red cummerbund; marked "1982 CPI Inc. 1982 CTNYNS Inc./1982 Knickerbocker Toy Co. Inc H-22" **$65.00**

Miss Hannigan: 7" (Carol Burnett); vinyl character head; plastic body; rigid vinyl limbs; rooted hair; painted eyes; closed mouth; original, purple dotted dress with ruffle and purple shoes; marked "1982 CPI Inc. 1982 CTNYNS Inc./1982 Knickerbocker Toy Co. Inc H-22" **$85.00**

Punjab: 7" (Geoffrey Holder); dark vinyl character head; dark plastic body; rigid vinyl limbs; molded and painted hair and facial features; closed mouth; original all-white suit with gold trim; marked "1982 CPI Inc. 1982 CTNYNS Inc./1982 Knickerbocker Toy Co. Inc H-22" **$85.00**

Composition Knickerbocker Value Comparisons

Size	Composition Dwarf (each)	Snow White	Girl
9"	400.00		
14"		650.00	
15"			500.00
20"		900.00	

Size	Blondie	Dagwood	Alexander	Cookie	Jiminy Cricket	Pinocchio	Donald Duck
9"			700.00				
10"				900.00	900.00	1,200.00	1,500.00
11"	2,000.00						
13"		1,400.00					
14"						1,900.00	

Molly: 5 3/4" (Toni Ann Gisondi); vinyl character head; plastic body; rigid vinyl limbs; rooted dark hair; painted eyes; open/closed, wide, smiling mouth; original, turquoise dress with calico sleeves and collar; marked "1982 CPI Inc. 1982 CTNYNS Inc./ 1982 Knickerbocker Toy Co. Inc H-17"..............................$45.00

Little House on the Prairie Child: vinyl head, hands, and legs; cloth body; rooted hair; painted eyes; smiling mouth; original cotton dress with name printed on front pocket; marked "1978 ED FRIENDLY PRODUCTIONS INC/LIC JLM/ Made in Taiwan T-2" on back of head; dress tagged "Little House on the Prairie Made by Knickerbocker Toy Co." ...$65.00

Soupy Sales: vinyl head; cloth body; molded and painted hair; character face; painted eyes; heavy brows; closed, smiling mouth; non-removable clothes with polka-dot bow tie. Marked "1965 Knickerbocker" on back of head, tagged "Soupy Sales/ 1966 Soupy Sales W.M.C."....................................$250.00

Holly Hobbie: 10 1/2"; all vinyl; jointed at neck, shoulder, and hip; rooted, long hair; round, freckled character face; painted features; closed mouth; original calico dress and sun bonnet; marked "KTD/GAC/1974"...................................$75.00

Gebrüder Knoch

❦

The Knoch brothers, Ernst and Christian, opened their porcelain factory at Neustadt, near Coburg, Germany in 1877. Ernst was the doll creator, while Christian's talents lent more to the business dealing. Max Oscar Arnold purchased the factory in 1919 and discontinued the manufacturing of dolls.

The Knoch factory produced both dolly faced and character dolls. It is interesting to study the style variations, particularly with regard to character dolls. Several models, although charming, lack detail and inspiration. At the same time, others are wonderfully artistic.

For many years, Gebrüder Knoch received credit for dolls now known to have been made by Gebrüder Kuhnlenz. Knoch dolls are usually incised with crossed-bones, frequently "Made in Germany," the initials "G K N, Ges N Gesch," and/or "dep." The German translation for crossed-bones is "gekreuzte knochen," thus a double play of the G K N (Gebrüder Knoch Neustadt). Known mold numbers include 179, 181, 190, 192,

18" Gebrüder Knoch #181 Dolly-Face child. Courtesy of David Cobb's Doll Auctions

12" Gebrüder Knoch character baby with painted eyes and open-closed mouth with two lower glazed teeth. Courtesy of McMaster's Doll Auction

193, 201(black), and 204 registered socket heads. Also, 203, 205, 216, 217, 218, 223, 230, 232, 237, and 246 were registered shoulder heads. Many early Knoch dolls may be unmarked.

Prices listed are for appropriately dressed dolls in good condition. Normal wear, slight damage, or well-made repairs to the body do not greatly affect the price. If the bisque is damaged or repaired, expect the value to be less than half the amounts listed. It is perfectly acceptable to show a missing or repaired finger or joint or a mended body.

Dolly-face: bisque socket head; jointed wood and composition body; good wig; glass eyes; open mouth; appropriately dressed; typically marked with crossed-bones, "G K N/Made in Germany," "dep," "179," "181," "190," "192," "193," "201," and possibly others.

Character dolls: socket or shoulder head; may have molded tears or bonnet; jointed wood and composition, kid or cloth body; solid dome or molded and painted hair; painted eyes; open/closed expressive mouth; appropriately dressed; typically marked with crossed bones, "G K N/ Made in Germany," "dep," "Ges No Gesch," "203," "205," "206," "216," "217," "218," "223," "230," "232," "237," "246," and possibly others.

Gebrüder Knoch Doll Value Comparison

Size	Dolly-Face	Character, Not Individually Listed*	201 (Black Child)	204 Socket head Character*
14"		1,400.00		1,900.00
16"			1,000.00	
18"	550.00	1,800.00		2,660.00
20"		2,200.00	1,500.00	
22"	700.00			
24"	750.00			

* Add an additional $1,000.00 for black version.

** Add an additional $700.00 for jointed toddler body.

Size	216 & 218 Molded Hair, Open/ Closed Mouth With Two Lower Teeth	223 Molded Tears On Both Cheeks	237 Molded, Decorated Bonnet	246 One Eye, Winking, Molded Cap
14"			1,000.00	
16"	2,400.00	3,200.00		3,300.00
18"	3,000.00		1,500.00	
20"				3,800.00

Koenig & Wernicke

There are several points of disagreement concerning the Koenig & Wernicke (also spelled Konig & Wernicke) doll factory of Waltershausen, Thüringia, Germany. Uncertainty exists regarding the identities of the founders and owners, in addition to the spelling of their names. One fact that is undisputed is the date of the company's founding—1911.

Koenig & Wernicke was originally Koenig & Rudolph of Waltershausen. This team was made up of Max Koenig (Konig), and Max and August Rudolph. One year later, in 1912, Max and August Rudolph left the company and their share was taken over by Rudolf Wernicke. Some reports state that Max and August retired. However, their names surfaced intermittently in the doll industry over the next ten years. Nevertheless, the Rudolphs were out and Wernicke was in.

Koenig & Wernicke's bisque doll heads were poured at the porcelain factories of Bahr and Pröschild, Hertel, Schwab & Company, and Armand Marseille. Koenig & Wernicke supplied dolls under the trade names "My Playmate" and "My Pride" to George Borgfeldt, New York. Koenig & Wernicke is best known for its well modelled and nicely decorated character babies, made of fine quality bisque.

Coincidentally, several mold numbers registered by Koenig & Wernicke are identical to Simon & Halbig mold numbers. There is no known relationship between the two companies.

Prices listed are for appropriately costumed dolls in good condition. Normal wear, slight damage, or well-made repairs to the body do not greatly affect the price. If the bisque is damaged

42" Koenig & Wernicke # 4711 holding a Knickerbocker mohair teddy bear. Courtesy of David Cobb's Doll Auctions

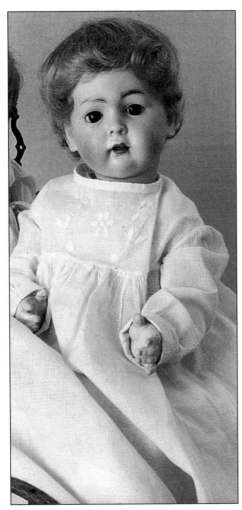

19" Koenig & Wernicke character baby. Courtesy of David Cobb's Doll Auctions

or repaired, expect the value to be less than half the amounts listed. It is perfectly acceptable to show a missing or repaired finger or joint, or a mended body.

Dolly Face: bisque socket head; jointed wood-and-composition body; good wig; glass eyes; open mouth; appropriately dressed; typically marked "4711," "K&W 1700," "K&W 4711." ***Note:*** *Glass eyes may be reflective and appear to follow you, however, the eyes do not move except to sleep.*

Character Baby: bisque socket head; composition, bent-limb baby body; good wig; glass eyes; open mouth; appropriately dressed; typically marked "Made in Germany," "98," "99," "179," "1040," "1090," "1570," "1590," "1070"; body may also be stamped "Germany/K&W." ***Note:*** *Glass eyes may be reflective and appear to follow you, however, the eyes do not move except to sleep.*

Character Child: very rare character bisque socket head; jointed wood-and-composition body; glass eyes; closed mouth; appropriately dressed; typically marked "199," "K&W 199," or "K & W" only. ***Note:*** *Glass eyes may be reflective and appear to follow you, however, the eyes do not move except to sleep.*

Koenig & Wernicke Value Comparisons			
Size	Dolly Face	Character Baby*	Character Child*
10"		600.00	1,600.00
12"		650.00	
14"		750.00	2,500.00
16"		850.00	3,200.00
18"	1,400.00	950.00	
20"	1,500.00	1,000.00	4,000.00
22"	1,600.00	1,200.00	
24"	1,700.00	1,400.00	4,500.00
26"	2,000.00	1,600.00	

* Add an additional $700.00 for jointed toddler body; $400.00 for reflective eyes.

Richard G. Krueger Inc.

Richard Krueger produced cloth dolls in New York City from 1920 through the 1930s. Krueger was also involved with King Innovations, the sole licensed manufacturer of soft-stuffed Kewpie dolls. This license was granted by Rose O'Neill and was fully protected by copyrights, trademarks, and United States patents.

Krueger produced a wide variety of dolls, including stuffed animals and rag dolls. Oilcloth was frequently used for the bodies and costumes. Most dolls are marked with a cloth label sewn either to the doll or its clothing.

Prices listed are for appropriately costumed dolls with good color and little or no fading. Slight wear and signs of aging, such as a settled body, do not greatly affect the price. If a doll is stained, torn, badly mended, or faded, expect the value to be less than half the amounts listed.

Also see Kewpies.

Pinocchio: pressed and molded cloth character face; attached ears; cloth body; jointed, wooden arms and legs; appropriately dressed; body labeled "Authentic Walt Disney/R. G. Krueger."

Dwarf: pressed and molded cloth face; side seams; velveteen body; arms stitched on at shoulders; polished cotton gauntlet hands; plush beard; painted facial features; clothing part of body structure; extra piece of velveteen forming belt and jacket tails at waist; "(Character Name)" stamped on top of hat in capital letters; marked with cloth body label "Authentic Walt Disney/Character/Exclusive/with R. G. Krueger, New York."

Oilcloth Child: heavy, buckram-type, mask face; side seams; flesh tone, soft cotton body and limbs; jointed at shoulder and hip; mitt hands with no stitching to indicate fingers; mohair wig; painted facial features; delicately-applied eyelashes; freckles across nose; closed, smiling mouth; appropriately dressed;

marked with body label "R Krueger/N.Y.C." and dress tag "Krueger, N.Y./Reg. U.S. Pat. Off. Made in U.S.A."

Cotton Child: mask-type face; cotton body; yarn hair; painted features; appropriately dressed; marked with "Krueger, N.Y./Reg. U.S. Pat. Off. Made in U.S.A."

Krueger Value Comparisons				
Size	Pinocchio	Dwarf (Each)	Oilcloth Child	Cotton Cloth
12"		300.00		175.00
12 1/2"			300.00	
15"	600.00			
16"			350.00	250.00

Complete set of Krueger Snow White and the Seven Dwarfs. Courtesy of David Cobb's Doll Auctions

Käthe Kruse

Käthe Kruse Dolls have been in production from 1910 to the present. Formerly located in Bad Kosen, Silesia, and Charlottenburg, Prussia, after World War II they moved to Donauworth, Bavaria. Artist Käthe Kruse founded the company. Legend tells that Käthe's husband was not in favor of his children playing with toys purchased at stores. To amuse her daughters, Käthe tied a towel to resemble a doll. The girls were happy for awhile, but eventually the towel came undone. Attempting to please her children, Käthe continued to improve her dolls, a task which ultimately developed into a successful business.

Käthe Kruse Dolls were made of waterproof treated muslin, cotton, wool, and stockinet. The earliest dolls were marked in black, red, or purple ink on the bottom of the foot with the name "Käthe Kruse" and a three- to five-digit number.

Käthe Kruse spent years developing a soft lifelike cloth doll that could withstand a child's loving. Daughter Hannah took over the doll manufacturing business after her mother's death in 1968.

Kruse was forced several times to bring litigation on infringement rights against competing doll manufacturers. While records indicate that she was always victorious, many Käthe Kruse-type Dolls were produced before a settlement was reached. Pay particular attention to markings on the bottom of the feet. Also, authentic Käthe Kruse Dolls typically have detailed toes. Sculpturing of the face and doll's decoration may also provide clues to its authenticity.

Prices listed are for originally costumed dolls with no damage. If torn, soiled, stained, repainted, or damaged in any way, expect to pay about one-half the amount listed.

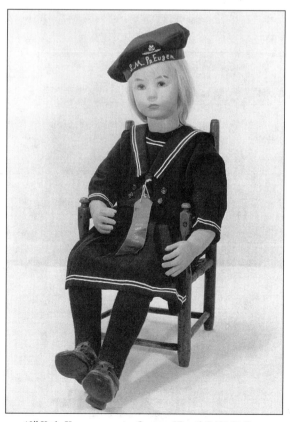

42" Käthe Kruse mannequin. Courtesy of David Cobb's Doll

Käthe Kruse Doll I. Courtesy of David Cobb's Doll Auctions

Doll I: 1910; all muslin; sturdy, toddler body; heavy, oil-painted hair; nicely painted eyes; closed mouth with pensive expression. This series can be identified by a center seam on the palm of the hand, three vertical seams on back of the head, and it may also have two chin seams.

Doll II: 1922; Schlenkerchen; all stockinet; arms and legs are supple and loose on soft body; heavy, oil-painted hair, nicely painted eyes with upper lashes; smiling, open/closed mouth. This series can be identified by one vertical seam on back of head.

Doll V and VI: 1925; all cloth; heavy, oil-painted hair; nicely painted facial features; closed, rather sad and pouty mouth; wigs added after 1930. Traumerchen have closed eyes with lashes. Du Mein have open eyes. Both dolls are found in both V and VI sizes. These dolls are often found weighted down with about five pounds of sand.

Doll VII: 1927, all cloth, heavy oil painted hair; nicely painted facial features, pensive face of Doll I or pouty Du Mein face, wigs were added to some dolls after 1929.

Doll VIII: 1929; all cloth; swivel head; human hair wig, or brush-stroked painted hair; painted facial features; closed mouth. Deutsches Kind can be identified by one vertical seam on back of head.

Doll IX: 1929; same as Doll VIII; Klein Deutsches Kind smaller size.

Doll X: 1935; swivel head; same type face as Doll I; smaller size.

Celluloid: 1936–1939; all celluloid; same characteristics as earlier cloth dolls; may have a turtle mark.

U.S. Zone/Germany: 1945–1951; very heavily painted; often with turtle mark.

Hard Plastic: 1952; pink muslin body; human hair wig; painted eyes.

Käthe Kruse Value Comparisons

Series	Size	Description	Excellent Condition
I, Early	16"	Wide hips	5,700.00
I, Later	17"	More slender hips	4,400.00
I, 1H	17"	Wigged	4,000.00
I, Bambino	8 1/2"	Special doll	2,600.00
II	13"	Schlenkerchen, smiling	12,000.00
V	17 1/2 to 19 1/2"	Du Mein, open eyes	7,800.00
V	17 1/2 to 19 1/2"	Traumerchen, closed eyes	7,500.00
VI	21 1/2 to 23 1/2"	Du Mein, open eyes	8,200.00
VI	21 1/2 to 23 1/2"	Traumerchen, closed eyes	8,000.00
VII	14"	Pensive or pouty, wide hips	3,000.00
VIII	21"	Deutscheskind, swivel head, wig	3,500.00
IX	14"	Klein Deutsches kind, swivel head, wig	2,200.00
X	14"	Swivel head, painted hair	2,200.00
Celluloid	16"	All celluloid	700.00
US Zone/Germany	14"	Very heavily painted	1,700.00
Hard Plastic	14"	Human hair wig, pink muslin body	600.00
Hard Plastic	20"	Human hair wig, pink muslin body	800.00
Contemporary	10"	Däumlinchen, Doggi, stuffed body	300.00
Contemporary	14"	Rumpumpel baby and toddler, stuffed body	500.00
Contemporary	14"	All hard plastic	200.00
Manniken	40" to 60"	Used in store display	3,000.00

Gebrüder Kuhnlenz

The firm of Gebrüder Kuhnlenz was founded by brothers Julius, Cuno, and Bruno Kuhnlenz in 1884. The Porzellanfabric (porcelain factory) was located in Kronach, Bavaria. Kuhnlenz dolls were long thought to be Gebrüder Knock or Gebrüder Krauss dolls. However, thanks to extensive research by Jurgen and Marianne Cieslik, we now know about Gebrüder Kuhnlenz and their wonderful dolls.

Kuhnlenz advertised "Doll heads with strange features." Perhaps "strange" is not exactly the correct term when discussing the lovely, unforgettable Kuhnlenz dolls. The bisque was quite pale; brows were heavy and close together; and frequently the dolls were found with very good quality paperweight eyes, finely lined in black, and long lashes. The open-mouth dolls have square, unglazed teeth, with lips more orange than red. Gebrüder Kuhnlenz also produced classic dolly-faced dolls with less dramatic expressions. Although they are utterly charming, they do not possess the same charisma as the "Strange Featured" dolls.

Many believe Gebrüder Kuhnlenz supplied doll heads for the French market. Few can dispute the fact that Kuhnlenz dolls share several French characteristics.

Mold numbers attributed to Gebrüder Kuhnlenz include 13, 21, 27, 28, 31, 32, 34, 36, 38, 41, 44, 47, 54, 56, 61, 68, 71, 72, 75, 76, 77, and 165.

Prices listed are for appropriately costumed dolls in good condition. Normal wear, slight damage, or well-made repairs to the body do not greatly affect the price. If the bisque is damaged or repaired, expect the value to be less than half the amounts listed. It is perfectly acceptable to show a missing or repaired finger or joint, or a mended body.

Also see All Bisque.

Closed Mouth Shoulder Head: pale bisque shoulder head; kid, often lady-type body; bisque arms; good wig; fine quality glass or paperweight eyes; softly feathered brows; delicately painted eyelashes; beautifully blushed; closed mouth; appropriately dressed; typically marked "G K 38."

Closed Mouth Socket Head: pale bisque socket head, jointed wood-and-composition body; good wig; fine quality glass or paperweight eyes; heavy feathered brows; closed mouth; appropriately dressed; typically marked "28," "31," or "32."

French Look: pale bisque socket head; French, jointed, wood-and-composition body; good wig; fine quality glass or paperweight eyes; feathered brows; closed mouth; appropriately dressed; typically marked "34."

Unique Look: bisque socket head; jointed wood-and-composition body; good wig; fine quality glass or paperweight eyes, finely lined in black; long lashes; heavy brows; open mouth; appropriately dressed; typically marked "GK," "41," "44," "54," or "56"

Dolly-Face Shoulder Head: bisque shoulder head; kid body, bisque arms; good wig; glass eyes, finely lined in black; heavy brows; open mouth; appropriately dressed, typically marked "13," "47," or "61."

Dolly-Face Socket Head: bisque socket head; jointed wood-and-composition body; good wig; glass eyes; feathered brows; open mouth; appropriately dressed; typically marked "G.K." or "165."

Tiny Doll: bisque socket head; five-piece composition or papier-mâché body with molded and painted shoes; mohair wig; glass eyes; open mouth; appropriately dressed; typically marked "44" and a sunburst.

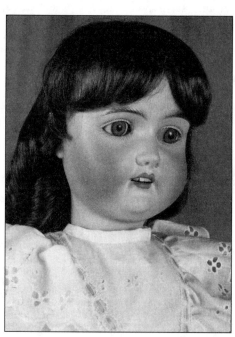

29" Kuhnlenz #165 Dolly-Face child. Courtesy of McMaster's Doll Auction

23" closed mouth Kuhnlenz character #32. Courtesy of David Cobb's Doll Auctions

	Closed Mouth, Shoulder Head, Kid Body	Closed Mouth, Socket Head, Jointed Body	French-Look, Closed Mouth, French Body*	Unique-Look, Open Mouth, Jointed Body	Dolly-Face, Shoulder Head, Kid Body	Dolly-Face, Open Mouth, Socket Head, Jointed Body	
Size							Tiny Doll
7 1/2"		1,300.00					300.00
14"	1,300.00	1,800.00	4,000.00				
16"	1,500.00	2,400.00		1,500.00	800.00	550.00	
18"	1,600.00	2,600.00	5,900.00	1,600.00	900.00	600.00	
20"	1,700.00	3,000.00	6,400.00	1,700.00	1,000.00	650.00	
22"	1,900.00		6,800.00	1,900.00		750.00	
24"	2,100.00			2,000.00			
28"				2,500.00		1,000.00	
30"						1,200.00	
32"						1,400.00	
34"						1,600.00	

Gebrüder Kuhnlenz Value Comparisons

* Add an additional $500.00 for black version.

A. Lanternier et Cie

 . Lanternier et Cie was a late arrival to the French doll scene. Although the company was founded in 1855, it was not until 1915 that it began producing doll heads.

17" Lanternier "JE Masson Lorraine." Courtesy of David Cobb's Doll Auctions

Many of the dolls produced by Lanternier have interesting and distinctive modelling. Others are less memorable. Considering this porcelain factory was located in Limoges, France, a city known worldwide for its porcelain products, the vast difference in the quality of the bisque is startling, ranging from very good to coarse and grainy.

Despite the varying quality of the dolls, particularly when compared to their German counterparts of the same era, Lanternier Dolls are undeniably popular. This may be the result of collectors' desire to own a first (or second or third) French doll and showing little regard for the variations in quality and excellence of production. Be patient and take the time to find a Lanternier doll that will satisfy both your taste and pocketbook. Lanternier et Cie. marks include trade names "Caprice," "Cherie," "Favorite," "La Georgienne," "Lorraine," "Masson," and "Toto," initials "CC," the signature of J. E. Masson, or the word "Limoges."

Prices listed are for appropriately costumed dolls in good condition. Normal wear, slight damage, or well-made repairs to the body do not greatly affect the price. If the bisque is damaged or repaired, expect the value to be less than half the amounts listed. It is perfectly acceptable to show a missing or repaired finger or joint, or a mended body.

Character Child: bisque head; jointed wood-and-composition body; good wig; jeweled eyes; open/closed mouth with molded upper and lower teeth; appropriately dressed; typically marked "Limoges" with anchor and "Toto."

Child: standard quality; bisque socket head; jointed wood-and-composition body; good wig; glass eyes lined in black; lower lashes painted straight with no slant; pierced ears; open mouth with molded teeth; appropriately dressed; typically marked "Fabrication Francaise," "Limoges" within a box, or "Limoges."

Child: better quality, nicely decorated bisque socket head; jointed wood-and-composition body; good wig; very good quality glass jeweled or paperweight eyes, lined in black; nicely painted lashes; pierced ears; open, slightly-smiling mouth; molded teeth; appropriately dressed; typically marked "Déposé Fabrication Francaise" within a box/"FAVORITE/J. E. Masson/AL & Cie/Limoges," "Cherie," or "Caprice."

Lady Lanternier: bisque socket head, designed by J. E. Masson; five-piece lady body; long, graceful arms and legs; good wig; glass eyes, lined in black; open/closed mouth with molded upper teeth; appropriately dressed; marked "J. E. Masson/LOR-RAINE/No. 0/A. L. & Cie/Limoges."

A. Lanternier et Cie Value Comparisons

Size	Character Child	Child, Standard Quality	Child, Better Quality	Lady Lanternier
12"	900.00			
14"	1,000.00			
16"	1,200.00	800.00	1,000.00	1,400.00
18"	1,400.00	850.00	1,100.00	1,600.00
20"	1,500.00	950.00		
22"		1,100.00	1,300.00	
24"		1,200.00		
26"		1,400.00	1,600.00	
28"		1,700.00	2,000.00	
30"		2,300.00	2,500.00	

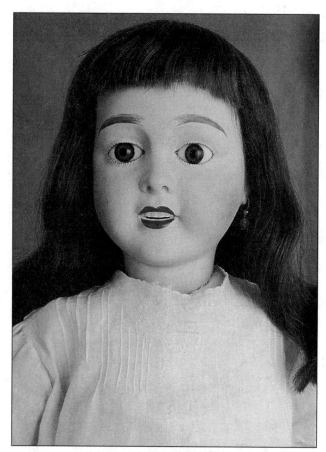

26" Lanternier "Favorite." Courtesy of David Cobb's Doll Auctions

Lenci

The Lenci Doll history of Turin, Italy, is well documented and quite interesting. Young Elana Konig Scavini was left alone when her husband, Enrico, went off to the war in 1918. Elana and her brother, Bubine Konig, made their first felt doll in the Scavini's apartment. Bubine steam-pressed the faces and Elana did the artistic work. This was the beginning of the world-famous Lenci doll.

There are at least two explanations for the name "Lenci." The more romantic is that Lenci was a nickname given to Elana by her husband before he went off to war. This may be true, for there is evidence that Elana used this name as early as 1915, when a gift was given her with the name "Lenci" engraved on it. However, the Lenci Company gives an entirely different explanation. According to the company records, the Lenci trademark was registered in 1919 as a child's spinning top with the words "Ludus Est Nobis Constanter Industria (taken from the Latin motto, freely translated to mean "To Play Is Our Constant Work."), forming the acronym "LENCI."

By the 1920s, the dolls produced by the Lenci factory had achieved worldwide recognition for their artistic beauty. Lenci was the first company to produce dolls using the pressed-felt method to give the faces dimensional character.

Lenci Dolls are often referred to in series, such as 'Mascotte' for the small 9-inch characters; 'Hard Faced' for composition, mask, or flocked plastic heads; and 'Bambino' for bent-limb babies. Code numbers are also commonly used; for example, children with hollow, felt torsos are in the 300 series, pouty-face dolls in the 1500 series, ladies or gentlemen in the 165 series, and girl dolls in the 700 series.

Lenci dolls may be marked with a hang tag, clothing label, or a purple or black "Lenci" stamp on the bottom of a foot. This stamp has a tendency to wear off easily.

Also see Boudoir Dolls.

Lenci Doll Characteristics

1. Zigzag stitching on back of neck, through tops of arms and legs, and occasionally at crotch.

2. Ears on larger dolls (over 10" tall) are double thickness of felt sewn together and then top stitched.

All original marked Lenci 22" with box, 17", and a 12". Courtesy of David Cobb's Doll Auctions

3. Human hair or mohair is attached in rows or strips.

4. Hollow cardboard bodies covered with felt or cloth; occasionally stuffed.

5. Well-shaped and proportioned arms and legs; slight elbow bend.

6. Nicely formed hands with separate thumb; mitt-type, stitched fingers, or separate fingers with third and fourth fingers stitched together.

7. Beautifully sculptured face with pleasingly round cheeks and soft expression.

8. Two white dots in each eye; one in upper right hand corner, and the other in lower left hand corner; or glass eyes.

9. Artistically applied two-tone lip color.

10. White, milk glass buttons on felt and/or organdy clothing; three or four holes in shoe buttons.

11. Scalloped top socks.

While ostensibly produced as playthings for children, their sophisticated design and cost resulted in many Lenci dolls being purchased as "playthings" for adults, which explains why so many vintage Lenci dolls are found in near mint condition.

There are many reports of Lenci-type dolls found with "Lenci" stamped on the foot. Rubber stamps are easily duplicated. The above characteristics can be used to separate fakes from authentic Lenci dolls..

Adult, Teenager, or Child: all felt; pressed face; jointed at neck, shoulder, and hip; mohair wig; painted, side-glancing eyes; closed mouth; original costume; typically marked with hang tag, clothing label, and/or "Lenci" stamped on foot, or unmarked.

Bambino: all felt; bent-limb body; pressed face; hand in fist position; mohair wig; painted, side-glancing eyes; closed mouth; original costume; typically marked with "Bambino" hang tag or "Bambino" clothing label.

Floppy Limb Felt Dolls: all felt; swivel neck; long arms and legs; mohair wig; felt disk eyes sewn to face; painted rosy cheeks; felt lips; original, felt costume; typically marked with hang tag attached to clothing.

Mascotte: loop at top for hanging; all felt; mohair wig; painted, side-glancing eyes; raised, sculptured eyebrows; closed mouth; surprised expression; original tagged costume.

Miniature: all felt; mohair wig; painted, round, side-glancing, surprised eyes; raised, sculptured brows; mouth with surprised "oh" expression; original tagged costume; heart-shaped wrist tag.

Hard Face: flocked hard plastic head; cloth body; felt limbs; mohair wig; painted eyes; small mouth; original, tagged costume; typically marked with hang tag, clothing label, and "Lenci/Made in Italy."

Chubby Cheeked: all felt; pressed felt, adorable character face; full, round cheeks; tiny nose; smile line under eyes; mohair wig, styled to emphasize and accentuate the chubby cheeks; painted, side-glancing eyes; small, closed mouth; original, tagged costume and accessories; typically marked with hang tag, clothing label, and "Lenci" stamped on foot or unmarked.

Contemporary: 1980 on; beautifully made, all jointed felt; mohair wig; painted, side-glancing eyes; closed mouth; original, tagged costume; typically marked with hang tag, clothing label, and "Lenci" along with production number stamped on foot; original, blue fabric-covered box and brightly colored, lithograph numbered, and signed certificate.

Other Lenci Dolls

Lenci Head: wearing hat with felt loop for hanging; used for decorative purposes..................................$150.00

Lenci Head: wrapped in felt petals forming flowers and painted into clay pot; several Lenci flowers in shades of yellow, green, and violet..................................$750.00

Lenci Head: with cap on top of basket as lid..............$150.00

Lenci Pan: all green pincushion; beautifully decorated with bright felt..................................$400.00

Purse: all felt lady with handle being part of doll; painted face with side-glancing eyes; beautifully dressed........................$500.00

Smooth Face Girl: pressed felt face, finished to resemble composition; painted eyes; rosy cheeks; closed mouth..$1,400.00

Lenci Value Comparisons

Size	Adult, Teenager, or Child	Bambino	Floppy Limb	Mascotte	Miniature	Hard Face
8–8 1/2"				600.00		
9–9 1/2"	700.00				550.00	
11–12"	1,000.00					300.00
13–14"	1,300.00	2,400.00				
15–16"	1,400.00	2,600.00				
17–18"	1,600.00	2,800.00				
19–20 1/2"	1,800.00	3,000.00				900.00
21–22"	2,200.00					
23–24"	2,400.00		250.00			
25–26 1/2"	2,700.00					
27–28 1/2"	3,000.00					
29–30 1/2"	3,200.00					
31–32 1/2"	3,400.00					
35"	3,800.00					
37"	4,000.00		350.00			
38"	4,200.00					
40"	4,600.00					

Size	Chubby Cheeked	Contemporary*	Sports Character	Brown/Black Island Character
13–14"		200.00		
15–16"			4,200.00	2,800.00
17–18"	3,500.00		4,600.00	
19–20 1/2"				3,500.00
21–22"		350.00	4,900.00	
23–24"			5,200.00	
27–28 1/2"		600.00		
31–32 1/2"			6,900.00	4,900.00

*Add an additional $200.00 for wide-awake or surprise eyes.

Size	Aviator (Amelia Earhart)	Tom Mix	Oriental	Indian Holding Papoose	Mozart, Bach, and Mendel	Wide-Awake	Googly Glass Eyes	Rudolph Valentino	Amor Black Cupid
16–17"			4,300.00						
18–19"	4,500.00	4,700.00	4,800.00	6,200.00	5,000.00		3,200.00		3,700.00
20–21"			5,200.00			3,200.00	3,500.00		
24–25"							3,800.00		
29–30 1/2"								15,000.00	

Lenci-Type Dolls

So popular and successful were the Lenci dolls that many companies could not resist the temptation to copy them. In many cases, they even copied the label designs. A sampling of companies that produced copies of Lenci dolls include: Alma, Alpha, Alexander, American Stuffed Novelty, Amfelt, Averill, Chad Valley, Celia, Davis, Deans, Eros, Fiori, Giotti, La Rosa, Magis, Perotti, Pori, Raynal, and Wellings.

Many Lenci-Type dolls are charming and very well made, however, they frequently lack the artistic appeal of the authentic Lenci dolls. One exception is R. John Wright, a gifted American artist and winner of the prestigious 'Jumeau Award' in the category of Outstanding International Doll Artist. Wright designs and creates extremely popular, contemporary, all felt dolls of superb quality.

Prices listed are for originally costumed dolls in very good to near mint condition. If torn, stained, moth-eaten, badly mended, faded, redressed, or undressed, expect the value to be less than half the amount listed. Character dolls elaborately costumed, historically noteworthy, or with exceptional visual appeal, may be valued much higher.

Child: all felt or cloth; mohair wig; painted features; nicely dressed in original felt or organdy costume; typically marked with cloth label, hang tag, wrist tag, or unmarked.

Novelty: all felt; mohair wig; painted features; often dressed in ethnic, military, or comic costumes; typically marked with cloth label, hang tag, wrist tag, or unmarked.

R. John Wright: all felt; swivel head; jointed limbs; stitched fingers; pressed and painted facial features; mohair wig; closed, pouty mouth; original, detailed costume; typically marked "Wright Little People," character name, and production number; clothing tagged "R. J. Wright," brass "RJW" button on clothing or doll.

Unmarked Lenci-type. Courtesy of McMaster's Doll Auction

Lenci-Type Value Comparisons			
Size	Child	Novelty	R. John Wright*
7 1/2"		75.00	
12"		150.00	
14"	750.00		
16"	850.00		1,400.00
18"	900.00		1,700.00
20"	950.00		2,100.00

* Add an additional $500.00–800.00 for popular personality or exceptional quality.

A. G. Limbach

This factory was founded in 1772 by Gotthelf Greiner, near Alsbach, Thüringia, Germany. A.G. Limbach was an early pioneer in the doll industry. The Sonneberg Museum has identified a china shoulder-head doll dating from 1850 as having been made by Limbach. The most beautiful of the Limbach bisque doll heads were made prior to 1899, when the production of bisque doll heads was temporarily discontinued.

Early dolls were marked with only the cloverleaf trademark and size number. Most were socket heads on composition bodies, although occasionally a bisque shoulder plate was used with a kid and/or cloth body.

The manufacture of bisque doll heads was resumed in 1919, when the trade name Norma, Rita, or Wally began to appear, along with the cloverleaf and crown mark. During the twenty-year interim, Limbach continued to manufacture small figurines, all bisque, and bathing dolls.

Prices listed are for appropriately costumed dolls in good condition. Normal wear, slight damage, or well-made repairs to the body do not greatly affect the price. If the bisque is damaged

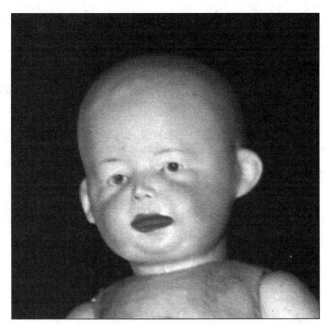

14" Limbach #8661 character baby. Courtesy of Ellen Schroy

Early Child: bisque socket head; full lower cheeks; jointed composition-and-wood or kid body with shoulder plate; good wig; large, oval-shaped eyes; open or closed mouth; appropriately dressed; typically marked with cloverleaf and size number only.

Dolly Face: bisque socket head, jointed wood-and-composition body; good wig; glass eyes; open mouth; appropriately dressed; typically marked "Wally," "Norma," or "Rita," (crown/cloverleaf) Limbach."

Character Baby: bisque socket head; composition bent-limb baby or composition body; solid dome or good wig; painted or glass eyes; closed or open mouth; appropriately dressed; typically marked "8682" (this doll is similar in appearance to character dolls produced by Swaine & Company) "8679" (this doll appears to be a more mature version of 8682), or 8661.

A. G. Limbach Value Comparisons

Size	Early Closed Mouth	Early Open Mouth	Dolly-Face Composition	Character Baby
12"	2,900.00	1,100.00		
14"	3,000.00	1,200.00	600.00	2,700.00
16"	3,100.00	1,300.00	650.00	
18"	3,200.00	1,400.00	700.00	
20"	3,300.00	1,500.00	725.00	4,200.00
22"	3,700.00	1,700.00	750.00	
24"	3,900.00	1,900.00	800.00	

or repaired, expect the value to be less than half the amounts listed. It is perfectly acceptable to show a missing or repaired finger or joint, or a mended body.

Also see All bisque, Parian.

Albert Marque

$\mathcal{A}$lbert Marque, a Parisian sculptor, designed the model for the A. Marque dolls, produced from 1910-1916. At a young age, Albert received critical acclaim for his Art Nouveau effigies of children. By the time he was twenty-five, he had displayed and won recognition for his works in bronze, marble, terra cotta, and plaster. It must have seemed a reasonable progression to include doll modelling to his repertoire.

In 1916, The Carnegie Museum purchased, for $35.00 each, five A. Marque dolls. They were beautifully dressed to portray Queen Isabel, Queen Marie, Queen Antoinette, Empress Josephine, and Empress Eugenie. The dolls arrived in custom-made boxes covered in fine French wallpaper. The Museum also purchased, for $20.00 each, thirty-five S. F. B. J. dolls, authentically dressed in regional costumes of Russia, Italy, Switzerland, England, and France. These dolls also arrived in custom-made boxes covered in fine French wallpaper. This event contributed greatly to the theory that S. F. B. J. produced the A. Marque doll, using the model designed by Albert Marque. The flaw to the deduction is the absence of the customary "S. F. B. J." mark. Perhaps a more logical explanation is the doll was simply made by the artist, thus explaining the very limited number of A. Marque dolls that are known to exist. There are only fifty authenticated examples. Of course, there may be one lying in a hidden corner of your attic, yet to be discovered!

Rare A. Marque. Photograph by P. Byron. Courtesy of Ellen Schroy

Reproductions of the A. Marque doll do exist. A careful inspection of the marking is essential. A true A. Marque was signed in script at a slant across the back of the head. There were no mold or size numbers. All known A. Marque dolls are twenty-two inches tall with the proportions of a tall, thin child (reproductions seem to be about nineteen inches tall). Exquisitely modelled bisque hands and forearms were connected to composition upper arms and strung onto a composition body with long, thin feet. The translucent, pale bisque head was a masterpiece of modeling. To avoid any undercuts, the mold was made in five sections. A careful inspection of the inside of the head should reveal the mold seams. The doll also has very good quality paperweight eyes, rich brown feathered brows, deep creased eyelids, black eyeliner, and lashes that skip over the crease line. The mouth is painted a deep vermilion red. A lighter red is used for eye-corner dots and nostrils. Original clothing is labeled Margaine Lacroix or Worth, and marked Eugene Alart shoes (leather soles incised with a standing girl and "Déposé" beneath).

Prices listed are for appropriately dressed dolls in good condition. Normal wear, slight damage, or well-made repairs to the body do not greatly affect the price. If the bisque is damaged or repaired, expect the value to be less. The A. Marque is so rare and desirable, serious collectors will forgive fine hairlines or professional repairs that do not jeopardize the integrity of the doll. The price should reflect the degree and extent of damage.

A. Marque: 22"; pale bisque socket head; long slender neck; broad forehead; pointed chin; wood and composition body with fine bisque lower arms; human hair wig; wide spaced paperweight eyes; closed mouth; appropriately dressed; marked "A. Marque" signature on a diagonal across back of head ....**$85,000.00.**

Armand Marseille

Armand Marseille founded his famous doll company in 1885, in Sonneberg and Köppelsdorf, Thüringia, Germany.

Armand Marseille was born in 1856 in St. Petersburg (Leningrad), Russia, where his father was an architect. Around 1860, the Marseille family left Russia, roamed Europe for a time, and eventually settled in Coburg, which was then Thüringia in Southern Germany. In 1884, Armand Marseille bought the toy factory of Mathias Lambert in Sonneberg, and the next year took possession of the Porcelain Factory of Lidbermann & Wegscher in Köppelsdorf.

From 1900 until 1930, Armand Marseille was one of the largest suppliers of bisque doll heads in the world, reportedly producing a thousand heads a day. Companies using Armand Marseille heads include Amberg, Arranbee, C. M. Bergmann, Borgfeldt, Butler Bros., Cuno & Otto Dressel, Eckart, Edelmann, Otto Gans, Goldberger, Hitz, Jacobs & Kassler, Illfelder, E. Maar, Montgomery Ward, Emil Pfeiffer, Peter Scherf, Seyfarth & Reinhardt, Siegel Cooper, E.U. Steiner, Wagner & Zetzsche, Wislizenus, and Louis Wolf.

Occasionally, a reproduction character doll will appear on the secondary market. Always inspect the markings. Check for names, initials, and dates that were not part of an A. M. marking. Bisque used by Armand Marseille was not silky-satin smooth. The decoration, though well done, did not have a perfect art-like application. Many of the reproductions appear to be precisely decorated. This was not the case with mass-produced dolls at that time.

Prices listed are for appropriately costumed dolls in good condition. Normal wear, slight damage, or well-made repairs to the body do not greatly affect the price. If the bisque is damaged or repaired, expect the value to be less than half the amounts listed. It is perfectly acceptable to show a missing or repaired finger or joint, or a mended body.

Also see Oriental, Googly-Eyed Dolls.

Standard Dolly-Face, Shoulder Head: bisque shoulder head; kid, cloth, or imitation leather body; good wig; glass eyes; may have fur brows; open mouth; appropriately dressed; typically marked "Made in Germany," "A. M.," "Armand Marseille," "270," "309," "370," "376," "920," "957," "2015," "3200," "Alma," "Darling," "Duchess," Floradora," "Lily," "Lissy," "Mabel," "My Dearie," "My Playmate," or "Rosebud."

Better Dolly-Face, Shoulder Head: bisque shoulder head; kid body; good wig; glass eyes; open mouth; appropriately dressed; typically marked "AM/DEP/Made in Germany," "Armand Marseille," "1374," "1890," "1892," "1894," "1895," "1896," "1897," "1899," "1900," "1901," "1902," "1903," "1905," "1909," "2000," "3091," "3093," "3095," "3200," "3300," "3500," "3700," "4008," "Baby Betty," "Beauty," "Jubilee," "Majestic," "Princess," or "Queen Louise."

Armand Marseille Dolly-Face, 31" Queen Louise, and 32" #390. Courtesy of David Cobb's Doll Auctions

Dolly-Face Socket Head: bisque socket head; jointed wood-and-composition body; good wig; glass eyes; open mouth; appropriately dressed; typically marked "Made in Germany/Armand Marseille," "384," "390,"' 390n," "391," "395," "1894," "1897," "2010," "3600," "Baby Betty," "Floradora," "Queen Louise," or "Rosebud." ***Note:*** *that several dolls share a name with shoulder heads.*

Character Lady: bisque, mature-lady socket head; five-piece, slender, composition, lady's body; good wig; glass eyes; soft brows; closed mouth; appropriately dressed; typically marked "400," "401," or "M. H."

Character Baby: bisque, character socket head; composition bent-limb baby body; appropriately dressed; typically marked "Germany A. M. DRGM," "259," "326," "327," "329," "347," "352," "360a," "750," "760," "790," "900," "927," "971," "980," "984," "985," "990," "991," "996," "1330," or "1333."

Infant (Dream Baby, Kiddie Joy, Our Pet): bisque socket head or flange neck; composition bent-limb baby or cloth body; appropriately dressed; typically marked "AM Germany," "341," "351," "342," or "Our Pet." A "K" at the end of the marking designates a composition body.

Named Character Baby: bisque socket head or flange neck; kid or cloth body; composition arms and straight legs or composition bent-limb baby body; painted hair or good wig; sleep eyes; soft brows; open or closed mouth; dimples; may have pierced nostrils; appropriately dressed; typically marked "Baby Gloria/A Germany M," "Melitta," "Ellar," "Phyllis," or "Gloria."

Character Doll: bisque, expressive character face; various body types; molded and painted hair or good wig; glass or painted eyes; open, closed, or open/closed mouth; appropriately dressed; typically marked with mold number (see chart) or "AM" only.

12" Armand Marseille #251/248 character baby. Courtesy of David Cobb's Doll Auctions

18" Armand Marseille #590 character child. Courtesy of David Cobb's Doll Auctions

Armand Marseille #990 character twin babies in a Whitney carriage. Courtesy of David Cobb's Doll Auctions

Armand Marseille Value Comparisons

Size	Dolly-Face Shoulder Head Kid Body Standard Quality	Dolly-Face Shoulder Head Kid Body Better Quality*	Dolly-Face Socket Head Composition Body*	Character Lady**	Character Baby Bent-Limb Baby Body	Open Mouth Infant Cloth Body
8"					450.00	300.00
10"	350.00	400.00	500.00	2,000.00	500.00	475.00
12"	375.00	450.00	525.00	2,500.00	550.00	500.00
14"	400.00	475.00	550.00	2,900.00	650.00	675.00
16"	425.00	500.00	575.00	3,400.00	850.00	700.00
18"	450.00	525.00	600.00	4,000.00	900.00	800.00
20"	500.00	575.00	650.00	4,800.00	950.00	900.00
22"	525.00	625.00	700.00	5,500.00	1,100.00	1,000.00
24"	600.00	675.00	750.00	6,500.00	1,200.00	
26"	650.00	750.00	900.00		1,400.00	
28"	700.00	800.00	1,000.00			
30"	750.00	900.00	1,400.00			
34"			1,900.00			
38"			2,600.00			
40"			2,800.00			
42"			3,000.00			

Size	Open Mouth Infant Composition Body	Closed Mouth Infant Cloth Body	Closed Mouth Infant Composition Body	Named Character, Cloth or Kid Body	Named Character, Composition Body
8"	350.00	375.00	450.00	850.00	950.00
10"	525.00	550.00	625.00	875.00	1,100.00
12"	550.00	575.00	650.00	900.00	1,300.00
14"	750.00	775.00	850.00	950.00	1,500.00
16"	800.00	850.00	925.00		1,600.00
18"	875.00	900.00	975.00	1,000.00	1,700.00
20"	975.00	1,000.00	1,100.00		1,800.00
22"	1,100.00	1,200.00	1,250.00		1,900.00
24"				1,500.00	

Add an additional $300.00 for black version of any doll.

* Add an additional $200.00–400.00 for nice, soft coloring or an exceptionally pretty doll.

** Add an additional $300.00 for high knee, flapper body.

Armand Marseille Character Value Comparisons

Size	233 OM, Glass Eyes	251/248 CM, Molded Tongue, Glass Eyes	328 OM, Glass Eyes	410 OM, 2 Rows of Teeth, Glass Eyes	580/590 O/CM, Glass Eyes	920 OM, Glass Eyes	970 Character
12"			650.00		1,600.00		
14"	650.00	4,000.00	700.00	2,400.00	1,800.00		
16"	750.00	4,600.00	950.00	2,700.00			
18"					2,400.00	900.00	800.00
20"	1,000.00	5,900.00	1,300.00			1,000.00	900.00
22"				3,800.00	3,200.00		

Armand Marseille Character Value Comparisons

Size	255 OM, 2 Rows of Teeth, Glass Eyes	230 CM, Fanny Solid Dome, Glass Eyes	231 CM, Fanny Wig, Glass Eyes	250/248 G.B. OM, Painted Eyes	300 MH CM, Glass Eyes	310 CM, Glass Eyes	340 OM, Glass Eyes	345 CM, Painted Eyes
9"					1,800.00	2,400.00		
10"				900.00				
12"				1,300.00				1,900.00
14"			6,800.00				3,200.00	2,300.00
16"	4,200.00	7,200.00	7,100.00	1,900.00				2,700.00
18"		8,900.00					4,300.00	
20"	5,000.00	9,500.00	9,500.00					

Size	350 CM, Glass Eyes	362 Black Character	372 OM, Glass Eyes	375 OM, Glass Eyes	451 OM, Glass Eyes	500 AM, 232 CM, Glass Eyes	520 AM, 232 CM, Glass Eyes	550 CM, Glass Eyes
10"	1,600.00						1,200.00	
12"			700.00			1,000.00		2,900.00
14"		1,100.00	1,000.00			1,300.00		
16"	2,900.00						2,000.00	
18"			1,200.00	1,200.00	1,200.00	1,900.00		4,000.00
20"	3,800.00							
22"				1,500.00			2,700.00	5,000.00
24"	4,700.00							

Size	560 AM, 232 O/CM, Painted Eyes	560a OM, Glass Eyes	570 AM, 232 O/CM, Glass Eyes	590 OM, Glass Eyes	600 AM, 234 CM, Painted Eyes	620 AM, 234 O/CM, Glass Eyes	640a AM, 234 CM, Painted Eyes
10"			1,200.00	900.00	900.00		
12"	1,000.00					1,000.00	
14"						1,400.00	
16"	1,700.00		2,000.00		1,300.00	1,700.00	1,800.00
18"				1,700.00			
20"							2,300.00
22"		1,600.00	2,700.00				

Size	700 CM, Glass Eyes	700 CM, Painted Eyes	710 CM, Glass Eyes	711 CM, Glass Eyes	800 AM, 234 O/CM, Glass Eyes	810 O/CM, Glass Eyes	820 O/CM, Glass Eyes	950 CM, Painted Eyes	Marked A.M. Only, Character Face
10"				1,600.00					
12"	6,000.00	4,700.00	2,400.00			2,600.00	1,900.00	1,000.00	
14"	7,000.00	6,100.00	3,000.00		2,500.00	2,900.00		1,900.00	
16"							3,000.00	2,500.00	7,500.00+
18"			4,100.00	4,900.00					

Add an additional $700.00 for jointed toddler body on any doll.

OM = Open Mouth

CM = Closed Mouth

O/CM = Open/Closed Mouth

A. M. = Armand Marseille

G. B. = George Borgfeldt

Mascotte

Bébés bearing the Mascotte label were produced by May Freres, Cie., from 1882 through 1901. Records indicate that Jules Steiner purchased May Freres and advertised Bébé Mascotte after 1897, as did Jules Mettais, Steiner's 1899 successor.

Reproductions and copies of Bébé Mascottes occasionally surface. Inspect the body and its markings. Look inside the thigh and upper arm joints. They should be smooth and not show signs of being turned. Close your eyes and use your fingers to lightly stroke the cheek; the bisque of an authentic Mascotte should be fine and creamy, but not silky-satin smooth. The feathered brows are a bit shiny and wide spaced.

Prices listed are for appropriately costumed dolls in good condition. Normal wear, slight damage, or well-made repairs to the body do not greatly affect the price. If the bisque is damaged or repaired, expect the value to be less than half the amounts listed. It is perfectly acceptable to show a missing or repaired finger or joint, or a mended body.

Bébé: bisque socket head; jointed wood-and-composition body; good wig; large, paperweight eyes; heavy, feathered, shiny brows; long, thick lashes; pierced ears (may be applied); closed mouth with two-tone paint; appropriately dressed; typically marked "M"; Mascotte body stamped "Bébé Mascotte/Paris"; also frequently found on a marked "Juneau" body.

Mascotte Bébé. Courtesy of David Cobb's Doll Auctions

Mascotte Value Comparisons	
Size	Bébé
10"	4,000.00
13"	4,200.00
15"	4,500.00
17"	4,900.00
19"	5,400.00
21"	5,800.00
23"	6,200.00
25"	6,800.00
27"	7,500.00

Mattel® Inc.

In 1945, Mattel established its headquarters in Hawthorne, California. The company, founded by Harold Matson and Elliot Handler, derived its name from a combination of letters from the two partners' names. Mattel, the world's largest toy manufacturer, is probably best known for Barbie, along with her friends and family. Initially Mattel produced dollhouse furniture. They expanded to include music boxes, guns, and a host of famous dolls such as Chatty Cathy, Sister Bell, Baby First Step, Cheerful-Tearful, Dancerina, and Talking Mrs. Beasley. Because of the innovative dolls created at Mattel, it is understandable that security is one of Mattel's top priorities. The company's research department, headed by a former missile engineer, is strictly off-limits to all but a few employees.

Many of Mattel's dolls have quickly attained collectible status. The high quality and imaginative concepts have no doubt contributed to this phenomenon. Mattel dolls are often action oriented. In addition to the walkers and talkers, there are singers, a bike rider, a doll that plays with puppets, another that juggles, and even one that moves her lips as she tells a secret. All Mattel dolls are well marked.

Prices listed are for dolls in near-mint, original condition. If damaged, redressed, or undressed, expect the value to be less than one half to one fourth the amounts listed.

Also see Barbie, Modern Collectibles.

Doug Davis, Spaceman: 6"; all vinyl; pose-able; molded and painted hair and features; marked "Mattel Inc./1967/Hong Kong" **$100.00**

Tiny Cheerful Tearful: 6 1/2"; all vinyl; rooted hair; painted eyes; open mouth; press tummy to change expression from glad to sad; marked "1966 Mattel Inc. Hong Kong"..................$75.00

Kretor and Zark the Shark: 7" Kretor and 12" Zark; Kretor's a vinyl frogman; Zark's a plastic shark that swims in the water and carries Kretor with him; pull-string activated; marked "6389-0150/2" on Kretor's left foot; "1970 Mattel Inc./Hong Kong/U.S. U For/Patented/Patented in Canada 1970" on Kretor's right foot; "1970 Mattel Inc./Hong Kong/U.S. Patent Pending" on Zark's underside; the set.................................$250.00

Gorgeous Creatures: 7 1/2"; animals in very womanly bodies; molded-on underwear; marked "Mattel, Inc. 1979 Philippines." ....

    Cow Belle: lavender and blue......................... $90.00
    Ms. Giddie Yup: (horse) hot pink 90.00
    Ms. Heavenly Hippo: yellow......................... 90.00
    Princess Pig: lavender and black................. 90.00

The Sunshine Family (9 1/2" Steve, 9" Stephie, and 3" Sweets): vinyl heads and arms; plastic bodies; jointed knees; rooted hair; insert eyes; marked "1973 Mattel Inc." on heads; "1973/Mattel Inc./Taiwan" on back; wrist tag "The Sunshine Family"; the set $165.00

Baby Go Bye Bye: 10"; vinyl head and limbs; plastic body; rooted, white hair; painted, blue eyes; open/closed mouth with two upper teeth; marked "1968 Mattel Inc./Hong Kong" $75.00

Buffie: 10", vinyl head; plastic body; vinyl limbs; rooted hair; painted eyes; open/closed mouth with two upper teeth; freckles across nose; holding 3 1/2" Mrs. Beasley doll; marked "1967/Mattel Inc./U.S. & For/Pats. Pend Mexico"......................$300.00

    Buffie: 6"; holding 2" Mrs. Beasley............ $400.00

Valerie: 10 1/2"; vinyl head and limbs; plastic body; rooted, blond hair; painted, blue eyes; open/closed mouth with two upper and two lower molded teeth; marked "1967 Mattel Inc./U.S. & For/Pat. Pend./Hong Kong"...............................$65.00

Baby Beans: 11", vinyl head; bean bag body; rooted, blond hair; painted features; pull-string talker; marked "Mattel/Baby Beans/1970" on tag sewn into seam $45.00

Baby Small Talk: 11", all black vinyl; rooted, black hair; painted, brown eyes; open/closed mouth with two upper and two lower teeth; pull-string talker; marked "1967 Mattel/Japan" on head $75.00

Baby Walk 'N Play: 11"; vinyl head; plastic body; vinyl limbs; rooted, yellow hair; painted eyes; open/closed mouth with two upper and two lower teeth; battery operated to play with yo-yo and paddle ball; marked "1967/Mattel Inc./Hong Kong" on head; 1967 Mattel Inc./US & Foreign Patented" on torso; dress tag reads "1968 Mattel Inc."...............................$45.00

Bouncy Baby: 11"; vinyl head; plastic body; vinyl limbs; rooted hair; painted eyes; open/closed mouth with two upper molded and painted teeth; spring action arms, legs, and head; giggles; marked "1968 Mattel Inc./Mexico/U. S. Patent Pending" on the back; dress tag reads "Bouncy Baby/1968 Mattel Inc./Hong Kong" $65.00

Small Talk Cinderella: 11"; all vinyl; rooted hair; big, painted eyes looking up; marked "Japan" on head; "1967 Mattel Inc./US & For/Pats. Pend./Mexico" on back; dress tag reads "Small Talk/1968 Mattel Inc. Hong Kong" $65.00

Sister Small Walk: 11 1/2"; vinyl head; plastic body; vinyl limbs; rooted, brown hair; painted, blue eyes; open/closed mouth with two upper and two lower molded and painted teeth; molded-on socks and shoes; marked "1967 Mattel Inc./U.S. & Foreign Patented/Other Patents Pending/U.S.A."..............$65.00

Gold Medal Big Jack: 12"; all rigid black vinyl; jointed at neck, shoulder, wrists, waist, hip, knees, and ankles; boxer; press back to make right arm move; marked "1971 Mattel, Inc./Hong Kong U. S. & Foreign Patented"..........................$250.00

Mattel Chatty Cathy all original with box, Chatty Cathy storybook, extra shoes, patterns for additional outfits, and rare shoehorn. Courtesy of McMaster's Doll Auction

Guardian Goddesses: 12"; adult figure; test market dolls only; Moonmystic and Sunspell; arms go up and down; when limbs are pulled, gowns fly off and reveal "Super Girl" outfit, 1979–1980...$500.00

Guardian Goddesses Outfits: Blazing Fire, Ice Empress, Lion Queen, and Soaring Eagle; each.................................$250.00

Talking Twin Kip: 12", vinyl head; cloth body; rooted, blond hair; painted eyes; two upper and two lower molded and painted teeth; pull-string talker; marked "1967 Mattel Inc., Japan" on head; "Mattel/Talking Twins 1970 Mattel Inc." on tag sewn into seam...$75.00

Baby Pattaburp: 13"; vinyl head; cloth body; vinyl limbs; rooted hair; sleep eyes with lashes; open mouth; mechanism causes her to burp when patted on back; marked "Quality Originals By Mattel/Baby Pattaburp/1963 Mattel Inc." on tag sewn into seam $50.00

Cheerful Tearful: 13"; vinyl head; plastic body; vinyl limbs; rooted hair; painted eyes; open mouth; moving left arm makes face change from sad to glad expression; marked "1965 Mattel Inc./Hawthorne Calif., U. S. Patents Pending/3036-014-1"
....$65.00

Baby Colleen: 14"; vinyl head; cloth body; rooted, orange hair; painted, blue eyes; pull-string talker; marked "Baby Colleen/1965 Mattel Inc." on tag sewn into seam; Sears exclusive
....$75.00

Shopping Sheryl: 14"; vinyl head; plastic body; jointed at shoulder, hip, waist, left wrist, and thumb; magnetic right hand; buttons on side of body operate thumb; rooted white hair; painted features; marked "1970 Mattel Inc./Hong Kong" on head; "Mattel Inc./Hong Kong/U.S. Patent Pending" on back
....$50.00

Love n' Touch Real Sisters: 15"; vinyl head; cloth body; vinyl hands; rooted hair; painted eyes; nicely modelled around eyes; marked "Mattel Inc. 1980 Taiwan" on head $75.00

Shrinking Violet: 15"; all cloth; yellow yarn hair; felt eyes, moveable lids; pull-string operates talker and facial movements. Cloth label sewn into seam marked "Mattel Shrinking Violet" and "63 The Funny Company All Rights Reserved Through Out The World" on reverse side.................$175.00

Baby Play A Lot: 16"; vinyl; rooted, blond hair; painted features; pull-string and start-switch on back activates doll to comb hair, brush teeth, do dishes, or play with one of twenty toys included in storage tray; marked "1971/Mattel Inc./Hong Kong/US Patent Pend" on back of head.............................$75.00

Saucy: 16"; vinyl head; plastic body; vinyl limbs; rooted hair; sleep eyes; rotating left arm causes eyes and mouth to form eight different expressions; marked "1972 Mattel Inc. Mexico" on head; "1972 Mattel Inc. Mexico/US Patent Pend." on back $125.00

Talking Baby Tenderlove: 16"; all vinyl; insert scalp with rooted white hair; painted eyes; open nurser mouth; pull-string talker in plastic hair ribbon on back of head; marked "677K 1969 Mattel Inc./Mexico".................$60.00

Talking Miss Beasley: 16"; vinyl head; blue and white polka-dot cloth body with apron; rooted, blond hair; painted features; black plastic glasses; pull-string talker; cloth tag "Mattel Miss Beasley" sewn into seam.................$400.00

Tippy Toes: 16"; vinyl head; plastic body; vinyl arms; rooted hair; painted eyes; open/closed mouth with two lower molded and painted teeth; battery operated to ride plastic tricycle; marked "Mexico" on head; "1967 Mattel Inc./Hawthorne Calif./Made in USA" on body; came with plastic tricycle..$65.00

Hi Dottie: 17"; vinyl head and left arm; plastic body; plastic right arm; rooted hair; painted features; plug in left hand to connect phone; marked "1969 Mattel Inc. Mexico" on head; "1971/Mattel Inc./Mexico/U. S. Patent Pend." on back $75.00

Peachy and Her Puppets: 17"; vinyl; rooted hair; painted features; pull-string to operate and make puppets talk; puppets include clown, girl, dog, and monkey; marked "1972 Mattel Inc./Mexico" on head; "1964 Mattel Inc./Hawthorne" on back $150.00

Sing-A-Song: 17"; vinyl head; plastic body; rooted, blond hair; painted, blue eyes; pull-string singer; marked "1969/Mattel Inc. Mexico" on head; "1964 Mattel Inc./Hawthorne" on back; dress tag reads "1968 Mattel Inc./Made in Hong Kong" $125.00

Sister Bell: 17"; hard plastic head; cloth body; glued-on, yellow, yarn hair; large, side-glancing, painted eyes; pull-string talker, eleven different phrases; marked "Mattel Inc./Hawthorne Calif." on head; "Mattel Inc. 1961" on tag sewn into seam..........$125.00

Teachy Keen: 17"; vinyl head; stuffed cloth body; rooted blond hair; painted features; dressed to teach skills of opening zippers, buckling shoes, tying, and buttoning; marked "Mattel/Teachy Keen/1969 Mattel Inc." on tag sewn into seam $60.00

Baby Secret: 18"; vinyl head; cloth body; vinyl hands; rooted hair; painted eyes; open mouth; pull-string talker, mouth moves as she talks; marked "Japan 1965" on head; "Baby Secret/Mattel Inc." on tag sewn into seam.................$125.00

Beany: 18"; vinyl head; cloth body; vinyl hands and feet; molded and painted, yellow hair; painted, side-glancing, blue eyes; open mouth with molded tongue, pull-string talker; marked "Mattel Inc. Toymakers/Bob Clampett – Hong Kong" on shoe; "Mattel 1969" on tag sewn into seam.................$85.00

Chatty Cathy: 20"; vinyl head; plastic body; vinyl limbs; rooted hair; sleep eyes with lashes; open/closed mouth with molded and painted teeth; marked "Chatty Cathy 1960/Chatty Baby 1961 By Mattel Inc./U.S. Pat. 301718/Other U.S. and For-

eign Pats. Pend./Pat'd in Canada 1962"; dress tag reads "Chatty Cathy Mattel" $350.00

Chatty Cathy black version.................$1,000.00

Cynthia: 20"; vinyl head; plastic body; rooted, blond hair; painted features; battery operated, talks with records; marked "1971 Mattel Inc./Hong Kong" on head; "1971 Mattel Inc./USA/U.S. Patent Pending" on back.................$125.00

Living Baby Tenderlove: 20"; one-piece vinyl body; rooted skull cap; painted features; open nurser mouth; marked "140/1970 Mattel Inc. Mexico/US and Foreign Patented".........$65.00

Scooby-Doo: 21"; vinyl head; cloth body; rooted hair; blue, sleep eyes with liner and eye shadow; closed mouth; pull-string on left hip; marked "Mattel/Scooby Doo 1964" on tag sewn into seam.................$250.00

Doctor Dolittle: 22"; vinyl head; cloth body; molded and painted realistic facial features; top hat; pull-string talker; marked "Dr. Dolittle/MCMLXVII Twentieth Century Fox/Film Corp. Inc." on tag sewn into seam $125.00

Dancerina: 24"; vinyl head; plastic body; vinyl arms; rooted hair; painted eyes; open/closed mouth; battery operated; activated by knob on top of head; marked "1968 Mattel" on head; "1968 Mattel" on body.................$150.00

Charmin Chatty: 25"; vinyl head and arms; plastic body; plastic legs; rooted hair; side-glancing, sleep eyes with lashes; closed, smiling mouth; record fits into slot on side of doll; pull-string operates talker; marked "Charmin Chatty 1961 Mattel, Inc.".................$200.00

Chatty Baby, 18"	$150.00
Tiny Chatty Baby, 15"	85.00
Tiny Chatty Baby Brother, 15"	100.00
Singing Chatty	200.00

Collector Doll Series

Classic Beauty: 1977–1978; vinyl head; plastic body; rooted hair; sleep eyes; very pretty facial modelling; dolls and clothing in excellent condition with wrist tag:

Cassandra: worldwide production of 2,761 .... $600.00

Cecelia: worldwide production of 3,005 .... 500.00

Catherine: worldwide production of 2,799 **500.00**

Cynthia: worldwide production of 3,731 ... 450.00

La Cheri Collection: also known as "French Country Garden Collection"; 18"; tagged with serial number and date; blue, burgundy, or pink dress:

1982: limited to 1,200 of each color........... $650.00

1983: limited to 2,000 of each color............ 500.00

Mariko Collection: 1983; 14"; ivory complexion of each doll; limited to 1,800 worldwide production:

Art: floral print dress $350.00

Drama: boy; striped pants 350.00

Mime: yellow dress 350.00

Music: lavender dress 350.00

Sekiguchi of Japan: Mattel owned exclusive distribution rights in the United States.

1982: mint $350.00

1983: mint 300.00

Kiddles

Dainty Deer Animiddle: 2"; all vinyl; fleece covering; deer outfit with antlers; orange hair; painted features; marked "1967 Mattel Inc.".................$250.00

Lolli Lemon: 2"; all vinyl; rooted, yellow hair; painted features; marked "Mattel Inc." on back.................$150.00

Liddle Locket: 2"; all vinyl; rooted, red hair; painted features; marked "Mattel Inc."; came in plastic locket **$100.00**

Calamity Jiddle Kiddle: 2 1/2"; all vinyl; rooted, blond hair; painted features; marked "1965/Mattel Inc./Japan"; came with large cowgirl hat and horse **$250.00**

Kiddle Kologne: 2 1/2"; all vinyl; rooted hair; painted features; marked "Mattel" on back; came in plastic cologne bottle **$100.00**

Bunson Burnie: 3"; all vinyl; rooted, red hair; painted features; marked "1966/Mattel Inc." **$45.00**

Rosemary Roadster: 3"; all vinyl; rooted, blond hair; painted features; marked "1966/Mattel Inc." **$250.00**

Liddle Red Riding Hiddle: 3 1/2"; all vinyl; rooted, blond hair; painted features; marked "1966/Mattel Inc." with chenille wolf..**$300.00**

Soapy Siddle: 3 1/2"; all vinyl; brown, rooted hair; painted features; wearing bathrobe; marked "Mattel Inc." on head **$100.00**

Telly Viddle Kiddle: 3 1/2"; all vinyl; rooted hair; painted features; marked "1965/Mattel Inc./Japan/15" on back; "Mattel/1965" on head **$200.00**

Howard Biff Boodle: 4"; all vinyl; rooted, blond hair; painted features; marked "1966/Mattel Inc." on back; came with plastic wagon **$150.00**

Suki Skididdle: 4"; all vinyl; rooted, blond hair; painted features; marked "1966/Mattel Inc." on back; came with plastic skiddle pusher..**$100.00**

Personality Dolls

Welcome Back Kotter Series: marked "Wolper-Komack" on head; "1973 Mattel Inc. Taiwan" on back:

> Barbarino..**$95.00**
> Epstein..75.00
> Washington..75.00
> Horshack...75.00
> Mr. Kotter...75.00

Mindy: 8 1/2"; rooted hair; open/closed mouth; marked "1979 P.P.C. Taiwan" on head; "1973 Mattel Taiwan" on back **$75.00**

Mork: 9"; molded hair; closed mouth; marked "1979 P.P.C. Taiwan" on head; "1973 Mattel Taiwan" on back..............**$75.00**

Lone Wolf: 9 1/2"; Indian; rooted hair; marked "1975 Mattel Inc." on head; "Hong Kong" sideways; "1971 Mattel Inc./Hong Kong U. S. & Foreign Patents" **$65.00**

Grizzly Adams: 10"; molded beard; marked "1971 Mattel Inc./U.S. & Foreign Patents/Hong Kong" on back..........**$60.00**

Jimmy Osmond: 10"; open/closed mouth and freckles; marked "22-1209/Mattel Inc./1966/Taiwan" on back......**$85.00**

Zeb McCahan: 10"; molded, blond hair and mustache; marked "1975 Mattel Inc." on head; "Hong Kong" sideways; "1971 Mattel Inc./Hong Kong U. S. & Foreign Patents"..**$85.00**

Julia: 11 1/2", from TV program *Julia*, starring Dianne Carroll; all black vinyl; bendable knees; rooted black hair; painted brown eyes; closed mouth; dressed in original 2-piece uniform; marked "1966 Mattel Inc." **$400.00**

Cheryl Ladd: 11 1/2"; bendable knees; green eyes; marked "Mattel 1966/Korea/13" **$95.00**

Debbie Boone: 11 1/2"; open/closed, smiling mouth; holding microphone; marked "RESI Inc. 1978 Taiwan" on head; "Mattel Inc. 1966 Taiwan" on back **$95.00**

Kate Jackson: 11 1/2"; brown hair and eyes; closed mouth; marked "Mattel Inc./1978" on head; "Mattel Inc./1966 Korea 13" on body..**$95.00**

Marie Osmond: 11 1/2"; dark, rooted hair; smiling; marked "Mattel Inc./1966/12 Korea" on back **$75.00**

Twiggy: 11 1/2"; short, blond, rooted hair; long lashes; marked "Mattel Inc./1969"..**$500.00**

Donny Osmond: 11 3/4"; molded, brown hair and eyes; open/closed, smiling mouth; marked "10-88-0S00S/Mattel Inc., 1968, Hong Kong"..**$75.00**

Shaun: 12"; holds plastic guitar; marked "Mattel Inc. 1979" on head; "Mattel Inc. 1975/Taiwan" across waist............**$175.00**

Mego

Mego marketed dolls during the 1970s and 1980s until going bankrupt in 1983. Mego is best known for its well-made and accurately costumed action figures and accessories. Particularly popular are the Super Heroes adapted from the famed D.C. Comics, and the celebrity stars. The KISS dolls are also a favorite with collectors; Originally retailing for less than $15.00 each in 1978, today the set of four in original boxes can command $800.00 or more.

Neal Adams, the well-known comic book artist, was responsible for much of Mego's packaging and toy artwork.

Prices listed are for dolls in near-mint, original condition. If damaged, redressed, or undressed, expect the value to be less than one half to one fourth the amounts listed.

Complete set of Kiss dolls (Ace, Peter, Gene, and Paul) in original condition. Courtesy of McMaster's Doll Auction

Mego Doll Value Comparisons		
Character Name	Size	Value
Action Jackson	8"	40.00
Dinah-mite	8"	60.00
Superman	8"	100.00
Batman (1st; removable cowl-mask)	8"	200.00
Batman	8"	150.00
Robin	8"	150.00
Aquaman	8"	100.00
Captain America	8"	100.00
Tarzan	8"	40.00
Spiderman	8"	75.00
Shazam	8"	100.00
Penguin	8"	100.00
Joker	8"	100.00
Riddler	8"	125.00
Mr. Mxyzptlk	8"	75.00
Waltons Mom & Pop, pair	8"	85.00
Grandma & Grandpa, pair	8"	85.00
Fighting Batman	8"	100.00
Fighting Robin	8"	100.00
Fighting Riddler	8"	100.00
Fighting Joker	8"	100.00
Jon, C.H.i.P.S.	8"	65.00
Ponch, C.H.i.P.S.	8"	65.00
Captain Patch	8"	85.00
Jean Lafitte	8"	85.00
Long John Silver	8"	85.00
Blackbeard	8"	85.00
Mighty Thor	8"	150.00
Conan	8"	150.00
The Thing	8"	30.00
Wonder Woman	8"	100.00
Super Girl	8"	150.00
Bat Girl	8"	100.00
Cat Woman	8"	100.00
Frankenstein	8"	50.00
Dracula	8"	50.00
Wolfman	8"	45.00
Mummy	8"	100.00
Wyatt Earp	8"	65.00
Cochise	8"	65.00
Davy Crockett	8"	65.00
Buffalo Bill Cody	8"	85.00
Wild Bill Hickok	8"	65.00
Sitting Bull	8"	85.00
Cornelius, Planet of the Apes	8"	150.00
Dr. Zaius	8"	150.00
Zira	8"	150.00
Soldier Ape	8"	150.00
Romulan	8"	800.00
Captain Kirk	8"	100.00
Mr. Spock	8"	95.00

Mego Doll Value Comparisons		
Character Name	Size	Value
Dr. "Bones" McCoy	8"	150.00
Lt. Uhura	8"	150.00
Mr. "Scottie" Scott	8"	150.00
Klingon	8"	75.00
Andorian	8"	600.00
Dorothy & Toto	8"	75.00
Cowardly Lion, Tin Woodsman, or Scarecrow	8"	75.00 each
Munchkins	8"	150.00 each
Glinda "The Good" Witch	8"	95.00
Wicked Witch	8"	100.00
King Arthur	8"	125.00
Sir Galahad	8"	125.00
Sir Lancelot	8"	125.00
Black Knight	8"	125.00
Ivanhoe	8"	125.00
Robin Hood	8"	150.00
Little John	8"	125.00
Friar Tuck	8"	125.00
Will Scarlet	8"	150.00
Green Arrow	8"	60.00
Green Goblin	8"	75.00
The Lizard	8"	100.00
The Falcon	8"	75.00
The Invincible Iron Man	8"	50.00
The Incredible Hulk	8"	100.00
Waltons, John Boy & Ellen, pair	8"	85.00
The Human Torch	8"	30.00
Mr. Fantastic	8"	30.00
Invisible Girl	8"	30.00
Neprunain	8"	70.00
The Keeper	8"	250.00
The Gorn	8"	100.00
The Cheron	8"	100.00
Zon, 1 Million BC	8"	100.00
Trag	8"	50.00
Grok	8"	50.00
Orm	8"	50.00
Alfalfa	8"	85.00
Spanky	8"	85.00
Darla	8"	85.00
Buckwheat	8"	100.00
Mickey	8"	40.00
Porky	8"	40.00
Galen	8"	45.00
General Ursus	8"	45.00
Peter Burke	8"	60.00
Alan Verdono	8"	60.00
Fonzie	8"	100.00
Richie	8"	75.00

Mego Doll Value Comparisons

Character Name	Size	Value
Potsy	8"	75.00
Kojack	8"	100.00
Captain	12"	100.00
Tenille	12"	100.00
Sonny	12"	150.00
Cher	12"	175.00
Diana Ross	12"	145.00
Jaclyn Smith	12"	75.00
Joe Namath	12"	200.00
Laverne	12"	125.00
Shirley	12"	125.00
Lenny	12"	125.00
Squiggy	12"	125.00

Mego Doll Value Comparisons

Character Name	Size	Value
Suzanne Somers	12"	75.00
Wonder Woman	12"	200.00
Llia, Captain Kirk, Mr. Spock, Star Trek	12"	150.00 each
Arcturian	12"	175.00
Maddie Mod	12"	65.00
Farrah Fawcett	12"	75.00
KISS, set	12"	800.00
Kriss	12"	200.00
Gene	12"	200.00
Ace	12"	200.00
Peter	12"	200.00

Metal-Head Dolls

The chief manufacturing center for Metal-Head Dolls was in Germany at Nossen, Saxony. The familiar tin heads, dating from the turn-of-the century, were cut and stamped from sheet metal then welded together. The inexpensive, pleasant-faced tin heads were sold separately; usually as replacements for the easily broken doll heads of bisque or china. This explains why metal heads are found on various body types.

Buschow & Beck purchased an established sheet-metal business in 1890, and they spent the next forty years fabricating metal doll heads. Their "Minerva" trademark is so well known that it became the standard for any Metal-Head Doll. Karl Standfuss dolls bore the trade name Juno, and Alfred Heller registered the trade name Diana.

Prices listed are for appropriately costumed dolls in good condition. If dented, chipped, or repainted, expect the value to be less than one half to one fourth the amounts listed.

Also see Gebeler Falk Doll Corp.

Shoulder head: metal shoulder head; kid or cloth body; molded and painted hair or good wig; painted or glass eyes; open or closed mouth; appropriately dressed; typically marked "Minerva" (over a helmet), "JUNO," or "DIANA."

Also see Gebeler Falk Doll Corp.

Metal-Head Value Comparisons

Size	Shoulder Head, Painted Eyes, Molded Hair	Shoulder Head, Glass Eyes, Molded Hair	Shoulder Head, Dolly-Face, Glass Eyes, Wig
12"	135.00	200.00	
14"	185.00	225.00	300.00
16"	200.00	250.00	325.00
18"	225.00	275.00	350.00
20"			375.00
22"	285.00	300.00	400.00

German tin heads with painted eyes and molded hair, and glass eyes with wigs. Courtesy of David Cobb's Doll Auctions

Modern Collectible Dolls

"**M**odern doll" is the term applied to any doll made after World War II. This section includes various dolls from numerous manufacturers not listed elsewhere. To simplify your search, the Collectible Category has been sub-divided into Hard Plastic/Vinyl and Contemporary Porcelain.

The hard plastic and vinyl dolls described within this section are among collectors' favorites. The attraction may be "I had that doll when I was a child" syndrome, the admiration of a subject, or simply the appeal of a particular doll.

The Home Shopping Channel and QVC have generated many new doll enthusiasts. Contemporary porcelain dolls from well-known and gifted artists have found their way into the hearts of collectors all over the world. Direct mail and the Internet have also been successful in recruiting new patrons. Add a "contemporary" doll to your collection because you adore it, just can't live without it, and have just the perfect place for it, but avoid buying it as an investment.

Prices listed are for original dolls in mint condition. If damaged, redressed, or undressed, expect the value to be less than one half to one fourth the amounts listed.

29" wax over porcelain Gloria Vanderbilt doll. Courtesy of Julia Burke

Hard Plastic/Vinyl

Adora Belle: 16 1/2"; all vinyl; jointed at neck, shoulder, and hip; good wig; big, acrylic-topped eyes; shy smile; original full dress; marked "MO" within a heart (a 1999 Marie Osmond doll for Knickerbocker Co.) **$85.00**

Alice in Wonderland: 8"; all quality vinyl; good wig; sleep eyes; closed mouth; classic Alice costume; marked "TONNER" (1997 Krupplebush Kids by Robert Tonner Doll Co.) **$85.00**

Annette Himstedt Children: 19"–31"; vinyl head and arms; cloth body; good wig; set eyes; closed or open/closed mouth; well-made appropriate costume; typically marked "Annette Himstedt/Puppen Kind," signature on neck, wrist tag with character name and clothing tag (designed by Annette Himstedt for Mattel)

    Timi, Toni, Panchita, Pancho, or Melvin$600.00
    Baby, Leischen, Tara, Annchen, Lona, or Kima
    .... 800.00
    Fiene, Kai, Janka, Liliane, Adriene, or Ayoka
    .... 1,200.00
    Neblina, Taki, Freeke, Bibbi, or Makimura
    .... 1,300.00
    Michiko, Malin, Frederike, or Tinka 1,500.00
    Kasimir.. 1,800.00

Barefoot Children: 26"; vinyl head and limbs with detailed bare feet; cloth body; human hair wig; set eyes; open/closed or closed mouth; appropriately designed children's costumes; marked "Annette Himstedt AH 1985/26.8.86" (designed by Annette Himstedt for Mattel)

    Fatou (Black) $1,300.00
    Paula (Pensive) 850.00
    Bastian (Boy)... 1,000.00
    Kathe (full pouty face)............................. 1,000.00
    Ellen (innocent and peaceful)................. 1,200.00
    Lisa (happy)... 950.00

Beatles: 5"; oversized vinyl heads; miniature plastic body; rooted hair; painted features; black suits; plastic guitars with "John," "Paul," "George," or "Ringo" written across the front; marked "Remco Ind.Inc.1964 (Seltael, Inc, NEMS) ..**$600.00 set**

Buddy Palooka: 16"; vinyl head; one piece latex body; molded and painted hair; big, side-glancing eyes; rosy cheeks; closed, smiling mouth; original red shorts and terry robe; marked "H Fisher/Personality Doll Corp//1953" or unmarked (original brightly colored lithograph box "It's A Boy! Buddy Palooka/ The Pride of the Palooka Family// America's Cutest Doll/Joe and Ann's New Little Champ)

    Mint in Box.. $800.00
    Doll only 400.00

Captain Kangaroo: 11"–21"; vinyl character modelled head and hands; cloth body; molded cap; hair and moustache; painted or insert eyes; open/closed smiling mouth; dressed in oversized pocket suit; marked "1961 ROBT. KEESHAN/ASSOC. INC." or " B B" (by Baby Barry Toy Co.)

    11"... $250.00
    15" 300.00
    21" 500.00

Carol Channing: 24"; vinyl head; hard plastic jointed body; rooted hair; sleep eyes with eye shadow; closed mouth; original evening dress with fabric flower corsage; marked "1961/KAY-SAM" (by Kay Sam Jolly Toy Co.)....................................**$300.00**

Caroline Kay: 20"; vinyl head; hard plastic body; beautifully modelled face; rooted, side-part hair; sleep eyes; closed, slightly-smiling mouth; cotton dress and organdy pinafore; marked "W. L. Wilson" (Assumed to be made by Playland Toy Corp. for which patent number 114706, fitting this dolls description, was granted on February 23, 1954) $600.00

Daisy May: 12"–20"; all vinyl; shapely, unjointed body; rooted hair; sleep eyes; closed mouth; original cut-off shorts and low-cut blouse; marked with cloth label "Exclusive License/ Baby Barry/Toy NYC/Al Capp/Dog Patch Family" (by Baby Barry Toy Co.)

> 12" $400.00
> 20" 550.00

Dawn Model Agency (Dawn, Angie, Glori, Dale [black version], April, Dinah, Melanie, Daphne): 6"; jointed at neck, shoulder, and hip; rooted hair; painted eyes; closed mouth; original "mod" outfit; marked production year (1969-1972) "Topper Corp/Hong Kong" and "H11A," "11C," "A11A," "K10," "H-7/110," "11-7," "878/K11A," "2/H-11," "A8-10," "H-17," "4/H 72," "543/H11a," "92/H-17," "154/S11," "51/D10," "4/H86," "K10/A," "AK11/H-7," and possibly others (by Deluxe Reading)..$125.00

Dick Clark (ABC Dance Band TV host): 26"; realistically modelled vinyl head and hands; cloth "to-autograph" body; molded and painted hair and eyes; open/closed smiling mouth with molded teeth; original suede saddle shoes, white shirt, tie, vest, gray suit with autograph pen in pocket; marked "JURO" (by Juro Novelty Co.)

> Mint.. $500.00
> With signatures 250.00

15" Dianna Effner Red Riding Hood.

Elmer Fudd: 8"; all vinyl; realistic characterization; carries shot gun; molded and painted hair; wide-open eyes; open/closed smiling mouth; appropriately costumed; marked "© WARNER BROS-SEVEN ARTS INC 1968//MADE IN HONG KONG" (by R. Dakin & Co.) $175.00

FayZah Spanos Babies and Children: 25"; quality vinyl head and limbs; cloth body; good wig; acrylic-topped eyes; open/closed mouth; nicely dressed; marked "FAYZAH SPANOS"..$250.00

Gay Bob: 12"; quality solid vinyl; multi-jointed, lifelike, pigeon-toed, anatomically correct male; flocked hair; painted eyes; pierced left ear; closed mouth; contemporary costume; unique "closet" box; marked "A Bartler Toy/Hong Kong"

> With box $400.00
> Without box 200.00

Gene®: 16"; jointed at neck, shoulder, and hip; rooted hair; beautifully-sculptured and dramatically-painted facial features; original, designer costume; marked "1995 Mel Odom/Ashton Drake" (designed by award winning artist Mel Odom for Ashton Drake)

> Early premier issue $750.00
> Later retired issue (depending upon costume)
> $200.00-400.00

Gerber Baby: 17"; vinyl head and hands; cloth body; sweet, classic character face; molded hair; rolling eyes; smiling open/closed mouth; body made of gingham to insinuate sleeper, with removable bib and skirt; marked "Gerber Products"//production year (by Atlanta Novelty, earlier dolls also by Sun Rubber and possibly others; markings and values may vary) ....$75.00+

GiGi (Juliet Prowse): 15"; vinyl head; hard plastic body; rooted hair; sleep eyes with eye shadow; closed mouth; red taffeta, lace-trimmed dress with bloomers and lace garter; marked "Kaysam 1961" (by Kay Sam Jolly Toy Co.) $75.00

Ginger: 21"; quality, brown vinyl head and limbs; cloth body; full wig; acrylic-topped eyes; closed mouth; nicely dressed; marked "Robert Tonner 1997" (by Robert Tonner Doll Co.)
....$300.00

Halco: 29"; hard plastic head and limbs; cloth body; mohair wig; flirty, sleep eyes; open mouth with teeth and felt tongue; nicely-made nylon dress with lace and fabric flower trim; unmarked; hang tag "Superb Halco Brand Beautiful Dolls, The Seal of Quality"..$650.00

Heidi Ott Children: 8"–16"; vinyl head and lower limbs; cloth body; molded and painted hair or human hair wig; nicely-designed original costumes; marked "Swiss design/ Heidi Ott"

> 8" $150.00
> 12" 175.00
> 16" 200.00

Hello Dolly (Carol Channing from David Merrick's musical *Hello Dolly*): 11"–24"; vinyl head; hard plastic jointed body; rooted hair; sleep eyes; closed mouth; original, fringe-trimmed, satin production costume long white gloves; marked "1373/K/1961" (by NASCO)

> 11" $100.00
> 24" 300.00

Hildegarde Günzel Children: 21"–30"; vinyl head and limbs; cloth body; good wig; set eyes; closed or open/closed mouth; nicely-designed costumes; marked "H. Günzel/China" (designed by Hildegarde Günzel for Alexander)

> Megan, Marissa, or Monica...................... $200.00
> Tricia, Chipie Baby, Lamponi, Matthias 450.00
> Marie or Binella 800.00

Honey West From Girl Private Eye (Anne Francis): 11" vinyl head; solid vinyl or hard plastic body; jointed at neck, shoulder, and hip; rooted, long, dark blond hair; painted eyes; closed mouth; original black judo leotard, vinyl boots, gold holster belt, and pistol (by Gilbert) $200.00

Hummel Dolls Peterle & Rose: 11"; realistically-modelled vinyl; molded and painted hair and facial features; exact replica of the famous Hummel figurines; nicely dressed in cotton and felt, including sandal-type shoes, top hat, and carrying basket of flowers; marked "original M T Hummel V GOEBEL," wrist tag "AUS DENHAUSE GOEBEL"................................**$125.00 pair**

John Travolta: 11 1/2"; vinyl head and jointed arms; hard plastic body; molded hair; painted eyes; open/closed smiling mouth with molded teeth; original bell-bottom pants and turtle-neck sweater; marked "32/HONG KONG" (by Chemtoy). **$125.00**

Julie Good-Krueger Children: 20"; all vinyl or vinyl head and limbs and cloth body; good wig; set eyes; closed or open/closed mouth; nicely dressed; marked "Julie Good-Krueger© (production date)"................................**$300.00**

Kimberly: 16"; all jointed vinyl; rooted hair; painted eyes; closed mouth; original school girl dress with matching clogs or classic cheerleading outfit; advertised as "she's really together—She's a real fashion setter"; marked "Tomy" (popular 1981 Tomy play doll) **$75.00**

Lee Middleton Babies or Toddlers: 11"–22"; realistically-modelled vinyl head and limbs; cloth body; rooted or molded hair; sleeping or set eyes; closed or open/closed mouth; nicely dressed with tiny Bible tied to wrist; marked character name and production number "Lee Middleton (date) (fish or Christian symbol) The Middleton Doll Co" and signature

11"	$100.00
20"	200.00
22"	250.00

Lil' Abner: 14"–21"; all vinyl; rooted hair; painted eyes; open/closed smiling mouth with molded teeth; original "Dog Patch" costume with oversized shoes; marked "Baby Barry Doll/25 1957" (by Baby Barry Toy Co.)

14"	$350.00
21"	500.00

Lilli: 11 1/2"; all quality vinyl; curvaceous body, jointed at neck, shoulder, and hip; rooted, long hair worn in a pony tail; heavily lined black and white painted eyes; closed mouth; fashionably dressed; marked "Germany" (by Bild Lilli) (very similar in appearance, in fact many believe Lilli was the impetus for Barbie®)

In original plastic tube with metal rod stand	$8,000.00
Without tube	5,000.00

Linda Williams from *Make Room For Daddy* (Angela Cartwright): 14"–30"; vinyl head; hard plastic jointed body; rooted hair worn in original ponytail; sleep eyes; open/closed smiling mouth with molded teeth; dressed in one of twelve original "school girl" outfits; marked "LINDA WILLIAMS" (by Natural Doll Company)

14"	$125.00
20"	200.00
30"	300.00

Lissi Dolls: 19 3/4"; vinyl head and limbs; cloth body; rooted hair; sleep eyes; closed or open/closed mouth with molded teeth; nicely dressed; marked "Anneliese S. Bätes" signature (may be any one of many names released by Lissi Dolls of West Germany) **$75.00**

Little Girl of Today: 23"; vinyl head and hand; cloth body; rooted human hair; well modelled child's face; sleep eyes; closed mouth; nicely designed and well-made nylon dress; marked "Fleischaker Novelty"................................**$400.00**

Little Iodine: 13"–21"; vinyl, character-modelled head; one piece latex body; deeply molded hair with large rolled loop for ribbon bow; painted eyes; wide, closed, smiling mouth; original cotton dress with bloomers showing (by Juro Novelty Co.)

13"	$75.00
18"	100.00
21"	150.00

Littlechap Family: 10"–14"; all jointed vinyl; molded or rooted hair; painted facial features; tagged clothes; marked "Remco Ind. Inc./1963//US & Foreign Pat/Pend. Hong Kong"

10" Libby	$125.00
12" Judy	125.00
13 1/2" Lisa	135.00
14" Dr. John	150.00

Lonely Lisa: 19"; vinyl head, arms, and legs; wire armature cloth body; rooted hair; large, painted, soulful eyes; closed mouth; dressed in typical '60s fashion; marked "Royal Doll/1965 (by Royal Doll Co.)"................................**$150.00**

LuAnn Simms: 14"; all hard plastic; jointed at neck, shoulder, and hip; dark saran wig; sleep eyes; open mouth with upper teeth; cotton dress, often with rickrack trim; marked "Made in USA," "170," or "180" (popular Arthur Godfrey TV personality made by Roberta, Horsman and Valentine for Belle Toys) **$400.00**

Mammy Yokum: 14"–23"; all vinyl, large-bosomed, unjointed body; character-modelled face with oversized nose and protruding chin, painted winking eye, closed mouth; original "Dog Patch" costume; marked "NY Doll Co. 3C// B B 25" (by Baby Barry Toy Co.)

14"	$350.00
21"	450.00
23" (with light-up nose)	500.00

Mammy Yokum: 21"; vinyl, character-modelled head and hands; cloth body; oversized nose; yarn hair; wide-open, painted eyes; closed, smiling mouth with corn-cob pipe; original felt "Dog Patch" costume; marked "Baby Barry/1952" (by Baby Barry Toy Co.)................................**$500.00**

Man From U. N. C. L. E. Illya Kuryakin (David McCallum) and Napoleon Solo (Robert Vaughn): 12"; jointed at neck, shoulder, and hip; hand-molded to hold cap-firing pistol; molded and painted hair; painted eyes; closed mouth; original costume with metal pistol adapter, pocket insignia, and Secret Agent Identification card; marked "K-78" or "K-50" (by Gilbert) ....**$200.00 each**

Complete set of Dolls by Jerri. Snow White and the 7 dwarfs, including rarely found Prince Charming and the Evil Witch. Courtesy of Trina Miller

Miss Seventeen: 15"; shapely body, jointed at neck, shoulder, and hip; insert skull cap hair pulled back tightly; painted eyes and earrings; closed mouth; original black swimsuit and long red cape; marked "US Patent 2925784/British Patent 804566/Made in Hong Kong" (by Marx) **$300.00**

Mr. Magoo: 16"; character modelled vinyl head; cloth body with stitched finger felt hands; molded hat, solid dome; weak, squinting eyes; open/closed smiling mouth; clothing forms body, with felt jacket added to side seams; marked with cloth label "1962/UPA Pictures, Inc./All Rights Reserved" **$250.00**

Old Cottage: 8"–9"; vinyl or hard plastic head; cloth body; soft wig; painted facial features; fanciful or historical costumes; marked with hang tag "Old Cottage Toys" or "Old Cottage Industries/Great Britain" (designed by Greta Fleischmann and daughter Susi) ...**$200.00–400.00, depending on character and costume**

Pappy Yokum: 14"–23"; all vinyl; character-modelled face with oversized nose; wide-open, painted eyes, closed, smiling mouth; original "Dog Patch" costume; marked "NY Doll Co. 3C//B B 25" (by Baby Barry Toy Co.)

14"	$300.00
21"	400.00
23" (with light-up nose)	450.00

Pinky Lee (NBC children's TV host): 25"; realistically-modelled vinyl head and hands; cloth body; molded and painted hat, painted or insert eyes; open/closed grinning mouth with molded teeth; original multi-miss-matched-plaid shirt and suit with large bow tie; marked "JURO CELEBRITY PRODUCTS" (by Juro Novelty Co.)..**$350.00**

Punky Brewster: 19"; vinyl; rooted hair; freckles; painted eyes; closed mouth; dressed as a child of the 1980s with vest, jeans, and a bandana tied around her leg; marked NBC inc. 1984 (by Galoob)...**$65.00**

Rags to Riches Doll (from CBS *Beat the Clock*): 14"–20"; all vinyl; jointed at neck, shoulder, hip, and waist; rooted hair; sleep eyes; closed mouth; original, two-piece dress unfolds to become full length gown; typically marked "1403 PAT PEND." (by Juro Novelty Co.)

14"	$150.00
20"	200.00

Robin Woods Child: 8"–17"; all jointed vinyl; good wigs; painted or sleep eyes; closed mouth; absolutely gorgeous multi-layered costumes; typically marked "Robin Woods" year (in 1992 Robin Woods accepted the position of Design Director for Alexander Doll Co. Prices listed are for dolls produced before that date)

8"	$95.00
14"	200.00
17"	300.00

Special series:

1986: Dancers in Action, Great Women in the Arts, and Little Miss Deb	**$600.00 each**
1987-1989: Christmas	400.00 each
1989-1990: Camelot Castle	350.00
1990: Camelot Series	400.00 each
1991: Shades of the Day	350.00
Disney Exclusive Editions (before or after 1992)	400.00

Sandra Sue: 8"; all excellent quality hard plastic; slender body, jointed at neck, shoulder, and hip; stitched wig; sleep eyes; painted, orangish-brown brows and lashes; closed mouth; beautifully-made, stylish costumes; unmarked, except for incised number inside arm or leg (by Richwood Toys Inc.) ....**$175.00, or more depending upon costume**

Teenage or Bride dolls: 15"–24" all hard plastic, jointed at neck, shoulder, and hip; good wig; sleep eyes; open or closed mouth; beautifully dressed; typically marked "Made in the U. S. A.," unmarked or letter or number only

15"	$350.00
16"–17"	400.00
18"	450.00
20"	600.00
22"	650.00
24"	750.00

Thumbs-Up: 7 1/2"; heavy, early latex (advertised as "Lasticoid, a flexible composition") molded, one piece or jointed at shoulder and hip; thumbs molded into a "thumbs-up victory sign"; long, blond wig; painted eyes; closed mouth; original satin frock, pinafore, and bonnet; marked with wrist tag "Manufacturer of this official Thumbs Up doll is participating in the Buy to Aid Britain Campaign by donating a portion of his profit on the sale to British American Ambulance Corps/Your $1.00 purchase of this doll helps in sending ambulances to Britain. An original creation of Margit Nilson Studios, 71 Fifth Ave., New York" later doll's wrist tag ".../Your $1.50 purchase of this doll helps in sending ambulances to Britain and Her Allies and Vitamins to the Undernourished Children of England" **$250.00**

Trolls: 1"-15"; comical characters; bushy hair; round, acrylic, insert eyes; wide, smiling, closed mouth; original felt costume; marked "Dam Thing"

1"–3"	$25.00
4"–6"	50.00
7"–10"	100.00
11"–12"	175.00
13"	200.00
14"	250.00
15"	350.00

Willie the Clown (Emmett Kelly): 14"–24"; all vinyl; molded hat; rooted hair; painted, droopy, or insert eyes; sad, closed mouth; dressed as unfortunate-downtrodden hobo; marked "B" or "B B" (by Baby Barry Toy Co.)

15"	$250.00
21"	300.00
24"	350.00

Contemporary Porcelain

Alice in Wonderland Set (Alice, White Rabbit, Mad Hatter, Queen of Hearts, Cheshire Cat, Duchess, and the Pig Baby): 25"–31"; expressive porcelain character heads; cloth bodies with wire armatures; Alice and Mad Hatter with wigs; others with molded and painted hair; painted eyes; Mad Hatter and Queen of Hearts with wide open/closed mouth, others with closed mouth; beautifully detailed character costumes; marked "W. © Silvestri ® 1985 Limited Edition" (designed by Faith Wick for Silvestri) ....**$3,500.00** complete set

Angie: 20"; beautiful black porcelain head and gracefully sculptured limbs; cloth body; stylish wig; acrylic-topped eyes; pierced ears; closed mouth; high fashion super model outfit; marked "LT/24" gold signature "1997" (designed by Anthony Mark Hankins for HSN)......................................**$250.00**

Ashton Drake Fairy-Tale: 14"; porcelain head, arms, and legs; cloth body; good wig; glass eyes; closed mouth; appropriate costume and accessories; marked "Dianna Effner/production number."

Red Riding Hood (first in the series)	**$175.00**
Cinderella (at the ball)	125.00
Cinderella (poor-girl)	150.00
Goldilocks	100.00
Rapunzel	100.00
Snow White	150.00

Austin: 26"; porcelain head and limbs; cloth body; good wig; acrylic-topped eyes; closed mouth; original costume; marked "1998 Pam Erff" production number (by Master Piece Gallery) **$85.00**

Baby Jill: 14"; porcelain socket head and limbs; seated cloth body; good wig; acrylic-topped eyes; pierced nostrils; closed, pouty mouth; nicely dressed; marked "Marion Blair 1999" production number..................**$150.00**

Bethany: 28"; porcelain head and limbs; cloth body; holding small porcelain baby; ringlet wig; acrylic-topped eyes; closed mouth; dressed in layers upon layers of lace trimmed chiffon adorned with silk ribbon and flowers; marked "Laura Cabale//1997" and production number (designed by Laura Cabale, dress designed by Kodene for Exclusively Yours) **$200.00**

Dolls by Jerry: 20"; all heavy porcelain; human hair wig; set glass eyes; closed mouth; marked with production year, signed Jerry McCloud, dated behind ear (by Jerry McCloud)........**$200.00**

FayZah Spanos Babies and Children: 20"–30"; uniquely modelled porcelain socket head and limbs; cloth body; wig; glass eyes; wide open/closed smiling mouth; beautifully dressed; marked character name, date "FAYZAH SPANOS"

> 20" $350.00
> 30" 450.00

Franklin Mint Ladies: 20"–22"; porcelain head and limbs; cloth body; nice wig; painted or glass eyes; closed mouth; beautifully costumed; marked "Franklin Mint"/date and/or production number ....**$300.00 and up, for dolls made before 1990, depending upon character and costume**

Gloria Vanderbilt: 29"; realistic wax over porcelain personality doll; human hair wig; fine quality blown glass eyes; closed mouth; beautifully styled, hand smocked dress with matching sweater; boxed with photograph of Gloria Vanderbilt from which the doll was modelled, certificate, flag, and specially designed stand **$600.00**

Gwen: 23"; porcelain head and limbs; cloth body; good wig; acrylic-topped eyes; closed mouth; original costume; marked "Treasures Forever" production number (designed by William Tung for the Treasures Forever Young Collection by Tuss, Inc.) **$85.00**

Hannah: 21"; porcelain socket head child; wooden, ball-jointed body with porcelain hands; good wig; glass eyes; closed mouth; original costumes; marked with character name and issue or style number (for example Hanna 13, Alice 38, Amy 4, and so on), "Lynne and Michael Roche/An Original Doll"

> **Early issue** **$1,400.00**
> **16"**... 900.00
> **6"** 400.00

Hildegarde Günzel Children: 25"–30" wax over porcelain head and limbs; cloth body; good wig; glass eyes; open mouth with wax over porcelain teeth and molded tongue; original, nicely-designed costumes; marked "H Günzel" possibly a production number or date

> **25"** **$1,200.00**
> **30"** 1,700.00

Marilou: 23"; porcelain; good wig; glass eyes; beautifully feathered brows; finely detailed, closed mouth with shaded lips; nicely designed period costume; marked "Jan McLean//1998" production number (by Exclusively Yours) **$400.00**

Martina or Marlene: 28"; porcelain head, hands, and legs; cloth body; good wig; glass eyes; open/closed mouth; nicely dressed; marked "R Schrott//1998//GACDO" (by the Great American Doll Co.) **$400.00**

Mother Teresa: 27"; realistically modelled porcelain head, hands, and lower legs; cloth body; gray wig; glass eyes; closed mouth; authentic white habit trimmed in blue; marked "Mother Teresa 1998 by Kelly RuBert" (20th anniversary 1979–1999 of Nobel Peace Prize by Collectible Concepts) **$350.00**

Noelle the Christmas Angel: 15"; porcelain in a pirouette pose; wig with blond curls; glass eyes; closed mouth; dressed in layers of diaphanous materials; marked "Noelle/Ann Timmerman" production number "1995" (designed by Ann Timmerman for the Little Bit of Heaven Collection from Georgetown Collection) **$165.00**

Picture Perfect Babies: 14 1/2"; distinctively modelled porcelain heads, arms, and legs; cloth bodies; molded and painted hair; glass eyes; closed or open/closed mouth; nicely costumed; marked "Yolanda Bello"/production number

> **Jason (first in the series)**........................... $400.00
> **Heather**... 200.00
> **Jennifer**.. 175.00
> **Matthew**... 150.00
> **Amanda**... 150.00
> **Sarah** 125.00
> **Jessica**.. 75.00
> **Lisa**... 100.00
> **Michael** 125.00
> **Emily** 100.00
> **Danielle**... 125.00

Royal Doulton: 8"–12"; porcelain heads and hands; cloth bodies with wire armatures; good wigs; painted eyes; closed mouth; wonderfully-detailed costumes; marked with the "Royal Doulton" stamp (designed by Eric Griffiths and costume designed by Peggy Nisbet)

> **8"** **$150.00**
> **12"** 250.00

Selena: 29"; exotic "café au lait" porcelain head and gracefully sculptured hands and lower legs; cloth body; good wig; acrylic-topped eyes; closed mouth; beautifully designed, multi-layered costume; marked "Tulay," signature, and a production number (from the 1998 Tulay Collection by Tuss Inc)....**$400.00**

Skippy: 11"; porcelain; painted hair and facial features; authentic aviator costume; marked "SKIPPY"/production number (produced with permission of the Dynamic Group in 1998 by HSN) **$75.00**

Sugar: 29"; porcelain; good wig; acrylic-topped eyes; very pouty, closed mouth; nicely-designed child's outfit; marked "1997 Donna RuBert," production number (designed by Donna RuBert for Collectible Concepts and a 1998 nominee for Porcelain Doll Of The Year Award in the $150.00–$350.00 category) **$250.00**

Molly-'es

Molly-'es is the trade name used by the International Doll Company, founded in 1929 by Marysia (Mollye) Goldman of Philadelphia, Pennsylvania.

Marysia was born in Russia around the turn-of-the-century. As a child, she fled with her parents to the United States. In 1919, she married Myer Goldman and began designing doll clothing shortly thereafter. The International Doll Company was originally a cottage-type industry, with neighborhood women sewing doll dresses in their homes. Eventually, Mollye opened a factory, which reportedly employed as many as 500 people. In addition to designing doll dresses for her own company, she also designed and manufactured costumes for other doll companies (most notably Ideal Toy Co., for whom Mollye designed the Shirley Temple doll's wardrobe).

In 1937, Mollye created a series of Hollywood Cinema dolls, dressed as stars and well-known personalities such as Irene Dunne, Jeanette McDonald, Betty Grable, June Allison, Olivia deHaviland, Joan Crawford, Queen Elizabeth, and Princess Margaret Rose. Mollye also created an entire group of dolls representing the characters from the movie *Thief of Baghdad*, considered by many to be Mollye's best work. The Sultan, with his beautifully hand-painted facial features, groomed beard, and satin costume, makes an impressive presentation. Mollye purchased good quality dolls of composition, hard plastic, and vinyl from various manufacturers, dressed them in her original costumes, and sold them under her name. Except for hang tags earlier Molly-'es Dolls are unmarked; later vinyl dolls were marked "Mollye" on the head.

Also see Raggedy Ann & Andy, Shirley Temple.

Cloth

Prices listed are for appropriately costumed dolls with good color and little or no fading. Slight wear and signs of aging, such as a settled body, do not greatly affect the price. If a doll is stained, torn, badly mended, or faded, expect the value to be less than half the amounts listed.

Child Mask-Type Face: all cloth stuffed body; mask-type face; yarn hair; painted eyes, long lashes; small, closed mouth; original costume; typically unmarked or hang tag only.

International Children Series: all cloth stuffed body; mask-type face; mohair wig; painted facial features; original, regional costume; typically unmarked or hang tag only.

Character: all cloth body; mask-type face; yarn hair; painted, big, round, side-glancing eyes; smiling, watermelon mouth; original costume; typically unmarked or hang tag only.

Composition

Prices listed are for appropriately costumed dolls in good condition. Slight crazing is acceptable and does not greatly affect the price. If badly crazed, cracked, peeling, or repainted, expect the value to be less than half the amounts listed.

Baby: all composition; jointed at neck, shoulder, and hip; molded and painted hair; sleep eyes; closed mouth; original outfit; typically unmarked or hang tag only.

17" hard plastic Molly-'es teen doll.

Lady/Teen: all composition; jointed at neck, shoulder, and hip; good wig; sleep eyes; real lashes; closed mouth; original outfit; typically unmarked or hang tag only.

Thief of Baghdad Series (Sultan, Thief, or Princess): all composition; jointed neck, shoulder, and hip; good wig, may have mohair beard and brows; detailed, painted eyes; closed mouth; original costumes; typically unmarked or hang tag only.

Hard Plastic & Vinyl

Prices listed are for dolls in near-mint, original condition. If damaged, redressed, or undressed, expect the value to be less than one half to one fourth the amounts listed.

Lady/Teen: all hard plastic; jointed at neck, shoulder, and hip; good wig; sleep eyes; closed mouth; beautifully designed, original costumes; typically marked "X," "200," unmarked, or hang tag only.

Child/Baby: all vinyl; jointed at neck, shoulder, and hip; rooted hair; sleep eyes; closed mouth; original costume; typically marked "Mollye," "15," or "450."

Molly-'es Doll Value Comparisons

Size	Cloth Child	Cloth International	Cloth Character-type	Composition Baby	Composition Lady/Teen	Composition "Baghdad Series"	Hard Plastic Lady/Teen	Hard Plastic Lady/Elaborate Gowns*	Vinyl Child & Baby
9"									100.00
12"									125.00
13"	200.00	125.00							
14"				250.00			350.00		
15"	225.00	150.00	250.00	300.00	550.00	750.00			
16"									145.00
17"							400.00		
18"	250.00		300.00	350.00	600.00			700.00	
19"						1,000.00			
20"							450.00	750.00	
21"				450.00	700.00			800.00	
23"								850.00	
24"	300.00		350.00						
25"							500.00		
27"		300.00			900.00				
28"							600.00	1200.00	
29"	350.00								

*Add an additional $300.00 for Dancing Deb posed on a revolving musical stand.

Morimura Brothers

Morimura Brothers, an 1870s Japanese import house, began producing dolls in 1915. With the onset of World War I, the flow of bisque dolls from Europe had virtually ceased. Morimura Brothers stepped in to supply Japanese-made bisque-head dolls to American customers during and immediately following World War I. Bisque doll heads manufactured by Morimura Brothers, while projecting a certain amount of charm, were frequently of poor quality. The company demonstrated a lack of the technical knowledge and experience needed to produce fine bisque dolls.

Morimura Brothers unabashedly set out to imitate the much-loved German doll and did, in fact, achieve a certain degree of success. There are many fine examples available, and as their German and French counterparts continue to escalate in price, Morimura Brothers dolls will undoubtedly become more popular.

Prices listed are for appropriately costumed dolls in good condition. Normal wear, slight damage, or well-made repairs to the body do not greatly affect the price. If the bisque is damaged or repaired, expect the value to be less than half the amounts listed. It is perfectly acceptable to show a missing or repaired finger or joint, or a mended body.

Also see Googly-Eyed Dolls.

Character Baby: bisque socket head; composition bent-limb baby body; good wig; glass eyes; open mouth; appropriately dressed; typically marked "M B" (within a circle), "Japan," "Nippon," "Yamato," "FY," "MB," or "JW."

Dolly Face: bisque shoulder or socket head; jointed composition or kid body; good wig; glass eyes; open mouth; appropriately dressed; typically marked "MB" within a circle, "NIPPON," "JW," "Yamato," "FY," or "MB."

Morimura Brothers babies from left to right: 10" marked "Nippon 22," 14" marked "M B A-9," 16" marked "Nippon 602/70018," and 11" marked "FY 215." Courtesy of David Cobb's Doll Auctions

Morimura Brothers Value Comparisons

Size	Character Baby, Standard	Character Baby, Exceptional	Dolly-Face, Standard	Dolly-Face, Exceptional
8"			150.00	325.00
10"	250.00		200.00	350.00
12"	300.00		250.00	400.00
14"	350.00	800.00	275.00	425.00
15"	400.00	1,000.00	300.00	450.00
18"	550.00	1,200.00	325.00	500.00
20"	650.00	1,250.00	350.00	550.00
22"	750.00	1,300.00	400.00	600.00
24"			450.00	700.00

Alexandre Mothereau

~◆~

Alexandre Celestin Triburee Mothereau, founder of this rather obscure French doll firm, produced Bébé Mothereau from 1880 until 1895. Not a great deal is known about Triburee, save the production of very rare and lovely bisque dolls on rather poorly proportioned bodies.

The bodies have turned-wooden upper limbs and rounded-joint lower limbs, with metal brackets to facilitate elastic stringing. They have very long and quite thin torsos, as well as extremely small hands and feet. Expect to find the familiar cork pate and the paperweight eyes, finely lined in black with delicately shadowed eyelids. The thin, feathered brows, however, are a departure from the quintessential French Bébé.

A careful examination is necessary to avoid purchasing a reproduction. The pressed, not poured, bisque should be fine and translucent, but not satiny and silk-like. The most helpful clue may be in the doll's height. Reproductions tend to be shorter than the incised number would indicate, for example #4 = 15", #6 = 17 1/2", #7 = 20", #8 = 22", #9 = 25", #10 = 29". Any deviation of more than one-inch should be considered suspicious.

Prices listed are for beautifully dressed dolls in good condition. Normal wear, slight damage, or well-made repairs to the body do not greatly affect the price. If the bisque is damaged or repaired, expect the value to be less. The Bébé Mothereau is so rare and desirable, serious collectors will forgive fine hairlines or professional repairs that do not jeopardize the integrity of the doll. The price should reflect the degree and extent of damage. It is perfectly acceptable to show a missing or repaired finger or a mended body.

Bébé Mothereau: pale pressed bisque socket head; jointed wood and composition French body with straight wrists; good human hair wig; paperweight eyes; delicately shadowed eyelids; thin feathered brows; pierced ears; closed mouth; marked (size number) "B M."

Beautiful and original #617 Mothereau Bébé. Courtesy of Christie's East Auctions

Bébé Mothereau Value Comparison	
Size	**Bébé**
15"	26,000.00
17"	27,000.00
20"	29,000.00
22"	33,000.00
25"	34,000.00
29"	38,000.00

Motschmann Baby

~◆~

For many years, collectors used the term "Motschmann Baby" for a vintage wax over papier-mâché doll. Christopher Motschmann received a patent for the first economically mass-produced voice box that could be placed within a doll's body. Dolls found stamped "Motschmann" were most likely produced within the operative patent years of 1857-1859. Old habits die hard, and many collectors still use the term "Motschmann Baby" when referring to a Sonneberg Täufling.

Also see Sonneberg Täufling.

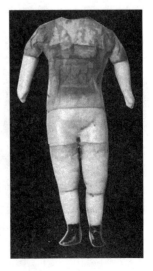

Body type often stamped Motschmann.

Multi-Faced Dolls

*V*intage Multi-Faced bisque dolls were made by various manufacturers. The dolls have two or more faces on a single head, usually within a molded bonnet that keeps all but one face hidden from view. Well known manufacturers include Carl Bergner, Max Frederick Schelhorn, and Fritz Bartenstein.

Two-faced dolls are usually found with opposing facial combinations: awake and asleep; white and black; youth and old age; or crying and laughing. Combination of faces on three-faced dolls include: awake, asleep, and crying; crying, laughing, and sleeping; black asleep, white awake, and mulatto crying; and even Red Riding Hood, Wolf, and Grandma.

Prices listed are for good quality, skillfully decorated dolls with no damage. Evaluate any Multi-Face Doll according to its uniqueness and visual appeal, as these factors greatly affect price. Inspecting the dolls can be difficult as one does not have access to the crown opening or the neck socket. Normal wear or well-made repairs to the body do not greatly affect price. If the bisque is damaged or repaired, expect the value to be about half the amount listed. It is perfectly acceptable to show a missing or repaired finger or a mended body.

Please note that examples of Multi-Faced Dolls may also be found elsewhere in this book, located in the sections devoted to their respective manufacturers.

Multi-Face: bisque socket and painted hair or mohair attached to molded hood or bonnet; painted or glass eyes, appropriately dressed; typically marked "CB," "HvB," "SH," "Shl," and possibly others.

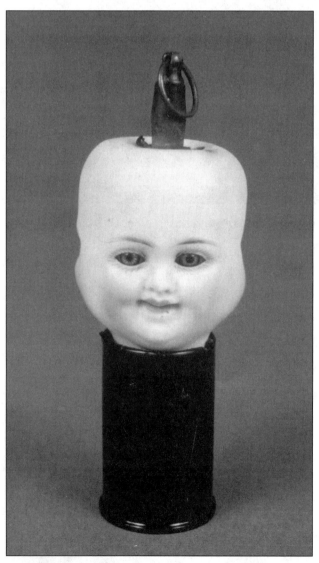

Carl Bergner multi-face doll, unattached. Courtesy of Helen Brooke

Multi-faced dolls. Courtesy of David Cobb's Doll Auctions

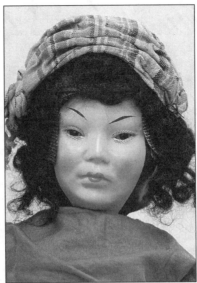
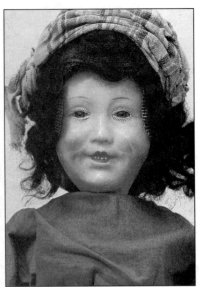

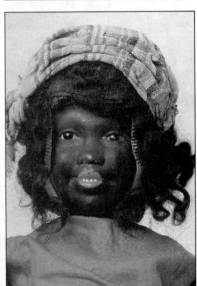

Series of photographs showing range of expressions from multi-face doll. Courtesy of David Cobb's Doll Auctions

Multi-Faced Dolls Value Comparisons

Size	Two-Faced Character, Standard	Two-Faced Character, Unusual	Two-Faced Character, Extraordinary	Three-Faced Character, Standard	Three-Faced Character, Unusual
12"	1,800.00	3,500.00	12,000.00	1,900.00	
15"	2,000.00	3,700.00		2,400.00	6,800.00
18"	2,400.00		17,000.00	2,600.00	

Munich Art Dolls

arion Kaulitz was the undisputed originator of Munich Art Dolls. At an awards ceremony in 1910, Kaulitz was credited with leading the Puppen Reform—a movement in Bavaria towards the creation of realism in dolls. Marie Marc-Schnur, Paul Vogelsanger, and Josef Wacherle designed the heads. Faces were hand painted by Marion Kaulitz, then dressed by Lillian Frobenius and Alice Hagemann. *Studio Talk* is quoted: "when the artistic conscience began to invade the doll industry it fell to some artists of Dresden and Munich to introduce the change." Their efforts attracted a great deal of attention in both artistic and commercial circles. In fact, the Munich Art Dolls undoubtedly inspired Kämmer & Reinhardt to manufacture character dolls.

The beautiful, child-like Munich Art Dolls, commonly dressed as French or German children, are extremely popular. They are admired not only for their appealing avant-garde naturalism, but also for their historically significant contribution to the evolution of doll making.

Prices listed are for originally costumed dolls in good condition. Slight crazing is acceptable and does not greatly affect the price. If badly crazed, cracked, peeling, or repainted, expect the value to be less than half the amounts listed.

Character Doll: composition head; ball-jointed composition body; molded and painted hair or good wig; artistically modelled and painted eyes with great detail; rosy cheeks, full, pouty, closed mouth; original costume; typically marked "K III," or "KI"; occasionally signed on neck.

Munich Art Dolls Value Comparisons	
Size	**Munich Art Doll**
13"	4,500.00
16 1/2"	6,000.00
17 1/2"	7,500.00
21 1/2"	9,700.00

Painted hair Munich Art Doll. Courtesy of Village Doll and Toy Shop, Becky and Andy Ourant, Adamstown, Pa.

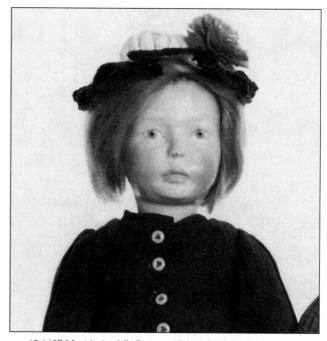

17 1/2" Munich Art doll. Courtesy of David Cobb's Doll Auctions

Nancy Ann Storybook Dolls

Hard plastic, painted lash Muffie with original box and additional outfit. Courtesy of McMaster's Doll Auction

second and third fingers molded together and curved inwards; excellent details on hands, wrists, and ears; and a slight blush on knees and wrists. Clothing snaps are usually small, with solid tops, and marked on the underside "Grippers SMCO."

Prices listed are for all original dolls with no damage. Values are determined by condition, scarcity of particular models, originality of accessorized costumes, and the presence of a wrist tag and original box.

Nancy Ann: 10"; all vinyl; jointed at neck, shoulder, and hip; rooted hair; sleep eyes with lashes; closed mouth; pierced ears; original costume; typically marked "Nancy Ann" **125.00**

Nancy Ann: 17 to 18"; all hard plastic with synthetic wig or vinyl head with rooted hair; jointed at neck, shoulder, and hip; sleep eyes with lashes; closed mouth; original costume; typically marked "17B" or "18B" or unmarked with hang tag only **1,000.00**

Muffie: 8"; all hard plastic; jointed at neck, shoulder, and hip; good wig; sleep eyes; closed mouth; original costume; typically marked "StoryBook Dolls California/Muffie" or "Muffie."

8" Muffie Value Comparisons (1953-on)	
Identification	**Value**
Painted lashes, no eyebrows, straight leg, non-walker (1953)	500.00
Molded lashes, painted eyebrows, straight-leg walker (1954)	400.00
Vinyl head, rooted saran hair, straight-leg or bent knee walker (1955)	250.00
Unmarked, molded lashes, wig, Muffie Around the World re-issue straight leg walker (1968)	150.00

Storybook Dolls

Painted Bisque: one piece head and body; jointed shoulder and hip; mohair wig; painted eyes; tiny closed mouth; original costume; see chart for various markings.

Judy Ann: classic characteristics with molded and painted bangs and white socks; see chart for various markings.

Hard Plastic: all hard plastic, or vinyl head with rooted hair; jointed at neck, shoulder, and hip; mohair or synthetic wig; painted or sleep eyes; closed mouth; original costume; see chart for various markings.

*N*ancy Ann Storybook Dolls were produced by a California-based company founded by Nancy Ann Abbott and her partner, A. L. Rowland, in 1936. These popular dolls were first made of painted bisque and later hard plastic. Abbott originally purchased dolls from overseas and repainted them. By 1938, the Nancy Ann Storybook Doll Company began producing dolls using clays imported from England.

During the 1960s, the company, which at its peak was producing over eight thousand dolls a day, began to experience technical problems. Doll production ceased not long after Abbott's passing in 1964. The dolls and clothing she designed are among the most outstanding produced during the 1950s and 1960s.

When Nancy Ann Storybook Dolls are mentioned, one immediately thinks of the adorable, little, all-painted bisque characters, which have endeared themselves to virtually every doll collector. Although not conventional antique bisque dolls, the 1940-era characters made of painted or sprayed clay-bisque, are so avidly sought after that they belong firmly in the legion of bisque doll collecting.

Characters portrayed by the 5 1/2 to 7 inch Nancy Ann Storybook Dolls from 1936 to 1947 are identified by a wrist tag and/or box. Only babies were produced the first year. Dolls had hip joints through 1942, when stiff-legged dolls were introduced. Clues to identifying the 17 to 18 inch hard plastic dolls include:

5 1/2" to 7" Storybook Doll Value Comparisons						
Date	**Child**	**Baby**	**Box**	**Clothing Closures**	**Identification**	**Value Estimates**
1936		Painted bisque, Mark I	Pink/Blue Marbleized, or color with starbursts	Silver pin	Gold foil stickers "Nancy Ann Dressed Dolls"	700.00
1937	Painted bisque, Mark I or II	Painted bisque, Mark I or II	Colored boxes with starbursts	Silver pin	Gold Foil Sticker "Nancy Ann Dressed Dolls"	1,000.00
1938	Painted bisque, Mark III "AMERICA" or "JUDY ANN USA"		Color boxes with starbursts*	Silver pin	Gold foil stickers "Judy Ann"	1,000.00

Original painted bisque Nancy Ann Storybook dolls. Courtesy of Pat Tyson

5 1/2" to 7" Storybook Doll Value Comparisons

Date	Child	Baby	Box	Clothing Closures	Identification	Value Estimates
1938	Painted bisque, Mark III	Painted bisque, Mark II or III	Colored boxes w/star-bursts	Silver or brass pin	Gold foil stickers "Storybook Dolls"	1,000.00
1939	Painted bisque, bangs, molded socks, Mark IV	Painted bisque, star-shaped hands, Mark IV	Colored box, small silver dots	Brass pins	Gold foil sticker "Storybook Dolls"	900.00
1940	Painted bisque, molded socks, Mark IV	Painted bisque, star-shaped hands, Mark IV	Colored box, white dots	Brass Pin	Gold foil sticker "Storybook Dolls"	450.00
1941-1942	Painted bisque, transition dolls Mark IV*	Painted bisque, some with star-shaped hands, some with firsts, Mark IV	White box, colored dots	Brass pin	Gold foil wrist tag with name	250.00
1943-1947	Painted bisque, One piece head, torso, and legs, Mark IV	Painted bisque, fist hands, Mark IV	White boxes, colored dots	Dull silver or brass pin, or ribbon ties	Gold foil wrist tag with name	175.00
1947-1949	Plastic, painted eyes, Mark V	Painted bisque body, plastic limbs, Mark IV	White box, colored dots, "Nancy Ann Storybook Dolls" printed between dots	Brass snaps	Gold foil wrist tag with name	150.00
1949-1953	Plastic, black sleep eyes, Mark V	Plastic, black sleep eyes, Mark V	Same as above.	Brass or painted snaps	Gold foil wrist tag with name	125.00
1953	Plastic, blue sleep eyes	Plastic, black sleep eyes	Same as above	Painted donut snaps	Gold foil wrist tag with name	100.00

* Add an additional $200.00 for "Pudgies" with chubby tummies.

Mark I = "Made in Japan," "87 Made in Japan," or "88 Made in Japan"

Mark II = "Made in Japan," "Japan," "AMERICA," "Made in Japan 1146," or "Made in Japan 1148"

Mark III = "STORYBOOK USA" or Story Book USA

Mark IV = "StoryBook Doll USA"

Mark V = "StoryBook Doll USA/Trade Mark Reg." Or "Nancy Ann Story Book Dolls/USA Trademark Reg."

Other Storybook Dolls

Prices listed are for original dolls in perfect, near-mint condition with boxes

Judy Ann in Fairyland in rare, red, book-shaped box
....$3,500.00
Roy Rogers and Dale Evans 2,900.00
Flower Girl..1,200.00

Easter Parade 1,300.00
Masquerade 1,500.00
Pirate 1,700.00
Margie Ann 900.00
Around the World 1,200.00
Sports Motif...1,900.00
Topsy and Eva 1,600.00
Oriental..2,500.00
Storybook Literary Set 6,000.00

Gebrüder Ohlhaver

There are conflicting dates as to the founding of the Gebrüder Ohlhaver doll factory in Sonneberg, Germany. Some sources give 1897 and others 1912. All agree, however, that in 1913 Ohlhaver was advertising "ball jointed dolls for sale." The owners of the company, Jonny Paulas Gerhard Ohlhaver, and Hinrick Ohlhaver, forever immortalized their names with their famous "Revalo" trademark, derived from the owners' names being phonetically spelled backwards.

The delightfully quaint faces of the Character dolls—along with the beguiling, slender-faced Revalo Child—are difficult for collectors to resist. Ohlhaver ordered its doll heads from several porcelain factories, including Ernst Heubach, Gebrüder Heubach, and Mengersgereuth—the latter distinguishable by an "X" within a circle mark. "Igodi," another commonly found mark, refers to a patented swivel head invented by Johann Gottleib Dierich in 1919. It appears on some heads produced by Ernst Heubach. Additional markings include the Ohlhaver trade names "Revalo," "My Queen Doll," and "Bébé Princess," in addition to mold numbers 150, 151, 10727, and 11010.

Prices listed are for appropriately costumed dolls in good condition. Normal wear, slight damage, or well-made repairs to the body do not greatly affect the price. If the bisque is damaged or repaired, expect the value to be less than half the amounts listed. It is perfectly acceptable to show a missing or repaired finger or joint, or a mended body.

Character Child: bisque socket head; jointed composition body; molded and painted hair; painted and highlighted intaglio eyes; open/closed mouth; appropriately dressed; typically marked "Revalo/(size number)/Dep."

Character Baby: bisque socket head; composition bent-limb baby body; good wig; glass eyes; winged, feathered brows; open mouth; appropriately dressed; typically marked "Germany Revalo."

Dolly Face: slender face; bisque socket or shoulder head; jointed composition or kid body; good wig; glass eyes; open mouth; appropriately dressed; typically marked "Germany Revalo."

17" Revalo sisters. Courtesy of McMaster's Doll Auction

Revalo Value Comparisons				
Size	Character Child**	Character Baby*	Dolly-Face Socket Head	Dolly-Face Shoulder Head
8"	900.00			
10"	950.00			
12"	1,100.00			
14"	1,300.00	800.00		
16"	1,500.00	900.00	800.00	550.00
18"		1,000.00	850.00	
20"		1,100.00	900.00	750.00
22"		1,200.00	1,000.00	800.00
24"			1,200.00	
26"			1,300.00	1,000.00
28"			1,500.00	

* Add an additional $700.00 for jointed toddler body.

** Add an additional $400.00–500.00 for molded hair bows.

Oriental Dolls

12" olive bisque Ellar by Armand Marseille with Bliss dollhouse. Courtesy of David Cobb's Doll Auctions

19" Simon & Halbig #1329 olive bisque in original elaborate hairstyle and costume. Courtesy of David Cobb's Doll Auctions

Many manufacturers made or handled dolls representing Oriental people. Oriental characteristics were achieved through the use of tinted bisque and by applying appropriate expressions to the face.

Also see Modern Collectibles, Nancy Ann Story Book, Mattel, Lenci, Horsman, Hasbro, Japanese Dolls, Door of Hope, Barbie, Cloth Dolls, Cabbage Patch, Artist Dolls, All Bisque.

Bisque

Prices listed are for appropriately costumed dolls in good condition. Normal wear, slight damage, or well-made repairs to the body do not greatly affect the price. If the bisque is damaged or repaired, expect the value to be less than half the amounts listed. It is perfectly acceptable to show a missing or repaired finger or joint, or a mended body.

Oriental Socket Head: expressive Oriental features; composition body; good wig; glass eyes; appropriately dressed; various manufacturers' markings include:

Armand Marseille: typically marked "353," "ELLAR."
Bähr & Pröschild: typically marked "220."
Belton-Type: typically marked "129" or "193."
Bru: typically marked "BRU JNE."
Bruno Schmidt: typically marked "500."

Ernst Heubach: typically marked "452."
Jumeau: closed mouth; typically marked "Tete."
Kestner: typically marked "243."
Schoeneau & Hoffmeister: typically marked "4900."
Simon & Halbig: typically marked "164," "1099," "1129," "1199," or "1329."
Theodor Recknagel: typically marked "Germany JS A (#) R."

Composition & Papier-Mâché

Prices listed are for appropriately costumed dolls in good condition. Slight crazing is acceptable and does not greatly affect the price. If badly crazed, cracked, peeling, or repainted, expect the value to be less than half the amounts listed.

Composition: composition head and limbs; cloth body or all composition; molded and painted hair, good wig, or solid dome with queue; expressive Oriental modelling; appropriately dressed; various markings or unmarked.

Papier-Mâché: papier-mâché head and limbs; cloth body; molded and painted hair, good wig or solid dome with queue; glass eyes; expressive, Oriental modelling; appropriately dressed;

various markings ("AMUSO 10062/Made in Germany") or unmarked.

Meiji Era Geisha: beautifully-made, oyster-shell composition doll; boxed with changeable, elaborate, coiffure arrangements; styled with ornamental braids, flowers, combs, tassels, bells and mirrors; unmarked.

Oriental Dolls Value Comparisons

Size	Armand Marseille (353)	Bähr Pröschild (220)	Belton-Type	Bru	Bruno Schmidt (500)	Ernst Heubach (452)	Jumeau Closed Mouth	Kestner (243)
8"	900.00							
10"	1,100.00		1,900.00			1,200.00		
12"	1,300.00		2,000.00					5,800.00
14"	1,500.00	3,400.00			2,600.00			6,200.00
16"	1,600.00	3,900.00	2,400.00		2,800.00			6,800.00
18"	1,700.00	4,500.00			3,200.00		57,000.00	7,500.00
20"		5,300.00		26,000.00	3,400.00	2,600.00	67,000.00	8,400.00
22"	1,900.00	5,800.00	2,900.00		3,700.00		72,000.00	
24"							77,000.00	
25"							82,000.00	

Size	Schoneau & Hoffmeister (4900)	Simon & Halbig 164, 1329	Simon & Halbig 1099, 1129, 1199	Theodor Reckna-gel (JS AR)	Papier-Mâché	Composition	Geisha with Changeable Wig
8"			1,600.00			200.00	
10"	1,100.00	1,800.00				250.00	700.00
12"	1,400.00	2,400.00	2,600.00			300.00	
14"	1,600.00	2,700.00	3,000.00	4,000.00	900.00	350.00	1,500.00
16"	2,000.00	2,900.00	3,400.00				
18"	2,300.00	3,200.00	3,800.00		1,200.00		
20"	2,700.00	3,700.00	4,500.00				2,300.00

Papier-Mâché Dolls

❧

Various German manufacturers made doll heads from the special type of composition known as papier-mâché. A 19th century dictionary defined papier-mâché as "a tough plastic material made from paper pulp containing a mixture of sizing, paste, oil, resin, or other substances or from sheets of paper glued and pressed together." The wood and rag fibers in paper were responsible for much of papier-mâché's strength. Papier-Mâché, carton paté (French) and holz-masse (German) are interchangeable terms for the paper-based composition.

Papier-Mâché Dolls were individually handmade as early as the 16th century. The development of the pressure-mold process in the early 1800s allowed papier-mâché dolls to be mass produced. It was in fact the pressure-molded papier-mâché dolls that helped lay the foundation for the great German doll industry.

Prices listed are for appropriately costumed dolls in good condition. Slight crazing is acceptable and does not greatly affect the price. If badly crazed, cracked, peeling, or repainted, expect the value to be less than half the amounts listed.

Also see Greiner, Cuno & Otto Dressel.

French-Type: papier-mâché shoulder head; pink, kid body; wooden limbs with no articulation; painted black pate; hair stippled around face; nailed-on human hair wig; glass, almond-shaped eyes; pierced nostrils; closed or open mouth with bamboo teeth; appropriately dressed; unmarked. ***Note:*** *Known as French type, although of German origin.*

Early Papier-Mâché: papier-mâché shoulder head; kid or cloth body; kid or wooden limbs; molded hair, styled close to head and painted black or nailed on wig; painted or glass eyes; single-stroke brows; oval-shaped face; may have pierced nostrils; closed mouth, appropriately dressed; typically unmarked.

Molded Hair Papier-Mâché/Milliner's Model: papier-mâché shoulder head; delicately modelled oval face; somewhat long neck; thin, tightly stuffed, kid body; wooden limbs with no articulation; may have strips of red, green, or blue paper covering

23" Early Papier-Mâché. Courtesy of Jean Campbell

junctures of wooden limbs and kid body; painted, flat shoes; stylishly molded and painted hair; painted eyes; closed mouth; appropriately dressed; unmarked. ***Note:*** *These dolls share many of the same characteristics as the earlier papier-mâché shoulder-head dolls. Classification is determined primarily by hairstyle. The U.F.D.C. named these demure little ladies, by popular vote, "Molded Hair Papier-Mâché's." The name, although accurate, does not seem popular with collectors. The term "Milliner's Model" apparently originated with the well-known doll historian, Eleanor St. George. According to her own account, there was no real basis for the term other than that she liked it. Evidence suggests that there were Milliner's Model dolls, but there is no reason to believe that they resembled the Molded Hair Papier-Mâchés.*

L. Moss: black papier-mâché character head: cloth body; molded and painted, tightly curled hair; glass eyes; molded tear on cheek; closed mouth; appropriately dressed; unmarked.

17", 12", 10", 8" unmarked Papier-Mâché showing several hairstyles. The doll on the left, pushing a buggy, is an 11" Ives Walker Papier-Mâché lady pushing a wooden buggy. Courtesy of David Cobb's Doll Auctions

Later Molded Hair: papier-mâché shoulder head; cloth body; leather hands; molded and painted wavy blond or black hair, reminiscent of the styles commonly found on china head dolls; short neck; rounded face; painted eyes; lightly feathered brows; closed mouth; typically marked "M & S Superior" or unmarked.

Papier-Mâché Value Comparisons

Size	French Type	Early, Papier-Mâché, Glass Eyes	Early, Papier-Mâché, Painted Eyes	Molded Hair/ Milliner's Model, Fancy Hair Style*	Molded Hair/ Milliner's Model Common Hair Style	L. Moss Black Character	Later Papier-Mâché
8"				1,000.00	600.00		
10"	1,400.00		900.00	1,300.00	700.00		
12"	1,600.00	1,400.00	1,000.00	1,500.00	800.00		
14"	1,800.00	1,600.00	1,100.00	1,900.00	950.00		400.00
16"	2,000.00	1,900.00	1,300.00	2,300.00	1,100.00		500.00
18"	2,300.00	2,100.00	1,400.00	2,700.00	1,300.00		550.00
20"	2,500.00	2,300.00	1,500.00	3,000.00	1,500.00		600.00
22"	2,800.00	2,500.00	1,700.00	3,300.00	1,700.00	8,000.00	700.00
24"	3,300.00	2,900.00	1,900.00	3,900.00	1,900.00	9,500.00	800.00
26"		3,300.00	2,200.00		2,400.00		850.00
28"		3,600.00					
30"						10,500.00	1,200.00
32"	3,800.00		3,100.00				

* Add an additional $200.00–400.00 for and unusual hairstyle or $400.00–800.00 for glass eyes.

Parian-Type Dolls

Various German porcelain factories produced Parian dolls from the late 1850s through the early 1880s. Parian is a generic term for the very pale or untinted bisque dolls of the 19th century. The term "Parian" has often been a source of confusion. How do Parian heads differ from other bisque heads? Actually, they don't. All glazed or unglazed "biscuit-mix" heads are porcelain. Many believe that the white bisque of the Parian dolls resembles the marble of Greek statues.

The exquisitely pale, high quality, unblemished porcelain with its beautiful modelling and delicate decoration is not to be confused with course, grayish "stone" or "sugar bisque." The Dresden porcelain factories were responsible for most of the early fine Parian doll heads. The hardness of the paste made it possible to cast intricately detailed molds. Artists were inspired to great flights of imagination when creating ornate laces and ruffles, and elaborate hairstyles that incorporated braids, ringlets, and curls. Even wreaths of flowers and jewels adorned these discriminating beauties. Soft coloring with touches of gold and luster decorated the lovely, marble-like heads. Although most Parians have painted eyes, some were given glass eyes, solid domes with wigs, plain, modest shoulder plates, pierced ears, and occasionally swivel necks. Any combination of these characteristics is possible.

Authentic Parian dolls are typically unmarked, or marked only with a number.

Prices listed are for beautifully dressed dolls in good condition. Normal wear or well-made repairs to the body do not greatly affect the price. Slight flakes from a delicate ruffle or petal of a flower would detract from the value in direct relation to the degree of damage. If the Parian is cracked or repaired or if significant damage to the trim exists, expect the value to be less than half the amounts listed. It is perfectly acceptable to show a missing or repaired finger or a mended body.

Parian-types 23" curly hair, black ribbon, painted features, and pierced ears; 19" braided hair, applied flowers, painted features, pierced ears, and beaded ruffled bodice; 19" uniquely styled hair, painted features, pierced ears, molded bodice with bow at neck; 18" Countess Dagmar, curly bangs with bow, plain molded bodice; 17" curly hair with black bow; and 12" Countess Dagmar. Courtesy of David Cobb's Doll Auctions

Parian Doll Value Comparisons

Description of Characteristics	Size	Value
Plain hairstyle, no decoration in hair nor on shoulder plate; may or may not have pierced ears; painted eyes	14" 18" 22"	500.00 600.00 750.00
Men's hairstyle; decorated shirt and tie shoulder plate; painted eyes	14" 18" 22"	900.00 1,600.00 2,400.00
Men's hairstyle; decorated shirt and tie shoulder plate; glass eyes	18" 22"	3,200.00 3,600.00
Molded head band, such as "Alice in Wonderland"-type, no decoration on shoulder plate; may or may not have pierced ears; painted eyes	14" 18" 22"	800.00 1,000.00 1,300.00
Solid dome, good wig; plain, modest shoulder plate; may or may not have pierced ears; painted eyes	14" 18" 22"	800.00 1,100.00 1,700.00
Solid dome, good wig; plain, modest shoulder plate; may or may not have pierced ears; glass eyes	14" 18" 22"	1,200.00 1,500.00 1,900.00
Curly hair style; bow on top; decorated shoulder plate with high neck ruffled blouse; broach; intaglio eyes; open/closed mouth; molded teeth; marked "8552" (Irish Queen by Limbach)	14" 18" 22"	900.00 1,300.00 1,900.00

17" Irish Queen Parian-type by Limbach and 15" Parian with applied gold luster head band. Courtesy of David Cobb's Doll Auctions

Parian Doll Value Comparisons

Description of Characteristics	Size	Value
Moderately fancy hairstyle; decorated shoulder plate; may or may not have pierced ears; painted eyes	14" 18" 22"	1,000.00 1,400.00 1,700.00
Moderately fancy hairstyle; decorated shoulder plate; may or may not have pierced ears; glass eyes	14" 18" 22"	1,100.00 1,700.00 2,000.00
Moderately fancy hairstyle; decorated shoulder plate; applied flowers or necklaces; pink luster hat, snood, or tiara; may or may not have pierced ears; painted eyes	14" 18" 22"	1,400.00 1,900.00 2,200.00
Moderately fancy hairstyle; decorated shoulder plate; applied flowers or necklaces; pink luster hat, snood, or tiara; may or may not have pierced ears; glass eyes	14" 18" 22"	1,800.00 2,300.00 2,700.00
Elaborate hairstyle, or explicitly detailed and decorated bonnet, and shoulder plate; may or may not have pierced ears; painted eyes	14" 18" 22"	1,600.00 2,200.00 2,500.00
Elaborate hairstyle, or explicitly detailed and decorated bonnet, and shoulder plate; may or may not have pierced ears; glass eyes	14" 18" 22"	2,200.00 2,900.00 3,400.00
Elaborate hairstyle and shoulder plate; swivel neck; may or may not have pierced ears; glass eyes	18" 22"	3,500.00 4,000.00

Patent Washable Dolls

*V*arious German manufacturers made Patent Washable Dolls after 1880. Unfortunately, these papier-mâché composition dolls are seldom found in good condition. The area around the eyes seems particularly susceptible to damage. Occasionally, however, a fine quality Patent Washable will be found with exceptionally beautiful modelling and decoration.

Prices listed are for appropriately costumed dolls in good condition. Slight crazing is acceptable and does not greatly affect the price. If badly crazed, cracked, peeling, or repainted, expect the value to be less than half the amounts listed.

Patent Washable: papier-mâché composition shoulder head; thin, cloth body; long, cloth limbs; composition papier-mâché forearms and lower legs; may have molded and painted boots; mohair or skin wig; bulgy, glass eyes; open or closed mouth; appropriately dressed; typically unmarked.

Rare 40" Patent Washable. Courtesy of McMaster's Doll Auction

Patent Washable Value Comparisons		
Size	Standard Quality Patent Washable	Extraordinary Quality Patent Washable
14"	300.00	750.00
20"	350.00	900.00
29"	600.00	1,600.00
38"	800.00	1,900.00

Peddlar Dolls

*D*uring the eighteenth and into the nineteenth century, Peddlar dolls were an important accessory in the most fashionable parlors. They were frequently created by the Lady of the house to exhibit her artistic talents. A Peddlar Doll served as a decorating accent, placed under a glass dome in a prominent location.

Itinerant traders traveled over Europe and the United States, but it was the English Peddler for whom there seemed a special fascination.

The weathered and wrinkled doll-faces were made of cloth, leather, wood, papier mâché, wax, cork, china, dried apples, and even breadcrumbs. The bodies were usually wooden or cloth-covered wire. "Notion Nannies," with traditional red cape, calico dress gathered to expose a black quilted slip, white apron, and black silk bonnet over a white laced mob cap were a particular favorite.

Although the majority of vintage Peddlar Dolls were homespun originals, C. H. White of Portsmouth, England advertised commercially supplied Peddlar Dolls. The marbleized paper-cover base and "C. H. White/Milton/Portsmouth" label allows for easy identification.

Wonderfully documented pair of Peddlar dolls by C. H. White c. 1810. Courtesy of Tom Gray

Deciding the age and authenticity of a Peddlar Doll can mean double-trouble! "Nanny" and her "Notions" are equally important. Evaluate the doll; bear in mind charm can be as important as condition. Also carefully study the wares, a few authentic antique miniatures added to a fraudulent doll is nonetheless nefarious.

The prices listed are for original dolls in good condition. Normal aging does not affect the price. Presentation, condition, and visual appeal are the determining value factors.

Peddlar Doll Value Comparison		
Size	Type or Style	Value
6"-14"	Hand-crafted; gnarled/cagey-face; original costume & miniatures	2,000.00
6"-14"	Specialized; hand-crafted; original costume & miniatures (Costermonger sells fruits or vegetables; Colporter [also spelled Colporteur] peddled religious goods; Tinker mender or metal wares)	2,500.00
6"-12"	Marked or known C.H. White; original costume & miniatures	2,500.00
6"-14"	Pair of Peddlar Dolls—Man and Woman as an obvious couple; original costume & miniatures	4,000.00
Any	Antique doll dressed and outfitted as a Peddlar Doll; original authentic costume & miniatures	1,000.00–3,000.00 plus current doll value

May have a mask made of wax, cloth, leather, or other material that was used to cover the original doll face. The masked Peddlar dolls are very rare and could easily double the value

Peggy Nisbet Limited

BR/314 & BR/315 the Pearly Queen and King. Courtesy of Nisbet Limited

The very English Peggy Nisbet began her journey into doll making history with a single doll in 1952.

Wishing to commemorate the coronation of Her Majesty Queen Elizabeth II, Peggy decided to make a doll. Just gaining permission to make such a doll would have been enough to discourage most people, but not Peggy Nisbet. Official approval was needed from Lord Chamberlain to model a likeness of any member of the royal family. After numerous letters, visits, and illustrations of Peggy's envisioned finished project, permission was granted. She immediately commissioned a 7 1/2-inch china doll from a local potter and set about creating an exquisitely costumed prototype. Relying totally upon home sewers copying the original prototype, 300 H. M. Queen Elizabeth II dolls were produced. Harrods Department Store purchased the entire lot, and Peggy Nisbet was on her way.

Over the years, Peggy Nisbet has gone through several trying times, both personally and professionally. With the determination the English are so famous for, she and her company never gave up. They always moved forward and never lost sight of her goals.

Recently Peggy Nisbet Limited and her subsidiaries have formed The House of Nisbet, under the direction of Peggy's son-in-law. In addition to the well-known petite fashion doll, bears, toys, and teaching accessories also bear the Nisbet name.

The small character dolls are marvels of costume design. Fabrics, style, accessories, and attention to detail place Nisbet dolls in a class of their own. Literally thousands of personalities have been introduced. All share a similar body type, but faces are astonishingly life-like in appearance. Whether Teddy Roosevelt, Margaret Thatcher, King Tutankhamen, or Bozo the Clown, the rendition is remarkable. Personal appeal and notoriety have a great deal of influence on the ever-fluctuating modern doll market. A doll that is worth very little can escalate over night (Princess Diana for instance), or it can lose its collectible appeal just as quickly (Prince Charles for instance). Please understand that I use these two dolls only to make a point. Recently both doll values have leveled off.

Prices listed are for dolls in mint, original condition with average appeal. Within a classification, any particular doll could be worth much less or much more. If damaged, redressed, or undressed, expect the value to be less than one fourth the amount listed.

Nisbet Collectible Character Dolls: 7-8"; vinyl; molded and painted character face; beautifully costumed and accessorized; wrist tag with character and history.

Peggy Nisbet Character Value Comparison				
Entertainment Personalities	Political Personalities	Royal Family, Past & Present	Historical and Literary	Regency/Guardsmen
150.00 (+/-)	125.00 (+/-)	200.00 (+/-)	100.00 (+/-)	125.00 (+/-)

Dr. Dora Petzold

Dr. Dora Petzold's composition character child dolls are surrounded by a landscape of mystery and charm. There are surprisingly few records and little information regarding Dr. Dora Petzold. The character heads have been reported as being made from silk, layers of paper, composition, and pressed cardboard—all of which are correct. The stockinette bodies have rather short torsos. Hands have separate free-form thumbs; the other fingers are only stitched. Legs have nicely-shaped calves.

A 1919 magazine, *Die Post,* reported on the Dora Petzold dolls. The article stated "...These are dolls for the high society, for the elegant world, for the boudoir, for the lady. Worked of velvet and silk...[they can be used] to decorate a room by placing them before an embroidered pillow and having them swing on the handrail of an armchair..." The author obviously thought Petzold dolls were extraordinary—an opinion shared by many.

Yet another quote, this one from Dr. Dora Petzold herself: "All Dora Petzold dolls are produced in my workshops under my personal directorship and after my personal designs and models. The body of the dolls consists of high quality knit wear and is stuffed so that all doll joints can be bent to imitate every human movement. The heads of Dora Petzold dolls are of unbreakable non-flammable material and painted with non-toxic colors which makes my dolls washable. The outfit of the dolls is fashioned after the best children's outfits and produced of the first class material. All these characteristics make a practical and at the same time very nice toy of my doll..."

Prices listed are for appropriately dressed dolls in good condition. Slight wear and signs of aging or well-made repairs to the body do not greatly affect price. If a doll is badly crazed, worn, stained, peeling, or repainted, expect the value to be less than half the amount listed.

Petzold Character: composition flange head; pink, stockinette body; jointed at shoulder and hip; mitt hands with stitched fingers and separate thumb; mohair wig; painted eyes; single-stroke brows; accent nostrils; closed mouth; molded dimples; appropriately dressed; stamped "Dora Petzold/Registered/Trade Mark/Doll/Germany."

Dora Petzold Value Comparisons	
Size	Petzold Character
18"	1,200.00
22"	1,400.00
25"	1,700.00

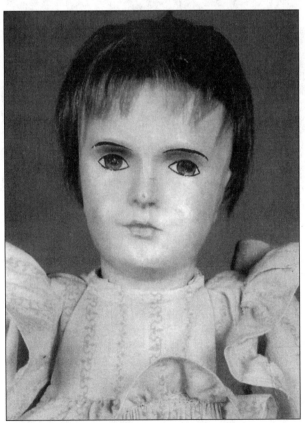

26" Dora Petzold character doll. Courtesy of McMaster's Doll Auction

Pintel & Godchaux

*I*n 1887, Henri Pintel and Ernest Godchaux formed the partnership of Pintel & Godchaux. They chose Montreuil-sous-Bois, France as the location for their new business, and continued operations there until becoming a member of S. F. B. J. in 1899.

22" early closed mouth Pintel & Godchaux. Courtesy Mrs. Adam Condo

Pintel & Godchaux registered the trade name "Bébé Charmat" in 1892. Prior to this they received a patent for a body with a diagonal hip joint. Several marked "P G" Bébés, presumably produced after the 1890 patent, are known to have this exclusive body type. Although unique and appropriate to the doll, the five-piece body does not pose or display as nicely as the more conventional jointed French body. In addition to a trade name or the initials "P G," a size number was also included in the marking. For example: #2 = 10 1/2", #6 = 16", and #13 = 24 1/2".

Prices listed are for appropriately dressed dolls in good condition. Normal wear, slight damage, or well-made repairs to the body do not greatly affect the price. If the bisque is damaged or repaired, expect the value to be less than half the amounts listed. It is perfectly acceptable to show a missing or repaired finger or a mended body.

Closed Mouth Bébé: bisque socket head; five piece composition or jointed wood and composition French body; good wig; paperweight eyes; long lashes; heavily feathered brows; pierced ears; closed mouth; appropriately dressed; typically marked "A/P (size number) G," "P G Déposé," or "C/P G."

Open Mouth Bébé: bisque socket head; five piece composition or jointed wood and composition French body; good wig; paperweight or glass eyes; feathered brows; pierced ears; open mouth with seven upper teeth; appropriately dressed: typically marked "A P G," "Déposé C/ P G," "B/P (size number) G."

Pintel & Godchaux Bébé Value Comparison

Size	Closed Mouth Bébé	Open Mouth Bébé
10 1/2"	3,000.00	
14"	3,200.00	
16"	3,400.00	1,900.00
18"	3,600.00	2,200.00
20"	3,800.00	2,600.00
22"	4,300.00	2,900.00
24"	4,900.00	

Rabery & Delphieu

This Paris, France doll manufacturer, named after founders Alexandre Rabery and Jean Delphieu, produced dolls from 1856 until 1899. After 1899, the company became part of the Societe Française de Fabrication de Bébés & Jouets (S.F.B.J.). Rabery and Delphieu were primarily interested in the production of doll bodies. In 1878, they exhibited their own dressed and undressed dolls at the Paris Exhibition. During the 1880s, Francois Gaultier supplied bisque heads and arms for Rabery & Delphieu Bébés.

Rabery & Delphieu Bébés were made using both pressed and poured bisque methods. They were marked "R.D." and a size number, ranging from 6/0 (11") to at least 4 (28").

The distinctive Rabery & Delphieu Bébés have very pale creamy bisque; unique, square-shaped facial modelling; large, almond-shaped, paperweight eyes, finely lined black; widely-arched, long, feathered brows; and pierced ears. The delicately colored, outlined, accented, and shaded lips have a high cupid's bow.

Earlier Rabery & Delphieu Bébés made of very pale, fine, smooth bisque. Later dolls have rosier and somewhat coarse bisque, less-delicately applied decoration, and rather obvious lashes, brows, and mouths.

Prices listed are for appropriately costumed dolls in good condition. Normal wear, slight damage, or well-made repairs to the body do not greatly affect the price. If the bisque is damaged or repaired, expect the value to be less than half the amounts listed. It is perfectly acceptable to show a missing or repaired finger or joint, or a mended body.

Bébé: bisque socket head; jointed wood-and-composition body with straight wrists; good wig; paperweight eyes; open or closed mouth; appropriately dressed; typically marked "R.D."; body stamped "Bébé Rabery."

26" Rabery & Delphieu Bébé. Courtesy of David Cobb's Doll Auctions

Rabery & Delphieu Bébé Value Comparisons

Size	Closed Mouth, Extraordinary Quality	Closed Mouth, Standard Quality	Open Mouth
11"	3,400.00		1,700.00
13"	3,500.00	2,500.00	1,800.00
15"	3,600.00	2,600.00	1,900.00
17"	3,900.00	2,800.00	2,100.00
19"	4,200.00	3,000.00	2,500.00
21"	4,500.00	3,300.00	2,600.00
23"	4,800.00	3,500.00	2,800.00
24"	5,400.00	3,900.00	3,000.00
26"	5,900.00	4,400.00	3,300.00
28"	6,400.00	4,700.00	3,400.00

Raggedy Ann & Andy®

*I*n 1915, Johnny Gruelle registered the trademark and patented a Raggedy Ann doll pattern. The story of Raggedy Ann & Andy is probably one of the best-loved American folk tales. Gruelle was born on Christmas Day, 1888. The Gruelle family was unusually gifted. His father and brother were both artists, and his sister, Prudence, was a dancer and concert singer. It came as no surprise that Johnny would also make an everlasting and far-reaching impression on the world.

Johnny and his wife Myrtle had three children—a daughter, Marcella, and two sons, Worth and Richard. It is obvious from his stories that Johnny loved children very much and wanted them protected from the harsh realities of an adult world. In *The Raggedy Ann Stories*, Johnny wrote "...Who knows, but that Fairyland is filled with old, lovable Rag Dolls—soft, floppy Rag Dolls who ride through all wonders of Fairyland in the crook of a dimpled arm, snuggling close to childish breast within which beats a heart filled with eternal sunshine." The love and tenderness that inspired such insight could only be that of an adoring father.

Marcella suffered a long and painful illness as a result of complications from a contaminated smallpox vaccination. Johnny spent hours telling his daughter wonderful stories about a land where dolls would come to life. About this same time, an old rag doll was found in his grandmother's attic. Johnny painted a face on the old rag doll, giving her renewed life and the name "Raggedy Ann." Marcella cherished her Raggedy Ann until her death in 1916. A grieving Johnny took Raggedy Ann to his office, where she became his constant companion. Although she failed to console him, she did inspire him. Whether as a self-prescribed therapy to lessen the pain of losing his daughter, or an attempt to immortalize her short life, Johnny Gruelle committed to writing the stories that had amused his daughter. Beginning with *The Raggedy Ann Stories*, published in 1918, he wrote twenty-five books about Raggedy Ann and her adventures before his untimely death in 1938. The Chicago firm of P. F. Volland published Gruelle's Raggedy Ann stories and suggested that a rag doll could help promote book sales.

The first Raggedy Anns were made by the Gruelle family. It is estimated that about 200 family-crafted Raggedy Anns were produced before the patent rights were given to Volland.

In 1920, Raggedy Ann's faithful companion and brother, Andy, first appeared. According to legend, Johnny was sitting in his office working on an illustration when a prim and proper little old lady suddenly appeared. She told him that she had been a neighbor and best friend to his mother when they were little girls. It was her mother that had made the girl rag doll for Johnny's mother, and had also made a boy doll for her. The two best friends had played many hours with their sister and brother rag dolls. She pulled a well-loved, old boy rag doll from her bag and gave it to Johnny, saying she was glad that the old rag dolls were together again. Johnny was touched by the story as he lovingly accepted the doll and turned briefly to place it beside Raggedy Ann. When he turned back, the old woman was gone. He never saw her again, but from that day forward Raggedy Andy has been a constant companion to Ann.

The early handcrafted Raggedy Ann & Andy dolls are undoubtedly very rare and infrequently found. The first mass-produced Raggedies, made by Volland, are uncharacteristic of the typical Raggedy Ann & Andy. They stand about 16" high and have rather long faces. Brown yarn hair usually surrounds the face only, which has button eyes and painted facial features. Vollands were stamped on the belly "Patented Sept 7, 1915." They also produced other characters from the Gruelle stories, such as Uncle Clem, Beloved Blindy, Johnny Mouse, Eddie Elephant, Percy Policeman, Cleety the Clown, Brown Bear, and Sunny Bunny. In 1934, Volland declared bankruptcy and the Exposition Doll and Toy Company assumed production of Raggedy Ann & Andy dolls.

Exposition Raggedies are almost as rare as the original family-crafted version. They are a bit more familiar in appearance, with painted eyes and facial features, and a more triangular nose. Exposition had the legal rights to produce Raggedy Ann & Andy dolls, however they voluntarily withdrew from their contract when the Gruelles became embroiled in a copyright suit. The legal battle was over production of an unauthorized Molly-'es version of Raggedy Ann & Andy.

Molly-'es Raggedies also have a perplexing history. By some accounts, mainly those of Mollye Goldman (owner of Molly-'es), Gruelle and Molly-'es entered into a friendly agreement. Johnny even paid for a holiday trip for the Goldmans. However, something went wrong and he changed his mind about having them produce Raggedy Ann & Andy. Conflicting stories state that

16" Volland Raggedy Ann & Andy. Courtesy of McMaster's Doll Auction

within a year of Volland's filing for bankruptcy, Molly-'es Doll Outfitters began producing Raggedy Ann & Andy dolls without permission from the Gruelle family, which had retained the copyright to the dolls, regardless of the manufacturer. Despite being confronted with the improper use of the Raggedy Ann name and her failure to obtain Gruelle's permission, Mollye continued to manufacture the dolls. The court battle lasted for three years, and in 1938 the Supreme Court ruled in favor of the Gruelle family. A month later, Johnny Gruelle died of a heart attack.

The Raggedy Anns and Andys produced by Molly-'es between 1935 and 1938 are among the most desirable Raggedies. Although unconventional in their appearance, none can resist their charm. Ranging in size from 17 to 22 inches, Molly-'es Raggedies were the first to have a heart printed on the chest. The bodies are more structured, allowing them to sit, and the legs are usually a multicolored striped material. They have dark, auburn yarn hair, and the facial features are painted with large black eyes and a triangular nose, outlined in black. In addition to Raggedy Ann & Andy, Molly-'es also made a 14" Baby Ann and Andy. Molly-'es were usually stamped on the chest "Raggedy Ann & Andy Dolls Manufactured by Molly-'es Doll Outfitters."

After winning the lawsuit, the Gruelle family entered into an agreement with the Georgene Novelties Company. Georgene continued to produce Raggedy Ann & Andy for the next twenty-five years. The earliest and most desirable Georgenes have black-outlined noses. Georgenes ranged in size 15 to 50 inches. The floppy cloth bodies were stitched at the knees and elbows, allowing them to bend. Although they usually have red and white striped legs, a few original Georgenes were made with legs of different materials. The yarn used for the hair changed color several times, from an almost strawberry blond to a deep orange, and all shades in between. Tin or plastic button eyes were added. The mouth was more defined. Most dolls have a curved- or wavy-line as opposed to a straight-line smile. Georgene also marketed a Beloved Belindy and an Awake/Asleep Raggedy Ann, with one side of the head sleeping and the other side awake. Georgene Raggedies have various cloth labels sewn into the side seam of the doll. Although wordy, all include "Johnny Gruelle's Own Raggedy Ann & Andy Dolls/and Georgene Novelties, Inc. New York City/Exclusive Licensed Manufacturer/Made in U.S.A."

The Knickerbocker Toy Company made a bid to the Gruelle family for the rights to Raggedy Ann & Andy in late 1962. When the contract with Georgene expired, Knickerbocker was awarded the license to manufacture Raggedies and use the Raggedy Ann & Andy names. Although most readily found in 12", 24", and 36" sizes, Knickerbocker Toy Company offered Raggedy Ann & Andy in an impressive range of sizes from a tiny three inches to a towering seventy-eight inches. Body construction remained the same, but all known Raggedies made by the Knickerbocker Toy Company have red and white striped legs and a heart imprinted on the chest. The yarn hair is redder, the eyes are black plastic disks, and the mouth is a straight-line smile. Knickerbocker Toy Company also produced Beloved Belindy, Camel with the Wrinkled Knees, and Raggedy Arthur. A vast assortment of Raggedy items was introduced, including: sleeping bags, marionettes, huggers, dress-me-dolls, musical Raggedies, tote bags, and "Flexies," (bendable Ann and Andy). Knickerbocker Toy Company tagged the clothing with at least six different versions in the twenty years manufacturing Raggedies. Although wordy, all include "Knickerbocker Toy Co./Raggedy Ann" or "Raggedy Andy"/country of origin.

In 1982, Warner Communications sold the Knickerbocker Toy Company, and with it the license for Raggedy Ann, to Has-

36" early Georgene Raggedy Ann & Andy, Ann with black-outlined nose and Andy without. Courtesy of Rusty Herlocher

bro Industries. Today Hasbro-Playskool Raggedies are either twelve or eighteen inches tall. The faces are silk screened and carry the Playskool label.

In 1993, Applause released a Raggedy Ann, Andy, and Baby Ann, copying the unauthorized Molly-'es as well as the more traditional Raggedy Ann & Andy with embroidered, stitched features. All the high quality Applause dolls range from seven to thirty-six inches and are tagged.

Johnny Gruelle's efforts to pay tribute to Marcella were well rewarded. Raggedy Ann walked into our hearts, hand-in-hand with her faithful Andy, and remains there still.

Reproduction Raggedy Ann & Andy dolls can be a problem. There is a very convincing reproduction Georgene presently circulating. Georgenes are tagged with a cloth label on the side seam. The reproductions are also made with what appears to be a well-worn tag on the side. Georgene's tags were white, whereas the copies have peach-colored tags of the same material from which the body is made. Carefully check the back of the head; reproduction dolls have a coarse, loosely-woven, red material covering beneath the yarn hair.

Another false representation uses an authentic Georgene, and outlines the nose with black fabric marker. The black outlining of the nose should show the same amount of wear and fading as the remaining face color. If the outline is darker than the other black details on the face, be suspicious. The worn, vintage look of the face is hard to copy. In addition to a good visual examination, smell the doll. Nothing can quite duplicate the scent acquired by a rag doll that has been around for sixty years. Several craft-type dolls boast of an "attic" smell, but these are only perfumed and don't have that true "I've been around a long time" smell. Inspect the seams. Recently-made dolls have strong seams that lack an aged look.

A large gathering of Knickerbocker and Georgene Raggedy Anns and Andys. Courtesy of Rusty Herlocher.

Finally, be aware of the potential problems with the hand-crafted Raggedy Ann & Andy dolls made from the McCall's pattern. To buy and/or sell the dolls is an infringement of the Gruelle copyright and therefore unlawful. McCalls has the right to print and sell the pattern for home use.

Prices listed are for originally dressed dolls in very good condition. Early Raggedies are forgiven for showing slight wear. If badly faded, stained, torn, or damaged, expect the value to be about half the amounts listed. It is perfectly acceptable to show normal signs of aging, such as a properly repaired seam or settled stuffing. Parenthetically, an early Raggedy in excellent condition is so very rare that it would easily be valued at two or three times the amounts listed.

First Gruelle Family Hand-Crafted Raggedy Ann: 1918; body with loosely-jointed limbs; stuffed with white cotton; long face with hand-painted features; brown yarn hair; candy heart in body (often sucked on by a child, so look for stains on the chest); homespun calico dress and white apron; typically marked with rubber-stamped date on tummy or back or unmarked; very rare.

Volland Raggedy Ann or Andy: 1920–1934; all cloth; movable arms and legs; brown yarn hair; painted features; button eyes; typically marked "Patented Sept. 7, 1915."

Exposition Doll and Toy Company: 1935; brown yarn hair; painted features; these extremely rare dolls were produced for only a few months; about one dozen dolls are known to be in collections.

Raggedy Ann & Andy Value Comparisons

Company Name	Size	Plain Nose Value	Black-Outlined Nose Value
Gruelle Family	16"; Ann only	8,500.00	8,500.00
Volland	16"; Ann or Andy	3,400.00	4,600.00
	14"; Beloved Belindy		3,800.00
	14"–18"; Character	3,000.00	
Exposition Doll		9,000.00	9,000.00
Molly-'es	17"–22"; Ann or Andy		2,500.00
	14"; Baby		3,500.00
Georgene	13"; Ann; Awake/Asleep	1,000.00	1,600.00
	14"–18"; Beloved Belindy		2,600.00
While Georgene manufactured Raggedys, the company rights were renewed in Johnny Gruelle's name, except in 1946. Tagged in part "...1946 by Myrtle Gruelle Silsby..." This tag adds an additional $200.00 to any doll.	15"; Ann or Andy	600.00	1,800.00
	19"; Ann or Andy	500.00	2,400.00
	24"; Ann or Andy	700.00	2,900.00
	31"; Ann or Andy	1,300.00	3,600.00
	36"; Ann or Andy	1,400.00	
	45"; Ann or Andy	1,600.00	
	50"; Ann or Andy	2,000.00	4,900.00
Knickerbocker Toy Co.	3"; Ann or Andy Huggers	200.00	
	6"; Ann or Andy	75.00	
	12"; Ann or Andy	150.00	
	15"; Ann or Andy	200.00	
	19"; Ann or Andy	275.00	
	24"; Ann or Andy	400.00	
	30"; Ann or Andy	700.00	
	36"; Ann or Andy	1,000.00	
	40"; Ann or Andy	1,400.00	
	45"; Ann or Andy	1,700.00	
	78"; Ann or Andy	2,500.00	
	15"; Beloved Belindy	1,500.00	1,500.00
Camel with Wrinkled Knees		500.00	
Raggedy Arthur		400.00	400.00
Applause	15"; Ann or Andy	65.00	

Molly-'es Raggedy Ann or Andy: 1935–1938; all cloth; often patterned materials; auburn yarn hair; printed features; black-outlined nose; heart on chest; typically marked "Raggedy Ann & Andy Dolls Manufactured by Molly-'es Doll Outfitters" or unmarked.

Georgene: 1938–1962; all cloth; stitched elbow and knee seams; printed heart on chest; silk-screen or printed features; button eyes; orangish-red yarn hair; Ann has a top-knot (few longer strands on top) to which a ribbon can be tied; typically marked with cloth label sewn into side "Johnny Gruelle's Own Raggedy Ann & Andy Dolls.../Georgene Manufacturers/Made in U.S.A."

Knickerbocker Toy Company Raggedy Ann or Andy: 1963–1982; silk-screen printed face; red shades of yarn hair; typically marked with cloth label "Raggedy Ann or Andy.../Knickerbocker Toy Co."/country of origin.

Hasbro/Playskool: currently available.

Applause: 1993; embroidered-type face play doll.

Other Raggedy Dolls

Prices listed are for original dolls in perfect, near-mint condition with boxes

Porcelain Limited Edition: 1983; 19"; by Ideal **$350.00**
Wendy Lawton's Marcella: 1987; 17"; by Wendy Lawton, porcelain Marcella holding a small Raggedy Ann..............**$750.00**
Anniversary Doll: 1992; 19"; by Applause
Ann **$250.00**
Andy 200.00

14" Molly-'es Raggedy Ann Baby. Courtesy of Rusty Herlocher

Molly-E Baby Ann: 1993; 13"; by Applause.............. $250.00
Mop Top Wendy and Billy: 1993; by Alexander Doll Co
....**$250.00 set**

Stamp Ann Doll: 1997; 17"; Copy of the commemorative stamp from the US Post Office..**$200.00**

Raleigh Dolls

*I*n 1916, Artist Jessie McCutcheon Raleigh founded the Raleigh doll company in Chicago, Illinois, shortly after the introduction of her critically acclaimed statuette "Good Fairy." Jessie wanted to produce a doll of superior quality; one that she believed would reflect her impeccable sense of art and the need for perfection. Producing such a doll proved more challenging than Jessie first anticipated. Unhappy with the products that were available, she enlisted the services of several large universities' research departments. Their assignment was to formulate a perfect composition for her dolls. Although a formidable task, Dr. W. P. Dun Lany, after extensive research, developed a material that met the high standard set forth by Mrs. Raleigh.

Talented sculptors, such as Emory Seidel, were commissioned to design realistic children, carefully following Raleigh's specifications. Extremely successful in her endeavors, the company produced aesthetically delightful Art Dolls.

The joints of the lightweight body were connected by metal springs attached to hardwood plugs imbedded into the composition. Often one arm was bent and the fingers curved so that the doll could hold an object. Students from the Chicago Art Institute often decorated the lovely hand-painted faces.

Raleigh dolls are unmarked. There are thousands of unmarked composition dolls, and only a few of these would be Raleigh's. However, a careful examination should allow easy

12" composition Raleigh baby with wig, holding a Steiff Leopard. Courtesy of McMaster's Doll Auction

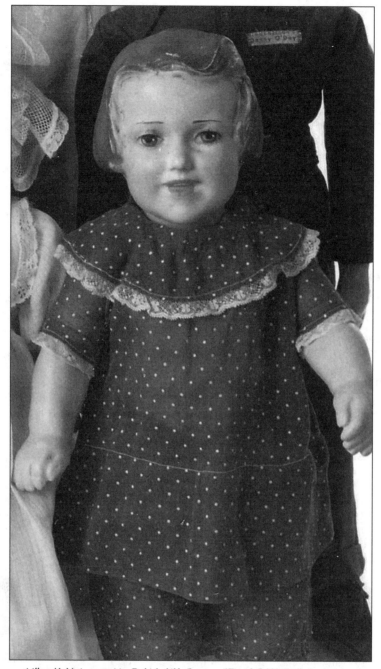

14" molded hair composition Raleigh child. Courtesy of David Cobb's Doll Auctions

identification. Simply remember to look for very lightweight, high quality composition, beautifully hand painted, unique plug and spring construction and realistic modelling.

A 1919 *Toys and Novelties* article aptly sums-up Raleigh Dolls by reporting "…The new dolls brought out by Jessie McCutcheon Raleigh this Christmas season…represent beauty in design, perfection of finish and daintiness in dress."

Prices listed are for appropriately costumed dolls in good condition. Very slight crazing is acceptable and does not greatly affect the price. If badly crazed, cracked, or repainted, expect the value to be less than half the amounts listed.

Raleigh Art Doll: all composition or composition head and limbs; cloth body; spring wire joints; molded and painted hair or good wig; nicely painted or sleep eyes; open/closed mouth may have molded and painted teeth; appropriately dressed; unmarked.

Raleigh Art Doll Value Comparison		
Size	**All Composition**	**Composition with Cloth Body**
10 1/2"	650.00	
11 1/2"	750.00	
12 1/2"	800.00	550.00
13 1/2"	900.00	
18"	1,300.00	
22"		600.00

Ravca Dolls

Wonderful group of 10" tagged Historical Ravca dolls. Courtesy of David Cobb's Doll Auctions

Ravca Dolls are known as the Real People Dolls. They are the artistic creations of Bernard Ravca, originally of Paris, France, and later the United States. After Ravca won first prize at the Paris Fair with his two life-sized figures of a Normandy peasant and his wife, the French government sent him to the United States. Fate intervened when, in 1939, Ravca arrived to exhibit his famous dolls in the French Pavilion at the New York World's Fair. The winds of war were gathering momentum in Europe, and while Ravca was representing his country in the United States, France fell under the heel of Nazi oppression, leaving Ravca an exile. He spent the next several years raising money for the Free French War Relief, and doing what he could for orphans of the resistance movement. Tragically, during Hitler's occupation of France, Ravca's entire family was lost, his studio pillaged, and his bank accounts seized. Bernard Ravca began life anew, and he became a United States citizen in 1947.

The sadness and loss that was so much a part of his life can be seen reflected in his work. The peasant with gnarled hands, stooped from a life of toil; aloof expressions on persons of royalty, far removed from ordinary life; corrupt political figures ridden with greed and ruthlessness—all are preserved in Ravca's lifelike soft sculptures. All facets of human nature are conveyed—some unpleasant emotions to be sure, but also joy and happiness. Ravca Dolls are far from dark and sinister; they show tremendous emotion and sensitivity. In the course of viewing and studying many Ravca Dolls while researching this book, it became evident that at least a few of the dolls credited to Bernard Ravca may, in fact, be the creations of his wife, Frances Elinor Ravca. While Ravca Dolls normally portray a realistic view of life, several dolls seem to have a more idealized view of how we wish life could be.

Ravca doll faces are made of silk stockinette stretched over sculpted cotton, with painted facial features. Cloth-covered wire armatures form the bodies. Occasionally, a composition of breadcrumbs and glue was used for heads, hands, or bodies. Dolls were marked with hang tags signed "Bernard Ravca," and/or with labels sewn into their perfectly accurate costumes.

While reproductions are not a problem, contemporary doll makers influenced by Ravca's creations have imitated his style with varying degrees of success. Since tags are often missing, it may be difficult to distinguish an original Ravca Doll from a copy. There is no positive way to identify an unmarked Ravca. Seek out, examine, and study as many authentic Ravca Dolls as possible to become familiar with his exquisitely detailed dolls.

Ravca Dolls are especially vulnerable to nose and chin rubs, which result in snags. Prices listed are for dolls in good condition. If damaged, repaired, or redressed, expect the value to be less than half the amounts listed.

Ravca Character: all cloth; silk stockinette drawn over face and arms; cloth-covered, straw-filled wire armature body; wool wig; beautifully painted facial features; original clothing; typically marked with hang tag "Original Ravca Fabrication Française," character name, and perhaps region; "Bernard Ravca" signature, printed clothing label, or unmarked.

Ravca Character Value Comparisons	
Size	Ravca Character
10"	400.00
15"	450.00
20"	600.00
30"	900.00
42"	3,500.00

Raynal

Eduard Raynal founded Les Poupées Raynal in Paris, France in 1922. Poupées Raynal may be found made of cloth, felt, and occasionally celluloid. The famed Rhone-Poulenc factory manufactured the specially-commissioned celluloid, Rhodoid, used by Raynal.

The Poupées Raynal appearance somewhat resembles a Lenci, but with a more sophisticated arrogance and less child-like qualities. Celluloid or

20" all original "Rhodoid" baby by Raynal Courtesy of David Cobb's Doll Auctions

squared-off felt mitt hands and long thin brows, painted wide on the forehead, characterize the doll. Look to the soles of the shoes for markings and "Les Poupées Raynal/Marque Déposé/Made in France" labels sewn into the clothing. Many dolls also wear a brass pendant inscribed "Les Poupées Raynal."

Prices listed are for dolls in original costume with good color and little or no fading. Slight signs of aging, such as a settled body, do not greatly affect the price. If a doll is stained, torn, mended, or faded, expect the value to be less than one half to one third the amounts listed.

Les Poupées Raynal: all cloth; felt or celluloid head; cloth body; slightly bent arms; mitt-type or celluloid hands; mohair or silk wig; painted, side-glancing eyes; upper lashes only; wide-spaced eyebrows; closed mouth with two-tone lips and white highlights on lower lip; original costume; typically marked "Raynal," letters may be placed so as to form a doll.

Les Poupées Raynal Value Comparison		
Size	All Cloth	Celluloid Head on Cloth Body
14"	600.00	
18"	900.00	750.00

Theodor Recknagel

34" Theodor Recknagel bisque Dolly-Face child. Courtesy of David Cobb's Doll Auctions

Production of dolls by Theodor Recknagel, located in Alexandrienthal, near Oeslau, Thüringia, Germany, began about 1893. While Recknagel's porcelain factory was founded in 1886, there is no evidence of doll production before 1893, when he registered two mulatto doll heads, which were tinted rather than painted.

Recknagel Dolls can be of the finest quality with extremely artistic application of decoration, or very coarse bisque with the facial features rather haphazardly applied.

Mold numbers registered by Recknagel include: R1, 21, 22, 23, 24, 25, 26, 27, 28, 29, 30, 31, 32, 33, 34, 35, 37, 39, 41, 43, 44, 45, 46, 47, 48, 49, 50, 53, 54, 55, 56, 57, 58, 86, 121, 126, 128, 129, 131, 132, 134, 135, 136, 137, 138, 226, 227, 1907, 1909, 1914, RIV, and R XII.

The four-digit mold numbers starting with a 19 do not appear to be a date. Often, in addition to, or occasionally in place of, a mold number, you may find "RA." Supposedly the initials of Recknagel/Alexandrienthal, they are sometimes reversed to "AR." "JK," "NG," or "NK" occasionally appear above the reversed "AR" marking. "NG" denotes a newborn with a flange neck, and NK denotes a newborn with a socket head.

Prices listed are for appropriately costumed dolls in good condition. Normal wear, slight damage, or well-made repairs to the body do not greatly affect the price. If the bisque is damaged or repaired, expect the value to be less than half the amounts listed. It is perfectly acceptable to show a missing or repaired finger or joint, or a mended body.

Also see Googly-Eyed, Oriental.

Dolly-Face: bisque socket head; jointed wood and composition body; good wig; glass eyes; open mouth; appropriately dressed; typically marked "1909 DEP R/A," "RA 1907," "1914," and possibly others.

Character Baby: bisque flange or socket head; cloth or composition bent-limb baby body; painted or glass eyes; open or closed mouth; appropriately dressed; typically marked "RA," "86," "121," "126," "127," "128," "129," "131," "132," "134," "135," "136," "137," "138," "1927," and possibly others.

Character Doll: bisque heads; varying characteristics, including molded bonnet, cap, and/or hair ornaments; painted eyes; closed or open/closed mouth; appropriately dressed; typically marked "AR," "RA," "22," "28," "43," "44," "55," and possibly others.

Max/Moritz: bisque character socket head; molded and painted hair and facial features; papier-mâché body; molded and painted hair and facial features; appropriately dressed; typically marked "31" or "32."

12" Theodor Recknagel bisque doll marked "R 5/0 A." Courtesy of David Cobb's Doll Auctions

Recknagel Bisque Doll Value Comparisons

Size	Dolly-Face, Socket Head, Composition Body, Better Quality	Dolly-Face, Socket Head, Composition Body, Standard Quality	Character Baby*	Character Dolls	Max/Moritz
8"			350.00	700.00	800.00
10"	350.00	200.00	375.00	900.00	1,000.00
12"	375.00	250.00	400.00	1,100.00	
14"	400.00	300.00	450.00	1,400.00	
16"	500.00	350.00	500.00	1,700.00	
18"	550.00	400.00	600.00	2,000.00	
20"	600.00	450.00	700.00		
24"	700.00	500.00			

* Add an additional $50.00–100.00 for Black version.

Reliable Toy Company Limited

A Canadian toy company founded in 1920, originally known as Canadian Statuary and Novelty Co., enjoyed a long and prosperous history manufacturing dolls.

Initially Reliable followed the example of other doll companies by assembling parts. Germany most often supplied the bisque heads, while the body parts were imported from the United States. Reliable began to produce original composition dolls in 1922. They were so successful that they outgrew their location, and in 1927 they moved to a larger factory. New and innovative methods of manufacturing helped Reliable become a worldwide distributor of composition dolls.

Perhaps best known for the typical Canadian style dolls, such as Indians and Mounties, Reliable also purchased doll molds from prominent U.S. doll manufacturers. They used these to produce a Canadian rendition of well-known dolls, with the stipulation that they would not import them to the United States.

As the popularity of plastic and vinyl grew, Reliable kept abreast of the changes and effortlessly converted to meet the demands.

There are three distinct classifications of Reliable Dolls: **The Common Novelty** includes Indian, Scottish Lad and Lassie, Topsy, Wettums, and Hiawatha; **The Better Quality Character** includes Royal Canadian Mounted Police, Baby Joan/Jean/Marilyn and Precious, Military Man, Sally Ann, and an Advertising Eskimo; **The Look-A-Likes** include Shirley Temple, Patsy, Barbara Ann Scott, Her Highness, and Snow White.

22" all original Reliable composition Shirley Temple. Courtesy of McMaster's Doll Auction

Prices listed are for original or appropriately costumed dolls in good condition. Slight crazing is acceptable and does not greatly affect the price. If badly crazed, cracked, peeling, or repainted, expect the value to be less than half the amounts listed.

Common Novelty: all composition or composition head and limbs; cloth body; molded and painted hair or inexpensive mohair wig; painted eyes; original costume; typically marked "Reliable," "Reliable/Made in/Canada," or unmarked; clothing tagged "Reliable."

Better Quality Character: all composition or composition head and limbs; cloth body; molded and painted hair or good wig; painted or sleep eyes; closed or open mouth with teeth; appropriately dressed; typically marked "Reliable," "Reliable/Made in/Canada."

Look-A-Like Dolls: all composition; jointed neck, shoulder, and hip; good wig; sleep eyes; open mouth with teeth; original or appropriate costume; typically marked "Reliable," may also show faint "Ideal."

Reliable Doll Value Comparison			
Size	Common Novelty	Better Quality Character	Look-A-Like
13"	200.00	325.00	
15"	265.00	450.00	700.00
17"		500.00	
22"			1,500.00

Grace Corry Rockwell

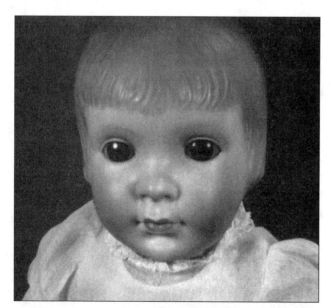

14" original composition Grace Corry Rockwell. Courtesy of Sotheby's Auctions

Located in New York City, Grace Corry Rockwell designed dolls for several manufacturers around 1920. Among her most popular dolls are Little Sister and Little Brother, designed for Averill Manufacturing. She also designed dolls for Century Doll Company, such as Fiji Wiji and a number of child dolls.

A bisque head character doll simply marked "Copr. by Grace C. Rockwell Germany" is no doubt her most famous and highly prized doll. It is assumed that Kestner produced the doll for Century Doll Company. The quality of bisque and nice application of decoration, coupled with the close association of Grace Corry Rockwell, Century Doll Company, and Kestner makes this a rather safe assumption.

Bisque

Prices listed are for appropriately costumed dolls in good condition. Normal wear, slight damage, or well-made repairs to the body do not greatly affect the price. If the bisque is damaged or repaired, expect the value to be less than half the amounts listed. It is perfectly acceptable to show a missing or repaired finger or joint, or a mended body.

Character Doll: bisque flange neck character head; cloth body; composition limbs; molded and painted hair or good wig; glass sleep eyes, painted upper and lower short lashes, very soft brows; closed mouth; appropriately dressed; typically marked "Copr. by/Grace C. Rockwell/Germany."

Composition

Prices listed are for appropriately costumed dolls in good condition. Slight crazing is acceptable and does not greatly affect the price. If badly crazed, cracked, peeling, or repainted, expect the value to be less than half the amounts listed.

Character Doll: composition flange neck, character head and arms; cloth body with crier box; composition or cloth legs; molded and painted hair and eyes; closed mouth; when dressed as a boy, "Little Brother"; and as a girl, "Little Sister"; and dressed as a nursery rhyme character, "Kiddie Karakter"; typically marked "©/By Grace Corry."

18" molded hair bisque character by Grace Corry Rockwell. Courtesy of Christie's East Auctions

Grace Corry Rockwell Value Comparison			
Size	Bisque Character	Composition Little Brother/ Sister*	Composition Kiddie Karakter*
14"	6,500.00	750.00	900.00
18"	7,500.00		
20"	8,500.00		

* The difference in the value of these dolls can only be interpreted by demand, appeal, and availability of the more rare Kiddie Karakter.

Mme. Rohmer

Marie Antoinette Leontine Rohmer of Paris, France operated her doll business from 1857 until 1880. She produced elegant Parisian fashion ladies, Poupée de Mode, of both china and bisque.

During the early years of production, Mme. Rohmer obtained several patents for improvements to doll bodies. The first, for articulated kid body joints, was followed by a patent for gutta percha or rubber doll arms. The final patent was for a new type of doll's head with a cord running through it into the body and out riveted holes in the front of the torso. This facilitated turning of the head in any direction and also secured the head to the body. Examples of bodies utilizing the first and last patents are occasionally found. Bodies with gutta percha arms are very rare. One explanation may be that they quickly deteriorated and were replaced with bisque. Almost fifty years after Mme. Rohmer registered her patent for articulated joints, Charles Fausel received a patent for a very similar universal joint in the United States.

The doll industry in the 19th century made great strides in manufacturing thanks to leaders such as Mme. Rohmer, who continually labored to improve the appearance and animation of her Poupée de Mode. At a time when men dominated the doll industry, Mme. Rohmer proved that women could also be quite successful.

Painted or glass eyed Rohmer Poupée de Modes are noted for their sensuous and somewhat dreamy expressions.

To positively identify a Rohmer, a careful examination of the body and head is essential. Look for a "Mme Rohmer/Brevete SGDG Paris" body stamp. The early dolls often had minute peppering of the porcelain. The neck socket of an authentic Rohmer doll had a kid-lined shoulder plate. Finally, Rohmer eye-

14" glass eye Rohmer Lady Poupée de Mode. Courtesy of David Cobb's Doll Auctions

lids were extremely well detailed. This detailing is often lost in a "mold-over" used for reproductions.

Prices listed are for appropriately costumed dolls in good condition. Normal wear, slight damage, or well-made repairs to the body do not greatly affect the price. If the bisque is damaged or repaired, expect the value to be less than half the amounts listed. It is perfectly acceptable to show a missing or repaired finger or joint, or a mended body.

Poupée de Mode: china or bisque swivel head; kid-lined shoulder plate; kid body may have eyelet holes at the abdomen and/or wooden joints at shoulder and knees; china or bisque arms; good wig; painted or glass eyes; rosy cheeks; closed mouth; appropriately dressed; typically stamped "Mme. Rohmer/Brevete SGDG Paris" on chest.

Rohmer Poupée de Mode Value Comparisons

Size	Painted-Eye Lady	Glass-Eye Lady
14"	5,700.00	6,200.00
16"	6,500.00	6,900.00
18"	7,500.00	8,200.00

Rollinson Dolls

Gertrude Rollinson of Holyoke, Massachusetts manufactured and sold dolls from 1916 until 1929. Mrs. Rollinson originally hand made cloth dolls with flat, painted faces for crippled children confined to hospitals. She continually experimented with sculpturing techniques until a satisfactory process was developed to produce three-dimensional features on a stockinette doll. So successful were her efforts that before long there was a great demand for her dolls. In 1916, Mrs. Rollinson commercialized her doll-making talents. A large-scale manufacturer was needed. Utley Company fulfilled that demand by producing thirty-five styles of Rollinson Dolls.

Rollinson Dolls can be found with three distinct hairstyles: short curls, long curls, or a short-straight Dutch-boy. Eyes were painted with highlighting detail; mouths were closed or open/closed with painted teeth; dolls were frequently given pierced nostrils. During production, each Rollinson Doll head received twenty coats of paint. After each coat, the head was dried in the sun and smoothed with sandpaper, resulting in a hard, durable, beautifully-polished, washable surface.

Look for a diamond-shaped stamp on the torso with "Rollinson Doll Holyoke Mass." around the border and a picture of a doll in the center.

Prices listed are for appropriately dressed dolls in good condition, slight wear and signs of aging such as a settled body do not greatly affect the price. If a doll is stained, torn, dented, cracked, peeling, or repainted, expect the value to be less than half the amounts listed.

Rollinson Child: all cloth; painted shoulder head and lower limbs; sateen-covered cloth body, stitched at shoulder, elbows, and knees; hands and feet stitched to show finger and toe details; painted hair or good wig; applied ears; painted eyes; closed mouth; appropriately dressed; typically stamped "Rollinson Doll Holyoke Mass" within a diamond on torso.

20" Rollinson child. Courtesy of McMaster's Doll Auction

Rollinson Child Doll Value Comparisons

Size	Cloth Child, Painted Hair	Cloth Child, Wigged
14"	1,200.00	1,400.00
16"	1,400.00	1,600.00
18"	1,600.00	1,800.00
20"	1,800.00	2,000.00
22"	2,000.00	2,200.00
24"	2,300.00	2,500.00
26"	2,500.00	2,800.00
28"	2,800.00	3,000.00

Sasha Dolls

Sasha Dolls were designed by Sasha Morgenthaler, an extremely gifted artist. Concentrating her efforts on making dolls, Sasha initially enjoyed a limited commercial success. Later, her dolls were mass-produced according to her artistic specifications and high standards. Gotz of Germany produced the first Sasha Dolls in 1964. Production problems occurred, prompting Ms. Morgenthaler to transfer the licensing rights to Trenton Toy, Ltd., Reddish, Stockport, England, which continued producing Sasha Dolls until the company went out of business in 1986.

All Sasha Dolls are similar in appearance, with wistful, serious expressions and a slightly darkened skin tone. The Gotz Dolls were marked "Sasha Serie" within a circle on the back of the head. Also, the upper eyelids of the Gotz dolls are painted with a curved eyelid, resulting in a somewhat unnatural appearance. Other Sasha Dolls are painted with a straighter eyelid line. All Sasha Dolls have a realistic body construction, allowing for a great range of movement. Later Sasha dolls are unmarked, save for a wrist tag.

A limited edition series of dolls was produced between 1981 and 1986. Because Trenton Toy, Ltd. went out of business in 1986, it is unlikely that the last doll of the series ever reached the planned production quantities.

There are no known reproduction Sasha Dolls. However, in 1995, Gotz once again released Sasha Dolls. The newly-introduced Sashas, although very similar in appearance to the earlier dolls, are easily recognized by their markings. The 1995 Sasha Dolls are marked with an incised circular logo between the shoulders, and the neck is incised "Gotz."

Prices listed are for dolls in near-mint, original condition. If damaged, redressed, or undressed, expect the value to be less than one half to one fourth the amounts listed.

Sasha Serie: 16"; similar in appearance to early Gotz; marked "Sasha Serie."

Trenton Toys, Ltd.: 16"; straight upper eyelid; marked with wrist tag only.

Bent-limb Baby: 12"; rigid plastic, jointed at neck, shoulder, and hip; cup-like hands; rooted hair; painted eyes; closed mouth; marked with wrist tag only.

20th Anniversary Sasha: 16"; black hair; copy of first Sasha doll; made by Trenton Toys, Ltd.; wearing blue corduroy dress.

Limited Edition Series: 16"; with certificate and wrist tag.

Velvet: girl; black hair; gray eyes; blue velvet dress; 1981, limited to 5,000.

Pintuck: girl; light hair; brown eyes; cotton dress with pin tucking; 1982, limited to 6,000.

16" early Trenton Toys Sasha dolls in original "crayon" tube box. Courtesy of McMaster's Doll Auction

Kiltie: girl; human hair; gray eyes; black watch tartan dress; amethyst necklace; 1983, limited to 4,000.

Harlequin: girl; long hair; straw hat; carrying wooden guitar; 1984, limited to 5,000.

Prince Gregor: boy; dark hair; tunic top; 1985, limited to 4,000.

Princess: girl; long, blond hair; blue eyes; pink dress; blue velvet cape; 1986, limited to 3,500.

Sasha Sari: 16"; wearing exquisitely-made sari from India; marked with wrist tag only.

Early Morgenthaler Original: 20"; original artist doll.

Sasha Dolls Limited Value Comparisons

Size	Black Baby	Sexed Baby, Before 1979	White Baby	White Child	Black Child	Marked "Sasha Series," Boy or Girl	20th Anniversary Sasha	1995 Sasha Doll
16"	300.00	400.00	250.00	300.00	350.00	2,200.00	400.00	300.00

Size	Early Original Sasha Doll	Velvet (1981)	Pintuck (1982)	Kiltie (1983)	Harlequin (1984)	Prince Gregor (1985)	Princess (1986)	Sasha Sari
16"		500.00	500.00	500.00	500.00	500.00	1,800.00	1,200.00
20"	9,000.00+							

Peter Scherf

20" Peter Scherf dolly-face child. Courtesy of David Cobb's Doll Auctions

24" Peter Scherf with beautiful bisque hands. Courtesy of David Cobb's Doll Auctions

listed. It is perfectly acceptable to show a missing or repaired finger or joint, or a mended body.

Dolly-Face: bisque shoulder head; kid body; riveted joints; nicely-molded bisque lower arms; good wig; glass, sleep eyes; open mouth; appropriately dressed; typically marked "P.Sch Germany."

| Peter Scherf Value Comparisons ||
Size	Dolly-Face Child
10"	250.00
12"	300.00
14"	350.00
16"	425.00
18"	475.00
20"	550.00
22"	650.00
24"	750.00
26"	800.00
28"	850.00
30"	1,000.00

This doll factory was founded in 1879 by Peter Scherf and located in Sonneberg, Germany, the famous "Town of Toys." Following Scherf's death in 1887, the business was divided among various family members. Bisque dolls continued to be supplied to the American market bearing Peter Scherf marks, or the trade name "The Fairy Kid," well into the 1920s. Doll heads were produced at Armand Marseille's porcelain factory.

Prices listed are for appropriately costumed dolls in good condition. Normal wear, slight damage, or well-made repairs to the body do not greatly affect the price. If the bisque is damaged or repaired, expect the value to be less than half the amounts

Bruno Schmidt

*I*n 1900, Bruno Schmidt founded his bisque doll factory in Waltershausen, Germany. Prior to 1900, Schmidt was in partnership with Hugo Geisler. When Geisler left the business, Schmidt changed the name to Bruno Schmidt. Schmidt's doll company manufactured and distributed some of the most desirable character dolls. Two of the best-known characters are Tommy Tucker (mold 2048) and his companion Wendy (mold 2033), which is decidedly more rare. Records indicate that Bruno Schmidt's character bisque heads were purchased exclusively from Bähr & Pröschild.

Bruno Schmidt eventually purchased the Bähr & Pröschild company. The heads produced by Bähr & Pröschild often bear both firms' trademarks, namely the heart and crossed swords, as well as two sets of mold numbers. The three-digit numbers were Bähr & Pröschild's; the four-digit mold numbers beginning with a "2" belonged to Bruno Schmidt. Mold numbers used by Bruno Schmidt include 2020, 2023, 2025, 2033, 2048, 2068, 2070, 2072, 2074, 2075, 2081, 2084, 2085, 2092, 2094, 2095, 2096, 2097, 2099, and 2154

Reproduction Bruno Schmidt doll molds are available. The majority of reproduction dolls are made by modern doll artists as legitimate copies. Most are proud of their work, and therefore, sign and date their creations. A careful examination of all markings is the first step in authenticating a bisque doll. It is also important to inspect the body, wig, and eyes, age and condition. Vintage Bruno Schmidt bisque dolls were of good quality, but did not have a silky, satin-smooth, creamy bisque, nor was the decoration precisely executed; reproduction dolls commonly have an exact look.

Prices listed are for appropriately costumed dolls in good condition. Normal wear, slight damage, or well-made repairs to the body do not greatly affect the price. If the bisque is damaged or repaired, expect the value to be less than half the amounts listed. It is perfectly acceptable to show a missing or repaired finger or joint, or a mended body.

Also see All Bisque, Oriental.

Character Doll: bisque socket head; jointed composition body; molded and painted hair or good wig; painted or glass eyes; open, closed, or open/closed mouth; appropriately dressed; typically marked "BSW" within a heart, and a number "2020," "2023," "2025," "2033," "2048," "2068," "2070," "2072," "2074," "2075," "2081," "2084," "2085," "2092," "2094," "2095," "2096," "2097," or "2099"; may also include a three-digit number, beginning with "5," such as 524, 537, 538, or 539.

Dolly-Face: bisque socket head; jointed composition body; good wig; glass eyes; open mouth; appropriately dressed; typically marked "B.S.W." within a heart, and/or "2154."

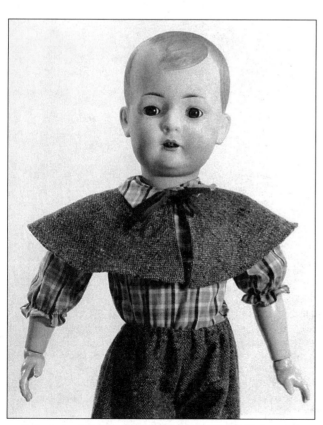

28" open mouth Bruno Schmidt character, #2048 Tommy Tucker. Courtesy of David Cobb's Doll Auctions

13" closed mouth Bruno Schmidt character, #2033 Wendy. Courtesy of David Cobb's Doll Auctions

Bruno Schmidt Character Dolls Value Comparisons

Size	2023, 2025, 2026 CM Glass Eyes	2023, 2025, 2026 CM, Painted Eyes	2033 CM, Glass Eyes	2048 CM, Glass Eyes	2048, 2094, 2096 OM, Glass Eyes	2072 CM, Glass Eyes	2072 OM, Glass Eyes	2092, 2097, 2099 OM, Glass Eyes
12"			17,000.00					
13"				2,200.00	1,500.00			
15"		4,400.00	26,000.00	3,200.00	2,000.00	4,400.00		850.00
18"	6,000.00	4,700.00			2,100.00	5,000.00	2,000.00	1,100.00
20"			35,000.00	4,100.00	2,200.00			
22"	8,000.00	5,400.00				5,700.00	2,500.00	1,500.00
24"			40,000.00	4,800.00	2,800.00			1,700.00

Add an additional $700.00 for jointed toddler body. Add an additional $200.00 for flirty eyes.

CM = Closed Mouth

OM = Open Mouth

Bruno Schmidt Child Doll Value Comparisons

Size	Dolly-Face
16"	700.00
18"	800.00
20"	1,000.00
22"	1,100.00
24"	1,400.00

Bruno Schmidt Child Doll Value Comparisons

Size	Dolly-Face
26"	1,500.00
28"	1,800.00
30"	2,400.00
32"	2,900.00

Add an additional $200.00 for flirty eyes.

Franz Schmidt

28" Franz Schmidt open mouth character baby, #1295 with original box. Courtesy of David Cobb's Doll Auctions

This bisque doll company was founded by Franz Schmidt in 1890 in Georgenthal, Thüringia, Germany. Franz Schmidt dolls are well known for their charming modelling and consistently excellent quality. The company also provided many innovations to the doll industry, including improved wooden body joints (1899); pierced nostrils (1912); movable tongue (1913); universal joints (1914); eye bar (1928); and doll voices (1928).

The Simon & Halbig porcelain factory supplied the bisque heads according to designs and specifications set forth by Schmidt. Two of their most famous sculptors were Traugott Schmidt and Albin Scheler.

Often, a small "z" is included in the marking of a Franz Schmidt Doll. It is assumed that this is an abbreviation for zentimeter—German for centimeter. Schmidt also appeared to have marked earlier bisque heads "S & Co." and later heads "FS & C."

Prices listed are for appropriately costumed dolls in good condition. Normal wear, slight damage, or well-made repairs to the body do not greatly affect the price. If the bisque is damaged or repaired, expect the value to be less than half the amounts listed. It is perfectly acceptable to show a missing or repaired finger or joint, or a mended body.

Dolly-Face: bisque socket or shoulder head; kid or jointed composition body; good wig; glass eyes; open mouth; appropriately dressed; typically marked "269," "293," "1180," "1250," "1253," "1370," "S & Co. Simon & Halbig," "FS & C Simon & Halbig," and possibly others.

Character Baby: bisque socket head; composition bent-limb baby body; good wig or solid dome; glass eyes; open mouth; often with pierced nostrils; appropriately dressed; typically marked "FS & C," "1271," "1272," "1295," "1296," "1297," "1310," and possibly others.

Character Doll: bisque socket head; jointed composition body; molded and painted hair or good wig; glass or painted eyes; open, closed, or open/closed mouth; appropriately dressed; typically marked "1262," "1263," "1266," "1267," "1286," and possibly others.

				Franz Schmidt Value Comparisons				
Size	Dolly-Face Kid Body	Dolly-Face Composition Body	Character Baby*	1262 O/CM, Painted Eyes	1263 CM, Painted Eyes	1266 O/CM, Painted Eyes	1267, 1270 CM, Painted Eyes	1286 OM, Smiling, Glass Eyes
12"	300.00	550.00	800.00					
14"	350.00	650.00	850.00					
15"						4,000.00		
16"	450.00	750.00	900.00	7,000.00	19,000.00	4,400.00		4,500.00
18"	500.00	800.00	1,000.00					
20"	550.00	850.00	1,200.00	15,000.00	24,000.00	5,300.00		5,200.00
22"	650.00	950.00	1,400.00				3,400.00	
24"	800.00	1,100.00	1,700.00	23,000.00	32,000.00			
26"	900.00	1,200.00	1,900.00				4,200.00	
28"		1,300.00	2,500.00					
30"		1,600.00						
36"		2,800.00						
42"		4,200.00						

*Add an additional $700.00 for jointed toddler or key-wound walker body, or add $400.00–600.00 for black version.

OM = Open Mouth

CM = Closed Mouth

O/C = Open/Closed Mouth

Schmitt et Fils

Schmitt et Fils, which translates to Schmitt and Sons, was located at Nogent-sur-Marne, Seine, and Paris, France. Maurice and Charles Schmitt manufactured bébés from 1863 to 1891.

Schmitt et Fils Bébés usually have pressed, rather than poured, bisque. The facial modelling consists of either a full, round face or a long-cheeked, oval shape. Lamb's wool wigs are not uncommon. Almond-shaped paperweight eyes possess great depth and richness of color. The eyeliner is black and thick, and the lashes are not necessarily long. Delicately shadowed eyelids match the soft cheek color as well as the blushed pierced ears. The mouth is closed, with a slender space between the lips and carefully painted outlines and shading. The enchanting facial modelling helps explain why Schmitt et Fils Bébés are numbered among the finest.

Avoid reproduction Schmitt et Fils Bébés by inspecting the markings, construction, and stamp, which may be found on the hip. The inside of the head should provide evidence of being pressed. The ears should show a light blush, a detail often overlooked on copies.

20" long face Schmitt et Fils Bébé, marked within a shield "SCH 9." Courtesy of David Cobb's Doll Auctions

Prices listed are for appropriately costumed dolls in good condition. Normal wear, slight damage, or well-made repairs to the body do not greatly affect the price. If the bisque is damaged or repaired, expect the value to be less than half the amounts listed. It is perfectly acceptable to show a missing or repaired finger or joint, or a mended body.

Bébé: bisque socket head; jointed wood-and-composition body; straight wrists; long, flat-bottom feet; good wig; oval-cut paperweight eyes, finely lined in black; blush eye shadow; thick, short lashes; feathered brows; pierced, lightly-blushed ears; closed mouth with slight space between lips; appropriately dressed; typically marked "SCH" and crossed hammers within a shield. **Note:** *Bébés may also be found with the neck ending in a dome shape that fits up into the neck socket, eliminating the line at the base of the neck. This arrangement is referred to as a "cup and saucer" neck.*

Schmitt et Fils Bébé Value Comparisons		
Size	Long-Face Bébé	Round-Face Bébé
12"	18,000.00	15,000.00
14"	20,000.00	
16"	24,000.00	20,000.00
18"	26,000.00	
20"	28,000.00	
22"	30,000.00	26,000.00
26"	32,000.00	

Add an additional $3,000.00 for a "cup and saucer" neck.

Schoenau & Hoffmeister

The Schoenau & Hoffmeister porcelain factory was located in Burggrub, Upper Franconia, Germany. Founded in 1901 by Arthur Schoenau and Carl Hoffmeister of Sonneberg, the factory produced bisque doll heads until 1953. By 1907, several disagreements erupted between the partners, the worst concerning the merits of socket versus shoulder heads. Although it seems a trivial thing, Carl Hoffmeister insisted upon producing bisque doll heads in the shoulder-head style, while Arthur Schoenau was equally determined to produce socket-head types. Unable to resolve their differences, the partnership was dissolved; Carl Hoffmeister left the firm and Arthur Schoenau became sole owner.

In 1909, a new partner, Magnus Leube, joined the firm. When Schoenau died in 1911, his son, Hans, took over as director of the company. Eventually, the directorship passed to Arthur's widow, Caroline, and to Curt Schoenau. Curt supplied Cäsar Schneider, their sculptor, with a photo of Princess Elizabeth. This was used as a model for the famous Princess Elizabeth Doll.

The Princess Elizabeth Doll is only one of the many dolls produced by Schoenau & Hoffmeister. The enviable record of designs included dolly-faces, ethnic characters, and fine portrait dolls. Trademarks included: "DALABA," an acronym for Das Lachende Baby (the laughing baby); "Hanna MB"; "My Cherub"; "Princess Elizabeth"; "Burggrub Baby"; "Bébé Carmencita"; "Künstlerkopf"; and "Viola." Registered mold numbers were: 169, 900, 914, 1400, 1800, 1904, 1906, 1930, 2500, 4000, 4001, 4500, 4600, 4700, 4900, 5000, 5300, 5500, 5700, and 5800 in conjunction with initials "SHPB" and a five-pointed star. After 1930, heads were incised with "Porzellanfabrik Burggrub" and perhaps "Special," "NKB," and "WSB."

Prices listed are for appropriately costumed dolls in good condition. Normal wear, slight damage, or well-made repairs to the body do not greatly affect the price. If the bisque is damaged or repaired, expect the value to be less than half the amounts listed. It is perfectly acceptable to show a missing or repaired finger or joint, or a mended body.

Also see Oriental, Hamburger.

Character Baby: bisque socket head; composition bent-limb baby body; good wig; glass eyes; open mouth; appropriately dressed; typically marked "S ★" with "P.B.H," "Porzellanfabrik Burggrub," "900," "169," "769," "Special," and "Burggrub Baby."

23" Schoenau & Hoffmeister Princess Elizabeth character toddler. Courtesy of David Cobb's Doll Auctions

Solid Dome Infant: bisque flange neck; cloth body; painted hair; small, glass, sleep eyes; closed mouth; appropriately dressed; typically marked "N.K.B.," may also have stamp in German. *Note: There are conflicting opinions on whether N.K.B. denotes flange neck or a factory location.*

Hanna Character Baby: bisque socket head; composition bent-limb baby body; good wig; large, somewhat-rounded glass eyes; no painted upper lashes; winged, feathered brows; open, slightly-smiling mouth; appropriately dressed; typically marked "S (star with PB) H/Hanna."

Das Lachende Baby (The Laughing Baby): bisque, full-faced socket head; composition bent-limb body; good wig; glass eyes; open, smiling mouth with two upper teeth (modelling resembles a happy baby, rather than a laughing one); appropriately dressed; typically marked "Porzellanfabrik/Burggrub/Das Lachende Baby/1930/Made in Germany/D.R.G.M."

Princess Elizabeth: bisque socket head; jointed composition body; blond mohair wig; oval, blue, sleep, slightly-squinting eyes; rosy cheeks; open, smiling mouth; very pretty expression; appropriately dressed; typically marked "Porzellanfabrik/Burggrub/Princess Elizabeth/Made in Germany."

Character Doll: bisque socket head; jointed composition body; good wig; deeply-cut, rounded eyes; winged brows; open mouth; wistful expression; typically marked "S (pb) within a star," "H," and "OX."

Dolly-Face: bisque shoulder or socket head; jointed composition or kid body; good wig; glass eyes; open mouth; appropriately dressed; typically marked "SH," a five-pointed star, "PB," "1400," "1800," "1904," "1906," "2500," "4500," "4700," "5300," "5700," or "5800."

"Künstlerkopf" (Art Doll Head): bisque, slender-face child doll; glass eyes; open mouth; appropriately dressed; typically marked "Künstlerkopf," and/or "4000," "4600," "5000," or "5500."

Schoenau & Hoffmeister Value Comparisons

Size	Character Baby	Solid Dome Infant	Hanna Character*	Das Lachlende Baby	Princess Elizabeth	Character H, OX Doll	Child Dolly-Face	Künstlerkopf (Art Doll) Child
10"		850.00						
12"	500.00	900.00				2,400.00		
14"	600.00	950.00	950.00	1,700.00	2,200.00		500.00	
16"	700.00		1,000.00	1,900.00	2,400.00		550.00	900.00
18"	800.00		1,200.00	2,100.00	2,500.00	3,200.00	600.00	
20"	850.00		1,400.00	2,500.00	2,700.00	3,600.00	700.00	
22"	900.00		1,600.00	2,800.00	2,900.00	4,000.00	800.00	
24"	1,000.00		1,700.00	3,000.00	3,200.00		900.00	1,400.00
26"	1,200.00		1,900.00				1,000.00	
28"	1,400.00						1,200.00	
30"	1,600.00						1,300.00	
32"							1,500.00	
34"							1,700.00	
36"							2,000.00	
38"							2,500.00	
40"							3,000.00	

*Add an additional $700.00 for jointed toddler body. Add an additional $300.00 for black version.

A. Schoenhut & Company

❧ ❦ ❧

Albert Schoenhut founded A. Schoenhut & Company in Philadelphia, Pennsylvania, in 1872, continuing a family tradition of toy makers. Grandfather Anton had carved wooden toys at his home in Württenberg, Germany. His son, Frederick, followed in his footsteps. Albert was destined to become a toy maker!

After venturing to the United States at the age of seventeen, Albert worked at different jobs, but by age twenty-two he established his own toy factory. Schoenhut's first toy was a piano.

The famous Humpty Dumpty Circus, introduced in 1903, probably included Schoenhut's first attempt at doll making. The ringmaster, lion tamer, lady circus rider, and gentleman and lady acrobats are identified solely by their characteristic painting and costuming. At about this same time, Schoenhut introduced the Chinaman, Hobo, Negro Dude, Farmer, Milkmaid, and Max and Mortiz. Rolly-Dollys were patented in 1908, as was Teddy Roosevelt and his "Teddy Adventures in Africa."

In 1909, Albert Schoenhut filed a patent application for his swivel, spring-jointed dolls, but the patent was not granted

Schoenhut piano, dolls, and props, including a 16" carved hair, intaglio eyes, incised #1911; 17" pouty boy and girl, both marked with "1933" and incised "1911"; 15" carved hair with ribbon; clowns and props on piano; 22" character girl with intaglio eyes, incised "1911"; 12" solid dome baby 1911 sticker; and a 22" Dolly-Face girl with open-closed mouth and painted teeth. Courtesy of David Cobb's Doll Auctions

until 1911. The metal joints had springs that compressed, rather than stretched when pulled. This added to the durability of the Schoenhut doll. In addition to the unique spring joints, the wooden dolls were painted entirely with oil colors. Their solid wood heads came with either mohair wigs or molded hair. Although collectors refer to this type of molded hair as carved hair, only the very crudest of features were carved, and then refined and finished by molding under pressure. The feet are of hardwood with two holes drilled into the soles to enable the doll to be placed on its stand and posed. One hole was drilled at an angle and one straight. The oblique hole allows the doll to hold its foot in the tip-toe position. The straight hole allows the doll to hold its foot resting flat.

Following his death in 1912, Albert Schoenhut was succeeded by his six sons—Harry, Gustav, Theodore, Albert Jr., William, and Otto. The new directors introduced an infant doll with curved limbs in 1913. It is identified by the © copyright symbol on its head.

The dolly-faced all-wooden dolls produced in 1915 had rounded eyes, advertised as "imitation glass," as opposed to intaglio eyes, and mohair wigs. The dolls came boxed in an accordion-type box with detailed instructions for posing. A round, tin doll stand with pins to accommodate the holes in the feet was

included. A series of 19" tall older boy dolls, called "Manikins," commonly dressed as athletes, was also introduced in 1915. Only 1,000 of the finely crafted male Manikins were produced. The bent-limb baby with split joints at the elbows and knees was also produced for the first time in 1915.

Walking dolls, jointed at the shoulder and hip only, were introduced in 1919. They were the first dolls without foot holes. In 1921, sleep eyes were added to the Schoenhut babies along with the dolly-faced dolls.

Cloth-bodied mama dolls, and a less expensive line of dolls with elastic joints, were marketed in 1924, but neither achieved the success of the earlier "All Wood Perfection Art Dolls."

In addition to producing finely crafted toys, A. Schoenhut & Company was a significant contributor to the beginning of the mass-marketed commercial doll industry in the United States. Although the majority of Schoenhuts are child dolls, none can argue the appeal of the character dolls, Nature Babies, or the desirable Manikins.

Schoenhut accessories, such as tin stands, name pins, and Schoenhut shoes, have been reproduced. The pins are printed "Made in U.S.A. Strong Durable and Unbreakable" around the outer edge, with a shield in the center that reads "Schoenhut All Wood Perfection Doll." The reproductions are quite "yellowed." In an attempt to make them appear old, the coloring has been overdone. The reproduction stands have a rather "pressed and rolled" look. Reproduction shoes are made using vintage doll shoes; authentic Schoenhut doll shoes often show slight corrosion around the rivet holes.

Prices listed are for originally costumed dolls in good to very good condition. Slight rubs and chips are becoming somewhat acceptable, as is very minimal paint touch-up. If repainted, badly chipped, or damaged, expect the value to be less than half the amount listed. Parenthetically, a doll in excellent condition would easily be double these amounts.

Character: all wooden, spring-jointed body; carved, molded (possibly with a ribbon or bow) hair or good wig; intaglio eyes; closed or open/closed mouth; appropriately dressed; typically marked with a paper label reading "Schoenhut Doll/Pat. Jan 17th 1911/U.S.A.," incised on back "Schoenhut Doll, Pat. Jan 17 '11 U.S.A./& Foreign Countries."

Bonnet Girl: molded and painted hair around face; cap molded to head; molded hair in back; intaglio, painted eyes; slightly open/closed mouth; cap with floral design; appropriately dressed; typically marked with paper label "Schoenhut Doll/Pat. Jan 17th 1911/U.S.A." on back.

Schnickel-Fritz: molded, wavy hair; squinting, painted eyes; toothy grin; appropriately dressed.

Tootsie Wootsie: lightly molded, short hair; small eyes; open/closed mouth; appropriately dressed.

Black Child: molded, curly hair; slightly side-glancing eyes; appropriately dressed.

Manikin: pensive expression, mature look; costumed in football, baseball, basketball, or circus outfit, complete with accessories.

Circus and Character Figures: small, comical, jointed characters; good modelling; painted features.

Early Humpty Dumpty Circus: complete with tent, animals, and figures **$3,800.00**

Later Humpty Dumpty Circus Parade: #18, complete with tent, animals and figures...**$2,500.00**

Schoenhut Baby: jointed toddler or bent-limb baby body; painted hair; painted eyes; open or closed mouth; appropriately dressed; typically marked "©," label reading "C" in center; H. E. Schoenhut 1913" printed on rim; "Schoenhut Doll/Pat. Jan 17th 1911/U.S.A." inscribed on shoulder; blue stamped "Patent applied for; Schoenhut Doll."

Schoenhut Humpty-Dumpty Circus, including: Chinese acrobats, lion tamer, clowns, Spark Plug, Barney Google, horse, donkey, elephant, dog, props, Maggie, and Jiggs. Courtesy of David Cobb's Doll Auctions

Dolly-Faced: all wooden, full spring-jointed body; good wig; painted rounded eyes; open/closed mouth with painted teeth; appropriately dressed; typically marked with "Schoenhut/Doll Pat. Jan 17 '11 U.S.A./& Foreign Countries" incised on back.

Walker Body: all wooden, jointed at shoulder and hip only; arms bent at elbows; no holes in feet; painted features; appropriately dressed; typically marked with label reading "C" in center; H. E. Schoenhut 1913" printed on rim; or "Schoenhut Doll/Pat. Jan 17 '11 U.S.A./& Foreign Countries."

Sleep-Eye Child: all wooden; good wig; sleep eyes; open mouth with teeth; appropriately dressed; typically marked "Schoenhut Doll/Pat. Jan 17th 1911/USA," "C" in center; "H. E. Schoenhut 1913" printed on rim.

Composition: all composition, jointed at neck, shoulder, and hip; molded and painted hair; painted eyes; small closed mouth;

appropriately dressed; typically marked with paper label reading "Schoenhut Toys/Made in U.S.A."

Mama Doll: hollow wooden head; cloth limbs; wooden hands; mohair wig; painted features; appropriately dressed; typically marked with Schoenhut stamp on head.

A. Schoenhut & Company Circus and Character Value Comparisons			
Lion Tamer, Rolly Polly, Clown	Farmer, Milk Maid	Ringmaster, Acrobat	Negro Dude, Maggie, Jiggs
450.00	500.00	550.00	700.00

A. Schoenhut & Company Early Character Value Comparisons							
Size	Character, Carved Hair and Intaglio Eyes	Character, Wig and Intaglio Eyes	Bonnet Bonnet Girl	Schnickel-Fritz	Tootsie Wootsie	Black Child	Manikins Men
14"	2,200.00	1,800.00	4,000.00				
16"	2,300.00	2,000.00		3,400.00	3,600.00	4,700.00	
19"	2,400.00	2,300.00	5,000.00				3,100.00
21"	2,500.00	2,500.00					

A. Schoenhut & Company Baby and Child Value Comparisons						
Size	Baby with Toddler Body	Baby With Bent-Limb Body	Dolly-Face	Walker	Sleep-Eye Child	All Composition	Mama Doll
11"	1,000.00	1,000.00		900.00			
13"						800.00	
14"	1,100.00		1,100.00	1,100.00	1,300.00		300.00
16"			1,300.00		1,400.00		350.00
17"	1,300.00	1,000.00		1,300.00			
19"		1,100.00	1,500.00		1,500.00		
21"			1,700.00		1,600.00		

Schützmeister & Quendt

23" Schützmeister & Quendt character baby #201, holding a Gebrüder Süssenguth "Peter Bear." Courtesy of David Cobb's Doll Auctions

Wilhelm Quendt and Philipp Schützmeister founded a porcelain factory in Boilstadt, Gotha, Germany, in 1889. In 1908, Quendt left and Schützmeister became sole owner. Following the company's acquisition by the Bing Concentra of Nürmberg in 1918, Schützmeister & Quendt limited its production to bisque doll heads for other members of the consortium, such as Welsch & Company and Kämmer & Reinhardt.

The firm's intertwined S & Q trademark can be found incised on heads, along with mold numbers 101, 102, 201, 204, 252, 300, 301, and 1376. Mold numbers 79, 80, and 81 were also registered in 1891, but there are no known or documented examples. According to the registration, they were dolly-face child dolls.

Prices listed are for appropriately costumed dolls in good condition. Normal wear, slight damage, or well-made repairs to the body do not greatly affect the price. If the bisque is damaged or repaired, expect the value to be less than half the amounts listed. It is perfectly acceptable to show a missing or repaired finger or joint, or a mended body.

Character Baby: bisque socket head; composition bent-limb baby body; good wig; glass eyes; open mouth; appropriately dressed; typically marked "S & Q" intertwined, "201," "204," "300," and "301."

Dolly-Face: bisque socket head; jointed composition body; good wig; glass eyes; open mouth; appropriately dressed; typically marked "S & Q" intertwined, "101," and "102."

Schützmeister & Quendt Value Comparisons

Size	Character Baby	Dolly-Face	Black Child
12"		500.00	
14"	750.00	650.00	
16"	850.00	750.00	
18"	950.00	800.00	
20"	1,000.00	900.00	
22"	1,200.00	1,000.00	2,600.00
24"		1,100.00	
26"		1,300.00	
30"		1,600.00	

* Add an additional $700.00 for jointed toddler body.

Sheppard & Co., Philadelphia Baby

The Philadelphia Baby, also known as the Sheppard Baby, is a life-size cloth doll. The dolls were sold at the J. B. Sheppard Linen Store on Chestnut Street in Philadelphia, hence the name. The designer, maker, and dates of origin are unknown. The doll is generally accepted as having been made around the turn-of-the-century. One creditable theory is that Elizabeth Washington, a student/artist at the Philadelphia School of Design, designed the Philadelphia Baby. Supposedly, J. B. Sheppard's Linen Store held a contest for the best-designed doll that could be used as a model for their baby clothes and also offered for sale. Elizabeth Washington's doll won the contest, and the Sheppard Store purchased the rights. There is no documentation to either validate or invalidate this story. We can, however, thank U.F.D.C. member Frances Walker for offering this explanation through her writings in the 1980s.

Philadelphia Babies range in size from 18 to 22 inches. The head, shoulders, forearms, and legs are painted in flesh-colored oil paints. The face is molded with large, deep eyes and well-modelled, heavy eyelids. The mouth is a "cupid's bow" with a deep indentation in the center of the lower lip. The chin is quite pronounced. The individually formed ears are applied. The entire face has a rather flattened appearance. The fingers curve slightly inwards, in mitten fashion with separate thumbs. The one-piece arms have no elbow seams. The legs are stitched at the knees, allowing flexibility. The toes are also stitched.

Prices listed are for appropriately dressed dolls in good condition. Slight wear and signs of aging or well-made repairs to the body do not greatly affect the price. If a doll is badly crazed, worn, stained, peeling, or repainted, expect the value to be less than half the amount listed.

Sheppard Baby: all cloth; oil-painted stockinette head and body, painted lower limbs; jointed at shoulder, hip, and knees; painted hair, brows, and eyes; molded eyelids; accented nostrils; applied ears; closed mouth with center lower lip indented; appropriately dressed; unmarked.

Character Baby: all cloth; oil-painted stockinette head and body, painted lower limbs; jointed at shoulder, hip, and knees; unique facial modelling; sculptured, broad, round face; soulful expression; flattened pug nose; painted hair, brows, and eyes; molded eyelids; accented nostrils; applied ears; open/closed mouth; impression of a protruding lower lip; appropriately dressed; unmarked.

21" Philadelphia Baby from Sheppard & Company. Courtesy of McMaster's Doll Auction

Sheppard Baby Value Comparisons		
Size	Sheppard Baby	Character Baby
18"	4,900.00	9,000.00
21"	5,200.00	9,500.00
22"	6,000.00	10,000.00

Simon & Halbig

he Simon & Halbig porcelain factory was located in Frafenhain and Hidburghausen, near Ohrdruf, Thüringia, Germany. Founded by Wilham Simon and Carl Halbig in 1839, it began producing dolls in the late 1860s or early 1870s.

Information about the early years of Simon & Halbig is quite elusive. The company's tinted and untinted bisque shoulder heads with molded hair and delicate decoration are typical of the prodigious number of fine-quality dolls they produced. Kid-bodied shoulder heads from the 1880s closely followed the French classic standard of large, often paperweight eyes, pierced ears, and heavy brows. A number of swivel heads on kid-lined shoulder plates were made entirely in the French manner.

Virtually any combination of features have been found with the Simon & Halbig mark, including solid dome, open pate or Belton-Type; molded and painted hair or wigged; painted, stationary, sleep paperweight or flirty eyes; open, closed, or open/closed mouths; and pierced or un-pierced ears. It was not unusual for a particular mold to have been produced with a variety of characteristics.

Simon & Halbig patented several new ideas, including eyes operated by a lever, movable eyelids, using threads for eyelashes, and neck socket glazing to reduce friction between the neck and the body socket.

Simon & Halbig not only produced a multitude of fine quality dolls from their own molds, but also produced dolls for several other manufacturers, such as C. M. Bergmann, Carl Berger, Cuno & Otto Dressel, Hamburger, Handwerck, Hulss, Kämmer & Reinhardt, Schmidt, and Wislizenus, and the French firms of Fleischmann & Bloedel, Jumeau, Roullet & Decamp, and S.F.B.J. While many of these manufacturers were supplied heads from several porcelain factories, Kämmer & Reinhardt depended entirely upon Simon & Halbig—a dependency that no doubt led to Kämmer & Reinhardt's acquisition of Simon & Halbig in 1920.

Most Simon & Halbig dolls are fully marked. The ampersand was added to the mark in 1905; hence, it is assumed that marks without the ampersand were produced before 1905.

Prices listed are for appropriately costumed dolls in good condition. Normal wear, slight damage, or well-made repairs to the body do not greatly affect the price. If the bisque is damaged or repaired, expect the value to be less than half the amounts listed. It is perfectly acceptable to show a missing or repaired finger or joint, or a mended body.

See Automata, Oriental.

Character Dolls

Due to the wide variety of Simon & Halbig character dolls, the following charts are arranged by mold numbers, with pricing of specific models corresponding to size.

Simon & Halbig child dolls 22" #719 and 17" flirty eyes, key-wind walker. Courtesy of David Cobb's Doll Auctions

15 1/2" Simon & Halbig open-closed smiling mouth character girl. Courtesy of David Cobb's Doll Auctions

Character Doll Value Comparisons

Mold #	Description	Size	Value
	Fashion doll; bisque socket head; bisque shoulder plate; kid lady's body; good wig, glass eyes; CM	12" 18"	3,200.00 4,000.00
	Fashion doll; bisque socket head; bisque shoulder plate; wooden lady's body; good wig, glass eyes; CM	10" 16"	5,000.00 6,800.00
Simon & Halbig	Child; jointed composition body; well defined eye and nose modelling; OM; tentative smile	28" 30"	34,000.00 41,000.00
SH	Shoulder head lady; glass eyes; molded hair with bow; pierced ears; CM	12" 16"	2,200.00 3,900.00
SH	Shoulder head lady; painted eyes; molded hair with bow; pierced ears; CM	12" 16"	1,800.00 3,600.00
SV IV	Jointed composition body; good wig, glass, stationary eyes; CM	14" 18"	22,000.00 33,000.00
110	Toddler; jointed composition body; glass eyes; O/CM smiling mouth with molded tongue and teeth	14"	6,500.00
120	Character baby face; glass eyes; OM	12" 21"	3,000.00 5,500.00
150	Jointed composition body; good wig; intaglio eyes; CM	16" 20" 26"	20,000.00 29,000.00 56,000.00
151	Jointed composition body; good wig; dimples; intaglio eyes; O/CM; smiling with teeth	14" 23"	8,300.00 17,000.00
152	Character face; long nose; molded eyelids; painted eyes; CM	18" 24"	18,000.00 28,000.00
153	Character face; molded hair; painted eyes; CM (Little Duke)	18"	46,000.00
172	Character baby; molded hair	14"	4,200.00
411	Fashion lady; bisque shoulder head; cloth lady's body; kid arms; glass eyes; good wig; O/CM with molded teeth	18"	5,200.00
600	Baby; good wig; dimples in chin; glass eyes; OM	16"	1,800.00
601	Character child; smiling with molded teeth; rounded, cut glass eyes; OM	31"	17,000.00
616	Baby; good wig; glass eyes; OM	20"	1,700.00
719	Jointed composition body; round face; glass eyes; OM	20" 23"	4,700.00 5,400.00
720	Kid body; glass eyes; CM	20"	2,400.00
739	Bisque; good wig; dolly-face; glass eyes; OM	24"	4,950.00
740	Kid body; glass eyes; CM	20"	2,300.00
749	Composition body; glass eyes; CM	20" 24"	4,300.00 4,800.00
905	Jointed composition body; good wig; glass eyes; CM	16"	3,800.00
908	Kid body; good wig; glass eyes; OM	16"	3,800.00
919	Child, glass eyes; CM	17" 20"	9,500.00 14,000.00
920	Shoulder head child; glass eyes; solid dome with wig; CM	18"	3,400.00
929	Child; glass eyes; CM	20"	5,200.00
939	Socket head child; glass eyes; OM	18" 27"	3,900.00 5,900.00
941	Kid body; good wig; glass eyes; OM	22"	1,800.00
949	Composition; glass eyes; CM	16" 20" 24"	2,900.00 3,400.00 4,200.00
950	Kid body; good wig; glass eyes; CM	14"	1,800.00
969	Bisque shoulder head; glass eyes; smiling OM	20"	3,500.00
979	Composition body; glass eyes; OM	18"	4,100.00
989	Composition body; glass eyes; CM	22" 24"	4,500.00 5,700.00
1009/1010	Shoulder head; good wig; glass eyes; OM	16" 20"	1,450.00 1,700.00
1039	Pull-string walker body; good wig; glass eyes; OM	22"	2,000.00
1039	Key-wind walker body; good wig; sleep eyes; OM	22"	2,600.00
1039	Jointed composition body; good wig; glass eyes; OM	16" 20" 24"	1,200.00 1,400.00 2,000.00
1139	Composition body; good wig; glass eyes; OM	24"	3,400.00

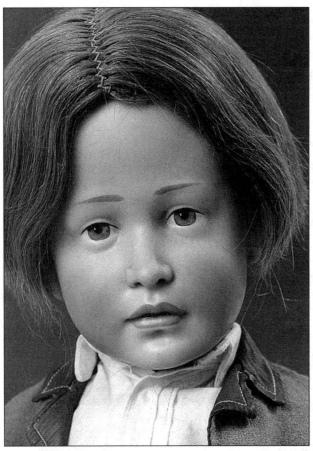

20" Simon & Halbig #150 painted eye character boy. Courtesy of David Cobb's Doll Auctions

26" Simon & Halbig solid dome #1498 character toddler. Courtesy of David Cobb's Doll Auctions

Character Doll Value Comparisons

Mold #	Description	Size	Value
1159	Lady's body; good wig; glass eyes; OM	12"	1,900.00
		16"	2,500.00
		22"	3,400.00
1160	Cloth or kid body; fancy mohair wig; glass eyes; CM (Little Women)	6"	550.00
		7"-8"	600.00
		10"-14"	700.00–950.00
1269	Composition body; good wig; sleep eyes; OM	18"	1,500.00
1279	Composition body; good wig; glass eyes; OM w/pursed lips, upper teeth	12"	2,600.00
		18"	3,800.00
		24"	5,600.00
1294	Baby; composition body; good wig; flirty eyes; OM	18"	1,200.00
		22"	1,700.00
		24"	2,000.00
1299	Baby/Child; good wig; glass eyes; OM	12"	1,700.00
		16"	1,900.00
1303	Older woman; may be darker-complexion character Indian; good wig; glass eyes; CM	14"	20,000.00
		21"	24,000.00
1304	White-faced clown; oval, glass eyes; arched brows; CM; smiling	13"	2,900.00
		22"	4,700.00
1305	Sharp-featured, older woman; glass eyes; O/CM; smiling	16"	15,000.00
		20"	29,000.00
1307	Long-face lady; glass eyes; CM	20"	22,000.00
1308	Coke Maker; composition body; head painted to show smudges; mohair wig; wearing original costume; glass eyes; smiling, CM*	14"	18,000.00
1339	Glass eyes; OM; "L.L. & S."	18"	1,400.00
		24"	2,600.00
1358	Beautiful ebony child; glass eyes; OM	19"	16,000.00

Character Doll Value Comparisons

Mold #	Description	Size	Value
1388	Composition body; good wig; glass eyes; O/CM, wide smile, molded teeth	24"	37,000.00
1398	Composition body; good wig; glass eyes; O/CM, wide smile, molded teeth	24"	26,000.00
1428	Crooked Smile; good wig; glass eyes; O/CM, impish	16" 21" 25"	3,900.00 4,800.00 5,200.00
1448	Composition body; good wig; pierced ears; glass sleep eyes; CM	15" 24"	26,000.00 38,000.00
1468	Child; sweet expression; glass eyes; CM	10" 12"	3,200.00 3,800.00
1469	Lady's body; good wig; glass eyes; CM	16"	5,000.00
1478	Glass eyes; CM	16"	12,500.00
1488	Character baby; glass eyes; O/CM	20"	6,100.00
1489	Baby; good wig; glass eyes; OM	22"	4,600.00
1498	Solid dome glass eyes; O/CM	16" 22"	5,400.00 7,000.00

Add an additional $300.00 for an open mouth doll with square teeth. Add an additional $700.00 for a jointed toddler body.

*Coke Maker's costume consists of a long black coat, black pants, red vest with two rows of brass buttons, and black felt hat.

OM = Open Mouth
CM = Closed Mouth
O/CM = Open/Closed Mouth

Child Dolls

Unique Face: bisque socket head; jointed composition body; good wig; glass eyes; feathered brows; pierced ears; open mouth; appropriately dressed; typically marked "Simon & Halbig," "S & H," "759," and "769."

Santa: bisque socket head; jointed composition body; good wig; glass eyes; pierced ears; open mouth; appropriately dressed; typically marked "Simon & Halbig," "S & H," "1248," or "1249."

Dolly-Face Socket Head: bisque socket head; jointed composition body; good wig; glass eyes; softly feathered brows; pierced ears; open mouth; appropriately dressed; typically marked "Simon & Halbig," "S & H," "540," "550," "570," "1079," "1078," and "Baby Blanche."

Dolly-Face Shoulder Head: bisque shoulder head; kid body; bisque arms; good wig; glass eyes; pierced ears; open mouth; appropriately dressed; typically marked "Simon & Halbig," "S & H," "1040," "1080," "1250," and "1260."

Child Doll Value Comparisons

Size	Unique Face	Santa	Dolly-Face, Socket Head, Composition Body	1078-1079 Dolly-Face, Socket Head, Composition Body	Dolly-Face, Shoulder Head, Kid Body
7"				700.00	
10"				800.00	
12"	1,700.00			850.00	
14"	1,800.00	1,300.00			900.00
16"	2,000.00	1,500.00		950.00	925.00
18"	2,400.00	1,600.00	900.00	1,100.00	950.00
20"		1,750.00	950.00	1,200.00	1,000.00
22"	2,900.00	2,000.00	1,000.00	1,300.00	1,100.00
24"		2,100.00	1,100.00	1,400.00	1,200.00
26"	3,400.00	2,300.00	1,200.00	1,600.00	1,300.00
28"		2,500.00		1,800.00	1,400.00
30"	3,800.00	2,700.00		2,100.00	1,600.00
32"		2,800.00		2,300.00	
34"		3,200.00		2,500.00	
36"		3,500.00		3,000.00	
38"		3,700.00		3,500.00	
40"	5,200.00			4,500.00	
42"				5,000.00	

Add an additional $300.00 for an open mouth doll with square teeth, or an additional $500.00 for black version.

Ella Smith Doll Company

According to legend, a neighbor girl brought Ella Smith a broken bisque doll to be repaired. When Ella saw how upset the little girl was, she set out to make a doll that could not be broken. She obviously succeeded. At one point, as the story goes, a truck ran over one of the dolls and didn't even crack the paint. Commonly known as Alabama Indestructible Dolls, they were produced from 1904 to 1924 in Roanoke, Alabama.

In obtaining the patent, Ella Smith describes her dolls as follows: "I make the body or trunk, the arms, hands, legs and feet of stuffed fabric and apply over the feet and hands as high up on the legs and arms as desirable one or more coats of flesh colored and preferably waterproof paint. The head, face, neck and bust are also fabric covered, and the neck or bust is secured to the trunk by suitable stitching. The outer fabric of the face covers and conforms to the curvature of a backing molded to conform to the contour of the human face. The fabric of the head is stitched up and stretched over a stuffed head portion forming a continuation of the stuffed body, and as a means for making the head rigid a rod or stick may be inserted through the head and passed down a suitable distance into the trunk or body. If desired, the doll may be provided with a wig. I prefer, however, to produce the appearance of hair by paint applied directly to the fabric and to render the head waterproof. The ears are preferably made of stuffed fabric and sewed to the side of the head, after which they are painted."

The Ella Smith Doll Company was housed in a factory built by Smith's husband. Each beautifully hand-crafted doll was stitched and painted by Mrs. Smith or one of her assistants, whose ranks at times numbered twelve or more. At the peak of production, it has been reported that as many as 6,000 dolls a year were made.

Ella Smith Dolls have heavily painted cloth bodies jointed at the hip and shoulder. The hair is usually painted in a short style, occasionally wigged. The faces are molded and painted with applied ears. Many have bare feet with stitched toes, but dolls with painted-on button slippers or low boots are more commonly found. The dolls were made to represent white or black children and babies. Stuffed through the top of the head, Alabama Indestructible Dolls are easily recognized by a stitched circular crown. Consider these characteristics in authenticating an Ella Smith Alabama Indestructible doll.

Prices listed are for appropriately dressed dolls in good condition. Slight wear and signs of aging such as a settled body do not greatly affect the price. If a doll is stained, torn, dented, cracked, peeling, or repainted, expect the value to be less than half the amount listed.

23" early Alabama Indestructible doll by Ella Smith. Courtesy of McMaster's Doll Auction

14" Ella Smith doll. Courtesy of Sotheby's Auctions

Early Doll: all painted cloth; applied ears; short, painted hair or good wig; painted shoes or bare feet; appropriately dressed; typically marked "Pat. Nov. 9 1912/No. 1/Ella Smith Doll Co." or "Mrs. S. S. Smith Manufacturer and Dealer to/The Alabama Indestructible Doll/Roanoke, Ala./Patented Sept. 26, 1905." **Note:** *Occasionally the date 1907 will appear on leg or torso.*

Later Doll: molded rather than applied ears; typically marked the same as early dolls.

Ella Smith (Alabama Indestructible Doll) Value Comparisons

Size	Early Applied Ears*	Early Applied Ears, Black	Later Molded Ears	Later Molded Ears, Black
12"	1,900.00			
14"	2,200.00	8,000.00		
15"			1,400.00	3,800.00

Ella Smith (Alabama Indestructible Doll) Value Comparisons

Size	Early Applied Ears*	Early Applied Ears, Black	Later Molded Ears	Later Molded Ears, Black
17"			2,000.00	4,000.00
18"	3,000.00	9,000.00		
19"				4,600.00
21"		12,000.00	2,900.00	
24"	3,900.00			
25"			3,400.00	
38"	12,000.00			

* Add an additional $500.00 for a wigged version.

Société de Fabrication de Bébés & Jouets

The Société de Fabrication de Bébés & Jouets (Society for the Manufacturer of Bébés and Toys) is commonly referred to as S.F.B.J. In 1899, the society signed an agreement for locations in Paris and Montreuil-sous-Bois, France.

French doll manufacturers struggled to compete with the German companies for years, until finally being forced to economize. Most of the premier French firms joined the S.F.B.J. syndicate. Many continued to produce the same dolls under S.F.B.J. that they had previously made as individual companies. Dolls produced under the amalgamation rarely met the high standards set by the original firms. Vast differences in quality are more obvious within S.F.B.J. than with any other manufacturer. Good examples are very good, and poor examples are very poor. Keep in mind that the S.F.B.J. heads were made in different porcelain factories, using different molds, which belonged to different companies.

Two types of dolls were produced by S.F.B.J. The familiar Bébé, similar in concept, if not in quality, to the earlier French Bébés, and charming, imaginative character dolls. The characters were modelled after real children with portrait-like detail as opposed to the idealized "dolly-face" Bébé. They were pouting, laughing, screaming, or smiling, as they portrayed baby or adolescent.

To distinguish a S.F.B.J. doll from one of the many reproductions, carefully inspect the markings. Another clue may be in the bisque. Gently run your fingers over the doll's cheek. Dolls produced by the S.F.B.J. will feel somewhat grainy, as opposed to the silky-smooth bisque used by contemporary doll makers.

21" S. F. B. J. #301 and 16" S. F. B. J. #60. Courtesy of David Cobb's Doll Auctions

24" S. F. B. J. 230 character boy, 24" S. F. B. J. Jumeau type Bébé #11. Courtesy of David Cobb's Doll Auctions

Quality and condition are equally important when considering a S.F.B.J. doll.

Prices listed are for appropriately costumed dolls in good condition. Normal wear, slight damage, or well-made repairs to the body do not greatly affect the price. If the bisque is damaged or repaired, expect the value to be less than half the amounts listed. It is perfectly acceptable to show a missing or repaired finger or joint, or a mended body.

Also see Googly-Eyed.

Jumeau-Type Bébé: bisque socket head; jointed composition body; very pretty, obviously Jumeau modelling; good wig; paperweight eyes; open mouth; appropriately dressed; typically marked "S.F.B.J." and/or size number only.

S.F.B.J. Bébé: bisque socket head; jointed composition body; good wig; glass eyes; open mouth; appropriately dressed; typically marked "S.F.B.J.," "S.F.B.J./301/Paris," "S.F.B.J./60/Paris," and "Bluette #301."

Character Dolls: bisque socket head; jointed body; molded and painted or flocked hair, or good wig; painted or glass eyes;

Wonderful group of S. F. B. J. character toddlers, including a 27" #252 pouty, 24" #247 Twirp, and 27" #236 Laughing Jumeau. Courtesy of David Cobb's Doll Auctions

open, closed, or open/closed mouth; appropriately dressed; typically marked "S.F.B.J./PARIS" and a mold number.

Société de Fabrication de Bébés & Jouets (S.F.B.J.) Value Comparisons

Size	Jumeau-Type	#60 (Glass Eyes)	#301
7"–8"		600.00	
10 1/2"–11" Bluette		1,200.00	1,400.00
12"		900.00	
14"	1,500.00	950.00	900.00
16"	1,800.00	1,000.00	1,000.00
18"	1,900.00	1,100.00	1,100.00
20"	2,100.00	1,200.00	1,500.00
22"	2,500.00	1,300.00	1,200.00
24"	2,200.00	1,400.00	1,300.00
26"	2,900.00	1,500.00	1,500.00
28"	3,200.00	1,600.00	2,000.00
30"	3,500.00		2,200.00
32"			2,400.00
34"			2,700.00
36"			3,000.00
38"			3,500.00

* Add an additional $500.00 for special clown facial paint.

Société de Fabrication de Bébés & Jouets (S.F.B.J.) Character Value Comparisons

Size	52 CM "O"-Shaped Upward Glancing Eyes Black	60 Painted Eyes	225 O/CM Molded Teeth	226 O/CM Full Cheeks Smiling	227 OM Character	229 OM Molded Teeth	230 OM Chin Dimples (May Be Marked "Jumeau")	233 O/CM Screamer	3 Interchangeable Heads, Molds 233, 235, and 237 Boxed Set
12"		600.00							
13"	2,600.00								
14"				2,600.00					14,000.00

Société de Fabrication de Bébés & Jouets (S.F.B.J.) Character Value Comparisons

Size	52 CM "O"-Shaped Upward Glancing Eyes Black	60 Painted Eyes	225 O/CM Molded Teeth	226 O/CM Full Cheecks Smiling	227 OM Character	229 OM Molded Teeth	230 OM Chin Dimples (May be marked "Jumeau")	233 O/CM Screamer	3 Interchangeable Heads, Molds 233, 235, and 237 Boxed Set
18"			2,300.00		2,700.00	4,100.00	2,300.00	6,000.00	
26"					3,600.00		2,800.00		

Size	Smiling 234 OM Movable Tongue	235 O/CM Squinting Eyes*	236 O/CM Laughing*	237 OM Wigged or Flocked Hair	237 OM Walker Body	238 OM Expressive Eyes Smiling	239 CM Street Urchin	242 Nursing Baby
14"							8,900.00	6,000.00
16"			1,700.00	2,900.00	3,600.00	3,400.00		7,500.00
18"	4,400.00						9,250.00	
20"		3,800.00	2,600.00					

Size	246 OM Round Child Face	247 Slight Overbite, Deeply Molded Eye Socket*	248 CM Pouty Fly-Away Brows	250 O/CM Smiling Lady/Young Girl	251 OM Slight Overbite, Deeply Molded Eyes, Cheek Dimples	252 CM* Pouty	262 OM Lower Lashes Only	287 O/CM Intaglio Eyes	Black Dolly-Face
12"								2,700.00	1,300.00
14"		2,200.00			2,450.00				
16"	3,900.00		14,000.00			5,300.00			2,400.00
18"		3,100.00		4,200.00			2,300.00		2,600.00

*Add an additional $700.00 for a jointed toddler body.

OM = Open Mouth

CM = Closed Mouth

O/CM = Open/Closed Mouth

Sonneberg Täufling

*S*onneberg Täufling, often referred to as Motschmann Babies, were made by various manufacturers in the Sonneberg area of Germany as early as 1851. Täufling simply means a baby dressed in a shift.

The idea of the Sonneberg Täufling came to Germany by way of Edmund Lindner, a Verleger (German merchant who buys manufactured goods or places orders). Lindner was in London in 1851 when he spied a new type of doll with Oriental facial characteristics and a distinct body construction. The shoulders, lower arms, hip section, and lower legs were made of composition and were connected by strips of cloth called floating joints.

Sonneberg Täufling dolls may be found stamped with the name Ch. Motschmann. Motschmann held the patent for the voice boxes often found within the doll bodies.

By the mid-1850s, doll manufacturer Henrich Stier had made several improvements to the Sonneberg Täufling, including coating the head with wax in order to produce a more lifelike appearance.

Prices listed are for dolls in good condition. Normal wear and signs of aging are to be expected and do not greatly affect price. The purist doll collector will look beyond the fine veining of the wax or slight nose rub to appreciate the doll as an essential link in the historical chain of the doll industry. If badly damaged or restored, expect to pay half the amount listed.

Also see Motschmann Baby.

Sonneberg Täufling: wax over composition, or papier-mâché shoulder head; cloth and composition body with floating joints; solid dome; painted wisps of hair above ears, or fine mohair wig; very oval-shaped glass, black, pupil-less eyes; no lashes; faint, single-stroke brows; closed or open mouth with bamboo teeth; appropriately dressed; unmarked.

18" Sonneberg Täufling. Courtesy of McMaster's Doll Auction

Sonneberg Täufling Value Comparisons	
Size	**Baby**
6"	900.00
8"	1,000.00
10"	1,200.00
12"	1,500.00
14"	1,700.00
16"	2,000.00
18"	2,200.00
20"	2,400.00
22"	2,900.00
24"	3,500.00
26"	3,800.00
28"	4,500.00

Soviet Union or Russian Dolls

Soviet Union or Russian dolls were made by various and unknown craftsmen. The evolution of Russian dolls can be linked to the country's changing political climate. An 1892 protest and declaration of the Russian Toy Congress warned "…against the large elegant French dolls that taught love of dress and suggested luxury…" This may well explain why Russian dolls are customarily dressed in simple, provincial peasant costumes.

Russian tea cozy. Courtesy of David Cobb's Doll Auctions

Wars and depressions were also responsible for many changes in both materials and types of dolls produced. Shortly after the Revolution, the Moscow Teachers Union issued a statement declaring, "… little girls should not be allowed to play with dolls. The doll represents a too bourgeois idea of family life…." With such sentiments, it is really rather remarkable that any Russian dolls were made.

The charming and modest cloth dolls continue to be popular with collectors, as well as the famous Russian Tea Cozy, the Trihedrals, and the Matryoshkas.

Peasants of Zagorsk and Bogorodskoye made the early Trihedrals using a hot iron. The all-wooden dolls were carved from a three-sided (or triangular, hence Trihedrals) piece of wood.

From the same regions around Moscow, Matryoshkas, or Nesting Dolls, were made in the homes of Russian citizens, a tradition practiced for several generations. Brightly painted dolls representing military leaders or Russian folklore characters were particular favorites.

Cloth

Prices listed are for appropriately dressed dolls with good color, little or no fading. If a doll is stained, torn, badly mended, or faded, expect the value to be less than half the amounts listed.

Russian Peasant Doll: stockinette face; cloth body, often with wooden legs or feet; stitched and painted facial features; yarn or painted hair; regional costumes; typically marked, stamped, or labeled "Made in Soviet Union."

Russian Tea Cozy: stockinette face; cloth upper body; large quilted skirt, forming lower body; stitched and painted facial features; yarn or painted hair; regional costumes; typically marked, stamped, or labeled "Made in Soviet Union."

Size	Better Quality Fine Detail Peasant Doll	Standard Quality Peasant Doll	Russian Tea Cozy
6"	125.00	85.00	
10"	200.00	145.00	
16"	400.00	250.00	
18"			350.00 +

Wooden

Prices listed are for dolls in good condition. If damaged, badly worn, repainted, or incomplete, expect the value to be less than half the amounts listed.

Trihedrals: all wooden with no joints; carved and painted facial features; carved and colorfully painted clothing and head wear; typically stamped "Soviet Union" (pre-Revolution Trihedrals are typically unmarked).

Matryoshkas: all wooden or papier mâché; opening mid point to reveal a smaller identical or related doll; descending and nesting in graduating sizes; brightly painted features and costumes in reds, greens, and oranges with hints of yellow and blue; highly reflective polished surface; typically stamped "Soviet Union" (pre-Revolution Matryoshkas are typically unmarked).

Size	Early or Better Quality Trihedrals	Standard Quality Trihedrals	Early Unmarked Matryoshkas	Marked Soviet Union Matryoshkas	Modern Political Matryoshkas
8"	400.00	100.00			
11"			1,700.00	350.00	
13"				450.00	100.00
15"			2,400.00		

Steiff

The German town of Gienger an der Brenz—the home of Margarete Steiff—dates back to the time of cobblestone streets and gingerbread houses. Born in 1847, Margarete Steiff contracted polio at the age of two, weakening her legs and right hand. This did not, however, dampen her spirits, for she was determined to learn to sew in order to support herself. As a young woman, she became an accomplished seamstress, having her own workshop where she made women's and children's clothing out of wool felt. In 1880, a flash of inspiration changed her life forever. Steiff designed and created a small felt elephant pincushion. She is quoted as writing in her diary: "...I quite casually came across a picture representing an elephant. Felt is quite the kind of material suitable for making small pattern animals, so I set to work, choosing for the purpose the best wool felt I could lay my hands on. The little elephant will make a lovely pincushion." This little elephant was very popular among the children of the neighborhood, who approached Steiff requesting copies of the little elephant to use as a plaything. It was then that she began commercially producing small, stuffed animals.

In 1897, Margarete's nephew, Richard, joined the family business. Richard had studied art in Germany and England. It was while he was in Stuttgart, Germany that the seeds for a popular toy were planted. Richard enjoyed sketching the bears housed at the Nills Animal Show. He was so taken with their antics that he filled several sketchbooks with his drawings. The sketches proved invaluable when he designed a small, jointed, mohair bear to debut at the 1903 Leipzig Toy Fair.

By coincidence, at about this same time, President Theodore Roosevelt traveled to Mississippi on a hunting expedition. One

14" Steiff lady and gentleman dolls. Courtesy Bill Neff

evening, a bear cub wandered into camp. Roosevelt refused to kill the young bear, instead chasing it back to its mother. The *Washington Post*'s political cartoonist, Clifford Berryman, a member of the hunting party, drew a cartoon of the President chasing the bear. From that day forward, the little bear called "Teddy's Bear" was in every cartoon Berryman did of President Teddy Roosevelt. President Roosevelt obviously enjoyed the kidding he received over the little bear. In 1906, at his daughter's wedding reception held at the White House, decorations were Steiff bears dressed as hunters and fishermen, chosen because of the President's love of the outdoors. This unofficial endorsement undoubtedly contributed to the unprecedented one million Steiff bears sold the next year.

Leadership of the Steiff company was passed to Margarete's nephews, following her death in 1909. The Steiff factory operated for many years as a cottage industry. Women would pick up the raw materials at the factory and return with a finished toy.

Steiff markings have changed several times. In 1892, a camel was used, but never registered. In 1898, the elephant with his trunk forming the letter "S" was used, but again without being registered. The Teddy Bear, introduced as "Petz," was never registered, explaining why numerous competing firms were able to manufacture "Teddy Bears." **Note:** *Steiff furnished the facts and information for this introduction. There may be conflicting facts and information elsewhere about "Teddy Bears."*

An application dated December of 1904 "for a button in the ear for toys of felt and similar material" put an end to Margarete's registration problems. She even wrote to her customers to inform them, "...From November 1, 1904 on, each of my products, without exception, shall have as my trademark a small nickel button in the left ear."

Although best known for their animals, Steiff also produced dolls advertised as "jovial lads and buxom maidens." Felt pressed heads with a seam down the middle of the face, mohair wigs, glass eyes, and large feet are classic Steiff doll characteristics.

In 1988, a new line of hard vinyl dolls was introduced to the United States. The dolls have hard vinyl heads and arms on cloth bodies with human hair wigs. They are well-dressed with the familiar button in the ear and a 24-karat gold-plated Steiff brooch.

Reproduction Steiff dolls are not as troublesome as copies. The copies may have a seam down the face and even resemble the characters. They do not have the Steiff ear-button or quality. The features on authentic Steiff dolls are often hand painted and embroidered, and seams are frequently hand sewn. The very qualities that make Steiff dolls so famous are exactly the things missing from a copy.

Prices listed are for originally costumed dolls in very good condition. If a doll is stained, torn, badly faded, mended, or redressed, expect the value to be less than one half to one third the amounts listed.

Also see Ideal.

Adult Doll: felt, velvet, or plush; seam down center of face; oversized nose; applied ears; very large feet; glass button eyes; painted or embroidered features; original costume; typically marked with ear-button.

Child Doll: felt, velvet, or plush; seam down center of face; jointed body; applied ears; glass button eyes; painted features; original costume; typically marked with ear-button.

Character Doll: felt, velvet, or plush; seam down center of face; applied ears; large feet; jointed body; glass button eyes; painted and embroidered features; original costume; typically marked with ear-button.

Vinyl Steiff Doll: vinyl head and arms; cloth body; marked with ear-button.

Tea cozy: Steiff doll topper; heavy quilted skirt; typically marked with ear-button..**$1,400.00**

Mickey & Minnie: 5"; pair; all felt; typically marked with ear-button...**$6,500.00**

Steiff Value Comparisons

Size	Adult	Child	Black Child	Military Officer/ Soldier	Mickey Mouse	Minnie Mouse	Clown
10"					1,900.00	2,300.00	
12"	2,100.00	1,500.00	2,200.00				
14"	2,500.00				2,600.00	3,000.00	2,800.00
18"	2,800.00	2,000.00	2,800.00	4,400.00			3,400.00
21"				4,700.00			
22"	3,500.00			5,600.00			

Size	Golliwog	Max and Moritz (pair)	Comic Characters, Elf/Chef	Vinyl Steiff
12"			1,300.00	400.00
14"	4,600.00			
16"		7,800.00	2,900.00	
16 1/2"	4,800.00			500.00
20"				700.00

Edmund Ulrich Steiner

*E*dmund Ulrich Steiner manufactured and distributed dolls from 1864 until 1916. Edmund came from a family with roots planted deeply in the doll industry. His father produced a high-grade doll, which was one of the first prominent lines to be marketed in the United States. His brother, Albert, was also well known within the doll business. Edmund, born in Germany, came to America as a young man from Sonneberg. Thüringia, Germany, and reportedly crossed the Atlantic eighty-four times in his career. He maintained a close association with the doll community in both his native country and the United States. He worked with a number of firms including Louis Wolf, Sanstag & Hilder, and Strobel & Wilken. Over the years, he registered several designs for bisque dolls, including Liliput, Daisy, and Majestic (Daisy and Majestic are registered trade names of other doll manufacturers, therefore care should be taken not to confuse a particular doll). Several companies, including Armand Marseille, manufactured Edmund Steiner's designs.

Many of Steiner's bisque-head dolls were marked with his initials within a diamond.

Prices listed are for appropriately costumed dolls in good condition. Normal wear, slight damage, or well-made repairs to the body do not greatly affect the price. If the bisque is damaged or repaired, expect the value to be less than half the amounts listed. It is perfectly acceptable to show a missing or repaired finger or joint, or a mended body.

Dolly-Face: bisque socket or shoulder head; jointed composition or kid body; good wig; glass eyes; open mouth; appropriately dressed; typically marked "Majestic/A M/Made in Germany," "Majestic," or "E. U. St." (within a diamond).

22" E. U. Steiner child doll. Courtesy of McMaster's Doll Auction

Edmund Ulrich Steiner Value Comparisons

Size	Dolly-Face, Kid Body	Dolly-Face, Composition Body
14"	350.00	
16"		500.00
18"	425.00	550.00
20"		600.00
22"	500.00	650.00
24"	575.00	700.00
26"		800.00

Hermann Steiner

14" Herm Steiner baby.

The factories of Hermann Steiner were located in Sonneberg, Neustadt, Thüringia, Germany, and in Bavaria. Although the company was founded in 1911, it did not produce dolls until 1920. This explains why the majority of dolls found with the Hermann Steiner mark are the character baby type, which was so popular and dominated the market at that time. Hermann Steiner had poor timing regarding the manufacture of bisque dolls, entering the market at the end of the era.

Prices listed are for appropriately costumed dolls in good condition. Normal wear, slight damage, or well-made repairs to the body do not greatly affect the price. If the bisque is damaged or repaired, expect the value to be less than half the amounts listed. It is perfectly acceptable to show a missing or repaired finger or joint, or a mended body.

Also see Googly-Eyed Dolls.

Character Baby: bisque socket or shoulder head; jointed composition or cloth body; solid dome with molded hair or good wig; painted or glass eyes; closed or open mouth; appropriately dressed; typically marked "Herm Steiner H S Germany," "H S," "246," and "131."

Dolly-Face: bisque socket head; jointed composition body; good wig; glass eyes; open mouth; appropriately dressed; typically marked "H S Germany" or "Herm Steiner Germany."

Herman Steiner Value Comparisons			
Size	Character Baby, Composition Body	Character Baby, Cloth Body	Dolly-Face
8"	400.00	350.00	
10"	450.00	400.00	425.00
12"	500.00	450.00	
14"	650.00	600.00	625.00
16"	750.00	700.00	725.00

Jules Steiner

Jules Nicholas Steiner founded his famous doll company in 1855, in Paris. Steiner was succeeded by Amédée La Fosse from 1892–1893 and, following his death, by his widow, who ran the business until 1899. From 1899 to 1901, Jules Mettais headed the company. He in turn was succeeded by Edmond Daspres from 1904 until 1908.

Many Steiner dolls are marked with the name "Bourgoin." Bourgoin was a Paris merchant dealing in porcelains and associated with Jules Steiner during the 1880s. Sometime after 1897, the Societe Steiner purchased May Freres Cie., the company responsible for the manufacture of Bébé Mascotte.

It was long believed that Steiner dolls were produced in Germany—a misconception possibly resulting from the Germanic name, or form distorted recollections. It is now generally accepted that the exquisite creations are unquestionably French. From the early dolls with their round faces and two rows of tiny, pointed teeth, to the later bébés with their captivating beauty, the Societe Steiner produced some of the most distinctively high-quality dolls of the 19th century, while under the leadership and creativity of its founder.

There is evidence that Steiner pressed their bisque doll heads even after other French manufacturers were routinely using the poured bisque method.

23" Jules Steiner "Figure B 4" bébé open mouth with two rows of teeth, lever eyes, and pierced ears. Courtesy of David Cobb's Doll Auctions

20" Jules Steiner "Figure A 13" closed mouth Bébé. Courtesy of David Cobb's Doll Auctions

Steiner bébés have been found in sizes ranging from 8 1/2 to 38 inches. A variety of markings will be found, including some that may seem strange:

FI, Fire, or Figure = Face or countenance

Bte = registered

Ste = Steiner

SUCCe = Successor

S.G.D.G. = registered but without government guarantee.

Markings usually include a size number and one of four letters: such as "A," "B," "C," "D," or "G," with "A" being the most commonly found.

When verifying the authenticity of a Steiner bébé, remember, most will have a pressed, rather than poured bisque head, and the pates are usually purple cardboard. Original Steiner bodies have a purple undercoat, which is often visible at the joints. Hands should have short, chubby fingers, all the same length, except the thumb. Le Parisien Bébé, have graceful hands with long, thin fingers. The big toe is often molded separately. Any of the molds may have sleep eyes, operated manually by a wire behind the ear, and often marked "J. Steiner."

The markings on Jules Steiner dolls can be confusing, as the heads often have both an incised mark and a stamped marking. The incised, in-the-mold mark is the more definitive labeling, although some prefer to use the stamp markings for identification.

Prices listed are for beautifully dressed dolls in good condition. Normal wear, slight damage, or well-made repairs to the body do not greatly affect the price. If the bisque is damaged or repaired, expect the value to be less than half the amounts listed. It is perfectly acceptable to show a missing or repaired finger or joint, or a mended body.

Also see Automata.

Early Round Face: very pale bisque socket head; jointed wood-and-composition body; stubby fingers; mohair or skin wig; bulgy, paperweight, almond-shaped eyes; light, pink-mauve eye shadow; thin brows; with or without pierced ears; closed or open mouth with eight upper and seven lower teeth; thin lips; appropriately dressed; typically unmarked; body may be stamped "J. Steiner fabricante," "J. Steiner fabricate, rue de Saintonge, No. 25 Paris, Prissette, Imp. Pass du Carre 17."

Täufling-Type Body: round, very pale bisque shoulder head with molded, full shoulder and upper body; bisque lower body/hip and tops of legs; cloth joints (same body-style as the Sonneberg Täufling); mohair or skin wig; bulgy, paperweight, almond-shaped eyes; light, pink-mauve eye shadow; thin brows; most without pierced ears; closed mouth; appropriately dressed; typically unmarked.

Series A or C Stamped in Red: bisque socket head; jointed wood-and-composition body; short, stubby fingers of same length, except for the thumb; straight wrists; human or mohair wig; round face with wide forehead and full cheeks; slight chin with hint of dimple; excellent-quality paperweight eyes with dark rims, or beautiful glass porcelain-encased sleep eyes, may be operated by a lever protruding from the back of the head; black lashes and outlined eyes; heavy brows with tiny brush strokes; light, pink-mauve eye shadow; pierced ears with light blush on rims; deep pink, closed mouth with high cupid's-bow upper lip and upturned corners; appropriately dressed; typically marked incised "Ste A" and size number or "Ste C" and size number, also stamped in red script "J. Steiner Bte SGDG J. Bourgoin" or "J. STEINER B.S.G.D.G."

Figure A, B, or C Bébé: bisque socket head; jointed wood-and-composition body; short, stubby fingers of same length, except for thumb; may have separate big toe; jointed or un-jointed wrists; human or mohair wig; purple, cardboard pate; somewhat-long, pretty, oval-shaped face; slight chin; beautiful, good-quality paperweight eyes; long, dark, thick lashes, beginning at the outer eye corners, may have a dot at the base of each; black-outlined eyes; heavy brows with tiny brush strokes (Steiner Bébé brows do not meet at bridge of nose as on other French dolls, but they tend to be longer at outer corner of eye); nicely-detailed, pierced ears with deep molding; deep pink, closed mouth with high cupid's-bow upper lip and upturned corners; appropriately dressed; body may have a label with a picture of a girl holding a flag; typically marked with incised:

Figure (A B or C) No. (Size Number)
J. Steiner Bte. S.G.D.G.
Paris

OR

Figure (A B or C) (Size Number)
J. Steiner Bte. S.G.D.G.
PARIS

OR

J. Steiner
Bte. S.G.D.G.
Paris
Fire (A B or C) (Size Number)

Stamp may or may not be present on head, body, or both:
"Le Petit Parisien"
Bébé Steiner
Medaille d'Or
Paris 1889

Le Parisien Bébé: bisque socket head; wood-and-composition body; longer, thin, very graceful fingers; big toe molded separately; jointed or un-jointed wrists (later Le Parisien may have mediocre-quality composition straight-limb body); human or mohair wig; cork or purple cardboard pate; somewhat rectangular-shaped face; slight chin; good quality, large, oval-shaped paperweight eyes; pronounced brows; beautifully-sculptured, pierced ears with intricate folds and canals; deep pink open or closed mouth, with high, cupid's-bow upper lip and upturned corners; appropriately dressed; typically marked incised:
(Size Number) OR A (Size Number)
Paris   Paris
Stamped in red block letters: Le PARISIEN
Body Stamped in purple:
Bébé Le Parisien
Medaille D'or
Paris

OR

Marque Déposés
Article
FRANCAIS (within a triangle in black)

19" Jules Steiner closed mouth Bébé Le Parisien size number 13. Courtesy of David Cobb's Doll Auctions

20" Jules Steiner open mouth Bébé Le Parisien size number 13. Courtesy of David Cobb's Doll Auctions

Jules Nicholas Steiner Value Comparisons

Size	Early Round Face, Closed Mouth	Early Round Face, Open Mouth	Täufling-Type*	Series A or C Stamped in Red	Figure A Closed Mouth Bébé	Figure B Closed Mouth Bébé	Figure C Closed Mouth Bébé	Figure Bébé Open Mouth	Le Parisien Bébé, Closed Mouth**	Le Parisien Bébé, Open Mouth
8 1/2"						3,600.00	7,000.00			1,900.00
9"				4,200.00						
10"				8,200.00		4,100.00	7,500.00		6,000.00	
11"		7,000.00				4,400.00	7,900.00			2,300.00
12"				4,600.00						
13"		7,500.00		8,300.00	5,000.00	4,700.00	8,100.00	5,000.00	6,400.00	
15"			7,200.00		5,600.00	5,400.00		5,700.00	6,800.00	2,800.00
16"		8,000.00		8,500.00			8,500.00			
17"			7,500.00		6,200.00			6,000.00	7,200.00	3,400.00
18"	15,000.00	9,000.00		10,000.00	6,600.00	6,200.00	8,900.00			
20"		9,500.00	8,000.00	11,500.00	6,900.00	6,500.00	9,700.00		7,600.00	
22"	19,000.00			12,000.00	7,200.00	6,900.00	10,500.00	6,700.00	8,300.00	3,700.00
24"				13,000.00	8,200.00	7,600.00	11,800.00	7,400.00	9,000.00	
26"										4,300.00
28"				14,000.00	9,900.00	9,000.00	12,500.00	8,000.00	11,000.00	
30"					10,500.00				13,000.00	4,900.00
32"								8,700.00		5,600.00
34"						10,000.00	17,000.00			
36"					13,000.00					
38"				27,000.00					15,000.00	

* Add an additional $1,000.00 for swivel neck.

** Deduct $1,000.00 for five-piece, straight-limb body.

Swaine & Company

Robert Swaine owned the Swaine & Company porcelain factory in Hüttensteinach, near Sonneberg, Germany. It produced quality dolls for a short period of time beginning in 1910. Made from high-grade bisque, the dolls were beautifully sculptured with fine modelling, and they exhibited extraordinary talent in the application of decoration. Faces were delicate, sweet, and uniquely Swaine. Many believe Swaine produced only one doll, "Lori," but with several expressions signified by letters "DI," DV," "DIP," and so on. Others contend that Swaine dolls were entirely different characters, only displaying the influence of a particular artist or sculpture.

Authentic Swaine dolls have a green ink "GESTCHUTZT GERMANY S & Co." stamp, in addition to the incised marking.

Prices listed are for appropriately costumed dolls in good condition. Normal wear, slight damage, or well-made repairs to the body do not greatly affect the price. If the bisque is damaged or repaired, expect the value to be less than half the amounts listed. It is perfectly acceptable to show a missing or repaired finger or joint, or a mended body.

23" Swaine & Co. character baby #232. Courtesy of McMaster's Doll Auction

Character Baby: bisque socket head; composition bent-limb baby body; solid dome or good wig; especially fine detailing around painted or glass eyes; open or closed mouth; appropriately dressed; typically marked with green stamp "GESTCHUTZT GERMANY S & Co." within a circle and incised "232," "Lori," "DIP," "DI," "DV," "BP," "BO," "S & C," "FP," "AP," or "Made in Germany S & C."

Swaine & Company Value Comparisons

Size	Lori Open/ Closed Mouth	232/Lori Open Mouth	DIP Closed Mouth	DV Open/ Closed Mouth	DI Open/ Closed Mouth	BP or BO Open/Closed Smiling Mouth	FP Open/ Closed Mouth	SC Child Doll	AP Painted Eyes Closed Mouth
8"		1,000.00					1,000.00		
10"		1,200.00					1,300.00	850.00	
12"			1,500.00	1,700.00	1,300.00				
14"	2,800.00	1,600.00	1,700.00	1,800.00	1,500.00	6,400.00		950.00	
16"	3,000.00	1,800.00	2,000.00	2,100.00		7,200.00			8,200.00
18"	3,500.00	2,100.00	2,300.00			8,200.00			
20"	3,700.00	2,300.00				8,800.00		1,200.00	
22"	4,000.00	2,800.00	3,000.00			9,500.00			
24"	4,500.00	3,200.00						1,700.00	
28"								2,500.00	

Add an additional $700.00 to any doll with jointed toddler body.

Shirley Temple

Ideal's composition Shirley Temple dolls including 18" all original Hawaiian, Marama; 15" and 17" original Shirley. Courtesy of David Cobb's Doll Auctions

The Christmas season of 2001 marked the 67th anniversary of Ideal's Shirley Temple Doll. In the midst of the Great Depression, when people needed an escape from the worries of their everyday lives, a darling child danced and sang her way into the hearts of the nation. Ideal's founder, Morris Michtom, once wrote, while negotiating the rights to the name Shirley Temple: "This nation needs a beautiful doll to cure this depression." Master doll artist, Bernard Lipfert, created the charming Shirley Temple doll to the specifications of Ideal, Michtom, and Shirley's mother (Mrs. Gertrude Temple). Mrs. Temple's approval was obtained only after more than twenty-eight molds were rejected.

The five-piece composition body was unusually well formed and lifelike with a rounded tummy, well-proportioned limbs, stocky legs, defined calves, and even dimples on the derriere. The flesh-colored composition was either light pink or with a delicate yellow cast. Two distinctly different topcoats were applied. Either a shiny high-gloss or a flat, matte-like finish softly blushed knees, elbows, and backs of the hands. The second and third fingers were molded together. Beautifully styled mohair wigs, ranging in shades from pale yellow to rich, golden-coppery blond, had spiral curls placed vertically around the head. The dolls had hazel, brown, or green eyes with either real or painted lashes and single-stroke brows. Shirley's orangish-red mouth was open with six upper teeth. Dimples on either side of her smile were the finishing touch.

At least four different markings were used on composition Shirley Temple Dolls. The first prototypes were marked "Cop./Ideal/N & T Co." on the head only. The second dolls, mostly 18- and 22-inch sizes, were marked "Shirley Temple" with the familiar "Ideal" within a diamond trademark below. The third mark was "Shirley Temple Corp. Ideal." Finally, the most commonly found "Shirley Temple" was marked with a size number in inches.

There are also genuine unmarked Shirley Temple Dolls. Some dolls were marked on both the head and body; others were marked on only the head or the body. During the process of assembling the dolls, various combinations occurred. It stands to reason that occasionally two unmarked pieces were joined together to create a genuine, unmarked Shirley Temple.

Mollye Goldman designed Shirley Temple outfits from 1934 to 1936. They include:

Baby Take A Bow: cotton dress of red or blue polka dots with white and red coin dot ruffled collar.

Bright Eyes: aviator costume with red, belted leather jacket and matching cap; also red plain dress with white collar and cuffs, red bow trim.

The Little Colonel: elaborate, organdy dress of either pink, green, lavender, or blue with attached slip, lace-trimmed tiered ruffles, lacy bloomers showing under dress, beautiful bonnet with plume, and fabric flower trim.

Curly Top: black velvet bodice and yellow or green taffeta skirt; embroidered flowers and appliqué trim; white fur coat, tam, and muff.

Our Little Girl: dress of either blue and white or red and white piqué with white Scottie dog appliqué.

The Littlest Rebel: cotton dress of either red and white, green and white, or brown and white with Peter Pan collar and pinafore.

Captain January: sailor suit.

Poor Little Rich Girl: silk, one-piece, polka-dot pajamas of either white and red or peach and blue.

Stowaway: two-piece, Oriental, navy, yellow, and red costume, trimmed with brass buttons.

Wee Willie Winkle: Scottish outfit.

Heidi: Dutch outfit with wooden shoes.

The Blue Bird: dress with blue skirt, white organdy blouse, red vest, and white apron with blue appliqué birds.

Texas Ranger: cowgirl ensemble, designed to coincide with the Texas Centennial (1936); plaid skirt; leather vest and chaps; holster with small gun; tan, cowgirl hat.

Clothing had two types of labels and pins. One type of label was blue and white rayon with "Shirley Temple" in red. The second type of label was similar but also had a blue eagle and the initials "N.R.A." (National Recovery Administration). Original pins were made of celluloid. The first had a happy, smiling face; the second had Shirley with her finger pointing to her face. Both read, "The World's Darling Genuine Shirley Temple Doll" around the outer edge.

Ideal also released a composition Baby Shirley Temple in 1935. However, Baby Shirley Temple Doll never received the level of success of the child dolls. Baby Shirley had a chubby, stuffed cloth body with composition bent arms and lower legs, molded hair or a blond mohair wig, sleep or flirty eyes, two upper and three lower teeth, and the famous Shirley Temple dimples on either side of her open, smiling mouth. They were marked "Shirley Temple" on the back of the head.

Ideal's composition Shirley Temple Dolls were so well marketed that they earned more than 45 million dollars in sales from their introduction in 1934 to their departure from the scene in 1939.

Shirley Temple Dolls, ranging in sizes from 12 to 36 inches, were reissued by Ideal in 1957. The dolls have a vinyl head; hard plastic body; rooted, dark blond, curly, synthetic hair; sleep or flirty eyes; and an open/closed, smiling mouth with molded and painted teeth. They were marked "Ideal Doll/ST - (size number)" on the back of the head and "ST - (size number)" on the shoulder. They also wore a gold, plastic pin with "Shirley Temple" written in script.

A special issue fifteen-inch vinyl doll marked "Hong Kong" was released for Montgomery Ward's 100th Anniversary in 1972. Then, in 1973, Ideal released a new Shirley Temple with an entirely different face. This sixteen-inch vinyl doll has stationary

Special release for Sears, Roebuck & Co. 1960. 36" vinyl Shirley Temple marked 35-38.2, valued at $2,000.00.

eyes and rooted hair. Eight- and twelve-inch dolls were reissued in 1982. Dolls, Dreams & Love, a company owned by Henry Garfinkle, released a special issue thirty-six-inch Shirley Temple doll in 1984 to commemorate the 50th anniversary of the original Shirley Temple Doll. This commemorative Shirley had rooted, blond, synthetic hair styled in long curls; hazel, sleep eyes; and an open/closed, smiling mouth with molded and painted teeth. It was marked "1984/Mrs. Shirley Temple Black/ Dolls, Dream & Love" on the back of the head.

During the late 1980s, the Danbury Mint began making fourteen-inch porcelain dolls, sculpted by Elke Hutchens. The dolls were available in several outfits and offered by direct mail. They were marked "Danbury Mint."

Shirley Temple Dolls have captured the hearts of collectors for over sixty-five years. She rekindles pleasant memories of bygone days with the sweet songs and adorable antics of a beautiful and talented little girl.

Copies of Shirley Temple Dolls are plentiful. Examples of copies include: Madame Alexander's Little Colonel; American Character's Sally Star; Arranbee's Nancy; Goldberger's Little Miss Charming; Horsman's Bright Star; Joy Doll's Miss World's Fairest; Regal's Kiddie Pal; and even Ideal's Ginger and Betty Jane Dolls. Because a royalty had to be paid for every genuine Shirley Temple Doll sold, it was more profitable for Ideal to issue a copy than a genuine Shirley Temple doll. Reliable of Canada was also licensed to make an authentic Shirley Temple Doll for the Canadian market.

Composition

Prices listed are for dolls in good condition with original costumes. Slight crazing is acceptable and does not greatly affect the price. If badly crazed, cracked, peeling, or repainted, expect the value to be less than half the amounts listed.

Ideal Shirley Temple: all composition; jointed at neck, shoulder, and hip; blond, mohair wig styled with curls; hazel, sleep eyes; painted lashes; single-stroke brows; rosy cheeks with dimples; open, slightly-smiling mouth; original, tagged "Shirley

Temple" outfit; typically marked "Shirley Temple" and size number on back of head and/or body; "Cop./Ideal/N & T Co." "Shirley Temple/Ideal" (within a diamond); "Shirley Temple Corp. Ideal"; and occasionally unmarked.

Baby Shirley Temple: composition head; cloth body and limbs; molded hair or wig; open mouth; original, tagged "Shirley Temple" outfit and pants; typically marked "Shirley Temple."

Brown Shirley Temple: represents Marama character from the movie *The Hurricane*; all brown composition; jointed at neck, shoulder, and hip; black yarn hair; painted, side-glancing eyes; open/closed mouth with painted upper teeth; original grass skirt and leis; flowers in hair; typically marked "Shirley Temple."

Vinyl and Plastic

Prices listed are for dolls in near-mint, original condition. If damaged, redressed, or undressed, expect the value to be less than one half to one fourth the amounts listed.

1957: vinyl head; hard plastic body; rooted, blond, curly, synthetic hair; brown, sleep eyes; open/closed, smiling mouth; nicely molded and painted teeth; dimples on side of mouth; original costume; gold, plastic script "Shirley Temple" pin; typically marked "ST-II."

1972: vinyl head; plastic body; made for Montgomery Ward; original costume; typically marked "Hong Kong."

1973: vinyl head; plastic body; rooted hair; stationary, brown eyes; open/closed mouth; molded and painted teeth; original costume; typically marked "1971/Ideal Toy Corp./ST-14-H-213."

1982: vinyl head; hard plastic body; original costume; typically marked "1982" on body and "1982 Ideal Toy Corp/S.T. 8-N-8371" on head.

1984: vinyl head; plastic body; original costume; typically marked "1984/Mrs. Shirley Temple Black/Dolls, Dreams & Love."

Porcelain

Prices listed are for original dolls in mint condition with boxes.
Display Doll: Marked "Danbury Mint."

Foreign Shirley Temple Dolls

United States patent laws did not protect against infringements by other countries.

Prices listed are for originally costumed dolls in Good to Very good condition.

Canadian: Reliable Doll Company had the legal rights to manufacture Shirley Temple dolls. Marked "Celichle."

French: stuffed felt swivel head stitched at back; cotton cloth body; jointed at shoulder and hip; celluloid hands; face and front of neck covered with sealing glaze and painted; blond, curly, mohair wig; painted, brown eyes, glancing slightly to side; single-stroke brows; detailed upper eyelid and lashes; open/closed, smiling mouth; finely-molded teeth; small dimples on either side of mouth; various costumes from Shirley Temple films; typically unmarked; (assumed to have been made by Edouard Raynal; not intended for export to the United States; very rare).

German: several German manufacturers produced Shirley Temple type dolls. The best known are the beautiful Armand Marseille composition molds 452 and 452H. All composition; socket head; jointed composition body; 452 wears wig; 452H has molded, curly hair; glass sleep eyes; rosy cheeks with hint of dimples; smiling, open mouth with teeth; appropriately dressed; typically marked "Armand Marseille 452 Germany" or "AM/452H/Germany."

Japanese: all composition; jointed at neck, shoulder, and hip; molded and painted, blond, curly hair; painted, brown eyes; long, painted upper lashes; open/closed, smiling mouth; white between lips to simulate teeth; original, pink-pleated, sleeveless dress, white socks, tie shoes; typically marked "S.T. Japan."

Foreign Shirley Temple Doll Value Comparisons				
Size	Canadian Composition	French Cloth	German Composition	Japanese Composition
10"				400.00
18"	1,500.00		1,700.00	
19"		1,700.00		
20"			2,000.00	
22"			2,400.00	

Shirley Temple Doll Value Comparisons									
Size	Ideal All Composition*	Baby Shirley	Brown Shirley	1957 Vinyl	1972 Vinyl	1973 Vinyl	1982 Vinyl	1984 Vinyl	Porcelain Danbury Mint
8"							100.00		
11"	1,300.00								
12"				300.00			125.00		
13"	1,200.00								
14"									250.00
15"	1,200.00			400.00	300.00				
16"	1,200.00	1,600.00				200.00			
17"	1,400.00			475.00					
18"	1,400.00	1,700.00	1,300.00						
19"				550.00					
20"		1,800.00							
21"		1,900.00							
22"	1,600.00								
23"		2,000.00							
25"	1,700.00	2,100.00							
27"	2,600.00								
36"								500.00	

Add an additional $300.00–800.00 for Texas Ranger or Curly Top costumed doll.

Terri Lee Company

Large group of 16" Terri Lee, 10" Tiny Terry Lee, and Baby Linda Lee, showing a few of the many outfits offered. Courtesy of David Cobb's Doll Auctions

*I*n 1946, when Mrs. Violet Gradwohl and ten employees ventured into the doll-making business in one room in Lincoln, Nebraska, the Terri Lee Company got its start. Mrs. Gradwohl was concerned with the quality of dolls being offered to children and wanted to manufacture a doll that could withstand all the "love" a child could inflict. Her first challenge was in finding a suitable plastic—one that was both lifelike and durable. The head was molded with closed mouth and painted eyes, thus eliminating eyes that could easily be broken.

Mrs. Gradwohl also wanted a wig that could be shampooed, combed, curled, and styled. She eventually received a patent for the process used to create artificial hair wigs woven from Celanese yarn. Once construction details of the Terri Lee Doll were settled upon, the only remaining area of concern was costuming. Mrs. Gradwohl decided that Terri Lee should have a beautiful wardrobe with all types of outfits made from the finest fabrics. Mrs. Gradwohl designed the clothing with her daughter, Terri Lee, for whom the dolls were named.

Every little girl needs companionship, and the Terri Lee Doll was no exception. Soon, brother, Jerri Lee, and friends Bonnie Lu, Patty Jo, Benjie, and Nanooh (an Eskimo child) were introduced. It is interesting to note that all the dolls used the same basic doll mold—the only difference being wig types or facial painting. Baby Linda, 11", also joined the family. She was closely followed by 10" Tiny Terri Lee and Tiny Jerri Lee. An entirely

new doll, Connie Lynn, also entered the scene. Reportedly, a birth certificate with fingerprints, footprints, and a lifetime guarantee was also issued with each doll. For a small fee (labor costs only), the company would restore "sick" or "injured" dolls.

Another innovative idea of Gradwohl's was a newsletter sent to the owner of Terri Lee dolls, keeping them informed of Terri Lee's latest fashions.

The Terri Lee Doll Company, despite its success, was plagued with misfortune. The factory in Lincoln burned to the ground, prompting its relocation to Apple Valley, California. In 1958, the California factory closed its doors for the last time.

Several copies of Terri Lee dolls have been produced. Many were made during the early 1950s at the peak of Terri Lee's popularity. They often have holes in their feet. Other differences include:

	Authentic Terry	Copies
Measurement at waist	9 3/4"	9 1/4"
Measurement at calf	5 1/2"	5 1/4"
Measurement of height	16"	15 1/2"

One well-known copy is Mary Jane, often called an unmarked Terri Lee walker. This is incorrect. Mary Jane is indeed unmarked and does in fact walk; however, she is not a Terri Lee even though she looks identical to the distinctive Terri Lee. Mary Jane was reportedly designed and manufactured by a former employee of Violet Gradwohl, advertised by Kathryn Kay-Toy Kreations, and dressed in a wardrobe designed by G. H. and E. Freydberg, the famous children's clothing designers.

Prices listed are for dolls in near-mint, original condition. If damaged, redressed, or undressed, expect the value to be less than one half to one fourth the amounts listed.

Also see Automata.

Composition Terri Lee: all composition; jointed at neck, shoulder, and hip; wiry hair wig; painted eyes; closed mouth; original tagged outfit; typically marked "Terri Lee, Pat Pending."

Hard Plastic/Vinyl: hard plastic; jointed at neck, shoulder, and hip; good wig; painted, distinctive facial features; large eyes; closed mouth; original tagged outfit; typically marked "Terri Lee Pat. Pending" on dolls made before 1949 and "Terri Lee" on dolls produced in 1949 and later years.

Gene Autry: molded and painted, brown hair; feathered brows; decal, blue eyes; open/closed mouth with painted teeth; original, tagged cowboy outfit; "Gene Autry" pin and "Terri Lee" label; typically marked "Terri Lee/Pat. Pending" on back.

Mary Jane: identical copy of Terri Lee; walker; sleep eyes; similar facial molding; original tagged "Mary Jane" costume; typically unmarked.

Terri Lee Family Value Comparisons

Size	Composition Terri Lee	Hard Plastic/ Vinyl Terri Lee	Gene Autry	Jerri Lee, Lambs-Wool Wig	Patti Jo	Benji, Bonnie Lu, or Other Friends	Nanook Eskimo	Tiny Terri Lee	Tiny Jerri Lee
10"								500.00	450.00
16"	700.00	800.00	3,700.00	900.00	1,600.00	1,000.00	2,000.00		

Size	Connie Lynn Baby	Mary Jane Sleep Eyes Copy	Vinyl So-Sleepy	Vinyl Baby Linda Lee
9 1/2"			300.00	
10"				300.00
17"		350.00		
19"	800.00			

A. Thuillier

Closed mouth A. Thuillier Bébé. Courtesy of Ellen Schroy

A. Thuillier, a.k.a. A. T., first appeared in the Paris annual register as a doll maker in 1875 and remained as such until 1893. Records indicate that François Gaultier provided at least some of the bisque heads used by Thuillier.

An interesting, and puzzling, circumstance surrounds a fashion type doll with a body labeled: "A. De La Thuillier (Thuilerie) Grand Magasin de Jouet Rue St. Honore' 366 Paris, English Spoken." An A. T. Fashion type! Perhaps Thuillier manufactured fashion-type dolls so rare that no conclusive evidence has surfaced; or a doll hospital furnishing parts labeled with the Thuillier name, or possibly Thuillier supplied Gaultier with bodies. It is such mysteries that entice and fascinate doll collectors.

Reproduction A. T. dolls do surface from time to time, whether originally intended to deceive or made purely for the enjoyment of the doll maker is unknown. Carefully examine the marking. An authentic A. T. doll will be incised with the initials "A. T." and a size number only. Thuillier bébés are made of very good, but not silky-smooth, bisque. An obvious clue may be in the size number. Reproductions tend to be one or more inches shorter than the incised number would indicate, for example #1 = 9"; #3 = 12"; #4 = 13"; #7 = 15 1/2"; #9 = 18"; #12 = 22 1/2" and #15 = 36 1/2".

Prices listed are for beautifully dressed dolls in good condition. Normal wear, slight damage, or well-made repairs to the body do not greatly affect the price. If the bisque is damaged or repaired, expect the value to be about half the amounts listed. It is perfectly acceptable to show a missing or repaired finger or joint or a mended body.

Early Closed Mouth Bébé: pale bisque socket head; jointed wood and composition French or kid body; good wig; cork pate; beautiful paperweight eyes, finely lined in black; short, thick, black lashes; delicate pink shadowed eye lids; softly feathered wide spaced brows; pierced ears; closed mouth with high cupid's bow and slight smile; appropriately dressed; marked "A. T."/size number only.

Later Closed Mouth Bébé: pale bisque socket head; jointed wood and composition French or kid body; good wig; cork pate; beautiful paperweight eyes, finely lined in black; long thick black lashes; somewhat heavy feathered brows; pierced ears; closed mouth; appropriately dressed; marked "A. T."/size number only.

Open Mouth Bébé: bisque socket head; jointed wood and composition French body; good wig; beautiful paperweight eyes; feathered brows; pierced ears; slightly open mouth with upper and lower teeth; appropriately dressed; marked "A. T."/size number only.

Open mouth A. Thuillier Bébé, note the two rows of teeth. Courtesy of David Cobb's Doll Auctions

A. T. Value Comparisons			
Size	Early Closed Mouth	Later Closed Mouth	Open Mouth
9"	37,000.00	22,000.00	
12"	39,000.00	22,000.00	
15 1/2"		28,000.00	
18"	48,000.00	30,000.00	14,000.00
22 1/2"	63,000.00	35,000.00	16,000.00
28"	73,000.00	42,000.00	
36 1/2"			29,000.00

Uneeda Doll Company

Uneeda Doll Company, founded in 1917 in New York, was also known as the Tony Toy Company of Hong Kong.

Since its inception, Uneeda has produced thousands of popularly priced dolls made from cloth, composition, hard plastic, and vinyl. The company's success in the doll industry was due to its production of good-quality dolls at competitive prices. Uneeda supplied jobbers, mail-order houses, and department stores with a complete line of well-made play dolls. Almost every little girl owned at least one Uneeda Doll.

By the 1930s, Uneeda was advertising over 400 different models of dolls, ranging in size from 14 to 28 inches. The dolls featured molded hair or wigs and painted or sleep eyes. Uneeda's Dollikins were probably the finest fully-jointed hard plastic dolls ever made. Dollikins featured a unique body construction jointed at the neck, shoulder, upper arms, elbows, wrists, waist, hip, knees, and ankles. The joints were hidden and allowed the doll to be gracefully posed in almost any position. Uneeda also advertised a "Magic Muscle" doll, which walked by means of a weighted, screw-type apparatus in its torso.

Uneeda Dolls are often found unmarked. Without their original wrist tags or boxes, they are virtually impossible to identify. Markings include "Uneeda" within a diamond, "Uneeda," "U," or "UN."

32" original Uneeda Pollyanna. Courtesy of David Cobb's Doll Auctions

This twentieth-century doll manufacturer is still producing play dolls. Born from the need for American-made dolls during World War I, Uneeda has proven that high quality and a fair price will be rewarded with success. Over the years, Uneeda has provided the world with many highly-collectible dolls, including personality dolls, babies, toddlers, mama dolls, boy dolls, and glamorous lady dolls.

Composition

Prices listed are for appropriately costumed dolls in good condition. Slight crazing is acceptable and does not greatly affect the price. If badly crazed, cracked, peeling, or repainted, expect the value to be less than half the amounts listed.

Rita Hayworth as Carmen: 14"; all composition; jointed at neck, shoulder, and hip; red, mohair wig; sleep eyes; exceptionally long lashes; gray eye shadow; closed mouth; original red dress with black lace overskirt and matching mantilla with silk flowers decorating both dress and scarf; gold shoes; typically unmarked; gold, fan-shaped wrist tag "The Carmen Doll/W. I. Gould & Co., Inc. Mfrd. by Uneeda Doll Co.,/Inspired by/Rita Hayworth's/Portrayal of Carmen/in/The Loves of Carmen." $600.00

Baby Sweetheart: 17"; all composition; jointed at neck, shoulder, and hip; deeply molded hair; sleep eyes; open mouth with metal tongue and two upper teeth; appropriately dressed; typically unmarked; hang tag "Everybody Loves Baby Sweetheart/Produced by Uneeda Doll Co." $500.00

Hard Plastic and Vinyl

Prices listed are for dolls in near-mint, original condition. If damaged, redressed, or undressed, expect the value to be less than one half to one fourth the amounts listed.

Tiny Time Teens: 5"; pose-able vinyl head; plastic body; rooted hair; painted features with real lashes; marked "U.D. Co. Inc./1967/Hong Kong." There are several dolls in this series, including Fun Time, Beau Time, Bride Time, Winter Time, Date Time, Party Time, Vacation Time, and Prom Time $45.00

American Gem Collection: 8 1/2"; rooted hair; painted features; nicely dressed; marked "U.D. Co. Inc./MCMLXXI/Made in Hong Kong" on head and body. Dolls include Georgia, Carolina, Patience, Prudence, Priscilla, and Virginia.....................$45.00

Little Sophisticates: 8 1/2"; mod dolls; vinyl head; plastic body; long, thin, vinyl arms; rooted hair; closed eyes with eye shadow; typically marked "Uneeda Doll Co. Inc./1967/Made in Japan" on head and back. Dolls include Kristina, Marika, Rosanna, Penelope, and Suzana...$35.00

Baby Sleep Amber: 11"; black vinyl head, arms, and legs; cloth body; rooted, black hair; sleep eyes; marked "Tony Toy/1970/Made in Hong Kong"...$25.00

Pri-Thilla: 12"; all vinyl; bent left arm; rooted hair; sleep eyes; open mouth; sucks thumb and blows up balloons; marked "4" on head...$75.00

Baby: 16"; all vinyl; rooted hair; sleep eyes; open, nurser mouth; marked "3TD11/Uneeda." $65.00

Magic Fairy Princess: vinyl head; hard plastic body; jointed at neck, shoulder, hip, and knees; rooted, pink hair; sleep eyes; closed mouth; original fairy costume of white satin top, white net tutu with glitter, plastic wings, and silver slippers; typically marked "Uneeda" on head, "210" on body.

18"	$200.00
32"	250.00

Janie: 8"; vinyl head; hard plastic body; rooted hair; sleep eyes; appropriately dressed; typically marked "U" $135.00

Original Girl Scout or Brownie costume
.... $250.00

Dollikins: vinyl head; hard plastic body; uniquely jointed at neck, shoulder, upper arms, elbows, wrists, waist, hip, knees, and ankles; rooted hair; sleep eyes; real lashes; pierced ears; closed mouth; polished fingernails and toenails; appropriately dressed; typically marked "Uneeda/25" on head.

8"	$100.00
12"	150.00
19"	250.00

Glamour Lady Bride Doll: 20"; vinyl head; hard plastic walker body; jointed at neck, shoulder, and hip; rooted hair; sleep eyes; real lashes; tiny, painted lower lashes; closed mouth;

original, bride gown with lace veil; marked "3" (in circle) "Uneeda" $85.00

Country Girl: 22"; vinyl head; hard plastic walker body; jointed at neck, shoulder, and hip; rooted hair; flirty, sleep eyes; real lashes; tiny, painted lower lashes; closed mouth; original, white and yellow, polka-dot dress and matching hat; marked "Uneeda" on head..$150.00

Toodles: 21"; vinyl head; hard plastic walker body; jointed at neck, shoulder, and hip; rooted hair; sleep eyes; real lashes; tiny, painted lower lashes; wide open/closed mouth; molded tongue; wearing original, soft cotton corduroy coat with lace trim and fabric flower corsage and matching hat; marked "Uneeda" on head...$175.00

Needa Toodles: 22"; hard plastic head; very unusual body with composition upper arms and legs; vinyl lower arms and legs; weighted, screw-type apparatus in torso causes doll to walk; saran wig; sleep eyes, real lashes; open/closed mouth; two upper teeth; hint of dimples; original dress and matching bonnet; marked "20" on head..$150.00

50th Anniversary Antebellum Southern Belle: 25"; all vinyl; rooted hair; sleep eyes; long lashes; eye shadow; closed mouth; marked "8/Uneeda Doll Co./1967" $125.00

Pollyanna: vinyl head; hard plastic jointed body; very blond, rooted hair; sleep eyes with lashes; eye liner; open mouth; painted teeth; marked "Walt Disney Prod./Mfd By Uneeda/ N.F."

11" $100.00
17" 125.00
31" 400.00

Freckles: 32"; vinyl head; hard plastic body; jointed at neck, shoulder, hip, and wrists; unique finger position; rooted hair; large, flirty, sleep eyes with lashes; freckles across nose and cheeks; open/closed mouth; four molded and painted upper teeth; original nylon dress with fitted waist and sash........$200.00

Saranade: 21"; vinyl head; hard plastic and vinyl body; rooted hair; sleep eyes; closed mouth; original, red and white cotton dress; marked "Uneeda Doll/1967"; phonograph and recorder with speaker in tummy...$250.00

Unis

𝒰nis is an acronym for the Union National Inter Syndicale, a mark found on various French dolls produced by Société Française de Fabrication de Bébés & Jouets (S.F.B.J.). These initials are often found within an oval and accompanied by numbers. The number to the left of the Unis mark represents the syndicale number (e.g. 71 was the number assigned to Chambre Syndicale). The number to the right of the Unis mark represents the manufacturer (e.g. 149 was the number assigned to S.F.B.J.). The number beneath the Unis mark represents the mold number (e.g. 60 or 301). You will notice that the Unis dolls have a slightly lower value than the S.F.B.J. dolls with the same mold numbers. This is because the later bisque dolls were usually made from a lesser-quality bisque than the earlier S.F.B.J. dolls. Facial decoration is also usually less detailed.

The Bluette booklet was first issued in 1916 and came out twice a year. It published patterns and advertised commercially made costumes for the Bluette doll, which incidentally frequently bore the Unis mark. Publication continued until 1960.

Bisque

Prices listed are for appropriately costumed dolls in good condition. Normal wear, slight damage, or well-made repairs to the body do not greatly affect the price. If the bisque is damaged or repaired, expect the value to be less than half the amounts listed. It is perfectly acceptable to show a missing or repaired finger or joint, or a mended body.

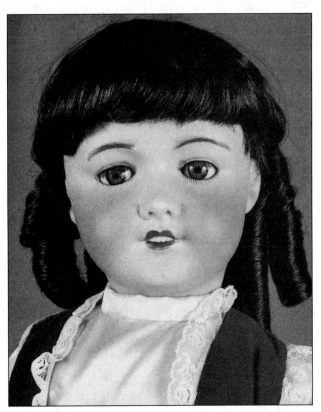

27" bisque "301 / 149" Unis France child doll. Courtesy of McMaster's Doll Auction

Bluette: bisque socket head; jointed composition body; good wig, styled in long braids; blue, stationary, glass, side-glancing eyes (not googly eyes); open mouth; appropriately dressed; typically marked "71/Unis" within an oval "/149/301"; hang tag "Marque Déposée Bluette 18 Rue Jacob Paris Vie."

Child: bisque socket head; jointed composition body; good wig; glass eyes; open mouth; appropriately dressed; typically marked "71/Unis France" within an oval "/149/301."

Princess Elizabeth: bisque socket head; jointed composition body; blond, mohair wig; glass eyes; open mouth; appropriately dressed; typically marked "71/Unis France" within an oval "/149/306/Jumeau/1938/Paris."

Composition

Composition dolls used the same molds as those used for bisque dolls, such as mold numbers 60 and 301. They have similar features, jointed bodies.

Prices listed are for appropriately costumed dolls in good condition. Slight crazing is acceptable and does not greatly affect the price. If badly crazed, cracked, peeling, or repainted, expect the value to be less than half the amounts listed.

Size	Bluette	Child*	Black Child	Princess Elizabeth	Composition Unis Doll
8"		550.00	600.00		
10"	1,200.00	600.00			
11"	1,400.00		700.00		
13"		700.00			
14"					350.00
15"		900.00	1,000.00	1,700.00	
16"					400.00
17"		1,100.00			
18"					500.00
20"				1,900.00	600.00
21"		1,300.00			
22"					700.00
23"		1,500.00			
24"				3,000.00	850.00
25"		1,600.00			
28"				3,200.00	
29"		1,700.00			

*Deduct $100.00 for painted eyes.

Van Rozen

J. Van Rozen, a Belgian refugee, designed doll heads in Paris, probably around 1910-1914. During World War I, Van Rozen escaped the political upheaval of her native Belgium for the safety offered in the avant-garde art communities of Paris. Noted for her bronze and terra cotta animal sculptures, her talents also included creating the most extraordinary character dolls known for their distinctively realistic expression. The dolls are so very rare that it is assumed she created them for special commissions only.

There is a haunting similarity between Van Rozen character faces and dolls produced by De Fussaeux in Belgium, just prior to World War I. To date, however, no connection has been established.

Van Rozen dolls are pressed, not poured, bisque-like ceramic. The modelling is superb with a great deal of attention to realism. A distinctive nose and chin line forms a unique profile, a characteristic overlooked by other doll makers. Eye cuts are somewhat slanted, and for lack of a better word, crinkled at the corners. Dolls are well marked with the Van Rozen name.

La Maison Bassier and La Maison Rowyaud served as Van Rozen's agents and distributed her dolls.

Prices listed are for appropriately costumed dolls in good condition. Normal wear, slight damage, or well-made repairs to the body do not greatly affect the price. If the bisque is damaged or repaired, expect the value to be less. A Van Rozen character is so rare and desirable, serious collectors will forgive fine hairlines or professional repairs that do not jeopardize the integrity of the doll. The price should reflect the degree and extent of damage. It is perfectly acceptable to show a missing or repaired finger or a mended body.

Van Rozen Character: course, chalky-feeling bisque-like ceramic socket head; jointed wood and composition French body; character modelling with fine detailing; good wig; glass eyes; feathered brows; closed or open/closed expressive mouth; appropriately costumed; marked "Van Rozen/France/Déposé."

Van Rozen Character Value Comparisons

Size	Van Rozen Character	Van Rozen Black Character
14"	18,000.00	22,000.00
17"	20,000.00	

Wonderful 17" Van Rozen character. Courtesy of Strong Museum, Rochester, NY.

Vogue Dolls, Inc.

*V*ogue Dolls was founded by Jennie H. Graves in Somerville, Massachusetts, shortly after Word War I. Graves never dreamed that her modest doll costuming business would grow to be the largest doll-only manufacturer in the world.

Originally intent on supplementing the family income, Graves set out to design and make doll clothing. After convincing several department stores to purchase her merchandise, she and her neighbors started designing and sewing doll clothing. The business' sole enterprise remained the production of doll clothing until the mid 1930s. Graves then decided to buy undressed quality bisque dolls from German manufacturers, design clothing for them, and then sell her creations at shops across the country. Graves' specially costumed dolls often retailed for $75.00 or more—an excessive price for a doll at that time. The political climate in Europe during the late 1930s forced Graves to look to the United States for her doll supply.

In 1948, the famous Ginny-type doll was born. The original miniature doll was an instant success, proving to be one of the most enduring little dolls of all time, originally introduced as a composition doll, known as "Toddles."

The darling little charmers wore a wide variety of well-made little girl outfits. Every year new outfits were added, including foreign and fantasy costumes. Early Toddles costumes had ribbon closures at the back of the garments. Later fashions closed with hooks and eyes. The earliest garments were not tagged. Later clothing had a cloth "Vogue" label. Very rarely, an original, round, paper "VOGUE" label is found attached to a garment. The dolls wore various styles of shoes, including slip-on pumps, center or side snap shoes, and Mary Janes from several colors of leatherette.

Vogue began producing hard plastic dolls in 1948. The first had painted, turquoise-blue eyes, looking to the left; wide-spaced upper lashes; and white highlights. In 1950, Ginny was given blue or brown sleep eyes with painted, wide-spaced lashes. In 1954, Ginny learned to walk while turning her head from side to side. In 1955, the sleep eyes were given molded lashes; and in 1957 knee joints were added.

Any doll as popular as Ginny needed a family. This may not seem unusual today, living in the world of Barbie and her extended family and friend list, but the idea of companion dolls during the 1950s was a novel idea.

Ginny's family included baby Ginnette, two teenage sisters, Jill and Jan, big brother Jeff, and baby brother Jimmy. Each version had its own wardrobe and accessories.

7" hard plastic painted lash Ginny with original box, in near mint condition. Courtesy of McMaster's Doll Auction

Over the years, Vogue diversified by introducing many new dolls, but production of Ginny Dolls remained constant. The perseverance may in part explain the dramatic increase in Ginny's collectible status.

Copies of the famous Ginny Dolls are numerous. Ginny is probably one of the most often-copied dolls ever produced. All Ginny Dolls were well marked, and a careful examination should ensure that you are purchasing an authentic Vogue's Ginny.

Bisque

Prices listed are for orginally costumed dolls in good condition. Normal wear, slight damage, or well-made repairs to the body do not greatly affect the price. If the bisque is damaged or repaired, expect the value to be less than half the amounts listed. It is perfectly acceptable to show a missing or repaired finger or joint, or a mended body.

Just Me: bisque socket head; jointed composition body; mohair wig; glass eyes; closed mouth; original tagged or untagged outfit; typically marked "Just Me A. M.," "A. M. 310/ 11 Just Me," or round hang tag "Vogue."

Vogue Bisque Value Comparisons

Size	Just Me	Painted Bisque Just Me
8"	1,900.00	1,400.00
9"	2,400.00	
11"	2,900.00	1,900.00
13"	3,700.00	

Composition

Prices listed are for dolls in good condition, costumed in their original tagged outfits. Slight crazing is acceptable and does not greatly affect the price. If badly crazed, cracked, peeling, or repainted, expect the value to be less than half the amounts listed.

Toddles: 8" all composition; jointed at neck, shoulder, and hip; mohair wig; large, round, painted eyes; closed mouth; original tagged outfit; typically marked "Vogue" on head, "Doll Co," or "Vogue" on back...$400.00

Child: all composition; jointed at neck, shoulder, and hip; good wig; sleep eyes; real lashes, with or without eye shadow; open mouth; appropriately dressed; typically marked "13," "15," or "20," or unmarked; paper tag reads "Vogue Dolls, Inc/Medford, Mass."

13"	$600.00
15"	700.00
20"	900.00

Hard Plastic & Vinyl

Prices listed are for dolls in near-mint, original condition. If damaged, redressed, or undressed, expect the value to be less than one half to one fourth the amounts listed.

#1 Ginny: 1948–1950; all hard plastic; jointed at neck, shoulder, and hip; molded hair under mohair wig; painted, side-glancing eyes; closed mouth; original, tagged outfit; typically marked "Vogue" on head and "Vogue Doll" on back; clothing tagged "Vogue Dolls."

#2 Ginny: 1950–1953; non-walker; all hard plastic; jointed at neck, shoulder, and hip; mohair wig with gauze strip forming cap of wig; sleep eyes; painted lashes; closed mouth; original, tagged outfit; typically marked "Vogue" on head and body; clothing tagged "Vogue."

#2 Ginny Poodle Cut: 1952 only; non-walker; all hard plastic; jointed at neck, shoulder, and hip; lamb's wool, bubble "Poodle" wig; sleep eyes; painted lashes; closed mouth; original, tagged outfit; typically marked "Vogue" on head and body; clothing tagged "Vogue."

#2 Ginny Fluffy Bunny: lamb's wool wig; original, tagged, fluffy bunny costume, complete with bunny ears.

#2 Crib Crowder Baby: bent-leg baby body.

#3 Ginny: 1954; straight-leg walker; all hard plastic; pin jointed; good wig; sleep eyes; painted lashes; closed mouth; original, tagged outfit; typically marked "Ginny" on head and "Vogue Dolls Inc./Pat #2687594/Made in USA" on body; clothing tagged "Vogue Doll."

#4 Ginny: 1955–1957; straight-leg walker; all hard plastic; pin jointed; good wig; sleep eyes; molded plastic upper lashes; closed mouth; original, tagged outfit; typically marked "Vogue" on head and "Ginny Vogue Dolls Inc./Pat. #2687594/Made in USA" on body; clothing tagged "Vogue Dolls."

#5 Ginny: 1957–1962; jointed-knee walker; all hard plastic; pin jointed; good wig; sleep eyes; molded plastic lashes; closed mouth; original, tagged outfit; typically marked "Vogue" on head and "Ginny Vogue Dolls Inc./Pat. #2687594/Made in U.S.A." on body; clothing tagged "Vogue Dolls Inc."

#6 Ginny: 1963; vinyl head; hard plastic body; rooted hair; sleep eyes; closed mouth; original, tagged outfit; typically marked "Ginny" on head and "Ginny Vogue Dolls Inc./Pat. No. 2687594/Made in U.S.A." on back; clothing tagged "Vogue Dolls Inc."

Modern Ginny: early 1970s; all vinyl; rooted hair; sleep eyes; closed mouth; original, tagged outfit; typically marked "GINNY" on head and "Vogue Dolls 1972/Made in Hong Kong/8" on body; clothing tagged "Made in Hong Kong."

Sassoon Ginny: 1978–1979; thin body and limbs.

Contemporary Ginny: made by Dankin.

Ginny Value Comparisons

Size	#1 Ginny Painted Eyes	#2 Ginny Sleep Eyes, Painted Lashes, Straight-Leg Non-Walker	#2 Ginny Poodle Cut	#2 Ginny Fluffy Bunny	#2 Ginny Crib Crow-der Baby	#3 Ginny Sleep Eyes, Painted Lashes, Straight-Leg Walker	#3 Ginny Black	#3 Ginny Queen	#4 Ginny Sleep Eyes, Molded Lashes, Straight-Leg Walker
8"	500.00	700.00	800.00	1,600.00	1,200.00	500.00	2,200.00	1,200.00	400.00

Size	#5 Ginny Sleep Eyes, Molded Lashes, Jointed-Knee Walker	#6 Ginny Vinyl Head, Rooted Hair	Modern Ginny, All Vinyl	Sassoon Ginny Painted Eyes	Sassoon Ginny Sleep Eyes	Contemporary Ginny
8"	300.00	200.00	100.00	75.00	65.00	30.00

Jill: all hard plastic; adult body; jointed at neck, shoulder, hip, and knees; high heel feet; saran hair; sleep eyes; molded lashes; pierced ears; closed mouth; appropriately dressed; typically marked "Vogue" on head and "Jill/Vogue Made in U.S.A. 1957" on body; clothing tagged "Vogue."

Li'l Imp: vinyl head; hard plastic, walker body; jointed at neck, shoulder, hip, and knees; dimples on back of hands; square arm hook is molded as part of arm (gently pull arm away from body to observe); orange hair; freckles; sleep eyes; open/closed mouth; appropriately dressed; typically marked "R & B" on head; clothing may or may not be tagged "Vogue."

Littlest Angel: vinyl head; hard plastic walker body; jointed at neck, shoulder, hip, and knees; rooted hair; sleep eyes; open/closed mouth; appropriately dressed; typically marked "R & B" on head; clothing may or may not be tagged "Vogue."

Child: all hard plastic; jointed at neck, shoulder, and hip; slender body; long legs; slightly bent arms; hands with first, second, and third fingers molded together; little finger molded separately; good wig; sleep eyes; real lashes; painted lower lashes; closed mouth; appropriately dressed; typically marked "14," "16," or other size number in inches on head and "Made in U.S.A." on back; clothing tagged "Vogue Dolls."

Jan: all vinyl; rigid body and limbs; jointed at neck, shoulder, swivel waist; high heel feet; rooted hair; sleep eyes; molded lashes; closed, smiling mouth; appropriately dressed; typically marked "Vogue" on head; clothing tagged "Vogue Dolls."

Jeff: vinyl head and limbs; plastic body; molded and painted hair; sleep eyes; molded lashes; appropriately dressed; typically marked "Vogue" on head; clothing tagged "Vogue Dolls."

Littlest Angel: all vinyl; bent-limb baby body; rooted hair; sleep eyes; real lashes; smiling, closed mouth; appropriately dressed; typically marked "Vogue Doll/1963" on head and back.

Angel Baby: all vinyl; bent-limb baby body; rooted strawberry blond hair; sleep eyes with lashes; smiling, closed mouth; appropriately dressed; typically marked "Vogue Doll/1965" on head.

Miss Ginny: all vinyl; jointed at neck, shoulder, and hip; teen body; rooted hair; sleep eyes; closed mouth; appropriately dressed; typically marked "Vogue Doll/1970"; clothing tagged "Vogue Dolls Inc."

Baby Dear: vinyl head and limbs; cloth body; rooted hair; painted eyes; closed mouth; newborn baby face; appropriately dressed; typically marked with cloth tag sewn into seam of body "Vogue Dolls, Inc." Back of left leg marked "E. Wilkins/1960."

Posie Pixie: vinyl head and gauntlet hands; cloth body; rooted hair; black, side-glancing eyes; open/closed mouth; appropriately dressed; typically marked "1964/Vogue/71" on head.

Ginny Baby: all vinyl; rooted hair; sleep eyes with lashes; open nurser mouth; appropriately dressed; typically marked "Ginny Baby/10/Vogue Doll Inc."

14" vinyl Baby Dear doll baby. Courtesy Vogue Dolls

Brickette: vinyl head and arms; plastic body; ball-jointed waist; long plastic legs; teen-type body; rooted hair; sleep/flirty eyes with lashes; smiling, closed mouth; appropriately dressed; typically unmarked. ***Note:*** *1961 original Brickette was issued in 16" and 22" sizes. It was reissued in 1980 in 18" size only.*

Note: *Several Vogue Dolls were original Arranbee Dolls. Vogue purchased Arranbee in 1957, but the dolls continued to be marked and sold as Arranbee until as late as 1961.*

Vogue Hard Plastic & Vinyl Value Comparison

Size	Jill	Jan	Jeff	Li'l Imp	Child	Littlest Angel	Angel Baby	Miss Ginny	Baby Dear	Posie Pixie	Ginny Baby	Brickette
10"	300.00		200.00									
10 1/2"				250.00								
11"						200.00						
13"		200.00				275.00			225.00			
14"					450.00		100.00					
15"								95.00				
16"					600.00							200.00
17"										100.00		
18"					800.00				350.00			75.00
22"											300.00	300.00
25"					125.00							
27"									600.00			

W. P. A. Dolls

18" Mother Goose and Goose W. P. A. doll in original, near mint condition. Courtesy of McMaster's Doll Auction

W. P.A. art dolls were made in the United States during the 1930s. Under Franklin D. Roosevelt's New Deal, the Works Progress Administration (W.P.A.) allowed the United States government to become a doll manufacturer. The W.P.A. provided work for artists and seamstresses struggling during the Depression. The objective of the project was to create cloth dolls representing characters from fairy tales and folklore, and historical figures from both the United States and various foreign countries. With the exception of Japan, most countries of the world were included. Japan's omission was undoubtedly due to strained international relations during that period in history. Completed dolls were loaned to major department stores for displays and to elementary schools to be used as visual aids.

Most of the dolls were approximately 12" tall and had cotton stuffed bodies. Torsos were made from four pieces of material. Three of the seams ran the entire length of the body; the front seam stopped at the neck. The separate arms were hand sewn to the body, but the legs were typically part of the body. The soft cotton stuffing made the doll's limbs flexible. Hands were mitten-shaped and generally without finger stitching. The yarn wigs were individually styled according to the character. Portrait printing techniques gave the flat faces a sculptured look. The head, neck, and arms were covered with flesh-colored oil paints. Legs and feet were not painted but were covered with stockings and shoes. Because each doll was hand crafted, variations did occur.

The quality, condition, artist's skill, and visual appeal make equally significant contributions to the value of a W.P.A. doll.

Prices listed are for appropriately costumed dolls with good color and little or no fading. Slight wear and signs of aging, such as a settled body, do not greatly affect the price. If a doll is stained, torn, badly mended, or faded, expect the value to be less than half the amounts listed.

Child/Adult: painted features; yarn hair; dressed appropriately for the character it represents; typically marked "Michigan W.P.A. Toy Project," "W.P.A. Museum Project Wichita," "Museum Project 1865 W.P.A.," "W.P.A. Toy Project, sponsored by Michigan State College," "W.P.A.," or "WPA Handicraft Project Milwaukee, Wisconsin."

Fairy Tale Character Set: cloth; yarn hair; oil-painted features. Examples include Mary and Her Lamb, Red Riding Hood and the Wolf, and Mother and Three Little Kittens; typically marked the same as child/adult above.

Nationality Doll and Famous Figures: all cloth; oil-painted features; examples include Denmark Couple, George and Martha Washington, and Paul Revere; typically marked the same as child/adult above.

Special Display Doll: all cloth; painted stockinette shoulder head; jointed at shoulder and hip; oil-painted features; hands stitched with fingers and separate thumb; yarn hair; typically marked the same as child/adult above.

W.P.A. Doll Value Comparisons

Size	Fairy Tale One Character	Fairy Tale Two to Three Characters	Fairy Tale Four or More Characters	Nationality Dolls	Famous Characters	Special Display Dolls
12"–18"	500.00–600.00	800.00–1,200.00 (Set)	2,000.00+ (Set)	200.00–300.00	400.00+	
22"–24"						2,000.00+

Wagner & Zetzsche

The company was founded by Richard Wagner and Richard Zetzsche, both of whom worked for Naumann Fischer before starting their own business on the first day of 1875 in Illmenau, Thüringia, Germany. Of the two partners, Zetzsche was the artist, responsible for designing and sculpting the dolls. Wagner was the practical one with the business sense. Four of the Zetzsche grandchildren—Harald, Hansi, Inge, and Barbele—were used as models for dolls.

Wagner & Zetzsche made doll bodies of cloth, leather, papier-mâché, and imitation leather. Numerous accessories, including more than 400 different designs of shoes, doll stockings, and wigs, were also made. Many of the marked Wagner & Zetzsche kid bodies are found with fine-quality bisque or china heads. Heads were supplied by Alt, Beck & Gottschalck, Buschow & Beck, Gebrüder Heubach, Armand Marseille, and possibly other manufacturers.

Around 1916, Wagner & Zetzsche acquired, from P. R. Zierow, of Berlin, the patent for a composition material and process called "Haralit". The material is often described as both a celluloid- and composition-like material. In truth, the material is more characteristic of composition. The character dolls of Harald, Inge, and Hansi were introduced as Haralit Art Dolls that same year. The company was in operation until at least 1938, as is evidenced by its advertisements of leather doll bodies.

Bisque

Prices listed are for appropriately costumed dolls in good condition. Normal wear, slight damage, or well-made repairs to the body do not greatly affect the price. If the bisque is damaged or repaired, expect the value to be less than half the amounts

17" closed mouth Wagner & Zetzsche #639. Courtesy of David Cobb's Doll Auctions

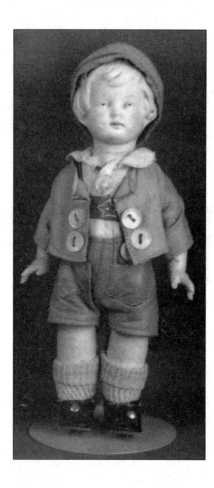

8" Hansi character doll of Haralit by Wagner & Zetzsche. Courtesy of David Cobb's Doll Auctions

listed. It is perfectly acceptable to show a missing or repaired finger or joint, or a mended body.

Closed Mouth: bisque turned shoulder head; kid body; good wig; glass eyes; feathered brows; closed mouth; appropriately dressed; typically marked with elaborately intertwined "W & Z," "639," "698."

Dolly-Face: bisque socket or shoulder head; jointed composition or kid body; good wig; glass eyes; open mouth; appropriately dressed; typically marked "WuZ," "10586," and "10585."

Haralit

Depending upon the condition, originality, and visual appeal of a Haralit doll, its value may be much higher—perhaps twice the amount given.

Prices given are for appropriately dressed dolls in good condition.

Harald or Hansi: Haralit character socket head; oilcloth body; jointed composition arms; several body variations exist; molded and painted hair; painted eyes; closed mouth; appropriately dressed; typically marked "1/Hansi/W.Z.," "1/Harald/W.Z."

Inge: Haralit character; appropriately dressed; typically marked "Inge/W.Z."

Barbele: Haralit character; appropriately dressed; typically marked "Barbele/W.Z."

	Wagner & Zetzsche Value Comparison					
Size	Closed Mouth, Kid Body	Dolly-Face, Kid Body	Dolly-Face, Composition Body	Haralit Character Harald or Hansi	Haralit Character Inge	Haralit Character Barbele
12"		700.00	800.00		1,100.00	1,900.00
12 1/2"				900.00		
14"	2,500.00	750.00		1,100.00	1,400.00	2,200.00
16"		800.00	950.00			
18"		900.00	1,100.00			
20"		1,000.00	1,200.00			
22"			1,300.00			
24"	3,800.00		1,500.00			
26"	4,500.00					

Izannah Walker

*I*zannah Walker made early American primitive sculpture dolls in Central Falls, Rhode Island. The dolls have heavily oil-painted features on slightly sculptured faces. They bear an uncanny resemblance to children in American folk art paintings.

All agree that Izannah Walker Dolls are wonderful, but few agree exactly when the dolls were first made. In June of 1873, Izannah Walker applied for a patent for her "Rag Dolls." According to patent law, it was illegal for her to have made her dolls for more than two years prior to her application date. Despite this, other possible dates abound. Mrs. Sheldon of the Chase Doll Company reported in *Doll Collectors of America* that the first Izannah Walker Doll was made in 1855. In *Your Dolls and Mine*, Izannah Walker's great niece, Janel Johl, states that the first Walker Dolls were made in 1840 (page 40); 1845 (page 39); 1848 (page 37), and 1855 (page 41). One solid bit of evidence does exist. The 1865 Census of Rhode Islands lists: "Walker, Izannah F., born of American parentage in Bristol, Rhode Island, living in the village of Central Falls in the town of Smithfield, occupation Doll Maker." These mysteries are what makes doll collecting so fascinating. One special lady, Mrs. Monica Bessette, has devoted years to answering these questions. We wish her luck, for her sake as well as ours!

Legend tells how Izannah Walker struggled to perfect her dolls. One problem in particular was how to create a surface resistant to cracking or peeling. One night, coming out of a deep sleep, Izannah sat up in bed and heard a voice say "USE PASTE." It was after this vision that she obtained her patent for making dolls. The patent application described layering and pressing cloth treated with glue in a heated two-part mold. The body was then sewn, stuffed, and glued around a wooden armature. Hands and feet were hand sewn. The entire doll was then hand painted in oil colors. The hair was painted with corkscrew curls or finely brush-stroked, short, straight hair. Other characteristics include applied molded ears, carefully stitched fingers, and either bare feet with stitched toes or painted-on high-laced shoes.

The quaint and charming beauty of an Izannah Walker doll is only surpassed by its historical significance. Although there are many copies of the type of cloth doll made by Izannah Walker, it is impossible to counterfeit the patina and softly-aged look of an authentic doll. Craft persons attempt to "age" dolls with coats of lacquer that cracks; although appealing and decorative, they do not really duplicate the aged look of the Walker dolls. If in doubt, smell the doll. Copies will have a chemical odor.

Prices listed are for appropriately dressed dolls in fair to good condition. Normal wear with crazing and slight rubs will not affect price. If the doll is badly worn, cracked, peeling, or has been repainted, expect the value to be less than half the amount listed.

Parenthetically, an Izannah Walker doll in very good condition is so very rare that it would easily be valued at three to four times the amount listed.

Izannah Walker: cloth doll; oil painted covering; painted hair with soft wisps and tiny curls around the face; molded facial features; large, luminous eyes; applied or molded ears; closed, slightly-smiling mouth; appropriately dressed; typically marked "Patented Nov. 4th 1873" or unmarked.

Early 20" Izannah Walker doll. Courtesy of McMaster's Doll Auction

	Izannah Walker Value Comparisons	
Size	**Izannah Walker Early Unmarked**	**After 1873 Patent**
15"	19,000.00	8,000.00
17"	20,000.00	8,500.00
18"	22,000.00	9,000.00
20"	25,000.00	10,000.00
21"	27,000.00	11,000.00
24"	30,000.00	15,000.00

Wax Dolls

26" wax over composition. Courtesy of McMaster's Doll Auction

There are three types of Wax Dolls: Wax-Over Dolls; Poured-Wax Dolls; and Reinforced-Wax Dolls.

New collectors often wonder how to tell the difference between the three types of Wax Dolls. Some clues that may be of help in distinguishing the different types are:

	Wax-Over	Poured-Wax	Reinforced-Wax
1. Wax Color	Clear	Tinted	Tinted
2. Hair	Wig or Molded	Inserted	Wig
3. Eyelids	None	Molded	Molded
4. Degree of Realism	Low	High	High
5. Molded Hair/Hat	Often Found	None Known	None Known
6. Hollow Poured Limbs	No	Yes	No

The most frequently found problem with any wax doll is restoration. A network of minute age lines on an original surface is always more desirable than a newly re-waxed surface. If the surface is perfectly smooth with no cracks, dents, or scuff marks, chances are it has been re-waxed. After studying Wax Dolls you begin to recognize the worn patina that vintage dolls acquire.

Occasionally someone will try to "fix" a Wax Doll by re-melting it with hot spoons or a curling iron or by having the head re-

dipped. Attempts at restoration are easily detected. Look for dirt embedded in the wax, a sure sign that someone has been reworking the wax. A clear wax outer layer on a poured wax doll is another sign, as the original wax was tinted. When re-waxing a doll, clear wax is often used as a top, sealing coat.

Prices listed are for appropriately dressed dolls in good condition. Normal wear such as slight veins or well-made repairs to the body do not greatly affect price. If a doll is badly cracked, warped, damaged, or has been restored, repaired or re-waxed, expect the value to be less than half the amount listed. It is perfectly acceptable to show a missing or repaired finger or toe.

Also see Boudoir Dolls.

Wax-Over Dolls

Wax-Over Dolls were made by various companies in England, France, and Germany during the 1800s and into the early 1900s. While dolls of many different materials were waxed over, papier-mâché/composition was by far the most frequently used.

An article published in the February 1875 edition of *St. Nicholas* magazine describes the process as follows: "...a frightful looking object she is, with color enough for a boiled lobster. When she has received her color and got dry...she proceeds to the next operator who is the waxer. In the kettle is boiling clear white beeswax, and into it Miss Dolly has been dipped, and is being held up to drain. If she had been intended for a cheap doll, she would have received but one dip, but being destined to belong to the aristocracy of the doll world, she received several dips, each one giving her a thin coat of wax, and toning down her flaming complexion into the delicate pink you see. The reason she was painted so red...is that she may have the proper tint when the wax is on. And now comes the next process which is coloring her face. In this room is a long table with several workmen, each of whom does only one thing. The first one paints Miss Dolly's lips and sets her down on the other side of him. The net one takes her up and puts on her eyebrows. The third colors her cheeks. The fourth pencils her eyelashes, and so she goes down the table, growing prettier at every step..."

It is interesting to note that this 1875 writing referred to beeswax. By the 1880s, paraffin or ozocerite, a wax made from the residue of petroleum, was used. The presence of beeswax can usually be detected by its distinct odor. Although perhaps less appealing and not nearly as lifelike as the lovely Poured-Wax or even the Reinforced-Wax Dolls, the Wax-Over Dolls stood a much better chance of surviving undamaged.

By the end of the 19th century, the quality of Wax-Over Dolls began to deteriorate. Nevertheless, many of the later Wax-Over Dolls are quite charming in their simplicity.

Early "English Split-Head": made in Germany and England; round face, Wax-Over shoulder head; cloth body with short leather arms; hair inserted in split in top of head; glass or sleep eyes operated by wire protruding from body midsection; sweet, smiling, closed mouth; appropriately dressed; typically unmarked.

Molded Hair or Bonnet: Wax-Over shoulder head with molded hair and/or bonnet; cloth body with wood or Wax-Over

Wax-Over Value Comparisons

Size	Early English Split-Head	Molded Hair or Bonnet	Extraordinarily Elaborate	With Wig, Exceptional Quality	With Wig, Standard Quality	Singing	Two-Faced
10"		400.00		500.00	200.00		
12"	900.00			525.00	300.00		
14"	1,000.00	450.00		550.00	400.00		
16"	1,100.00	550.00	3,500.00	650.00	450.00		1,200.00
18"	1,300.00	600.00		700.00	500.00		
20"	1,400.00	650.00	3,700.00	750.00	525.00		
22"	1,500.00	700.00		800.00	550.00	2,200.00	
24"	1,600.00	800.00	4,500.00	900.00	600.00	2,600.00	
26"	1,700.00				650.00	3,000.00	
28"	2,000.00	900.00			700.00		
30"	2,200.00	1,000.00		1,100.00	750.00		
32"		1,100.00		1,200.00	800.00		
34"					850.00		
36"					1,000.00		
38"					1,200.00		

limbs; glass eyes; closed mouth; appropriately dressed; typically unmarked.

Extraordinarily Elaborate: intricately styled hair with ornamentation or elaborately-styled bonnet; glass eyes; closed mouth; appropriately dressed; typically unmarked.

With Wig: Wax-Over shoulder head; cloth body; wooden, Wax-Over, or china limbs; good wig; glass eyes; open or closed mouth; appropriately dressed; typically unmarked. ***Note:*** *May be of standard quality or exceptional quality. Exceptional quality dolls are heavily waxed and nicely decorated. Evaluate a wigged Wax-Over Doll carefully to assign value.*

Singing Doll: very pretty Wax-Over shoulder head; cloth body; kid arms; stitched fingers; good wig; glass eyes; closed mouth; music box in torso with push bellows mechanism; appropriately dressed; typically marked "William Webber/Patented 1882/(name of tune)."

Two-Faced Doll: (one sleeping and other crying, or one sleeping and other awake and smiling); Wax-Over shoulder head; molded bonnet hides one of the rotating head-faces; cloth body; Wax-Over limbs; insert glass eyes; closed mouth; appropriately dressed; typically unmarked or body may be signed "Bartenstein."

Poured-Wax Dolls

Wax Dolls were produced as early as the Middle Ages in Italy and other parts of Europe. The wax dolls produced in England during the 19th century are a particular favorite. Poured-Wax dolls are so lifelike that many shun them for being "too morbid." On the other hand, connoisseurs of fine Wax Dolls view them as having utter realism. By the mid-1800s, Wax Dolls were being produced as toys. While it is hard to believe that these exquisite creations were ever meant to be played with by children, their original price tags ensured that they could be owned by only the very privileged.

The time required to make a Poured-Wax doll was lengthy. First, a clay sculpture was crafted and a plaster of Paris mold was made. This was accomplished by burying the clay head halfway in sand and then pouring plaster over the top. When the mold hardened, it was removed from the sand. The procedure was repeated for the other half of the head. The wax, originally bees-

26" Lucy Peck poured wax doll, wired sleep eyes with heavy lids, inserted human hair. Courtesy of McMaster's Doll Auction

wax and later paraffin, was placed in a cloth sack and boiled in water. It was then skimmed and placed in another sack. This purifying process was repeated at least four or five times. Purified carnauba wax, with its high melting temperature, was then added to the paraffin for stability. The wax was then bleached by cutting it into strips and placing it on porcelain slabs in the sun. The wax had to be kept cool; therefore, the porcelain slabs floated on water in order to keep the wax from melting. This bleaching process took about a week. After bleaching, the wax was colored by boiling it with lead dyes or vermilion. The melted wax was then poured into heated molds. Molds had to be heated in order to prevent ridges from forming when the wax was initially poured into the molds. After a few seconds, the two mold halves were fastened tightly together, and turned and rotated so that the melted wax could evenly coat over the mold's entire internal surface. The molds were removed when the wax congealed. While the wax was still warm, glass eyes were inserted and the eyelids molded. Next, the features were painted and hair inserted. Finally, the completed head was attached to a cloth body with wax limbs.

Most Poured-Wax Dolls are unmarked; occasionally a doll was stamped or engraved with a signature. Some believe Poured-Wax Dolls have a "pugged" look. Whether marked or unmarked, pugged or not pugged, the lovely Poured-Wax Dolls are easily identified. The method used for attaching the hair, the finely molded eyelids, tinted wax, and well-defined Poured-Wax arms and legs are all obvious indications.

Poured-Wax: lifelike shoulder head with well-molded plate; cloth body; hollow, poured-wax, molded arms and legs; human or fine mohair wig; glass eyes; deeply-molded eyelids; closed mouth; appropriately dressed; typically unmarked, name engraved on shoulder plate, or body stamped "Montarari," "Pierrotti," "Marsh," "Peck," "Meech," Morrell," "Edwards," or "Cremer."

Poured-Wax Value Comparisons

Size	Exceptional Quality	Standard Quality
14"	1,700.00+	900.00
18"	2,200.00+	1,100.00
20"	2,600.00+	1,300.00
24"	3,500.00+	1,500.00
26"	3,700.00+	1,900.00
30"	4,200.00+	

Reinforced-Wax Dolls

Reinforced-Wax Head Dolls are generally accepted as having been made in Germany from about 1860 until 1890. They share many characteristics with Poured-Wax dolls. The method for making Reinforced-Wax heads begins with the Poured-Wax process. The head is then reinforced from within by means of a thin layer of plaster of Paris or with strips of cloth soaked in composition. The intention of this reinforcement is to give the head added strength. Don't confuse Reinforced-Wax with Wax-Over Dolls. An examination of the inside of the head would distinguish the two, but that is not always convenient or practical.

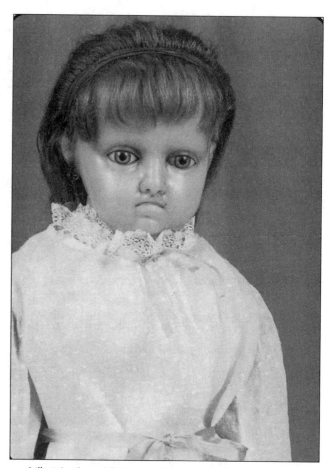

24" reinforced wax doll. Courtesy of McMaster's Doll Auction

Reinforced-Wax: very good to fair quality, shoulder head; cloth body; wax-over forearms; composition legs, molded and painted boots; good wig; glass eyes, molded lids; may have pierced ears; closed mouth; appropriately dressed; typically unmarked.

Reinforced-Wax Value Comparisons

Size	Very Good Quality	Fair Quality
12"		400.00
14"		450.00
16"	1,250.00	550.00
18"	1,600.00	
20"	1,800.00	700.00
24"	2,400.00	
26"		850.00

Norah Wellings

Norah Wellings was the chief designer at Chad Valley for several years, until she and her brother, Leonard, began manufacturing cloth dolls in 1926. The company, known as the Victoria Toy Works, was located in Arleston, England. Hundreds of different types of dolls portraying children, adults, fantasy characters, and ethnic groups were introduced. Made from excellent-quality velvet, velveteen, plush, and felt, these dolls ranged in height from 6 to 36 inches.

Most of Norah Wellings' dolls were marked with a cloth label sewn to the bottom of the foot. Occasionally the tag will be missing.

To help identify an unmarked Norah Wellings doll, look for these distinguishing characteristics:

1. The felt has a slightly rough feel.
2. Nicely painted, side-glancing eyes with one white dot in upper left-hand corner, or glass eyes.
3. Pale and slightly dotted, small eyebrows.
4. Small, heart-shaped mouth with thin red accent line.
5. Double-stitched ears.
6. Somewhat large hands with stitching indicating second and third fingers.
7. Seam on front and back of each leg.
8. No ankle seam.

Following the death of her brother in 1960, Norah closed the business and retired.

Prices listed are for originally costumed dolls with good color and little or no fading. Slight wear and signs of aging, such as a settled body, do not greatly affect the price. If a doll is stained, torn, badly mended, or faded, expect the value to be less than half the amounts listed.

Child: stockinette mask face; cloth body; jointed at shoulder and hip; felt arms and legs; mohair wig; painted or glass eyes; closed mouth; appropriately dressed; typically marked with cloth label; "Made in England/by/Norah Wellings."

Island Doll or Black Ethnic: all brown velvet; stitched at shoulder and hip; black mohair wig; painted, brown, side-glancing or glass eyes; wide, toothy, grinning mouth; appropriately dressed; typically marked with cloth label "Made in England/by/Norah Wellings."

Military: sculptured face; velvet body; mohair wig; painted, side-glancing or glass eyes; authentic military uniform; typically marked with cloth label "Made in England/by/Norah Wellings"; wrist tag "Force Comforts Committee an agreed percentage of the manufacturer's sales of the R.A.F. mascot doll is contributed to the Royal Air Comforts Fund."

Novelty Souvenir: stitched, long, thin, floppy limbs and over-sized hands; typically marked with cloth label "Norah Wellings/Wellington England." **Note:** *Thousands of these small dolls were sold around the world. Ocean liners, steamships, and gift shops offered Canadian Mounties, Little Pixie People, and tourist-type dolls.*

Norah Wellings Value Comparisons

Size	Child	Island or Black Character	Authentic Military	Novelty Souvenir
16"	900.00	450.00	550.00	
18"	1,000.00	500.00	600.00	
20"	1,100.00	550.00		
22"	1,200.00	600.00		
24"	1,400.00	700.00		
26"	1,600.00	800.00		
28"	1,800.00	900.00		
30"	2,200.00			
36"		1,400.00		

Add an additional $100.00–200.00 to any doll with glass eyes.

18" Norah Wellings felt mask child and 12" sculptured face sailor.
Courtesy of David Cobb's Doll Auctions

Norah Wellings Value Comparisons

Size	Child	Island or Black Character	Authentic Military	Novelty Souvenir
6"				150.00
8"				200.00
10"	600.00	300.00	350.00	250.00
12"	700.00	350.00	400.00	
14"	800.00	400.00	500.00	

Wilson Novelty Company

*I*n 1930, John Wilson founded the Wilson Novelty Company in Watsontown, Pennsylvania. The devastating effects of the Depression left this small central Pennsylvania town in desperate need. The old adage, "necessity is the mother of invention" was especially true in the creation of the little Wilson Walkies, also known as Watsontown Walkers. The little dolls had a tremendous responsibility placed upon their sloping shoulders, to save the small town, and that is exactly what they did!

Pair of Wilson Walkies. Courtesy of Bill Neff

The first Walkies were rather crude in design and appearance. They had cardboard cone bodies, pipe cleaner arms, and hand painted faces on a round wooden head. They were dressed in scraps of fabric and paper, and balanced in such a way that their wooden legs, moving inside the cone body, allowed them to walk along in a distinctive Walkie gait. Early Walkies were stamped "Made in U.S.A.," a mark that was used until 1938. Although the early Walkies were a bit short on quality, their charm and appeal were overwhelming. The company continued to grow and in the process refined the appearance of their walking Wilsons.

Walkies made between 1938 and 1940 were marked "Made in U.S.A. Pat. Pending." For a brief time in 1941, the mark was changed to "Made in U.S.A. Pat'd 12-18-40." By the mid-1940s, the Walkies could boast of nicely applied decal faces and wooden arms while retaining their cone bodies and wooden legs. At least twenty-five different characters were produced, ranging in height from three-inch animals with four legs to the rare, ten-inch characters. Included in their roster were the well-known Disney characters as well as King Features Syndicate's Popeye, Wimpy, and Olive Oyl. Also popular were the clowns, soldiers, sailors, bunnies, penguins, Santas, mammies, and many other wonderful characters. Walkies produced between 1940 and 1950 were marked "U.S. Patent Number 214027." Thanks, in part, to F. W. Woolworth's five and ten cents store marketing, the Wilson Novelty Company manufactured 13,000 Wilson Walkies a day. In 1949, just one year after the death of its founder, the Wilson Novelty Company was sold to a Canadian business; and in 1951, the production of the Walkies had come to an end.

Over the years, Wilson Novelty Company introduced several toys (such as a pop gun that shot out an American flag), but none could equal the popularity of the dear little walkers. Wilson Walkies have walked their way into the hearts of many collectors. Their happy faces and endearing waddle gaits are hard to resist.

Reproduction Wilson Walkies can be found. Hand crafted in similar fashion to the original Walkies, reproductions are brightly painted and marked on the foot with initials and possibly an eight-digit number.

Prices listed below are for dolls with no damage.

	Wilson Novelty Company Value Comparisons				
Size	Collectible Characters	Disney and Cartoon Characters	Military and Common Characters	Four-Legged Animals	Character Walkies
3"				300.00	
4"	200.00	300.00	150.00		
10"					500.00

Adolf Wislizenus

*I*n 1851, a doll and toy factory was founded by Gottlob Schafft in Waltershausen, Thur, Germany. In 1870, Adolf Wislizenus became a partner; by 1878 he was the sole owner.

In 1894, the company again changed ownership, when William Heincke became the new proprietor. Records indicate that in 1909 A. Wislizenus was owned by Hans Heincke, who retained ownership until the doll factory went into bankruptcy in 1931. König & Wernicke acquired the bankrupt estate. A. Wislizenus was a doll factory, not a porcelain factory; therefore, it was necessary for them to purchase their bisque doll heads elsewhere. Bähr & Pröschild, Simon & Halbig, and (after 1910) Ernst Heubach all supplied bisque heads for A. Wislizenus dolls.

It is believed that early in Adolph Wislizenus' ownership, he brought Jumeau's ball-jointed doll body to Waltershausen to study and adapt it for his own use. The Wislizenus factory eventually specialized in extraordinary ball-jointed bodies. Subsequent owners continued to improve designs. Several ingenious body types were registered; however, they are rarely found. This indicates that they were not overly popular at the time. One such doll body, DRGM 27 589, had an unusual construction with a somewhat long, thin torso with a molded rib cage and a diagonal hip joint, which allowed a full range of motion. Another unique body, DRGM 68 035, has a shapely torso with an indented waist and prominent rib cage. Upon closer inspection, it becomes evident that there are no ball joints showing. The elbows, although able to move in a natural manner, have the joint hidden within the upper arm. The hip joint is even more unusual, with the lower body coming down over the joints. The body construction allows a wide variety of lifelike movements.

A particularly confusing mark is the number "110" with a superimposed "5" over the "0." Many try in vain to determine whether their doll is actually a "110" or a "115" when in fact it is both.

Prices listed are for appropriately costumed dolls with good color and little or no fading. Slight wear and signs of aging, such as a settled body, do not greatly affect the price. If a doll is stained, torn, badly mended, or faded, expect the value to be less than half the amounts listed.

Dolly-Face: bisque socket head; jointed composition body; good wig; glass eyes; feathered brows; open mouth; unglazed porcelain teeth; appropriately dressed; typically marked "A. W. Special/Germany" or "A. W. Heubach-Kopplesdorf Germany."

Unique-Bodied Child: bisque socket head; unusual composition body; long, thin torso, concealed joints; good wig; glass eyes, heavily feathered brows; open mouth; appropriately dressed; typically marked "252 dep," "B. P. 289," or "S.H./A.W."

Character Baby: bisque socket head; composition bent-limb baby body; good wig; glass or painted eyes; open mouth; appropriately dressed; typically marked "A. W. Germany."

110 Character Baby: bisque socket head; jointed composition body; solid dome; painted hair; painted or glass eyes; defined eye lids; open/closed mouth with two molded upper teeth; appropriately dressed; typically marked "110. (5 superimposed over 0) Germany," body stamped "AW/W/DR6M421481."

24" Adolf Wislizenus, #110 solid dome character boy with open-closed mouth, molded teeth, intaglio eyes. Courtesy of David Cobb's Doll Auctions

Adolf Wislizenus Value Comparisons

Size	Child Dolly-Face	Unique-Bodied Child	Character Body	110/5 Character Painted Eyes	110/5 Character Glass Eyes
12"	500.00				
15"			550.00	1,800.00	4,800.00
16"	700.00				
18"			700.00		5,600.00
20"	750.00		1,000.00	2,500.00	
22"			1,600.00		
24"	900.00	3,000.00	1,700.00	3,100.00	
26"			2,100.00		8,000.00
28"	1,400.00				

Wooden Dolls

*A*nyone can pick up a stick and make a doll. Early English and German wooden dolls were handmade by unknown craftsmen. Accurately documented dolls from the 1600s have been reported; however, fewer than thirty of these early treasures are known to exist. Later wooden dolls of the 18th century, although far from common, are more plentiful.

Many early Wooden Dolls have remained in families where they have been passed down through generations as priceless treasured heirlooms. One such example is the Letitia Penn Doll. William Penn, then proprietor of Pennsylvania, brought this famous little Wooden Doll to America from Europe. His daughter, Letitia, presented it as a gift to Miss Rankin, the daughter of a Quaker friend. This doll is presumed to have resided in the United States longer than any other doll. She has stood as a silent witness to what must have been some intriguing times.

Another famous doll makes her home in a museum in Salisbury, England. She is a perfectly preserved Wooden Doll that belonged to Marie Antoinette. Remarkably, this doll still has her entire ensemble—made by Marie Antoinette while she sat in prison awaiting execution in 1793.

There are many fine examples of beautifully carved Wooden Dolls from Germany and Switzerland. Generally, Wooden Dolls have had a retrograde development, having declined, rather than improved, in quality. The crude peg Wooden Dolls made until quite recently give evidence to this statement.

Reproductions, or copies, are rather common with Wooden Dolls. Often, these copies are made for pleasure by a craftsperson, and therefore are not intended to be fraudulent. The modest price that most Wooden Dolls carry also makes the work and risk involved in reproduction rather pointless. Of course, early English William and Mary and Queen Anne-type Wooden Dolls are far from modest in price, but the patina of an authentic example is difficult, if not impossible, to duplicate. This knowledge, coupled with the fact that the earliest wooden Dolls are so very rare that only reputable antique dealers would be likely to handle them, should allow you to feel secure in the purchase of older Wooden Dolls.

Prices listed are for dolls in good condition.

English

William and Mary: 1680–1720; carved, one-piece head and torso with unique facial expression; human hair or flax nailed to head for wig; painted almond-shaped eyes with little detail; single-stroke brows extend from curve of nose and end at outer corner of eye; well-defined nose, mouth, ears, and rosy cheeks; limbs attached by various pinning and jointing methods; upper arms usually made of bound linen; carved wooden lower arms and hands; separate fingers and thumbs; often detailed fingernails; upper and lower legs, usually wooden with well-carved toes; entire body covered with gesso base layer, delicately painted

Early English Wooden dolls.

with flesh color and varnished; dressed in fashionable period costume; unmarked.

Queen Anne: 1700–1750; more stylized, less individual appearance; great craftsmanship; one-piece head and body; linen upper arms nailed to shoulders; shaped bosom, very narrow waist; rounded fingers with fingernails; hips curved on each side to accommodate pegged tongue-and-groove joints; human hair or flax wig nailed to head; oval, almost egg-shaped head; bulbous glass or painted oval eyes; brows and lashes indicated by a series of dots; well-defined nose and ears; closed mouth; rosy cheeks; entire body covered with gesso base layer; painted, very pale flesh color and varnished; dressed in fashionable period costume; unmarked.

Georgian: 1750–1800; one-piece carved head and body; somewhat rounded head; torso has rounded chest, narrow waist, square-ish hips, and flat back; upper arms of linen stitched to torso through hole drilled in shoulders; lower arms and hands carved with separate flat fingers and thumbs, and covered in kid with fingers exposed; legs carved to fit into carved slots of hips with pegged tongue-and-groove joints; human hair or flax wig nailed to head; well-defined nose and mouth; inserted lozenge-shaped glass eyes; brows and lashes indicated by a series of dots; closed, small mouth; entire body covered with gesso base layer; painted, very pale flesh color and varnished; dressed in fashionable period costume; unmarked.

Early 19th Century: 1800–1840; carved, one-piece head and torso; base of torso forms a point; arms attached to body with piece of linen; legs carved to fit against either side of pointed torso; then pegged with one single peg going first through one leg, then torso, and into other leg; stitched flax or human hair wig glued to head; nicely painted facial features; painted, over-sized, oval-shaped eyes; single-stroke brows; no ears; closed mouth; dark, rosy cheeks; upper body and lower limbs covered with gesso layer; painted a flesh color and varnished; typically dressed in gown much longer than legs, often with matching bonnet; unmarked.

English Wooden Dolls Value Comparisons				
Size	William and Mary	Queen Anne	Georgian	Early 19th Century
14"	50,000.00	20,000.00	37,000.00	2,000.00
17"	65,000.00			
18"		22,000.00	6,000.00	
20"				4,600.00
24"		28,000.00	7,000.00	

German

Early to Mid-19th Century: 1810–1840; carved, one-piece head and torso; often with high or Empire waist; all wooden arms; tongue-and-groove joints applied to shoulders and elbows (despite the relatively unrefined workmanship, the joints are quite efficient), allowing easy mobility. Finishing techniques were less sophisticated than earlier English dolls, but faces reflect a more delicate look with carved and painted hair, at times in elaborate styles, with curls around the face and the important addition of a hair comb carved into the back of the head. (Collectors often speak of "yellow tuck comb" when they are referring to this particular characteristic.) The nose was most often a wedge inserted into the face and heavily painted, making it less obvious, but still somewhat sharp in appearance. Earrings were common as were closed mouths. The costly gesso base layer was entirely omitted, with heavy paint applied directly to the wood and only on exposed areas. Fashionably dressed in period costume. Unmarked.

Later 19th Century: 1840–1900; carved, one-piece head and torso; very similar to the Early to Mid-19th Century doll in body configuration and facial features; artist's application of facial decoration progressively deteriorated until, by the end of the century, the painting was quite crude; other noticeable changes include the elimination of the hair comb, and the hair styles tend to be less elaborate with perhaps only a bun or carved side curls; fashionably dressed in period costumes; unmarked.

Bohemian Wooden Doll: turned wooden head; kid joints arms and legs to carved, red-painted torso; small waist; spoon-like hands; carved nose; painted facial features; appropriately dressed; unmarked.

Late 19th Century: carved wooden shoulder head and limbs; cloth body; simple, carved hair style; painted eyes; closed mouth; appropriately dressed; unmarked.

Peg Wooden or Dutch Wooden: after 1900; simple construction; jointed and fastened with wooden pegs; sharp, little carved noses, protruding from simple, round faces; painted, black hair; painted facial feature; stick-type limbs; spoon-like hands; painted white lower legs; black shoes; appropriately dressed; unmarked.

Bébé Tout en Bois (Dolls All of Wood): 1900–1914; manufactured by F. M. Schilling, its subsidiary Rudolf Schneider, and possibly others. Nicely carved head, resembling dolly-faced or character baby; fully jointed wooden or cloth body with wooden arms and legs; good wig; glass eyes; painted brows and lashes; open mouth with teeth; appropriately dressed; typically marked with the trademark "Angle," a sticker in three languages "Tout Bois, Holz, All Wood," or unmarked.

Early German wooden doll.

German Wooden Dolls Value Comparisons

Size	Early to Mid-19th Century	Later 19th Century No Comb	Bohemian, Kid Joints, Red Torso	Late 19th Century Cloth Body	Peg Wooden or Dutch Wooden	Bébé Tout en Bois
8"	1,200.00	400.00				
9"				500.00		
12"	1,800.00	550.00		550.00	100.00	
14"						650.00
16"		700.00				900.00
17"				700.00		
18"	2,400.00					1,000.00
20"		900.00	850.00			1,200.00
22"	3,200.00					
24"			1,000.00	1,100.00		

Swiss

Early 1900s: socket head or shoulder head; beautifully carved with wonderfully expressive face; all wood or cloth body with wooden limbs; carved and painted hair, often with intricate detailing; painted eyes with tiny lines going through iris to look like threading, usually with reflective white dot in middle; closed mouth; often wearing regional costumes; typically stamped "Made in Switzerland," unmarked, or wrist tag only.

Swiss Wooden Dolls Value Comparisons

Size	Value
10"	350.00
12"	500.00
14"	750.00
18"	1,000.00
20"	1,200.00

Contemporary

Commercial or Factory made wooden dolls are comparatively rare. The best known are Anri, Dolfi, Raike, and Harold Nabber's Kids.

Prices listed are for dolls in original near-mint condition.

Anri: beautifully hand carved and painted; fully articulated; carved hair or good wigs; nicely dressed; typically marked "Anri" and production number; wrist tag with artist name/"St. Christina South Tyrol Italy."

Dolfi: beautifully hand carved and painted; similar in construction and appearance to Anri.

Raike: best known for his bears and other animals, Robert Raike also introduced a limited number of dolls; carved heads and limbs; cloth body; carved hair or good wig; insert or painted eyes; closed mouth; nicely dressed; typically marked "Robert Raikes/production number"; body labeled "Applause."

Size	Anri	Dolfi	Raike
12"			200.00
14"	500.00		250.00
16"		550.00	350.00

Nabber Kid: originally handmade by Harold Nabber while working as a pilot and merchant in Anchorage, Alaska; from 1988–1994 produced at his factory in Prescott, Arizona; happy, chubby-cheeked characters; fully articulated; large, painted eyes; adorable, child-like costumes; typically marked "Harold Nabber Original," "Nabber Kid," or other variations; hang tag "Nabber Kid" or "Wild Woods Baby."

Production Year	Nabber Kid	Value
1987	Molli	3,900.00
1988	Jake	1,500.00
	Max	1,200.00
1989	Ashley	1,000.00
	Millie	700.00
1990 *	Maurice	900.00
	Sussi	800.00
	Frieda	700.00
	Walter	600.00
1991 *	Peter	500.00
	Pam	500.00
	Darina	500.00
1992	Henry**	800.00
	Sami	400.00
	Samantha	400.00
	Freddi	400.00
	Amy	350.00
	Heide	450.00
1993	All characters	400.00

* Add an additional $300.00 for Arizona Finish (heavy satin finish).

** Add an additional $500.00 for special Diver Suit.

Manufacturer Mold Numbers

Mold numbers organized by chapter

Alexander Doll Company: none

Henri Alexandre: none

All-Bisque: 123; 124; 890; 891

Allied Imported: none

Alt, Beck & Gottschalk: 630; 639; 698; 772; 870; 882; 890; 894; 898; 911; 916; 938; 974; 978; 980; 989; 990; 996; 998; 1000; 1002; 1004; 1028; 1030; 1046; 1054; 1056; 1062; 1064; 1112; 1123; 1142; 1154; 1210; 1214; 1218; 1222; 1226; 1234; 1235; 1254; 1288; 1322; 1326; 1352; 1357; 1358; 1359; 1361; 1362; 1367

Amberg: 972; 973; 983

American Character: none

Max Arnold: none

Arranbee Doll Company: 210; 341; 351

Arrow Novelty Company: none

Artist Dolls: none

Automata: 1; 2; 3; 3000

Averill Manufacturing Company: 1005; 1386; 1402; 1714; 1717; 3653

Babyland Rag: none

Bähr & Pröschild: 201; 204; 207; 212; 213; 217; 219; 220; 224; 225; 226; 227; 230; 239; 244; 245; 247; 248; 251; 252; 253; 259; 260; 261; 263; 264; 265; 269; 270; 273; 275; 277; 278; 281; 283; 287; 289; 292; 297; 300; 302; 305; 306; 309; 313; 320; 321; 323; 324; 325; 330; 340; 342; 343; 348; 350; 374; 375; 376; 378; 379; 380; 381; 389; 390; 393; 394; 424; 425; 441; 482; 499; 500; 520; 525; 526; 529; 531; 535; 536; 537; 539; 541; 546; 549; 554; 557; 568; 571; 581; 584; 585; 587; 600; 604; 619; 620; 624; 640; 641; 643; 644; 645; 646; 678; 707; 799

Barbie: none

E. Barrois: none

Beecher Baby: none

Belton-Type: none

C.M. Bergmann: 612; 1916

Bing Brothers: none

George Borgfeldt & Co.: 251; 326; 327; 329; 1369; 1410; 1418; 1923

Boudoir Dolls: none

Jne Bru & Cie: none

Albert Brückner: none

A. Bucherer: none

Cabbage Patch Dolls: none

Cameo Doll Company: 71 (s)

Campbell Kids: 1910

Catterfelder Puppenfabrik: 200; 201; 207; 208; 217; 219; 220; 262; 263; 264; 270; 1100; 1200; 1357

Celluloid: none

Century Doll Company: 277; 281

Chad Valley, Ltd.: none

Martha Chase: none

China Heads: none

Cloth Dolls: none

Dewees Cochran: none

Columbian Dolls: none

Composition: none

Modern Collectible Dolls: none

Dean's Rag Book Co.: none

DEP Dolls: none

Doll House Dolls: none

Door of Hope Dolls: none

Cuno & Otto Dressel: 93; 1348; 1349; 1468; 1469; 1776; 1848; 1849; 1893; 1896; 1898; 1912; 1914; 1920; 1922; 2736

Eden Bébé: none

Eegee: none

Effanbee: 162; 166; 176; 172; 174

Eisenmann & Co.: none

Joel Ellis: none

J.K. Farnell & Company: none

French Bébé: none

French Fashion-Type: none

Ralph A. Freundlich, Inc.: none

Fulper Pottery Company: none

German Bisque: 50; 51; 101; 132; 136; 216; 223; 230; 806; 44611

E. Gesland: none

Godey Lady Dolls: none

William Goebel: 34; 73; 89; 120; 123; 124; 330; 350; 521

Googly-Eyed Dolls: 19; 47; 82; 83; 84; 85; 86; 87; 88; 111; 122; 131; 163; 165; 172; 173; 175; 178; 179; 180; 200; 208; 210; 217; 221; 222; 223; 240; 241; 242;

Shepard & Co. Philadelphia Baby: none

Rabery & Delphieu: none

Raggedy Ann & Andy: none

Ravca Dolls: none

Theodor Recknagel: 21; 22; 23; 24; 25; 26; 27; 28; 29; 30; 31; 32; 33; 34; 35; 37; 39; 42; 43; 44; 45; 46; 47; 48; 49; 50; 53; 54; 55; 56; 57; 58; 86; 121; 126; 127; 128; 129; 131; 132; 134; 135; 136; 137; 138; 226; 227; 1907; 1909; 1914; 1927

Grace Corry Rockwell: none

Mme. Rockwell: none

Rollinson Doll: none

Sasha Dolls: none

Peter Scherf: none

Bruno Schmidt: 2020; 2023; 2025; 2026; 2033; 2048; 2051; 2068; 2070; 2072; 2074; 2075; 2081; 2084; 2085 2092; 2094; 2095; 2096; 2097; 2099; 2154

Franz Schmidt: 269; 293; 1180; 1250; 1253; 1262; 1263; 1266; 1267; 1268; 1271; 1272; 1295; 1296; 1297; 1310; 1370

Schmitt et Fils: none

Schoenau & Hoffmeister: 169; 769; 900; 914; 1400; 1800; 1904; 1906; 1930; 2500; 4000; 4001; 4500; 4600; 4700; 4900; 5000; 5300; 5500; 5700; 5800

Schoenhut: none

Schuetzmeister & Quendt: 101; 102; 201; 204; 300; 301

Simon & Halbig: 120; 150; 151; 152; 153; 172; 411; 540; 550; 570; 600; 616; 719; 720; 739; 740; 749; 759; 769; 939; 949; 905; 908; 919; 929; 941; 950; 969; 979; 989; 1009; 1010; 1039; 1040; 1079; 1080; 1139; 1159; 1160; 1248; 1249; 1250; 1260; 1269; 1279; 1294; 1299; 1303; 1307; 1308; 1339; 1388; 1398; 1428; 1448; 1468; 1469; 1478; 1488; 1489; 1498

S.F.B.J.: 60; 226; 227; 229; 230; 233; 235; 236; 237; 238; 239; 242; 245; 247; 248; 250; 251; 252; 262; 287; 301

Ella Smith Doll Company: none

Sonneberg Täufling: none

Steiff: none

Edmund Ulrich Steiner: none

Hermann Steiner: 131; 246

Jules Steiner: none

Swaine: 232

Shirley Temple: 452; 8371

Terry Lee: none

Uneeda Doll Company: 3; 4; 8; 20; 25; 210

Unis: 60; 71; 149; 301

Van Rozen: none

Vogue Dolls, Inc.: 10; 13; 14; 15; 20; 71; 310; 2687594

W.P.A.: 1865

Wagner & Zetzsche: 639; 698; 10585; 10586

Izannah Walker: none

Wax Dolls: none

Norah Wellings: none

Wilson Novelty Company: 214027

Adolf Wislizenus: 110/115; 252; 289; 421481

Wooden Dolls: none

Glossary

Applied Ears—Ears that are molded separately and affixed to the head.

Appropriately Dressed—Clothing that fits the time period and doll style.

Ball Jointed Body—Doll body of wood-and-composition, jointed at shoulder, elbows, wrists, hip, and knees, allowing movement.

Bébé—French dolly-faced doll.

Bent-Limb Baby Body—Five-piece baby body of composition with curved arms and legs, jointed at shoulder and hip.

Bisque—Unglazed porcelain.

Blown Glass Eyes—Hollow eyes of blue, brown, or gray.

Breather Dolls—With pierced or open nostrils.

Brevete—French marking indicating a registered patent.

Bte—Patent registered.

Caracul—Lamb's skin used to make wigs.

Character Doll—Dolls molded to look lifelike; may be infants, children or adults.

Child Doll—Typical "dolly-face" dolls.

China—Glazed porcelain.

Composition—A wood-based material.

Crazing—Fine lines that develop on the painted surface of composition.

D.E.P.—A claim to registration.

Dolly-Face—Typical child doll face.

D.R.G.M.—German marking indicating a registered design.

Feathered Brows—Eyebrows painted with many tiny strokes.

Five-Piece Body—Body composed of torso, arms, and legs.

Fixed Eyes—Eyes set in a stationary position.

Flange Neck—Doll's neck with ridge and holes at the base for sewing onto a cloth body.

Flirty Eyes—Eyes that move from side to side when head is moved.

Flocked Hair—A coating of short fibers glued to a doll's head to represent hair.

Ges (Gesch)—German marking indicating a registered design.

Googly Eyes—Large, round eyes looking to the side.

Gutta-percha—A pinkish-white rubbery, hard, fibrous substance once used to make dolls, bodies, and parts.

Hard Plastic—Material used after 1948. Very hard with excellent impressions and good color.

Hina-Ningyo—Japanese festival doll.

Huminals—Figures having both human and animal characteristics.

Ichimatus—Japanese play doll.

Intaglio Eyes—Sunken, rather than cut, eyes that are then painted.

Kabuto—Japanese warrior or helmet for a Japanese warrior.

Kid Body—Doll body made of leather.

Lady Doll—Doll with adult face and body proportions.

Magic Skin—A rubbery material used for dolls. They age poorly, becoming dark, and deteriorating as the surface turns soft and sticky.

Mask Face—A stiff face that covers only the front of a doll's head.

Mohair Wig—Wig made from very fine goat's hair.

Mold Number—Impressed or embossed number that indicates a particular design.

Open Mouth—Lips parted with opening cut into the bisque. Teeth usually show.

Open/Closed Mouth—Molded mouth appears open, but no opening cut into the bisque.

Painted Bisque—Paint that is not baked into body; brighter in color, but can be rubbed off.

Painted Eyes—Flat or rounded, and painted eyes.

Paperweight Eyes—Blown glass eyes with an added crystal to the top resulting in a look with depth and great realism.

Papier-mâché—Material made of paper pulp and glue.

Pate—Covering for the opening in a doll head. May be made of cardboard, cork, or plaster.

Peppering—Tiny black specks in the slip of many older bisque or China dolls.

Personality Doll—Dolls molded and fashioned to resemble a famous person.

Pierced Ears—Holes in a doll's ear lobes. Hole goes all the way through the lobe.

Pierced-in Ears—Hole for earring passing through doll's ear lobe and straight into doll's head.

Pouty—Closed mouth doll with a solemn or petulant expression.

Pug or Pugged Nose—Small, button, slightly turned-up nose.

Queue—Oriental hairstyle of a single plat.

Regional Costume—A traditional costume worn in specific region or country.

Reproduction—A doll produced from a mold taken from an existing doll.

Rub—A spot where the color has worn away.

Sakura-Ningyo—Traditional Japanese cherry doll.

S.G.D.G.—Registered, but without government guarantee.

Shoulder Head—Head and shoulder in one piece.

Shoulder Plate—Shoulder portion with socket for head.

Socket Head—Head with neck that fits into a shoulder plate or the opening of a body.

Solid-dome—Head with no crown opening. May have painted hair or wear a wig.

Stationary Eyes—Glass eyes that do not sleep; also known as staring eyes.

Stockinette—Soft jersey fabric used for dolls.

Toddler Body—A short, chubby body of a toddler; often diagonal joints at hips.

Turned Head—Shoulder head with head slightly turned.

Vinyl—Material used after 1950.

Walker Body—Head moves from side to side when legs are made to walk.

Watermelon Mouth—A closed, smiling mouth, usually with a single line.

Weighted Eyes—Sleep eyes that operated by means of a weight attached to a wire frame holding the eyes.

Bibliography

Anderton, Johana Gast. *More Twentieth Century Dolls From Bisque To Vinyl.* Volume I (A-H) Volume II (I-Z), Revised edition. Wallace-Homestead, 1979.

——*Twentieth Century Dolls From Bisque To Vinyl.* Wallace-Homestead, 1974.

Cieslik, Jurgen and Marianne. *German Doll Encyclopedia 1800–1939.* Hobby House Press, 1985.

——*German Doll Marks & Identification Book.* Hobby House Press, 1990.

Coleman, Dorothy S. *Lenci Dolls.* Hobby House Press, 1977.

Coleman, Dorothy S., Elizabeth A. Coleman, and Evelyn J. Coleman. *The Collector's Encyclopedia of Dolls.* Crown Publishers, 1968.

——*The Collector's Encyclopedia of Dolls.* Volume II. Crown Publishers, 1986.

Fraser, Antonia. *Dolls, Pleasures and Treasures.* Weidenfeld and Nicolson, 1963.

Gibbs, Patikii. *Horsman Dolls, 1950-1970.* Collector Books, 1985.

Goodfellow, Caroline. *The Ultimate Doll Book.* Hobby House Press, 1993.

Herlocher, Dawn. *200 Years of Dolls,* Antique Trader, 1996.

——*Doll Makers and Marks,* Antique Trader, 1999.

Heyerdahl, Virginia Ann (ed.). *The Best of Doll Reader.* Volumes I-IV. Hobby House Press, Inc., 1982, 1986, 1988, 1991.

Hunter, Marsha. *Madame Alexander Cloth Dolls.*

Izen, Judith. *A Collector's Guide to Ideal Dolls.* Collector Books, 1994.

Jacobs, Laura. *Barbie: What A Doll!* Artabras, 1994.

Johl, Janet Pagter. *Still More About Dolls.* H. L. Lindquist Publications, 1950.

Judd, Polly. *Cloth Dolls. 1920s and 1930s. Identification and Price Guide.* Hobby House Press, 1990.

Judd, Polly and Pam. *Composition Dolls: 1928-1955.* Hobby House Press, 1991.

——*Compo Dolls: 1909-1928.* Volume II. Hobby House Press, 1994.

——*Glamour Dolls of the 1950s and 1960s: Identification and Values.* Revised edition, Hobby House Press, 1993.

——*Hard Plastic Dolls: Identification and Price Guide.* Third revised edition. Hobby House Press, 1993.

——*Hard Plastic Dolls II: Identification and Price Guide.* Revised Edition. Hobby House Press, 1994.

King, Constance Eileen. *The Collectors History of Dolls.* Bonzana Books, 1977.

Lavitt, Wendy. *Dolls.* Alfred A. Knopf. 1983.

Mandeville, A. Glenn. *Alexander Dolls Collector's Price Guide.* Second edition. Hobby House Press, 1995.

——*Doll Fashion Anthology and Price Guide.* Fourth revised edition. Hobby House Press, 1993.

Manos, Paris and Susan. *The Wonder of Barbie: Dolls and Accessories 1976–1986.* Collector Books, 1987, 1993 value update.

Merill, Madeline Osborne. *The Art of Dolls 1700–1940.* Hobby House Press.

Merill, Madeline O., and Nellie W. Perkins. *The Handbook of Collectible Dolls.* Volumes 1, 2, and 3. Woodward and Miller, 1969, 1974.

Reinelt, Sabine. *Magic of Character Dolls.* Hobby House Press, 1993.

Revi, Albert Christian. *Spinning Wheel's Complete Book of Dolls.* Galahad Books, 1975.

Richter, Lydia. *China, Parian, and Bisque German Dolls.* Hobby House Press, 1993.

——*Treasury of French Dolls.* HP Books, 1983.

——*Treasury of German Dolls.* HP Books, 1984.

Smith, Patricia R. *Antique Collector's Dolls, First Series.* Volume I (1975, 1991 value update), Volume II (1976, 1991 value update). Collector Books.

——*Collector's Encyclopedia of Madame Alexander Dolls 1965-1990.* Collector Books, 1991, 1994 value update.

——*Modern Collector's Dolls.* Volumes I, II, III, IV, V and VI. Collector Books, 1973, 1975, 1976, 1979, 1984, 1991, 1993, 1994, 1995, value updates, Series I-VI.

——*Modern Collector's Dolls, Seventh Series.* Collector Books, 1995.

St. George, Eleanor. *Old Dolls.* Gramercy Publishing Co., 1960.

——*The Dolls of Yesterday.* Charles Schribner's Sons, 1948.

Theriault, Florence. *More Dolls: The Early Years 1780-1910.* Gold Horse Publishing, 1992.

——*Theriault's Doll Registry.* Gold Horse Publishing, 1984.

Westenhouser, Kitturah B. *The Story of Barbie.* Collector Books, 1994.

Index

More Information About Your Prized Dolls

Warman's® Dolls
by R. Lane Herron
For both doll collectors and dealers, this is the most complete and useful guide available, covering dolls dating from 1822 to the late 1950s. All of the most collectible lines, for example, Bru, Jumeau, and Lenci are included. Provides detailed descriptions, reproduction alerts, collecting hints, and historical backgrounds that will make you an expert in this popular collectible area.
Softcover • 8-1/4 x 10-7/8
224 pages
450 b&w photos
40 color photos
Item# WDOLL • $22.95

2002 Price Guide to Limited Edition Collectibles
7th Edition
edited by Mary L. Sieber and the staff of *Collector's Mart* magazine
Bigger and better than ever, this handy collector's guide will help you determine the value of your treasured collectibles with information on edition limit, issue price, year of issue, series name and artist's name. Representing more than 370 companies with more than 65,000 listings and 130,000 prices, this is the authority on contemporary collectibles, including bells, cottages, dolls, figurines, plates, prints, steins and ornaments.
Softcover • 6 x 9 • 928 pages
200 b&w photos
8-page color section, 30 color photos
Item# LEP07 • $19.95

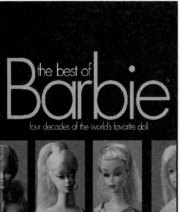

The Best of Barbie®
Four Decades of America's Favorite Doll
by Sharon Korbeck
Enchanting. Gorgeous. Presenting America's favorite doll with striking photography, insightful commentary and historical tidbits. Come and explore the most sought after and valuable Barbie Dolls from 1959 to 2000 with descriptions and more than 1,200 listings to help you easily identify your dolls and price your collection.
Hardcover • 8-1/4 x 10-7/8
256 pages
350 color photos
Item# BBARB • $39.95

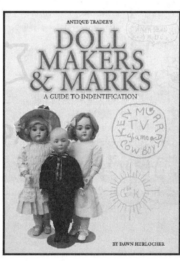

Antique Trader® Doll Makers & Marks
A Guide to Identification
by Dawn Herlocher
This comprehensive resource covers 3,000 dolls manufactured by the world's leading doll makers with detailed charts, listings, line-drawings and background information, detailing each doll manufacturer's production history, particular mold characteristics, size numbers and tips on how to spot reproductions.
Softcover • 8-1/2 x 11
400 pages
140 color & b&w photos
2,000 illustrations
Item# AT0004 • $29.95

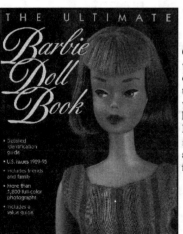

The Ultimate Barbie® Doll Book
by Marcie Melillo
Complete descriptions, values, model numbers, dates and markings for more than 1,000 dolls will assist you in identification of these highly sought after dolls. Barbie and all her friends issued in 1959 through 1995 are photographed in 1,800 full color photographs.
Hardcover with jacket
8-1/2 x 11 • 280 pages
1,800 color photos
Item# UBD01 • $39.95

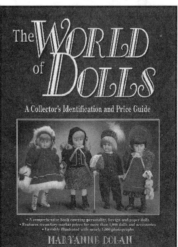

The World of Dolls
A Collectors' Identification and Price Guide
by Maryanne Dolan
This book is an invaluable reference and price guide. It includes secondary market prices for more than 1,000 dolls and doll-related items and covers doll artists; foreign dolls; doll accessories; paper dolls; and personality dolls from the 1920s to today.
Softcover • 8-1/2 x 11
368 pages
300 b&w photos
28 color photos
Item# CHADO • $24.95

To order call **800-258-0929** Offer ACB2
M-F 7am - 8pm • Sat 8am - 2pm, CST

Krause Publications, Offer ACB2
P.O. Box 5009, Iola WI 54945-5009
www.krausebooks.com

Shipping & Handling: $4.00 first book, $2.25 each additional. Non-US addresses $20.95 first book, $5.95 each additional.

Sales Tax: CA, IA, IL, NJ, PA, TN, VA, WI residents please add appropriate sales tax.

Satisfaction Guarantee: If for any reason you are not completely satisfied with your purchase, simply return it within 14 days of receipt and receive a full refund, less shipping charges.

Must-Have References for All Collectors

Antique Trader®
Antiques & Collectibles
Price Guide
edited by Kyle Husfloen
You will discover many of the current "hot" areas in collecting in this comprehensive guide to antiques and collectibles. Features more than 18,500 listings complete with current pricing and a detailed description of each item. Some added features include a listing of names and addresses of the numerous special contributors to the edition and access to a free online price guide.
Softcover • 6 x 9 • 1,048 pages
4,300+ b&w photos
16-page color section
Item# AT2002 • $16.95

Antique Trader®
Jewelry Price Guide
edited by Kyle Husfloen, Contributing Editor Marion Cohen
In the respected tradition of the Antique Trader Antiques and Collectibles Price Guide, this new price guide gives jewelry dealers, appraisers, and collectors the same comprehensive coverage, detailed descriptions and reliable pricing. You'll find 3,500 pieces individually priced and listed in an easy-to-use format. Three major sections describe: fine antique jewelry, 1800 to 1920; modern jewelry, 1920 to present day; and costume jewelry, some now priced to rival even fine antiques.
Softcover • 6 x 9 • 304 pages
400 b&w photos
16-page color section
Item# ATJE1 • $17.95

Warman's®
American Furniture
edited by Ellen T. Schroy
If you have ever brought home a piece of furniture then began to research its style and value, this new book in the Warman's line is for you. It features more than 20,000 price listings, hundreds of photos and hand-drawn illustrations of everything from beds and cupboards to sofas and tables. It also includes other helpful advice and tips to help you understand your furniture and the current antiques marketplace.
Softcover • 8-1/2 x 11
352 pages • 275+ b&w photos • 16-page color section
Item# WAFT • $24.95

Maloney's
Antiques & Collectibles
Resource Directory
6th Edition
by David J. Maloney Jr.
The most comprehensive antiques and collectibles resource directory is better than ever with contact information for more than 23,250 resources in nearly 3,200 specialty categories. From collector clubs, specialty periodicals, dealers, collectors, experts, buyers and appraisers, to parts suppliers, reproduction sources, repair/restoration/ conservation specialists, and auction services, you'll find it here. Listings are organized by subject and are cross-referenced to make it easy for you to locate the resource you need.
Softcover • 8-1/4 x 10-7/8 • 976 pages
Item# DMAL6 • $32.95

Warman's® American
Pottery & Porcelain
2nd Edition
by Susan & Al Bagdade
The only book of its kind, this price guide profiles nearly 150 potteries and their wares, categorized by art pottery, dinnerware, general, and utilitarian. Potteries are arranged alphabetically and each includes a history, dates of operation, references, museums and up-to-the-minute price listings-nearly 12,000 in all. This updated edition features new categories of advertising and souvenir pieces, American Bisque Co., Autumn Leaf, Sascha Brastoff, Camark, head vases, Josef Originals, Kay Finch and Morton Pottery.
Softcover • 8-1/2 x 11
304 pages • 300 b&w photos • 16-page color section, 64 color photos
Item# WAPP2 • $24.95

2002 Toys & Prices
9th Edition
edited by Sharon Korbeck & Elizabeth A. Stephan
With more than 30,000 listings and 80,000 values, 2002 Toys & Prices is the most comprehensive price guide for postwar toys on the market. Detailed descriptions, up-to-date prices and brand new to this edition-an index, make this the guide toy collectors need.
Softcover • 6 x 9 • 960 pages
700 b&w photos
8-page color section
Item# TE09 • $18.95

To order call **800-258-0929** Offer ACB2
M-F 7am - 8pm • Sat 8am - 2pm, CST

Krause Publications, Offer ACB2
P.O. Box 5009, Iola WI 54945-5009
www.krausebooks.com

Shipping & Handling: $4.00 first book, $2.25 each additional. Non-US addresses $20.95 first book, $5.95 each additional.

Sales Tax: CA, IA, IL, NJ, PA, TN, VA, WI residents please add appropriate sales tax.

Satisfaction Guarantee: If for any reason you are not completely satisfied with your purchase, simply return it within 14 days of receipt and receive a full refund, less shipping charges.